Fodor's

ESSENTIAL
CHILE

D0912527

Welcome to Chile

A long sliver of land wedged between the Andes and the Pacific, Chile packs a wealth of diverse landscapes in its narrow borders. In the north, the Atacama Desert enthralls with the world's highest geyser field and alpine salt flats dotted with flamingos. Vibrant beaches, first-rate vineyards, and bustling cities like Santiago and Valparaíso make it easy to tap into the good life in central Chile. In Patagonia, outdoor enthusiasts revel in exciting adventures, from climbing snow-capped volcanoes to trekking through the majestic Torres del Paine National Park.

TOP REASONS TO GO

★ **Stunning Scenery:** Postcard-perfect backdrops from Chiloé to San Pedro de Atacama.

★ **Wine:** Full-bodied reds and crisp whites flourish in wineries on the Andes foothills.

★ **Patagonia:** Immense blue glaciers, dramatic mountain peaks, and crystalline lakes.

★ **Outdoor Activities:** Hiking and spotting unique wildlife are just a few top options.

★ **Easter Island:** Mesmerizing stone moai loom large on this remote island.

★ **The Central Coast:** Alluring beaches, fresh seafood, and Valparaíso's colorful hills.

Contents

1 EXPERIENCE CHILE 7
17 Ultimate Experiences. 8
What's Where 14
What to Eat and Drink in Chile 16
Best Chilean Wineries 18
Best Things to Do in Patagonia 20
Chile Today. 22
History of Chile 25
What to Watch, Read,
and Listen To 27

2 TRAVEL SMART 29
Know Before You Go 30
Getting Here. 32
Essentials 36
Helpful Phrases in Spanish 44
Great Itineraries 46
On the Calendar 50
Contacts 52

3 SANTIAGO 53
Welcome to Santiago 54
Planning 57
Santiago Centro 62
La Alameda 71
Bellas Artes and Lastarria. 74
Parque Forestal 77
Bellavista and
Parque Metropolitano. 80
Parque Quinta Normal Area 84
Vitacura. 86
Las Condes. 90
Providencia 94
Side Trips from Santiago 99

4 THE CENTRAL COAST. 109
Welcome to the Central Coast 110
Planning 113
Valparaíso. 116
Viña del Mar 128
Casablanca Wine Valley 134
Quintay 135
Algarrobo 136
Isla Negra. 139
Concón 141
Maitencillo. 144
Zapallar. 147

5 EL NORTE CHICO 149
Welcome to El Norte Chico 150
Planning 153
La Serena 155
Vicuña 159
Pisco Elqui 163
Ovalle. 166

Parque Nacional
Bosques de Fray Jorge. 169
Reserva Nacional
Pingüino de Humboldt. 170
Parque Nacional
Llanos de Challe 171
Copiapó 172
Parque Nacional
Nevado Tres Cruces 174
Bahía Inglesa. 176
Parque Nacional Pan de Azúcar 178

6 EL NORTE GRANDE 179
Welcome to El Norte Grande 180
Planning 183
Antofagasta 186
Chacabuco 188
Calama. 189
San Pedro de Atacama. 191
Geysers del Tatio 200
Reserva Nacional Los Flamencos. . . . 202
Iquique. 202
Mamiña 206
Pica. 207
Reserva Nacional
Pampa del Tamarugal 207
Gigante de Atacama 208
Arica. 209
Parque Nacional Lauca 212
Reserva Nacional Las Vicuñas 213
Salar de Surire 214

7 THE CENTRAL VALLEY 215
Welcome to the Central Valley. 216
Planning 219
Rancagua 222
San Fernando and Nearby. 225
Santa Cruz 227
Curicó. 233
Lago Vichuquén 234
Talca. 235

8 THE LAKE DISTRICT 241
Welcome to the Lake District. 242
Planning 244
Temuco 246
Parque Nacional Conguillío 252
Curacautín and Nearby 253
Villarrica 254
Pucón. 257
Parque Nacional Huerquehue 262
Parque Nacional Villarrica 263
Lican Ray 265
Valdivia 266
Huilo Huilo 274

Lago Ranco and Nearby............ 274
Osorno............................ 276
Parque Nacional Puyehue.......... 279
Puerto Octay...................... 280
Frutillar.......................... 281
Puerto Varas...................... 283
Ensenada......................... 288
Parque Nacional
Vicente Pérez Rosales............. 289
Puerto Montt...................... 290
Cochamó.......................... 295

9 CHILOÉ......................... 297
Welcome to Chiloé................. 298
Planning.......................... 301
Ancud............................. 303
Quemchi.......................... 306
Quicaví........................... 307
Dalcahue.......................... 307
Isla Quinchao..................... 309
Castro............................. 310
Chonchi........................... 314
Parque Nacional Chiloé............ 316
Queilén........................... 317
Quellón........................... 318

10 THE SOUTHERN COAST......... 321
Welcome to the Southern Coast..... 322
Planning.......................... 325
Chaitén........................... 326
Parque Nacional
Pumalín Douglas Tompkins......... 330
Futaleufú......................... 332
La Junta.......................... 335
Puerto Puyuhuapi................. 335
Parque Nacional Queulat.......... 337
Coyhaique......................... 338
Puerto Chacabuco
and Puerto Aysén................. 345
Parque Nacional
Laguna San Rafael................ 348
Lago General
Carrera and Nearby............... 349
Parque Nacional Patagonia........ 350

11 SOUTHERN CHILEAN PATAGONIA
   AND TIERRA DEL FUEGO........ 353
Welcome to Southern Chilean
Patagonia and Tierra del Fuego...... 354
Cruising and Land
Tour Company Profiles............. 357
Planning.......................... 362
Puerto Natales.................... 365
Parque Nacional Torres del Paine... 372
Punta Arenas, Chile............... 376
Puerto Hambre.................... 383

El Calafate and Parque
Nacional los Glaciares, Argentina ... 384
El Chaltén, Argentina.............. 394
Ushuaia, Argentina................ 396
Parque Nacional
Tierra del Fuego, Argentina......... 406
Puerto Williams, Chile............. 409

12 EASTER ISLAND................ 411
Welcome to Easter Island.......... 412
Planning.......................... 415
Hanga Roa........................ 418
The Southeastern Circuit.......... 428
The Western Circuit............... 431

INDEX........................... 437

ABOUT OUR WRITERS.......... 447

MAPS

Santiago Centro and La Alameda......64
Bellas Artes, Lastarria,
and Parque Forestal................. 78
Vitacura........................... 87
Santiago Side Trips................ 100
Valparaíso..................... 118–119
Viña del Mar...................... 129
The Southern Beaches............. 137
The Northern Beaches............. 145
The Elqui Valley and
the Limarí Valley.................. 167
Copiapó Valley.................... 172
Nitrate Pampa.................... 186
San Pedro and the
Atacama Desert................... 191
Iquique and Nearby................ 203
Arica and Nearby.................. 209
Rapel Valley...................... 221
Valle Curicó and Valle Maule....... 235
La Araucanía...................... 247
Lago Villarrica.................... 255
Los Lagos and Los Ríos............ 266
Valdivia.......................... 268
Puerto Varas and Lago Llanquihue... 284
Chaitén, Futaleufú,
and Puerto Puyuhuapi............. 327
Coyhaique and Nearby............. 345
Parque Nacional Laguna San Rafael. 347
Puerto Natales and Nearby......... 366
Parque Nacional Torres del Paine ... 374
Punta Arenas..................... 378
Hanga Roa........................ 420
The Southeastern Circuit.......... 429
The Western Circuit............... 433

Chapter 1

EXPERIENCE CHILE

17 ULTIMATE EXPERIENCES

Chile offers terrific experiences that should be on every traveler's list. Here are Fodor's top picks for a memorable trip.

1 San Pedro de Atacama

In the heart of the Atacama Desert, San Pedro is renowned for its breathtaking scenery. Explore erupting geyser fields and blue alpine lakes, and watch colorful sunsets across lunar-like landscapes. (Ch. 6)

2 Churches and Wizards in Chiloé

Indigenous and colonialist histories collide in this picturesque archipelago that's home to 70 wooden churches and, locals say, several wizards. (Ch. 9)

3 Valparaíso

A UNESCO World Heritage site, the port town of Valparaíso charms with its candy-color metal houses, street art, dramatic hills, and funiculars. (Ch. 4)

4 Santiago

Surrounded by the Andes, Chile's vibrant capital is filled with top-notch museums, colorful crafts markets, colonial buildings, and trendy restaurants. (Ch. 3)

5 Wineries

Sample rich reds and crisp whites at the vineyards that line Chile's Central Valley. The often stunning settings and generous tasting sessions are added bonuses. (Ch. 3, 4, 7)

6 Wildlife Spotting

Chile's ecosystems support a variety of wildlife. Expect to see penguins and guanacos (above) in Patagonia and alpacas and flamingos in the Atacama Desert. (Ch. 6, 11)

7 Seafood

You're never far from the ocean in Chile. Local restaurants serve delicious seafood throughout the country, from Patagonian king crab (centolla) to mouthwatering stews. (Ch. 1)

8 Pablo Neruda's Houses

Even those unfamiliar with Neruda's poetry will be captivated by the whimsical objects and architecture at his houses in Santiago, Valparaíso, and Isla Negra (below). (Ch. 3, 4)

9 Torres del Paine

This national park is Chile's premier destination for hikers and nature lovers. Its aquamarine lakes, abundant wildlife, and jagged peaks are spectacular. (Ch. 11)

10 Lakes and Volcanoes

Whether you prefer fishing, hiking, kayaking, climbing, or horseback riding, Chile's snowcapped volcanoes and glistening lakes offer outdoor activities for everyone. (Ch. 8)

11 Easter Island

Wandering among the mysterious moai, the colossal stone statues that keep watch over the most isolated island in the world, is truly awe-inspiring. (Ch. 12)

12 Beaches

Take your pick of gorgeous beaches—from the glamorous strands along the Central Coast to windswept beauties in the south—on the long Pacific coastline. (Ch. 4, 5, 6)

13 Patagonia's Glaciers

Between the regions of Aysén and Magallanes, witness the majesty of ice cathedrals and gaze into their deep blue caverns on a hiking or kayaking adventure. (Ch. 11)

14 Fiestas Patrias

Expect big street parties, traditional rodeos, cueca dancing, lots of empanadas, flag-waving, and plenty of pisco sours during this national holiday on September 18. (Ch. 2)

15 Pisco, Elqui

Chile's pisco heartland is in the town of Pisco, in Elqui, where the lion's share of Chile's clear grape brandy originates. Try it in a pisco sour on a hot summer evening. (Ch. 5)

16 Termas

Chileans love a good terma (thermal bath). Pick between well-run large resorts found in Chillán and Puyuhuapi or natural pools in Colina, Polloquere, and Puyehue. (Ch. 10)

17 Road Trip Down Ruta 5

Chile's main highway, the Ruta 5, stretches from beyond the Atacama Desert to the gateway of Patagonia and makes for an epic road trip. The highway passes through wine valleys, forests, and salt flats. (Ch. 10)

WHAT'S WHERE

1 Santiago. Although it doesn't get the same press as Rio or Buenos Aires, this metropolis is just as cosmopolitan as its flashier South American neighbors. Ancient and modern stand side by side, and the Andes are ever present to the east.

2 The Central Coast. Anchoring the coast west of Santiago, port city Valparaíso has stunning views from atop its more than 40 hills. Next door, Viña del Mar has nonstop nightlife and popular beaches.

3 El Norte Chico. A land of dusty brown hills, the "little north" stretches for some 700 km (435 miles) north of Santiago. The lush Elqui Valley grows the grapes used to make *pisco*. Astronomers flock here for the clear night skies.

4 El Norte Grande. Stark epitomizes Chile's great north, a region bordering Peru and Bolivia. This is the driest place on Earth, site of the stunning landscapes of San Pedro de Atacama.

5 The Central Valley. Chile's wine country lies south of Santiago, from the Valle Maipo to the Valle Maule. Some

of the world's best wines come from this fertile strip of land.

6 The Lake District. The austral summer doesn't get more glorious than in this compact stretch of land between Temuco and Puerto Montt. It has fast become vacation central, with resorts such as Pucón and Villarrica.

7 Chiloé. More than 40 islands sprinkled across the Golfo de Ancud make up the archipelago of Chiloé. Dozens of wooden churches, constructed during the colonial era, dot the landscape.

8 The Southern Coast. This stretch of coastline between the Lake District and Patagonia is one of the Earth's most remote regions. Anchoring its spine is the Carretera Austral, an epic road trip.

9 Southern Chilean Patagonia. Chile's south-ernmost region is home to some of the most stunning landscapes on the planet, including the majestic Torres del Paine.

10 Easter Island. The world's most remote island astounds with archaeology, trekking, and diving. Learn the mysterious history of the Rapa Nui and the iconic moai, but be prepared to leave with more questions than answers.

What to Eat and Drink in Chile

CURANTO

The ritual of cooking Chiloé's famous dish is an event in itself: the stew is prepared outdoors buried in a pit lined with red-hot stones. Layers of shellfish, sausage, smoked pork ribs, potatoes, and pulses are added, then covered with sodden earth to create a kind of pressure cooker.

ASADO

Asados (barbecues) are a national pastime, and any excuse is used to start up the grill. The Chilean barbecue starts with *choripan*, a spicy sausage served in a bun and topped with *pebre*, a mixture of tomatoes, cilantro, onions, and chilies, as well as mayonnaise.

MERKÉN

Although Chilean cuisine is not renowned for its spice, the indigenous Chilean seasoning, *merkén*, is used to flavor everything from peanuts to meats. Hailing from the native Mapuche tribe in southern Chile's IX region, it is a powdered mixture of *cacho de cabra*-chili, toasted coriander seeds, and salt.

MANJAR

Made from boiled condensed milk, this caramel-like sweet substance is used as a filling for everything from *alfajores* (two cookies sandwiched together and covered in chocolate) and *cuchuflis* (thin wafers rolled into cylinders) to crepes. It's commonly used as an ice-cream flavor.

CORN

Corn is a versatile ingredient used in many Chilean comfort food dishes. In summer, when it's in season, try *humitas*, a lightly seasoned corn paste wrapped in corn leaves, normally eaten plain or sprinkled with sugar as a main course, and *pastel de choclo*, a mixture of minced beef, chicken, olives, hard-boiled egg, and raisins, topped with a layer of creamy mashed corn and served in a heavy clay bowl.

SANDWICHES

One of the most popular fast foods is the essential sandwich. Try the *churrasco* sandwich (thin strips of beef on your choice of white sliced bread or in an oversize bun) and *lomito* (a pork sandwich). Don't forget to add *ají chileno*, a spicy local version of ketchup.

EMPANADAS

You can order an empanada as a starter or a main course, or buy them from small supermarkets to eat on the go. These rectangular doughy packages come most commonly as *empanadas de pino*, filled with meat, onions, olives, egg, and raisins, or *queso*, filled with cheese; or occasionally *mariscos* (shellfish).

Empanadas

SEAFOOD
A trip to Punta Arenas would not be complete without trying *centolla* (king crab), nor should you leave Easter Island without savoring a yellowfin tuna ceviche. Many coastal towns have a central fish market where you can buy fresh catch or enjoy a *paila marina* (a seafood stew).

SOPAIPILLAS
This tasty circular snack is made from pumpkin dough, then deep-fried. Chileans serve it warm and douse it with sweet or savory toppings such as honey, *pebre* salsa, or mayo.

PISCO SOUR
Chile's national drink is a grape brandy usually mixed with lime, egg white, and sugar. It's best sampled where it is developed: Pisco, in the Elqui Valley.

CHILEAN WINE
Several stellar wine regions exist in Chile: Central Maipo and Alto Maipo are the cradle of Chile's Cabernets. Colchagua Valley wines often make top world's best lists, especially their Malbec and Carménère (Chile's signature grape). More than 30 varieties of grapes grow in Curicó. Finally, Maule Valley is Chile's largest wine region.

COMPLETO
One of the most popular fast foods in Chile is the complèto, an enormous, loaded hot dog in a bun smothered with toppings like tomatoes, avocado, mayo, and sauerkraut.

CHIRIMOYA
Walk into one of the *ferias* (street markets) in the summer and you will be overwhelmed by the colors and smells of all the fresh fruit. Try a custard apple (*chirimoya*), with its mottled green skin and creamy texture—divine on its own or made into juices or to flavor ice cream.

Best Chilean Wineries

VIÑA SANTA RITA

Located a 45-minute drive from Santiago in Maipo, 1880-founded Viña Santa Rita today houses a boutique hotel set among 40 hectares of vineyards, a neo-Gothic chapel, Roman-style baths, and a 3,000-exhibit Andean museum—a most immersive experience in Maipo. Day-trippers can take a cellar tour, which includes a cheese-paired wine tasting, while aspiring vintners can create their own blend out of the 33 varieties cultivated here to take home. (Ch. 3)

CASAS DEL BOSQUE

Food is a focal point at Casablanca-based Casas del Bosque, which is surrounded by pine forest and olive groves. Work up an appetite cycling around the vineyards before taking a cooking class or devouring a four-course tasting menu at the winery's Tanino restaurant. The kitchen can also rustle up gourmet sandwiches for a picnic, best savored with a bottle of refreshing house Sauvignon Blanc. (Ch. 4)

CLOS APALTA

This stunning winery near Colchagua holds its own Denomination of Origin thanks to its microclimate. Grand Marnier heiress Alexandra Marnier Lapostolle cultivates organic and biodynamic vineyards to create Bordeaux-style red blends as well as Chilean red favorite Carménère. (Ch. 7)

VILLARD FINE WINES

At a family-run winery in a country where corporations are the norm, Thierry Villard and his son Jean-Charles make the effort to personally show visitors around their vineyard and cellar room. There you can live the winemaker experience, sampling vintages directly from tanks or barrels. Sharing lunch with the family—a three-course paired affair that includes their renowned Tanagra blend—ensures an insider's perspective. (Ch. 4)

VIÑA VIU MANENT

Clamber into a horse-drawn carriage for a scenic vineyard tour in Colchagua Valley before tasting Viu Manent's big red portfolio, including the first Malbec to be produced in Chile. At in-house restaurant Rayuela Wine and Grill, celebrity chef Pilar Rodríguez uses a traditional clay oven to cook. (Ch. 7)

VIÑA MONTES

One of Chile's most renowned wineries, Colchagua-based Montes produces a stellar cast of iconic labels, such as Alpha M and Purple Angel, that you can sample in a premium tasting. You can also book a table at Francis Mallmann's Fuegos de Apalta feng shui–inspired restaurant or opt for a picnic. (Ch. 7)

Viña Undurraga

VIÑA VIK
Nestled on top of a hill in the Cachapoal Valley, Viña Vik produces few vintages, but it's worth the visit for the fantastic architecture. Big budgets should book a night in a glass-walled bungalow. Despite the wild setting, guests can keep busy dining at the three restaurants, perusing the contemporary art collection, or rejuvenating at the wine spa. (Ch. 7)

ITATA EXPEDICIONES
While not a winery per se, this tour company organizes visits around Itata, a southern wine region five hours south of Santiago, where the vintages are exciting wine critics. The area is home to a cluster of small and very promising viñas located on unusual volcanic soils and led by passionate viticulturists, and many projects rescue and regenerate abandoned vines. Unusual grapes to sample include Pipeño, Criolla, and Carignan—ones for real wine aficionados. (Ch. 4)

VIÑA UNDURRAGA
Founded in 1885, this Maipo-based viña is one of Chile's oldest. While it's a behemoth on the winemaking map with six vineyards spanning 1,350 hectares, intimate corners are revealed on a guided tour, such as the 19th-century cellars that still age Undurraga's Reserva line. Splash out on the Founders Tour tasting, which includes four premium wines and a cheese plate. (Ch. 3)

BODEGAS RE
Blending ancient winemaking practices with contemporary enological thinking, this gem in the Casablanca Valley is run by the ninth and 10th winemaking generations of the Morandé family. Made in clay amphorae, fascinating blends include Pinotel (Pinot Noir and Muscatel). (Ch. 4)

Best Things to Do in Patagonia

LEARN ABOUT MAPUCHE CULTURE
The town of Temuco, gateway to the Lake District, and its environs are one of the best places in the region to immerse yourself in ancestral travel and learn about the Mapuche, Chile's most populous indigenous culture. Cultural exchanges include weaving in hand looms, staying in a runa center, or preparing *digüeñe* (mushroom) empanadas.

TRAVEL TO THE LAND OF FIRE
Accessible by car or train, Parque Nacional Tierra del Fuego in Argentina is the southernmost national park in the world. Here you can discover breathtaking wildlife refuges, mountain-ringed lakes, strikingly green lagoons, peat bogs, and wild cherry forests.

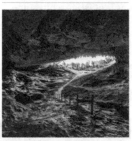

VISIT THE PREHISTORIC CUEVA DEL MILADÓN
Gateway town to Parque Nacional Torres del Paine, Puerto Natales is also a jumping-off point to visit the Mylodon Cave Natural Monument. Once inhabited by prehistoric mylodons, this vast cavern is 200 meters (656 feet) deep, 80 wide and 30 high, and excavations reveal both human and animal archaeology and paleontology.

HIKE TO GLACIAR GREY
The Patagonia ice field covers much of the southern end of the Andean mountain range, straddling the Argentina–Chile border. Perhaps the most stunning glacier is Glaciar Grey at Parque Nacional Torres del Paine, with its fragmented icebergs, an easy and rewarding site to hike or kayak.

MEET PENGUINS IN ISLA MAGDALENA
Home to 150,000 Magellanic penguins, this one-square-kilometer island is the site of one of the largest such colonies in southern Chile. It's an easy boat ride away from Punta Arenas. The best time to see penguins is from November through February, during milder weather.

SNAP COLORFUL STILT HOUSES IN CASTRO

On the island of Chiloé, take a full day to photograph the rows of multicolor homes on stilts, called *palafitos*, in Castro, capital of the island. Just as vibrant are the 70 UNESCO World Heritage site churches in the surrounding towns, which are equally deserving of your time.

GET CLOSER TO WILDLIFE

Binoculars always come in handy, and there's no shortage of wildlife spotting, including condors and guanacos (a smaller cousin of the alpaca and llama) at Parque Nacional Torres del Paine, Chile's most popular national park. Also look out for rhea, much like a road runner, striding across the rugged terrain, and puma, not as elusive as you'd think.

TREK PARQUE NACIONAL TORRES DEL PAINE

Chile's most popular national park offers classic hikes and wild rock climbing, whose end goals offer spectacular views of waterfalls and glaciers. Its most spectacular attractions are its lakes of turquoise and emerald waters and the Cuernos del Paine ("Paine Horns"), the geological showpiece of the immense granite massif.

VISIT PATAGONIA'S NEWEST NATIONAL PARK

A vast and remote area consisting of half a million acres, Parque Nacional Patagonia officially came into existence in 2019. The land, first purchased by the Tompkins Foundation, was developed as a conservation area and then donated back to the Chilean government to become a park. Part of its mission is rewilding species.

FEEL THE HEAT AT VOLCÁN OSORNO

Visible from every point in Osorno in the Lake District, the volcano is located on the southeastern shore of Lago Llanquihue. Reaching a height of 2,661 meters (8,730 feet) above sea level, it takes around six hours to ascend, best undertaken in an organized group with a local guide.

Chile Today

POLITICS

While the Chile of today is a democratic and peaceful country, it wasn't always that way. A military dictatorship led by General Augusto Pinochet shaped the country for 17 years, from 1973 until a return to democracy in 1990. Since then, this isolated nation at the end of the world has made great strides on several fronts. The World Bank classifies Chile's national economy as upper-middle income with only moderate debt, a drastic change from 30 years ago. Corruption is lower here than anywhere else in South America, one of the factors contributing to the country's political stability and economic development. On the political front, Chileans have democratically elected eight presidents since 1990, including Chile's first female president, Michelle Bachelet, who was elected twice, and the more conservative billionaire Sebastián Piñera, who governed Chile from 2010 to 2014, and again from 2017 to 2021. The most recent election was held in December 2021, when 56 percent of Chileans elected left-wing legislator Gabriel Boric as president. Once a student activist who rose to prominence during the anti-government protests, Boric is Chile's youngest president (then 35 years old) with a mandate to tackle poverty and fight "the privileges of the few," in his words. Though income inequality is a significant concern, the number of people living below the poverty line in Chile was reduced by 18.1% (from 26% to 7.9%) from 2000 to 2017, although it had risen to 10.8%.

As for confronting Chile's recent torrid past, humans rights abusers from the dictatorship continue to be prosecuted, though the Chilean Supreme Court often reduces their sentences. These lenient decisions on ensuring punishments do not fit the crime continues to divide Chileans today.

THE ENVIRONMENT

Unfortunately, Chile faces an array of environmental issues ranging from deforestation to intense mining, while air pollution is a serious problem in capital city Santiago. Between 1985 and 1995, some 2 million hectares of forest were lost to the pulping industry, causing high levels of soil erosion while mining aftercare is given far less attention than the actual extraction of natural resources such as copper and silver. Booming industries close to Santiago ensure the country's smog levels rank among the world's highest. Measures taken by the government to combat these issues include a carbon tax and district energy strategies. Chileans are now taking a more serious attitude toward climate change after joining the Paris Agreement in 2017, and in 2021 Chile passed the Energy Efficiency law, which will reduce emissions by 2% a year until 2030. However, with just 10% of the nation's trash recycled, there's still plenty of work to be done.

Things are looking up for the country's national parks though. Via the Rewilding NGO, formerly known as Land Conservation Trust, North Americans and former CEOs of the outdoor clothing company Patagonia Inc., Kristine and Douglas Tompkins, purchased vast swaths of land and recuperated them to create—then gift to the government—national parks. After donating such projects to Chile since 2005, the Tompkins's latest additions to the country's seven-strong national parks family are Pumalín Douglas Tompkins (named for the late cofounder), 988,000 acres near Puerto Montt, and Patagonia, 752,504 acres near the Aysén region, which received national park status in 2019.

WOMEN AND THE FAMILY

Over the past decade, women in Chile have become increasingly influential in both the government and the private sector. When the country's first female president, Michelle Bachelet, began her first term in 2006, she launched a campaign to promote gender equality in Chile and named women to a number of influential posts in her cabinet. During her second term between 2013 to 2017, she proposed legislation on women's sexual reproductive rights and same-sex marriage, which is considered ground-breaking for this predominantly Catholic nation. Despite many advances, salaries for men and women remain unequal in Chile, and men typically occupy the most influential positions, particularly in the private sector.

Two government policies have had a particularly important impact on women and the family in Chile. In November 2004, divorce became legal, then in 2006, state-run hospitals were given clearance to distribute the morning-after pill free of charge. Before legalizing divorce, Chile was one of the few countries in the world to prohibit this practice, which resulted in many Chileans forming new families without legally divorcing. Those who could afford it had their marriages annulled. These new policies have directly challenged the influence of the Roman Catholic Church in Chile (about 60% of Chileans are Catholic) and were resisted by the powerful conservative sectors of the Chilean population.

CHILEAN IDENTITY

Due in part to its overall economic success, Chilean identity is in flux. While Chileans are proud of their nationality and celebrate the *fiestas patrias* (independence-day holidays) with fervor, they also increasingly value cultural and material imports from abroad. Many Chileans flock to malls to buy the latest technological toys, and SUVs are common, despite high gas prices. Many members of the expanding middle class are moving to the suburbs and sending their children to private, bilingual schools; incorporating English words into conversations and having coffee at Starbucks have become status symbols.

Other sectors of the Chilean population, however, resist these influences, including members of the political left and indigenous groups. A number of popular Chilean artists have also commented on Chile's increasingly materialistic and outward-looking culture, including writer Alberto Fuguet and musicians Los Chancho en Piedra and Joe Vasconcellos.

An interesting example of these tensions in Chilean identity is the annual pre-Christmas charity event, the Teletón. Modeled on telethons in the United States, the Teletón is billed as "27 hours of love" and presided over by Chilean TV personality Don Francisco. Despite its growing commercialization—companies showing off with big donations to strengthen their branding—the event is remarkable not only because it raises large sums of money for children with disabilities, but also because almost all Chileans watch it and contribute funds, despite class, ethnicity, or geographic differences. The Teletón is truly an expression of modern *chilenidad* (Chileanism).

EXPORT INDUSTRIES

Chilean export industries continue to be a crucial source of jobs and national income. Foremost among these are the nation's copper mines, which are more productive than any others in the world. In 2020, Chilean copper exports reached US$32.2 billion; mining products constituted 50% of the Chilean export market and 10% of the country's GDP. Chile's principal nonmineral exports include wine, wood, fruit, vegetables, and fish. The top three markets for Chilean exports are China (23%), the United States (19%), and Brazil (8%).

Despite the positive economic impacts of Chile's vibrant export sector, the success of these businesses has also resulted in domestic conflicts. The mining and salmon industries have been criticized for negative environmental effects. The Mapuche, Chile's most significant indigenous group, have challenged the construction of hydroelectric plants in the south on environmental, territorial, and cultural grounds. And following the infamous mining accident of 2010, when 33 Chilean miners found themselves trapped underground for more than two months before their miraculous rescue, workers have raised concerns about mine safety, as well as pertinent questions about working conditions and higher wages.

CHILE ON THE INTERNATIONAL STAGE

Since its return to democracy in 1990, Chile has been active in international politics and trade relations. A strong proponent of free trade, Chile has signed more than 26 Free Trade Agreements (FTAs) with 65 countries. It participates actively in United Nations agencies and has sent Chilean soldiers on UN peacekeeping missions in countries such as Haiti and Iraq.

Despite its increasingly important role on the global stage, Chile's relations with its immediate neighbors are somewhat contentious. Chile and Argentina have ongoing disputes over natural gas, and Bolivia and Chile have maintained only consular relations since 1978 due to a long-standing conflict over Bolivia's sea access. After Peru elevated its dispute over the demarcation of the coastline between the two countries to The Hague, the court ruled against Chile in 2014. While Chile lost 8,000 square miles of maritime territory, it was able to keep its rich coastal fishing waters. The case has been in the hands of the International Court of Justice since 2015.

HEALTHY EATING

Facing an ever-growing obesity epidemic (nearly one-third of adult Chileans and one-quarter of children are considered obese or overweight), the Chilean government stepped in to regulate the packaging, marketing, and labeling of food sold in Chile, particularly junk food and sugary cereals. A bill was introduced in the Chilean legislature in 2007, requiring the removal of cartoon characters from food boxes and the addition of black warning labels for foods that are high in fat, sugar, salt, and calories. Due to intense opposition from major corporations, it took nearly a decade for the rules to finally be enacted (they became law in 2016), but now Chile is on the forefront of the push against the obesity epidemic. The sale of junk food is also prohibited in schools, and advertising for candy and junk food is banned during television programs aimed at young viewers. Obesity rates have yet to fall (and many think the new president will push back on these regulations), but a visit to a Chilean grocery store can be quite the experience for those used to the colors and logos (and lack of black warning labels) found in most Western grocery stores.

History of Chile

PRECOLONIAL CHILE

The indigenous groups living in Chile before the arrival of the Spanish can be categorized as the pre-Incan cultures in the north, the Mapuche in the region between the Choapa River and Chiloé, and the Patagonian cultures in the extreme south. Although the Incan Empire extended into Chile, the Mapuche successfully resisted their incursions; there is a debate about how much of Chile the Incans conquered.

The **geoglyphs** constructed between AD 500 and 1400 in the mountains along ancient northern trade routes are some of the most important in the world. The **Chinchorro mummies,** relics of the Chinchorro people who lived along the northern coast, are the oldest in the world, dating from 6000 BC. They are visible at the Museo Arqueológico de San Miguel de Azapa near Arica. The **Museo Arqueológico Gustavo Le Paige** in San Pedro de Atacama has an impressive collection of precolonial and colonial objects.

In Temuco, the **Museo Regional de la Araucanía** provides a fairly good introduction to Mapuche art, culture, and history. Temuco and its environs also offer a sense of modern Mapuche life. Farther south, the **Museo Salesiano de Maggiorino Borgatello** in Punta Arenas has an interesting collection of artifacts from various Patagonian cultures. Finally, in Santiago, the **Museo Chileno de Arte Precolombino** has an excellent collection of indigenous artifacts from Mexico to Patagonia.

COLONIAL CHILE

While Ferdinand Magellan and Diego de Almagro both traveled to Chile earlier, it was Pedro de Valdivia who founded Santiago in 1541. Before being killed in battle by a Mapuche chief, Valdivia established a number of other important towns in Chile as well. Yet the Mapuche successfully resisted Spanish conquest and colonization, ruling south of the Bío Bío River until the 1880s.

The **Plaza de Armas** is where Pedro de Valdivia founded Santiago in 1541. The **Iglesia San Francisco** is Santiago's oldest structure, dating from 1586, although it was partially rebuilt in 1698 and expanded in 1857. The **Casa Colorada** is a well-preserved example of colonial architecture. It was the home of Mateo de Toro y Zambrano, a Creole businessman and Spanish soldier, and now houses the Museo de Santiago. On Chiloé near Ancud, the **San Antonio Fort,** constructed in 1786, is all that remains of Spain's last outpost in Chile.

INDEPENDENCE

September 18, 1810—Chilean Independence Day—is when a group of prominent citizens created a junta to replace the Spanish government. However, full independence was achieved several years later in 1818 with the victory of the Battle of Maipú by Bernardo O'Higgins and José de San Martín. Chiloé remained under Spanish control until 1826.

The **Temple of Maipú** on the outskirts of Santiago was constructed in honor of the Virgin of Carmen, patron saint of Santiago, after the Battle of Maipú. While the original temple was destroyed, its foundations still exist near the new structure built in the 1950s.

The **Palacio Cousiño** in Santiago, built by one of Chile's most important families in 1871, provides an excellent sense of how the elite lived in an independent, modernizing Chile.

MILITARY DICTATORSHIP

In 1973, Chile's first socialist president, Salvador Allende, was overthrown by a military coup by the Chilean Air Force. Some of the bullet holes from their bombardment of the **Palacio de La Moneda,** where Allende committed suicide after refusing to surrender, can still be seen. Today, this building is the site of the country's presidential offices; construction first began on it in 1784.

A junta led in part by Augusto Pinochet, the commander-in-chief of the Chilean army, seized power and began to detain thousands of people whom they considered potential subversives, including political activists, journalists, professors, and trade unionists. The junta used the **Estadio Nacional** in Santiago as a prison camp and torture site for tens of thousands of detainees. The stadium is considered a national site and has since been renovated and expanded. First-division soccer matches and large concerts are now held in this stadium.

The most important site used by the Chilean secret police to torture and interrogate political prisoners during the Pinochet era is on the outskirts of Santiago. Once a spot where artists and progressives would meet up, **Villa Grimaldi** held more than 4,000 detainees in the mid-1970s. Today, it is a memorial site and peace park featuring a wall of names of its prisoners and a memory room containing personal items and mementos of the people who "disappeared" at Villa Grimaldi.

Two other prominent sites that the Pinochet regime used for torture and imprisonment are found in the Atacama Desert to the north of Santiago. In **Chacobuco,** a ghost town roughly 70 km (43 miles) north of Antofagasta in El Norte Grande, the regime established a notorious prison camp, and the artwork of its former inhabitants still lines the walls. Farther north, around 168 km (100 miles) north of Iquique, **Pisagua** was where the Pinochet regime established a camp for missing persons and political prisoners. The camp still haunts the small town even now.

One of the largest cemeteries in Latin America, the **Cementerio General de Santiago,** is an important national monument that reveals a lot about traditional Chilean society. Most Chilean presidents are buried here, with the notable exception of Pinochet. Salvador Allende, who was originally buried in a makeshift grave outside of Viña del Mar, was transported here when democracy was restored to the country. His grave, along with the memorials for those disappeared during the Pinochet regime, make this cemetery an important pilgrimage site.

A NEW CONSTITUTION

In late 2019, protesters took to the streets across Chile in what's been seen as the country's largest social uprising of the past 30 years. It escalated into clashes with police forces and raised questions regarding human rights. A year later, in a referendum, Chileans approved the idea of a new, post-Pinochet constitution, making Chile the first country in the world with a constitution drafted by an equal number of women and men from all social, cultural, and sexual orientations; it will be voted upon in 2022.

What to Watch, Read, and Listen To

RESIDENCE ON EARTH
This breakthrough work by Nobel laureate Pablo Neruda, arguably Chile's most famous literary figure, is a collection of poems that explore life in Latin America. After reading Neruda's work, visit the poet's three homes: Casa de Isla Negra on Isla Negra, La Sebastiana in Valparaíso, and and La Chascona in Santiago.

THE HOUSE OF THE SPIRITS
Isabel Allende's spiritual story of four generations of a Chilean family is filled with magic, history, and drama. It was also adapted for a 1993 movie.

DISTANT STAR
This searing short novel by Roberto Bolaño takes place in the first years of Pinochet's military dictatorship. It follows Alberto Ruiz-Tagle (aka Carlos Wieder), an air force pilot and poet who comes under fire for his provocative skywriting.

MACHUCA
A socially conscious film written and directed by Andrés Wood explores the lives of two youths from very different backgrounds right before the military coup.

THE MOLE AGENT
Nominated for best documentary at the 2021 Oscars, this moving work from director Maite Alberdi is set at a senior citizens' home and readdresses what it means to make a documentary. Also check out her 2014 award-winning film La Once ("Tea Time").

ISABEL
This HBO miniseries released in 2021 is about renowned Chilean writer Isabel Allende—at once the niece of a former president, a diplomat's daughter, and in her own right a feminist and one of the Spanish language's most important literary agents. Known for her magical realism, Allende is just as compelling on-screen as in her fiction.

CASO 63
A psychological podcast thriller recounting conversations between a psychiatrist and her enigmatic "time traveling" patient, Caso 63 has become the most listened to fictitious podcast in Latin America. Created by Julio Rojas, it has been picked up in Brazil and India, and hits the U.S. in 2022.

CHICAGO BOYS
In this 2015 documentary by journalist Carola Fuentes and director Rafael Valdeavellano, a group of economists shares how they, with the support of Augusto Pinochet in the 1970s, used Chile to conduct radical economic experiments using Milton Friedman's policies. It is essential viewing that will help all visitors understand Chile today.

UN VERDOR TERRIBLE
Shortlisted for the International Booker Prize in 2021, Benjamín Labatut's work, which translates to "A Terrible Greenness," challenges readers to think about physics and history.

COLONIA DIGNIDAD: A SINISTER SECT
The true story of Nazi German lay preacher Paul Schäfer, who migrated to Chile to found a sect backed by Augusto Pinochet in the 1960s, is told by those who lived—and survived—in this 2021 Netflix docuseries that features unseen archival material. The horrors continue to make headlines today, as Colonia Dignidad's survivors fight for compensation.

THE CHILEAN KITCHEN
Covering 75 seasonal recipes from tomato shrimp stew to the tempting dulce de leche thousand-layer cake, this 2020-published cookbook brings together Pilar Hernández's family recipes that are honed by longtime U.S. transplant and Chilean foodie Eileen Smith.

PIPEÑO, UNA MEMORIA QUE PORFÍA

One for wine lovers, this romantic documentary directed by Marcelo Gotelli (translated as "Pipeño: Memory That Prevails") casts an eye on winemaking in Itata, examining the remote region's cultures and traditions as lived by its charismatic vignerons and how they create Pipeño. It's available on YouTube with Spanish subtitles.

CIELO

Become entranced by the starry skies of the Atacama Desert in this visually stunning 2017 documentary by Alison McAlpine, called both a "cinematic reverie" and a "love poem to the night sky."

CHILEAN POET: A NOVEL

Alejandro Zambra, one of contemporary Chile's greatest authors, explores relationships and, of course, poetry in this brilliantly written novel. If you enjoy Zambra's work, also check out novels *Multiple Choice* and *Bonsai,* as well as "My Documents," a finalist for the Frank O'Connor International Short Story Award.

DESOLACIÓN

No exploration of Chilean poetry would be complete without reading the work of Gabriela Mistral, the first Latin American author to receive the Nobel Prize in literature. This moving collection of Mistral's early work from 1922 explores topics such as family and religion.

Chapter 2

TRAVEL SMART

Updated by
Mark Johanson

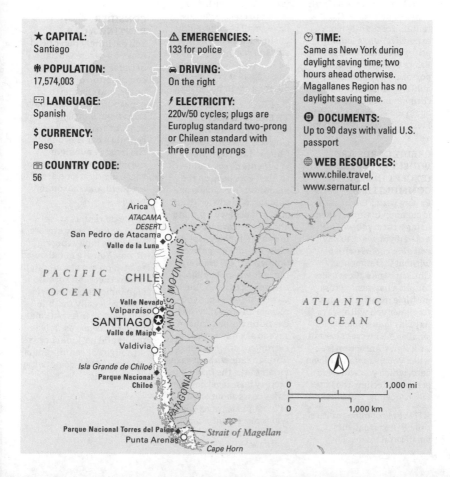

★ **CAPITAL:**
Santiago

♙ **POPULATION:**
17,574,003

🗨 **LANGUAGE:**
Spanish

$ **CURRENCY:**
Peso

☎ **COUNTRY CODE:**
56

⚠ **EMERGENCIES:**
133 for police

🚗 **DRIVING:**
On the right

⚡ **ELECTRICITY:**
220v/50 cycles; plugs are
Europlug standard two-prong
or Chilean standard with
three round prongs

🕒 **TIME:**
Same as New York during
daylight saving time; two
hours ahead otherwise.
Magallanes Region has no
daylight saving time.

🛂 **DOCUMENTS:**
Up to 90 days with valid U.S.
passport

🌐 **WEB RESOURCES:**
www.chile.travel,
www.sernatur.cl

Arica
ATACAMA
DESERT
San Pedro de Atacama
Valle de la Luna

PACIFIC
OCEAN

CHILE

ANDES MOUNTAINS

ATLANTIC
OCEAN

Valle Nevado
Valparaíso
SANTIAGO
Valle de Maipo

Valdivia

Isla Grande de Chiloé
Parque Nacional
Chiloé

PATAGONIA

0   1,000 mi

0   1,000 km

Parque Nacional Torres del Paine
Punta Arenas

Strait of Magellan

Cape Horn

Know Before You Go

Do you need to speak Spanish? Can you drink the water? Will you need to rent a car for your trip? You may have a few questions before you head out on vacation to Chile. We've got answers and a few tips to help you make the most of your visit.

CHILE IS EXPENSIVE.

Chile is among the most expensive countries in Latin America. Food costs are often on par with North America or Europe. Car rentals are slightly more expensive, while lodging prices are much cheaper. Prices of hotels and transportation go up considerably from mid-December through mid-March and again in September over the Fiestas Patrias celebrations.

CREDIT CARDS ARE WIDELY ACCEPTED (EXCEPT IN REMOTE COMMUNITIES).

Paying with a credit card is common in Chile. When using a card, you will be asked if you want to pay *con o sin cuotas* (with or without installments). Chilean banks allow users to split a payment across multiple months, but as a foreigner you will always pay *sin cuotas*. Some smaller businesses also add a foreign transaction fee when you use a non-Chilean card, which you will have to accept or decline (the latter will cancel the transaction).

ATMs are common in cities, though less frequent in small rural towns. They usually have an option for English. Fees for drawing money from a foreign card are quite high (up to US$10). When paying with cash, it is best to ensure you always have small change. Many businesses do not keep a stocked drawer and will not be able to provide you with change when you use a big bill for a small purchase.

THERE ARE WAYS TO SAVE MONEY.

One way to save is to eat Chilean fast food. Stop at a *fuente de soda* (diner) to feast for cheap on the ubiquitous empanada or a churrasco sandwich (thin strips of beef with tomatoes and mashed avocado). Or, take a tax holiday. Hotels in Chile do not charge taxes (known as IVA) to foreign tourists when they show their passport and Tourist Card (a slip of paper you receive on arrival). When checking the price, make sure to ask for the *precio extranjero, sin impuestos* (foreign rate, without taxes). Finally, take the fancy bus. Luxury bus travel between cities costs about one-third of what plane travel costs and is more comfortable, with reclining seats, movies, and snacks.

PACK YOUR BEST OUTDOOR GEAR.

Many of Chile's attractions are outdoors, so packing sturdy, all-weather gear is a good idea. Sunglasses, a hat, and sunscreen are all essential because the ozone layer over Chile is particularly deteriorated. Layers are needed throughout the year as temperatures always drop considerably at dusk. For your electronic gear, keep in mind that you will need a two-pronged plug adapter and that voltage in Chile is 220 volts, 50 cycles (220V 50Hz).

CONSIDER RENTING A CAR.

You definitely don't need to rent a car in Santiago because you can take a combination of taxis, buses, and the metro to get around town. For day trips from Santiago to the coast or wine country, renting a car is probably the most convenient option, although buses to these destinations are also frequent and reasonably priced.

If you do rent a car, be aware of one-way streets and signs indicating right of way. You are not allowed to turn on red at a stoplight unless there is a specific sign indicating otherwise. To drive legally in Chile you need an international driver's license as well as your valid national license, although car rental companies and police do not often enforce this.

DRIVING CONDITIONS VARY.

The main highways in Chile (including the Pan-American) are in excellent condition. They are kept that way because of expensive tolls: you must pay to use them, particularly in greater Santiago. Rural roads in Patagonia and on the Altiplano of the Atacama Desert are often unpaved and can be quite challenging with potholes, water crossings, and no guardrails.

In general, drivers in Chile are quite courteous and not overly aggressive. Santiago can be a bit hectic at rush hour, but elsewhere in the nation, lengthy traffic jams are uncommon.

YOU CAN DRIVE BETWEEN CHILE AND ARGENTINA.

Yes, you can drive between Chile and Argentina, but there are a few things to keep in mind. First, because it is an international border, be sure to have your passport, along with your driver's license. Also, special insurance is required.

If you rent a car, the rental company will provide you with a permit to drive into Argentina (for an extra price, of course), which includes all the necessary paperwork to cross the border (including the insurance). The permit must be requested several days in advance of the day the rental begins. The rental car must be returned in Chile, and the permit is valid for one exit to Argentina and one entrance into Chile. Common border crossings include the route from Santiago to Mendoza, Valdivia to Bariloche, and Punta Arenas to El Calafate.

U.S. CITIZENS NO LONGER HAVE TO PAY A RECIPROCITY FEE UPON ENTERING CHILE.

Formerly, all U.S. citizens entering Chile for the first time had to pay a reciprocity fee of US$161 before passing customs. Because the United States made Chile a country eligible for its U.S. Visa Waiver Program, Chile has dropped the reciprocity fee for U.S. citizens. You will receive a free stamp in your passport that allows you entry for up to 90 days.

THERE ARE SOME THINGS YOU CAN'T BRING TO CHILE.

Chile has some of the world's strictest customs regulations in order to protect its vital agriculture industry. All plant or animal products must be declared at the border; some will not be allowed into the country. This includes items made from wood, and fruits, vegetables, cheese, grains, and seeds.

BRUSH UP ON YOUR SPANISH.

It is always helpful to speak the language of the country where you are traveling, but you can likely get by in Chile without it. In Santiago, there is often at least one person who can speak English in restaurants, hotels, and shops. However, if you plan on traveling to less tourist-oriented destinations, fewer people will speak English, and you may need to resort to nonverbal means of communication or trying out those basic Spanish phrases you've learned. In general, the level of English-language comprehension in Chile is far lower than elsewhere in Latin America.

YES, YOU CAN DRINK THE WATER.

Visitors seldom encounter problems with drinking the water in Chile. Almost all drinking water receives proper treatment and is unlikely to produce health problems. But its high mineral content—it's born in the Andes—can disagree with some people. In any case, a wide selection of still (*sin gas*) and sparkling (*con gas*) bottled waters is available.

THE TIMES ARE CHANGING.

Major social and political shifts are happening in Chile today. A new constitution was formed after widespread protests in late 2019; it was the first to be drafted by an equal representation of all sexes, cultures, and social groups in Chile. A young left-wing president, Gabriel Boric, was elected in 2022 to reflect the progressive movement. Boric plans to tackle inequality and poverty.

Getting Here

Air

Traveling between the Americas is usually less tiring than traveling to Europe or Asia because you cross fewer time zones. Miami (8½ hour flight), New York (11 hours), Dallas (9½ hours), and Atlanta (9½ hours) are the primary departure points for flights to Chile from the United States, though there are also frequent flights from Los Angeles, Houston, and Toronto. Other international flights often connect through major South American cities like Buenos Aires, São Paulo, and Lima.

Citizens of the U.S., Canada, Australia, and a handful of other nations formerly had to pay hefty reciprocity fees to enter Chile. These are no longer required, and you will not have to pay anything upon arrival.

Always confirm international flights at least 72 hours ahead of the scheduled departure time. This is particularly true for travel within South America, where flights tend to operate at full capacity and passengers often have a great deal of baggage to process.

LATAM is the largest carrier in South America and is based in Chile. It offers the LATAM pass frequent flyer program, where customers can earn miles (actually, kilometers) by flying with LATAM partners like Delta Air Lines or through car rentals or hotel stays with affiliated companies.

AIRPORTS

Most international flights head to Santiago's Arturo Merino Benítez International Airport (SCL; also known as Nuevo Pudahuel Airport) about 30 minutes west of the city. Domestic flights leave from the adjacent terminal. Expect long customs queues on arrival and remember that it's prohibited to bring fresh produce (dairy, fruit, meat, jams) into Chile.

FLIGHTS

American Airlines is the North American carrier with the most flights to Chile, including direct service from Dallas, New York, and Miami; Delta flies from Atlanta. United flies from Houston. LATAM flies nonstop to Santiago from Miami, New York, and Los Angeles. Air Canada flies nonstop from Toronto. Most of the major Central and South American airlines also fly to Santiago, including Aerolíneas Argentinas, Avianca, and Copa.

LATAM, Sky, and JetSmart have daily flights from Santiago to most cities throughout Chile.

⭕ Boat

Boats and ferries are the best way to reach many places in Chile, such as Chiloé and the fjords of Patagonia. They are also a great alternative to flying when your destination is a southern port like Puerto Natales or Punta Arenas. Navimag and Transbordadora Austral Broom are the main companies operating routes in the south. Both maintain excellent websites with complete schedule and pricing information. You can buy tickets online, or book through a travel agent.

CRUISES

Several international cruise lines, including Celebrity Cruises, Holland America, Norwegian Cruise Lines, and Princess Cruises call at ports in Chile or offer cruises that start in Chile. Itineraries typically start in Valparaíso, following the coastline to the southern archipelago and its fjords. Some companies, such as Silversea Cruises, have itineraries that include Antarctica. Victory Adventure Expeditions and Aurora Expeditions are tour companies that offer cruises to Antarctica.

You can spend a week aboard the luxury *Skorpios,* which leaves from Puerto Montt and sails through the archipelago to the San Rafael glacier. In Punta Arenas, you can board *Cruceros Australis* and motor through the straights and fjords to Ushuaia and Cape Horn.

🚌 Bus

Long-distance buses are safe and affordable. Luxury bus travel between cities costs about one-third that of plane travel and is more comfortable, with wide reclining seats, movies, drinks, and snacks. The most expensive service offered by most bus companies is called *cama premium* or simply *premium,* which indicates that the seats fold down into an almost horizontal bed. Service billed as *semi-cama, ejectivo,* and *cama* are other comfortable alternatives.

Without a doubt, the low cost of bus travel is its greatest advantage; its greatest drawback is the time you need to cover the distances involved. A trip from Santiago to San Pedro de Atacama, for example, takes about 23 hours. Be sure to get a receipt for any luggage you check beneath the bus and keep a close watch on belongings you take on the bus.

Tickets are sold online, at bus company offices, and at city bus terminals. Note that in larger cities there may be several bus terminals (Santiago has three major terminals, for example), and some small towns may not have a terminal at all: pickups and drop-offs are at the bus line's office, invariably in a central location. Expect to pay with cash, as only the large bus companies such as Pullman Bus and Turbus accept credit cards.

Reservations are recommended all year round but are essential for holidays and travel during high season. You should arrive at terminals extra early for travel during peak seasons when the terminals can be packed with travelers.

Pullman Bus and Turbus are two of the best-known companies in Chile. Their websites are Spanish-only.

🚗 Car

Certain areas of Chile are most enjoyable when explored on your own in a car, such as the beaches of the Central Coast, the wineries of the Central Valley, the Atacama Desert in the north, and the Lake District in the south.

Drivers in Chile are not particularly aggressive, but neither are they particularly polite. Some common-sense rules of the road: Before you set out, establish an itinerary. Be sure to plan your daily driving distance conservatively, as distances are always longer than they appear on maps. Google maps is sufficient but not always faultless, so seek out a CHILETUR guide and map (Spanish only) from a gas station if you are heading off the radar. Bring enough change to pay tolls on highways.

Obey posted speed limits and traffic regulations, and keep your lights on during the day as well as the night. And above all, if you get a traffic ticket, don't argue—and plan to spend longer than you want settling it.

Getting Here

GASOLINE

Most service stations are operated by an attendant and accept credit cards. They are open 24 hours a day along the Pan-American Highway and in most major cities, but not in small towns and villages. Attendants will often ask you to glance at the zero reading on the gas pump to show that you are not being cheated. A small tip is expected if attendants clean your windows or check your oil level.

PARKING

You can park on the street, in parking lots, or in parking garages in Santiago and large cities in Chile. Expect to pay anywhere from 500 to 3,000 pesos approximately, depending on the length of time. For street parking, a parking attendant (either official or unofficial) will be there to direct and charge you. You should tip the unofficial parking attendants, called *cuidadores de autos*; 1,000 pesos is a reasonable tip for two to three hours.

ROAD CONDITIONS

Between May and September, roads and underpasses can flood when it rains. It can be dangerous, especially for drivers who don't know their way around. Avoid driving if it has been raining for several hours.

The Pan-American Highway runs from Arica in the far north down to Puerto Montt and Chiloé, in the Lake District. Much of it is now two-lane and bypasses most large cities. The Carretera Austral, a partially unpaved road that runs for 1,240 km (770 miles) as far as Villa O'Higgins in Patagonia, starts just south of Puerto Montt. A few stretches of the road are broken by water and are linked only by car ferries (check ferry schedules before departing as times may change or become less frequent depending on the season). Some parts of the Carretera can be washed away in heavy rain; it is wise to consult local police for details.

Many cyclists ride without lights in rural areas, so be careful when driving at night, particularly on roads without street lighting. This also applies to horse- and bull-drawn carts.

ROADSIDE EMERGENCIES

Car-rental agencies typically provide emergency assistance to clients in need. Ensure that you have the 24-hour number before leaving with your vehicle. If you are driving long distances and concerned about an accident, be sure to book with a company that maintains offices throughout the country.

RULES OF THE ROAD

Keep in mind that the speed limit is 60 kph (37 mph) in cities and 120 kph (75 mph) on highways unless otherwise posted. The police regularly enforce the speed limit, handing out tickets to speeders.

Right-hand turns are prohibited at red lights unless otherwise posted. Seat belts are mandatory in the front and back of the car, and police give on-the-spot fines for not wearing them. There is a zero tolerance alcohol policy for drivers in Chile. If the police find you with more than 0.03 milligrams of alcohol in your blood, you will be considered to be driving under the influence and arrested.

Plan to rent snow chains for driving on the road up to the ski resorts outside Santiago. Police will stop you and ask if you have them—if you don't, you will be forced to turn back.

It is obligatory to keep your headlights lit during the day and night.

CAR RENTAL

On average it costs 30,000 pesos (about US$40) a day to rent the cheapest type of car with unlimited mileage. Vehicles with automatic transmissions tend to be more luxurious and can cost twice as much as the basic rental with manual transmission. Many companies list higher rates (about 20%) for the high season (December–February). Hertz, Avis, and Budget have locations at Santiago's airport and elsewhere around the country.

To access some of Chile's more remote regions, it may be necessary to rent a four-wheel-drive vehicle, which can cost 80,000 pesos (about US$100) a day. You can often get a discounted weekly rate. The rate you are quoted usually includes basic insurance, but make sure to find out exactly what the insurance covers and to ask whether there is a deductible you will have to pay in case of an accident. You can usually pay slightly more and have no deductible. An obligatory extra that all companies charge for rentals out of or returning to Santiago is TAG, an electronic toll-collection system used in that city. This charge is currently about 5,000 pesos (about US$7) per day. If you don't want to drive yourself, consider hiring a car and driver through your hotel concierge, or make a deal with a taxi driver for some extended sightseeing at a longer-term rate.

Major international rental companies (Avis, Budget, Hertz, Europcar) operate in Chile, but local companies are sometimes a cheaper option. Rosselot, Econorent, and Chilean are reputable local companies with offices in Santiago and other cities.

To drive legally in Chile you need an international driver's license as well as your valid national license, although car rental companies and police do not often enforce this regulation. The minimum age for driving is 18, but to rent a car you have to be 22 (or 23 depending on the company).

Train

Good train service is a thing of the past in Chile, though there is still limited service from Santiago to cities south of the capital. EFE offers two daily departures between Santiago and Chillán (and points in between), with additional bus service to Concepción. Reservations can be made via the company's website or in person.

Essentials

Dining

The restaurants that we list are the cream of the crop in each price category. It is customary to tip 10% in Chile; tipping above this amount is uncommon among locals. Servers will typically ask if you'd like to include the *propina* (gratuity) and will automatically add 10% to the bill if you agree. Credit cards are widely accepted in all cities, but when visiting smaller towns and rural areas, always bring enough cash.

Chileans like to eat at least three staple meals a day. You can expect a typically light breakfast to be served between 7 am and 10 am; lunch is usually eaten between 1 pm and 3 pm; and dinner won't usually be served before 8 pm, often running till midnight. In between lunch and dinner, many Chileans will have *once,* a light fourth meal that includes tea, breads, and sweets.

Reservations are advisable but generally not necessary unless you are visiting a popular restaurant or are taking a large group.

The dress code for lunch is fairly casual, but eating out in the evening is often a special occasion. Chileans can be conservative with dress; baring a lot of flesh might attract scornful looks or meandering gazes.

🛏 Lodging

The lodgings that we list are the cream of the crop in each price category. All hotels listed have private bath unless otherwise noted. In Chile, a national rating system is used, classifying hotels on a scale of one to five stars. The rating is determined by SERNATUR, the national tourism agency, and is based on the services offered and the physical attributes of the hotel and its property. The system is somewhat perfunctory, however, and doesn't allow for true qualitative analysis.

It's always good to look at any room before accepting it. Expense is no guarantee of charm or cleanliness, and accommodations can vary dramatically within one hotel. If you ask for a double room, you'll get a room for two people, but you're not guaranteed a double mattress. If you'd like to avoid twin beds, ask for a *cama matrimonial.*

Hotels in Chile do not charge taxes (known as IVA) to foreign tourists. When checking the price, ask for the *precio extranjero, sin impuestos* (foreign rate, without taxes). If you are traveling to Chile from neighboring Peru or Bolivia, expect a significant jump in prices. Also, note that you can always ask for a *descuento* (discount) out of season or sometimes midweek during high season.

HOTELS

Chile's urban areas and resort areas have hotels that come with all of the amenities that are taken for granted in North America and Europe, such as room service, a restaurant, and a swimming pool. Elsewhere you may not have television or a phone in your room, although you will usually find them somewhere in the hotel. Rooms that have a private bath may have only a shower, and in some cases, there will be a shared bath in the hall. In all but the most upscale hotels you may be asked to leave your key at the reception desk whenever you leave.

RESIDENCIALES

Private homes with rooms for rent, *residenciales* (also called *hospedajes*) are a unique way to get to know Chile, especially if you're on a budget. (Many rooms cost less than US$30 per night.) Sometimes residenciales and hospedajes are small, with basic accommodations and not necessarily in private homes. Some will be shabby, but others can be substantially better than hotel rooms. Staying in these types of accommodations allows you to interact with locals (though they are unlikely to speak English). Contact the local tourist office for details on residenciales and hospedajes.

MOTELS

If you spot motels while road tripping in Chile—often recognizable by their signage of palm trees and neon hearts—you should think twice before heading in for the night. Motels in Chile are usually used for their pay-per-hour love pads and range from seedy and shabby to over-the-top with themed decor.

⊙ Electricity

Unlike the United States and Canada—which have a 110- to 120-volt standard—the current in Chile is 220 volts, 50 cycles alternating current (AC). The wall sockets accept plugs with two round prongs.

Consider making a small investment in a universal adapter, which has several types of plugs in one lightweight, compact unit. Most laptops and mobile phone chargers are dual voltage (i.e., they operate equally well on 110 and 220 volts) and so require only a plug adapter. These days the same is true of small appliances such as hair dryers. Always check labels and manufacturer instructions to be sure. Don't use 110-volt outlets marked "for shavers only" for high-wattage appliances such as hair dryers.

⊕ Emergencies

The numbers to call in case of emergency are the same all over Chile and work from both cell phones and landlines. Operators will generally not speak English, however; your embassy is your best bet for most emergencies.

⊕ Health

From a health standpoint, Chile is one of the safer countries in which to travel. To be on the safe side, take the normal precautions you would traveling anywhere in South America.

COVID-19 has disrupted travel since March 2020, and travelers should expect sporadic ongoing issues. Always travel with a mask in case it's required, and keep up to date on the most recent testing and vaccination guidelines for Chile.

In Santiago there are several large private clínicas, and many doctors speak at least a bit of English. In most other large cities there are one or two private clinics where you can be seen quickly. Generally, hospitales (hospitals) or postas (centers for emergency first aid) are for those receiving free or heavily subsidized treatment, and they are often crowded with long lines of patients waiting to be seen.

Altitude sickness—which causes shortness of breath, nausea, and splitting headaches—may be a problem in some areas of the North or hiking in the Andes. The best way to prevent puna is to ascend slowly and acclimate, spending at least one night at a lower altitude if possible. If symptoms persist, return to lower elevations. Over-the-counter medications to help prevent altitude sickness

Essentials

are available. If you have high blood pressure and/or a history of heart trouble, you should check with your doctor before traveling to high altitudes.

When it comes to air quality, Santiago ranks as one of the most polluted cities in the world. The reason is that the city is surrounded by two mountain ranges that keep the pollutants from cars and other sources from dissipating. The pollution is worst in winter.

What to do? First, avoid strenuous outdoor exercise and the traffic-clogged streets when air-pollution levels are high. Santiago has a wonderful subway that will whisk you to almost anywhere you want to go. Spend your days in museums and other indoor attractions. And take advantage of the city's many parks.

Visitors seldom encounter problems with drinking the water in Chile. Almost all drinking water receives proper treatment and is unlikely to produce health problems. But its high mineral content—it's born in the Andes—can disagree with some people. In any case, a wide selection of still (*sin gas*) and sparkling (*con gas*) bottled waters is available.

Food preparation is strictly regulated by the government, so outbreaks of food-borne diseases are rare. But use common sense. Don't risk restaurants where the hygiene is suspect or street vendors where the food is allowed to sit around at room temperature.

SHOTS AND MEDICATIONS

All travelers to Chile should get up-to-date COVID, tetanus, diphtheria, and measles boosters, and a hepatitis A inoculation is recommended. Children traveling to Chile should have current inoculations against mumps, rubella, and polio. Always check with your doctor before leaving.

If you have traveled to an area at risk for yellow fever transmission within five days before entering Chile, you may be asked to show proof that you have been vaccinated against the disease.

The Hanta virus, a serious respiratory disease, exists in Chile, particularly in rural areas where rats are found (long-tailed rats are the most common carriers). Pay particular attention to warnings in campgrounds, and make sure to keep camping areas as clean as possible.

According to the Centers for Disease Control and Prevention (CDC), there's some risk of food-borne diseases such as hepatitis A and typhoid. There's no risk of contracting malaria, but a very limited risk of dengue fever, another insect-borne disease, on Easter Island. Chile is one of the few South American countries free of Zika.

The best way to avoid insect-borne diseases is to prevent insect bites by wearing long pants and long-sleeve shirts and by using insect repellents with DEET. If you plan to visit remote regions or stay for more than six weeks, check with the CDC's International Travelers Hot Line.

OVER-THE-COUNTER REMEDIES

Mild cases of diarrhea may respond to Imodium (known generically as loperamide). Pepto Bismol is not available in Chile (though Maalox is), so pack some chewable tablets. Drink plenty of purified water or tea—chamomile (*manzanilla* in Spanish) is a soothing option. You will need to visit a *farmacia* (pharmacy) to purchase medications such as *aspirina* (aspirin), which are readily available.

📦 Mail

The postal system (CorreosChile) is efficient and reliable; on average, letters take about 10 days to reach the United States, Europe, Australia, and New Zealand. They will arrive sooner if you send them *prioritario* (priority) post. You can send them *certificado* (registered), in which case the recipient will need to sign for them. Vendors often sell stamps at the entrances to larger post offices, which can save you a potentially long wait in line—the stamps are valid, and selling them this way is legal. There are no mailboxes in Chile. You must mail letters from a post office or through your hotel. Post offices are open from 9 to 6 or 7 on weekdays and from 10 to 2 on Saturday.

Postage on regular letters and postcards to the United States and Europe costs around 1,000 pesos but depends on the destination and origin.

Correo Central—Santiago's main post office—is housed in the ornate Palacio de los Gobernadores, in Santiago Centro on the north side of the Plaza de Armas. It is open weekdays 9–6:30. There is a second downtown branch near the Palacio de la Moneda, as well as one in Providencia near the Manuel Montt metro stop and one near the Escuela Militar station in Las Condes.

💲 Money

Unlike in some other South American countries, U.S. dollars are rarely accepted in Chile. (The exception is larger hotels, where prices are often quoted only in dollars.) Credit cards are accepted in most resorts and in many shops and restaurants in major cities, though you should always carry some local currency

for minor expenses like taxis and tipping. Once you stray from the beaten path, you can often pay only with pesos.

Typically you will pay 2,500 pesos for a cup of coffee, 3,000 pesos for a glass of beer in a bar, 3,000 pesos for a ham sandwich, and 2,000 pesos for an average museum admission.

Prices throughout this guide are given for adults. Substantially reduced fees are almost always available for children, students, and senior citizens.

■ TIP→ **Banks never have every foreign currency on hand, and it may take as long as a week to order. If you're planning to exchange funds before leaving home, don't wait until the last minute.**

ATMS AND BANKS

Automatic teller machines, or *cajeros automáticos,* dispense only Chilean pesos and are ubiquitous. Although most have instructions in English, not all are linked to the Plus and Cirrus systems. Look at the stickers on the machine to find the one you need. Most ATMs in Chile have a special screen—accessed after entering your PIN—for foreign-account withdrawals. In this case, you need to select the "extranjeros/foreign clients" option from the menu. ATMs offer excellent exchange rates because they are based on wholesale rates offered only by major banks.

Your own bank will probably charge a fee for using ATMs abroad; the foreign bank you use will also charge a fee, which can be up to 7,000 pesos. Nevertheless, you'll usually get a better rate of exchange at an ATM than you will at a currency-exchange office or even when changing money in a bank. And extracting funds as you need them is a safer option than carrying around a large amount of cash.

Essentials

■TIP➔ PINs with more than four digits are not recognized at ATMs in Chile. If yours has five or more, remember to change it before you leave.

Banco de Chile is probably the largest national bank; its website lists branches and ATMs by location if you click on the *surcursales* (locations) link, then the *cajeros automáticos* link. Banco Santander is another fairly common option.

CREDIT CARDS

It's a good idea to inform your credit-card company before you travel, especially if you're going abroad and don't travel internationally often. Otherwise, the credit-card company might put a hold on your card owing to unusual activity—not a good thing halfway through your trip. Record all your credit-card numbers—as well as the phone numbers to call if your cards are lost or stolen—in a safe place, so you're prepared should something go wrong. Both MasterCard and Visa have general numbers you can call (collect if you're abroad) if your card is lost, but you're better off calling the number of your issuing bank, since MasterCard and Visa usually just transfer you there.

If you plan to use your credit card for cash advances, you'll need to apply for a PIN at least two weeks before your trip. Although it's usually cheaper (and safer) to use a credit card abroad for large purchases (so you can cancel payments or be reimbursed if there's a problem), note that some credit-card companies *and* the banks that issue them add substantial percentages to all foreign transactions, whether they're in a foreign currency or not. Check on these fees before leaving home, so there won't be any surprises when you get the bill.

Dynamic currency conversion programs are becoming increasingly widespread. Merchants who participate in them are supposed to ask whether you want to be charged in dollars or the local currency, but they don't always do so. And even if they do offer you a choice, they may well avoid mentioning the additional surcharges. The good news is that you *do* have a choice. And if this practice really gets your goat, you can avoid it entirely thanks to American Express; with its cards, DCC simply isn't an option.

Credit cards are widely accepted in hotels, restaurants, and shops in most cities and tourist destinations. Fewer establishments accept credit cards in rural areas. You may get a slightly better deal if you pay with cash (ask about discounts), and some businesses charge an extra fee for paying with a non-Chilean credit card.

Chile has implemented a security system for credit-card transactions called PinPass, which requires you to enter a previously established PIN in a handheld machine. As a foreigner, you should explain that you haven't activated your PinPass, and the merchants should be able to process the transaction with your signature.

Credit card receipts in Chile have a line for signatures as well as for national ID numbers, or RUTs. You may be asked to put your passport number on this second line; otherwise, you can leave it blank.

CURRENCY AND EXCHANGE

The peso is the unit of currency in Chile. Note that Chilean currency may be written as $1,000 or CLP$1,000. Chilean bills are issued in 1,000, 2,000, 5,000, 10,000, and 20,000 pesos, and coins come in units of 1, 5, 10, 50, 100, and 500 pesos. Note that getting change for larger bills, especially from small shop-keepers and taxi drivers, can be difficult. Make sure to get smaller bills when you exchange currency. Always check exchange rates in newspapers or online for the most current information; at this writing, the exchange rate was approxi-mately 800 pesos to the U.S. dollar.

Common to Santiago and other mid- to large-size cities are *casas de cambio,* or money-changing stores. Naturally, those at the airport will charge premium rates for convenience's sake. It may be more economical to change a small amount for your transfer to the city, where options are wider and rates more reasonable. Note that exchange houses will not accept damaged or overly creased dollar notes.

The U.S. State Department warns travel-ers that Chilean banks, casas de cambio, and businesses may refuse US$100 bills due to past problems with counterfeiting. Chilean banks and police officers have been trained by the U.S. Secret Service to identify counterfeit bills, but some places still won't accept them. If you plan to exchange U.S. currency, bring bills smaller than US$50.

🖰 Packing

You'll need to pack for all seasons when visiting Chile, no matter what time of year you're traveling. Outside the cities, especially in the Lake District and South-ern Chile, long-sleeve shirts, long pants, socks, sneakers, a hat, a light waterproof jacket, a bathing suit, and insect repellent are all essential. Light colors are best, since mosquitoes avoid them. If you're

visiting Patagonia or the Andes, bring a jacket and sweater or a fleece pullover. A high-factor sunscreen is essential at all times, especially in the far south where the ozone layer is much depleted.

Other useful items include a screw-top water bottle that you can fill with purified water, a money pouch, a travel flashlight and extra batteries, a medical kit, binoc-ulars, and a good day pack. A sarong or light cotton blanket can have many uses: beach towel, picnic blanket, and cushion for hard seats, among other things. You can never have too many large resealable plastic bags, which are ideal for storing food, protecting things from rain and damp, and quarantining stinky socks.

Since it's sometimes hard to get a bottle of shampoo through customs these days, an easy workaround (and load-lightener) is to buy a handful of shampoo packets (about the size of a ketchup packet) in any Chilean drug store or street market. Of course, many better hotels will provide shampoo and soap. Though Chile's bathrooms are generally well stocked with toilet paper, it's still not a bad idea to have a small packet of tissues in your pocket.

🌐 Passports and Visas

While traveling in Chile you might want to carry a copy of your passport and leave the original in your hotel safe. If you plan on paying by credit card you will often be asked to show identification (the copy of your passport or a driver's license, for example). Citizens of the United States, Canada, Australia, New Zealand, and the United Kingdom need only a passport to enter Chile for up to 90 days. Keep hold of the Tourist Card you receive on

Essentials

arrival; you'll need to hand it over when you leave. The Tourist Card is also needed to avoid the 19% hotel tax domestic tourists have to pay.

➕ Safety

The vast majority of visitors to Chile never experience a problem with crime. Violent crime is a rarity; far more common is pickpocketing or thefts from purses, backpacks, or rental cars. Be on your guard in crowded places, especially markets, bus stations, and at festivals. It's best to avoid wearing flashy jewelry and handling money in public. Always remain alert for pickpockets, and take particular caution when walking alone at night, especially in the larger cities.

Large-scale protests have become common in Chile ever since the mass social uprising of October 2019. These demonstrations can turn violent fast and are best avoided. Social unrest is also on the rise in parts of the Araucanía and Biobio Regions as indigenous Mapuche clash with farmers, forestry workers, and security forces. Check the current state of affairs before traveling to this area.

Volcano climbing is a popular pastime in Chile, with Volcán Villarrica, near Pucón, and Volcán Osorno the most popular. But some of these mountains are also among South America's most active volcanoes. CONAF, the agency in charge of national parks, cuts off access to any volcano at the slightest hint of abnormal activity. Check with CONAF before heading out on any hike in this region.

Many women travel alone or in groups in Chile with no problems. Chilean men are less aggressive in their machismo than men in other South American countries (they will seldom, for example, approach a woman they don't know), but it's still an aspect of the culture (they may make comments when a woman walks by). Single women should take caution when walking alone at night, especially in larger cities.

In the event of an earthquake in Chile, exercise common sense (don't take elevators and move away from heavy objects that may fall, for example) and follow instructions if you are in a public place (metro, museum, etc.). If you are in a coastal location, listen for tsunami sirens, or simply follow the tsunami evacuation route (indicated by signs in the streets) or head to high ground. Chile is well prepared for earthquakes and has strict building codes that ensure minimal damage.

💲 Taxes

A 19% value-added tax (called IVA in Chile) is added to the cost of most goods and services in Chile; often you won't notice because it's included in the price. When it's not, the seller gives you the price plus IVA. At many hotels you may receive an exemption from the IVA if you show your Tourist Card and pay in American dollars (or with a credit card in U.S. dollars).

⑨ Tipping

In restaurants and for tour guides, a 10% tip is usual, unless service has been deficient. Taxi drivers don't expect to be tipped. Visitors need to be wary of parking attendants. During the day, they should only charge what's on their portable meters when you collect the car, but, at night, they will ask for money—usually 1,000 pesos. This is a racket but, for your car's safety, it's better to comply.

⦿ Visitor Information

The national tourist office, Servicio Nacional de Turismo, or SERNATUR, with branches in Santiago and major tourist destinations around the country, is often the best source for general information about a region. The SERNATUR office in Santiago is open 9–6 weekdays, and 10–2 on Saturday. The hours of SERNA-TUR's regional offices vary but can be found on its website.

Municipal tourist offices, often located near a central square, usually have better information about their town's sights, restaurants, and lodging. Many have shorter hours or close altogether during low season, however. Some regional offices do not have English-speaking staff.

📅 When to Go

High Season: Across Chile, high season runs from December to March, peaking during January and February, except in Santiago, which tends to empty as most Santiaguinos take their summer holiday.

Low Season: May to September is considered the low season. The wettest months are June and July. During this time, places like Chiloé and Patagonia can feel forlorn, though the Atacama Desert is at its prime. Note that domestic travel booms, briefly, during the Fiestas Patrias celebrations in mid-September.

Value Season: The high season tapers off in March, and April is an excellent time to visit for more tranquility. November is also quiet, but colorful. Expect vast north-to-south climatic differences because Chile's distances span the equivalent of Cancún to Hudson Bay.

Helpful Phrases in Spanish

BASICS

Hello	Hola	**oh**-lah
Yes/no	Sí/no	see/no
Please	Por favor	pore fah-**vore**
May I?	¿Me permite?	may pair-**mee**-tay
Thank you	Gracias	**Grah**-see-as
You're welcome	De nada	day **nah**-dah
I'm sorry	Lo siento	lo see-**en**-toh
Good morning!	¡Buenos días!	**bway**-nohs **dee**-ahs
Good evening!	¡Buenas tardes! (after 2pm)	**bway**-nahs-**tar**-dess
	¡Buenas noches! (after 8pm)	**bway**-nahs **no**-chess
Good-bye!	¡Adiós!/¡Hasta luego!	ah-dee-**ohss/ah** -stah **lwe**-go
Mr./Mrs.	Señor/Señora	sen-**yor**/ sen-**yohr**-ah
Miss	Señorita	sen-yo-**ree**-tah
Pleased to meet you	Mucho gusto	**moo**-cho **goose**-toh
How are you?	¿Que tal?	keh-tal

NUMBERS

one	un, uno	oon, **oo**-no
two	dos	dos
three	tres	tress
four	cuatro	**kwah**-tro
five	cinco	**sink**-oh
six	seis	saice
seven	siete	see-**et**-eh
eight	ocho	**o**-cho
nine	nueve	new-**eh**-vey
ten	diez	dee-**es**
eleven	once	**ohn**-seh
twelve	doce	**doh**-seh
thirteen	trece	**treh**-seh
fourteen	catorce	ka-**tohr**-seh
fifteen	quince	**keen**-seh
sixteen	dieciséis	dee-**es**-ee-**saice**
seventeen	diecisiete	dee-**es**-ee-see-**et**-eh
eighteen	dieciocho	dee-**es**-ee-**o**-cho
nineteen	diecinueve	dee-**es**-ee-new-**ev**-eh
twenty	veinte	**vain**-teh
twenty-one	veintiuno	**vain**-te-**oo**-noh
thirty	treinta	**train**-tah
forty	cuarenta	kwah-**ren**-tah
fifty	cincuenta	seen-**kwen**-tah
sixty	sesenta	sess-**en**-tah
seventy	setenta	set-**en**-tah
eighty	ochenta	oh-**chen**-tah
ninety	noventa	no-**ven**-tah
one hundred	cien	see-**en**
one thousand	mil	meel
one million	un millón	oon meel-**yohn**

COLORS

black	negro	**neh**-groh
blue	azul	ah-**sool**
brown	marrón	mah-**ron**
green	verde	**ver**-deh
orange	naranja	na-**rahn**-hah
red	rojo	**roh**-hoh
white	blanco	**blahn**-koh
yellow	amarillo	ah-mah-**ree**-yoh

DAYS OF THE WEEK

Sunday	domingo	doe-**meen**-goh
Monday	lunes	**loo**-ness
Tuesday	martes	**mahr**-tess
Wednesday	miércoles	me-**air**-koh-less
Thursday	jueves	hoo-**ev**-ess
Friday	viernes	vee-**air**-ness
Saturday	sábado	**sah**-bah-doh

MONTHS

January	enero	eh-**neh**-roh
February	febrero	feh-**breh**-roh
March	marzo	**mahr**-soh
April	abril	ah-**breel**
May	mayo	**my**-oh
June	junio	**hoo**-nee-oh
July	julio	**hoo**-lee-yoh
August	agosto	ah-**ghost**-toh
September	septiembre	sep-tee-**em**-breh
October	octubre	oak-**too**-breh
November	noviembre	no-vee-**em**-breh
December	diciembre	dee-see-**em**-breh

USEFUL WORDS AND PHRASES

Do you speak English?	¿Habla usted inglés?	**ah**-blah oos-**ted** in-**glehs**
I don't speak Spanish.	No hablo español	no **ah**-bloh es-pahn-**yol**
I don't understand.	No entiendo	no en-tee-**en**-doh
I understand.	Entiendo	en-tee-**en**-doh
I don't know.	No sé	no **seh**
I'm American.	Soy americano (americana)	soy ah-meh-ree-**kah**-no (ah-meh-ree-**kah**-nah)
What's your name?	¿Cómo se llama ?	koh-mo seh **yah**-mah
My name is . . .	Me llamo . . .	may **yah**-moh
What time is it?	¿Qué hora es?	keh **o**-rah es
How?	¿Cómo?	**koh**-mo
When?	¿Cuándo?	**kwahn**-doh
Yesterday	Ayer	ah-**yehr**
Today	hoy	oy
Tomorrow	mañana	mahn-**yah**-nah
Tonight	Esta noche	es-tah **no**-cheh
What?	¿Qué?	keh
What is it?	¿Qué es esto?	keh es **es**-toh

English	Spanish	Pronunciation
Why?	¿Por qué?	pore **keh**
Who?	¿Quién?	kee-**yen**
Where is ...	¿Dónde está ...	dohn-deh es-**tah**
... the train station?	la estación del tren?	la es-tah-see-**on** del trehn
... the subway station?	estación de metro	la es-ta-see-**on** del **meh**-tro
... the bus stop?	la parada del autobus?	la pah-**rah**-dah del ow-toh-**boos**
... the terminal? (airport)	el aeropuerto	el air-oh-**pwar**-toh
... the post office?	la oficina de correos?	la oh-fee-**see**- nah deh koh-**rreh**-os
... the bank?	el banco?	el **bahn**-koh
... the hotel?	el hotel?	el oh-**tel**
... the museum?	el museo?	el moo-**seh**-oh
... the hospital?	el hospital?	el ohss-pee-**tal**
... the elevator?	el ascensor?	el ah-sen-**sohr**
Where are the restrooms?	el baño?	el **bahn**-yoh
Here/there	Aquí/allí	ah-**key**/ah-**yee**
Open/closed	Abierto/cerrado	ah-bee-**er**-toh/ ser-**ah**-doh
Left/right	Izquierda/derecha	iss-key-**eh**-dah/ dare-**eh**-chah
Is it near?	¿Está cerca?	es-**tah** sehr-kah
Is it far?	¿Está lejos?	es-**tah** leh-hoss
I'd like ...	Quisiera ...	kee-see-**ehr**-ah
... a room	un cuarto/una habitación	oon **kwahr**-toh/**oo**-nah ah-bee-tah-see-**on**
... the key	la llave	lah **yah**-veh
... a newspaper	un periódico	oon pehr-ee-**oh**-dee-koh
... a stamp	un sello de correo	oon **seh**-yo deh korr-**eh**-oh
I'd like to buy ...	Quisiera comprar ...	kee-see-**ehr**-ah kohm-**prahr**
... soap	jabón	hah-**bohn**
... suntan lotion	crema solar	**kreh**-mah soh-**lar**
... envelopes	sobres	**so**-brehs
... writing paper	papel	pah-**pel**
... a postcard	una tarjeta postal	**oon**-ah tar-**het**-ah post-**ahl**
... a ticket	un billete (travel)	oon bee-**yee**-teh
	una entrada (concert etc.)	**oona** en-**trah**-dah
How much is it?	¿Cuánto cuesta?	**kwahn**-toh **kwes**-tah
It's expensive/ cheap	Es caro/barato	es **kah**-roh/ bah-**rah**-toh
A little/a lot	Un poquito/mucho	oon poh-**kee**-toh/ **moo**-choh
More/less	Más/menos	**mahss**/**men**-ohss
Enough/too (much)	Suficiente/	soo-fee-see-**en**-teh/
I am ill/sick	Estoy enfermo(a)	es-**toy** en-**fehr**-moh(mah)
Call a doctor	Llame a un medico	**ya**-meh ah oon **med**-ee-koh

English	Spanish	Pronunciation
Help!	Socorro	soh-**koh**-roh
Stop!	Pare	**pah**-reh
DINING OUT		
I'd like to reserve a table ...	Quisiera reservar una mesa ...	kee-**syeh**-rah rreh-sehr-**bahr** oo-nah **meh**-sah ...
... for two people.	para dos personas.	**pah**-rah dohs pehr-**soh**-nahs
... for this evening.	para esta noche.	**pah**-rah **ehs**-tah **noh**-cheh
... for 8 PM	para las ocho de la noche.	**pah**-rah lahs **oh**-choh deh lah **noh**-cheh
A bottle of ...	Una botella de ...	**oo**-nah bo-**teh**-yah deh
A cup of ...	Una taza de ...	**oo**-nah **tah**-sah deh
A glass of ...	Un vaso (water, soda, etc.) de...	oon **vah**-so deh
	Una copa (wine, spirits, etc.) de...	**oona coh**-pah deh
Bill/check	La cuenta	lah **kwen**-tah
Bread	El pan	el pahn
Breakfast	El desayuno	el deh-sah-**yoon**-oh
Butter	La mantequilla	lah man-teh-**kee**-yah
Coffee	Café	kah-**feh**
Dinner	La cena	lah **seh**-nah
Fork	El tenedor	el ten-eh-**dor**
I don't eat meat	No como carne	noh koh-moh **kahr**-neh
I cannot eat ...	No puedo comer ...	noh **pweh**-doh koh-**mehr**
I'd like to order ...	Quiero pedir ...	**kee**-yehr-oh peh-**deer**
I'd like ...	Me gustaría ...	Meh goo-stah-**ee**-ah
I'm hungry/thirsty	Tengo hambre/sed	**Tehn**-goh **hahm**-breh/seth
Is service/the tip included?	¿Está incluida la propina?	es-**tah** in-cloo-**ee**-dah lah pro-**pee**-nah
Knife	El cuchillo	el koo-**chee**-yo
Lunch	La comida	lah koh-**mee**-dah
Menu	La carta, el menú	lah **cart**-ah, el meh-**noo**
Napkin	La servilleta	lah sehr-vee-**yet**-ah
Pepper	La pimienta	lah pee-mee-**en**-tah
Plate	plato	**plah**-toh
Please give me ...	Por favor déme ...	pore fah-**vor deh**-meh
Salt	La sal	lah sahl
Spoon	Una cuchara	**oo**-nah koo-**chah**-rah
Sugar	El ázucar	el ah-**su**-kar
Tea	té	teh
Water	agua	**ah**-gwah
Wine	vino	**vee**-noh

Great Itineraries

The City, the Beach, and the Desert in 10 Days

DAYS 1–3: SANTIAGO

No matter where you fly from, you'll likely arrive in Chile's capital early in the morning. Unless you can sleep the entire night on a plane and arrive refreshed at your destination, reward yourself with a couple of hours' shut-eye at your hotel before setting out to explore the city.

The neighborhoods, small and large, that make up Santiago warrant at least a day and a half of exploration. A trip up one of the city's hills—like **Cerro San Cristóbal** in Parque Metropolitano or **Cerro Santa Lucía**—lets you survey the capital and its grid of streets. Any tour of a city begins with its historic center; the cathedral and commercial office towers on the **Plaza de Armas** reflect Santiago's old and new architecture, while the nearby bohemian quarter of **Bellavista,** with its bustling markets and colorful shops, was built for walking. But Santiago's zippy, efficient metro can also whisk you to most places in the city and lets you cover ground more quickly. Avoid taking the metro during the morning and evening rush hour when trains fill well beyond capacity.

If you're here in the winter, gloomy smog can hang over the city for days at a time. Your first instinct may be to flee, and one of the nearby wineries in the **Valle de Maipo** will welcome you heartily. If it's winter and you brought your skis, **Valle Nevado,** Chile's largest downhill resort area, lies a scant 65 km (40 miles) outside Santiago.

DAYS 4–6: VALPARAÍSO AND THE CENTRAL COAST

A 90-minute drive west from Santiago takes you to the Central Coast. You'll be confronted with one of Chilean tourism's classic choices: Valparaíso or Viña del Mar. If you fancy yourself one of the glitterati, go for Viña and its chic cafés and restaurants and miles of beach. But "Valpo" offers you the charm and allure of a port city, rolling hills, and cobblestone streets with better views of the sea.

Here's a solution: Why not do them both? Only 10 km (6 miles) separate the two cities, and it's easy to travel between them, whether by taxi or the regional light rail system. Besides, they offer their own distinct charms.

Spend the first day in **Valparaíso,** where you can ride the funiculars up the city's many hills, wander through streets lined with brightly painted houses, and feast on some of the country's freshest seafood near the port. Don't miss a visit to **La Sebastiana,** one of Pablo Neruda's houses. The poet's bedroom window offers one of the best panoramic views of Valparaíso that you'll encounter.

The following day, make your way to **Viña del Mar** and prepare to soak in the rays. Some of the best and most glamorous beaches in the country can be found here. When you've had enough sun, you can stroll through the numerous shopping galleries in downtown Viña.

Round out your visit the following day with a trip to the charming coastal town of **Isla Negra,** 90 km (56 miles) south of Valparaíso. The unmistakable highlight is another of Pablo Neruda's houses, easily the best of his three residences. It's chock-full of artifacts and curios from his many travels and overlooks a rough part of the Pacific Ocean. Head back to Santiago at night in preparation for the next leg of the journey.

DAYS 7–10: SAN PEDRO DE ATACAMA

You certainly *could* drive the nearly 1,500 km (900 miles) to Chile's vast El Norte Grande, but a flight from Santiago to **Calama,** then a quick overland drive to **San Pedro de Atacama** will take you no more than 3½ hours. This is one of the most-visited towns in Chile, and for good reason: it sits right in the middle of the Atacama Desert, with sights all around.

You'll need at least two days here to do justice to the alpine lakes, ancient fortresses, vast salt flats, and surreal landscapes dotted with snow-capped volcanoes. Your best bet is to find a reputable tour agency in San Pedro—and there are many—and make at least two day trips: one to the **Geysers del Tatio,** which requires a pickup around 4 in the morning; and one to the **Reserva Nacional Los Flamencos,** where you can watch flamingos fly over jagged salt flats and cobalt lakes.

Just remember that you'll be in a high-altitude zone, so it's best to take it easy during your first day here, wandering through the charming town and popping into the numerous gift shops. Don't miss the stunning sunsets over the nearby **Valle de la Luna**.

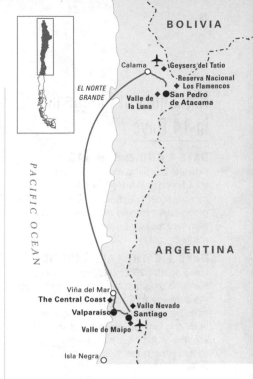

TRANSPORTATION

It's quite easy, and even preferable, to explore Santiago, Viña del Mar, and Valparaíso using public transportation, and a car is not needed in San Pedro de Atacama if you use tour agencies. Once in San Pedro de Atacama, you can hook up with various tour agencies to visit sights not accessible by bus. There are frequent flights from Santiago to Calama and back.

Highlights of Patagonia in 14 Days

DAYS 1 AND 2: SANTIAGO

Arrive in Santiago early the morning of your first day. After a brief rest, set out to explore the city's museums, shops, and green spaces using the power of your own two feet and the capital's efficient metro.

DAYS 3–6: THE LAKE DISTRICT

Head south 675 km (420 miles) from Santiago on a fast toll highway to **Temuco,** the gateway to Chile's Lake District, or even better, take one of the frequent hour-long flights. Temuco and environs are one of the best places in the region to learn about the indigenous Mapuche culture.

About an hour south, and just 15 minutes apart on the shores of **Lago Villarrica,** lie the twin resort towns of **Pucón** (more high-end) and **Villarrica** (more low-key). Base yourself in the latter if you're in peso-saving mode. Drive south through the region from the graceful old city of **Valdivia** to **Puerto Montt,** stopping at the various resort towns along the way. Frutillar, Puerto Octay, and Puerto Varas still bear testament to the Lake District's German-Austrian-Swiss immigrant history. Be sure to make time for one of the region's many hot springs.

DAYS 7–9: CHILOÉ

From Puerto Montt, drive or take a bus 65 kilometers (40 miles) southeast toward Pargua and catch the ferry to Chiloé. Base yourself in **Castro,** the capital, which allows for easy side trips through the island. Take a full day to photograph the rows of multicolor homes on stilts, called *palafitos,* in Castro, and then visit the UNESCO World Heritage–listed churches in surrounding towns.

For those seeking to get away from it all, set out for a day hike in **Parque Nacional Chiloé,** with its heavily forested trails and dramatic lookout points. Roughly 29 km (18 miles) southwest of the town of Ancud, you can visit **Puñihuil** and its colony of Humboldt and Magellanic penguins. Don't forget to dine on the island's famous *curanto* (a traditional seafood and meat dish) at night.

DAYS 10–14: PARQUE NACIONAL TORRES DEL PAINE

After taking a return ferry and bus ride back to Puerto Montt, take a spectacular morning flight over the Andes to the Patagonian city of **Punta Arenas.** On the next day take a bus north to **Puerto Natales,** gateway to the **Parque Nacional Torres del Paine.** You'll need at least two days to wander through the wonders of the park. On your final day, head back to Punta Arenas, stopping en route at one of the penguin sanctuaries, and catch an afternoon flight to Santiago.

The Ultimate Chilean Wine Trip in 6 Days

DAYS 1 AND 2: SANTIAGO AND THE MAIPO VALLEY

Start your oenophile adventure in the capital city of **Santiago**; some of Chile's best wineries are only a cork's throw away in the **Maipo Valley**. Look for bilingual tour availability and accessibility to public transit. The most fun time of year to visit is during the February to March harvest season, as many festivals and celebrations are held with unique opportunities to participate.

Book your winery tours at least 24 hours ahead to ensure the availability of an English-speaking guide. Private, personalized tours may be available depending on the establishment. Our top recommendations include **Viña Undurraga**, started and run by the same family since 1885; **Viña Concha y Toro**, Chile's largest wine producer and perhaps its most entertaining winery tour, with a visit to the Casillero del Diablo, the famed wine cellar where the devil supposedly dwells; and **Viña Santa Rita**, with an impressive on-site museum and Pompeiian-style manor.

DAYS 3 AND 4: CASABLANCA VALLEY

From Santiago, it's a mere 45-minute drive to the **Casablanca Valley**. Just three decades ago, the land here was considered inhospitable for vineyards, but now winemakers have discovered that the valley's proximity to the sea is its main asset, because cooler temperatures give the grapes more time to develop flavor as they ripen.

The three can't-miss vineyards in this area are **Casas del Bosque**, which offers a vineyard tour in an old wagon; **Viña Matetic**, whose stunning bodega resembles a bunker worthy of a James Bond villain; and **Emiliana Organic Vineyards**, the world's largest organic winery, where alpacas "mow" the impeccable grounds.

If you grow tired of vineyard-hopping, make your way to **Viña del Mar**, a mere 30 kilometers (18.6 miles) away from the heart of the valley. It's a great place to spend the night while exploring Casablanca Valley. You can walk along the beach in the morning and then indulge in the vibrant nightlife when you've returned in the evening.

DAYS 5 AND 6: COLCHAGUA VALLEY

From Santiago, drive 90 minutes south to the **Colchagua Valley**. Stay overnight at an inn or B&B in **Santa Cruz**, the main town of the valley, with an attractive central square and several craft shops. There are numerous vineyards to visit throughout this valley, but one of the better ones to start with is **Viña Montes**. It's known for its deep reds, crisp whites, and feng shui design principles. Nearby, **Viña Lapostolle-Clos Apalta** is housed in one of the most handsome pieces of architecture in Chile: barrel-stave-shape beams rise above the vineyards, creating a wooden nest for the winery, which is built into a hillside to facilitate the gravity-flow process.

Be sure to make time to visit **Viña Santa Cruz**, which is really an entire wine complex. It features a cable car, astronomical center, and indigenous museum. Plan to spend several hours here.

TRANSPORTATION

Most organized tours are offered as either half- or full-day, and include guides as well as meals. If you prefer the independence of a self-guided tour, rent a vehicle in Santiago. From Santiago to Casablanca, take a public bus and then taxi from the terminal to the wineries.

On the Calendar

January

Santiago a Mil International Theater Festival. One of the largest performing arts festivals in Latin America, Santiago a Mil fills the Chilean capital with music, dance, theater, opera, ballet, and circus for three weeks each January. Many performances are free and take place in parks and plazas across the city. www.teatroamil.cl

El Festival del Huaso de Olmué. Folk music takes center stage at this traditional mid-January festival held in the small city of Olmué, about an hour east of Valparaíso. Encompassing four days of *cueca* dancing, folk singing, and poncho flaunting, the event is also broadcast live on TV across Chile. ⊕ www.festivaldelhuaso.cl

February

Festival Internacional de la Canción in Viña del Mar. Chile's equivalent of Eurovision, this annual event is one of Latin America's most important music festivals, launching the careers of celebrities like Shakira and Sofía Vergara (a former host). ⊕ www.festivaldevinachile.cl

Carnaval Andino con la Fuerza del Sol in Arica. Chile's northernmost city hosts the nation's largest carnival celebration, which draws many indigenous Aymara down from their Andean homes. ⊕ www.aricafuerzadelsol.cl

Tapati Rapa Nui. This annual festival is a two-week celebration of Easter Island's Polynesian heritage. Rooms on the island often sell out weeks in advance.

La Semana Valdiviana in Valdivia. Brightly lit boats take to the Calle-Calle River in a floating parade through this southern university town. There is also a craft fair, beauty contest, and large fireworks display. www.nochevaldiviana.cl

March

Fiesta De La Vendimia De Colchagua. Chile's most important wine region celebrates harvest season over a long weekend in early March with food, music, and plenty of vino. ⊕ www.colchaguavalley.cl

April

Campeonato Nacional de Rodeo in Rancagua. Rodeo season culminates with this championship event in Rancagua, where *huasos* (cowboys) dress up and often end the day stomping *cueca* (a local folk dance). ⊕ www.caballoyrodeo.cl

May

Día de las Glorias Navales. The Day of Naval Glories (May 21) commemorates the Battle of Iquique, a turning point in the War of the Pacific, which pitted Chile against Peru and Bolivia (both of whom ultimately lost large swaths of the Atacama Desert as a result). The holiday is celebrated throughout Chile with military parades, speeches, and sporting events, including boat races.

June

We Tripantu (the Mapuche New Year).
We Tripantu coincides with the winter solstice in the Southern Hemisphere and is a time of gathering for Chile's largest indigenous community. Celebrated in Temuco, Santiago, and other areas with large Mapuche communities, it typically involves songs, dances (like the *purrún* and the *mazatún*), a communal meal, and offerings to the land.

July

Fiesta de La Tirana. The tiny town of La Tirana in Chile's northern Tarapacá region hosts the country's most important folklore festival with lavish parades, colorful outfits, and plenty of devil masks. *www. fiestadelatirana.cl*

August

Santiago International Film Festival (SANFIC). One of the most prestigious film festivals in South America, the week-long SANFIC has helped put Chilean cinema on the map by displaying the works of local auteurs alongside top international talent. ⊕ www.sanfic.com

September

Fiestas Patrias. On September 18, Chileans all over the country celebrate their independence day with traditional activities and food. Large *fondas* (street fairs) take place in regional parks and plazas in the week leading up to the date.

November

Festival Puerto de Ideas. This week-long festival draws artists, scientists, writers, and other big thinkers to Valparaíso for a program filled with workshops, panel discussions, cultural exhibitions, and musical performances.⊕ www.puerto-deideas.cl

December

Año Nuevo. The neighboring cities of Valparaíso and Viña del Mar fill to the brim as tourists from near and far flock to the coast for Chile's largest New Year's Eve celebration. The extravagant fireworks display can be seen as far north as Reñaca and Concón.

Contacts

Air

AIRPORT Arturo Merino Benítez International Airport. ✉ *Pudahuel, Pudahuel* ☎ *2/2690–1796* ⊕ *www. nuevopudahuel.cl.*

AIRLINES Aerolíneas Argentinas. ☎ *800/333–0276 in North America, 2/2210–9300 in Chile* ⊕ *www.aerolineas.com.ar.* **American Airlines.** ☎ *800/433–7300 in North America, 2/2938–1417 in Chile* ⊕ *www.aa.com.* **Avianca.** ☎ *800/284–2622 in North America, 2/3322–5802 in Chile* ⊕ *www.avianca.com.* **Copa.** ☎ *800/359–2672 in North America, 2/2573–9318 in Chile* ⊕ *www. copaair.com.* **Delta Air Lines.** ☎ *800/221–1212 for U.S. reservations, 800/241–4141 for international reservations, 800/202–020 in Chile* ⊕ *www.delta.com.* **LATAM.** ☎ *866/435–9526 in U.S., 600/526–2000 in Chile* ⊕ *www.latam.com.* **Sky.** ☎ *600/600–2828 in Chile* ⊕ *www.skyairline. com.* **JetSmart.** ☎ *600/600–1311 in Chile* ⊕ *www. jetsmart.com.*

⭕ Boat

Navimag. ☎ *2/2411–2600 in Santiago* ⊕ *www.navimag.com.* **Transbordadora Austral Broom.** ☎ *61/272–8100* ⊕ *www.tabsa.cl.*

INTERNATIONAL CRUISE LINES Celebrity Cruises. ☎ *888/751–7804* ⊕ *www. celebritycruises.com.* **Norwegian Cruise Line.** ☎ *866/234–7350* ⊕ *www. ncl.com.* **Princess Cruises.** ☎ *800/774–6237* ⊕ *www. princess.com.* **Victory Adventure Expeditions.** ☎ *9/8836–7614 in Chile* ⊕ *www.victory-cruises. com.*

CHILEAN CRUISE LINES Cruceros Australis. ☎ *800/743–0119 in North America, 2/2797–1000 in Chile* ⊕ *www.australis. com.* **Skorpios.** ☎ *305/285–8416 in U.S., 2/2477–1900 in Chile* ⊕ *www.skorpios. cl.*

Bus

Pullman Bus. ☎ *600/600–0018* ⊕ *www.pullmanbus. cl.* **Turbus.** ☎ *600/660–6600* ⊕ *www.turbus.cl.*

🚗 Car

MAJOR RENTAL AGENCIES Avis. ☎ *800/352–7900 in U.S., 2/2795–3900 in Chile* ⊕ *www.avis.com.* **Budget.** ☎ *800/214–6094 in U.S., 2/2795–3974 in Chile* ⊕ *www.budget.com.* **Hertz.** ☎ *800/654–3131 in U.S., 2/2601–0477 in Chile* ⊕ *www.hertz.com.* **Europcar.** ✉ *Aeropuerto*

Balmaceda and Errázuriz 454, Coyhaique ☎ *67/267–8640* ⊕ *www.europcar.cl.*

LOCAL AGENCIES Econorent. ☎ *2/2299–7100* ⊕ *www.econorent.cl.* **Chilean Rent-a-Car.** ✉ *Bellavista 0183, Bellavista* ☎ *2/2963–8760* ⊕ *www. chileanrentacar.cl.* **Rosselot.** ✉ *Comodoro Arturo Merino Benítez International Airport, Santiago* ☎ *9/6207–1468* ⊕ *www. rosselot.cl.*

🇺🇸 U.S. Embassy

United States. ✉ *Av. Andrés Bello 2800, Las Condes* ☎ *2/2330–3000* ⊕ *cl. usembassy.gov.*

➕ Emergencies

Ambulance. ☎ *131.* **Fire.** ☎ *132.* **Police.** ☎ *133.*

📍 Visitor Information

SERNATUR. ☎ *2/2731–8336* ⊕ *www.sernatur.cl.*

Chapter 3

SANTIAGO

Updated by
Sorrel Moseley-Williams

⊙ Sights	🍽 Restaurants	🛏 Hotels	👜 Shopping	🍸 Nightlife
★★★★★	★★★★★	★★★★☆	★★★★☆	★★★★☆

WELCOME TO SANTIAGO

TOP REASONS TO GO

★ **The Andes:** Towering, jagged peaks over 4,572 meters (15,000 feet) high keep you oriented in Santiago, where "uptown" is always due east, toward the mountains.

★ **Great crafts markets:** Fine woolen items, lapis lazuli jewelry, carved wooden and terra-cotta bowls, and other handicrafts from the length of the country are bountiful in Santiago.

★ **Vibrant food scene:** Never considered a gourmet destination, change is afoot in Santiago. Restaurants showcase some of Chile's finest agricultural products with innovative and traditional preparations, and many local ingredients are now given reputable "Denomination of Origin" status.

★ **World-class wineries:** Santiago is in the Maipo Valley, the country's oldest wine-growing area, home to some of Chile's largest and most traditional wineries. Concha y Toro and Santa Rita are within an hour's drive of the city, as is the lovely Casablanca Valley.

1 Santiago Centro. The areas around La Moneda presidential palace and the Plaza de Armas are where you find most of the monuments and museums as well as innovative spaces such as Centro Cultural La Moneda.

2 La Alameda. Also known as Avenida Libertador Bernardo O'Higgins, La Alameda marks the southern boundary of Santiago Centro and is lined with sights like the San Francisco church, the Universidad de Chile, and Gabriela Mistral Cultural Center.

3 Bellas Artes and Lastarria. Bellas Artes houses a cluster of restaurants, stores, and two art museums. Given its proximity to Parque Forestal, there is always a throng of people out and about. Lastarria, named after the area's famed cobblestone street, has now become a focal point for foodies.

4 Parque Forestal. A leafy park along the banks of the Río Mapocho gives this tranquil district its name. It's a prime spot for luxury and boutique hotels. Families and sporty types make the most of the green space on weekends.

5 Bellavista and Parque Metropolitano. On the north side of the Río Mapocho, Bellavista is a bohemian district of cafés, small restaurants, shops, and one of the homes of poet Pablo Neruda.

6 Parque Quinta Normal Area. Slightly off the beaten track in western Santiago, the Quinta Normal is one of the largest parks in the city and home to four museums, including one featuring old locomotives.

7 Vitacura. Well-heeled Vitacura is home to swanky restaurants, highrises, and posh boutiques.

8 Las Condes. This business area, specifically Isidora Goyenechea street, has upscale eateries, boutiques, and a few high-end hotels.

9 Providencia. This is where most tourists go out at night. It's slightly less historical than the center and is divided into smaller neighborhoods linked by a metro station.

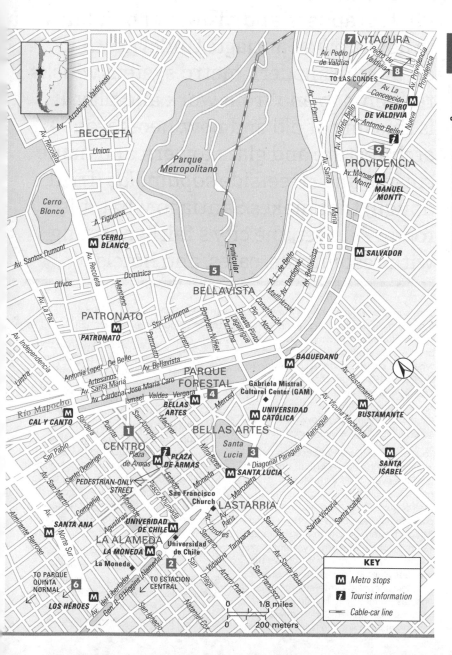

RECOLETA

Union

Av. Arzobispo Valdivieso

Av. Recoleta

Cerro
Blonco

Av. Santos Dumont

Av. Recoleta

Av. La Paz

A. Figueroa

CERRO
BLANCO

Dominica

Olivos

Menarao

Parque
Metropolitano

Av. El Cerro

VITACURA

Av. Pedro
de Valdiva

TO LAS CONDES

Av. La
Concepción

PEDRO
DE VALDIVIA

Av. Andrés Bello

Av. Antonio Bellet

Pedro de
Valdivia

Av. Providencia

Providencia

Nueva

PROVIDENCIA

Av. Manuel
Montt

MANUEL
MONTT

Av. Santa

María

SALVADOR

Funicular

A. L. de Bello

Av. Dardignac

Matilinkraut

Av. Bellavista

BELLAVISTA

Constitución

Pío Nono

Ernesto Pinto
Lagarrigue

Purísima

PATRONATO

Av. Independencia

Lastra

PATRONATO

Sta. Filomena

Antonia Lopez – De Bello

Artesanos
Av. Santa María

Patronato

Loreto

Bombero Núñez

Av. Bellavista

Río Mapocho

CAL Y CANTO

Av. Cardenal José María Caro

Ismael

Valdés

Vergara

PARQUE
FORESTAL

BELLAS
ARTES

Merced

Gabriela Mistral
Cultural Center (GAM)

BAQUEDANO

Av. Vicuña Mackenna

Av. Bustamante

Av. Santa

BUSTAMANTE

UNIVERSIDAD
CATÓLICA

San Antonio

Mosquero

Puente

Bandera

San Pablo

San Domingo

San Martín

Almirante Barroso

SANTA ANA

Av.

Compañía

Agustinas

UNIVERDIAD
DE CHILE

LA ALAMEDA

LA MONEDA

La Moneda

CENTRO

Plaza
de Armas

PLAZA
DE ARMAS

PEDESTRIAN-ONLY
STREET

Paseo Ahumada

Estado

San Francisco
Church

Universidad
de Chile

Miraflores

Moneda

Av. Andrés

Serrano

Av. Paris

LASTARRIA

BELLAS ARTES

Santa
Lucía

Diagonal Paraguay

SANTA LUCIA

Marcoleta

Vidaurre

Tarapaca

San Diego

Av. del Libertador
Gen'l. B. O'Higgins/ Alameda

TO PARQUE
QUINTA
NORMAL

LOS HÉROES

TO ESTACIÓN
CENTRAL

Nataniel Cox

San Isidoro

Arturo Prat

Santa Victoria

Santa Isabel

San Francisco

Santa Rosa

Lira

Rancagua

SANTA
ISABEL

Norte Sur

KEY	
M	Metro stops
i	Tourist information
--	Cable-car line

0 ___ 1/8 miles
0 ___ 200 meters

Plazas, parks, and fountains share space with street performers, urban photographers, and historical buildings in downtown Santiago. Underneath it all, an ultramodern metro system whisks residents to and from work and play. It is this mix of old and new, neo-baroque architecture and glass towers, and haute cuisine and streetside *sopaipillas* (fried dough) that makes Santiago what it is today. All over, the city's fairly bursting with restaurants, cafés, and hotels.

Santiago has come a long way from the triangular patch of land hemmed in by the Río Mapocho (which has since been rerouted and has only one branch), when the city was founded by Pedro de Valdivia in 1541. Today the area of the original municipality is known as Santiago Centro and is just one of 32 *comunas* (districts)—each with its own distinct personality—that make up the city.

You'd never confuse Patronato (in Recoleta), a neighborhood north of downtown (and the river), filled with Moorish-style mansions built by families who made their fortunes in textiles and currently a place to buy inexpensive clothing and eat Middle Eastern or Korean food, with Las Condes, where modern skyscrapers built by international corporations crowd the avenues along with brand-name shops. The chic shopping centers of Providencia and Las Condes have little in common with the beer garden–style sidewalk restaurants that line Pío Nono, the main street in Bellavista, nor the crafts fair to the left side of the Pío Nono Bridge.

In the city, the comuna names rule conversation and can make or break friendships. The most moneyed semi-central districts like Las Condes, Vitacura, and to a lesser extent, Providencia and Ñuñoa are considered part of the *barrio alto* (literally "high neighborhood, referring to both topography and social strata). It's considered more bohemian to live and spend time in Santiago Centro, particularly the neighborhoods of Lastarria, Barrio Bellavista, Bellas Artes, near Parque Forestal, or even down in Barrio Brasil, where some of the city's oldest architecture is found.

That is not to say that well-heeled Santiaguinos do not spend time downtown. Santiago Centro is central to many businesses, and all the bank branches and government architecture are here, including the stock market (though trading is mostly done online now). It's also home to several arts and performance spaces including the Universidad de Chile Theater, Municipal Theater, and the Gabriela Mistral Cultural Center.

Parks are a major meeting point for friends and families in the city, including Parque Quinta Normal (at the metro of the same name), Parque O'Higgins, where the military parade is held every year for Fiestas Patrias, Parque Forestal, and Parque Metropolitano, commonly referred to as Cerro San Cristobal, the larger of the two hills that overlooks the city. Farther uptown in Vitacura, Parque Bicentenario, with its waterfowl feeding ponds and dog park, attracts families with children. In most city parks you can find people playing *fútbol*, riding bikes, or just enjoying the green space as a retreat from what can be a busy city.

And it is busy. Santiago and its metropolitan region today are home to 8 million people—well over a third of the country's total population. The city continues to spread outward to the barrios altos east of the center, and all over the city there are cranes, signaling the rise of new office and apartment buildings. The tallest building in Santiago and in South America—making it a good orientation landmark—is the nearly 1,000-foot-tall Costanera Center, steps from the Tobalaba metro station and home to a flashy, upscale mall, which some consider a shrine to Chilean consumerism.

Yet residents are just as likely to run into each other at the supermarket, Vega, weekend fruit and vegetable markets called *ferias,* or in the neighborhood plaza. When they do, they stop to greet each other and talk for at least a minute or two, because even though at times it's a hectic city, in many ways Santiago is just a giant small town at heart.

Planning
When to Go

Santiaguinos tend to abandon their city every summer during the school holidays that run from the end of December to early March. February is a particularly popular vacation time, when seemingly everyone is out of town. If you're not averse to the heat, this can be a good time for walking around the city; otherwise, spring and fall are better choices, as the weather is more comfortable. Santiago is at its prettiest in spring, when gentle breezes sweep in to clean the city's air of winter smog and when the violet-hued jacaranda and the yellow-blooming *aromo* (a type of acacia) begin to flower.

Spring and fall are also good times to drive up through the Cajón del Maipo, when the scenery is at its peak. In spring, the plum and cherry trees are in bloom, and in fall, you get some foliage change, and maybe an early snow. Also in fall, the vineyards around the city celebrate *vendimia*—the grape harvest—with colorful festivals that are an opportunity to try traditional Chilean cuisine as well as some of the country's renowned wines. Winters in the city aren't especially cold—temperatures rarely dip below freezing—but days can be gray and gloomy, and air pollution is at its worst, making it a good time to head to the coast or mountains.

Planning Your Time

Santiago is a compact city, small enough to visit all the must-see sights in a few days. Consider the weather when planning your itinerary—on the first clear day your destination should be Parque Metropolitano, where you are treated to exquisite views from Cerro San Cristóbal. After a morning gazing at the Andes, head back down the hill and spend the afternoon wandering the bohemian streets of Bellavista, with a visit to Nobel laureate Pablo Neruda's Santiago residence, La Chascona. Check out one of the neighborhood's colorful eateries, or take a side trip down to Patronato for a falafel or some cheap clothes shopping.

The next day, head to Parque Forestal, a leafy park that runs along the Río Mapocho. Be sure to visit the lovely old train station, Estación Mapocho. After lunch at the Mercado Central, or across the river at Vega or Vega Chica, cover the city's colonial past in Santiago Centro. Requisite sights include the Plaza de Armas, where the cathedral and old post office are, and the nearby Museo Chileno de Arte Precolombino. Stop for coffee or tea in Lastarria or Bellas Artes and do some wandering in Plaza Mulato Gil de Castro and the connected Lastarria or Bellas Artes neighborhoods, ending at the culture and arts center GAM. On your third day explore the sights along La Alameda, especially the presidential palace of La Moneda and the landmark church, Iglesia San Francisco. For a last look at the city, climb Cerro Santa Lucía. That night go for dinner and drinks in trendy Las Condes or more upscale Vitacura.

Getting Here and Around

AIR

Santiago's Comodoro Arturo Merino Benítez International Airport is about a 30-minute drive west of the city. An official taxi or private transfer from the airport to Centro is about 20,000 pesos (slightly more to Providencia and Las Condes); get tickets from the counters before entering the arrivals hall. A shared transfer (which departs when there are enough passengers) costs about 7,000 pesos; get this also from the counters. The cheapest option is to take one of two buses—Turbus or Centropuerto—that depart from the airport to Pajaritos and

Los Héroes metro stations (Los Héroes is more centrally located), for about 1,500 pesos one way, per person, or 2,800 pesos round-trip. These buses leave from the departures terminal.

AIRPORT CONTACT Comodoro Arturo Merino Benítez International Airport. ⊠ *Av., Armando Cortínez Norte, Pudahuel* ☎ *2/2690–1796* ⊕ *www.nuevopudahuel.cl.*

AIRPORT TRANSFERS CentroPuerto. ☎ *2/2601–9883* ⊕ *www.centropuerto. cl.* **Taxi Oficial.** ☎ *2/1601–9880.* **Transvip.** ☎ *2/2677–3000* ⊕ *www.transvip.cl.*

BUS

Buses are relatively efficient and clean, although very crowded at peak times. Fares on the subway and buses are paid using the same prepaid smart card (most easily acquired in subway stations), called a BIP (say: BEEP). The BIP card (*la tarjeta bip!*) itself costs 3,000 pesos. You can also buy single-use tickets for the metro, but not for the bus. Fares vary from 640 to 800 pesos, depending on the time of day, and transfers taken (one free transfer from bus to bus; one paid transfer from bus to metro within 120 minutes). At night, most tourists stick to the subway for simplicity's sake; however, if you do not have enough money on your BIP card, you can use the bus at night in an emergency by showing your BIP card.

BUS DEPOTS Terminal Alameda. ⊠ *La Alameda 3750, Estación Central* ☎ *2/2822–7500.* **Terminal Los Héroes.** ⊠ *Tucapel Jiménez 21, Santiago Centro* ☎ *2/2420–0009.* **Terminal San Borja.** ⊠ *San Borja 184, Estación Central* ☎ *2/2776– 0645* ⊕ *www.terminaldebuses.com/ terminales-de-buses.* **Terminal Santiago.** ⊠ *La Alameda 3850, Estación Central* ☎ *2/2376–1750.*

BUS LINES Turbus. ⊠ *Martínez 800, Estación Central, Estación Central* ☎ *600/660–6600, 2/2822–7500* ⊕ *www. turbus.cl.*

CAR

You don't need a car to explore Santiago if you're not going to venture outside the city limits, as most of the downtown sights are within walking distance of each other. A car is the best way to see the surrounding countryside, and the highways around Santiago are excellent. There is an iPhone and Android app called Carretera that helps estimate cost of travel in Chile, calculating cost of gasoline and tolls.

SUBWAY

Santiago's subway system is the best way to get around town. The metro costs between 640 and 800 pesos per ride (depending on time of day and bus transfers). You can buy a single-use ticket or a BIP smart card (la tarjeta bip!). The metro is safe but gets very crowded at peak hours, and you should keep a hand on your valuables. The system operates weekdays 5:40 am–11:30 pm and weekends 8 am–11 pm, with some variation depending on the metro line. Metro opening and closing hours are listed at each station above the turnstiles.

TAXI

Taxis are plentiful, especially outside of bus stations and in touristy neighborhoods. The taxi services Uber and Cabify have caught on, though some people prefer to use the app SaferTaxi to ensure that there is a record of their journey. If taking a taxi, be prepared with small bills, as some drivers may not have change. Tipping is not required, but it is customary to round to the closest 500 pesos.

TAXI COMPANIES Andes Pacífico.
✉ José Pedro Alessandri 30, Ñuñoa ☎ 2/2912–6000 ⊕ www.andespacifico. cl. **Apoquindo.** ✉ Bilbao 7202, Las Condes ☎ 2/2210–6200 ⊕ www.transporte-sapoquindo.cl. **Italia.** ✉ Coquimbo 1469, Santiago Centro ☎ 2/2591–8900 ⊕ www. ritalia.cl. **Neverías.** ✉ Apoquindo 4830, Office 22/23, Las Condes ☎ 2/2207–0003 ⊕ www.neverias.cl. **Radio Taxi Las Condes.** ✉ Badajoz 12, Las Condes ☎ 2/2211–4470 ⊕ www.radiotaxilascondes.cl.

Pedro de Valdivia wasn't very creative when he mapped Santiago, sticking to the simple grid pattern typical of most colonial towns. The city didn't grow much larger before the meandering Río Mapocho impeded these plans, but you may be surprised at how orderly the city remains. It's difficult to get lost downtown, using the Andes as your compass on the east.

Much of the city, especially districts such as Bellavista, is best explored on foot. The subway is the quickest, cleanest, and most economical way to get around. To travel to more distant neighborhoods, or get anywhere at night after the subway closes, it's probably best to hail a taxi.

Dining

Menus cover the bases of international cuisines, but don't miss the local bounty—seafood delivered directly from the Pacific Ocean. One local favorite is caldillo de congrio, the hearty fish stew celebrated by poet Pablo Neruda in his "Oda al Caldillo de Congrio." (The lines of the poem are, in fact, the recipe.) A pisco sour—a cocktail of grape brandy, egg white, and lemon juice—is a great aperitif for any meal, especially when accompanied by a plate of machas a la parmesana, surf clams served au gratin, baked in lemon juice or with white wine, butter, and grated cheese.

Tempted to try heartier Chilean fare? Pull up a stool at one of the counters at Vega Central and enjoy a traditional pastel de choclo, pie filled with ground beef, chicken, olives, and a boiled egg, topped with mashed corn. Craving seafood? Head to the Mercado Central, where fresh fish is brought in each morning. Want a memorable meal? Trendy restaurants are opening every day in neighborhoods like Bellavista, where hip Santiaguinos come to check out the latest hot spots.

In the neighborhood of Vitacura, a 20- to 30-minute taxi ride from the city center, a complex of restaurants called Borde Río attracts an upscale crowd, but other reservations-only restaurants worth a look are on Alonso de Córdova and Nueva Costanera. El Golf, an area including Avenida El Bosque Norte and Avenida Isidora Goyenechea in Las Condes, has numerous restaurants and cafés. The emphasis is on creative cuisine, so familiar favorites are given a Chilean twist. This is one of the few neighborhoods where you can stroll between restaurants until you find exactly what you want.

Santiaguinos dine a little later than you might expect. Most fancy restaurants don't open for lunch until 1. (You may startle the cleaning staff if you rattle the doors at noon.) Dinner begins at 7:30 or 8, although most places don't get crowded until after 9. Many eateries close for a few hours before dinner and on Sunday night. People do dress smartly for dinner, but a coat and tie are rarely necessary. Avoid shorts, sneakers, and athletic gear, and you should be fine in most places.

Restaurant reviews have been shortened. For full information, visit Fodors.com.

What It Costs in Chilean Pesos (in Thousands)			
$	$$	$$$	$$$$
AT DINNER			
Under 7	7–10	11–15	over 16

Lodging

Santiago's accommodations range from luxurious *hoteles* to comfortable *residenciales,* which can be homey bed-and-breakfasts or simple hotel-style accommodations. All the construction in the past decade means competition between hotels is steep, but they still fill in the high summer season and when large trade fair or business conventions occur (March is a peak month). Outside these dates, you can often find a room for up to 20% less than the advertised rack rates, particularly if you stay for more than a couple of days. Call several hotels and ask for the best possible rate. It's a good idea to reserve in advance during the peak seasons (January, February, July, and August).

Some hotels, particularly more expensive ones, quote prices in U.S. dollars rather than pesos. Visitors from abroad are exempt from the 19% sales tax, provided they pay in foreign currency or with an overseas credit card.

Hotel reviews have been shortened. For full information, visit Fodors.com.

What It Costs in Chilean Pesos (in Thousands)			
$	$$	$$$	$$$$
FOR TWO PEOPLE			
Under 50	51–95	96–125	over 126

Nightlife

Bars and clubs are scattered all over Santiago, but a handful of streets have such a concentration of establishments that they resemble block parties on Friday and Saturday nights. Pub crawls along Avenida Pío Nono and neighboring streets in Bellavista yield venues aimed at a young crowd (the drinking age is 18). Across the river and farther west, Lastarria hosts a busy bar scene. To the east in Providencia, the area around Manuel Montt and Tobalaba metro stations attract a slightly older and well-heeled crowd.

What you should wear depends on your destination. In general, the dress gets smarter the farther east you move, but remains casual.

⚠ Note that establishments referred to as "nightclubs" are almost always female strip shows. The signs in the windows usually make it quite clear what goes on inside. The same is true for certain cafés with blacked-out windows, called "cafés con piernas" (literally: coffee with legs).

Performing Arts

From the dozens of museums scattered around the city, it's clear Santiaguinos also have a strong love of culture. Music, theater, and other artistic endeavors supplement weekends spent dancing the night away.

Provided that you understand at least a little Spanish, you may want to take in a bit of Chilean theater. Performances take place all year, mainly from Thursday to Sunday around 8 pm.

For film lovers, Santiago's many cinemas screen movies in English with Spanish subtitles. Movie listings are posted in El Mercurio and other dailies. Admission is generally between 1,500 and 3,000 pesos, with reduced prices for matinees. The newest multiplexes—with mammoth screens, plush seating, and fresh popcorn—are in the city's malls, but don't overlook the offerings at the Centro Cultural La Moneda or el Biografo if you want more artsy or themed films.

Shopping

Vitacura is, without a doubt, the destination for upscale shopping. Lined with designer boutiques with SUVs double-parked out front, Avenida Alonso de Córdova is Santiago's equivalent of Fifth Avenue in New York City or Rodeo Drive in Los Angeles. "Drive" is the important word here, as nobody strolls from place to place. Although buzzing with activity, the streets are strangely empty. Here you'll see names like Emporio Armani, Louis Vuitton, and Hermès. Other shops

are found on nearby Avenidas Vitacura and Nueva Costanera.

Providencia, another popular shopping district, has rows of smaller, less luxurious boutiques. Avenida Providencia slices through the neighborhood, branching off for several blocks into the parallel Nueva Providencia. Shops continue east to Tobalaba metro, after which Avenida Providencia changes its name to Avenida Apoquindo and the neighborhood turns into Las Condes. To be on the cutting edge, head south to Avenida Italia (close to Salvador), where there are several blocks of shops stretching south from Bilbao. Converted row houses and workshops have been given over to (mostly) home design stores, cafés, and restaurants with courtyards in back. Girardi street also has several antiques dealers.

Bohemian Bellavista attracts those in search of the perfect thick woolen sweater or the right piece of lapis lazuli jewelry. Santiago Centro is more down to earth, while the Mercado Central just north of Parque Forestal sells ocean-related products, and nearby markets Vega Chica and Vega Central sell cheese, fruit, meat, eggs, vegetables, cleaning supplies, signs, and many other items. Shops are grouped together by type.

Shops in Santiago are generally open weekdays 10–7 and Saturday 10–2. Malls are open daily 10–10.

Safety

Despite what Chileans claim, Santiago is no more dangerous than most other large cities and considerably less so than many other Latin American capitals. As a rule of thumb, watch out for your property, preferably keeping physical contact with it, but unless you venture into some of the city's outlying neighborhoods, your physical safety is unlikely to be at risk. Beware of pickpockets particularly in the Centro, near Los Leones metro, and on

3

Santiago **PLANNING**

buses. Don't keep valuables in outside pockets, and exercise caution when using smartphones in very busy areas.

Visitors should be wary of parking attendants. During the day, they should charge only what's on their portable meters when you collect the car, but at night they ask for money—usually 1,000 or 2,000 pesos—in advance. This is a racket, but for your car's safety it's better to comply.

Tours

Sernatur, the national tourism service, maintains a listing of experienced individual tour guides, who run half-day tours of Santiago and the surrounding area.

Chilean Travel Services

GUIDED TOURS | Chilean Travel Services handle tours of Santiago and other parts of Chile. ⊠ *Antonio Bellet 77, Office 101, Providencia* ☎ *2/2251–0400* ⊕ *www. ctsturismo.cl.*

FoodyChile

GUIDED TOURS | The name of Kylie Sheriff's tour company is a play on words, meaning both ".foodie Chile" and "food and Chile." Tours, booked online only, are always small, personalized, and focus on consumables, including wine, craft beer, and sweets. There are lunches and dinners hosted in private homes, as well as market tours. Kylie also runs wine excursions under the name Chile Wine Trails. ⊠ *Providencia* ☎ *9/5119–4956* ⊕ *www. foodychile.com* ✉ *From US$110.*

Travesia Tour Chile

SPECIAL-INTEREST TOURS | This Santiago-based tour operator can arrange full-day trips with round-trip transportation to the skiing and wine regions outside of the city. ⊠ *Agustinas 1185, Of. 95, Santiago Centro* ☎ *2/3277–0373* ⊕ *travesia-tourchile.cl* ✉ *From 25,000 pesos.*

Turismo Cocha

GUIDED TOURS | One of the biggest players in the Chilean tourism industry, Cocha books tours inside and outside of Chile, as well as hotels, airfare, and cruises. Single-day city tours are available, but the main focus is on multiday tours with lodging at three-, four-, and five-star hotels. The main office is in El Golf (Las Condes), but there are 13 offices around the city, including one at the airport that's open 24 hours. ⊠ *El Bosque Norte 0430, Las Condes* ☎ *2/2464–1300* ⊕ *www. cocha.com* ✉ *From 72,000 pesos.*

Upscape

ADVENTURE TOURS | This adventure tour company prides itself on running tours no one else does, such as heli-skiing at Ski Arpa and thematic tours of Santiago, including Jewish culture, bicycling, and food. The company also organizes multiday trips inside and outside of Santiago, extending to the north and south of the country and beyond to Argentina and Uruguay. ⊠ *Tegualda 1352, Providencia* ☎ *2/2244–2750* ⊕ *www.upscapetravel. com* ✉ *From US$74.*

Essentials

VISITOR INFORMATION Sernatur. ⊠ *Av. Providencia 1550, Providencia* ☎ *2/2731–8336* ⊕ *www.sernatur.cl.*

EMERGENCY SERVICES Ambulance. ☎ *131.* Fire. ☎ *132.* Police. ☎ *133.*

Santiago Centro

Shiny new skyscrapers may have sprouted up in neighborhoods to the east, but Santiago Centro has its share of construction going on, too. During the past decade, the population downtown has nearly doubled, but that's for the whole comuna, not just the *casco histórico*, which is close to the Alameda and runs from La Moneda up to about Santa Lucía. Take the metro down here, not a taxi, for easy transportation, as the usual traffic headaches apply to downtown Santiago.

TIMING AND PRECAUTIONS
In this part of the city you can find interesting museums, performance spaces, galleries, imposing government buildings, and bustling commercial streets. Don't worry about getting lost in a sprawling area—it takes only about 15 minutes to walk from one edge of the historic center to the other.

Sights

Correo Central
GOVERNMENT BUILDING | Housed in what was once the ornate Palacio de los Gobernadores, this building dating from 1715 is one of the most beautiful post offices you are likely to see. It was reconstructed by Ricardo Brown in 1882 after being ravaged by fire and is a fine example of neoclassical architecture, with a glass-and-iron roof added in the early 20th century. It has occasional exhibits in the main hall, plus an extensive collections of stamps from around the world and other postal and telegraph memorabilia in the adjoining Postal and Telegraph Museum (free admission). ⊠ *Plaza de Armas 989, at Puente, Santiago Centro* ☎ *2/2956–5145* ⊕ *www.correos.cl* ☺ *Museum: weekends* Ⓜ *Plaza de Armas.*

Ex Congreso Nacional
NOTABLE BUILDING | Once the meeting place for the National Congress (the legislature moved to Valparaíso in 1990), this palatial neoclassical building became the Ministry of Foreign Affairs for a time but was returned to the Senate for meetings after the Ministry moved to the former Hotel Carrera in Plaza de la Constitución in December 2005. The original structure on the site, the Iglesia de la Compañía de Jesús, was destroyed by a fire in 1863 in which 2,000 people perished. Two bells from that church now grace the elaborate gardens. To coordinate a tour, email protocolostgo@senado.cl with at least two days' notice. More formal attire is appreciated, and neither shorts nor baseball caps are permitted. The tour is free and lasts approximately 30 minutes. ⊠ *Catedral 1158, entrance on Morande, Santiago Centro* ☺ *Closed weekends* Ⓜ *Plaza de Armas.*

★ Gabriela Mistral Cultural Center (GAM)
CONVENTION CENTER | This giant cultural center just steps from the Universidad Católica metro houses some of Santiago's most interesting indigenous arts exhibits and offers a packed cultural itinerary, including theater. There is a large atrium between the two halves of the building with a colorful skylight, restaurant, and café. Outside the building, to the north side is an amphitheater that is occasionally used to host events. An antiques market takes place on the west side of the building Tuesday through Saturday, if it's not raining. **Tip:** A helpful tourism office is located here. ⊠ *Alameda 227, Santiago Centro* ☎ *2/2566–5500* ⊕ *gam.cl* Ⓜ *Universidad Católica.*

Londres 38 Espacio de Memorias
NOTABLE BUILDING | This lovely facade on Calle Londres holds dark secrets: Londres 38 was a clandestine torture center for 98 people for three years during Chile's 27-year dictatorship, beginning in 1973. Rooms include a tiny bathroom, where multiple DNA was recovered that helped to identify victims; a video shows the work forensic scientists undertook. Simple signs add to the sad and dignified ambience that holds a torrid past and now plays its part as a space for memory. ⊠ *Londres 38, Santiago Centro* ☎ *2/26320–7859* ⊕ *www.londres38.cl* ☺ *Closed Fri.–Mon.* Ⓜ *Universidad de Chile.*

Metropolitan Cathedral
RELIGIOUS BUILDING | Conquistador Pedro de Valdivia declared in 1541 that a house of worship would be constructed at this site bordering the Plaza de Armas. The first adobe building burned to the ground, and the structures that replaced it were

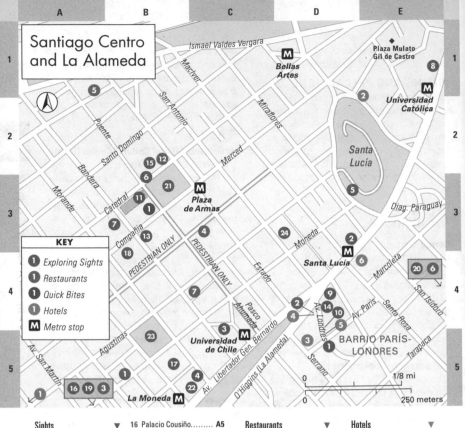

Santiago Centro and La Alameda

Sights ▼

1 Barrio París-Londres... **D5**
2 Biblioteca Nacional **D3**
3 Bolsa de Comercio **C4**
4 Centro Cultural La Moneda **C5**
5 Cerro Santa Lucía **D3**
6 Correo Central **B3**
7 Ex Congreso Nacional **B3**
8 Gabriela Mistral Cultural Center (GAM) **E1**
9 Iglesia San Francisco .. **D4**
10 Londres 38 Espacio de Memorias.. **D4**
11 Metropolitan Cathedral **B3**
12 Municipalidad de Santiago............. **B2**
13 Museo Chileno de Arte Precolombino **B3**
14 Museo de Arte Colonial San Francisco........... **D4**
15 Museo Histórico Nacional **B2**

16 Palacio Cousiño........ **A5**
17 Palacio de La Moneda **B5**
18 Palacio de los Tribunales de Justicia.. **B4**
19 Parque O'Higgins **A5**
20 Persa Bío Bío............. **E4**
21 Plaza de Armas **B3**
22 Plaza de la Ciudadanía **B5**
23 Plaza de la Constitución............. **B5**
24 Teatro Municipal........ **D3**

Restaurants ▼

1 Blue Jar.................. **B5**
2 Bristol **D4**
3 Confitería Torres **A5**
4 Dominó................... **C3**
5 Mercado Central........ **A1**
6 Pulpería Santa Elvira............... **E4**
7 Salvador Cocina y Café **B4**

Quick Bites ▼

1 Faisan D'Or **B3**

Hotels ▼

1 Happy House Hostel.... **A5**
2 Hotel Foresta............. **E1**
3 Hotel Fundador.......... **D5**
4 Hotel Plaza San Francisco........... **D5**
5 Hotel Vegas.............. **D5**
6 Mercure Santiago Centro.......... **E4**

The two halves of the Gabriela Mistral Cultural Center are separated by an atrium with a colorful skylight.

destroyed by the earthquakes of 1647 and 1730. The finishing touches of the neoclassical cathedral standing today were added in 1789 by Italian architect Joaquín Toesca. Be sure to check out the baroque interior stained-glass-topped arched colonnade, and look out for the sparkling silver altar of a side chapel in the south nave. ⊠ *Plaza de Armas 444, Santiago Centro* ☎ *2/2671–8105* Ⓜ *Plaza de Armas.*

Municipalidad de Santiago

NOTABLE BUILDING | Today's city hall for central Santiago can be found on the site of the colonial city hall and jail. The original structure, built in 1552, survived until a devastating earthquake in 1730. Joaquín Toesca, the architect who also designed the presidential palace and completed the cathedral, reconstructed the building in 1785, but it was destroyed by fire a century later. In 1891, Eugenio Joannon, who favored an Italian Renaissance style, erected the structure standing today. On the facade hangs an elaborate coat of arms presented by

Spain. The interior now houses a tourist office as well as a small gallery and souvenir shop. The tourism office runs free tours on Monday, Wednesday, and Friday at 10 am with no previous registration required. ⊠ *Plaza de Armas, Santiago Centro* Ⓜ *Plaza de Armas.*

Museo Chileno de Arte Precolombino

HISTORY MUSEUM | This well-endowed collection of artifacts of the region's indigenous peoples, much of it donated by the collector Sergio Larraín García-Moreno, is displayed in the beautifully restored Royal Customs House that dates from 1807. The permanent collection, on the upper floor, showcases ceramics and textiles from Mexico to Patagonia. Unlike many of the city's museums, the displays here are well labeled in Spanish and English. Guided tours in English are available at no extra cost, but must be booked in advance. There is a shop with a good selection of on-topic books and an airy café as well. ⊠ *Bandera 361, at Av. Compañía, Santiago Centro* ☎ *2/2928–1500 general, 2/2929–1522 tours* ⊕ *www.*

precolombino.cl ✉ *5000 pesos; free 1st Sun. of every month* ⊘ *Closed Mon.* Ⓜ *Plaza de Armas.*

Museo Histórico Nacional

The colonial-era Palacio de la Real Audiencia served as the meeting place for Chile's first Congress in July 1811. The building then functioned as a telegraph office before the museum moved here in 1911. It's worth the small admission charge to see the interior of the 200-year-old structure, where exhibits tracing Chile's history from the preconquest period to the 20th century are arranged chronologically in rooms centered on a courtyard. Keep an eye out for Allende's eyeglasses. Ask for the English brochure and free audio guide, and if you are not heights-averse, take a tour up the tower for a bird's-eye view of the Plaza de Armas, cathedral, and downtown Santiago. ✉ *Plaza de Armas 951, Santiago Centro* ☎ *2/2997–8930* ⊕ *www.mhn.gob. cl* ⊘ *Closed Mon.* Ⓜ *Plaza de Armas.*

Palacio de los Tribunales de Justicia

GOVERNMENT BUILDING | During Augusto Pinochet's rule, countless human-rights demonstrations were held outside the Courts of Justice, which house the country's Supreme Court. The imposing neoclassical interior is worth a look, but the guards reserve the right to admission and prefer more formal attire (no shorts, flip-flops, tank tops). It is open for visits from 9 to 2. ✉ *Av. Compañía 1140, Santiago Centro* Ⓜ *Plaza de Armas.*

Parque O'Higgins

CITY PARK | Named for Chile's first president and national hero, whose troops were victorious against the Spanish, this park has plenty of open space for everything from ball games to military parades and a dedicated picnic area complete with barbecues. Street vendors sell *volantines* (kites) in the park year-round; breezy September and early October comprise prime kite-flying season, especially around September 18, Chile's national holiday. There are pedalcab and

rollerblade rentals on weekends, a competitive rollerblade track, and a terrain park with a deep bowl for skateboarders and rollerbladers. The park has a beautiful covered pool, which costs 7,000 pesos for an hour-long pass; goggles and bathing cap are required. Both the Movistar Arena and Cúpola Multiespacio theater are also located at this park. ✉ *Autopista Central between Av. Blanco Encalada and Av. Rondizonni, Santiago Centro* ☎ ✉ *Free* Ⓜ *Parque O'Higgins.*

★ Plaza de Armas

PLAZA/SQUARE | This square has been the symbolic heart of Chile—as well as its political, social, religious, and commercial center—since Pedro de Valdivia established the city on this spot in 1541. The Palacio de los Gobernadores, the Palacio de la Real Audiencia, and the Municipalidad de Santiago front the square's northern edge. The dignified cathedral graces the western side of the square. The plaza has historically been very lively, with chess players in a gazebo, street performers playing in the bandstand, and caricaturists. Recent improvements have increased the number of trees and installed Wi-Fi. ✉ *Compañía at Estado, Santiago Centro* Ⓜ *Plaza de Armas.*

Santiago's Plaza de Armas is the symbolic heart of Chile.

Persa Bío Bío

MARKET | A meatpacking district that's slowing undergoing gentrification, Barrio Franklin hands its streets over to pedestrians and turns into a vast flea market on weekends. Take the metro to Estación Franklin, then start walking down Calle Placer. Here, you can pick up anything from wine to vinyls, vintage clothes, and household supplies from hawkers who have lovingly laid out their wares on a mat on the sidewalk to 300 established storefronts such as antiques dealers located within old warehouses. Check out Factoria Franklin, home to handcraft gin distillery Quintal and AFA Galería art gallery at Franklin 741. There's also plenty of street food to be enjoyed, from *lomito completo* sandwiches to small bowls of ceviche. The vibe is relaxed and live bands often perform a set. With plenty to feast your eyes on, as with any busy space, keep an eye on personal belongings. ✉ *Calle Placer, Santiago Centro* 🕒 *Closed Mon. to Thurs.* [M] *Franklin, Bío Bío.*

🍴 Restaurants

★ Blue Jar

$$$ | **CHILEAN** | Simple but creative dishes using the best and freshest Chilean ingredients appeal to local office workers and visitors alike at this popular downtown spot, where lunch patrons often enjoy a sandwich or soup-salad combo. The menu changes seasonally, with dishes like chicken cashew curry and venison with caponata sharing menu space with grilled bass and chia polenta cake. **Known for:** reservations necessary for busy lunches; specialty coffee; early dinners (closes at 9 pm except first Thursday of each month). [$] *Average main: pesos11000* ✉ *Amanda Labarca 102 at Moneda, Santiago Centro* ☎ *2/96155–4650* 🌐 *www.bluejar.cl* 🕒 *Closed weekends* [M] *Moneda.*

Bristol

$$$ | **CHILEAN** | This restaurant inside the sophisticated Hotel Plaza San Francisco serves creative seafood dishes like marinated scallops over octopus carpaccio and cold tomato-and-pepper sauce. Frequented by local business people, Bristol has won several awards and often makes it onto top lists in local media. **Known for:** creative menu; seafood; efficient service. $ *Average main: pesos15000* ✉ *Hotel Plaza San Francisco, Alameda 816, Santiago Centro* ☎ *2/2630–4516* ⊕ *www. plazasanfrancisco.cl* Ⓜ *Universidad de Chile.*

★ **Confitería Torres**
$$$ | CHILEAN | Opened in 1879, this is the oldest restaurant still operating in Chile and remains one of the city's most traditional dining rooms, with red-leather banquettes, mint-green ceramic floors, and huge chandeliers with tulip-shaped globes. Classic dishes such as *lomo al ajo arriero* (sirloin sautéed with peppers and garlic) are menu staples; if you're after a quick bite, order the Sandwich Barros Luca, as this is where it was created. **Known for:** classic dishes; quick bites; traditional decor. $ *Average main: pesos12000* ✉ *Alameda 1570, Santiago Centro* ☎ *2/2688–0751* ⊕ *www. confiteriatorres.cl* ⊘ *Closed Sat. and Sun.* Ⓜ *Moneda.*

Dominó
$ | CHILEAN | A Chilean institution, this 70-year-old fast-food chain is impeccably clean, and the service is fast and friendly. It's the place to try an *Italiano* (a hot dog with tomatoes and avocado) or *chacarero* (hot dog or beef sandwich with green beans, tomato, and chili pepper). **Known for:** no frills; fast food; cheap eats. $ *Average main: pesos5000* ✉ *Huérfanos 1296, Santiago Centro* ☎ *2/2963–7695* ⊕ *www.domino.cl* ⊘ *Closed Sat. and Sun.*

Mercado Central
$$$ | SEAFOOD | Where better than to sample fresh Chilean seafood and eat where the locals eat than at Santiago's fish market? Bustling and loud, the market has an ambience you'll want to soak up, whether you visit Donde Augusto and La Joya del Pacífico in the center or at a

smaller, less touristy, and cheaper spot such as Marisol or Francisca. **Known for:** cash-only at smaller restaurants; fantastic seafood; casual dining. $ *Average main: pesos14000* ✉ *San Pablo 967, Santiago Centro* ☎ ⊘ *No dinner* Ⓜ *Cal y Canto.*

★ **Pulpería Santa Elvira**
$$ | CHILEAN | Behind an anonymous-looking front door lies this charming restaurant, a short drive south of Santiago Centro. Choose your table from the various salons, including the adorable patio or a more private dining space, then pick your dishes from the short yet eclectic blackboard. **Known for:** simple, seasonal dishes; local ingredients; outdoor dining. $ *Average main: pesos9500* ✉ *Santa Elvira 475, Santiago Centro* ☎ *9/4111– 6000* ⊕ *www.pulperiasantaelvira.cl* ▤ *No credit cards* ⊘ *Closed Mon. and Tues.* Ⓜ *Avenida Atta.*

★ **Salvador Cocina y Café**
$$ | CHILEAN | This tucked-away two-story downtown lunch spot offers unmissable weekday set menus with appetizer, main dish, iced tea, and choice of coffee or dessert for 9,900 pesos. Dishes adopt modern spins on Chilean and international favorites, such as grain salad with *mote* (hulled wheat kernels), beef carpaccio, kidneys in cream sauce, or spinach-filled pasta. **Known for:** reasonable prices; adventurous meat dishes; great lunch set menu. $ *Average main: pesos7700* ✉ *Bombero Ossa 1059, Santiago Centro* ☎ *2/95817–9777* ⊕ *www.salvadorcocinaycafe.cl* ⊘ *Closed weekends. No dinner* Ⓜ *Universidad de Chile.*

☕ Coffee and Quick Bites

Faisan D'Or
$ | CAFÉ | Pause for a coffee or a cold beer at one of the sidewalk cafés on the west side of Plaza de Armas and let the hustle and bustle of the city flow past you. The coffee is best at the Faisan D'Or, which serves a typical *cortado* (coffee with warm milk). **Known for:** central location;

coffee; lively energy. $ Average main: pesos3000 ⊠ Plaza de Armas 430, Santiago Centro ☎ 2/2696–4161 ▭ No credit cards.

 Hotels

Happy House Hostel
$ | HOTEL | From the gorgeous baroque facade with balconies to the original ceiling medallion from which the chandelier in the giant salon and living room hangs, it's clear that Happy House Hostel is something special. **Pros:** close to nightlife and Barrio Yungay; historical architecture; a beautiful plaza. **Cons:** can be a little chilly in winter (but you'll be loaded up with comforters); walls not thick to keep out noise; a bit farther afield from some sights. $ Rooms from: pesos40000 ⊠ Moneda 1829, Barrio Brasil ☎ 2/2688–4849 ⊕ www.happyhousehostel.com ↝ 25 rooms ⦿ Free Breakfast Ⓜ Los Héroes.

Hotel Foresta
$ | HOTEL | Staying in this seven-story hotel across the street from Cerro Santa Lucía is like visiting an elegant old home that has seen better days. **Pros:** larger suites optional; great location near the quaint cafés and shops of Plaza Mulato Gil de Castro; rooftop restaurant and bar with a view. **Cons:** dated look; no online booking; rooms are small. $ Rooms from: pesos54000 ⊠ Victoria Subercaseaux 353, Santiago Centro ☎ 2/2639–6261 ↝ 35 rooms ⦿ Free Breakfast Ⓜ Bellas Artes.

Hotel Fundador
$$ | HOTEL | On the edge of the quaint Barrio París-Londres, this hotel has rooms that, although small, are airy and attractive. **Pros:** free Wi-Fi; tucked away from downtown traffic noise; on the doorstep of a subway station. **Cons:** rooms a bit dated; few restaurants or bars in the immediate vicinity; not an area for a stroll at night. $ Rooms from: pesos64500 ⊠ Paseo Serrano 34, Santiago Centro ☎ 2/2387–1200 ⊕ www.fundador.cl ↝ 119 rooms, 28 suites ⦿ Free Breakfast Ⓜ Universidad de Chile.

★ Hotel Plaza San Francisco
$$$ | HOTEL | Across from Iglesia San Francisco, this sophisticated business hotel has everything traveling executives need: spacious rooms with large beds and double-paned windows to keep out the downtown noise, a sparkling indoor pool, a fitness club, and even an art gallery. **Pros:** clean quiet rooms; helpful English-speaking staff; on-site restaurant offers interesting cuisine. **Cons:** street-facing rooms can get noisy; on-site restaurant expensive; nightlife and other good restaurants are a metro or taxi ride away. $ Rooms from: pesos96000 ⊠ Av. Bernardo O'Higgins (Alameda) 816, Santiago Centro ☎ 2/2639–3832 ⊕ www.plazasanfrancisco.cl ↝ 146 rooms ⦿ Free Breakfast Ⓜ Universidad de Chile.

Hotel Vegas
$ | HOTEL | This colonial-style building, adorned with a bullet-shaped turret, sits in the heart of the charming Barrio París-Londres. **Pros:** spacious rooms; good location for downtown sightseeing; free Wi-Fi. **Cons:** no elevator or parking; cramped lobby, bar, and café; some rooms smell musty. $ Rooms from: pesos45000 ⊠ Londres 49, Santiago Centro ☎ 2/2638–3225 ⊕ www.hotelvegas.net ↝ 20 rooms ⦿ Free Breakfast Ⓜ Universidad de Chile.

Mercure Santiago Centro
$$ | HOTEL | It's hard to beat the location of this business traveler–minded hotel, which is close to Cerro Santa Lucía. **Pros:** clean and relatively quiet; central location; within walking distance from many points of interest downtown. **Cons:** lighting in some rooms not good; some rooms more outdated than others; a bit impersonal. $ Rooms from: pesos90000 ⊠ La Alameda 632, Santiago Centro ☎ 2/2595–6622 ⊕ all.accor.com ↝ 142 rooms ⦿ Free Breakfast.

Nightlife

CUECA CLUBS

El Huaso Enrique

THEMED ENTERTAINMENT | This classic of Barrio Yungay predates the current immigration of hipsters and the revitalization of the neighborhood. For nearly 70 years, the kitchens have turned out Chilean specialties such as the heavy-hitting *chorrillana,* a plate of French fries covered in stewed onions and sausage, and topped with a fried egg. They also teach classes in the stompiest style of Chile's national dance, the *cueca brava.* Classes are Wednesday through Saturday at 7:30 pm and cost 4,000 pesos. Given the timing, it's best to dance first, then eat. ⊠ *Maipú 462, Santiago Centro* ☎ *9/2070–1885* ⊕ *www.elhuasoenrique. cl* Ⓜ *Quinta Normal.*

★ La Chiminea

THEMED ENTERTAINMENT | Hidden on a side street downtown, you might be forgiven for thinking that La Chiminea was just a hole in the wall. Besides towering plates of French fries and happy-hour specials, this place has an undying love of all things Chilean, especially cueca. Come here with nothing but a competitive spirit and a hanky, a dance essential. Classes run Monday and Thursday at 8 pm and cost 2,500 pesos. ⊠ *Príncipe de Gales 90, Santiago Centro* ☎ *2/2697–0131* Ⓜ *La Moneda.*

 Performing Arts

Ballet de Santiago

The Teatro Municipal has its own company, the Ballet de Santiago, which performs regularly, often with guest soloists. ⊠ *Plaza Alcalde Mekis, Agustinas 794, Santiago Centro* ☎ *2/2463–1000* ⊕ *www. balletdesantiago.com.*

Movistar Arena

MUSIC | Movistar Arena, a covered stadium inside Parque O'Higgins, is a frequent venue for concerts by popular singers and groups, principally those on international tours. It seats 12,000, though seats to the side of the stage have poor acoustics. ⊠ *Av. Beaucheff 1204, Santiago Centro* ☎ *2/2770–2300* ⊕ *www.movistararena.cl.*

★ Teatro Municipal

MUSIC | Home to the national opera company, Santiago's 19th-century Teatro Municipal also presents excellent classical concert and ballet by internationally recognized artists from March to December. Opened in 1857, it was designed by French architects and has had several major renovations since. The Renaissance-style building hosts one of the city's most refined monuments with a lavish interior that deserves a visit. The cobblestone path around the building completes the picture. ⊠ *Plaza Alcalde Mekis, Agustinas 794 at San Antonio, Santiago Centro* ☎ *2/2463–1000* ⊕ *www. municipal.cl.*

Shopping

ANTIQUES

Galpón de Anticuarios Los Reyes

ANTIQUES & COLLECTIBLES | West of Estación Mapocho and at the end of Avenida Brasil, this complex is filled with antiques dealers. They are used to foreigners coming and poking around, some of whom have been known to fill entire containers with jewelry, chandeliers, ceramics, and crystalware to bring back home.

■ **TIP→ Take a quick peek across the street to the skate park at Parque de Los Reyes, where some of the best skateboarders in Chile practice on weekends.** ⊠ *Av. Brasil 1157 at Balmaceda, Santiago Centro* ☎ *2/2688–1348* ⊕ *www.galpondelosreyes.cl.*

CLOTHING
Donde Golpea El Monito

MEN'S CLOTHING | In the countryside, men often wear *texanos* (cowboy hats), *paños* (formal hats), and *chupallas* (flat-brimmed hats). If you've ever wondered where to buy these proper toppers, head to Donde Golpea El Monito. At this downtown shop, in business for a century, the store's friendly staff shows customers the differences between each hat and how to wear them. Also for sale are spurs, ponchos, and other *huaso* (Chilean cowboy) essentials. ⊠ *21 de Mayo 707, Santiago Centro* ☎ *2/2638–7120* ⊘ *Closed Sun.*

SHOPPING MALLS
Mall VIVO del Centro

MALL | Santiago's downtown mall includes sporting goods stores, a food court with fast food restaurants, and public bathrooms. It's close to the Mercado Central and has free Wi-Fi in the rest areas and food court. ⊠ *Puente 689, Santiago Centro* ☎ *2/2611–2005* ⊕ *www.vivoelcentro.cl.*

La Alameda

Avenida Libertador Bernardo O'Higgins, more frequently called Alameda, is the city's principal thoroughfare. Along with the Pan-American Highway (Avenida Norte Sur) and the Río Mapocho, it forms the wedge that defines the city's historic district. Many of Santiago's most important buildings, including landmarks such as the Iglesia San Francisco, stand along the avenue. Others, like Teatro Municipal, are just steps away.

TIMING AND PRECAUTIONS

You could spend an hour alone at the Palacio de la Moneda—try to time your visit with the changing of the guard, which takes place every other day at 10 am on weekdays, and 11 on weekends. Under the Plaza de la Constitución, which is on the Alameda side of the Moneda, there's the Centro Cultural La Moneda—a culture, arts, and exhibition space with a few shops and cafés. Across the Alameda, take at least 1½ hours to explore Iglesia San Francisco, the adjacent museum, and the Barrio París-Londres. You could easily spend a bookish half hour perusing the stacks at the Biblioteca Nacional, where you can also take advantage of free Wi-Fi. Plan for an hour or more at Cerro Santa Lucía with its splendid view of the city and adjacent crafts markets.

Sights

Barrio París-Londres

NEIGHBORHOOD | Many architects contributed to what is frequently referred to as Santiago's Little Europe, among them Alberto Cruz Montt, Jorge Elton Alamos, and Sergio Larraín. The string of small mansion houses lining the cobbled streets of Calles París and Londres sprang up in the mid-1920s on vegetable patches and gardens once belonging to the convent adjoining Iglesia San Francisco. The three- and four-story town houses are all unique; some have brick facades, while others are done in Palladian style. ⊠ *Londres at París, Santiago Centro.*

Biblioteca Nacional (*National Library*)

LIBRARY | Near the foot of Cerro Santa Lucía is the block-long classical facade of the National Library. Moved to its present premises in 1925, this library, founded in 1813, has one of the oldest and most extensive collections in South America. The second-floor Sala José Toribio Medina (closed Saturday), which holds the most important collection of early Latin American print work, is well worth a look. The three levels of books, reached by curved-wood balconies, are lighted by massive chandeliers. The café on the ground floor is a quiet place to linger over a coffee. There is free Wi-Fi throughout the building. ⊠ *La Alameda 651, Santiago Centro* ☎ *2/2997–8818* ⊕ *www.*

bibliotecanacional.cl 🍴 *Free* ◷ *Closed Sat. afternoon, Sun.* Ⓜ *Santa Lucía.*

Bolsa de Comercio

NOTABLE BUILDING | Chile's stock exchange is housed in a 1917 French neoclassical structure with an elegant clock tower surmounted by an arched slate cupola. Business is now done electronically, but you can visit the old trading floor with its buying and selling circle called *rueda*. You must leave your ID at the door. ✉ *La Bolsa 64, Santiago Centro* ☎ *2/2399–3000* ⊕ *www.bolsadesantiago.com* 🍴 *Free* Ⓜ *Universidad de Chile.*

Centro Cultural La Moneda

ARTS CENTER | Tucked away underneath the Plaza de la Ciudadanía is the Centro Cultural La Moneda, a fantastic arts center that puts on an array of interesting exhibitions and art workshops. It's also home to the national Cineteca, which regularly screens Chilean movies and documentaries (tickets cost 2,500 pesos). The Artesanías de Chile crafts shop there showcases top-quality work, and the Tienda Centro Cultural is a good place to buy unusual souvenirs and jewelry. There's also a restaurant, a café, and a bookshop. ✉ *Plaza de la Ciudadanía 26, La Alameda* ☎ *2355–6500* ⊕ *www.cclm.cl* 🍴 *Free* ◷ *Closed Mon.*

★ Cerro Santa Lucía

CITY PARK | The mazelike park of Santa Lucía is a hangout for park-bench smoochers and photo-snapping tourists. Walking uphill along the labyrinth of interconnected paths and plazas takes about 30 minutes, or you can take an elevator two blocks north of the park's main entrance (no fee). The uppermost lookout point affords an excellent 360-degree view of the entire city; two stairways lead up from the Plaza Caupolicán esplanade; those on the south side are newer and less slippery. Be careful near dusk as the park, although patrolled, attracts the occasional mugger. There is a tiny tourism office near the Alameda entrance, open weekdays, but closed

Soccer in Chile

Chile's most popular spectator sport is soccer, but a close second is watching the endless bickering among owners, trainers, and players whenever a match isn't going well.

Estadio Nacional Julio Martínez Prádanos. First-division fútbol matches, featuring the city's handful of local teams, are held in the Estadio Nacional Julio Martínez Prádanos, southeast of the city center in Ñuñoa. Soccer is played year-round, with most matches taking place on weekends. The stadium is also a major concert venue. ✉ *Av. Grecia 2001, Ñuñoa* ☎ *2/2238–8102.*

for lunch from 2 until 3 pm, and a small indigenous crafts fair called the Centro de Exposición de Arte Indígena (or Gruta Welén) in a natural cavern carved out of the western flank of the hill. ✉ *Santa Lucía at La Alameda, Santiago Centro* ☎ *2/2664–4206* Ⓜ *Santa Lucía.*

Iglesia San Francisco

CHURCH | Santiago's oldest structure, greatest symbol, and principal landmark, the Church of San Francisco is the last trace of 16th-century colonial architecture in the city. Construction began in 1586, and although the church survived successive earthquakes, early tremors took their toll and portions had to be rebuilt several times. Today's neoclassical tower, which forms the city's most recognizable silhouette, was added in 1857 by architect Fermín Vivaceta. Inside are rough stone-and-brick walls and an ornate coffered wood ceiling. Visible on the main altar is the image of the Virgen del Socorro (Virgin of Perpetual Help) that conquistador Pedro de Valdivia carried for protection and guidance. ✉ *La Alameda 834, Santiago Centro* ☎ *2/2638–3238* Ⓜ *Santa Lucía, Universidad de Chile.*

Museo de Arte Colonial San Francisco

ART MUSEUM | This monastery adjacent to Iglesia San Francisco houses the best collection of 17th-century colonial paintings on the continent. Contained in rooms that wrap around the courtyard are 54 large-scale canvases portraying the life of St. Francis, painted in Cusco, Peru, as well as a plethora of religious iconography and an impressive collection of silver artifacts. Most pieces are labeled in Spanish and English. Peacocks roam the central courtyard. ⊠ *La Alameda 834, Santiago Centro* ☎ *2/2639–8737* ⊕ *www.museosanfrancisco.com* ✉ *1000 pesos* ⊗ *Closed Sun. and Mon.* Ⓜ *Santa Lucía, Universidad de Chile.*

Palacio Cousiño

HISTORIC HOME | Dating from the early 1870s, this fabulous mansion was built by the wealthy Cousiño-Goyenechea family. All that mining money allowed them to build this palace with amenities such as one of the country's first elevators. The elegant furnishings were—of course—imported from France. Extensive refurbishments to all four salons were done in 2017. Email ahead for 45-minute tours in English that take place daily. ⊠ *Dieciocho 438, La Alameda* ☎ *2/2386–7448* ✉ *palaciocousino@gmail.com* ✉ *4000 pesos* ⊗ *Closed Sat.–Mon.* Ⓜ *Toesca.*

Palacio de La Moneda

CASTLE/PALACE | Originally the royal mint, this sober neoclassical edifice designed by Joaquín Toesca in the 1780s and completed in 1805 became the presidential palace in 1846, serving that purpose for more than a century. It was bombarded by the military in the 1973 coup, when Salvador Allende defended his presidency against the assault of General Augusto Pinochet before he committed suicide there. Free tours can be arranged by email with at least two days' notice—tell them you want to see the Salón Blanco if you'd like to go upstairs. ⊠ *Plaza de la Constitución, Moneda between Teatinos and Morandé, Santiago Centro* ☎ *2/2690–4000* ✉ *visitas@presidencia.cl* ⊕ *www.gob.cl* Ⓜ *La Moneda.*

Plaza de la Ciudadanía

PLAZA/SQUARE | On the south side of the Palacio de la Moneda, this well-kept plaza was inaugurated in 2006 as part of a public works program in preparation for the celebration of the bicentenary of Chile's independence in 2010. There are attractive water fountains and a statue of former president Jorge Alessandri. The Centro Cultural La Moneda is located underneath the plaza. ⊠ *Plaza de la Ciudadanía 26, Santiago Centro* ☎ ⊕ *www.ccplm.cl* Ⓜ *La Moneda.*

★ Plaza de la Constitución

PLAZA/SQUARE | Palacio de la Moneda and other government buildings line Constitution Square, the country's most formal plaza. The changing of the guard takes place every other day at 10 am within the triangle defined by 12 Chilean flags. Adorning the plaza are four monuments, each dedicated to a notable national figure: Diego Portales, founder of the Chilean republic; Jorge Alessandri, the country's leader from 1958 to 1964; Eduardo Frei Montalva, president from 1964 to 1970; and Salvador Allende (1970–73). ⊠ *Moneda at Morandé, Santiago Centro* Ⓜ *La Moneda.*

Teatro Municipal

PERFORMANCE VENUE | The opulent Municipal Theater is the city's cultural center, home to the opera as well as ballet and classical music performances. Designed by French architects, the theater opened in 1857, with major renovations in 1870 and 1906 following a fire and an earthquake. The Renaissance-style building is one of the city's most refined monuments with a lavish interior that deserves a visit. The cobblestoned walk around the building completes the picture. For greater insight, email ahead for a guided general tour in English. ⊠ *Plaza Alcalde Mekis, Av. Agustinas 794, at Av. San Antonio, Santiago Centro* ☎ *2/2463–1000*

⊕ *www.municipal.cl* ✉ *General tour 6000 pesos; private tour 30000* Ⓜ *Universidad de Chile, Santa Lucía.*

Shopping

Centro Artesanal Santa Lucía

MARKET | This souvenir market just across the Alameda from the base of Cerro Santa Lucía has some indigenous and locally made crafts, including some (not the finest quality) lapis lazuli items. Get your ears or navel pierced as well. It's open daily 11–7. As you should in all crowded and touristy areas, keep an eye on valuables. ✉ *Alameda and Diagonal Paraguay, La Alameda.*

Bellas Artes and Lastarria

This contiguous area is really two neighborhoods, but elements of modern and artsy Bellas Artes and the more traditional and cobblestoned Lastarria flow in and out of each other. Bellas Artes went from seedy to universally popular within a decade and is now full of budget-friendly empanada joints, pizza places, ice-cream parlors, and all-natural food shops.

Mostly cobblestoned Lastarria, which has been given city cultural heritage status, starts at Merced and extends south to the imposing new Gabriela Mistral Cultural Center. It's a better-heeled crowd in Lastarria, and the area has more upscale dining. Both areas have street-level commerce with clothing boutiques and art suppliers, and are popular among Chileans and foreigners.

TIMING AND PRECAUTIONS

You can't go wrong with a late afternoon in Bellas Artes, as restaurants and streetside cafés fill up with people off work early. In Plaza Mulato Gil de Castro, allot at least 30 minutes for the Museo de Artes Visuales and adjoining Sala

Museo Arqueológico. Because both of these areas are busy and attract people who've come to spend money, simple precautions like keeping your purse in your lap, not on the back of your chair, are recommended. Consider coming down into Lastarria after a walk up Cerro Santa Lucía, the smaller of the two hills that overlooks the city.

Sights

★ Museo de Artes Visuales

ART MUSEUM | This dazzling museum has one of Chile's finest collections of contemporary Chilean art and it displays the combined private holdings of Chilean industrial moguls Manuel Santa Cruz and Hugo Yaconi. The building itself is a masterpiece: six gallery levels float into each other in surprising ways. The wood floors and Plexiglas-sided stairways create an open and airy space where you might see—depending on what's on display when you visit—paintings and sculptures by Roberto Matta, Arturo Duclos, Gonzalo Cienfuegos, Roser Bru, José Balmes, and Eugenio Dittborn, among others. Pick up artsy souvenirs from Tienda Mulato or refuel at the café next to the entrance. ✉ *José Victorino Lastarria 307, at Plaza Mulato Gil de Castro, Lastarria* ☎ *2/2664–9337* ⊕ *www.mavi.cl* ✉ *Free* ☾ *Closed Mon.* Ⓜ *Universidad Católica.*

Sala Museo Arqueológico de Santiago

HISTORY MUSEUM | This archaeological museum is devoted specifically to the indigenous peoples of Chile and more than makes up for its small size with the quality of the exhibits, labeled in English and Spanish. Artifacts include an outstanding collection of the Andean headwear used to distinguish different ethnic groups, pottery, jewelry, and a collection of the woven bags used by Andean peoples to carry the coca leaves that sustained them during their long treks at high altitudes. It is located inside the Museo de Artes Visuales, and one entry fee pays for both visits. ✉ *José*

A work of art in itself, Museo de Artes Visuales is a prime spot to snap photos.

Victorino Lastarria 307, 2nd fl., Lastarria ☎ *2/2664-9337* ⊕ *www.mavi.cl/mas* 🖼 *Free* ⊘ *Closed Mon.* Ⓜ *Universidad Católica.*

🍴 Restaurants

★ Bocanariz

$$$ | **CHILEAN** | A haven with wine aficionados, trendy Bocanariz in Lastarria has Chilean fare, but it's best known as a superior place to sample *vino chileno*. Waitstaff at this tastefully designed and somewhat romantic venue are all sommeliers, and they serve 300 wines on any given evening, many by the glass or small pour. **Known for:** wine flights; wine by the glass; tapas. 💲 *Average main: pesos13000* ✉ *José Victorino Lastarria 276, Lastarria* ☎ *2/2638-9893* ⊕ *www.bocanariz.cl* ⊘ *Closed Sun.*

Castillo Forestal

$$$ | **FRENCH** | French fare is on the menu at this spacious national heritage converted castle with a turret room and gorgeous terrace. At lunch, sample the set brasserie menu with seafood tartare and duck, or for something lighter and also less expensive, try a turkey club or Mediterranean sandwich on focaccia with fresh Chilean mozzarella. **Known for:** great wine list; park views; French cuisine. 💲 *Average main: pesos12900* ✉ *Cardenal José María Caro 390, across from Bellas Artes museum, Parque Forestal* ☎ *9/4444-8531* ⊕ *www.castillo-forestal.cl* ⊘ *Closed Mon.*

Les Assassins

$$$ | **FRENCH** | Although at first glance this appears to be a rather somber bistro, nothing could be further from the truth. The service is friendly and the Provence-influenced food—such as the mouthwatering steak au poivre and beef Bourguignon—is first-rate. **Known for:** tasty meat dishes; exceptional French fare; great service. 💲 *Average main: pesos12000* ✉ *Merced 279B, Parque Forestal* ☎ *2/2638-4280* ⊘ *Closed Sun.* Ⓜ *Universidad Católica.*

Hotels

★ Hotel Ismael 312

$$ | HOTEL | This well-placed and well-run design hotel with a personal touch has expansive views over Parque Forestal and a rooftop pool from which to enjoy it. **Pros:** welcoming staff; unbeatable location; high design elements. **Cons:** no parking; rooms overlooking the street (as opposed to the park) do not have much of a view; the rooms can feel a bit sterile. [$] *Rooms from: pesos95000* ✉ *Ismael Valdes Vergara 312, Parque Forestal* ☎ *2/2616–7600* 🌐 *www.hotelismael312.com* 🛏 *45 rooms* 🍴 *Free Breakfast.*

★ Hotel Magnolia

$$$$ | HOTEL | A welcome addition to the neighborhood, this beautifully restored 1929 mansion is perfectly located on the cusp of both Lastarria and Bellas Artes, a stone's throw from Santa Lucía hill. **Pros:** abundant breakfast; great location; stylish and practical communal areas. **Cons:** some rooms are dark; you have to ring the bell to get in after midnight; some amenities lacking for what you expect of a higher-end hotel (e.g., no slippers or free coffee in room). [$] *Rooms from: pesos170000* ✉ *Huérfanos 539, Lastarria* ☎ *2/2664–4043* 🌐 *www.hotelmagnolia.cl* 🛏 *42 rooms* 🍴 *Free Breakfast* [M] *Bellas Artes.*

★ The Singular

$$$$ | HOTEL | This luxury lodging in Lastarria is a smart spot that's well furnished, with a modern, mainly European style. **Pros:** spa with massages, sauna, and steam room; courtyard for leisurely breakfasts; stylish and spacious rooms. **Cons:** breakfast can get crowded; no daytime access to rooftop terrace; exposed concrete of old buildings visible from rooftop deck. [$] *Rooms from: pesos200000* ✉ *Merced 294, Bellas Artes* ☎ *2/2306–8820* 🌐 *thesingular.com/hotel/santiago* 🛏 *62 rooms* 🍴 *Free Breakfast* [M] *Bellas Artes.*

Nightlife

BARS AND CLUBS

El Diablito

DANCE CLUBS | Identifiable by the leering devil on the sign, El Diablito is one of the only divey places left in Lastarria/Bellas Artes, whose decor sports spurs, stirrups, and other metal items. If you want to see what this area felt like about 10 years ago, before gentrification, this is a good spot to try. It's popular for drinks after work or late at night. ✉ *Merced 336, Parque Forestal* ☎ *2/2638–3512.*

★ José Ramón 277

BREWPUBS | A leader on the local craft beer scene, this friendly *chopería* (pub) serves an array of brews on tap and classic Chilean sandwiches—the pulled pork and avocado is a delight—to soak up the alcohol. Hipsters and local Lastarria residents come together at wooden tables to enjoy a pint or two; early birds will appreciate the breakfast menu, from 8 am. ✉ *José Ramón Gutiérrez 277, Lastarria* ☎ *9/4258–1689* [M] *Universidad Católica.*

Performing Arts

El Biógrafo

FILM | Most of the city's art cinemas tend to screen international favorites. The old standby is El Biógrafo, which shows foreign films on its single screen in the cute cobblestoned neighborhood of Lastarria. There is a café upstairs with a nice rooftop deck, decent food, and good drinks for pre- and postscreening. ✉ *José Victorino Lastarria 181, Santiago Centro* ☎ *2/2633–4435* 🌐 *www.elbiografo.cl* [M] *Universidad Católica or Bellas Artes.*

Sala La Comedia

THEATER | The well-respected theater company by the name of ICTUS performs in the Sala la Comedia, a theater just outside the Lastarria neighborhood. The company's been around for more than 50 years and is one of the most important independent groups in the country. ⊠ *Merced 349, Santiago Centro* ☎ *2/2639–1523* ⊕ *www.teatroictus.cl.*

Shopping

BOOKS
La Tienda Nacional
SOUVENIRS | For independent books from local authors, including kids' books and locally designed toys, head here. There are also postcards and posters with historical Chilean motifs, indie rock and folk bands from the '70s, and today's music, films, and documentaries for sale. ⊠ *Merced 369, Lastarria* ☎ *2/2638–4706* ⊕ *www.latiendanacional.cl* Ⓜ *Bellas Artes.*

WINE
★ Santiago Wine Club
WINE/SPIRITS | Take your most finicky wine-loving friends to this small storefront in Barrio Lastarria to try its highly rated, indie, terroir, and signatures wines, many of which are fairly hard to find elsewhere. The knowledgeable owners usually have a bottle or two on the go to sample. ⊠ *Rosal 386, Lastarria* ☎ *2/2639–3085* ⊕ *www.santiagowineclub.cl* Ⓜ *Bellas Artes or Universidad Católica.*

Parque Forestal

You wouldn't think building-happy Santiago would let the prime real estate that is Parque Forestal go without construction, but the narrow strip of land was left over after a canal was built in 1891 to tame the unpredictable Río Mapocho. The area quickly filled with the city's refuse. A decade later, under the watchful eye of Enrique Cousiño, it was transformed into the leafy Parque Forestal. It was and still is enormously popular with Santiaguinos, and recent investments have cleaned it further, installed playgrounds for children, and created a bike path along the northern edge.

On weekends, the area near the Contemporary Art Museum fills with jugglers, people doing aerial silks, and those skilled in acrobatics. The eastern tip of the park, near Plaza Baquedano (also referred to as Plaza Italia, though that plaza is farther north) is distinguished by the Wagnerian-scale *Fuente Alemana* (German Fountain), donated by the German community of Santiago. The bronze-and-stone monolith commemorates the centennial of Chilean independence.

TIMING AND PRECAUTIONS
You can have a pleasant, relaxing day strolling through the city's most popular park, losing yourself in the art museums and exploring the Mercado Central. You can easily spend an hour or two in the Museo Nacional de Bellas Artes and the Museo de Arte Contemporáneo. The Vega Chica, Tirso de Molina, and Vega Central markets are usually crowded, so keep an eye on your personal belongings. When they close around sunset, it's best to return to more lively neighborhoods south of the river.

◉ Sights

Centro Cultural Estación Mapocho
TRAIN/TRAIN STATION | This mighty edifice, with its trio of two-story arches framed by intricate terra-cotta detailing, is as elegant as any train station in the world. The station was inaugurated in 1913 as a terminus for trains arriving from Valparaíso and points north, but after trains were diverted to Estación Central, the space was turned into one of the city's principal arts and conference centers. The Centro Cultural Estación Mapocho houses two restaurants, a café, a large exhibition hall, and arts space. The cavernous station that once sheltered steam engines now hosts musical performances and other events, such as the Cumbre Guachaca, a celebration of city-meets-down-home-country culture, usually held in April. ⊠ *Plaza de la Cultura, Independencia at Balmaceda, Parque Forestal*

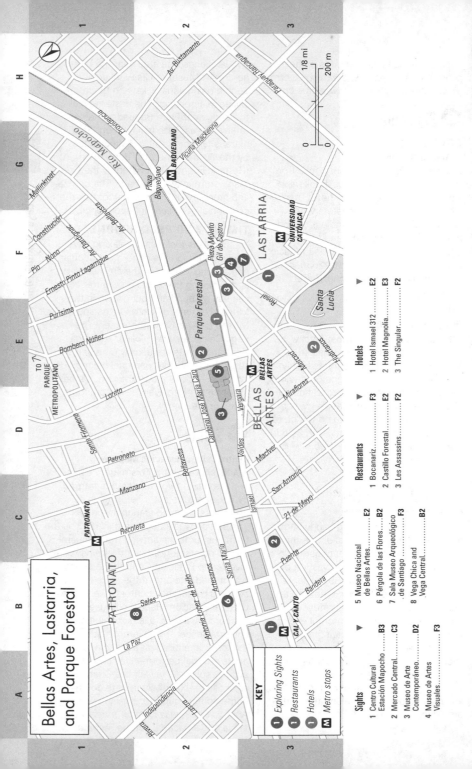

Bellas Artes, Lastarria, and Parque Forestal

KEY

1 Exploring Sights
1 Restaurants
1 Hotels
M Metro stops

Sights ▶

1 Centro Cultural
Estación Mapocho **B3**
2 Mercado Central **C3**
3 Museo de Arte
Contemporáneo **D2**
4 Museo de Artes
Visuales **F3**
5 Museo Nacional
de Bellas Artes **E2**
6 Pérgola de las Flores **B2**
7 Sala Museo Arqueológico
de Santiago **F3**
8 Vega Chica and
Vega Central **B2**

Restaurants ▶

1 Bocanariz **F3**
2 Castillo Forestal **E2**
3 Les Assassins **F2**

Hotels ▶

1 Hotel Ismael 312 ....**E2**
2 Hotel Magnolia **E3**
3 The Singular **F2**

1/8 mi
200 m

TO
PARQUE
METROPOLITANO

PATRONATO
CAL Y CANTO
BELLAS ARTES
LASTARRIA
BAQUEDANO
UNIVERSIDAD CATÓLICA

Parque Forestal
Plaza Mulato Gil de Castro
Plaza Baquedano
Santa Lucía
Río Mapocho

Av. Bustamante
Vicuña Mackenna
Providencia
Mallinkrodt
Constitución
Pío Nono
Av. Bellavista
Ernesto Pinto Lagarrigue
Purísima
Bombero Núñez
Loreto
Santa Filomena
Patronato
Manzano
Recoleta
La Paz
Salas
Antonia López de Bello
Artesanos
Santa María
Puente
Bandera
21 de Mayo
Ismael
San Antonio
Maciver
Valdés
Cardenal José María Caro
Vergara
Miraflores
Namur
Huérfanos
Merced
Rosal
Parque Bustamante

☎ 2/2787–0000 ⊕ www.estacionmapo-cho.cl ☒ Station free, exhibition fees vary ◌ Closed Mon. Ⓜ Puente Cal y Canto.

Mercado Central

MARKET | At the Central Market you'll find a matchless selection of edible products from the sea. Depending on the season, you might see the delicate beaks of picorocos, the world's only edible barnacles; erizos, the prickly-shelled sea urchins; or heaps of giant mussels. If the seafood doesn't capture your interest, the architecture may: the lofty wrought-iron ceiling of the structure, reminiscent of a Victorian train station, was prefabricated in England and erected in Santiago between 1868 and 1872. Diners are regaled by minstrels in the middle of the market, where a few larger restaurants compete for customers. You can also find a cheap meal at the smaller restaurants around the edge of the market. ✉ Ismael Valdés Vergara 900, Parque Forestal ☎ 2/2696–8327 ⊕ www.mercadocentral.cl Ⓜ Puente Cal y Canto.

Museo de Arte Contemporáneo

ART MUSEUM | The elegant Museum of Contemporary Art, set in a classic building, showcases modern Latin American paintings, photography, and sculpture. The museum is run by the art school of Universidad de Chile and isn't afraid to take risks. Look for Fernando Botero's pudgy Caballo (Horse) sculpture out front, and drop in at its café serving gourmet coffee and homemade treats. There is a second location of this museum near Quinta Normal, and a bus-turned-café called Central Placeres or simply La Micro ("the bus," in Chilean slang) parked outside. ✉ Ismael Valdés Vergara 506, Parque Forestal ☎ 2/2977–1755 ⊕ www.mac.uchile.cl ◌ Closed Mon. Ⓜ Bellas Artes.

Museo Nacional de Bellas Artes

ART MUSEUM | Unfortunately, Chile's main fine arts museum now has only a small part of its excellent collection of Chilean paintings on display, confining it to just six small rooms on the first floor. The rest of the museum is given over to temporary exhibitions of varying interest. The elegant, neoclassical building, which was originally intended to house the city's school of fine arts, has an impressive glass-domed ceiling, which illuminates the main hall. Guided tours are available in Spanish only, with reduced schedules in January and February.

■ TIP➜ Walk through to the Museo de Arte Contemporáneo, housed in the same building. ✉ At José M. de la Barra 650, Parque Forestal ☎ 2/2997–8000 ⊕ www.mnba.gob.cl ☒ Free ◌ Closed Mon. ☞ Guided tours daily in Spanish; reserve ahead to mediacion.educacion@mnba.cl Ⓜ Bellas Artes.

Pérgola de las Flores

MARKET | Santiaguinos come to the Pérgola de las Flores (literally: "gazebo of flowers") markets to buy wreaths and flower arrangements for decoration or to bring to the city's two nearby cemeteries. La Pérgola de las Flores, a famous Chilean musical and movie, is based on the conflict that arose in the 1930s when the mayor of Santiago wanted to shut down the market, which at that time was located near the Iglesia San Francisco on the Alameda; find a chatty florist at one of the two open-air markets—Pérgola San Francisco and Pérgola Santa María, each with about 40 vendors—and you may learn all about it. ✉ Av. La Paz at Artesanos, Recoleta ☎Ⓜ Puente Cal y Canto.

Vega Chica and Vega Central

MARKET | From fruit to furniture, meat to machinery, these lively markets stock just about anything you can name. Alongside ordinary items you can find delicacies like piñones, giant pine nuts found on monkey-puzzle trees. If you're undaunted by crowds, try a typical Chilean meal in a closet-size eatery, or picada in the Vega Central, chowing down on brothy cazuela (a typical meat and vegetable soup) or a plate of fried fish. For greater selection and a little more space, go to the second floor of the Vega Chica (now called Tirso de Molina) where Chilean, Colombian, Thai, Mexican, and Peruvian food is dished out in large portions at fair prices. As in any other crowded market, be extra careful with your belongings. ✉ *Antonia López de Bello between Av. Salas and Nueva Rengifo, Recoleta* Ⓜ *Patronato or Puente Cal Y Canto.*

Bellavista and Parque Metropolitano

If you happen to be in Santiago on one of those lovely winter days when the sun comes out after rain has cleared the air, head straight for Parque Metropolitano. In the center is Cerro San Cristóbal, a hill reached via funicular railway, taxi, a 45-minute trail, or an hour-plus uphill walk on the main road. Atop the hill are spectacular views of the city below the snow-covered Andes Mountains.

In the shadow of Cerro San Cristóbal is Bellavista. The neighborhood has but one sight—poet Pablo Neruda's hillside home of La Chascona—but it's perhaps the city's best place to wander. Strike out on your own, or start out in Patio Bellavista (an open-air mall/arcade); either way you're sure to find interesting shops, small art galleries, souvenirs, and food to suit most budgets and tastes.

TIMING AND PRECAUTIONS

Plan on devoting an entire day to visiting Parque Metropolitano's major attractions. During the week the park is almost empty, and you can enjoy the views in relative solitude. If you decide to walk (or cycle) up from the Bellavista side, take the road about 5 km (3 miles), or take a right at a sign about half a mile in that says Zorro Vidal and follow the path for a hike about 40 minutes to the top. This is best done on weekends. Avoid walking down the hill if you decide to watch the sunset from the lofty perch—the area is not well

patrolled. Give yourself at least an hour to wander through Bellavista, and another hour for a tour of La Chascona.

Sights

★ Cerro San Cristóbal

VIEWPOINT | FAMILY | This large, iconic hill within the centenary Parque Metropolitano is one of the most popular tourist attractions in Santiago. From the western entrance at Plaza Caupolicán (Pío Nono), you can take a steep but enjoyable one-hour walk to the summit, or take the funicular, a historic monument that opened in 1925. The *teleférico* (cable car) ascends from the eastern entrance, seven blocks north of Pedro de Valdivia metro stop. ✉ *Cerro San Cristóbal, Bellavista* ☎ *2/2730–1331* ⊕ *www. parquemet.cl* 🖰 *Round-trip teleférico 6900 pesos* 🕑 *Closed: park, after 8 pm; funicular, after 6:45 pm* Ⓜ *Baquedano, Pedro de Valdivia.*

Jardín Botánico Mapulemu

GARDEN | Gravel paths lead you to restful nooks in the Mapulemu Botanical Garden, dedicated to more than 70 native Chilean species. Every path and stairway seems to bring you to better views of Santiago and the Andes. On weekends, the Instituto Nacional de Deportes conducts classes starting at 9:30 am. These free municipality-run seminars may include yoga, Zumba, aerobics, aeroboxing, or *bicicleta estática*, a spinning-like activity. There are also paid yoga classes on Sundays from 10 to noon. The easiest access is from the Pedro de Valdivia side. ✉ *Cerro San Cristóbal, Bellavista* ☎ *2/2730–1331* 🖰 *Free* Ⓜ *Pedro de Valdivia.*

★ La Chascona

HISTORIC HOME | This house designed by Nobel Prize–winning poet Pablo Neruda was dubbed the "Woman with the Tousled Hair" after Matilde Urrutia, his third wife. The two met while strolling in nearby Parque Forestal, and for

Take a funicular ride to the hilltop of Cerro San Cristóbal for views of the city.

years the house served as a romantic hideaway before they married. The pair's passionate relationship was recounted in the 1995 Italian film *Il Postino*. Audio guides are available in English, Spanish, French, Portuguese, and German, and the house is visually fascinating, with winding garden paths, stairs, and bridges leading to the house and its library, which is stuffed with books. There's Neruda's old bedroom in a tower and a secret passageway. Scattered throughout are collections of butterflies, seashells, wineglasses, and other odd objects that inspired Neruda's tumultuous life and romantic poetry. Although not as magical as Neruda's house in Isla Negra, La Chascona still sets your imagination dancing. The house is on a little side street leading off Constitución. ⊠ *Fernando Márquez de la Plata 0192, Bellavista* ☎ *2/2777–8741* ⊕ *www.fundacionneruda.org* ✉ *Audio guide 8000 pesos; students 2500 pesos* ⊙ *Closed Mon.* Ⓜ *Baquedano.*

★ Patio Bellavista

RESTAURANT | This multilevel complex of bars, eateries, cafés, and souvenir shops is a Bellavista centerpoint. The patio houses a tourist office, free concerts or *cueca* (national dance) performance in the central plaza, a live music space, a theater, galleries, and restaurants dealing in Peruvian cuisine such as Tambo, as well as Italian, French, and Middle Eastern eateries. The patio is open daily from 8 am until 2 am; shops open 10–9. ⊠ *Pío Nono 73, Bellavista* ☎ *2/2249–8700* ⊕ *www.patiobellavista.cl* Ⓜ *Baquedano.*

Plaza Tupahue

PLAZA/SQUARE | **FAMILY** | The main attraction in summer of this area inside Parque Metropolitano is the delightful Piscina Tupahue, an 82-meter (269-foot) pool with a rocky crag running along one side. Beside the pool is the 1925 Torreón Victoria, a stone tower surrounded by a trellis of bougainvillea. If Piscina Tupahue is too crowded, try the nearby Piscina Antilén. From Plaza Tupahue you can follow a path below to Plaza de Juegos

Infantiles Gabriela Mistral, a popular playground. ✉ *Cerro San Cristóbal, Bellavista* ☎ *2/2730–1300* 🎟 *Piscina Tupahue 4000 pesos; piscina Antilén 7500 pesos* ⏲ *Pool closed Mon.* [M] *Pedro de Valdivia.*

Zoológico Nacional

ZOO | **FAMILY** | The zoo is a good place to see Chilean birds and animals, such as puma and condor, that you might not otherwise encounter. As is often the case with many older zoos, the animals aren't given much room. ✉ *Cerro San Cristóbal, Bellavista* ☎ *2/2730–1368* 🌐 *www.parquemet.cl/zoologico-nacional* 🎟 *Adults 4000 pesos; children 2000 pesos* ⏲ *Closed Mon.* [M] *Baquedano.*

🍴 Restaurants

★ Como Agua Para Chocolate

$$$ | **CHILEAN** | Originally inspired by Laura Esquivel's romantic 1989 novel *Like Water for Chocolate,* this Bellavista standout focuses on Chilean dishes made with "life, love, vigor, and passion" as per the book. Reserve the "bed table" if you want to be showy (it has a headboard but is not actually a bed). **Known for:** crowds; merluza; romantic ambience. [$] *Average main: pesos13000* ✉ *Constitución 88, Bellavista* ☎ *2/2777–8740* 🌐 *www.comoaguaparachocolate.cl* ⏲ *Closed Sun. lunch* [M] *Baquedano.*

El Mesón Nerudiano

$$$ | **CHILEAN** | Evoking another time and place, El Mesón Nerudiano centers around traditional recipes, poetry, music, and live theater, all in homage to Chile's greatest poet, Pablo Neruda. A stone's throw from La Chascona, Neruda's house-turned-museum, this restaurant has a menu with Chilean favorites, including *caldillo de congrio,* a fish soup cooked from the recipe given in one of Neruda's poems. **Known for:** literary inspiration; traditional ambience; popular with tourists. [$] *Average main: pesos12000* ✉ *Dominica 35, Bellavista* ☎ *2/2737–1542* 🌐 *www.elmesonnerudiano.cl* ⏲ *Closed Mon.*

Galindo

$$ | **CHILEAN** | Starting life as a canteen for local workmen, Galindo today draws artists and the young Bellavista crowd, who come for traditional Chilean fare in an old adobe house. Although it gets crowded, it's a great place to try traditional dishes like *pastel de choclo* or a hearty *cazuela,* a typical meat and vegetable soup. **Known for:** casual atmosphere; Chilean classics; reasonable prices. [$] *Average main: pesos8000* ✉ *Dardignac 098, Bellavista* ☎ *2/2777–0116* 🌐 *www.galindo.cl* [M] *Baquedano.*

La Bodeguilla

$$$ | **SPANISH** | Stop by this authentic Spanish restaurant after visiting Cerro San Cristóbal for tasty tapas like *chorizo riojano* (a piquant sausage), *pulpo a la gallega* (octopus with peppers and potatoes), and *queso manchego* (a mild white cheese) or for the house specialty—*cabrito al horno* (oven-roasted kid goat). Wine aficionados will appreciate the extensive list of vino chileno. **Known for:** casual vibe; small bites to share; extensive wine list. [$] *Average main: pesos13000* ✉ *Av. Domínica 5, Bellavista* ☎ *9/6769–2872* ⏲ *Closed Sun. and Mon.* [M] *Baquedano.*

Peumayén

$$$ | **CHILEAN** | Taking inspiration from ancestral dishes made in all the regions of Chile, there's a historical theme at Peumayén, where every meal starts with a colorful "bread basket," a slate plate with examples from the north to the south of Chile. Entrées designed for sharing include guanaco meat; horse meat, lamb, fish, and the much-celebrated potato continue the ancestral theme. **Known for:** outdoor seating; unique and tasty meat dishes; traditional decor. [$] *Average main: pesos12900* ✉ *Constitución 136, Bellavista* ☎ *9/4958–0141* 🌐 *www.peumayenchile.cl* ⏲ *Closed Sun. and Mon.* [M] *Baquedano.*

Uncle Fletch

$$ | **AMERICAN** | **FAMILY** | Hereford beef burgers, onion rings, and three kinds of veggie burgers all share space at this American-style restaurant owned by a French expatriate. These are some of the best burgers in the city, with patties made from meat, mushroom, chickpea, quinoa, or shrimp. **Known for:** casual dining; fast food; great burgers. $ Average main: pesos9900 ✉ Dardignac 0192, Bellavista ☎ 9/4297–4299 ⊕ www.uncle-fletch.com Ⓜ Baquedano.

🛏 Hotels

★ The Aubrey

$$$$ | **HOTEL** | One of the city's favorite luxury boutique hotels, this hotel was formed in 2009 when two 1920s mansions next to Cerro San Cristóbal were joined together, giving it ample outdoor space, including a pool and an indoor-outdoor patio bar. **Pros:** 20% discount on rooms in winter; well lit; knowlegeable and friendly staff. **Cons:** noise from nearby bars can make its way in; aromas from the nearby zoo can waft in; less expensive rooms lack hillside views and private terraces. $ Rooms from: pesos177000 ✉ Constitución 317, Bellavista ⊕ www.theaubrey.com ⬎ 15 rooms ⏐◌⏐ Free Breakfast.

El Castillo Rojo

$$$ | **HOTEL** | This boutique hotel in a red castle just off the beaten path in Bellavista is a step back in time, in all the right ways. **Pros:** superior customer service; great location in Bellavista; attention to detail. **Cons:** limited breakfast; main areas can be dark; decoration feels fussy at times. $ Rooms from: pesos106000 ✉ Constitución 195, Bellavista ☎ 2/2352–4500 ⊕ www.castillorojohotel.com ⬎ 19 rooms ⏐◌⏐ Free Breakfast.

★ Loreto Hotel

$$ | **HOTEL** | This historic house nestled between Bellavista and Recoleta neighborhoods has a great location and yet isn't close enough to hear any of the noise. **Pros:** quiet; great breakfast buffet; very helpful staff. **Cons:** some rooms are very small (ask for a larger one); no elevator; you need to take a taxi at night. $ Rooms from: pesos88000 ✉ Loreto 170, Bellavista ☎ 2/2777–1060 ⊕ www.loretohotel.cl ⬎ 28 rooms ⏐◌⏐ Free Breakfast.

🍸 Nightlife

BARS AND CLUBS

La Casa en el Aire

LIVE MUSIC | Located within Patio Bellavista, La Casa en el Aire is a great place to catch live bands. There's also a larger venue with a terrace at Antonia López de Bello 0125. If your Spanish is good, you can listen to storytelling and stand-up, too, or even perform. There's a happy hour daily from 4 to 9. ✉ Constitución 40, Local 56, Bellavista ☎ 2/2243–6902 ⊕ www.lacasaenelaire.cl.

La Peña de Nano Parra

CAFÉS | This brightly colored house in Bellavista is a great place to take in local music with a down-to-earth and generally young, local crowd. Peñas are traditional watering holes where la nueva canción chilena, a kind of Latin American resistance folk music, was first popularized. Due to their historically political nature, peñas became clandestine during the dictatorship. ✉ Ernesto Pinto Lagarrigue 80, Bellavista ☎ 9/6586–6832.

Sarita Colonia

BARS | Three floors of fun await at Sarita Colonia, the only Peruvian drag bar and restaurant in Chile. Named after a Peruvian saint for the poor, Sarita Colonia is brimming with kitsch religious artifacts and is one of the most fun places in Bellavista for a night out. Order a ceviche or the Peruvian classic lomo saltado. The bar serves delicious pisco sours. ✉ Loreto 40, Bellavista ☎ 2/2881–3937 ⊕ www.saritacoloniarestoran.cl ⊗ Closed Sun. dinner and Mon. Ⓜ Bellas Artes.

SALSA CLUBS
Havana Salsa
DANCE CLUBS | If you're itching to dance salsa or merengue plus enjoy food and a show, come to this club Thursday, Friday, or Saturday night. It starts with an all-you-can-eat buffet of Cuban specialties, and at midnight, there's a 40-minute show with sensual professional dancers. Only after that does the dance floor open to the public. ✉ *Domínica 142, Bellavista* ☎ *9/8457–4556* ⊕ *www.havanasalsa.cl* ☞ *13900 pesos with buffet; 6000 pesos without.* Ⓜ *Baquedano.*

Salsoteca Maestra Vida
DANCE CLUBS | This gay-friendly small club gets full quickly, but salsa dancers say it's the best in Santiago. Classes for beginners to advanced are 3,000 pesos and run Wednesday through Friday from 8. Come alone or with a partner. Pisco cocktails from 3,500 pesos. ✉ *Pío Nono 380, Bellavista* ☎ *2/2735–7416* ⊕ *www. maestravida.cl.*

 ## Shopping

MARKETS
Feria Artesanal Pío Nono
MARKET | Bellavista's colorful Feria Artesanal Pío Nono, held in the park at the start of Avenida Pío Nono, comes alive every night of the week. The area, particularly the south end of Pío Nono, is even busier on weekends, when vendors gather in Parque Domingo Gómez, in the shadow of the Universidad de San Sebastián Building to display handicrafts. It can be hit or miss for quality, but you can't beat it for convenience. ✉ *At Pío Nono and Bellavista, Bellavista.*

Parque Quinta Normal Area

Just west of downtown is shady Parque Quinta Normal, a 75-acre park with three museums within its borders, another just across the street, and two more down the block. This is an especially-good place to take kids. The park was created in 1841 as a place to experiment with new agricultural techniques. It's great for quiet strolls, except on weekends, when you have to maneuver around noisy families. Pack a picnic or a soccer ball and fit right in. *The park is closed on Mondays.*

Near the park is the Museo de la Memoria, a museum in memory of the dictatorship, and the modern Biblioteca de Santiago. Closer to the Alameda is the arts and performing center Matucana 100 and the Quinta Normal branch of the Museo de Arte Contemporáneo, both of which have outdoor cafés.

TIMING AND PRECAUTIONS
Except on Monday, you can visit the museums in and around the park, stroll along a wooded path, take a pedal boat in the lagoon, rent a pedal car, or take the motorized pretend train around the park all within a couple of hours. Check out the dilapidated greenhouse midpark for photo ops.

 ## Sights

Barrio Concha y Toro
NEIGHBORHOOD | Don't be put off by the shops selling car parts at the entrance to this intimate neighborhood on the north side of La Alameda between avenues Brasil and Ricardo Cumming. Developed in the 1920s on land belonging to a mining branch of the Concha y Toro family— another branch founded the winery of

the same name—the neighborhood has short winding streets spanning out from a central plaza with a fountain and an eclectic mixture of neoclassical, art deco, and Baroque houses, many designed by the same architects who worked on Barrio París-Londres. There is a restaurant, café, and occasional street fairs on weekends. ⊠ *Barrio Concha y Toro, Santiago Centro* Ⓜ *República.*

★ Cementerio General

CEMETERY | This necropolis in the northern part of the city reveals a lot about traditional Chilean society. Through the lofty stone arches of the main entrance are well-tended paths lined with marble mausoleums and squat mansions belonging to Chile's wealthy families. The 8- or 10-story "niches"—concrete shelves housing thousands of coffins—resemble middle-class apartment buildings. Their inhabitants lie here until the rent runs out and they are evicted. Look for former President Salvador Allende's final resting spot; a map at the main entrance to the cemetery can help you find it. Fifty-minute Human Rights Tours in Spanish run weekdays at 6 pm. General tours are weekdays (except Wednesday) by prior arrangement and last 90 minutes. Two 75-minute night tours are available at 8:45 pm for kids and adults. All tours require online reservations and are either free or cost between 4,000 and 6,000 pesos. ⊠ *Av. Prof. Alberto Zañartu 951, main entrance at La Paz, Recoleta* ☎ *2/2637–7800* ⊕ *http://tour.cementeriogeneral.cl* ☒ *Free* Ⓜ *Cementerios.*

Estación Central

NOTABLE BUILDING | Inaugurated in 1897, Central Station is the city's last remaining train station, serving the south as far as Chillán. The greenish iron canopy of the station that once shielded the engines from the weather is flanked by two lovely beaux arts edifices. A lively market keeps this terminal buzzing with activity. The grand entrance has a colorful, illuminated carousel and a couple of cafés. As in any busy place, keep a close watch on valuables. ⊠ *Alameda 3170, Estación Central* ☎ *600/585–5000* ☒ *Free* Ⓜ *Estación Central.*

Museo Artequín

ART MUSEUM | FAMILY | The resplendent Pabellón París outside the Parque Quinta Normal grounds houses this interactive museum that teaches the fundamentals of art to children, but the pavilion itself—with its glass domes, Pompeian-red walls, and blue-steel columns—is the real jewel. Designed by French architect Pierre-Henri Picq, it housed Chile's exhibition in the 1889 Paris International Exposition (where Gustave Eiffel's skyline-defining tower was unveiled); the structure was later shipped to Santiago. On weekdays, school groups explore the two floors of reproductions of famous artworks hung at kid-height as well as the virtual reality salon. There are occasional interactive exhibits and workshops, plus an on-site café. ⊠ *Av. Portales 3530, Parque Quinta Normal* ☎ *2/2681–8656* ⊕ *www.artequin.cl* ☒ *2000 pesos; free Sun.* ☾ *Mon. and Feb.* Ⓜ *Quinta Normal.*

Museo de Ciencia y Tecnología

SCIENCE MUSEUM | FAMILY | Children can spend a happy half hour at this small science-and-technology museum's interactive exhibits, while adults can peruse its collection of old phonographs, calculators, and computers. A small part of the Museo Infantil's (Children's Museum) collection was also moved to this museum after the 2010 earthquake, and there are exhibits for ages three and up on astronomy and vision. ⊠ *Parque Quinta Normal, Parque Quinta Normal* ☎ *2/2681–6022* ⊕ *www.corpdicyt.cl* ☒ *1000 pesos* ☾ *Closed Mon.* Ⓜ *Quinta Normal.*

★ Museo de La Memoria y Los Derechos Humanos

HISTORY MUSEUM | This museum is a powerful testimony to the coup that established the Chilean dictatorship of Augusto Pinochet; the resulting detention, torture, and murder of Chilean citizens; and the country's historic vote to return to democracy. There is a heavy audio-visual component, with moving letters by children about the events of the times. Some images and artifacts here might be challenging for children to process, but it's an important part of Chilean history and arguably the country's best museum. It is just across the street from the Parque Quinta Normal, and there is also an entrance in Quinta Normal metro station. Daily tours in English begin at 11 am, noon, and 3:30 pm; audio guides in several languages are available for 2,000 pesos. ⊠ *Matucana 501, Parque Quinta Normal* ☎ *2/2597–9600* ⊕ *www.museodelamemoria.cl* ☜ *Free* ☉ *Closed Mon.* Ⓜ *Quinta Normal.*

★ Museo Ferroviario

OTHER MUSEUM | FAMILY | Chile's once-mighty railroads have been relegated to history, but this acre of Parque Quinta Normal keeps the memory alive. Sixteen steam locomotives and four passenger coaches are set within quiet gardens with placards in Spanish and English. You can board several of the trains. Among the collection is one of the locomotives used on the old cross-Andes railway to Argentina, which operated between Chile and Argentina from 1910 until 1971. Guided tours are available. ⊠ *Av. Las Palmeras, Parque Quinta Normal* ☎ *2/2681–4627* ⊕ *www.corpdicyt.cl/ mferroviario* ☜ *800 pesos* ☉ *Closed Mon.* Ⓜ *Quinta Normal.*

Museo Nacional de Historia Natural

HISTORY MUSEUM | FAMILY | The National Natural History Museum is the centerpiece of Parque Quinta Normal. French architect Paul Lathoud designed the building for Chile's first international exposition in 1875. Damaged by successive earthquakes, the neoclassical structure was rebuilt and enlarged. There are large dioramas of stuffed animals against painted backdrops, descriptions of wrongs committed against indigenous people, and occasionally, paleontologists working in glass-walled exhibits. The skeleton of an enormous blue whale hangs in the central hall, delighting children of all ages. Exhibits are labeled only in Spanish, but audio guides in English are available. ⊠ *Parque Quinta Normal* ☎ *2/2997–9229* ⊕ *www.mnhn.cl* ☜ *Free* ☉ *Closed Mon.* Ⓜ *Quinta Normal.*

🎭 Performing Arts

★ Matucana 100

THEATER | Over the past several years, Matucana 100, a converted train warehouse, has become one of the main anchors of the area surrounding Quinta Normal Park. On weekends there are outdoor dance events, and Matucana 100 frequently host fairs, art installations, and film festivals. Cafe 100—housed in a converted bus, continuing the public transport theme—sells specialty coffee and coconut water, a good complement to the nearby Soul Kitchen food truck, which serves a hearty Sunday brunch until 4 pm. ⊠ *Matucana 100, Quinta Normal* ☎ *2/2964–9250* ⊕ *www.m100. cl* ☞ *Closed Mon. and Tues.* Ⓜ *Quinta Normal or Estación Central.*

Vitacura

Vitacura is not only Santiago's top shopping spot, it is also—with its tree-shaded streets, gardens, and wide sidewalks—a great place for a stroll, especially on a Saturday morning when residents are out jogging, walking their dogs, or simply picking up a newspaper and some fresh *marraquetas,* Chile's favorite bread rolls. Parque Bicentenario is a great place for a run, or taking kids to feed the fish, geese,

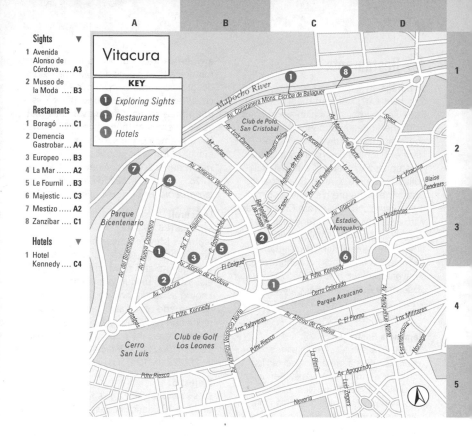

Sights ▼

1 Avenida
  Alonso de
  Córdova..... **A3**
2 Museo de
  la Moda **B3**

Restaurants ▼

1 Boragó **C1**
2 Demencia
  Gastrobar... **A4**
3 Europeo **B3**
4 La Mar **A2**
5 Le Fournil .. **B3**
6 Majestic **C3**
7 Mestizo **A2**
8 Zanzíbar **C1**

Hotels ▼

1 Hotel
  Kennedy **C4**

and other birds that live in the pond there (animal feed is sold on-site).

Sights

Avenida Alonso de Córdova

STREET | In Vitacura, you can wrap yourself in style on and near Avenida Alonso de Córdova. This wide street, home to high-end chain stores, is where the well-heeled shop for more expensive items. Look sharp and ring the bell at these stores, as they usually keep their doors locked (not just anybody gets in). ✉ *Santiago.*

Museo de la Moda

OTHER MUSEUM | FAMILY | The Fashion Museum, opened in 2007 by a son of Jorge Yarur Banna, one of Chile's most successful textile barons, hosts small but choice exhibitions mostly featuring women's dresses that date to the 1600s. Housed in the Yarur family's former home, designed by Chilean architects in the style of Frank Lloyd Wright in the early 1960s, the museum offers a fascinating insight into the lifestyle of the Chilean oligarchy in the run-up to the upheaval of Salvador Allende's socialist government and the ensuing military coup. The main rooms feature original furnishings, while the pink 1958 Ford Thunderbird driven by Yarur's wife is parked in a courtyard.

■ **TIP→ Call before visiting; the museum can close for up to two months between exhibitions.**

El Garage café, open daily, serves light meals and snacks at reasonable prices. ✉ *Av. Vitacura 4562, Vitacura* ☎ *2/2219–3623* ⊕ *www.museodelamoda.cl* ✉ *3000 pesos* ⊘ *Closed Mon.* Ⓜ *No metro.*

🍴 Restaurants

★ Boragó
$$$$ | **CHILEAN** | Concept meets Chilean ingredients (many of which are foraged from the Andes and the length of the coast) at this award-winning establishment, where diners enjoy a 15- to 18-step tasting menu that has sustainability at its core. One of Chef Rodolfo Guzmán's signature dishes is a spin on the *curanto* clambake from Chiloé, made with Patagonian rainwater and served in what looks like a small clearing in a tiny thicket. **Known for:** unforgettable experience; fine dining; tasting menu. $ *Average main: pesos110000* ✉ *San Josemaría Escrivá de Balaguer 5970, Vitacura* ☎ *2/2953–8893* 🌐 *www.borago.cl* 🕒 *No lunch; closed Sun.*

Demencia Gastrobar
$$ | **CHILEAN** | Small sharing plates with Asian flair plus a fantastic cocktail list make for a fun and tasty experience at Demencia. Chef Benja Nast plays with colors and flavors (think: scallops in a fresh herb salsa with a chili pepper kick). **Known for:** light bites; sake-based drinks; trendy hot spot with music. $ *Average main: pesos9000* ✉ *Av. Vitacura 3520, Vitacura* ☎ *9/7760–5761* 🌐 *www.demenciagastrobar.com* 🕒 *Closed Sun.*

Europeo
$$$$ | **SEAFOOD** | Seafood receives top billing at this trendy yet relaxed eatery on Santiago's swankiest shopping avenue. Try the shellfish risotto topped with a fish stock foam or wild game, such as venison ragout. **Known for:** posh crowd; seafood and wild game; efficient service. $ *Average main: pesos18000* ✉ *Av. Alonso de Córdova 2417, Vitacura* ☎ *2/2208–3603* 🌐 *www.europeo.cl* 🕒 *Closed Sun. No lunch Mon.*

★ La Mar
$$$$ | **SEAFOOD** | Opened by Peruvian culinary legend Gastón Acurio, this restaurant with a busy roadside location is bright and airy, with turquoise chairs and a white canvas roof over the terrace that mimics a boat's sails. For your palatable delight, tuck into Peru's emblematic ceviches—you're spoiled with choices due to the seven different varieties that you can enjoy at the fish counter. **Known for:** top-notch pisco sours; seafood; elevated Peruvian classics. $ *Average main: pesos20000* ✉ *Nueva Costanera 4076, Vitacura* ☎ *2/2206–7839* 🌐 *www.lamarcebicheria.cl* 🕒 *No dinner Sun.*

Le Fournil
$$$ | **BISTRO** | **FAMILY** | This restaurant features Mediterranean fare and is a great place for a carry-out breakfast or a light quiche and salad lunch. Le Fournil also offers a unique version of pizza, known as *tartine,* which uses its own homemade bread as a base. **Known for:** quick and easy dining; on-site bakery; Chilean specialty pizza. $ *Average main: pesos11000* ✉ *Av. Vitacura 3841, Vitacura* ☎ *2/2228–0219* 🌐 *www.lefournil.cl.*

Majestic
$$$$ | **INDIAN** | Santiago's first Indian restaurant, Majestic is considered by some to be the best. Whether you order a simple lentil dahl or sophisticated curries, you're in for an authentic meal surrounded by tapestries and shiny adornments. **Known for:** reasonable prices; spicy food; Indian cuisine. $ *Average main: pesos17000* ✉ *Av. Kennedy 5600, Vitacura* ☎ *2/3245–0337* 🌐 *www.majestic.cl* [M] *Manquehue.*

Mestizo
$$$ | **CHILEAN** | Sporting views over Parque Bicentenario, this is a great spot for a leisurely lunch or a generous pisco sour as the sun sets between the hills in summer. The eclectic menu brings together some of the best of Chilean and Peruvian cuisine, with an emphasis on fish, as well as *plateada,* a slow-cooked cut of beef on a bed of mashed potatoes and basil. **Known for:** great views; outdoor seating; seafood. $ *Average main: pesos14000* ✉ *Av. Bicentenario 4050, Vitacura* ☎ *9/6843–7146* 🌐 *www.mestizorestaurant.cl.*

The restaurant La Mar by Gastón Acurio is known for Peruvian classics such as ceviche and pisco sours.

Zanzíbar

$$$$ | **ASIAN** | The decor here is fun, if a bit over-the-top. Tables are fanciful, with designs made from pistachio nuts, red peppers, and beans; and bright mosaic floors and dozens of silver lanterns create a sensual ambience and conjure up an exotic atmosphere for dishes taking origin from Africa and Asia, such as the flavorful Szechuan shrimp and Indonesian satay. **Known for:** pan-African and Asian cuisine; buzzy atmosphere; rooftop dining. [$] *Average main: pesos15500* ✉ *Borde Río, Av. Monseñor Escrivá de Balaguer 6400, Vitacura* ☎ *2/2218–0118* 🌐 *www.zanzibar.cl* ⏲ *No dinner Sun.*

Hotels

Hotel Kennedy

$$ | **HOTEL** | Located on the main road out to the mountains, Hotel Kennedy with its glass tower is popular with skiers who prefer to make the 45-minute journey each day rather than pay higher hotel prices up by the slopes. **Pros:** helpful staff; Aquarium restaurant, featuring good international cuisine and a cellar full of excellent Chilean wines; free Wi-Fi. **Cons:** not all staff speak English; Wi-Fi connection slow; now more than 20 years old, the hotel is showing its age. [$] *Rooms from: pesos59000* ✉ *Av. Kennedy 4570, Vitacura* ☎ *2/2290–8100* 🌐 *www.hotelkennedychile.com* 🛏 *133 rooms* 🍴 *Free Breakfast* [M] *No metro.*

Nightlife

El Toro

DANCE CLUBS | This spacious gay resto-bar welcomes everyone and is open every night except Sunday. From your table, you may spot models and other members of the "*farandula*" (Chilean celebrities) who frequent the place. Lunch is well priced, with dishes such as eggplant lasagna or ají de gallina (Peruvian chicken stew) available for around 9,000 pesos. It functions as a bar-restaurant until 2 am, but may close earlier on quieter nights like Monday or Tuesday. ✉ *Av. Alonso de Córdova 3788, Vitacura* ☎ *2/2761–5954* 🌐 *www.eltoro.cl* ⏲ *Closed Sun.*

Shopping

ANTIQUES

Centro Comercial Lo Castillo

ANTIQUES & COLLECTIBLES | Some nice antiques shops are found in the basement of the Centro Comercial Lo Castillo, which is quite small and, apart from a cinema and the antique shops, sells mostly women's wear and jewelry. It's one block up from the corner of Avenida Alonso de Córdova. The indoor shopping arcade dates back to the '80s and is *caracol-*, or snail-like, in its spiral layout. Le Fournil restaurant, just across Avenida Vitacura in Paseo Mañío on the fifth floor, is a good place for a coffee or light meal. ⊠ *Candelaria Goyenechea 3820, Vitacura* ☎ *2/2570–9232* ☉ *Closed Sun.*

CLOTHING

Casimires Ingleses Matilde Medina

MIXED CLOTHING | Yards and yards of cashmere fill the window of Casimires Ingleses Matilde Medina. The owner imports her beautiful scarves and sweaters from England and sells fine dress shirts, which are also imported. ⊠ *Av. Vitacura 3660, Vitacura* ☎ *2/220–7146* ⊕ *www.casimiresingleses.com* ☉ *Closed Sun.*

Hermès

MIXED CLOTHING | Looking a bit like a fortress, Hermès occupies some prime real estate on Alonso de Córdova, Santiago's main upscale international brand shopping drag. ⊠ *Av. Alonso de Córdova 2526, Vitacura* ☎ *2/2374–1576* ⊕ *www.hermes.com* ☉ *Closed Sun.*

GALLERIES

Galleries are scattered around the city, and admission is usually free. The newspaper *El Mercurio* lists current exhibitions in its Saturday supplement *Vivienda y Decoración*.Bellavista, which is full of small galleries and where restaurants often put on exhibitions, is the place to scout the work of young artists, but Vitacura is the heart of the more consolidated gallery scene.

Galería Animal

ART GALLERIES | See works by local artists at Galería Animal, a spacious, luminous gallery in Vitacura. The large-scale pieces include sculpture and other types of installations. ⊠ *Nueva Costanera 3731, Vitacura* ☎ *2/2371–9090* ⊕ *www.galeria-animal.cl.*

Galería Aninat

ART GALLERIES | Javiera García-Huidobro and Isabel Aninat curate works of both established and emerging Chilean artists at this Vitacura gallery, which has three rooms to browse. ⊠ *Av. Alonso de Córdova 4355, Vitacura* ☎ *2/2481–9870* ⊕ *www.aninatgaleria.org* ☉ *Closed Sun.*

HANDICRAFTS

La Blanquería

CRAFTS | This shop sells a wide variety of wool carpets and other weavings designed and produced in Chile. ⊠ *Store 115, 2nd fl., Vitacura* ☎ *2/3457–5719* ⊕ *www.lablanqueria.cl* ☉ *Closed Sun.*

WINE

La Vinoteca

WINE/SPIRITS | Proudly proclaiming itself Santiago's first fine wine shop, La Vinoteca stocks vintages from all over Chile and abroad, as well as beer and liquor. There is an outlet at the airport for last-minute purchases and another shop 14 blocks down Manuel Montt from Providencia. ⊠ *Av. Nueva Costanera 3955, Vitacura* ☎ *2/2953–6290* ⊕ *www.lavinoteca.cl* ☉ *Closed Sun.*

Las Condes

One of Santiago's swankier residential neighborhoods and home to the banking district, Las Condes is home to a swath of stores, accommodations, and restaurants nestled among the high-rises; it's also considered one of the capital's safer areas. Its northern location means it's a great base for easy access to the ski resorts.

🍴 Restaurants

Le Due Torri

$$$ | ITALIAN | For excellent homemade pastas such as *agnolotti,* stuffed with ricotta cheese and spinach, head to this longtime Italian-owned favorite that's been feeding regulars for more than 60 years. The rear of the dining room, with its small cypress trees and corner pergola, is traditional, while seating in the front is more contemporary. **Known for:** pasta; casual setting; authentic Italian. [$] *Average main: pesos13000* ✉ *Av. Isidora Goyenechea 2908, Las Condes* ☎ *2/2231–3427* 🌐 *www.leduetorri.cl* [M] *Tobalaba.*

Matsuri

$$$$ | JAPANESE | With a sleek design that calls to mind Los Angeles as much as Tokyo, this Nikkei restaurant in the Mandarin Oriental is one of Santiago's most stylish eateries. Comprising a sushi bar and two tatami rooms (no shoes allowed, but slippers are provided) with sliding screens for privacy, Matsuri also has two grill tables. **Known for:** sushi; popularity on weekends; stylish setting. [$] *Average main: pesos18000* ✉ *Mandarin Oriental Santiago, Av. Kennedy 4601, Las Condes* ☎ *2/2950–3088* 🕒 *Closed Sun.*

★ Olam

$$$$ | CHILEAN | A delectable seafood-forward menu and stylish location on the first floor of 45 By Director hotel have won Olam a cluster of awards since it opened in 2019. A palette of grass green and white in the dining room makes for a fresh, romantic ambience, while haute cuisine by Spanish-born chef Sergio Barroso Urbano showcases the best of contemporary Chilean cooking while keeping a zero waste philosophy at its heart. **Known for:** beautiful presentation; fine dining; sharing plates. [$] *Average main: pesos16000* ✉ *45 By Director Hotel, Carmencita 45, Las Condes* 🌐 *olam.cl* 🕒 *Closed Sun.*

🛏 Hotels

45 By Director

$$$ | HOTEL | Following a substantial redesign accompanied by a name change, this Chilean hotel chain is appealing to a trendier and younger clientele, offering perks like an iPad to control blinds. **Pros:** walking distance to the mall, coffee shops, and restaurants; spacious and comfy suites; friendly staff. **Cons:** some designated smoking areas; the lobby shares an entrance with a bar and can be noisy; room gadgets might not suit everyone. [$] *Rooms from: pesos103000* ✉ *Carmencita 45, Las Condes* ☎ *2/2498–3000* 🌐 *45bydirector.com* 🛏 *49 rooms* 🍴 *Free Breakfast* [M] *El Golf, Tobalaba.*

Mandarin Oriental Santiago

$$$$ | HOTEL | The soaring spire of the Mandarin Oriental resembles a rocket, and you might feel like an astronaut when you're shooting up a glass elevator through a 24-story atrium. **Pros:** three excellent restaurants; garden and swimming pool are particularly lovely; great views of Andes. **Cons:** one of city's main shopping malls about a 15-minute walk away; fee for Internet; out of the way and not much else close by. [$] *Rooms from: pesos210000* ✉ *Av. Kennedy 4601, Las Condes* ☎ *2/2950–3088* 🌐 *www.mandarinoriental.com/santiago/las-condes/luxury-hotel* 🛏 *310 rooms* 🍴 *Free Breakfast* [M] *No metro.*

MR. Express

$$ | HOTEL | This "express" version of the larger MR Hotel (on Avenida Pedro de Valdivia) lacks the frills, but rooms are tastefully modern and bright with plenty of space. **Pros:** free Wi-Fi; convenient for fashionable Las Condes but priced lower; close to Costanera Center. **Cons:** some rooms are very small; staff can be on the dry side; although all windows have double glass, rooms on Avenida Apoquindo still get traffic noise (those at the back are quieter). [$] *Rooms from: pesos68000* ✉ *Vecinal 40 at Av. Apoquindo, Las*

Condes ☎ 2/2663–3152 🌐 www.mrhoteles.cl/hoteles/mrexpress 🛏 53 rooms 🍴 Free Breakfast [M] El Golf, Tobalaba.

NH Collection Plaza

$$$ | **HOTEL** | Santiago's World Trade Center is also home to the NH, a combination that makes sense to many corporate travelers. **Pros:** spacious rooms; all the comfort and facilities of a top hotel (such as concierge service) at a more modest price; easy walk to the metro. **Cons:** rooms are gradually being overhauled so not all are the same standard; teething troubles with service following new (2017) ownership; the presence of the nearby Costanera Center and an increase in car ownership snarls traffic during peak commuting hours. [$] *Rooms from: pesos 11000 ✉ Av. Vitacura 2610, Las Condes ☎ 2/2433–9000 🌐 www.nh-collection.com 🛏 159 rooms 🍴 Free Breakfast [M] Tobalaba.*

The Ritz-Carlton

$$$$ | **HOTEL** | The rather bland brick exterior of this 15-story hotel, the first Ritz-Carlton in South America, belies the luxurious appointments within, such as the mahogany-paneled walls, cream marble floors, and enormous windows characterizing the splendid two-story lobby. **Pros:** personalized service; prime location on Avenida Apoquindo; close to the El Golf business and restaurant area. **Cons:** staff can be snooty; Wi-Fi is free in only some room categories; some find the elaborate decoration fussy and oppressive. [$] *Rooms from: pesos 157000 ✉ El Alcalde 15, Las Condes ☎ 2/2470–8500 🌐 www.ritzcarlton.com/en/hotels/santiago 🛏 205 rooms 🍴 Free Breakfast [M] El Golf.*

Santiago InterContinental

$$$$ | **HOTEL** | Attendants wearing top hats usher you into the two-story marble lobby of one of the city's top hotels. **Pros:** heated indoor pool; easy walking distance from the El Golf business and restaurant area; concierge. **Cons:** small breakfast salon for such a large hotel; some rooms have not been renovated and are outdated, requiring regular maintenance; bad traffic congestion around the hotel. [$] *Rooms from: pesos 160 ✉ Av. Vitacura 2885, Las Condes ☎ 2/2394–2000 🌐 www.intercontisantiago.com 🛏 382 rooms 🍴 Free Breakfast [M] Tobalaba.*

Santiago Marriott Hotel

$$$$ | **HOTEL** | The first 25 floors of this gleaming copper tower house the Marriott, which welcomes guests into its impressive two-story, cream marble lobby with full-grown palm trees in and around comfortable seating areas. **Pros:** activities like wine tastings and live music; excellent, friendly service; concierge. **Cons:** some rooms could use an upgrade; free Internet not included for all; removed from the action in a suburban neighborhood. [$] *Rooms from: pesos 144000 ✉ Av. Kennedy 5741, Las Condes ☎ 2/2426–2000 🌐 www.santiagomarriott.com 🛏 280 rooms 🍴 Free Breakfast [M] No metro.*

W Santiago

$$$$ | **HOTEL** | Located in the heart of the fashionable El Golf business and restaurant district, South America's first W Hotel set a new standard of luxury and service in Santiago when it opened, and its smart, contemporary decoration still makes the city's other five-star hotels look staid. **Pros:** great shops inside the hotel (clothing, jewelry, crafts); excellent location; heated outdoor pool. **Cons:** Internet is free in lobby and some common areas, but there's a charge for in-room usage; not everyone is comfortable with the bath and shower integrated into the bedroom; expensive. [$] *Rooms from: pesos 165000 ✉ Isidora Goyenechea 3000, Las Condes ☎ 2/2770–0000 🌐 www.wsantiagohotel.com 🛏 196 rooms 🍴 Free Breakfast [M] El Golf.*

Nightlife

BARS AND CLUBS
Irish Geo Pub
BARS | Close to the main drag of Avenida El Bosque Norte, this is an honest-to-goodness pub serving Irish food and beer. The upstairs, downstairs, and outside area often fill with expats and their friends. ⊠ *Encomenderos 179, Las Condes* ☎ *2/2233–6675* ⊕ *www. flannerys.cl.*

Nkiru
COCKTAIL LOUNGES | A large dose of New York City spirit in the form of a hip-hop soundtrack and subway street art makes for a distinctly urban drinking experience at cocktail bar Nkiru. Located on the ground floor of 45 By Director hotel, it attracts a young, hip crowd keen for signature cocktails. ⊠ *45 By Director, Carmencita 45, Las Condes* ⊕ *www. nkiru.cl* ⊗ *Closed Sun.* ☞ *Dress code means no sandals or caps.*

Performing Arts

Cine Hoyts Parque Arauco
FILM | Cine Hoyts Parque Arauco is the city's most modern cinema, with 3D and deluxe seating. Be sure to check to see if movies are subtitled (*subtitulada*) or dubbed (*doblada*), especially for kids' movies. The website shows the current listings. ⊠ *Parque Arauco mall, Av. Kennedy 5413, Las Condes* ☎ *600/500–0400* ⊕ *www.cinehoyts.cl.*

Cinemark Alto Las Condes
FILM | Among the best theaters in town is the Cinemark Alto Las Condes. Its dozen screens, some of which are 3D or XD, show the latest releases. The most expensive seats, in the premier class (for selected screenings), come with their own lounge, recline like spacious airline seats, and have a leg rest. ⊠ *Alto Las Condes mall, Av. Kennedy 9001, Las Condes* ☎ *600/586–0058* ⊕ *www. cinemark.cl/theatres/alto-las-condes.*

Shopping

Coquinaria
FOOD | This gourmet food shop is packed with temptations such as fresh pasta and cheeses not easily found elsewhere in Santiago. ⊠ *Isidora Goyenechea 3000, Las Condes* ☎ *2/2307–3000* ⊕ *www. coquinaria.cl* Ⓜ *El Golf.*

MARKETS
★ Centro Artesanal Pueblito Los Dominicos
MARKET | This crafts "village" inside a former cloister houses some 50 stands filled with goods made of fine leather and wool, semiprecious stones (including lapis lazuli), and *greda* (Chile's version of terra-cotta). There's also a display of cockatoos and other live birds. It's a nice place to visit, especially on weekends when traveling musicians entertain the crowds. It's open daily 10–8 in summer and 10–7 in winter, and there are two cafés serving traditional Chilean food. Next door is an attractive whitewashed church dating from the late 18th century. The complex is a bit far afield but easily accessed by the metro of the same name. ⊠ *Av. Apoquindo 9085, Las Condes* ☎ *9/9253–3863* ⊕ *www.pueblo-losdominicos.cl* ⊗ *Closed Sun.* Ⓜ *Los Dominicos.*

SHOPPING MALLS
Alto Las Condes
MALL | This mall has more than 200 shops, three department stores, a multiplex cinema, indoor food court, and an outside patio lined with restaurants. Also here is Jumbo, a good super-market that carries excellent Chilean wines. ⊠ *Av. Kennedy 9001, Las Condes* ☎ *2/2299–6965* ⊕ *www.altolascondes.cl* Ⓜ *No metro.*

★ Costanera Center
MALL | This mall organizes stores by type and has 12 movie screens, free Wi-Fi, and a wide variety of food. You can't miss the building, which stands 62 stories (the mall is on the first six floors); it is the highest building on the continent.

■ **TIP→ Once you're done shopping, catch the sunset at Sky Costanera on the 62nd floor (10,000 pesos).** ✉ *Andres Bello 2425, Las Condes* ☎ *2/2916–9226* 🌐 *www.costaneracenter.cl* [M] *Tobalaba.*

Providencia

A residential neighborhood, bustling Providencia lines two eponymous avenues and features a mixture of high-rises and two-story buildings. There's plenty of accommodations to suit all budgets, plus a great selection of cafés and restaurants offering classic Chilean fare to creative paired tasting menus.

👁 Sights

Parque de las Esculturas

CITY PARK | Residents in Providencia know this as one of the city's most captivating—and least publicized—public parks. Its gardens are filled with sculptures by Chile's top artists and because of its pastoral atmosphere, the park is popular with joggers and cuddling couples. In the center is a wood pavilion that hosts art exhibitions. The park also hosts a jazz festival every January, and a little farther west of the entrance is one of the free exercise stations that dot the city. ✉ *Pedro de Valdivia and Santa María, Providencia, Providencia* [M] *Los Leones.*

🍴 Restaurants

★ Ambrosía Bistro

$$$ | **CHILEAN** | An intimate yet smart spot attracting foodies and office workers, this sister restaurant to acclaimed Ambrosía in Vitacura is setting palates on fire. Grab a comfy bar stool to watch chef Carolina Bazán and team in action in the open kitchen, where they focus on Chilean ingredients; the menu changes weekly, but if possible order the citrus ceviche or steak from the dry-aged beef fridge. **Known for:** large portions to share; seafood and dry-aged beef; extensive by-the-glass wine list curated by top sommelier Rosario Onetto. [$] *Average main: pesos12000* ✉ *Nueva de Lyon 99, Providencia* ☎ *2/2233–4303* 🌐 *www.ambrosiabistro.cl* 🕒 *Closed Sun.* [M] *Pedro de Valdivia.*

Barandiarián

$$$ | **PERUVIAN** | Founded by a chef to the Peruvian embassy, Barandiarián serves traditional favorites, like *ají de gallina* , a mild creamy chicken stew, lomo saltado, and ceviche among other meat, fish, shellfish, and pasta dishes. The restaurant has an outdoor layout with parasols covering tables that surround a small swimming pool, all to the backdrop of a vast image of Machu Picchu. **Known for:** seafood; Peruvian-inspired cuisine; casual ambience. [$] *Average main: pesos11500* ✉ *Manuel Montt 315, Providencia* ☎ *2/2236–6854* 🌐 *www.barandiaran.cl* 🕒 *No dinner Sun.*

Cafetería Voilà

$ | **VEGETARIAN** | Well-priced daily specials attract a mixed crowd eager to enjoy a wide selection of salads, such as pasta salad with pesto, bean salad, and chicken or fish (optional)—all served over a plate of mixed greens. Those on a budget will appreciate that a lunch will only cost around 5,000 pesos. **Known for:** budget meals; amazing salads; vegetarian-friendly dishes. [$] *Average main: pesos6000* ✉ *Padre Mariano 125, Providencia* ☎ *2/2341–5907* 🕒 *No dinner weekends.*

Divertimento Chileno

$$$ | **CHILEAN** | **FAMILY** | A favorite with Chilean politicians, journalists and, on Sunday, local families, this restaurant serves both homemade pasta—the spinach and ricotta ravioli served with butter and sage is excellent—and traditional Chilean fare such as *pastel de choclo* (beef and corn casserole). For alfresco dining, book a table in the tranquil tree-shaded setting at the base of San Cristóbal hill. **Known for:** outdoor dining; Italian fare; child friendly. [$] *Average main: pesos12000*

✉ *Av. El Cerro 722, Providencia* ✣ *at Av. Pedro de Valdivia Norte* ☎ *2/7135–5664* 🌐 *www.divertimento.cl* [M] *Pedro de Valdivia.*

Eladio

$$ | **CHILEAN** | **FAMILY** | A vast, rather retro space on the fifth floor of an office block, Eladio invites you to enjoy a succulent *bife de chorizo* (sirloin), mouthwatering *costillas de cerdo* (pork ribs), or just about any other meat with a good bottle of Chilean wine. Finish with a slice of *amapola* (poppy-seed) sponge cake. **Known for:** excellent wine list; traditonal Chilean meat dishes; no-reservations policy. [$] *Average main: pesos11000* ✉ *Nueva Providencia 2250, 5th fl., Providencia* ☎ *2/2231–4224* 🌐 *www.eladio.cl* 🕒 *Closed Sun.* [M] *Los Leones.*

El Cid

$$$$ | **CHILEAN** | The culinary centerpiece of the Sheraton has an excellent lunch buffet, which includes unlimited wine. The dining room, which overlooks the pool, has crisp linens and simple place settings because all the excitement here is provided by the famous grilled seafood—king crab, prawns, squid, and scallops with a sweet, spicy sauce. **Known for:** great service; sophisticated ambience; seafood. [$] *Average main: pesos18000* ✉ *Sheraton Santiago Hotel and Convention Center, Av. Santa María 1742, Providencia* ☎ *2/2233–5000* 🌐 *marriott.com* [M] *No metro.*

El Huerto

$$ | **VEGETARIAN** | One of Santiago's most established vegetarian restaurants, this wood-paneled eatery in the heart of Providencia serves both vegetarian- and vegan-friendly fare, including hearty soups and fresh-squeezed juices. The vegan set lunch is a good value, and the three-step menu that changes daily consists of an appetizer, main course, and dessert for 8,900 pesos. **Known for:** vegetarian and vegan selections; set lunch menu. [$] *Average main: pesos7000* ✉ *Orrego Luco 054, Providencia* ☎ *2/2231–4443* 🌐 *www.elhuerto.cl* 🕒 *No dinner Sun.* [M] *Pedro de Valdivia.*

Fuente Alemana

$$ | **CHILEAN** | **FAMILY** | Grab a vast, overflowing sandwich that Chileans consider unique to their country. The soda fountain has been serving up a *lomito completo* with thin tender slices of pork with sauerkraut, mayonnaise, and tomato sauce since 1954; also try a *chacarero,* with slices of beef with tomatoes, green beans, and chili pepper—get it "*sin ají*" if you don't like spicy food. **Known for:** sandwiches; good prices; fast food. [$] *Average main: pesos7000* ✉ *Pedro de Valdivia 210, Providencia* ☎ *2/2639–3231* 🌐 *www.falemana.cl* 🕒 *Closed Sun.* [M] *Baquedano.*

Guappo Bistro

$$$ | **ITALIAN** | Expect enormous flavors from this tiny bistro, whose patio is considerably larger than its interior. A young husband-and-wife team run Guappo, cooking solid and delicious Mediterranean fare such as gnocchi and Sicilian-style eggplant stew, all nicely plated and well priced. **Known for:** Italian classics; outdoor dining; tiramisu. [$] *Average main: pesos12000* ✉ *Av. Pocuro 3091, Providencia* ☎ *2/2929–8316* 🌐 *www.guappobistro.cl* 🕒 *Closed Mon.* [M] *Francisco Bilbao.*

Le Flaubert

$$ | **FRENCH** | With table lamps casting a warm glow and walls covered with black-and-white photographs, this little eatery could be in any small town in France. The menu of the day, written on a blackboard, might tempt you with such dishes as a traditional coq au vin that's cooked to perfection. **Known for:** afternoon tea; friendly service; garden patio. [$] *Average main: pesos10000* ✉ *Orrego Luco 0125, Providencia* ☎ *2/2231–9424* 🌐 *www.leflaubert.cl* 🕒 *No dinner Sun. and Mon.* [M] *Pedro de Valdivia.*

★ Liguria

$$$ | CHILEAN | This extremely popular restaurant and bar is always packed with a young crowd, so you might have to wait to be seated in the chandelier-lighted dining room or at one of the tables on the sidewalk. A large selection of Chilean wine accompanies such favorites as *cazuela* (a stew of beef or chicken and potatoes) and *mechada* sandwiches (thinly sliced beef). **Known for:** Chilean fare; lively ambience; cocktails. $ *Average main: pesos11000* ⊠ *Av. Providencia 1373, Providencia* ☎ *2/2235–7914* ⊕ *www.liguria.cl* ⊘ *Closed Sun.* Ⓜ *Manuel Montt.*

Normandie

$$$ | FRENCH | This unassuming French restaurant with a slightly haphazard decor has service as friendly as the food is good. Join the regulars at the wooden bar for a steaming bowl of onion soup and beef Bourguignon with French fries (made from real potatoes) in winter, or a glass of wine at one of the pavement tables in summer. **Known for:** alfresco dining; French cuisine; extensive Chilean wine list. $ *Average main: pesos9900* ⊠ *Providencia 1234, Providencia* ☎ *2/2236–3011* ⊕ *www.normandie1234. cl* ⊘ *Closed Sun.* Ⓜ *Manuel Montt.*

Coffee and Quick Bites

Felix Café

$ | CAFÉ | A specialty coffee shop founded by two food and travel journalists looking for a plan B, Felix's great brews, vegan cakes, and pastries have captured the hearts of local residents. Enjoy a brownie with a flat white on the outside forecourt; the quiet street offers welcome respite from the busy avenue, a stone's throw away. **Known for:** coffee and pastries; neighborhood following; central location. $ *Average main: pesos2500* ⊠ *Coyancura 2223, Providencia* ☎ *9/7548–4482* ⊕ *instagram.com/felixcafe.cl* ⊘ *Closed Mon.*

Hotels

Chilhotel

$$ | HOTEL | Good midrange hotels are few and far between in Santiago, and this small, family-owned, funky old house set on a quiet side street is one of them. **Pros:** free Wi-Fi; excellent service closely supervised by owners; a 10-minute metro ride from downtown. **Cons:** spartan; no elevator; small rooms. $ *Rooms from: pesos55000* ⊠ *Cirujano Guzmán 103, Providencia* ☎ *2/2235–0713* ⊕ *www. chilhotel.cl* ⮑ *17 rooms* � O ⊘ *Free Breakfast* Ⓜ *Manuel Montt.*

Carménère EcoHotel

$$$$ | B&B/INN | In an airy house on a quiet street, this eco-friendly B&B evokes a country house in southern Chile. **Pros:** excellent breakfast; lots of care taken with decorations, plants, and food; personal touches include handmade chocolates on pillows. **Cons:** Wi-Fi can be spotty; some rooms are poky; on occasion the whole property is rented out, leaving no rooms for other guests. $ *Rooms from: pesos168000* ⊠ *María Luisa Santander 0292, Providencia* ☎ *2/2204–6372* ⊕ *www.hotelcarmenere. com* ⮑ *5 rooms* ⊘ *Free Breakfast.*

Four Points by Sheraton

$$$ | HOTEL | The heart of Providencia's shopping district is just steps away from this hotel, which is a favorite with savvy business visitors to the city. **Pros:** good, helpful staff; excellent value for money; a desk in each room. **Cons:** sometimes it's noisy from the street and a/c; restaurant just okay; free Internet only in the lobby, hourly charge in rooms. $ *Rooms from: pesos72000* ⊠ *Av. Santa Magdalena 111, Providencia* ☎ *2/2750–0300* ⊕ *www. fourpointssantiago.com* ⮑ *128 rooms* ⊘ *Free Breakfast* Ⓜ *Los Leones.*

★ Hotel Orly

$$$ | HOTEL | This sweet and economical treasure in such a convenient location in the middle of Providencia is a real find. **Pros:** free parking; excellent maintenance;

free Wi-Fi. **Cons:** rooms are outdated; bathrooms are cramped; difficult to get a room on short notice. $ *Rooms from: pesos98000* ✉ *Av. Pedro de Valdivia 027, Providencia* ☎ *2/2630–3000* 🌐 *www.orly-hotel.com* 🛏 *28 rooms* 🍴 *Free Breakfast* [M] *Pedro de Valdivia.*

Italia Suite Bed & Breakfast
$ | **B&B/INN** | Stay in one of Santiago's most interesting design neighborhoods at this cozy B&B in Barrio Italia, a vibrant subsection of Providencia known for its design shops and antique stores. **Pros:** free Wi-Fi; neighborhoody feeling; attentive hosts. **Cons:** owners speak little English; breakfast is not very creative; not on the main L1 metro line. $ *Rooms from: pesos30000* ✉ *Tegualda 1846, Providencia* ☎ *2/2505–9530* 🌐 *www.italiasuite.com* 🛏 *9 rooms* 🍴 *Free Breakfast* [M] *Irrarazaval.*

★ Le Rêve
$$$ | **HOTEL** | This classic 20th-century French house is a charming boutique hotel with comfortable rooms that all but guarantee a good night of sleep—after all, the name in French means "the dream." It's big enough not to feel closed in, and there are garden and street views from the spacious and stylish three floors. **Pros:** excellent buffet breakfast; self-serve snacks in the kitchen until 1 am; great location close to restaurants. **Cons:** breakfast time can be very busy; street-facing rooms particularly susceptible to noise; some noise from nearby restaurants. $ *Rooms from: pesos115000* ✉ *Orrego Luco 023, Providencia* ☎ *2/2757–6000* 🌐 *www.lereve.cl* 🛏 *31 rooms* 🍴 *Free Breakfast* [M] *Los Leones or Pedro de Valdivia.*

Santiago Park Plaza
$$$$ | **HOTEL** | Although this hotel bills itself as English in style, it's removed the formerly oppressive dark furnishings, making the lobby and restaurant larger and airier. **Pros:** close to Costanera Center mall; in the heart of Providencia with a metro station at the doorstep; free Wi-Fi. **Cons:** hit-and-miss service; room decor dated; breakfast not impressive. $ *Rooms from: pesos131000* ✉ *Av. Ricardo Lyon 207, Providencia* ☎ *2/2372–4000* 🌐 *www.parkplaza.cl* 🛏 *104 rooms* 🍴 *Free Breakfast* [M] *Los Leones.*

Sheraton Santiago Hotel and Convention Center
$$$$ | **HOTEL** | Popular with business executives who value its efficiency, elegance, and impeccable service, the modern rooms at the Sheraton have elegant linens and are decorated with rich fabrics; ask for one overlooking the San Cristóbal Hill. **Pros:** free Wi-Fi in lobby; excellent amenities; concierge service. **Cons:** some rooms are outdated; minimum three-hour charge in rooms for Wi-Fi; a taxi ride away from the nearest metro station and restaurant and shopping areas. $ *Rooms from: pesos175000* ✉ *Av. Santa Maria 1742, Providencia* ☎ *2/2233–5000* 🌐 *www.marriott.com/hotels/travel/sclsi-sheraton-santiago-hotel-and-convention-center* 🛏 *525 rooms* 🍴 *Free Breakfast* [M] *Pedro de Valdivia.*

Nightlife

BARS AND CLUBS

Club de Jazz de Santiago
LIVE MUSIC | Open since 1943, Santiago's foremost jazz club has hosted the genre's greats like Louis Armstrong and Herbie Hancock, as well as esteemed Chilean performers. Performances take place between Wednesday and Saturday, and cost between 5,000 and 7,000 pesos. While you're clicking your fingers, order pizza, pasta, and other Italian dishes from La Fábrica, with which the club shares a roof. ✉ *Ossa 123, La Reina* ☎ *2/2830–6208* 🌐 *www.clubdejazz.cl* [M] *Plaza Egaña.*

Fausto Discotheque
DANCE CLUBS | The venerable gay disco Fausto, in business for more than 40 years, has polished wood paneling that calls to mind a gentlemen's club. It has a

few different sections, a show at 2 am, and offers free admission to men during their birthday month. There are occasional theme parties and entertainers. Unlike many other gay clubs in Santiago, Fausto attracts a more solidly thirties-and-up crowd. Fausto is open until 4 am or later. ✉ *Av. Santa María 0832, Providencia* ☎ *2/2777–1041* ⊕ *www.fausto.cl* ⏲ *Closed Tues.*

 Performing Arts

Ballet Nacional Chileno
The venerable Ballet Nacional Chileno, founded in 1945, performs at CEAC U Chile (ex-Teatro Universidad de Chile) near Plaza Baquedano. ✉ *Av. Providencia 043, Providencia* ☎ *2/2978–2480* ⊕ *www.ceacuchile.com/ballet-nacional-chileno.*

CEAC U Chile
MUSIC | The Coro Sinfónico and the Orquesta Sinfónica, the city's highly regarded chorus and orchestra, perform near Plaza Baquedano at the Centro de Extensión Artística y Cultura (CEAC) Universidad de Chile. Other functions such as ballet and quartets and solo vocal performances take place throughout the year. This venue is also home to the Ballet Nacional Chileno. ✉ *Av. Providencia 43, Providencia* ☎ *2/2978–2480* ⊕ *www.ceacuchile.com* Ⓜ *Baquedano.*

Festival Internacional de Jazz de Providencia
MUSIC | This jazz festival, along with a handful of other open-air concerts, are held in early evenings in summer in the lovely Parque de las Esculturas sculpture park, tucked in between the Mapocho River and Cerro San Cristóbal. Arrive there by walking over the bridge from Pedro de Valdivia. ✉ *Av. Santa María 2205 between Av. Pedro de Valdivia Norte and Padre Letelier, Providencia* ☎.

Festival Internacional Teatro a Mil
THEATER | In January, the year's best plays are performed at Estación Mapocho and other venues around Santiago in a well-organized program called the Festival Internacional Teatro a Mil. The name refers to the admission price of 1,000 pesos (just under $2), although many now cost between 6,000 and 8,000 pesos. Regardless, some spectacles, particularly the often large-scale opening and closing events near La Moneda Palace, are free. ✉ *Santiago* ☎ *2/2925–0310* ⊕ *www.fundacionteatroamil.cl.*

Teatro Oriente
MUSIC | A national monument, the Teatro Oriente hosts dance, music, and theater for all ages, and special programming for children and senior citizens. ✉ *Pedro de Valdivia 099, Providencia* ☎ *2/2385–6350* ⊕ *www.teatrooriente.cl.*

 Shopping

GIFTS
Manao
LEATHER GOODS | This leather goods shop sells colorful bespoke purses, bags, and accessories with material sourced from Chile, Argentina, and Brazil. The craftsmanship is all Chilean though, with owner Paola Vidal behind all the designs and much of the handiwork. She can make custom items, though these will take a few days to stitch together. ✉ *Condell 1447, Providencia* ☎ *9/9987–0084* ⊕ *www.manaodiseno.cl* ⏲ *Closed Sun. and Mon.*

JEWELRY
Blue Stone
JEWELRY & WATCHES | This is one of the top-end stores in which to buy lapis lazuli, the blue stone for which Chile is famous. Unlike other stores that have dozens of the same items, each piece of jewelry here is unique, as are decorative items for the table, including sets of cutlery inlaid with lapis lazuli and home furnishings such as copper vessels from replicas of original designs by indigenous peoples of Chile. ✉ *Los Araucanos 2020, Providencia* ☎ *2/2232–2581* ⊕ *www.bluestone.cl.*

⚡ Activities

Sunday is the day for sports. In the prosperous eastern part of the city, jogging and cycling are popular, while in-line skating and e-scooters have caught on. Some streets are closed to traffic across Las Condes, Providencia, and Santiago Centro. People also take *fútbol* (soccer) games quite seriously. Head to an open park to check out some local pickup games, and try Parque de Los Reyes (near Barrio Brasil) if you want to see *futbolito* (soccer played on a minipitch) at play.

ATHLETIC CLUBS AND SPAS

All of Santiago's larger hotels have health clubs on the premises, usually with personal trainers on hand to assist workouts. Even if you aren't staying at a particular hotel, you can usually pay for a day pass to use the facilities.

BICYCLING

Santiago has no shortage of public parks, and they provide good opportunities to see the city. If you're ambitious, you can pedal up Cerro San Cristóbal, the city's largest hill. On Sunday, several roads are given over to bikes, such as busy Balmaceda that runs alongside Parque Forestal.

★ La Bicicleta Verde

BIKING | One of the top indie tour providers in Santiago, this shop with a storefront just across the river from Bellas Artes rents singles and tandems, starting at 5,000 pesos for a half day, and offers different thematic (historical, political, wine-based) bike tours. ⊠ *Almirante Montt 471, Recoleta* ☎ *2/2570–9939* ⊕ *www.labicicletaverde.com* Ⓜ *Bellas Artes.*

HORSE RACING

Betting on horses is popular in Santiago, which is the reason you see so many teletrak betting offices. The city has two large racetracks.

SKIING
KL Ski Rental

SKIING & SNOWBOARDING | If you're planning on hitting the slopes, KL Ski Rental not only rents skis and snowboards but also arranges transportation to and from the nearby resorts. ⊠ *Augusto Mira Fernández 14248, Las Condes* ☎ *2/2217–9101, 877/260–5447 in U.S.* ⊕ *www.kladventure.com.*

SOCCER

Chile's most popular spectator sport is soccer (*fútbol*), but a close second is watching the endless bickering among owners, trainers, and players whenever a match isn't going well.

Estadio Nacional Julio Martínez Prádanos

SOCCER | First-division fútbol matches, featuring the city's handful of local teams, are held in the Estadio Nacional Julio Martínez Prádanos, southeast of the city center in Ñuñoa. Soccer is played year-round, with most matches taking place on weekends. The stadium is also a major concert venue. ⊠ *Av. Grecia 2001, Ñuñoa* ☎ *2/2238–8102.*

Side Trips from Santiago

For more than a few travelers, Santiago's main attraction is its proximity to the continent's best skiing. The snowcapped mountains to the east of Santiago have the largest number of runs, not just in Chile or South America, but in the entire Southern Hemisphere. The other attraction is that the season lasts from June to September and, in some places, October, so savvy skiers can take to the slopes in Chile when people back home are hitting the beach. It's no wonder that skiing aficionados and pros from around the world head to Chile.

The wineries around Santiago make for interesting day- or multiday trips. These winemakers provide the majority of the country's excellent exports, and you might find the source of your favorite

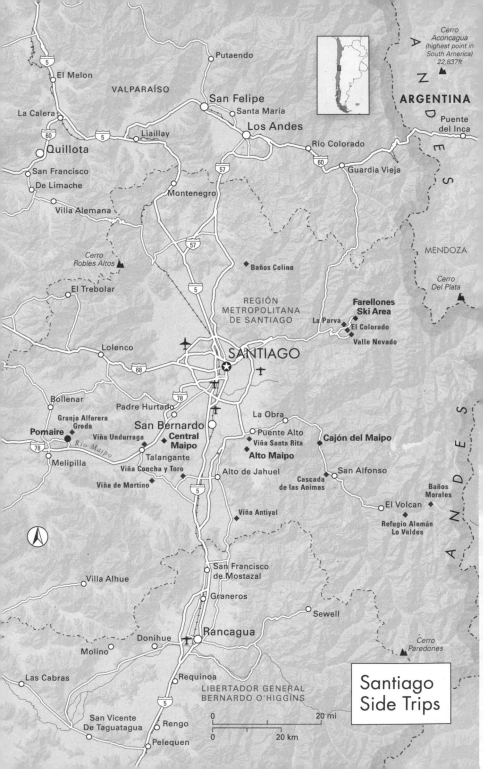

Chilean *vino* back home just a short jaunt from the capital. The Casablanca Valley, west of Santiago, on the road to Valparaíso, is where some of the country's best white wines are produced.

The Cajón del Maipo in the Andes makes for a relaxing trip to soak in hot springs, take a hike, or wander through the crafts village of Pomaire, 70 km (43 miles) west of Santiago.

Central Maipo

40 km (25 miles) southwest of Santiago.

The Central Maipo Valley is home to some of the most traditional wineries in Chile. In the lowest part of the valley, close to the coast, are the newcomers, producing lighter red wines from grapes cooled by sea breezes, as well as some Sauvignon Blancs.

GETTING HERE AND AROUND
The Autopista del Sol (Ruta 78) from Santiago to the port of San Antonio runs through the heart of the Maipo Valley, but vineyards are too far off the highway to be reached by public transport. Drive to these vineyards, take an organized tour with Chile Wine Trails (www.chilewine-trails.com), or combine local transportation with taxis or colectivos (shared taxis) to get to your destination.

 Sights

Viña De Martino
WINERY | The De Martino family has been making wine in Isla de Maipo since 1934 and were the first in Chile to bottle Carménère, now Chile's signature grape. The winery is a strong proponent of organic viticulture. Its winemaking team has done groundbreaking work in seeking out the country's finest terroirs. Tours and tastings are run at a variety of price points and interest levels, and there's an elegant lunch for a minimum of seven people and buffet for less.

Several vegetarian entreé options are available alongside meat and seafood. ⊠ *Manuel Rodríguez 229, Isla de Maipo* ☎ *2/2577–8837* ⊕ *www.demartino.cl* ⊠ *From 10000 pesos* ⊘ *Closed Sun.* ⚲ *Reservations essential.*

Viña Undurraga
WINERY | Don Francisco Undurraga Vicuña founded this traditional winery in 1885 in the town of Talagante, 34 km (21 miles) southwest of Santiago. Today you can tour the gardens—designed by George Dubois, who planned Santiago's Parque Forestal—or take a look at the facilities and enjoy a tasting. Reserve ahead for a spot on a tour in English or Spanish. Viña Undurraga is along the way to Pomaire, so you might visit both in the same day. Private tours for a minimum of two participants begin weekdays at noon and must be reserved two days in advance at a cost of 28,000 pesos per person. ⊠ *Camino a Melipilla Km 34, Talagante* ☎ *2/2372–2850* ⊕ *www.undurraga.cl* ⊠ *15000 pesos for group tours; 28000 pesos for private* ⚲ *Tours daily at 10 and 3.*

Alto Maipo

39 km (24 miles) southeast of Santiago.

Some of Chile's finest red wines hail from the Alto Maipo, the eastern sector of the Casablanca Valley. There are a number of wineries—old and new, big and small—snuggled up into the foothills of the Andes Mountains.

GETTING HERE AND AROUND
The only easy ways to reach the Antiyal and Santa Rita vineyards in the Alto Maipo are by car or again, on an organized wine tour. Pirque can be reached by taking Línea 4 of the metro to Puente Alto; from there it is only a short taxi ride, and there are also frequent colectivos (shared taxis).

Tours of Viña Antiyal focus on environmentally friendly and biodynamic winegrowing.

Sights

★ Viña Antiyal

WINERY | Chilean winemaker Alvaro Espinoza and his wife, Marina Ashton, harvested their first organically grown grapes from biodynamically managed vines in their own front yard in 1998 and Chile's first ultrapremium "garage wine" was born. They've grown since then and have more land higher in the mountains but still produce just 25,000 bottles (each numbered by hand) of their red-blend Antiyal. Tours are personalized, with emphasis on environmentally friendly and biodynamic winegrowing. Llamas, alpacas, geese, and the family dog wander the vineyards. Visits should be arranged at least 24 hours in advance. Antiyal has also opened a small B&B on-site. Contact them through the winery to arrange a stay. ⊠ *Padre Hurtado 68, Buin* ☎ *2/2821–4224* ⊕ *www.antiyal.com* ✉ *From 30000 pesos* ⊗ *Closed Sun.* ⚲ *Reservations essential.*

★ Viña Concha y Toro

WINERY | Chile's largest producer is consistently good in every price range, from inexpensive table wine to some of Chile's finest—and priciest—labels. Melchor de Concha y Toro, who once served as Chile's minister of finance, built the *casona,* or manor house, in 1875. He was among the first to import French vines, making this a cutting-edge winery since its foundation in 1883. The typical hour-long tour includes a stroll through the century-old gardens and vineyards, a look at the modern facilities, and a visit to the Casillero del Diablo, the famed cellar where Don Melchor kept his finest stock. There is a sound-and-light show in the dark here that appeals to lovers of kitsch. Tastings of three wines are included. Reserve a few days ahead for weekdays or a week ahead for popular weekend hours. Close to Puente Alto metro, the vineyard is easily reached by private or colectivo from the end of the line, though the complimentary wine glass is unlikely to survive the way home. ⊠ *Av. Virginia Subercaseaux 210, Pirque*

☎ 2/2476–5269 ⊕ www.conchaytoro.com
🍴 Regular tour 18000 pesos; Marqués
de Casa Concha tour 25000 pesos
🔑 Reservations essential ☞ English
general tours at 10:20, 11:30, 1, 2:30,
3:10, 3:40, and 4; Marqués de Casa
Concha tour (includes more tastings with
a sommelier) in English daily at 4.

★ Viña Santa Rita

WINERY | Chile's third-largest winery,
on a sprawling estate with an impressive museum, dates to 1880, when
everything from vines to winemakers
was brought from France. The Pompeiian-style manor now houses the pricey
16-room Casa Real Hotel, owned by, but
operated separately from, the winery.
The house, its neogothic chapel, and
the park that surrounds them are strictly
off-limits to all but the hotel's guests,
though on tours you get a good peek. The
on-site Andean Museum, with its small
collection of pre-Columbian artifacts and
textiles, is open to the public free of
charge and highly recommended. Winery
tours take you down into the musty fan
vault cellars, now national monuments,
which were built by French engineers in
1875 using a limestone-and-egg-white
stone masonry technique called cal y
canto. Stop in for a lunch at Doña Paula
for a formal meal, or stick to the snack
bar for lighter fare. There are nine tours
to choose from, including winemaker,
picnic, bike, and Carménère. You must
reserve a week ahead for tours. ⊠ Camino Padre Hurtado 0695, Alto de Jahuel
☎ 2/2362–2594 weekdays or 2/2362–
2590 weekends ⊕ www.santarita.com
🍴 Tour 15000 pesos; tours of grounds,
but not wine cellars free with lunch at
Casa de Doña Paula. Ultra premium tour
70000 pesos, includes top-range wines
and cheese platter. English general tours
at 10:30 and 2:30.

🍴 Restaurants

Restaurant Doña Paula

$$$$ | CHILEAN | A century-old colonial
building with thick adobe walls houses
Viña Santa Rita's restaurant, which
serves a three-course set menu at lunch;
dishes might include tuna tartare or rib-
eye. Beneath the exposed beams of the
peaked wooden ceiling, the restaurant is
decorated with old religious sculptures
and portraits, including one of Paula
Jaraquemada, who owned the land at
the time of the revolution. **Known for:**
classic winery dining; traditional décor;
minimum charge for lunch. $ Average
main: pesos31000 ⊠ Viña Santa Rita,
Camino Padre Hurtado 0695, Alto de
Jahuel ☎ 2/2362–2590 ⊕ www.santarita.
cl/visitanos/gastronomia ⊙ Closed Mon.
No dinner.

Pomaire

50 km (31 miles) west of Santiago.

You can easily spend a morning or
afternoon wandering around the quaint
village of Pomaire, a former settlement
of indigenous people founded in 1771
comprising a few streets of single-story
adobe dwellings. On weekends Pomaire
teems with people wandering around,
shopping, and having lunch in one of the
rather touristy country-style restaurants
with red-and-white checked tablecloths
and clay ovens specializing in empanadas
and other typical Chilean foods.

Pomaire is famous for its brown greda, or
earthenware pottery, which is ubiquitous
throughout Chile. Pastel de choclo is
nearly always served in a round, simple
clay dish—they're heavy and retain the
heat, so the food arrives at the table
piping hot.

The village bulges with bowls, pots, and
plates of every shape and size, not to
mention piggy banks, plant pots, vases,
and the unmissable "chanchito de la

Known for its Carménère, Viña Santa Rita is Chile's third-largest winery.

suerte," three-legged pigs that make great souvenirs. Most shops at the top of the main street sell the work of others; walk farther down or into the side streets and find the workshops they buy from (prices are cheaper there).

GETTING HERE AND AROUND

Pomaire is easy to find. It's clearly signposted to the right off the Autopista del Sol (Ruta 78). You can also take the Ruta Bus 78 buses, which depart frequently from Terminal San Borja in downtown Santiago and leave you at the turnoff to Pomaire, 2 km (1 mile) from the village. Once you get to the tiny village, it's small enough to get around on foot. To return to Santiago, simply walk back to the highway and hail the first bus, or in the late afternoon, wait at the church and take a bus back to Santiago (earlier in the day you have to make a connection in Melipilla).

Sights

Granja Alfarera Greda

OTHER ATTRACTION | **FAMILY** | Take a pottery-making course at this workshop, run by local artisans especially for visitors. Suitable for both children ages five and up and adults, the two-hour course starts with a video in English, followed by instruction in the use of a pottery wheel, and winds up with an insight into the techniques used by the area's indigenous peoples. ⊠ *Av. Bernardo O'Higgins 260, Pomaire* ☎ *9/9879–3533* ⊕ *www.greda.cl* ✉ *4000 pesos* ☞ *4 classes weekdays, 6 classes on weekends.*

Restaurants

La Greda

$$$ | **CHILEAN** | Named for the earthenware pottery that made this village famous, La Greda is a great place for grilled meats. Try the *filete de la greda,* a steak covered with a sauce of tomatoes, onions, and mushrooms, and topped with cheese; or try a complete *menú,* with drink, main, side, and coffee included. **Known for:** traditional Chilean cooking; outdoor dining; grilled steak. [$] *Average main: pesos12500* ✉ *Manuel Rodríguez 251, at Roberto Bravo, Pomaire* ☎ *9/7185–0905* 🌐 *www.lagredapomaire.com* ⏲ *No dinner.*

San Antonio

$$ | **CHILEAN** | **FAMILY** | The food is much the same here as elsewhere in Pomaire, but San Antonio has a number of perks, particularly for families with children. There's a children's menu and, on weekends, everyone who eats here can take the free pottery course at the Granja, just across the road. **Known for:** nearby swimming pool for customer use (for a small fee); kid-friendly atmosphere; classic Chilean cuisine. [$] *Average main: pesos9000* ✉ *Roberto Bravo 320, Pomaire* ☎ *9/5207–1142* 🌐 *www.restaurantsanantonio.cl.*

Cajón del Maipo

60 km (37 miles) southeast of Santiago.

The Cajón del Maipo, a narrow valley deep in the Andes, is irresistible for those who want to soak in natural hot springs; stroll through picturesque mountain towns, where low adobe houses line the roads; or just take in the stark but majestic landscape. In summertime, *humitas,* or fresh corn (unfilled) tamales are a popular snack or meal. There are hot springs at Baños Morales, just below the Refugio Lo Valdés, and higher up the valley at Baños de Colina. The dirt road is rough (and impassable in winter), but the pools of steaming water and the spectacular setting are well worth the effort when the weather is in your favor.

GETTING HERE AND AROUND

To reach Cajón del Maipo, head south on Avenida José Alessandri until you reach the Rotonda Departamental, a large traffic circle. There you take Camino Las Vizcachas (aka Camino Cajón del Maipo), following it south into the valley.

Travesía Tour Chile sells round-trip tickets from Santiago to Lo Valdés Mountain Center in Cajón del Maipo, Baños Morales, and the Baños de Colina hot springs. Full-day excursions for each circuit leave Bandera 642 in Centro at 7 am. A round-trip day ticket to Cajón del Maipo and Embalse El Yeso is 28,000 pesos. Prior booking is essential, and you should sit on the right side of the van for a good view of the river on the ascent.

Sights

Baños Colina

HOT SPRING | These hot springs high in the mountains at 3,500 meters (11,483 feet) above sea level are a series of natural pools down which water drops, cooling gradually. The road is rough and often impassable in winter and there is little infrastructure, but the view and clear skies are spectacular, including from the astronomical observatory located here. Rustic lodging and camping is available. Do not confuse these rustic springs with Termas de Colina, which are similarly named but located north of the city. ✉ *Camino Cajón del Maipo, 104 km (65 miles) from Santiago, Baños de Colina* ☎ 🌐 *www.cajondelmaipo.com/banos_colina.php.*

Baños Morales

HOT SPRING | Two pools in the tiny village of Baños Morales, where the Morales and Volcán rivers meet, are pleasantly warm, not hot, and rich in iodine and other minerals. You can hike from this area as well. Be warned that surprise winter storms can trap you here. The village has some rustic lodging, but many people prefer to come for the day. ✉ *Camino Cajón del Maipo, 92 km (57 miles) from Santiago, Baños Morales* ☎ 🌐 *www.cajondelmaipo.com/banos_morales.php.*

Cascada de las Animas

RESORT | **FAMILY** | This small tourist complex in the shadow of the mountains has a swimming pool and picnic area for short stays, as well as lodgings for longer sojourns. This is also a great base for exploring the Cajón. Accommodations come in several forms, including campsites, lodge suites, and freestanding cabins with rustic wood furniture. From here, multiday horseback-riding trips, guided hikes, and rafting excursions are available, as is transportation from Santiago. ⊠ *Camino al Volcán 31087, San Alfonso* ☎ *2/2861–1303* ⊕ *www.cascadadelasanimas.cl* ✉ *20000 pesos for admission to swimming pool and picnic area in high season; 10000 in low season.*

Refugio Alemán Lo Valdés

RESORT | The Alemán Lo Valdés Mountain Center, built in 1932, provides basic, well-priced lodgings and organizes activities such as trekking and horseback riding in the mountains. It is open year-round and has a restaurant that also serves day visitors until 8 pm; meals won't cost more than 9,500 pesos. If you'd prefer to do your own hike, the center can give you a map and instructions. ⊠ *Km 77, Camino Cajón del Maipo, Lo Valdés* ☎ *9/3429–9019* ⊕ *www.refugioalemanlovaldes.com.*

Farellones Ski Area

32 km (20 miles) east of Santiago.

Rub shoulders with pro skiers at three world-class ski resorts (El Colorado, La Parva, and Valle Nevado) that lie just outside Santiago near the village of Farellones. With a total of 176 groomed runs for all levels, the resorts cover 34,500 acres (El Colorado is the largest), providing more than enough space to ski or board. Farellones, with some unremarkable shops, restaurants, and hotels, lies at the base of the Cerro Colorado mountain. Shorten your drive by parking at Curva 17 parking lot of Valle Nevado and taking the gondola up to midmountain from there. All ski areas rent equipment, for about 24,000 (basic) to 34,000 (professional) pesos per day.

GETTING HERE AND AROUND

It can take up to two hours to reach these ski resorts, which lie 48–56 km (30–35 miles) from Santiago. The road is narrow, winding, and full of Chileans racing to get to the top. If you decide to drive, make sure you have a four-wheel-drive vehicle or snow chains, which you can rent along the way or before you leave Santiago from international car rental agencies (such as Hertz or Avis). Chains are installed for about 10,000 pesos. Don't think you need them? There's a police checkpoint just before the road starts to climb into the Andes, and if the weather is rough they make you turn back.

To reach these areas by car, follow Avenida Kennedy or Avenida Las Condes eastward until you leave Santiago. Here, you begin an arduous journey up the Andes, making 40 consecutive hairpin turns. The road forks when you reach the top, with one road taking the relatively easy 16-km (10-mile) route east to Valle Nevado, and the other following a more difficult road north to Farellones and La Parva.

Several bus companies run regularly scheduled service to the Andes in winter. Skitotal buses depart from the company's office on Avenida Apoquindo and head to all the ski resorts. Buses depart as they fill, starting at 7:30 am; and the last trip up departs at 8:30. A round-trip ticket costs around 17,000 pesos to Farellones, La Parva, and El Colorado, and 19,000 pesos to Valle Nevado. You can arrange for private transfer with them as well, which varies in price for round-trip from 130,000 for one to three passengers, to 180,000 for 6 to 10 passengers. The company Travesía Tour Chile offers similar services to the resorts year-round. Skitotal also offers hotel-to-slopes or airport-to-slopes service.

ESSENTIALS

BUS CONTACTS Skitotal. ⊠ *Apoquindo 4900, Las Condes* ☎ *9/9509–4823* ⊕ *www.skitotal.cl.*

Hotels

La Cornisa

$$$$ | **HOTEL** | This quaint old inn on the road to Farellones gives you easy access to the slopes with its free shuttle to and from the nearby ski areas. **Pros:** breakfast and dinner included; cozy, intimate ambience; outdoor hot tub. **Cons:** Wi-Fi can be very slow; some rooms are small and cramped; not as close to the slopes as the ski resorts themselves. [$] *Rooms from: pesos269000* ✉ *Av. Los Cóndores 636, Farellones* ☎ *2/2321–1172* 🌐 *www.es.lacornisa.cl* 🛏 *10 rooms* 🍴 *Free Breakfast.*

Puerta del Sol

$$$$ | **RESORT** | The largest of the Valle Nevado hotels, Puerta del Sol can be identified by its signature sloped roof. **Pros:** giant Jacuzzi; only 160 feet from the ski slopes; interconnecting rooms good for families. **Cons:** check-in and check-out are very busy; Jacuzzi packs out early in the evening; rooms are quite small and basic. [$] *Rooms from: pesos481000* ✉ *13 km (8 miles) beyond La Parva, Lo Barnechea* ☎ *2/2477–7005, 800/669–0554 toll-free in U.S.* 🌐 *www.vallenevado.com* ⏲ *Closed Oct.–May* 🛏 *124 rooms* 🍴 *Free Breakfast.*

Tres Puntas

$$$$ | **RESORT** | It bills itself as a hotel for young people, though Tres Puntas may remind you of a college dormitory. **Pros:** friendly staff; slopes are a quick walk away; free Wi-Fi in lobby. **Cons:** check-in and check-out is laborious; dated decor could use an overhaul; rooms are very cramped. [$] *Rooms from: pesos322000* ✉ *13 km (8 miles) beyond La Parva, Farrellones, La Parva* ☎ *2/2477–7000, 800/669–0554 toll-free in U.S.* 🌐 *www.vallenevado.com* ⏲ *Closed Oct.–May* 🛏 *82 rooms* 🍴 *Free Breakfast.*

LA PARVA

Condominio Nueva Parva

$$$$ | **APARTMENT** | The best place to stay in La Parva is this complex of spacious, modern apartments that sleep six to eight people. **Pros:** modern apartments; right next to the ski slopes; free Wi-Fi. **Cons:** no supermarkets nearby; only well priced for groups of six people; minimum one-week stay. [$] *Rooms from: pesos558000* ✉ *Nueva La Parva 77, La Parva* ☎ *2/2339–8490* 🌐 *www.laparva.cl* ⏲ *Closed Oct.–May* 🛏 *38 apartments* 🍴 *No Meals.*

VALLE NEVADO

Three hotels dominate Valle Nevado, an international resort; staying at one gives you access to the facilities at the other two. The three hotels share restaurants, which serve almost every type of cuisine. Rates include lift tickets, breakfast, and dinner. Peak season is July and August; you can find deals in June and September.

Valle Nevado

$$$$ | **RESORT** | The resort's most extravagantly priced lodge provides ski-in–ski-out convenience. **Pros:** rooms have balconies; close to El Plomo mountain; free Wi-Fi. **Cons:** slow Wi-Fi connection; restaurants get busy and require reservations; expensive, particularly if you plan to be out on the slopes all day. [$] *Rooms from: pesos194000* ✉ *13 km (8 miles) beyond La Parva, Farellones* ☎ *2/2477–7000, 800/669–0554 toll-free in U.S.* 🌐 *www.vallenevado.com* ⏲ *Closed spring–fall* 🛏 *53 rooms* 🍴 *All-Inclusive.*

Activities

SKIING

El Colorado

SKIING & SNOWBOARDING | The closest ski area to Santiago, El Colorado has 2,718 acres of groomed runs—the most in Chile. There are 19 ski lifts here and 112 runs for beginners through experts, as well as the best snowpark in South America, which has six jumps. The beginner runs are at the base of the mountain near the village of Farellones. There are sled tracks and a few other activities for nonskiers. A few restaurants and pubs are located nearby, but most are down in the village of Farellones. The ski season runs from mid-June through September, depending on snowfall. ✉ *On road between Farellones and La Parva, Lo Barnechea* ☎ *9/7897–7534* ⊕ *www. elcolorado.cl* 🍽 *Lift tickets 38000–45000 pesos.*

La Parva

SKIING & SNOWBOARDING | This colorful conglomeration of private homes set along a handful of mountain roads with stunning views of Santiago is home to a resort with 40 trails, mostly for intermediate skiers. The more adventurous (and advanced) can take part in heli-skiing on the resort's 1,800-plus acres. ✉ *3 km (2 miles) up road from Farellones, La Parva* ☎ *2/2964–2100* ⊕ *www.laparva.cl* 🍽 *Day pass from 52000 pesos.*

Valle Nevado

SKIING & SNOWBOARDING | Chile's largest ski region is a luxury resort area with 17 ski lifts that connect to 34 runs covering 22,200 acres. Intended for skiers who like a challenge and attracting international ski teams, this resort has few beginner slopes. Two of the extremely difficult runs from the top of Cerro Tres Puntas are called Shake and Twist. If that doesn't intimidate you, then you might be ready for some heli-skiing. The helicopter whisks you to otherwise inaccessible peaks where you can ride a vertical drop of up to 2,500 meters (8,200 feet). A ski school at Valle Nevado gives pointers to everyone from beginners to experts. Many visitors are European, as are the ski instructors, though Brazilians come to Chile for the skiing as well. ✉ *13 km (8 miles) beyond La Parva, Lo Barnechea* ☎ *2/2477–7000* ⊕ *www.vallenevado. com* 🍽 *64000–80000 pesos* 🕐 *Closed Oct.–mid-June.*

Chapter 4

THE CENTRAL COAST

4

Updated by
Mark Johanson

● Sights	🍴 Restaurants	🛏 Hotels	◉ Shopping	🍸 Nightlife
★★★★★	★★★★☆	★★★☆☆	★★★☆☆	★★★★☆

WELCOME TO THE CENTRAL COAST

TOP REASONS TO GO

★ **Riding the ascensores:** Valparaíso's steep hills are smoothed out a bit by its 19th-century *ascensores,* or funiculars, that shuttle locals between their jobs near the port and their homes in the hills.

★ **Beautiful beaches:** Thousands of Santiaguinos flock to the Central Coast's beaches every summer, where hundreds of seafood restaurants of all types and sizes serve the masses.

★ **Superb shopping:** The streets of Cerro Alegre and Cerro Concepción in Valparaíso are lined with shops selling everything from finely wrought jewelry to hand-tooled leather, while Viña has everything from large department stores and outlet malls to trendy shops and boutiques.

★ **Seafood straight from the net:** Almost every town on the Central Coast has its own wharf where fishermen land with the day's catch. Bustling with shoppers, the *caleta* offers an excellent biology lesson on the diversity of sea life in addition to, of course, many a gastronomic treat.

The Central Coast lies two hours west of Santiago, across the Coastal Mountains. Dominated by the overlapping cities of Valparaíso and Viña del Mar, this is where stressed Santiaguinos come to sunbathe, party, and gorge on seafood every moment they can. In the summer, even the smallest resort can heave with visitors, but outside of January and February they can be quiet.

Two of Neruda's three homes—La Sebastiana, nestled in the hills of Valparaíso, and his beach-side abode in small-town Isla Negra—are found along Chile's Central Coast. The sundry objects he collected in his vast travels around the globe inhabit his former residences and give each one a life of its own.

1 Valparaíso. The winding streets of Valparaíso, a once wealthy port, are filled with historic monuments recalling their 19th-century glory. A cultural renaissance has been under way ever since UNESCO listed the city as a World Heritage Site in 2003.

2 Viña del Mar. Neighboring Valparaíso, Viña del Mar has one of the country's largest casinos, elegant hotels, and a sharp nightlife scene that make it an excellent place to blow off some steam.

3 Casablanca Wine Valley. Chile's most lauded valley for white wines, located along the road between Santiago and the coast.

4 Quintay. A forgotten former whaling station south of Valparaíso.

5 Algarrobo. Don't miss the relaxed charms of this southern beach town.

6 Isla Negra. Where South America's most famous poet, Pablo Neruda, had his seaside retreat.

7 Concón. A busy northern beach resort.

8 Maitencillo. Easygoing beach on the northern coast popular with affluent families.

9 Zapallar. This stunning northern beach town is an exclusive seaside resort for Santiago's rich and powerful.

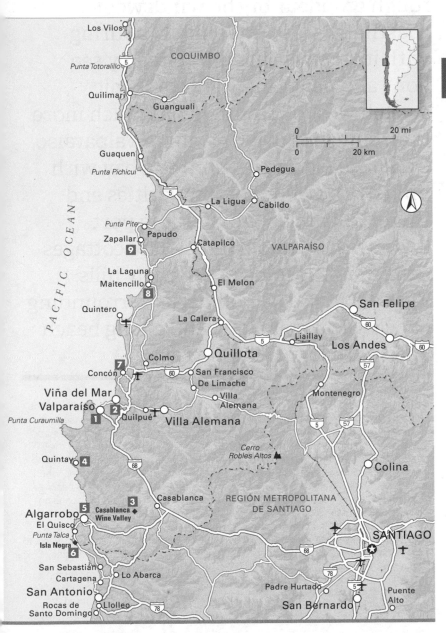

Most people head to the Central Coast for a single reason: the beaches. The rough grandeur of the windswept coastline here is undeniably alluring with its rocky islets inhabited by sea lions and penguins. Yet this scenic stretch west of Santiago has much more than sun and surf. Charming Valparaíso, Chile's quirkiest city, shares a bay with Viña del Mar, but the similarities end there. Valparaíso is a bustling port town with a jumble of colorful cottages nestled in the folds of its many hills. Viña del Mar has lush parks surrounding neoclassical mansions and a long beach lined with luxury high-rises.

The *balnearios* (small beach towns) to the north and south of the twin cities have their own character, often defined by coastal topography. You can take a sunset stroll along the stone path built between the mansions and rocks that jut out into the Pacific in Zapallar; watch or join the surfers in Maitencillo; indulge yourself in the culinary delights of Concón; gawk at the sculpted bodies that strut around Reñaca's hip beach; visit a former whaling station in quaint Quintay; discover Pablo Neruda's infatuation with the sea in Isla Negra; and take a dip in clear-blue and, yes, chilly water in Algarrobo's el Canelillo.

Proximity to Santiago has resulted in the development—and in some cases over-development—of these towns as summer resorts. At the beginning of the 20th century, Santiago's elite started building vacation homes here. Soon after, when trains connected the capital to beaches, middle-class families started spending their summers at the shore. Improved highway access in recent decades has allowed Chileans of all economic levels to enjoy the occasional beach vacation.

Late December through mid-March, when schools let out for summer vacation and Santiago becomes torrid, the beaches are packed. Vacationers frolic in the chilly sea by day and pack the restaurants and bars at night. The rest of the year, the coast is relatively deserted and, though often cool and cloudy, a pleasantly tranquil place to explore. For a taste of local life, check out the *caletas* (coves) where boaters gather to unload their catch. They're usually the site of small fishing cooperatives and are always colorful and lively places to visit.

MAJOR REGIONS

Viña del Mar and Valparaíso (Vineyard of the Sea and Paradise Valley, respectively) each maintain an aura that warrants their dreamy appellations. Only minutes apart, these two urban centers are nevertheless as different as sister cities can be. Valparaíso won the heart of poet Pablo Neruda, who praised its "cluster of crazy houses;" it continues to be a disorderly, gritty, bohemian, and ultimately charming town. Still an active port, its lack of beaches keeps things more urban, if not urbane.

Viña del Mar, Valparaíso's glamorous sibling, is a clean, orderly, and elegant city with miles of beige beach, a glitzy casino, manicured parks, and shopping galore. Viña, together with nearby Reñaca, is synonymous with the best of life for vacationing Chileans. Its beaches gleam, its casino rolls, and its discos sizzle.

Once a dominion of solitude and sea, the **Southern Beaches**, a stretch of coastline south of Valparaíso, have seen much development, not all of it well planned, over the past few decades. A succession of towns here caters to the beach-bound hordes in January and February and becomes a sleepy retreat for most of the rest of the year. None of the towns are terribly attractive, but a few of the beaches are. In the off-season, it'll give you a good feel for rural life in this neck of the woods. The main reason to visit—and it's a great one—is to take a look at poet Pablo Neruda's hideaway in Isla Negra, where you can see the various treasures he collected during his lifetime.

On the **Northern Beaches**, to the north of Viña del Mar, the Pacific collides with the rocky offshore islands and a rugged coastline broken here and there by sandy bays. The coastal highway runs from Viña del Mar to Papudo, passing marvelous scenery along the way. Between Viña and Concón, it winds along steep rock faces, turning inland north of Concón, where massive sand dunes give way to expanses of undeveloped coastline, reminiscent of northern California's coast. The farther north you drive, the greater the distance between towns, each of which is on a notably distinct beach. Whether as a day trip from Viña or on a series of overnights, this stretch of coast is well worth exploring.

Planning

When to Go

It seems that all of Chile heads to the coast in the summer months of January and February. This can be a great time to visit, with the weather at its warmest and the nightlife at its steamiest. But it's also a tough time to find a room, especially on weekends. Make reservations as far in advance as possible. Spring (October and November) and fall (April and May) can be perfect times to visit, when the days are warm and breezy and the nights cool. Consider visiting during the shoulder months of December and March too, which have decent weather and also provide relative solitude in which to explore.

FESTIVALS AND SEASONAL EVENTS

The star-making Festival Internacional de la Canción (International Song Festival) takes place the third week of February in Viña del Mar. The concerts are broadcast live for an audience of millions across Latin America. Most towns have colorful processions on Día de San Pedro (June

29). A statue of St. Peter, patron saint of fishermen, is typically hoisted onto a fishing boat and led along a coastal procession. When the clock strikes midnight on New Year's Eve, the bay that runs from Valparaíso to Concón plays host to one of the world's most spectacular fireworks shows.

Planning Your Time

Plan to spend at least two days in Valparaíso, where you can ride a few funiculars and explore the cobbled streets. While you're there, a good day trip is an excursion to Pablo Neruda's waterfront home nearby in Isla Negra. You'll want to take a day or so to stroll around the bustling beach town of Viña del Mar. After that you can drive north along the coastal highway, stopping for lunch in either Concón or Maitencillo. From there you can return to Viña del Mar or continue on to spend a night in Zapallar.

Getting Here and Around

AIR
The Central Coast is served by LATAM Airlines, and a host of other carriers, via Santiago's Aeropuerto Internacional Arturo Merino Benítez, a 1½-hour drive from either Viña del Mar or Valparaíso.

BUS
There is hourly bus service between Santiago and both Valparaíso and Viña del Mar. Turbus, Pullman, and other companies leave from Santiago's Terminal Alameda, but it's best to take buses from metro station Pajaritos and avoid most of the capital's traffic. Smaller companies serving the other beach resorts depart from Santiago's Terminal San Borja.

To get to Concón you can take a *micro* or *liebre* (local bus) from Viña del Mar. Valparaíso's bus terminal is your best bet for reaching the smaller beach towns farther north or south of the twin cities.

Plan ahead, as the buses may fill up, especially in summer.

BUS CONTACTS Turbus. ☎ *600-660–6600* ⊕ *turbus.cl.* **Sol del Pacífico.** ☎ *32/279–5700* ⊕ *soldelpacifico.cl.* **Pullman Bus.** ☎ *600–600–0018* ⊕ *pullmanbus.com.* **Condor Bus.** ✉ *Valparaíso* ☎ *9/3426–4597* WhatsApp ⊕ *condorbus.cl.*

CAR
Because it's so easy to get around in Valparaíso and Viña del Mar, there's no need to rent a car unless you want to travel to other towns on the coast.

RENTAL CARS Rosselot. ✉ *Av. Colón 2409, Valparaíso* ☎ *32/314–0351* ⊕ *rosselot.cl/rent-a-car.*

TRAIN
The bright, spacious Tren Limache–Puerto (formerly known as Metro Valparaíso) links Valparaíso with Viña del Mar. It runs every 12 minutes from 6 am to 11:30 pm on weekdays, and from 7:30 am to 11:30 pm on weekends and holidays. Check out the website to plan your trip: efe.cl

Restaurants

Dining is one of the great pleasures of visiting the Central Coast. It's not rare to see fishermen bringing the day's catch straight to the restaurants that inevitably line the shore. Your server will be happy to share with you which fish were caught fresh that day. Try *corvina con salsa margarita* (sea bass in shellfish sauce) or *ostiones a la parmesana* (scallops served with melted Parmesan cheese). The more daring can also try a batch of raw shellfish bought direct from the fishermen's nets and served with a dash of lemon. With the exception of major holidays or fancier restaurants, reservations are almost never required here. Many restaurants still close between lunch and dinner: from 3 or 4 to 7 or 8.

Beachgoing in Chile

To the vast majority of Chileans, summer holiday means one thing: heading to the beach. Whether on the edge of a southern rainforest, one of the north's deserted coves, or one of the pleasant towns of the Central Coast, beaches all over the country are packed from late December to early March. Chile is not, however, your standard beach destination. Even where the water is safe enough to enter, the icy Humboldt Current, rushing up from the deep south slightly north of Antarctica, means only the brave (and typically the local) can bear more than a few seconds up to their chests.

Outside of the water, wandering vendors constantly appear, plying ice cream, drinks, *palmeras* (a heart-shape puff pastry), and other goodies. And watch out for the *promotoras*, scantily clad men and women promoting everything from batteries to beer. Where permitted, Chileans will set up a *parrilla* for one of their famous

asados to grill meat and sausages over a charcoal fire. The athletic may go for a game of *paleta*, batting a tennis ball back and forth with a small wooden racket, or the occasional *pichanga* (pick-up soccer game). If you want to escape the crowds, try walking along to the next beach, which may be surprisingly empty though just a few hundred meters away. The southern end of Maitencillo or the north of Papudo are particularly suitable for exploration.

Strong sun protection in Chile is essential due to a hole in the ozone layer in this part of the world. Even if the day begins in a fog, the mist quickly burns off, leaving you vulnerable to the sun's rays. Be sure to pack a hat, strong sunblock, and something to cover you up. You might even consider a beach umbrella, often available to rent right on the sand. Once the sun goes down, temperatures can fall quickly as sea breezes pick up, so bring a light jacket or sweater as well.

Restaurant reviews have been shortened. For more information, visit Fodors.com.

Hotels

Because the central beach resorts were developed by and for the Santiago families who summer here, they are dominated by vacation homes and apartments, although new, often upmarket hotels have been built especially around Valparaíso, Viña del Mar, and Concón. *Cabañas,* somewhat rustic cabins with a kitchenette and one or more bedrooms, are designed to accommodate families on tighter budgets. An even more affordable option is a *residencial*

(guesthouse), often just a few rooms for rent in a private home.

Hotel reviews have been shortened. For more information, visit Fodors.com.

What It Costs in Chilean Pesos (in Thousands)			
$	$$	$$$	$$$$
RESTAURANTS			
Under 6	6–8	9–11	over 11
HOTELS			
Under 46	46–75	76–105	over 105

Valparaíso is known for its colorful street murals.

Valparaíso

10 km (6 miles) south of Viña del Mar;
120 km (75 miles) west of Santiago.

Valparaíso's dramatic topography—42 *cerros*, or hills, overlooking the ocean—makes the use of winding pathways and wooden *ascensores* (funiculars) necessary to get around. The slopes are covered by candy-color houses, most of which have exteriors of corrugated metal peeled from shipping containers eons ago when Valparaíso was the busiest port in South America. The opening of the Panama Canal in 1914 heralded the end of the city's glory days. Yet, while changing trade routes and industrial decline may have diminished its importance, it remains one of Chile's principal ports and cultural hubs.

Most shops, banks, and other businesses cluster along the handful of streets called *El Plan* (the flat area) that are closest to the shoreline. *Porteños* (port residents) live in the surrounding hills

where, amid an undulating array of colorful abodes, you'll also find the city's best bars and restaurants. Head to the top of the dozens of stairways between *El Plan* and the hills and you'll find *paseos* (promenades) with spectacular views; many are named after prominent British and Yugoslavian immigrants. Neighborhoods take the name of the hill they cover.

With the jumble of power lines overhead and the hundreds of buses that slow down—but never completely stop—to pick up agile riders, it's hard to forget you're in a city. Still, walking is the best way to experience Valparaíso. Be careful where you step, though, as there are *quiltros* (street dogs) taking siestas on nearly every sidewalk.

GETTING HERE AND AROUND

By car from Santiago, take Ruta 68 west through the coastal mountains and the Casablanca Valley as far as you can go until the road descends into Valparaíso's Avenida Argentina, on the city's eastern edge. If you don't have a car, Turbus,

Pullman, and Condor buses leave several times an hour for Valparaíso and Viña del Mar from Santiago. Buses depart from both Terminal Alameda (the Universidad de Santiago Metro station) and Terminal Santiago (Estación Central station), but it's best to save yourself a crawl through Santiago by catching a bus from the smaller, safer, and more modern station outside the Pajaritos Metro stop on the city's western edge.

If you're using Valparaíso as your hub, you can take Pullman Bus to get to most coastal towns south of the city. Sol del Pacífico heads north to Cachagua, Zapallar, and other towns. Valparaíso has two information booths: one at Muelle Prat that is supposedly open daily 10–2 and 3–6 (although in real life the hours vary wildly).

BUS CONTACTS Valparaíso Bus Terminal. ⊠ *Av. Pedro Montt 2860, Valparaíso* ☎ *32/293–9695* ⊕ *vlpo.cl/2020/04/24/ terminal-rodoviario.*

TOURS
Valpo Street Art Tours
WALKING TOURS | Valparaíso is globally famous for its prismatic street murals; to see the most iconic ones you'll want to sign up for a tour. Founder Al Ramirez also runs Chilean Cuisine Cooking Classes (cookingclasseschile.com). ⊠ *Paseo Barbosa 151, Cerro Alegre* ⊕ *valpostreetart.com* 🖃 *From $25.*

ESSENTIALS
VISITOR INFORMATION Tourism Office. ⊠ *Condell 1490, Valparaíso* ☎ *32/293-9262* ⊕ *vlpo.cl.* **Valparaíso Municipal Tourism Kiosk at Muelle Prat.** ⊠ *Muelle Prat, Valparaíso* ⊕ *vlpo.cl.*

Sights

Ascensor El Peral
NOTABLE BUILDING | In Valparaíso, riding one of the city's 30 *ascensores* (funiculars) is a must. El Peral, built in 1902 and now a national monument, is one of the five currently operating (another five are

under repair). For just 100 pesos, it runs a very steep 52 meters (172 feet) from the Palacio de Justicia (court house) on the northeastern side of Plaza Sotomayor, up to the gorgeous Paseo Yugoslavo on Cerro Alegre, where the Palacio Baburizza houses a fine arts museum. ⊠ *Plaza Sotomayor, Cerro Alegre* ⊕ *ascensoresvalparaiso.org* 🖃 *100 pesos.*

Ascensor Reina Victoria
NOTABLE BUILDING | FAMILY | This steep 40-meter (131-foot) funicular, built in 1902 and named for Queen Victoria of England, who died a year earlier, connects Avenida Elías near Plaza Aníbal Pinto with the very popular Cerro Alegre. Once atop the hill, you'll come out to a small plaza where you can swoosh down a small metallic slide if your inner child so desires. ⊠ *Elías, Cerro Alegre* ⊕ *ascensoresvalparaiso.org* 🖃 *100 pesos.*

★ Cerro Concepción
VIEWPOINT | Either walk up from Plaza Aníbal Pinto or ride the Ascensor Concepción (due to reopen in 2024) to one of the most popular of Valparaíso's famous *cerros* (hills). The greatest attraction is the view, which is best appreciated from Paseo Gervasoni, a wide promenade to the right when you exit the ascensor, and Paseo Atkinson, one block to the east. Over the balustrades that line the promenades are amazing vistas of the city and bay. Nearly as fascinating are the narrow streets above them, some of which are quite steep. Continue uphill to Cerro Alegre, which has a bit of a bohemian flair. ⊠ *Ascensor Concepción, Esmeralda 916, Valparaíso.*

Galería Municipal de Arte
ART MUSEUM | This crypt in the basement of the Palacio Lyon hosts temporary exhibits by top-caliber Chilean artists that are displayed on stone walls under a series of brick arches. It's easy to miss the entrance, which is on Calle Condell just beyond the Museo de Historia Natural de Valparaíso. ⊠ *Condell 1550, Valparaíso* ⊕ *vlpo.cl/category/exhibiciones* 🖃 *Free* 🕑 *Closed Sun.*

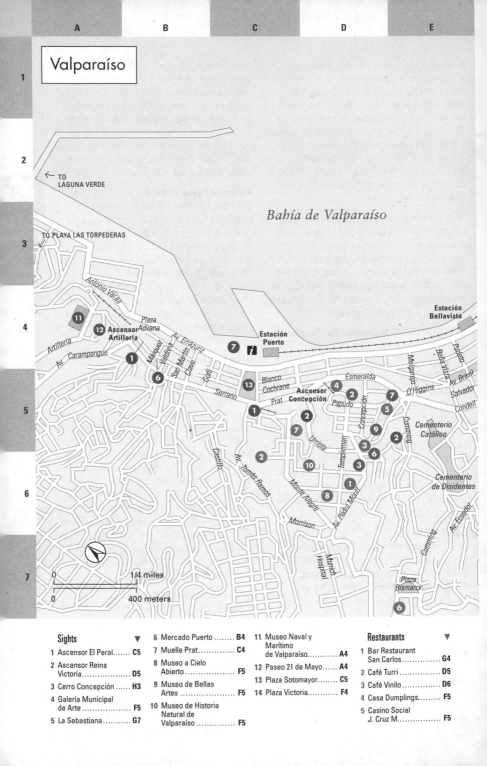

Valparaíso

← TO
LAGUNA VERDE

Bahía de Valparaíso

TO PLAYA LAS TORPEDERAS

Estación
Bellavista

Plaza
Advana

Ascensor
Artillería

Estación
Puerto

Blanco
Cochrane

Ascensor
Concepción

Esmeralda

Prat

Cementerio
Católico

Cementerio
de Disidentes

Munich
Hospital

Plaza
Bismarck

0   1/4 miles

0   400 meters

Sights ▼

1 Ascensor El Peral....... **C5**
2 Ascensor Reina
 Victoria.................. **D5**
3 Cerro Concepción **H3**
4 Galería Municipal
 de Arte **F5**
5 La Sebastiana **G7**

6 Mercado Puerto **B4**
7 Muelle Prat.............. **C4**
8 Museo a Cielo
 Abierto **F5**
9 Museo de Bellas
 Artes **F5**
10 Museo de Historia
 Natural de
 Valparaíso **F5**

11 Museo Naval y
 Marítimo
 de Valparaíso............ **A4**
12 Paseo 21 de Mayo...... **A4**
13 Plaza Sotomayor........ **C5**
14 Plaza Victoria............ **F4**

Restaurants ▼

1 Bar Restaurant
 San Carlos............... **G4**
2 Café Turri **D5**
3 Café Vinilo **D6**
4 Casa Dumplings......... **F5**
5 Casino Social
 J. Cruz M................. **F5**

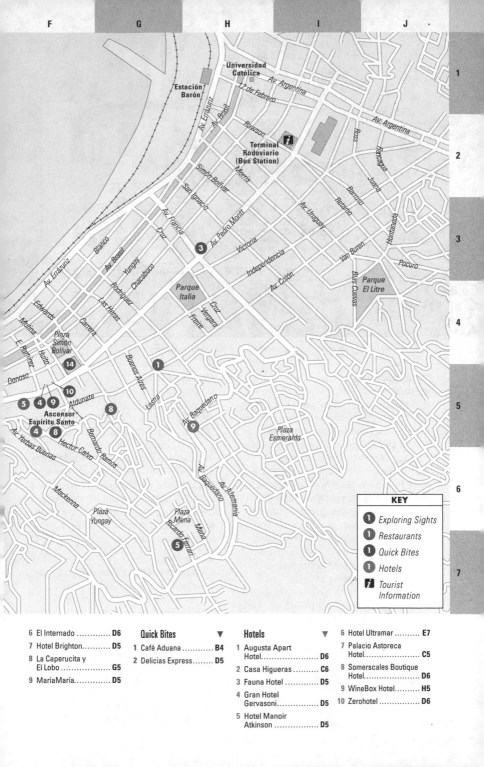

KEY

- **1** Exploring Sights
- **1** Restaurants
- **1** Quick Bites
- **1** Hotels
- **i** Tourist Information

6 El Internado **D6**
7 Hotel Brighton........... **D5**
8 La Caperucita y
   El Lobo **G5**
9 MaríaMaría............. **D5**

Quick Bites ▼
1 Café Aduana **B4**
2 Delicias Express........ **D5**

Hotels ▼
1 Augusta Apart
   Hotel.................... **D6**
2 Casa Higueras **C6**
3 Fauna Hotel **D5**
4 Gran Hotel
   Gervasoni............... **D5**
5 Hotel Manoir
   Atkinson **D5**

6 Hotel Ultramar **E7**
7 Palacio Astoreca
   Hotel..................... **C5**
8 Somerscales Boutique
   Hotel..................... **D6**
9 WineBox Hotel.......... **H5**
10 Zerohotel **D6**

You can visit one of poet Pablo Neruda's homes, La Sebastiana, in Valparaíso.

★ La Sebastiana

HISTORIC HOME | FAMILY | Tired of the frenetic pace of Santiago, poet Pablo Neruda longed for a calmer place overlooking the sea, and he found it here in the house that Spanish architect Sebastián Collado began building for himself but never finished. Neruda bought it with friends in 1959 and restored the upper floors in his own eclectic style, complete with curving walls, narrow winding stairways, and a tower. The view from the house is spectacular, but the real reason to visit is to see Neruda's extravagant collection of thousands of diverse objects. The house is a shrine to his many cherished belongings, including a beautiful orangish-pink stuffed bird he brought back from Venezuela, a carousel horse, and the pink-and-yellow barroom stuffed with kitsch. ⊠ *Ferrari 692, Valparaíso* ☎ *32/225–6606* ⊕ *fundacionneruda.org* 💲 *7000 pesos* ⊙ *Closed Mon.*

Mercado Puerto

MARKET | Built in 1922 and shuttered after the earthquake of 2010, Mercado Puerto officially reopened in 2020 following a 10-year-long restoration. This historic building now houses not only fruit and vegetable stands but also more than two dozen arts and crafts vendors, gourmet grocers, and trendy cafés. The revival of the old market is part of a larger scheme to spruce up the greater Barrio Puerto neighborhood. ⊠ *Valdivia 269, Valparaíso* ⊕ *instagram.com/mercadobarriopuerto.*

Muelle Prat

MARINA/PIER | FAMILY | Valparaíso's main wharf, Muelle Prat, bustles with activity. Vendors hawk their offerings, from trinkets and snacks to face painting and temporary tattoos, and owners of the dozens of bobbing *lanchas* (small boats) dwarfed by enormous cargo ships call out departure times for the next tour of the bay. At 4,000 pesos, a half-hour tour is a great way to experience the activity in the port, see a spectacular view of the city, and even get a close-up view of a sea lion colony. Here you'll also find a tourist information office and a row of souvenir shops. ⊠ *Av. Errázuriz at Plaza Sotomayor, Valparaíso* Ⓜ *Estación Puerto.*

Museo a Cielo Abierto
(*The Open Sky Museum*)

PUBLIC ART | This "museum" is actually a winding walk past 20 official murals (and dozens of unofficial ones) by some of Chile's best painters. There's even one by the country's most famous artist, Roberto Matta. The path is not marked, there's no fixed route, and much of the signage has disappeared over the years. The point is to get lost in the city's history and culture. ⊠ *Ascensor Espíritu Santo up to Cerro Bellavista, Valparaíso.*

★ Museo de Bellas Artes

HISTORIC HOME | The art nouveau Palacio Baburizza, built in 1916, houses the city's fine-arts museum. Former owner Pascual Baburizza donated this large collection of European paintings to the city. The fanciful decorative exterior is reminiscent of the style of Spanish architect Antoni Gaudí—note the bronze children dancing around the portico. The paintings and the impressive mansion itself take you on a historical journey through Chile's past. Fans of contemporary art should check out the free temporary exhibitions in the basement. ⊠ *Ascensor El Peral to Paseo Yugoslavo, Paseo Yugoslavo 176, Cerro Alegre* ☎ *32/225–2332* ⊕ *museobaburizza.cl* ☒ *2000 pesos, 4000 pesos for foreigners with audio guide included* ⊗ *Closed Mon.*

Museo de Historia Natural de Valparaíso

HISTORY MUSEUM | **FAMILY** | Within the Palacio Lyon, one of the few buildings to survive the devastating 1906 earthquake is this small but interesting natural history museum. With a focus on land and sea animals, it's a good place to take children. ⊠ *Condell 1546, Valparaíso* ☎ *32/254–4840* ⊕ *mhnv.cl* ☒ *Free* ⊗ *Closed Sun. and Mon.*

Museo Naval y Marítimo de Valparaíso

HISTORY MUSEUM | Take the Ascensor Artillería up to Paseo 21 de Mayo for a great view of the port and then head to this large neoclassical mansion that once housed the country's naval academy. It now contains a maritime museum, with displays that document the history of the port and the ships that once defended it. Cannons positioned on the front lawn frame the excellent view of the ocean. ⊠ *Paseo 21 de Mayo N° 45, Valparaíso* ☎ *32/253-7018* ⊕ *museomaritimo.cl* ☒ *3100 pesos.*

Paseo 21 de Mayo

VIEWPOINT | Ascensor Artillería pulls you uphill to Paseo 21 de Mayo, a wide promenade lined by a long row of booths selling crafts and souvenirs and surrounded by well-tended gardens and stately trees. From here you can survey the working port and much of the city through coin-operated binoculars. A gazebo—a good place to escape the sun—seems to be hanging in midair. Paseo 21 de Mayo is located in the middle of Cerro Playa Ancha, one of the city's more colorful and less touristy neighborhoods. ⊠ *Ascensor Artillería at Plaza Aduana, Valparaíso.*

Plaza Sotomayor

PLAZA/SQUARE | Valparaíso's impressive Plaza Sotomayor serves as a gateway to the bustling port. The **Comandancia en Jefe de la Armada**, headquarters of the Chilean navy, is a grand periwinkle building that rises to a turreted pinnacle over a mansard roof. At the eastern end of the plaza the **Monumento de los Héroes de Iquique** honors Arturo Prat and other heroes of the War of the Pacific. At the southern end, the **Ministerio de las Culturas, las Artes y el Patrimonio** often hosts art exhibitions. A crafts and products fair also happens weekly during the warmer months. Beware of traffic in the middle of the square; cars and buses come suddenly from all directions. ⊠ *Av. Errázuriz at Sotomayor, Valparaíso.*

Chilean Coastal Cuisine

"In the turbulent sea of Chile lives the golden conger eel," wrote Chilean poet Pablo Neruda in a simple verse that leaves the real poetry for the dinner table. To many, dining is the principal pleasure of a trip to the Central Coast. Along with that succulent conger eel (*congrio* as it's known in these parts), menus here typically offer *corvina* (sea bass), a whitefish called *reineta*, and *lenguado* (sole). The appetizer selection, which is invariably extensive, usually includes *machas* (razor clams), *ostiones* (scallops), *camarones* (shrimp), and *jaiba* (crab).

Fish and meat dishes do not usually include *agregados* (side dishes), so if you want French fries, mashed potatoes, a salad, or *palta* (avocado), you have to order them separately. Bread, lemons, and a sauce called *pebre* (a mix of tomato, onion, cilantro, parsley, and chili) are always brought to the table. Valparaíso is also known for a hearty, cheap meal called *chorillana*—a mountain of thinly sliced steak, onions, cheese, and eggs on a bed of French fries that is generally placed in the center of the table to be shared by the group.

Plaza Victoria

PLAZA/SQUARE | FAMILY | Most Chilean cities have a Plaza de Armas that serves as the center of urban life, but Valparaíso has this, the "Victory Plaza," which dates back to the early 19th century. It was once the favored venue for bullfights and public executions, but today it's a lovely park graced by a large fountain. The fountain is bordered by four female figures representing the seasons and two black lions that look across the street to the neo-Gothic cathedral and its unusual freestanding bell tower. ⊠ *Condell at Molina, Valparaíso.*

Beaches

If it's beaches you're after, head to Viña del Mar or one of the other resort towns along the coast.

Laguna Verde

BEACH | In a somewhat secluded cove 14 km (9 miles) southwest of Valparaíso, Laguna Verde is a stunning and largely uncrowded stretch of yellow-sand coastline that's worth the visit if you have some time to spend. You can get there via a one-hour local bus ride or can rent a car for the half-hour trip. Better yet, rent

a four-wheel-drive vehicle to be able to explore the surrounding area. It's rustic, but there are now a few restaurants, food trucks during the summer months, basic services, and cabins ranging from spartan to spectacular. **Amenities:** food and drink; free parking. **Best for:** solitude; sunset; walking. ⊠ *47 Av. Principal, Valparaíso.*

Playa Las Torpederas

BEACH | Valparaíso's only true swim-worthy beach is set in a sheltered crescent of yellow sand west of the port. Although less attractive than other beaches up and down the coast, it's a fast and easy getaway from the busy port and does have very calm water. **Amenities:** food and drink; free parking. **Best for:** sunset; swimming. ⊠ *Altamirano 22100, Valparaíso.*

🍴 Restaurants

Bar Restaurant San Carlos

$ | CHILEAN | If you were to ask a local to take you to a traditional restaurant, chances are you would wind up here. Now operated by the third generation of the same family, this small establishment will take you back in time with its long wooden bar, older gentlemen playing dominoes, and very traditional Chilean fare. **Known for:** the adventurous cow's feet dish; cuisine cooked in a traditional cazuela; old-school atmosphere. [$] *Average main: pesos6000* ✉ *Las Heras 685, at Colón, Valparaíso* ☎ *32/223–4043.*

Café Turri

$$$$ | **SEAFOOD** | Near the top of Ascensor Concepción, this 19th-century mansion is one of the city's best-known restaurants. The traditional menu has a French twist; onion soup with Gruyère and foie gras sit alongside excellent seafood. **Known for:** traditional fine dining; an awesome view; excellent seafood. [$] *Average main: pesos12500* ✉ *Templeman 147, at Paseo Gervasoni, Cerro Concepción* ☎ *32/225–2091, 32/236–5307* 🌐 *www.turri.cl.*

Café Vinilo

$$ | **CHILEAN** | Serving traditional Chilean cuisine with a contemporary touch, Café Vinilo prides itself on making its own bread and desserts. They also work directly with their food suppliers, so you can rest assured the rock fish ceviche on your plate was likely caught that same morning by a diver in Quintero, an hour's drive north along the coast. **Known for:** jazz music ambience; youthful atmosphere; fresh seafood. [$] *Average main: pesos7000* ✉ *Almirante Montt 448, Cerro Alegre* ☎ *32/223–0665* 🌐 *cafevinilo.cl.*

Casa Dumplings

$$ | **ASIAN** | This cozy "dumpling house" near the Museo a Cielo Abierto is a soothing oasis of tranquil music, woodsy vibes and excellent Asian street food. It's a great alternative to all the seafood and sandwich restaurants nearby with a completely different menu and aesthetic. **Known for:** curries, noodles, and dumplings; afternoon tea; peaceful ambience. [$] *Average main: pesos7000* ✉ *Cerro Bellavista, Héctor Calvo 308, Valparaíso* ☎ *32/360–5906* 🌐 *instagram.com/casadumplings.*

Casino Social J. Cruz M

$$$ | **CHILEAN** | This eccentric restaurant is a Valparaíso institution thanks to its legendary status for inventing the *chorillana* (thinly sliced beef with fried onions and eggs served atop French fries), a dish that is meant to be eaten communally. There's no menu—choose either a plate of *chorillana* for two or three, or *carne mechada* (stewed beef) with a side of French fries, rice, or tomato salad. **Known for:** shared tables and dishes; home of the Chilean classic chorillana; very casual dining. [$] *Average main: pesos9000 (shared plate)* ✉ *Condell 1466, Casa 11, Valparaíso* ☎ *32/259–6166* 🌐 *jcruz.cl* 💳 *No credit cards.*

El Internado

$$ | **CHILEAN** | Boasting what is arguably one of the best terraces in town, this two-story hilltop behemoth is one of the trendiest spots to watch the sunset with a pisco sour and a ceviche. Yet it's much more than just a bar and restaurant; you can also listen to live music, view art exhibitions, or shop for gifts at the on-site design store. **Known for:** craft cocktails; sunset views over the harbor; creative Chilean sandwiches. [$] *Average main: pesos8000* ✉ *Paseo Dimalow 167, Cerro Alegre* ☎ *32/335–4153* 🌐 *elinternado.cl.*

Hotel Brighton

$$ | **ECLECTIC** | Seemingly dangling from the edge of Cerro Concepción, the bright yellow Hotel Brighton and its restaurant have an amazing view from the black-and-white-tiled terrace. The limited menu specializes in seafood, with such standards as *ostiones a la parmesana* (scallops on the half shell with Parmesan), as well as pizzas and burgers. **Known for:** sweeping views; relaxed and inviting atmosphere; live music on weekends. [$] *Average main: pesos8000* ✉ *Paseo Atkinson 151, Cerro Concepción* ☎ *32/222–3513* 🌐 *brighton.cl.*

★ La Caperucita y El Lobo

$$$$ | **CONTEMPORARY** | This place is one of those delightful little restaurants that seems to have it all—great food and an excellent view of the bay in a warm and intimate setting. Seafood plays a key role here, but the carefully constructed menu also features dishes like rabbit, lamb, and steak, along with some vegetarian options. **Known for:** lots of local charm; excellent seafood and other meat options; nice views. [$] *Average main: pesos12000* ✉ *Ferrari 75, Cerro Florida, Valparaíso* ☎ *32/317–2798* 🌐 *lacaperucitayellobo.cl* 🕑 *Closed Mon.*

★ MaríaMaría

$ | **BAKERY** | This cutesy cafe is Valpo's yummiest breakfast, brunch, or lunch spot with homemade sourdough breads, sweet treats, silky lattes, fresh kombuchas, and health-focused bites. Sit in the brick-red bakery to watch the action or at a table on the tree-shaded street out front. **Known for:** trendy vibe; creative baked goods; healthy lunches. [$] *Average main: pesos3000* ✉ *Beethoven 286, Cerro Concepción* 🌐 *instagram.com/mariamaria_valpo* 🕑 *Closed Mon. and Tues.*

☕ Coffee and Quick Bites

Café Aduana

$ | **CAFÉ** | This trendy café with exposed brick walls, colorful murals, and hardwood floors is one of the best reasons to leave the hills for the flatland of Barrio Puerto. In addition to a fine array of coffees and baked goods, you'll also find soups, salads, and sandwiches that offer superb value for money. **Known for:** espresso coffees; slick design; historic building. [$] *Average main: pesos4000* ✉ *Cochrane 25, Valparaíso* ☎ *32/225–0706* 🕑 *Closed Sat. and Sun.*

Delicias Express

$ | **CHILEAN** | This long-running bakery on the road up to Cerro Alegre prepares more than 80 different varieties of empanadas, including surprising combos like cheese, salmon, and capers or cheese, mango, and pineapple. The dough is crispy, the service is friendly, and the line out front moves fast. **Known for:** mural-covered exterior; unique empanadas; good value. [$] *Average main: pesos2000* ✉ *Urriola 358, Cerro Alegre* ☎ *32/223–7438* 🕑 *Closed Sun.*

🛏 Hotels

Augusta Apart Hotel

$$$ | **APARTMENT** | Floor-to-ceiling glass windows give the spacious suites on the upper levels of this 6-room apart-hotel soaring views over Cerro Alegre. **Pros:** fantastic service; large rooms; ground floor suite with private patio. **Cons:** you can hear footsteps of guests sleeping above; in-room kitchen is basic; not all rooms have views. [$] *Rooms from: pesos90,000* ✉ *San Enrique 577, Cerro Alegre* ☎ *9/9079–9608* 🌐 *augustavalparaiso.cl* 🛏 *6 rooms* 🍴 *Free Breakfast.*

★ Casa Higueras

$$$$ | **B&B/INN** | The hills of Valparaíso have enjoyed a boom of boutique hotels in the last decade, but this one is a cut above the rest. **Pros:** pampering staff; a rare spot of luxury in Valparaíso; convenient location. **Cons:** some rooms are a little noisy; limited on-site parking; the rest of the street could benefit from a paint job. [$] *Rooms from: pesos200000* ✉ *Higueras 133, Cerro Alegre* ☎ *32/249–7900* 🌐 *casahigueras.cl* 🛏 *20 rooms* 🍴 *Free Breakfast.*

★ Fauna Hotel

$$$ | **HOTEL** | As the name suggests, Fauna stays true to its natural surroundings: the floors, stairs, and handrails are made from recycled native wood, adobe is used generously in the architecture, and the span of the hotel's interior streetside wall, extending some two floors, is actually the exposed containment wall originally constructed to keep Cerro Alegre standing. **Pros:** trendy restaurant; unique design; centrally located. **Cons:**

no elevator, so stairs could be a problem for some; no access by vehicle; lots of foot traffic outside. $ *Rooms from: pesos100000* ✉ *Pasaje Dimalow 166, Cerro Alegre* ☎ *32/327–0719* ⊕ *faunahotel.cl* ⟻ *22 rooms* ⦿ *Free Breakfast.*

Gran Hotel Gervasoni

$$ | B&B/INN | Set in a sprawling Victorian mansion that spreads across five floors built in the 1870s, the Gervasoni is a chance to step back in time to Valparaíso's more elegant past. **Pros:** attentive staff; a chance to imagine life in Valparaíso's Victorian apogee; convenient location. **Cons:** some of the rooms are a bit tired; views are spoiled by a concrete office block; very steep stairs. $ *Rooms from: pesos60000* ✉ *Paseo Gervasoni 1, Cerro Concepción* ☎ *32/223–9236* ⊕ *hotelgervasoni.com* ⟻ *15 rooms* ⦿ *Free Breakfast.*

Hotel Manoir Atkinson

$$ | B&B/INN | One of the first boutique hotels to spring up on fashionable Cerro Concepción, this cozy house lies at the end of Paseo Atkinson, near many local attractions. **Pros:** friendly and attentive owner/hosts; many of Valparaíso's best restaurants are just a block or two away; peaceful location. **Cons:** Wi-Fi can be spotty; parking is an issue; despite location, many of the rooms lack sea views. $ *Rooms from: pesos65000* ✉ *Paseo Atkinson 165, Cerro Concepción* ☎ *45/298–4820* ⊕ *hotelatkinson.cl* ⟻ *6 rooms* ⦿ *Free Breakfast.*

Hotel Ultramar

$$ | B&B/INN | Behind a staid-looking brick facade, there's an ultramodern yet simple interior in this early 20th-century building on Cerro Carcel. **Pros:** free parking; eye-popping views of the bay from terrace; friendly, helpful staff. **Cons:** traffic noise at night; not very kid-friendly; location is a bit far from the action. $ *Rooms from: pesos65000* ✉ *Peréz 173, Cerro Cárcel, Valparaíso* ☎ *32/221–0000* ⊕ *hotelultramar.com* ⟻ *16 rooms.*

Palacio Astoreca Hotel

$$$$ | HOTEL | Complete with a piano bar, wine cellar, spa, massage room, indoor heated swimming pool, wood-fire heated hot tub, and indoor garden, this luxurious hotel aims to please. **Pros:** wonderful spa on-site; a beautiful setting in a renovated Victorian mansion; convenient, peaceful location. **Cons:** parking is limited and tricky; spotty Wi-Fi; a bit pricey. $ *Rooms from: pesos130000* ✉ *Calle Montealegre 149, Cerro Alegre* ☎ *32/327–7700* ⊕ *hotelpalacioastoreca.com* ⟻ *23 rooms* ⦿ *Free Breakfast.*

Somerscales Boutique Hotel

$$$ | B&B/INN | Perched high atop Cerro Alegre, between ascensores El Peral and Reina Victoria, this palm-shaded mansion has an unobstructed view of the sea. **Pros:** beautiful garden; light, bright rooms; in the heart of hip Valpo. **Cons:** furnishings a bit dated; no air-conditioning in rooms; a steep climb back to your room at night. $ *Rooms from: pesos100000* ✉ *San Enrique 446, Cerro Alegre, Valparaíso* ☎ *32/233–1006* ⊕ *hotelsomerscales.cl* ⟻ *8 rooms* ⦿ *Free Breakfast.*

★ WineBox Hotel

$$ | HOTEL | This one-of-a-kind, brightly colored apart-hotel is one of the most creative lodgings in the country: in honor of the city's role as a working port, it was built from 25 recycled shipping containers, and its rooftop terrace provides a 360-degree view of the bay and entire city. **Pros:** creative, container hotel design; all rooms include original artwork; wine bar/restaurant and shop on-site. **Cons:** far from main sites; not the best setting for nondrinkers; weekend terrace parties mean it can get noisy. $ *Rooms from: pesos65000* ✉ *Av. Baquedano 763, Cerro Mariposa, Valparaíso* ☎ *9/5824–4497* ⊕ *facebook.com/wineboxvalparaiso* ⟻ *21 rooms* ⦿ *No Meals* ⟻ *No children allowed.*

Zerohotel

$$$ | **B&B/INN** | Set in one of the quieter corners of bustling Cerro Alegre, this former Dutch diplomat's residence dating to to the 1880s has been transformed into a chic boutique hotel. **Pros:** very stylish; a quiet, relaxing corner on Cerro Alegre's normally bustling streets; can arrange local experiences. **Cons:** presents some difficulty for people with mobility problems; no on-site parking (paid parking is available nearby with reservations); no restaurant. [$] *Rooms from: pesos105000* ✉ *Lautaro Rosas 343, Cerro Alegre* ☎ *32/211–3113* 🌐 *zerohotel.com* 🛏 *9 rooms* 🍴 *Free Breakfast.*

🍸 Nightlife

Valparaíso has an inordinate number of late-night establishments, which run the gamut from pubs to tango bars and salsa dance clubs. Thursday through Saturday nights most places get crowded between 11 pm and midnight and young people stay out until dawn. The main concentrations of bars and clubs are around Plaza Anibal Pinto and along Avenida Errázuriz nearby, though many long-running establishments shut down during the pandemic and never reopened. Cerros Concepción, Alegre, and Bellavista have quieter options, many with terraces perfect for admiring the city lights.

Tango dancing is so popular in Valparaíso that you might think you were in Buenos Aires. Then there's the *cueca brava,* a common Chilean song and dance (also called *cueca urbana* or *cueca chora* in these parts); it's undergone a revival in recent years, taking on a much more modern and urban slant.

BARS

Bar de Pisco

COCKTAIL LOUNGES | True to its name, this venue specializes in pisco, the national drink distilled from grapes. There are more than 30 different brands available at this stylish bar, which is attached to Café Vinilo, where bartenders serve up deliciously creative cocktails, such as *apiado,* which includes a celery-based liquor. ✉ *Almirante Montt 448, Cerro Alegre* ☎ *32/223–0665.*

★ **Bar del Tio**

COCKTAIL LOUNGES | The cheap prices at this trendy, split-level bar belie the top quality of the world-class cocktails whipped up by some of Chile's best bartenders. A few sips and you'll view pisco in an entirely new light. Craft Chilean beer, artisan wine, and delicious bar food make this a crowd-pleasing spot to start or end your Valpo evening. ✉ *Almirante Montt 67, Valparaíso* ☎ *2/3271–9479* 🌐 *facebook.com/bardeltio* 🕒 *Closed Sun. and Mon.*

Bar Victoria

BARS | Fishing nets hanging from the ceiling, brightly polished wood floors, and black-and-white photos on the walls give this bar-restaurant an old-fashioned feel. Patrons come for a bite to eat, from *chorrillana* (French fries topped with eggs, onions, and beef) to ceviche, and then stay for the beer on tap. ✉ *Salvador Donoso 1540, Valparaíso* ☎ *32/245–9387.*

Casa Cervecera Altamira

BREWPUBS | This low-lit bar with exposed brick walls under the Ascensor Reina Victoria makes the Central Coast's best craft beers, as well as a killer gin and tonic with its home-distilled Altamira Gin. The music is funky, the service is grand, and the elevated pub grub is delicious. Don't forget to check out the small beer museum in the back. ✉ *Elias 126, Valparaíso* ☎ *9/9109–6457* 🌐 *cerveceraaltamira.cl* 🕒 *Closed Sun.*

DANCE CLUBS

Some of the city's hottest dance clubs are found on the streets southeast of Plaza Sotomayor near the waterfront. There is also a cluster of bars along the streets that lead uphill from Plaza Anibal Pinto.

LIVE MUSIC
Bar Liberty
LIVE MUSIC | Founded in 1897, this traditional *porteño* hangout claims to be the oldest bar in the city. It's an iconic spot for folk music and *cueca* dancing with all the salty sailors, sticky tables, and memorabilia-stuffed walls to prove it! ⊠ *Barrio Puerto, Almirante Riveros 9, Valparaíso* ☎ *9/9170–0171.*

Brighton
LIVE MUSIC | On Cerro Concepción, Brighton has live Latin music on Friday and Saturday nights, starting at 11 pm. Its black-and-white tile terrace overlooks the city's glittering lights. ⊠ *Paseo Atkinson 151, Cerro Concepción* ☎ *32/222–3513.*

El Rincón de Las Guitarras (Casa de Cueca)
LIVE MUSIC | Get a double shot of *porteño* (port city) nightlife at this classic restaurant with two rooms that feature two different acts simultaneously. Go ahead and try the traditional Chilean food, but the real reason to come is for the *cueca*, Chile's national dance. Forget everything you might know about the traditional folklore show. This is the gutsy, gritty, eye-to-eye, forehead-to-forehead *cueca chora*, which has undergone a revival in the past few decades. If you want a table, you'll need to come early—and plan on staying into the wee hours. ⊠ *Freire 431, Valparaíso* ☎ *32/223–4412* ☞ *Live music Thurs.–Sun.*

Performing Arts

Parque Cultural Valparaíso (Ex-Cárcel)
ARTS CENTERS | In 1999, Valparaíso's prison population was moved to a new facility on the outskirts of town, and the old prison (Ex Cárcel), built in 1906, was basically abandoned until opened to the community as a museum and was occasionally used for plays and concerts. In 2011, it was renovated for use as a cultural park with excellent spaces for art exhibitions and theater performances. You'll find drumming groups practicing on the lawn and the occasional arts fair. ⊠ *Calle Cerro Carcel 471, Valparaíso* ☎ *32/235–9400* ⊕ *parquecultural.cl.*

Teatro Municipal de Valparaíso
THEATER | Off Plaza O'Higgins, the lovely old Municipal Theater hosts symphonies, films, and ballet, opera, and theater performances. ⊠ *Uruguay 410, Valparaíso* ⊕ *facebook.com/municipalvalpo.*

⬤ Shopping

Outside of Santiago, there are more boutique shops in Valparaíso than anywhere else in Chile. If it's handicrafts you're looking for, head to the bohemian neighborhoods of Cerro Concepción and Cerro Alegre. There are dozens of workshops where you can watch artisans ply their crafts.

Galería de Arte Bahía Utópica
ART GALLERIES | With several small rooms displaying the works of local painters and sculptures, this is one of the best galleries in town for affordable (and portable) art. You'll also find creative postcards and other gifts. ⊠ *Almirante Montt 372, Cerro Alegre* ☎ *32/273–4296* ⊕ *bahiautopica.cl.*

Galería Espacio Rojo
ART GALLERIES | This quirky gallery displays the works of 60 Chilean artists, including many who painted the murals you see on nearby buildings. There are also kitschy gifts and one-of-a-kind souvenirs. ⊠ *Miramar 175, Cerro Alegre* ☎ *32/324–0437* ⊕ *galeriaespaciorojo.com.*

Mercado Moderno Valparaíso
WOMEN'S CLOTHING | One of the best clothing boutiques on the Central Coast with flowing gowns, designer ponchos, colorful jewelry, and made-in-Chile handbags. Send a message on WhatsApp to make an appointment. ⊠ *Lautaro Rosas 450, Cerro Alegre* ☎ *9/9885–4237* ⊕ *mm450.cl/en/our-boutique/* ⊙ *By appointment.*

Ripley

DEPARTMENT STORE | One of the country's major department store chains, Ripley is across from Plaza Victoria. The fifth floor has a food court. ⊠ *Plaza Victoria 1646, Valparaíso* ☎ *600/230–0222* ⊕ *ripley.cl.*

Activities

BOATING

Muelle Prat Boat Tours

BOATING | FAMILY | Boat operators at Muelle Prat offer 30-minute tours of the bay for 4,000 pesos. If you have several people, consider hiring your own boat for 30,000 pesos. ⊠ *Av. Errázuriz at Plaza Sotomayor, Valparaíso* ⊠ *From 4000 pesos.*

SOCCER

Estadio Elías Figueroa Brander

SOCCER | Valparaíso's major sports stadium is known by many names, including most commonly as the Playa Ancha Stadium, but the city's first-division soccer team, the Santiago Wanderers, call it home. It was originally inaugurated in 1931; it was closed for renovations in 2012 and reopened in 2014. ⊠ *Av. Guillermo González de Hontaneda 1310, Valparaíso* ☎ *32/234-7056* ⊕ *santiago-wanderers.cl.*

Viña del Mar

120 km (75 miles) northwest of Santiago.

Viña del Mar has high-rise apartment buildings that tower above its excellent shoreline, which boasts miles of beige sand combed by heavy surf. Just back from the sea are wide boulevards lined with perky palms, lush parks, and crumbling mansions. Clean and orderly, the city has long been more popular with Chileans than foreigners, who tend to fall for the anything-goes appeal of neighboring Valparaíso.

Viña, as it's popularly known, has the country's oldest casino, excellent hotels, and an extensive selection of restaurants. To some, all this means that Viña del Mar is modern and exciting; to others, it means the city is lacking in character. But there's no denying that Viña del Mar has a little of everything—trendy boutiques, beautiful homes, interesting museums, a casino, varied nightlife, and, of course, one of the best beaches in the country.

GETTING HERE AND AROUND

From Santiago, take Ruta 68 west through the Coastal Mountains, turning off to Viña del Mar as the vineyards of the Casablanca Valley give way to eucalyptus forests. The spectacular twisting access road (Agua Santa), through hills dotted with Chilean palm trees, drops you on Avenida Alvarez, just a couple of blocks from downtown Viña del Mar. Turbus, Condor, and Pullman all run buses to Viña del Mar from the station outside the Pajaritos metro stop. Viña del Mar has the best tourist office on the coast, offering fistfuls of helpful maps and brochures.

ESSENTIALS

VISITOR INFORMATION Viña del Mar main office. ⊠ *Arlegui 715, Viña del Mar* ✛ *Beside Hotel O'Higgins across from park* ☎ *32/218–5712* ⊕ *visitevinadelmar.cl.*

Sights

Casino Viña del Mar

CASINO | Built in 1930 in a neoclassical style that wouldn't be out of place in a James Bond movie, Chile's oldest casino has a restaurant, bar, and cabaret, as well as roulette, blackjack, and 1,500 slot machines. It's open nightly until the wee hours of the morning most of the year. There's a 3,500-peso cover charge, and keep in mind that people dress up to play here, especially in the evening. ⊠ *Av. San Martín 199, Viña del Mar* ☎ *600/700-6000* ⊕ *enjoy.cl.*

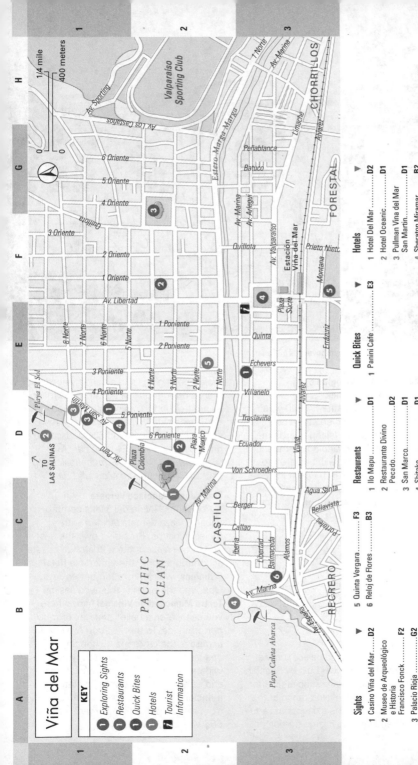

Viña del Mar

KEY

- ① Exploring Sights
- ① Restaurants
- ① Quick Bites
- ① Hotels
- 🖪 Tourist Information

PACIFIC OCEAN

Playa Caleta Abarca

Valparaíso Sporting Club

FORESTAL

CHORRILLOS

RECREO

CASTILLO

Sights ▶

1 Casino Viña del Mar......D2
2 Museo de Arqueológico e Historia Francisco Fonck......F2
3 Palacio Rioja......G2
4 Plaza José Francisco Vergara......F3
5 Quinta Vergara......F3
6 Reloj de Flores......B3

Restaurants ▶

1 Ilo Mapu......D1
2 Restaurante Divino Pecado......D2
3 San Marco......D1
4 Shitake......D1

Quick Bites ▶

1 Panini Cafe......E3

Hotels ▶

1 Hotel Del Mar......D2
2 Hotel Oceanic......D1
3 Pullman Viña del Mar San Martín......D1
4 Sheraton Miramar......B2
5 Tres Poniente......E2

Palacio Rioja houses a decorative-arts museum.

★ Museo de Arqueológico e Historia Francisco Fonck

HISTORY MUSEUM | FAMILY | A 500-year-old stone *moai* (a carved stone head) brought from Easter Island guards the entrance to this archaeological museum. The most interesting exhibits are the finds from Easter Island, which indigenous people call Rapa Nui, such as wood tablets displaying ancient hieroglyphics. The museum, named for groundbreaking archaeologist Francisco Fonck—a native of Viña del Mar—also has an extensive library of documents relating to the island. Other fun but freaky exhibits include shrunken heads, insects, and all sorts of stuffed birds and animals. ⊠ *4 Norte 784, Viña del Mar* ☎ *32/268–6753* ⊕ *museofonck.cl* ⊠ *3000 pesos.*

Palacio Rioja

ART MUSEUM | This grand palace, now a national monument, was built by Spanish banker Francisco Rioja immediately after the earthquake that leveled much of the city in 1906. It contains a decorative-arts museum showcasing a large portion of Rioja's belongings and a conservatory, so there's often music in the air. Performances are held in the main ballroom. You'll find a nice café in the back with seating under the trees in beautifully landscaped grounds. ⊠ *Quillota 214, Viña del Mar* ☎ *32/218–4690* ⊕ *www.museopalaciorioja.cl* ⊠ *Free* ⊗ *Closed Mon. and Tues.*

Plaza José Francisco Vergara

PLAZA/SQUARE | Viña del Mar's central square, Plaza Vergara is lined with majestic palms. Presiding over the east end of the plaza is the patriarch of coastal accommodations, the venerable **Hotel O'Higgins**, which has seen better days. Opposite the hotel is the neoclassical **Teatro Municipal de Viña del Mar**, where you can watch a ballet, theater, or music performance. To the west on **Avenida Valparaíso** is the city's main shopping strip, a one-lane, seven-block stretch with extra-wide sidewalks and numerous stores and cafés. Some of the city's stateliest mansions lie on the streets just back from the plaza. ⊠ *Plaza Vergara, Arlegui 687, Viña del Mar.*

Quinta Vergara

GARDEN | FAMILY | Lose yourself on the paths that wind amid towering araucaria and other well-marked trees on the grounds that contain one of Chile's best botanical gardens. An amphitheater here holds an international music festival, Festival Internacional de la Canción de Viña del Mar, in February. There is also an arts-focused kids' museum, Museo Artequin, which is highly interactive. ⊠ *Av. Errázuriz 563, Viña del Mar* ☎ *32/218–5720* ⊕ *quintavergara.cl* ⊠ *Free.*

Reloj de Flores

CLOCK | FAMILY | Built for the 1962 World Cup, this functional flower clock has been tick-tocking away for six decades. The botanical landmark is not only one of the most photographed sites on the Central Coast; it's helped Viña del Mar foster a reputation as La Ciudad Jardín ("The Garden City"). ⊠ *Alamos 590, Viña del Mar* Ⓜ *Miramar.*

Beaches

Las Salinas

BEACH | FAMILY | Just north of town a white arch announces the tiny family-friendly Balneario Las Salinas beach area, a crescent of yellow sand that has the calmest water in the area. **Amenities:** food and drink; parking; toilets. **Best for:** sunset; swimming; walking. ⊠ *Jorge Montt 12021, Viña del Mar.*

Playa Caleta Abarca

BEACH | FAMILY | One of Viña's most popular beaches, smack in the center of town, Playa Caleta Abarca's golden sands are crowded with sun worshippers in midsummer, making it a great place for people-watching. **Amenities:** food and drink; lifeguards. **Best for:** swimming. ⊠ *Avenida España s/n, Viña del Mar* ⊕ *Just south of Sheraton Hotel, across from Reloj de Flores.*

★ Playa El Sol

BEACH | FAMILY | Just north of the rock wall along Avenida Peru and flanked by the old Muelle Vergara is a stretch of sand that draws hordes of people from December through March. This is Viña del Mar's main beach, and it goes by many names the longer you walk: Acapulco, Blanca, Los Cañones, Marineros. It's great for swimming and people-watching as well as for exploring the artisan fair nearby. **Amenities:** food and drink; parking; showers; toilets. **Best for:** sunset; walking. ⊠ *San Martín 1130, Viña del Mar.*

🍴 Restaurants

★ Ilo Mapu

$$$$ | CHILEAN | If your travels don't include the Mapuche heartland of La Araucanía, head to this artfully designed restaurant in Viña for a vital introduction to the little-appreciated cuisine of Chile's largest indigenous group. Start with one of the myriad tasting boards before seguing into the mains, which feature everything from wild boar to antioxidant-rich *maqui* berries and *piñón* seeds from ancient araucaria trees. **Known for:** endemic Chilean ingredients; fusion Mapuche cuisine; artful plating. Ⓢ *Average main: pesos13000* ⊠ *6 Norte 228, Viña del Mar* ☎ *32/269–1564* ⊕ *ilomapu.cl* ☉ *Mon. and Tue.*

Restaurante Divino Pecado

$$$$ | SEAFOOD | Facing the casino, this elegant seafood restaurant specializes in made-from-scratch pasta, crab casseroles, tuna tartare, and fresh-caught fish draped in creative sauces. There's a rare-in-Chile English-language menu, and you can expect impeccable service from the career waiters. **Known for:** seafood straight from the fishermen; refined European ambience; extensive wine list. Ⓢ *Average main: pesos12000* ⊠ *San Martín 180, Viña del Mar* ☎ *32/297–5790* ⊕ *divinopecado.cl* ☉ *Mon.*

San Marco

$$$$ | **ITALIAN** | More than six decades after Edoardo Melotti emigrated here from northern Italy, his restaurant maintains a reputation for first-class food and service. The menu includes traditional gnocchi, as well as pasta stuffed with shrimp, *carne mechada* (shredded beef), or pear, walnut, and ricotta. **Known for:** elegant ambience; traditional Northern Italian cuisine; extensive wine list. $ *Average main: pesos13000* ⊠ *Av. San Martín 597, Viña del Mar* ☎ *32/297–5304* ⊕ *ristorantesanmarco.cl.*

Shitake

$$ | **JAPANESE** | With so much fresh fish available, it's no wonder that sushi and sashimi have caught on with locals. In fact, it's hard to find a block downtown that lacks a Japanese restaurant, but a favorite is Shitake, which occupies a few gold and beige rooms on Avenida San Martín. **Known for:** local favorite; fresh sushi made for sharing; Ecuadorean shrimp tempura. $ *Average main: pesos8000* ⊠ *Av. San Martín 421, Viña del Mar* ☎ *9/9779–5089* ⊕ *shitake.cl.*

 Coffee and Quick Bites

Panini Cafe

$ | **CAFÉ** | Whether you like your coffee prepared in a Chemex or espresso machine, brewed hot or cold, you can find it at this friendly café, which also serves up incredibly cheap panini sandwiches, salads, and traditional Chilean cakes. **Known for:** great value for money; lively terrace; strong cold-brew coffee. $ *Average main: pesos2500* ⊠ *Arlegui 495, Viña del Mar* ☎ *32/311–0853* ⊕ *paninicafe.cl* ⊗ *Closed Sat. and Sun.*

Hotels

★ Hotel Del Mar

$$$$ | **RESORT** | A rounded facade, echoing the shape of the adjacent Casino Viña del Mar, means that almost every room at this elegant oceanfront hotel has unmatched views. **Pros:** free access to the casino; notable in-house restaurant; pure luxury in every direction. **Cons:** no coffee or tea in the room means guests must wait for restaurant to open; can be a pretty busy place; constant chiming of gaming machines may grate on your nerves. $ *Rooms from: pesos140000* ⊠ *Av. San Martín 199, Viña del Mar* ☎ *600/700–6000* ⊕ *enjoy.cl* ⮫ *60 rooms* ⦿ *Free Breakfast.*

Hotel Oceanic

$$$$ | **B&B/INN** | Built on the rocky coast between Viña and Reñaca, this boutique hotel has luxurious rooms with gorgeous ocean views. **Pros:** peaceful setting on city's edge; ocean views from hotel terraces; on-premise spa for massage and pampering. **Cons:** no air-conditioning in rooms; standard rooms do not have an ocean view; beyond the city limits, making a vehicle necessary for getting around town. $ *Rooms from: pesos110000* ⊠ *Av. Borgoño 12925, north of town, Reñaca* ☎ *32/283–0006* ⊕ *hoteloceanic.cl* ⮫ *30 rooms* ⦿ *Free Breakfast.*

Pullman Vina del Mar San Martín

$$$ | **HOTEL** | The slick and modern Pullman boasts all the things you'd expect of a glossy chain hotel, including a pool, fitness center, rooftop terrace, bar, and attractive restaurant. **Pros:** Jacuzzi tubs; rooftop bar overlooking the sea; beach access. **Cons:** standard rooms have no sea views; room design is a bit generic; bars nearby can be noisy on weekends. $ *Rooms from: pesos100,000* ⊠ *Av San martin 667, Viña del Mar* ☎ *32/381–7100* ⊕ *all.accor.com* ⮫ *160 rooms* ⦿ *No Meals.*

★ Sheraton Miramar

$$$$ | **RESORT** | This sophisticated city hotel certainly earns its name, as you can do almost everything here while you gaze at the sea. **Pros:** the beach is right next door; first-class city hotel with spectacular views; elegant and luxurious. **Cons:** access to the hotel by car is tricky;

a bit of a walk to main drag; area around the hotel is partially blighted by one of Viña's main access roads. $ *Rooms from: pesos200000* ✉ *Av. Marina 15, Viña del Mar* ☎ *32/238–8600* ⊕ *marriott.com* ⇥ *142 rooms* ⚭ *Free Breakfast.*

Tres Poniente

$ | B&B/INN | Come for the personalized service and for many of the same amenities you'll find at larger hotels at a fraction of the cost. **Pros:** tasty breakfast; good value on a quiet backstreet; friendly, helpful staff. **Cons:** no elevator; plumbing can be noisy in some rooms; a long walk from the beach or Viña's main attractions. $ *Rooms from: pesos45000* ✉ *3 Poniente 70, between 1 and 2 Norte, Viña del Mar* ☎ *32/247–8576* ⊕ *hotel3poniente.cl* ⇥ *11 rooms* ⚭ *Free Breakfast.*

Nightlife

Viña's nightlife varies considerably according to the season, with the most glittering events concentrated in January and February. There are nightly shows and concerts at the casino and frequent performances at Quinta Vergara. During the rest of the year, things get going only on weekends. Aside from the casino, late-night fun is concentrated in the area around the intersection of Avenida San Martín and 4 Norte, as well as the intersection of Von Schroeder and Avenida Valparaíso. Viña residents tend to go to Valparaíso for live music, since it has a much better selection.

BARS

Barbones Bar

BARS | A trendy take on the classic Chilean dive, this bustling backstreet bar boasts a dozen local craft beers on tap and more than 100 pisco labels, which it claims is the largest selection in Chile. Overflowing sandwiches, deep-fried empanadas, and massive *chorrillanas* (French fries topped with cheese, meat, onions, and fried eggs) help soak up all

the alcohol. ✉ *7 Norte 444, Viña del Mar* ☎ *9/5342–2688* ⊕ *barbones.cl.*

DANCE CLUBS

Café Journal

DANCE CLUBS | This long-running bar and nightclub may be tucked into a 100-year-old building, but it never seems to go out of fashion. DJs rattle the walls of two dimly lit dance floors each weekend, while emerging rock bands take to the stage at the attached concert hall. During the week, you can expect live-streamed soccer matches, cover bands, stand-up comedy, and an eclectic cast of characters. ✉ *Av Agua Santa 4, Viña del Mar* ☎ *32/266–6654* Ⓜ *Miramar.*

Shopping

Avenida Valparaíso

NEIGHBORHOODS | Viña's main shopping strip is Avenida Valparaíso between Cerro Castillo and Plaza Vergara, where wide sidewalks accommodate throngs of mostly local shoppers. Stores here sell everything from shoes to cameras, and there are also sidewalk cafés, bars, and restaurants. ✉ *Viña del Mar.*

Espacio Urbano

MALL | For one-stop shopping, locals head to the mall. Espacio Urbano, on the north end of town, is a longtime favorite. ✉ *Av. Benidorm 805 at 15 Norte, Viña del Mar* ☎ *2/3252–7259* ⊕ *espaciourbano.cl/centro-comercial/15-norte.*

Falabella

DEPARTMENT STORE | This popular department store is located south of Plaza Vergara. ✉ *Sucre 250, Viña del Mar* ☎ *600/390–6500* ⊕ *falabella.com.*

Feria Artesanal Muelle Vergara

CRAFTS | On the beach, near the pier at Muelle Vergara, the Feria Artesanal Muelle Vergara is a crafts fair open daily in summer and on weekends the rest of the year. ✉ *Viña del Mar.*

Mall Marina

MALL | Viña's largest shopping center, Mall Marina, offers the wide range of department stores, boutiques, restaurants, and movie theaters you'd expect in any major city. ⊠ *14 Norte 821, Viña del Mar* ☎ *32/216–1203* ⊕ *mallmarina.cl.*

Activities

GOLF

Granadilla Country Club

GOLF | You can play 18 holes Tuesday through Sunday at the Granadilla Country Club. It's an established course in Santa Inés—a 10-minute drive from downtown. The greens fees are 72,000 pesos, and they rent clubs for 15,000 pesos, but you need to make a reservation. ⊠ *Camino a Granadilla s/n, Av Santa Inés s/n, Viña del Mar* ☎ *32/278–0686* ⊕ *www.granadilla.cl* 🏌 *18 holes, 6443 yards, par 72.*

HORSE RACING

Valparaíso Sporting Club

HORSE RACING | Horse racing is hosted here every Wednesday. The Clásico del Derby, Chile's version of the Kentucky Derby, takes place the first Sunday in February. Rugby, polo, cricket, and other sports are also played here. The site is a favorite for other large-scale events too. ⊠ *Av. Los Castaños 404, Viña del Mar* ☎ *32/265–5610* ⊕ *sporting.cl.*

SOCCER

Estadio Sausalito

SOCCER | Everton is Viña del Mar's soccer team. Matches are held at the 20,000-seat Estadio Sausalito, which hosted World Cup matches in 1962 and the Americas Cup in 1991 and 2015. ⊠ *Laguna Sausalito, Viña del Mar* ☎ *9/5423–9401* ⊕ *tiendaeverton.cl.*

Casablanca Wine Valley

Don't miss the chance to stop at the many wineries along the road between Santiago and the coast. As you come out of the Zapata Tunnel (at km 60 on Ruta 68), the importance of wine production to the local economy will be obvious. Vineyards carpet the floor of the Casablanca Valley for as far as the eye can see. Up until the mid-1980s, most enologists considered this area inhospitable for wine grapes, yet today it is at the forefront of the country's wine industry. Experts have come to recognize the valley's proximity to the sea as its main asset, because cooler temperatures give the grapes more time to develop flavor as they ripen.

Many of the wineries are open to visitors and offer activities such as tours, tastings, picnics on the grounds, lunch at an on-premises restaurant, or an overnight stay (all for a price, of course). Although most offer tours on a daily basis, it's best to call ahead to ensure someone is available to show you around.

GETTING HERE AND AROUND

Most of the vineyards are a bit of a trek from the main highway, so having a bus drop you off on the side of the road probably isn't the best way to go. If you drive, plan to spend several hours touring and tasting the wines, and give yourself time for the alcohol to leave your system as Chile has a strict zero-tolerance policy on drinking and driving. Alternately, indulge freely and spend the night, or take one of many guided tours.

TOURS

If you want to visit more than one winery, the **Ruta del Vino de Casablanca** (32/274–3755) offers a number of tour options departing from the main plaza in Casablanca.

Sights

Casas del Bosque
WINERY | Nestled among rolling vine-covered hills just outside the town of Casablanca, Casas del Bosque offers tastings and tours as well as creative options such as biking through the vineyard, being a winemaker for a day, cooking classes, and more. During March and April, the main harvest months, you can learn even more about the production process with the chance to pick your grapes and take them for selection and pressing. Like many wineries in the valley, Casas del Bosque has its own restaurant, Tanino. ✉ *Hijuelas No. 2, Centro Ex Fundo Santa Rosa, Casablanca* ☎ *2/2480–6946 Restaurant, 2/2480–6941 Tours* 🌐 *casasdelbosque.cl* 🎟 *Tours from 12500 pesos.*

Casa Valle Viñamar
WINERY | For those who like their wines cold and bubbly, look no further than this *espumante* (sparkling wine) specialist, which offers tastings in a stunning pearly-white mansion on a hill overlooking the valley. The winery also houses one of Casablanca's most renowned restaurants, Macerado, which pairs local wines with local produce. ✉ *Camino interior Nuevo Mundo s/n, Casablanca* ✣ *Ruta 68, Km. 7* ☎ *9/7831–4823 Restaurant, 32/331–3387 Tours* 🌐 *vinamar.cl.*

★ **Emiliana Organic Vineyards**
WINERY | Emiliana is the world's largest organic winery, and it preaches its green ethos all across this stunning property, where chickens help with pest control and alpacas mow the lawn. Emiliana also produced the first biodynamic wine in Latin America, and you can try it on a tour or tasting. Stop by as well for organic picnics and a chance to mix your own wine blends. ✉ *Ruta 68, km 60.7, Casablanca* ☎ *2/2353–9151* 🌐 *emiliana.cl.*

Viña Matetic
WINERY | The biodynamic Viña Matetic straddles the border between the Casablanca Valley and the adjacent San Antonio Valley and may take the prize for having the region's most stunning bodega. Set into a ridge overlooking vines on both sides, it aims to harmonize with the gorgeous setting, with sloping passageways revealing glimpses into the barrels stored below. Just down the road, the winery's restaurant looks out over beautifully manicured gardens, in the middle of which is a restored guesthouse with 10 elegantly decorated rooms. ✉ *Fundo Rosario, Lagunillas, Casablanca* ☎ *2/2611–1501* 🌐 *matetic.com* 🎟 *Tours from 17000 pesos; Tastings from 7000 pesos.*

Hotels

Hotel La Casona
$$$$ | **RESORT** | La Casona is a stately boutique hotel tucked into a colonnaded colonial estate on the vast grounds of the Matetic Vineyards. **Pros:** stunning location within the vines; organic meals; access to on-site winery. **Cons:** far from other wineries; inconsistent customer service; quite pricey. [$] *Rooms from: pesos425000* ✉ *Fundo El Rosario s/n, Lagunillas* ☎ *2/2604–9076* 🌐 *matetic.com* 🛏 *10* 🍴 *All-Inclusive.*

Quintay

40 km (25 miles) south of Valparaíso.

Not too long ago, migrating sperm whales were a common sight along the beaches at Quintay, although they were all but exterminated by the whaling industry that sprang up here in 1943. Whaling was banned in 1967, and Quintay returned to being a quiet fishing village. If you wonder what the Central Coast was like before condos began springing up, head to this charming spot.

GETTING HERE AND AROUND

From Valparaíso, follow Ruta 68 toward Santiago until you reach Las Tablas. Then turn onto Ruta F-800, which winds down through the hills to Quintay. From Santiago, follow Ruta 68, turn off at the Quintay-Tunquén exit, and follow F-800 to the coast.

Sights

Quintay Whaling Station

FACTORY | Fundación Quintay looks after this former whaling station, which operated from 1943 to 1967 and processed approximately 13,700 whales. It's been converted into a quaint museum that gives you a window into this coastal town's past. The museum, along with the skeletal remains of a whale, are just a stone's throw away from the handful of brightly colored fishing boats at the wharf. ⊠ Caleta Quintay, Quintay 🕾 32/236–2511 ⊕ fundacionquintay.com 🗐 1000 pesos.

Beaches

Playa Grande

BEACH | FAMILY | Vacation apartments keep creeping closer to the beach, which gets its fair share of sun worshippers in summer. There are two ways to reach Playa Grande: through the town, following Avenida Teniente Merino, or through the gated community of Santa Augusta. **Amenities:** food; parking (fee); toilets. **Best for:** sunset; surfing; swimming; walking. ⊠ Quintay.

 Restaurants

Pezcadores

$$$ | SEAFOOD | Echoing the colors of the fishing boats below, this seafood restaurant is painted vivid shades of yellow, green, and red. The restaurant's proximity to the caleta (cove) means the fish on your plate was probably pulled from the water early that morning. **Known for:** bustling fishing pier atmosphere; fresh and tasty fish; nice wine list. 🟤 Average main: pesos9000 ⊠ Avenida Costanera s/n, Quintay 🕾 32/236–2068 ⊕ pezcadores.cl ⊗ Closed Mon. and Tue.

Activities

DIVING

Austral Divers

SCUBA DIVING | Austral Divers offers diving courses for all levels, kayaking, and other water excursions from its beachside office. ⊠ Caleta Quintay, Quintay 🕾 9/9885–5099, 9/9477–8409 ⊕ australdivers.cl.

Chile's coastline has several interesting shipwrecks. Two are off the shores of Quintay, including Indus IV, a whaling ship that went down in 1947.

Algarrobo

35 km (22 miles) south of Quintay.

The first sizable town south of Valparaíso, Algarrobo has a winding coastline with several yellow-sand beaches that attract throngs of sun worshippers. The pine forest behind two of its more popular beaches, El Canelo and Canelillo, is also worth exploring.

GETTING HERE AND AROUND

From Valparaíso, follow Ruta 68 toward Santiago and turn off onto Ruta F90 just after Casablanca. From there it is approximately 35 km (22 miles) to Algarrobo. Pullman and Turbus travel regularly to Algarrobo from the Alameda Terminal (Universidad de Santiago Metro station) in Santiago. Most of Algarrobo's main beaches lie within easy walking distance of the town. Regular buses run from here along the coast to El Quisco and Isla Negra farther south.

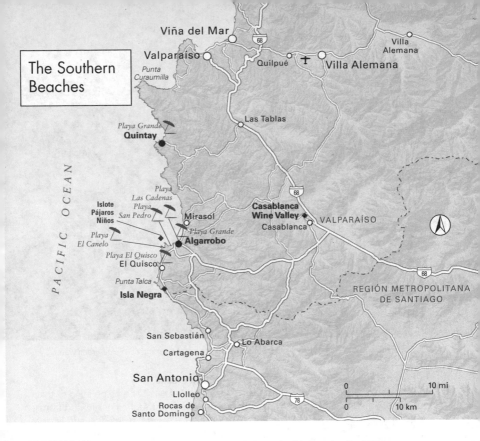

The Southern Beaches

Viña del Mar

Valparaíso

Punta
Curaumilla

Quilpué

Villa Alemana

Villa
Alemana

PACIFIC OCEAN

Playa Grande
Quintay

Las Tablas

*Playa
Las Cadenas*

*Playa
San Pedro*

**Islote
Pájaros
Niños**

Mirasol

*Playa
El Canelo*

Playa Grande
Algarrobo

Playa El Quisco
El Quisco

Punta Talca

Isla Negra

**Casablanca
Wine Valley**

Casablanca

VALPARAÍSO

REGIÓN METROPOLITANA
DE SANTIAGO

San Sebastián

Cartagena

Lo Abarca

San Antonio

Llolleo

Rocas de
Santo Domingo

0   10 mi

0   10 km

ESSENTIALS

**VISITOR INFORMATION Municipal Tourist
Office.** ✉ *Av. Peñablanca 250, Algarrobo*
☏ *35/220–0100* ⊕ *municipalidadalgarrobo.
cl.*

Sights

Club de Yates Algarrobo

MARINA/PIER | This private yacht club next
to Playa San Pedro organizes and participates in numerous regattas throughout
the year. It also has sailing classes and
a lively clubhouse. ✉ *Carlos Alessandri
2447, Algarrobo* ☏ *35/248–2074* ⊕ *cya.cl.*

Islote Pájaros Niños

ISLAND | Just offshore from the Cofradía
Náutica, this tiny island and penguin
sanctuary shelters 20 species of marine
birds, including some 60 Humboldt
penguins. The upper crags of the island

are dotted with hundreds of little caves
dug by the penguins using their legs and
beaks. Though only members are allowed
in the marina, a path leads to the top of
a nearby hill from which you can watch
the flightless birds through binoculars.
✉ *Algarrobo* ⊕ *monumentos.gob.cl.*

Beaches

El Quisco

BEACH | **FAMILY** | South of Algarrobo, El
Quisco is a long beach of pale sand
guarded on either end by stone jetties. In
the middle of the beach is a boulder with
a 15-foot-high, six-pronged cactus sculpture perched atop it. South of the beach
is the blue-and-yellow cove, where boats
anchored offshore create a picturesque
composition. Easily reached by all forms
of transportation, the beach is packed
on sunny summer days, when tourists

Playa El Canelo, one of Algarrobo's prettiest beaches, has rocky shores and calm blue-green water.

outnumber *quisqueños* (locals) about 10 to 1. **Amenities:** food and drink. **Best for:** sunset; swimming; walking. ⊠ *Algarrobo.*

★ Playa El Canelo

BEACH | Algarrobo's prettiest beach is Playa El Canelo, located in a secluded cove south of town. It's actually two beaches in one, divided only by a small outcrop of rocks. The idyllic spot with fine yellow sand, calm blue-green water, and a backdrop of pines is blissfully quiet most of the year, but gets very crowded in January and February. From Algarrobo, follow Avenida Santa Teresita south to Avenida El Canelo and the pine forest of Parque Canelo, or from the main coastal road, take Bahía Mansa to Valle Verde. Because it's in a fairly tight cove, it's a great place for swimming, but other activities include boat rides, zip lines, body boarding, and walking the trails along the upper cliffs. **Amenities:** food and drink; parking (fee). **Best for:** sunset; surfing; swimming. ⊠ *Algarrobo.*

Playa Grande

BEACH | FAMILY | The beige sand of this nice beach stretches northward from town for several miles. The surf is usually rough—though beautiful—and therefore not apt for swimming. It's a great place for a long walk on the beach, and you'll often see people fishing. Massive condominium complexes scattered along the beach spill hundreds of vacationers onto it every summer. **Amenities:** food and drink. **Best for:** sunset; walking. ⊠ *Camino Algarrobo Mirasol, Algarrobo.*

Playa Las Cadenas

BEACH | Toward the northern end of town, where the promenade that runs between the beach and the long row of waterfront properties ends, Playa Las Cadenas is a popular, smaller spot to spread a beach towel. The calm and relatively shallow water makes it a good place for swimming. The name, translated to "Chain Beach," refers to the thick metal links lining the sidewalk, which were recovered from a shipwreck off Algarrobo Bay. **Amenities:** food and drink; toilets.

Best for: sunset; swimming. ⊠ *Av. Carlos Alessandri 1928, Algarrobo.*

Playa San Pedro

BEACH | FAMILY | The most popular beach in town is tiny Playa San Pedro; a statue of Saint Peter in the sand next to the wharf marks the spot. It's small, but the waters are surrounded by a rocky barrier that keeps them calm and good for swimming. **Amenities:** food and drink. **Best for:** sunset; swimming; walking. ⊠ *Av. Carlos Alessandri, Algarrobo ⊹ Just south of Club de Yates.*

 **Restaurants**

A Toda Costa

$$$$ | SEAFOOD | Head north of town to this hot spot right on the beach for the best seafood in town. The extensive menu includes the classics like razor clams Parmesan and crab gratin as well as more creative fare. **Known for:** vegetarian options; creative and tasty seafood; great ocean view. $ *Average main: pesos12000* ⊠ *Av. Costanera s/n, Albarrobo Norte, Algarrobo* ☎ *9/4424–5850* ⊕ *atodacosta.cl.*

 Hotels

Pao Pao Lodge

$$ | B&B/INN | FAMILY | The pine cabanas here range from cozy studios to two-bedroom apartments complete with wooden decks and hot tubs. **Pros:** idyllic spot for rest and relaxation; rural setting makes it ideal for families; pool on-site. **Cons:** gets quite noisy during peak season; pool could be a bit cleaner; cabins are close together. $ *Rooms from: pesos55000* ⊠ *San Gerónimo s/n, Algarrobo* ☎ *9/3063–0898* ⊕ *paopaolodge.cl* ⇥ *22 cabins* ⦿| *No Meals.*

San Alfonso del Mar

$$$ | APARTMENT | FAMILY | If you want to swim in the sea but aren't keen to brave the polar temperatures of Chilean waters, try this set of imposing apartment buildings on Algarrobo's northern edge with its eight-hectare, 1,000-meter, turquoise-blue seawater pool that stretches the length of the complex. **Pros:** everything you need is close at hand; avoid the chilly Humboldt Current in style; world's largest man-made pool. **Cons:** lack of coordination between management and owners make it difficult to resolve any problems; swimming is not allowed in the large pool; if you do feel the need to stray, it's a long walk to town. $ *Rooms from: pesos90000* ⊠ *G-98-F 886, Algarrobo* ☎ *9/9233–1864* ⊕ *sanalfonso.cl* ⇥ *160 apartments* ⦿| *No Meals.*

 Activities

DIVING

Buceo Algarrobo

SCUBA DIVING | Pablo Zavala teaches diving and runs expeditions to half a dozen dive spots from the Club de Yates. ⊠ *Av. Carlos Alessandri 2447, Algarrobo* ☎ *9/9435–4835* ⊕ *buceoalgarrobo.cl.*

Isla Negra

6 km (4 miles) south of El Quisco; 61 km (38 miles) south of Valparaíso.

"I needed a place to work," Chilean poet and Nobel laureate Pablo Neruda wrote in his memoirs. "So I found a stone house facing the ocean, in a place nobody knew about." That place, of course, was Isla Negra. Neruda bought his house here in 1939 and became enamored with the raw beauty of its setting: "Isla Negra's wild coastal strip, with its turbulent ocean, was the place to give myself passionately to the writing of my new song."

GETTING HERE AND AROUND

From Algarrobo, head out as if returning to Santiago but turn southward at the crossroads on the road marked El Quisco. Follow the coastal road for about

Neruda's Inspiration

First, let's clear up one thing: Isla Negra may mean "Black Island," but this little stretch of rugged coastline is not black, and it's not an island. This irony must have appealed to Nobel Prize–winning poet Pablo Neruda, who made his home here for more than three decades.

Of his three houses, Pablo Neruda was most attached to Isla Negra. "Ancient night and the unruly salt beat at the walls of my house," he wrote in one of his many poems about his home here. It's easy to see how this house, perched high above the waves crashing on the purplish rocks, could inspire such reverie.

Neruda bought the place in 1938. Like La Sebastiana, his house in Valparaíso, it had been started by someone else and then abandoned. Beginning with the cylindrical stone tower, which is topped by a whimsical weather vane shaped like a fish, he added touches that could only be described as poetic. There are odd angles, narrow hallways, and various nooks and crannies, all for their own sake.

What is most amazing about Isla Negra, however, is what Neruda chose to place inside. There's a tusk from a narwhal in one room, and figureheads from the fronts of sailing ships hanging overhead in another. There are huge collections ranging from seashells to bottles to butterflies. And yet it is also just a house, with a simple bedroom designed so he could gaze down at the sea when he needed inspiration.

9 km to the small village of Isla Negra. The path leading down to Neruda's house begins from the main road just after a row of stores selling handicrafts and souvenirs. Local buses run regularly along the coastal road between Algarrobo and San Antonio.

◉ Sights

★ Casa-Museo Isla Negra

HISTORIC HOME | Perched on a bluff overlooking the sea, this house is a shrine to the life, work, and many passions of the Chilean poet and Nobel laureate Pablo Neruda. Throughout the house, you'll find displays of treasures—from bottles and maps to seashells and a narwhal tusk—he collected over the course of his remarkable life. Although he spent much time living and traveling abroad, Neruda made Isla Negra his primary residence later in life. He wrote his memoirs from the upstairs bedroom to the sound of the crashing waves and dictated the final pages to his wife there before departing for the Santiago hospital where he died (supposedly of cancer, though rumors abound that he was actually poisoned). Neruda and his wife are buried in the prow-shaped tomb area behind the house.

Just before Neruda's death in 1973, a military coup put Augusto Pinochet in command of Chile. He closed off Neruda's home and denied all access, but Neruda devotees still chiseled their tributes into the wooden gates surrounding the property. In 1989 the Neruda Foundation, started by his widow, restored the house and opened it as a museum. Here his collections are displayed as they were while he lived. The living room contains—among numerous other oddities—a lapis lazuli and quartz fireplace and a number of figureheads from ships hanging from the ceiling and walls.

You can visit the museum with an audio guided tour, available in English, Spanish, French, German, and Portuguese (included in the admission price) that describes Neruda's many obsessions, from the positioning of guests at the dinner table to the east–west alignment of his bed. Objects had a spiritual and symbolic life for the poet, which the tour makes evident. Reservations are not required for the tour, but space is filled on a first-come, first-served basis, so plan on coming early and be prepared for a long wait during the busy summer months. ✉ *Poeta Neruda s/n, Isla Negra* ☎ *35/246–1284* 🌐 *fundacionneruda.org* 🎫 *7000 pesos* 🕒 *Closed Mon.*

🍴 Restaurants

El Rincón del Poeta
$$$$ | SEAFOOD | Inside the entrance to the Neruda museum at Isla Negra, this small restaurant has a wonderful ocean view, with seating both indoors and on a protected terrace. The name translates as the Poet's Corner, a theme continued in the small but original menu filled with classic Chilean dishes. **Known for:** another ode to the poetry of Pablo Neruda; excellent seafood, including Neruda's favorite fried conger eel; views of pounding waves. $ *Average main: pesos12000* ✉ *Casa-Museo Isla Negra, Poeta Neruda s/n, Isla Negra* ☎ *35/246–1774* 🌐 *elrincondelpoeta.cl* 🕒 *Closed Mon.*

Concón

15 km (9 miles) north of Viña del Mar, along Avenida Borgoño.

How to explain the lovely name Concón? One theory is that in the language of the Changos, *co* meant "water," and the duplication of the sound alludes to the confluence of the Río Aconcagua and the Pacific. When the Spanish arrived in 1541, Pedro de Valdivia created an improvised shipyard here that was destroyed by Native inhabitants, leading to one of the first known clashes between indigenous and Spanish cultures in central Chile.

Concón has been a seaside resort for Santiaguinos for a century, first with large stately homes surrounded by well-tended gardens or perched among the rocks just meters from the sea. Many of these still exist and jostle for space among a growing number of high-rise apartment buildings, all vying for a share of the impressive ocean views. Concón has also declared itself the Gastronomic Capital of Chile—a claim that seems a bit of an exaggeration, although it may well have more restaurants per capita than any other Chilean town, many of which are great for seafood. The other main attractions include its beaches as well as the rugged coastal scenery along the road that connects it to Reñaca. The wetlands and sand dunes north of town get less attention but are equally impressive.

GETTING HERE AND AROUND

Concón occupies a long stretch of coast just south of where the Aconcagua River spills into the Pacific. It's 15 km (9 miles) north of Viña del Mar along the spectacular Avenida Borgoño (check out the houses built into the cliffs), passing through Reñaca along the way. If coming direct from Santiago, follow Ruta 5 north until Km 109 and take the road to Quillota all the way to the coast. Part of the route is called the Ruta Las Palmas, named for the giant smooth-trunked Chilean palm trees that produce tiny coconuts called *coquitos*. Buses leave regularly from Viña del Mar's Plaza Vergara and Santiago's Terminal Alameda.

Mantagua Wetlands at Posada del Parque is a bird-watcher's paradise.

Sights

★ Mantagua Wetlands at Posada del Parque

NATURE PRESERVE | One of Chile's most important wetlands lies along the northern bank of the Aconcagua River, and a good place to explore it—especially for bird-watchers and photographers—is the Posada del Parque, 5 km (3 miles) north of Concón. This family-run lodge works hard to protect and educate visitors about the wetlands and offers guided or independent bird-watching, nature hikes, and kayaking, as well as simple but delicious home-cooked meals and a few very nice rooms to stay overnight. ✉ *Camino Concón-Quintero Km 5 (Ruta F30E), Concón ✛ 3 miles north of mouth of Aconcagua River* ☎ *9/3375–4049* ⊕ *posadadelparque.cl.*

Parque Nacional La Campana

NATIONAL PARK | This national park about 45 minutes east of Concón by car holds the largest remaining forests of Chilean wine palms, which tower above the arid peaks of the Cordillera de la Costa. To immerse yourself in these massive palms, head to the northern Palmas de Ocoa Sector. If you want to instead follow in Charles Darwin's footsteps to the top of the park's namesake peak, Cerro La Campana, head to the southern Granizo Sector near the village of Olmué (which is famous for its annual folk music festival). Note that the hike to this 1,880-meter summit is a 11.5km (7.1 mile) full day affair along the largely shade-less Sendero El Andinista. ✉ *Olmué, Concón* ☎ *33/244-1342* ⊕ *www.conaf.cl* ✉ *3100.*

Roca Oceánico

NATURE SIGHT | This massive promontory covered with scrubby vegetation has footpaths winding throughout that afford excellent views of Viña del Mar, Valparaíso, and the sea churning against black volcanic rock below, as well as pelicans and other sea birds soaring and diving headlong into the sea. ✉ *Concón ✛ 6.5 km (about 4 miles) north of Las Salinas in Viña del Mar* ✉ *Free.*

Beaches

Playa Amarilla

BEACH | **FAMILY** | One of Concón's most popular beaches, Playa Amarilla's yellow sand and relatively calm waters make it a favorite with families, many of whom own or rent apartments in the stair-stepped high-rise buildings across the street. The street-level promenade makes for a nice stroll and a beautiful spot to sit and watch people, or the sunset. There are plenty of options for eating, ranging from kiosk snacks to formal dining. **Amenities**: food and drink; lifeguards; toilets. **Best for**: sunsets; swimming. ⊠ *Av. Borgoño 175, Concón.*

Playa La Boca

BEACH | **FAMILY** | At the northern end of town is the sprawling gray-sand Playa La Boca, named for the *boca* (mouth) of the Aconcagua River, which flows into the Pacific here and sometimes makes the water murky. The long, regular curl to the waves makes it a favorite spot for paddleboarding and beginning surfers (there are numerous places to take lessons along the beach). The southern end has a large parking lot with prices that vary throughout the year, and the northern end has a children's park and horse and kayak rentals. There's a very long stretch of seafood restaurants in between. **Amenities:** food and drink; water sports. **Best for:** sunset; surfing; walking. ⊠ *Av. Borgoño s/n, Concón.*

Playa Los Lilenes

BEACH | The westernmost beach in Concón, the tiny Playa Los Lilenes is set in a yellow-sand cove with calm waters. It's good for swimming and family outings. **Amenities:** food and drink. **Best for:** swimming. ⊠ *Av. Borgoño 20500, Concón.*

★ **Playa Ritoque**

BEACH | Just north of the Mantagua Wetlands, a long stretch of enormous dunes and golden sands hugs the coastline for 7 km (4 miles) up to the small hamlet of Ritoque. Much of this beautiful beach is too open for safe swimming, though ideal for strolling, sunbathing, fishing, and in some areas, surfing. Watch out for all-terrain vehicles and the occasional horse cruising along the more secluded sections. To swim, head to the small cove in front of Ritoque where there are restaurants, kiosks, and a hotel. **Amenities:** food and drink; parking. **Best for:** solitude; sunset; surfing; walking. ⊠ *Concón.*

 Restaurants

Aquí Jaime

$$$$ | **SEAFOOD** | Owner Jaime Vegas is usually on hand here, seating customers and scrutinizing the preparation of such house specialties as *ensalada de mariscos Aquíjaime* (a seafood salad mix of abalone, crab meat, shrimp, scallops, fried calamari, and clams with melted Parmesan cheese), *arroz a la valenciana* (paella packed with seafood), and *ceviche de centolla* (king crab ceviche). Perhaps this is why the small restaurant perched on a rocky promontory next to Caleta Higuerillas has one of the best reputations in the region. **Known for:** hands-on owner and chef; fantastic seafood; ocean views. Ⓢ *Average main: pesos16000* ⊠ *Av. Borgoño 21303, Concón* ☎ *32/281–2042* ⊕ *aquijaime.cl.*

 Hotels

★ **Hotel Boutique Casadoca**

$$$$ | **B&B/INN** | This delightful seafront property, tucked into a lovingly restored 1940s-era home, pairs the intimacy of a B&B with the amenities of a luxury hotel. **Pros:** sea views in four of the six rooms; private parking; 400-thread-count sheets and duvets. **Cons:** setting is urban, despite seafront location; must cross a busy road to get to the beach; no elevator. Ⓢ *Rooms from: pesos110000* ⊠ *Av. Borgoño 22090, Concón* ☎ *32/281–1400* ⊕ *casadoca.cl* ⊅ *6 rooms* ⦵*l Free Breakfast.*

Playa Ritoque is a lovely spot to watch the sun set.

La Ritoqueña Eco Hotel de Playa

$$$ | **B&B/INN** | This stylish property on Playa Ritoque has three two-floor cabins with separate rooms on each level and a shared bathroom in between, making it idea for two couples or a family. **Pros:** youthful vibe; unrivaled beach access; bountiful breakfasts. **Cons:** cramped common area; rooms are on the small side; shared bathroom. [$] *Rooms from: pesos160000* ✉ *Ritoque sitio 70, Quintero, Concón* ☎ *9/6121–2436* 🌐 *laritoquena.com* 🛏 *6* 🍴 *Free Breakfast* ☞ *Price is for 2 rooms (4 people).*

Radisson Blu Acqua Hotel & Spa Concón

$$$$ | **HOTEL** | Rising out of a craggy headland with spectacular views up and down the coast, this hotel blends almost seamlessly into its surroundings. **Pros:** great spa on-site; escape the summer crowds of larger towns, while still just a walk from the beach; spectacular views. **Cons:** indoor pool can be cold; parking is limited; hard floors and cool atmosphere not for everyone. [$] *Rooms from: pesos140000* ✉ *Av. Borgoño 23333, Concón, Concón* ☎ *32/254–6400* 🌐 *radissonhotelsamericas.com* 🛏 *66 rooms* 🍴 *Free Breakfast.*

Activities

HORSEBACK RIDING

Punta Piedra

FOUR-WHEELING | This long stretch of beach (not apt for swimming) begins just north of the mouth of the Aconcagua River and ends at Playa Ritoque. It offers a wide assortment of entertainment, with four-wheeling along the dunes a particularly popular activity. There is also paragliding, a go-kart course, horseback riding, and more. ✉ *Concón.*

Maitencillo

42 km (26 miles) north of Concón.

This town—really a string of cabanas, houses, and eateries spread along the 4-km (3-mile) Avenida del Mar—tends to attract Chile's*nouveau riche*. Two long

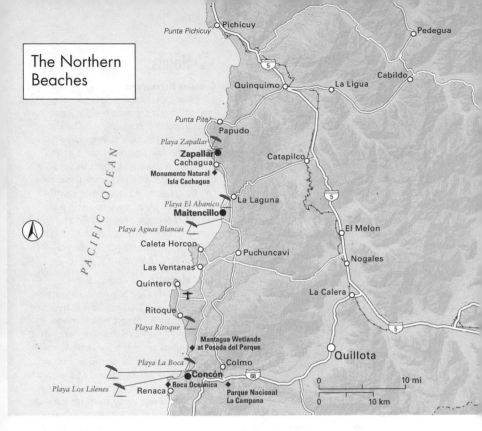

The Northern Beaches

beaches are separated by an extended rocky coastline that holds the local *caleta*. To complement the abundant sand and surf, there's a decent selection of restaurants, bars, and accommodations. The windswept coast south of the town is almost completely undeveloped and a magnet for seabirds; it's also ideal for surfing, paddleboarding, and paragliding.

GETTING HERE AND AROUND

From Concón, follow Ruta F30 E north turning inland from the coast past Quintero until signs show the turnoff for Maitencillo and La Laguna. If coming from Santiago, take Ruta 5 Norte and exit at the turn for Catapilco (just after the El Melón Tunnel), and follow the road to the coast.

🏖 Beaches

Playa Aguas Blancas

BEACH | The light-gray sand of the long and narrow Playa Aguas Blancas lies to the south of a rock outcropping, protected from the swells, and consequently is decent for swimming (and fishing). A constant stiff breeze and the cliffs leading down to the beach also make it ideal for paragliding. **Amenities:** food and drink. **Best for:** sunset; swimming; walking. ✉ *Maitencillo*.

Playa El Abanico

BEACH | This nice stretch of light-gray-sand beach on the northern end of town has the best of both worlds—the waves are big enough for light surfing, bodyboarding, and paddleboarding, but not big enough to be dangerous for swimmers. Lifeguards are on duty, beachgoers can rent lounge chairs and sun umbrellas, and beachside restaurants offer drinks and light meals. **Amenities**: food and drink; lifeguards; water sports. **Best for**: sunsets; surfing; swimming. ✉ *Av. del Mar 1350, Maitencillo.*

🍴 Restaurants

La Canasta

$$$ | **MEDITERRANEAN** | Serpentine bamboo tunnels connect rooms through La Canasta, and slabs of wood suspended by chains serve as tables, creating a scene that could be straight from *The Hobbit*. A small menu changes regularly but includes dishes such as *cordero a la ciruela* (lamb with plum sauce) and *corvina queso de cabra* (sea bass with goat cheese). **Known for:** eclectic cocktail menu; frequently changing menu featuring unique twists on Chilean classics; playful and surprising decor. [$] *Average main: pesos11000* ✉ *Av. del Mar 592, Maitencillo* ☎ *9/9546-1713* 🌐 *lacanastarestobar.cl.*

Mar Central

$$$ | **SEAFOOD** | With its trendy decor and swanky seafront setting, Mar Central looks a lot more expensive than it actually is. Instead, it eschews the heavily marked-up seafood dishes of other spots nearby by offering fish tacos, crab sandwiches, octopus fried rice, and other casual fair, alongside killer cocktails like the Elqui Mule (a twist on the traditional Moscow Mule with pisco from the Elqui Valley). **Known for:** great prices; open-air setting over the Pacific; crowd-pleasing seafood dishes. [$] *Average main: pesos9000* ✉ *Av. del Mar 2730, Maitencillo* ☎ *9/8249–2263* 🌐 *facebook.com/marcentral.maitencillo* 🕒 *Closed Tues. and Wed.*

🛏 Hotels

Cabañas Hermansen

$$$ | **B&B/INN** | **FAMILY** | Set in an overgrown garden, these cabanas feel far away from everything, but in reality, they're just across from the beach. **Pros:** cozy cabins perfect for families; the best place to escape the crowds without leaving Maitencillo; friendly, helpful staff. **Cons:** heating can be an issue during cooler months; sketchy Wi-Fi; you have to cross a busy road to reach the beach. [$] *Rooms from: pesos82000* ✉ *Av. del Mar 592, Maitencillo* ☎ *32/277–1028* 🌐 *hermansen.cl* 🛏 *16 cabins* 🍽 *No Meals.*

Hotel Marbella

$$$$ | **RESORT** | Golf fairways, pine trees, and ocean vistas surround this five-story white-stucco resort building; the spacious, colorful rooms are decorated with original art and have large terraces with views of Maitencillo Bay. Some meals are included, served at the circular Mirador Restaurant, which specializes in seafood. **Pros:** away from the crowds; stunning setting; plenty to do. **Cons:** could use some refurbishing; unreliable Wi-Fi; distance from the beach—you need a car if you also want to explore the coast. [$] *Rooms from: pesos165000* ✉ *Carretera Concón–Zapallar, Km 35, Maitencillo* ☎ *32/279–5900* 🌐 *marbella.cl* 🛏 *85 rooms* 🍽 *Free Breakfast.*

🏃 Activities

GOLF

Marbella Country Club

GOLF | The Marbella Country Club has 27 holes of golf—without a doubt some of the best on the coast—in an exclusive environment replete with massage facilities and a swanky clubhouse restaurant. The tennis and paddle-tennis courts are available only to members and to guests of the Marbella resort. Greens fees for hotel guests are 40,000 pesos. ✉ *Camino Concón–Zapallar, Km 35, Maitencillo*

🖅 *32/346–9874* ⊕ *marbellacountryclub.cl* 🖅 *Greens fee 40000 pesos* 🏌️. *27 holes; 93 hectares; 3 circuits of 9 holes.*

HANG GLIDING

Parapente Aventura

HANG GLIDING & PARAGLIDING | *Parapente,* Spanish for paragliding, is a seated version of hang gliding and quite popular in many places along the Chilean coast. Parapente Aventura has classes and two-person trips for beginners. ✉ *Cerro Tacna, Calle Los Laureles 22-9, Maitencillo* 🖅 *9/9547–5955* ⊕ *parapenteaventura. cl.*

SURFING

Escuela De Surf Maitencillo

SURFING | This is Maitencillo's longest-running and most respected surf school, which offers equipment rentals and both group and private classes (from 16,000 pesos). You can also rent standup paddleboards or take paddleboarding lessons. ✉ *Av. del Mar 1442, Maitencillo* 🖅 *9/9885–6456* ⊕ *escuelasurfmaitencillo. cl.*

Zapallar

15 km (9 miles) north of Maitencillo.

An aristocratic enclave for the past century, Zapallar doesn't promote itself as a vacation destination. In fact, it has traditionally been reluctant to receive outsiders. The resort is the brainchild of Olegario O'Valle, who owned property here. In 1893, following an extended stay in Europe, O'Valle decided to recreate the Riviera on the Chilean coast. He allotted plots of land to friends and family with the provision that they build European-style villas. Today the hills above the beach are dotted with these extravagant summer homes. Above them are the small, tightly packed adobes of a working-class village that has developed to service the mansions.

GETTING HERE AND AROUND

From Maitencillo, follow Ruta F30 E north over the clifftops until signs indicate the turn for Zapallar. If coming from Santiago, take Ruta 5 Norte, exit at the turnoff for Catapilco, and follow the road to the coast.

Sights

Caleta de Zapallar

MARINA/PIER | At the south end of Playa Zapallar is a rocky point that holds Caleta de Zapallar, where local fisherfolk unload their boats, sell their catch, and settle in for games of dominoes. The view of the beach from the caleta is simply gorgeous. On the other side of the point, a stunning trail leads over the rocks to rugged but equally impressive views. ✉ *Zapallar.*

Monumento Natural Isla Cachagua

ISLAND | This 4.5-hectare protected island off the coast of Cachagua, a few miles south of Zapallar, is one of the world's most important Humboldt penguin breeding grounds. No one is allowed on the island, but you can see it from the beach below Cachagua, though you need binoculars to watch the penguins wobble around. For a closer look, hire a boat at the Caleta de Zapallar. ✉ *Zapallar* ⊕ *www.conaf.cl/parques/ monumento-natural-isla-cachagua.*

Plaza Mar Bravo

PLAZA/SQUARE | **FAMILY** | Up the hill from Caleta de Zapallar is this plaza. Translated as the "Rough Sea Square," the park has a nice ocean view and a playground. In January and February, there are often mule rides for kids as well. ✉ *Zapallar.*

Beaches

★ Playa Zapallar

BEACH | Zapallar's raison d'être is a crescent of golden sand kissed by blue-green waters, with a giant boulder plopped in the middle. Cropped at each end by rocky points and backed by large pines and rambling flower gardens, it's arguably the loveliest beach on the Central Coast. **Amenities:** food and drink. **Best for:** snorkeling; sunset; swimming. ✉ *Zapallar.*

🍴 Restaurants

★ El Chiringuito

$$$$ | **SEAFOOD** | Pelicans, gulls, and cormorants linger among the fishing boats anchored near this remarkable seafood restaurant. Because it's next door to the fishermen's cooperative, the seafood is always the freshest in town. **Known for:** beach views; nice variety of fresh seafood; marine-inspired decor. [$] *Average main: pesos16000* ✉ *Caleta de Zapallar s/n, Zapallar* ☎ *33/274–1024* 🕓 *No dinner weekdays Mar.–Nov.*

🛏 Hotels

Hotel Casa Zapallar

$$$$ | **B&B/INN** | This architectural gem in the heart of Zapallar is a tranquil oasis of style and sophistication. **Pros:** custom-made toiletries; high design aesthetic; restaurant focused on local ingredients. **Cons:** pricey; a 15-minute walk to the beach; no ocean views. [$] *Rooms from: pesos215000* ✉ *Diego Sutil 292, Zapallar* ☎ *9/4228–3810* 🌐 *www.hotelcasazapallar.com* 🛏 *7 rooms* 🍽 *Free Breakfast.*

★ Isla Seca

$$$$ | **B&B/INN** | Bougainvillea and cypress trees surround two identical moss-green buildings with well-appointed, spacious rooms. **Pros:** private trail leading to the beach; quiet and rather secluded; gorgeous ocean views from many rooms. **Cons:** customer service could be improved; pricey; not all rooms have ocean view. [$] *Rooms from: pesos160000* ✉ *Camino Costero Ruta F-30-E No. 31, Zapallar* ☎ *33/274–1226* 🌐 *hotelislaseca.cl* 🛏 *40 rooms* 🍽 *Free Breakfast.*

Chapter 5

EL NORTE CHICO

Updated by
Matt Maynard

● Sights	● Restaurants	● Hotels	● Shopping	● Nightlife
★★★★★	★★★★☆	★★★★☆	★★★★★	★★★☆☆

WELCOME TO EL NORTE CHICO

TOP REASONS TO GO

★ **Sugar-sand beaches:** Soft sand and turquoise waters make El Norte Chico's beaches among Chile's best. In summer (January and February) you may have to fight for a place in the sun.

★ **Starry skies:** Thanks to some of the clearest skies in the world, Chile's northern desert is a top destination for international stargazers and scientists. A number of astronomical observatories in El Norte Chico arrange tours.

★ **Mountains and nature:** Explore Parque Nacional Fray Jorge with its ghost-like fog, the petrified forest of Monumento Nacional Pichasca, the barren desert landscape of the Parque Nacional Pan de Azúcar, and the altiplanic beauty of Parque Nacional Nevado Tres Cruces.

★ **Wine and pisco:** No trip to El Norte Chico is complete without sampling its most famous export, pisco. The liquor's muscat grapes flourish in this temperate climate, which is also ideal for wine-grape growing (particularly Pinot Noir).

1 La Serena. The bustling regional capital of the Elqui Valley.

2 Vicuña. A mountain town well situated for stargazing and accessing the Elqui Valley.

3 Pisco Elqui. This historic mountain hamlet is home to the pisco grape.

4 Ovalle. The Limarí Valley's main town is a good jumping-off point for nearby sites that feature ancient rock art and mysterious carvings.

5 Parque Nacional Bosques de Fray Jorge. An easily accessible national park where an oasis of lush forest is nourished by coastal condensation.

6 Reserva Nacional Pingüino de Humboldt. A rich archipelago where penguin- and whale-watching tours can be organized.

7 Parque Nacional Llanos de Challe. The rare desert-in-bloom phenomenon can turn the scorched Atacama Desert technicolor in this national park.

8 Copiapó. The northernmost city in the Copiapó Valley, this inland mining town lies at the end of the world. Here the semi-arid El Norte Chico gives way to the Atacama Desert.

9 Parque Nacional Nevado Tres Cruces. This high altitude national park is the throne room for majestic Andean peaks.

10 Bahía Inglesa. Breathtaking white-sand beaches with turquoise water provide an opportunity to kick back.

11 Parque Nacional Pan de Azúcar. Dramatic cliffs and wildlife abound in this coastal wilderness area.

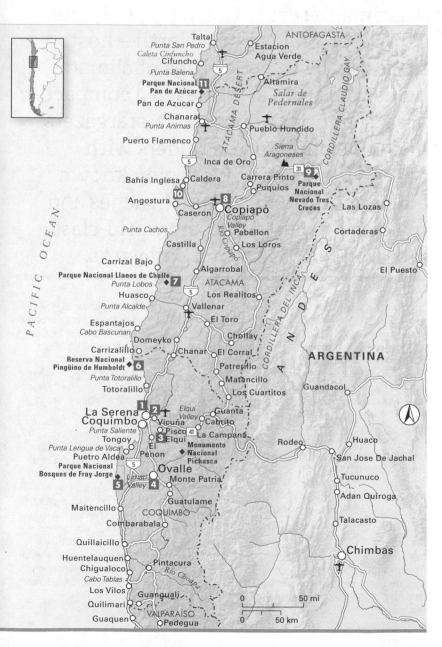

Between the fertile central valley to the south and the vast expanse of the Atacama Desert to the north, El Norte Chico—or Chile's Little North—hosts a fantastically eclectic range of climates, landscapes, and activities in a compact area. Among the burnt hills, stargazers and wine buffs rub shoulders with adrenaline seekers in a region known equally for its white-sand beaches and towering mountains as its world-class research telescopes and vineyards.

These varied landscapes and ecosystems, unsurprisingly, are home to a diverse range of flora and fauna. Visitors with the will to tear themselves away from the beaches can tour rocky offshore islands that shelter colonies of penguins and sea lions or cruise the clear, cool waters of the marine reserves where sperm whales and bottlenose dolphins flourish. Shimmering mountain lakes are home to huge flocks of flamingos. Even the parched earth flourishes twice a decade in a phenomenon called *el desierto florido,* or the flowering desert. During these years, the bleak landscape gives way to a riot of colors—flowers of every hue imaginable burst from the normally infertile soil of the plain.

In a land where water is so precious, it's not surprising that the people who migrated here never strayed far from its rivers. In the south, La Serena sits at the mouth of the Elqui River. El Norte Chico's most important city, La Serena is the region's cultural center as well, with colonial architecture and a European flavor. Nearby, in the fertile Elqui Valley, farmers in tiny villages grow grapes to make pisco, the potent brandy that has become Chile's national drink. Those in search of archaeological wonders head to Valle del Encanto, a large collection of ancient petroglyphs.

On El Norte Chico's northern frontier is the Río Copiapó. This is the region that grew up and grew rich during the silver boom. The town of Copiapó, this area's most important trade center, makes an excellent jumping-off point for exploring the hinterland. Heading into the Andes mountains you reach the world-class Parque Nacional Nevado Tres Cruces. Heading toward the ocean, you come to Parque Nacional Pan de Azúcar, where you'll find some of El Norte Chico's most stunning coastal scenery.

MAJOR REGIONS

El Norte Chico is a vast region spreading some 700 km (435 miles) between Río Aconcagua and Río Copiapó. Ideally, you need more than one base to explore the entire area.

In the south, La Serena is a good place to start if you're going to **the Elqui Valley**. This surprisingly lush, green land along the Río Elqui grows everything from olives to avocados to papayas. The most famous crop is the grape variety distilled to make Chile's national drink—pisco.

The Elqui Valley is renowned not only for its grapes, but also for its unusually clear skies, which have brought scientists from around the world to peer through the telescopes of the area's many observatories. It's easy to see where Nobel Prize–winning Chilean poet Gabriela Mistral, raised in the valley, got her inspiration.

The Limarí Valley is where you want to be if your destination is Valle del Encanto. The region is perfect for grape growing and the source of some of Chile's newest and most exciting wines. It is also home to the only lapis lazuli mine in the country.

The Copiapó Valley, once known as Copayapu, meaning "cup of gold" in the Andean Quechua language, is a copper mining region. The center is Copiapó, a hot inland town where the mining industry's newly minted wealthy are building hotels and homes. It's a convenient stop if you're headed to Parque Nacional Pan de Azúcar or Parque Nacional Nevado Tres Cruces. Just 15 minutes outside of Copiapó is the desert, where quail and lizards scamper beneath the shadows of cacti.

Planning

When to Go

During the summer months of January and February, droves of Chileans and Argentines flee their stifling hot cities for the relative cool of El Norte Chico's beaches. Although it is an exciting time to visit, prices go up and rooms are hard to find. Make your reservations at least a month in advance. For a little tranquility, it is better to visit when the high season tapers off in March. Near the coast, temperatures can be chilly due to the wind and famously cold sea, but the weather inland is mild all year; temperatures can drop quite a bit at night or when you head to the mountains. The almost perpetually clear skies explain why the region has the largest concentration of observatories in the world.

Planning Your Time

Six days should give you time for a quick road trip to see the best the region has to offer if you don't mind driving long distances at a stretch; if you have the time, allow yourself rest days to enjoy each place in more detail. Start by visiting the Valle del Encanto near Ovalle to see the petroglyphs, and then go to nearby Viña Tabalí vineyard, ending the day with a relaxing dip in the hot springs at the Termas de Socos. The next morning, head toward the coast to La Serena and spend the day exploring the whitewashed churches and lively markets of this quaint colonial town. On the third day, journey to the idyllic and mystical village of Pisco Elqui to relax with a massage and obligatory pisco sour before spending the evening stargazing. The following morning, head north on a road trip into the Atacama Desert toward Copiapó. Spend day five exploring Parque Nacional Nevado Tres Cruces and spend your last day at Bahía Inglesa, sunbathing on some of the region's most beautiful and deserted beaches as well as visiting the Parque Nacional Pan de Azúcar.

Getting Here and Around

AIR

While El Norte Chico lacks an international airport, both LAN and Sky do operate several flights daily from Santiago to La Serena and Copiapó. Round-trip flights to El Norte Chico can be as cheap as 40,000 pesos if booked in advance but much more expensive in high season and for late availability. Buses from not-too-distant Santiago are far and away the best option both for seeing the landscape change and reducing the carbon footprint of travel.

AIR CONTACTS La Florida Airport (LSC). ⊠ *Ruta 41* 🕾 *51/227–0353.* **LAN.** ⊠ *Balmaceda 406, La Serena* 🕾 *600/526–2000* ⊕ *www.lan.com.* **Sky.** ⊠ *Colipi 526, Copiapó* 🕾 *600/600–2828* ⊕ *www. skyairline.cl.*

BUS

Every major city in El Norte Chico has a bus terminal, and there are frequent departures to other cities as well as smaller towns in the area. Overnight buses are a great option for travelers keen to keep moving. Choose the premium *salon cama* option for a spacious reclining seat. Keep in mind that there may be no direct bus service to the smallest villages or more remote national parks.

BUS CONTACTS Turbus. 🕾 *600/660–6600* ⊕ *www.turbus.cl.*

CAR AND TAXI

Because of the distances between cities, taking overnight buses between the major cities combined with guided tours or car hire once you arrive is the best option for touring El Norte Chico. Many national parks can be visited only by car, preferably a four-wheel-drive vehicle. Within cities, local buses or metered taxis are another option for getting around. Bridging the gap between buses and taxis is a *colectivo,* a shared taxi that picks up several people going in the same direction. Colectivos charge a fixed rate per person regardless of the number of passengers and run regularly during business hours. Fares begin at around 800 pesos per person for inner-city trips.

Restaurants

Although El Norte Chico is not known for gastronomy, the food here is simple, unpretentious, and often quite good. Along the coast, you'll find abundant seafood. Don't pass up the *caldillo de congrio* (conger eel stew) or *choritos al vapor* (mussels steamed in white wine). Inland you come across country-style *cabrito* (goat), *conejo* (rabbit), and *pichones escabechados* (baby pigeons). Don't forget to order a pisco sour, the frothy concoction made with a grape-based brandy distilled in the Elqui or Limari Valley.

People in El Norte Chico generally eat a heavy lunch around 2 pm that can last two hours, followed by a light dinner around 9 pm. Reservations are seldom needed, except in the fanciest restaurants. A 10% tip is expected and will be automatically added to your bill.

Restaurant reviews have been shortened. For full information, visit Fodors. com.

Hotels

The good news is that lodging in El Norte Chico is relatively inexpensive. Your best bet is often the beach resorts, which have everything from nice cabañas to high-rise hotels. Farther inland, the region is experiencing a boom in boutique hotels and innovative rental properties, meaning lodging in style in beautiful surroundings is more affordable than ever.

Almost all lodging options listed offer breakfast included in the price.

Hotel reviews have been shortened. For full information, visit Fodors.com.

What It Costs in Chilean pesos (in thousands)

$	$$	$$$	$$$$
RESTAURANTS			
Under 6	6 –9	10–13	over 13
HOTELS			
Under 51	51–85	86–115	over 115

Health and Safety

Naturally, in the desert, drinking plenty of nonalcoholic fluids is crucial, as is protecting your face and body from the sun's powerful rays. Get a good pair of sunglasses for driving, as the glare can be intense. Keep in mind that pisco sours, though they may go down as smooth as lemonade, are a powerful drink, so a moderate intake is recommended.

Tours

You're welcome to tour many of the region's pisco distilleries. Several of them are more than 100 years old, with the oldest distillery in Pisco Elqui in the Elqui Valley. The Solar de Pisco Elqui has been entirely renovated since it began operations, but you can still take a tour of the old plant and learn how pisco is made. This is where the famous Tres Erres brand is distilled. In Pisco Elqui you also find Los Nichos, a quaint 130-year-old distillery open to the public, whereas nearby Vicuña is home to Chile's most popular brand, Capel. To escape the crowds, head to the Pisquera Aba distillery near Vicuña or ask at your hotel about less frequently visited distilleries in the Limarí Valley.

La Serena

480 km (300 miles) north of Santiago.

Steeped in history, Chile's second-oldest city, La Serena, wears three distinct faces today. On one hand, it charms visitors with its European-style old quarter. On the other, it dazzles with a dash of modern pomp and convenience through its upmarket beachfront—a great place to indulge in sunshine and luxurious hotels and restaurants. Additionally, since 2019, it has been the site of some of Chile's most vehement protest during the ongoing *estallido social* (social crisis) leaving a wake of political graffiti, some slightly battered shopfronts, and empty plazas.

Nevertheless, the city's location within easy striking distance of many top regional attractions makes it a good base to explore the budding astronomy, viticulture, and wildlife of El Norte Chico. Deciphering the political street art with a tour guide is to take a journey into the important long-term transformations occurring in this complex country.

One of the most stunning features amid La Serena's streets and hidden plazas is the number of churches: there are more than 30, and many date as far back as the late 16th century. Most have survived fires, earthquakes, and devastating pirate attacks, all common threats in the turbulent decades after conquistador Juan Bohón founded the city in 1544.

The preservation of colonial architecture, and its continuance, is thanks to Gabriel González Videla, who was president of Chile from 1946 to 1952.

■ TIP→ **Take care of banking or medical needs in La Serena, as there are fewer services in other towns in the area.**

GETTING HERE AND AROUND

La Serena is almost exactly 300 miles north of Santiago via Ruta 5, the Pan-American Highway. A direct bus trip takes about seven hours from the capital, and there are some that travel via Ovalle (from which it's an hour or less to La Serena). La Serena's bus terminal on Avenida Amunátagui is a 15-minute walk or a five-minute ride from downtown (colectivos 21 and 44 make the trip for less than a dollar). Daily flights from Santiago take about an hour to reach La Serena's La Florida Airport, which is 20 to 30 minutes from downtown via car or taxi. The Pan-American Highway runs right through town if you follow Avenida Francisco de Aguirre toward the ocean. The Elqui Valley is just an hour to the east of La Serena via Route 41.

BUS CONTACTS La Serena Bus Station.
⊠ *Av. El Santo and Amunátegui, La Serena* ☎ *51/222–4573.*

TOURS

From La Serena, tours can be arranged for regional highlights including the Elqui Valley, several observatories, and the Reserva Nacional Pingüino de Humboldt, a nature reserve where you can see the endangered Humboldt penguin as well as various types of birds, sea lions, dolphins, and the occasional whale. Historical tours of La Serena and the adjacent port city of Coquimbo are available from almost all local operators.

Elqui Valley Tour

GUIDED TOURS | This small but professional operator runs regular tours to the Reserva Nacional Pingüino de Humboldt, the Omega Observatory, the Elqui Valley, and La Serena. When there is sufficient demand, they also lead excursions to areas of Parque Nacional Fray Jorge and Valle de Encanto, as well as the nearby town of Andacollo. ⊠ *La Serena* ☎ *9/7374–2208* ⊕ *goelqui.cl* ⊠ *From 35000 pesos.*

Ingservtur

GUIDED TOURS | This local tour operator organizes visits to sites of historical interest in La Serena, nearby observatories, the Elqui Valley, Valle del Encanto, and the Reserva Nacional Pengüino de

Humboldt. ⊠ *La Serena* ☎ *9/9333–0412* ⊕ *www.ingservtur.cl* ⊠ *From 40000 pesos.*

★ Tembeta Tours

CULTURAL TOURS | This long-standing local tour operator provides impassioned, comprehensive, and professional tours of the Coquimbo region from their base in La Serena. Bringing the region's rich history to life on multisensory adventures, they particularly excel at highlighting oft overlooked treasures, such as Coquimbo's coastal, most northerly commune of La Higuera. ⊠ *La Serena* ☎ *9/9012–8608* ⊠ *From 40000 pesos.*

ESSENTIALS

VISITOR INFORMATION Sernatur. ⊠ *Matta 461, 1st fl., La Serena* ☎ *51/222–5199* ⊕ *www.sernatur.cl.*

Sights

Iglesia Catedral

CHURCH | With its central location in the beautiful Plaza de Armas, this imposing cathedral—the largest church in La Serena—is a great place to start your city tour. French architect Jean Herbage built the behemoth using stone from the Soldado mine in 1844 in the so-called Serena style of arches and columns, but it wasn't until the turn of the 20th century that the bell tower was added. The church is open to the public. ⊠ *Plaza de Armas, Cordovez and Balmaceda, La Serena* ☎.

Iglesia San Francisco

CHURCH | One of La Serena's oldest churches, Iglesia San Francisco has a Baroque facade and thick stone walls. The exact date of the church's construction is not known, as the city archives were destroyed in 1680, but it's estimated that the structure was built sometime between 1585 and 1627. The church is open to the public. ⊠ *Balmaceda 640, La Serena* ☎.

Iglesia Santo Domingo

CHURCH | This impressive church was built in 1673 and then rebuilt after a pirate attack in 1755. Its Italian Renaissance–style facade is eye-catching, and its best feature is the elegant bell tower. ⊠ *Pedro Pablo Muñoz and Cordovez, La Serena.*

Memorial en Homenaje a los Detenidos Desaparecidos y Ejecutados Políticos de la IV Región

MONUMENT | A reminder of Chile's recent tragic past, this memorial is dedicated to the "disappeared" of the area, the prisoners and politicians who went missing during the Pinochet regime in the 1970s and '80s. More than 60 people, many of whom died in their early twenties, are listed on the large stone monument. ⊠ *Adjacent to Parque Japonés on steps leading up to Pedro Pablo Muñoz street, La Serena.*

★ Museo Arqueológico de La Serena

HISTORY MUSEUM | Housing many fascinating artifacts and one of the world's best collections of precolonial ceramics, this museum is a must-see for anyone interested in the history of the region. Reopened in 2021 after a 10-year restoration, the museum's new curation contains a beautifully housed collection of Diaguita and Molle pottery, an Easter Island *moai* (carved stone head), bones of the mysterious American Horse, and a raft made of seal skins sown together with cactus spines. ⊠ *Cordovez and Cienfuegos, La Serena* ✥ *a short walk from Mercado La Recova* ☎ *51/267–2243 tickets* ⊕ *www.museoarqueologicolaserena.gob.cl* ⊠ *Free* ☉ *Closed Mon.*

Museo Histórico Gabriel González Videla

Former president Gabriel González Videla is known for his vigorous renovation of La Serena, as well as for prompting the exile of senate member Pablo Neruda. The museum is housed in his former home and also contains works by Chilean artists. ⊠ *Matta 495, La Serena* ☎ *51/256–2572* ⊕ *www.museohistoricolaserena.gob.cl* ⊠ *Free* ☉ *Closed Sun.*

Museo Mineralógico Ignacio Domeyko

OTHER MUSEUM | One of the most complete mineral collections in the world is on display here. Exhibits highlight fossils and minerals from the surrounding region. ⊠ *University of La Serena, Benavente 980, La Serena* ☎ *51/220–4096* ⊠ *500 pesos* ☉ *Closed weekends.*

Parque Japonés

CITY PARK | This park was a collaboration between a local mining company and its Japanese trading partners as a symbol of friendship between the two nations. Within it, you'll find Kokoro No Niwa, a Japanese garden filled with koi ponds, intricate bridges, and a network of walking paths. ⊠ *Eduardo de la Barra 25, La Serena* ✥ *At bottom of hill inside Parque Pedro de Valdivia* ☎ *51/221–7013* ⊠ *1000 pesos* ☉ *Closed Mon.*

Beaches

While vacationing Chileans often flock to La Serena for the beaches, it's usually just for sunbathing and water sports, not for swimming. High winds and strong currents tend to make swimming quite dangerous here, so be sure to heed any warning signs that may be posted on the beach before venturing into the water.

La Herradura

BEACH | Well sheltered within a small cove, La Herradura—or the Horseshoe—is a small but attractive beach that enjoys calm waters and lies within easy striking distance of Coquimbo. These days it is best known as a holiday destination or as a prime windsurfing, kayak, or stand-up paddleboarding spot, but the area's history as a fishing cove can still be seen in the brightly colored boats tethered out in the calm waters of the bay. **Amenities:** food and drink; parking (fee). **Best for:** snorkeling; sunset; surfing; swimming; windsurfing. ⊠ *La Serena.*

Playa Peñuelas

BEACH | Stretching along the city's coastline up to neighboring Coquimbo, this sandy city beach is La Serena's star attraction and a popular spot for families, surfers, and couples, who come to enjoy the great views over the bay at sunset. Like many city beaches, though, it suffers from mild trash problems in parts and is overrun with tourists during the summer high season. Be sure the beach is marked with a sign that says *Playa Apta* before swimming, as the high waves and fierce currents often make it a dangerous place for swimmers. **Amenities:** food and drink; lifeguards (summer only); parking (fee); toilets. **Best for:** sunset; surfing; walking. ⊠ *La Serena.*

★ Playa Totoralillo

BEACH | Even though it's a bit of a trek, this stunning package of bleach-white sand, turquoise water, and rocky desert scenery is worth the trip. The 17-km (10-mile) journey south from Coquimbo is more than made up for by the natural advantages of the beach and the perfect conditions for swimming, diving, fishing, and snorkeling. **Amenities:** food and drink (summer only); parking (fee). **Best for:** snorkeling; sunset; surfing; swimming; walking. ⊠ *La Serena.*

🍴 Restaurants

Donde el Guatón

$$ | **CHILEAN** | Popular with locals, this rustic restaurant is housed in a building from 1840 and today serves delicious Chilean food. The early republic-themed decor and waiters clad in the traditional garb of the Chilean cowboy, or *huaso,* narrowly avoid coming off as contrived, but ultimately present a fitting backdrop for the plethora of hearty local fare. **Known for:** romantic ambience; sweet-corn pie; barbecued meats. $ *Average main: pesos8000* ⊠ *Brasil 750, La Serena* ☎ *51/221–1519* ☾ *No dinner Sun. Closed after 8 pm.*

La Mía Pizza

$$$ | **ITALIAN** | Just across the road from the beach and with great views across the bay, this restaurant serves a range of renditions of Italian classics appealing to holidaymakers and the business lunch crowd alike. The extensive menu includes locally sourced delights such as *cordero* Sebastián (lamb in a red wine and mushroom sauce, served with potatoes and polenta), as well as traditional Italian staples. **Known for:** beach views; family-friendly setting; outdoor terrace. $ *Average main: pesos10000* ⊠ *Av. Del Mar 2100, La Serena* ☎ *51/221–2891,* ☾ *No dinner Sun.*

☕ Coffee and Quick Bites

Terracota Café

$$ | **CAFÉ** | Conveniently located near the La Serena bus terminal, this smart café is ideal for grabbing a snack before continuing your journey. It has good coffee and a selection of desserts, including homemade gluten- and lactose-free ice creams. **Known for:** peace and quiet; small bites; breakfast and soups. $ *Average main: pesos6000* ⊠ *Las Rojas Oriente 1642, La Serena* ☎ *9/9761–4550* ⊕ *mybakarta.com/Terracota-Cafe.*

🛏 Hotels

Costa Real

$$$ | **HOTEL** | Centrally located and replete with all the modern touches you might expect from an executive-class hotel—business center, meeting rooms, and Wi-Fi access throughout—Costa Real is an eminently efficient, practical option for any visit to La Serena. **Pros:** big and comfortable beds; modern and clean; good restaurant. **Cons:** no air-conditioning; surroundings battered by social crisis protests; roadside rooms are noisy. $ *Rooms from: pesos86000* ⊠ *Av. Francisco de Aguirre 170, La Serena* ☎ *51/222–1010* ⊕ *www.costareal.cl* ⇨ *51 rooms* ❙◎❙ *Free Breakfast.*

Enjoy Coquimbo Hotel de la Bahía

$$$ | HOTEL | Every room has a sea view at this hotel that towers over the far end of the Avenida del Mar. Part of the exclusive Enjoy Casino & Resort chain, it also sits head and shoulders above its competition in every way, from its imposing modern lobby to five-star accommodations and service. **Pros:** excellent spa; a sea view from every room; top-tier facilities and service. **Cons:** average restaurant; out-of-the-way location (it's technically in Coquimbo); can be noisy at night. $ *Rooms from: pesos86000* ✉ *Av. Peñuelas Norte 56, La Serena* ☎ *9/7399–7890* ⊕ *www.enjoy.cl* ⇩ *121 rooms* ❙❍❙ *Free Breakfast.*

Hotel Club La Serena

$$$ | HOTEL | FAMILY | Defining itself in opposition to its more luxurious, high-end rivals, this hotel offers a professional but somewhat understated, four-star setting for business delegations in the off-season before letting its hair down for a few months each summer to cater to the die-hard beachcombers who descend on the conveniently located complex. **Pros:** on-site restaurant; across from the beach; amazing views. **Cons:** basic furnishings in rooms; far from the main area of the beach; rooms are rather small. $ *Rooms from: pesos90000* ✉ *Av. del Mar 1000, La Serena* ☎ *51/222–1262* ⊕ *www.clublaserena.com* ⇩ *98 rooms* ❙❍❙ *Free Breakfast.*

Nightlife

Ovo Lounge

DANCE CLUBS | Vast, modern, and unashamedly generic, Ovo Lounge is a decent option for mainstream music until late every Thursday through Saturday. This chain club tends to attract a slightly more affluent crowd in the 25- to 35-age range. ✉ *Av. Peñuales Norte 56, La Serena* ⊕ *instagram.com/ovonightclubcq.*

Shopping

Mall Plaza La Serena

MALL | This sprawling, modern, 70-store mall is home to coffee and wine shops, international brands, and two movie theaters. ✉ *Alberto Solari 1400, La Serena* ☎ *2/2585–7000* ⊕ *www.laserena. mallplaza.cl.*

★ Mercado La Recova

CRAFTS | On the corner of Cienfuegos and Cantournet, this modern market housed in a pleasant neoclassical building sells dried fruits, handicrafts, and lapis lazuli jewelry. The Diaguita-style ceramics and the trinkets made from *combarbalita*, the locally mined marblelike rock, are particularly stunning. Don't forget to pick up some of the region's famous papayas, goat cheese, olive oil, and *copao* (a native fruit born from cacti). ✉ *Cantournet and Cienfuegos, La Serena.*

Vicuña

62 km (38 miles) east of La Serena via Ruta 41.

As you head into the Elqui Valley, the first town you come to is Vicuña, famous as the birthplace of one of Chile's most important literary figures, Gabriela Mistral. Her beautiful, haunting poetry often looks back on her early years in the Elqui Valley. Mistral's legacy is unmistakable as you wander through town. In the Plaza de Armas, for example, there is a chilling stone replica of the poet's death mask.

GETTING HERE AND AROUND

Vicuña is about an hour's drive or bus ride from La Serena, a straight shot on Route 41. Enjoy the views of the vineyards as you make the slight climb from the coast. The tiny bus terminal in Vicuña is serviced by a number of regular buses, vans, and colectivos.

Stargazing in El Norte Chico

With some of the clearest skies in the Southern Hemisphere, El Norte Chico is home to observatories with many of the world's most powerful telescopes, several of which give guided tours by appointment. A boom in tourist-friendly observatories in the Elqui Valley means visitors have ample opportunity to peer into the depths of the universe for themselves.

Cerro Tololo Observatory. Perched at 2,200 meters (7,200 feet), Cerro Tololo Observatory runs free tours of its two principal telescopes on Saturdays. During January and February, priority is given to nonspecialist visitors— although high demand means it's worth reserving at least a month in advance—while the rest of the year the observatory tours cater principally to delegations. Tours should first be requested by phone or email; once the reservation has been made, permission certification can be picked up at the observatory's offices in Las Serena on the corner of avenidas Huanhalí and J. Cisternas. Tours may be canceled in bad weather. ⊠ *Rte. 41, 80 km (50 miles) east of La Serena, Colina El Pino, Vicuña* ☎ *51/220–5200* ⊕ *www.ctio.noao.edu* ⊠ *Free.*

Gemini South Observatory. With one of the largest telescopes in the world, an 8.1-meter (26.5 feet) Cassegrain, this observatory 10 kilometers (6 miles) from Cerro Tololo is operated by a consortium of six nations. Tours are free of charge on Friday mornings and can be tailored to the interests of the group (usually between 10 and 25 people). Email at least a month in advance to request a place on the tour. Priority is given to student and scientific delegations. ⊠ *Rte. 41, 90 km (55 miles) south-east of La Serena, Cerro Pachón, Vicuña* ☎ *51/220–5600* ⊕ *www.gemini.edu* ⊙ *Closed June–Aug.*

Las Campanas Observatory. This observatory of the Carnegie Institute of Washington, 170 km (105 miles) north of La Serena, has twin 6.5-meter Magellan telescopes (internationally recognized as the best natural imaging telescopes) as well as two others. Free tours of the facilities take place on Saturday between 10 and 2:30, but due to high demand visitors are advised to make reservations several weeks in advance. Preference is given to school groups and delegations. ⊠ *Vallenar, Atcama* ☎ *51/220–7301* ⊕ *www.lco.cl.*

La Silla Observatory. Administered by the 15-member European Southern Observatory (ESO), La Silla Observatory is one of the largest and most important observatories in the Southern Hemisphere. Free tours are available of the three principal telescopes each Saturday at 2 pm, except during July and August, due to the risk of snowstorms in this period. Note that bookings are accepted only if made via the online visitor form. ⊠ *Pan-American Hwy., about 130 km (80 miles) north of La Serena, signposted just after turnoff for Incahuasi and before reaching Vallenar, La Higuera* ☎ *2/246–3100* ⊕ *www.ls.eso.org.*

Colectivos run 24 hours and can be flagged down at designated stops; they also have a large stand inside the Vicuña bus terminal. To take the colectivo from La Serena to Vicuña, go to the main office at Domeyko 565 or flag the colectivo from the corner of Cienfuegos and Cantournet, outside La Recova market.

BUS CONTACTS Bus Station. ✉ *Av. Bernardo O'Higgins, at Arturo Prat, Vicuña.*

ESSENTIALS
VISITOR INFORMATION Vicuña Tourist Information. ✉ *At bottom of Torre Bauer, opposite Plaza de Armas, Vicuña* ☎ *51/267–0308.*

Sights

★Alfa Aldea
OBSERVATORY | Although there are more established observatories in the area, Alfa Aldea has made its mark on the astronomy world due to the flawless attention to detail and excellent customer service. With a glass of wine in hand, embark on a journey to the beginning of time as the dome above you transforms into an interactive and 3D exploration. While lounging among comfortable seating, carpeted floors, and blankets, a bilingual astronomer explains the inner workings of the universe. Afterward, you pop outside beneath the stars to peep at constellations, nebulas, planets, and the moon with a real telescope before listening to light transformed into sound waves by a radio telescope, one of the very few available to tourists in the area. You will need to book your visit here in advance. ✉ *Parcela 17, La Vinita, Vicuña* ☎ *51/241–2441* ⊕ *www.alfaaldea.cl* 🖾 *10000 pesos.*

Centro Turístico Capel
DISTILLERY | Visiting a pisco vineyard is a great way to learn about the history of a product that has come to define the Elqui Valley, not to mention the perfect excuse to enjoy a relaxing glass of this tasty, fruity, aromatic drink in beautiful surroundings. At Centro Turístico Capel, just across the Elqui River from Vicuña, you can tour the bottling facility, well-groomed gardens, and artisan's gallery before tasting several piscos. ✉ *Camino a Peralillo s/n, Vicuña* ☎ *51/255–4337* ⊕ *www.centroturisticocapel.cl* 🖾 *Standard tour 4000 pesos.*

Cerro de la Virgen
VIEWPOINT | Devotees of the Virgen de Lourdes, the town's patron saint, consider this hill a place of pilgrimage. Overlooking the city, it affords a great view of Vicuña. It's a 2-km (1-mile) hike north of the city via a poorly maintained trail that can be litter strewn, yet the summit is well worth it.

■**TIP**➜ **Head up in the evening to see the surrounding hills in the Elqui Valley bathed in deep reds and oranges by the setting sun.** ✉ *Vicuña.*

Iglesia de la Inmaculada Concepción
CHURCH | A huge steeple tops this 1909 church facing the central square. It has some pretty ceiling paintings and an image of the Virgen del Carmen carried by Chilean troops during the War of the Pacific. The wooden, fire-engine-red Torre Bauer, next to the church, was prefabricated in Germany. ✉ *Gabriela Mistral 315, Vicuña* ☎.

Museo Gabriela Mistral
OTHER MUSEUM | An expansive tribute to Vicuña's favorite daughter, the Gabriela Mistral Museum gathers a wide array of artifacts from the writer's life, including handwritten letters, poems, and a signed copy of *Canto General* given to her by her compatriot and fellow Nobel Prize winner, Pablo Neruda. A pleasant garden behind the main salon pays tribute to Mistral's love of nature. ✉ *Gabriela Mistral 759, Vicuña* ☎ *51/241–1223* ⊕ *www.mgmistral.cl* 🖾 *Free* ◷ *Closed Mon.*

Observatorio Cerro Mamalluca
OBSERVATORY | The most welcoming of the Elqui Valley observatories and the one that attracts the most visitors, Mamalluca

is 9 km (6 miles) north of Vicuña. On the Basic Astronomy tour, visitors are given an introductory talk before stargazing on the terrace and taking turns looking through a 12-inch digital telescope at sights including the moons of Jupiter and the rings of Saturn. Another tour focuses more on the Andean interpretation of the constellations. Tours should be booked at least a month in advance during spring and summer. You can either make your own way to the observatory or contract transport from the tour office in Vicuña at 5,000 pesos per person. ✉ *Tour office, Gabriela Mistral 260, Vicuña* ☎ *51/267–0331* 🎟 *12000 pesos.*

★ Pangue Observatory

OBSERVATORY | One of the many tourist observatories to pop up across the region catering to the growing numbers of visitors keen to catch their own glimpse of the mysteries of the universe, Pangue—17 km (11 miles) south of Vicuña—boasts more firepower than most, with arguably the most powerful telescope in the region. Through the 16- and 25-inch telescopes, you can view solar systems, planets, galaxies, and nebulae. The standard tour allows enough time to see eight to 10 such phenomena, while budding stargazers are welcome to bring their own list, and tour guides can help you find them. Tours can be organized from the tour office at San Martín 233 in Vicuña and are available in English, French, and Spanish. Note that tours do not run for the week around each full moon. ✉ *17 km north of Vicuña, Ruta Antakari D445, Vicuña* ☎ *51/241–2584* 🌐 *observatoriodelpangue.blogspot.com* 🎟 *From 24000 pesos* 🕑 *Closed July and Aug.*

Pisquera Aba

DISTILLERY | This small, family-run distillery is known for producing several premium piscos that are consistently winning awards and international accolades. The free 40-minute tour includes a tasting; make sure you try the variety made with maqui, a berry native to the southern forests of Chile and Argentina. The distillery is located just off the road between Vicuña and Pisco Elqui. ✉ *Fundo San Juan, sector El Arenal, Km 66 Ruta 41, Vicuña* ☎ *51/241–1039* 🌐 *www.pisquera-aba.cl* 🎟 *Free.*

Viña Cavas del Valle

WINERY | A pleasant stop along the drive between Vicuña and Pisco Elqui, this family-owned boutique vineyard uses natural processes to produce several much-praised wines. Production is limited, and the wine is sold only here at the vineyard. Tours by the affable staff include a visit of the original ancestral home, which now houses the wine cellar. Tours are free but purchase of the wine tasting glass is necessary and not included in the cost. ✉ *Ruta R-485, at Km 14.5; 1 km (1/2 mile) before Montegrande from Vicuña, Vicuña* ☎ *56/9–7476–8200* 🌐 *www.cavasdelvalle.cl* 🎟 *Free.*

🍴 Restaurants

Delicias del Sol

$$ | **CHILEAN** | Just outside of Vicuña is the small settlement of Villa Seca that has attracted attention in Chile due to their use of solar-powered ovens. Delicias del Sol is one such restaurant serving Chilean-style lunches and desserts all cooked outside beneath the sun's rays. **Known for:** unique, eco-friendly dining experience; ice-cold papaya juices; sun-baked fudge brownies. [$] *Average main: pesos7000* ✉ *Chiloe 164, Villa Seca, Vicuña* ☎ *51/198–2184, 9/32303382.*

🛏 Hotels

★ Hostal Valle Hermoso

$ | **B&B/INN** | Set in a beautiful turn-of-the-century house that seeps history and has some of the most reasonable rates in town, it's no wonder that Hostal Valle Hermoso has become a favorite with visitors. **Pros:** near major museums; beautiful building; great value. **Cons:** no

Colectivos run 24 hours and can be flagged down at designated stops; they also have a large stand inside the Vicuña bus terminal. To take the colectivo from La Serena to Vicuña, go to the main office at Domeyko 565 or flag the colectivo from the corner of Cienfuegos and Cantournet, outside La Recova market.

BUS CONTACTS Bus Station. ☒ *Av. Bernardo O'Higgins, at Arturo Prat, Vicuña.*

ESSENTIALS
VISITOR INFORMATION Vicuña Tourist Information. ☒ *At bottom of Torre Bauer, opposite Plaza de Armas, Vicuña* ☎ *51/267–0308.*

◉ Sights

★ Alfa Aldea
OBSERVATORY | Although there are more established observatories in the area, Alfa Aldea has made its mark on the astronomy world due to the flawless attention to detail and excellent customer service. With a glass of wine in hand, embark on a journey to the beginning of time as the dome above you transforms into an interactive and 3D exploration. While lounging among comfortable seating, carpeted floors, and blankets, a bilingual astronomer explains the inner workings of the universe. Afterward, you pop outside beneath the stars to peep at constellations, nebulas, planets, and the moon with a real telescope before listening to light transformed into sound waves by a radio telescope, one of the very few available to tourists in the area. You will need to book your visit here in advance. ☒ *Parcela 17, La Vinita, Vicuña* ☎ *51/241–2441* ⊕ *www.alfaaldea.cl* ☒ *10000 pesos.*

Centro Turístico Capel
DISTILLERY | Visiting a pisco vineyard is a great way to learn about the history of a product that has come to define the Elqui Valley, not to mention the perfect excuse to enjoy a relaxing glass of this tasty, fruity, aromatic drink in beautiful surroundings. At Centro Turístico Capel, just across the Elqui River from Vicuña, you can tour the bottling facility, well-groomed gardens, and artisan's gallery before tasting several piscos. ☒ *Camino a Peralillo s/n, Vicuña* ☎ *51/255–4337* ⊕ *www.centroturisticocapel.cl* ☒ *Standard tour 4000 pesos.*

Cerro de la Virgen
VIEWPOINT | Devotees of the Virgen de Lourdes, the town's patron saint, consider this hill a place of pilgrimage. Overlooking the city, it affords a great view of Vicuña. It's a 2-km (1-mile) hike north of the city via a poorly maintained trail that can be litter strewn, yet the summit is well worth it.

■**TIP**→ **Head up in the evening to see the surrounding hills in the Elqui Valley bathed in deep reds and oranges by the setting sun.** ☒ *Vicuña.*

Iglesia de la Inmaculada Concepción
CHURCH | A huge steeple tops this 1909 church facing the central square. It has some pretty ceiling paintings and an image of the Virgen del Carmen carried by Chilean troops during the War of the Pacific. The wooden, fire-engine-red Torre Bauer, next to the church, was prefabricated in Germany. ☒ *Gabriela Mistral 315, Vicuña* ☎ .

Museo Gabriela Mistral
OTHER MUSEUM | An expansive tribute to Vicuña's favorite daughter, the Gabriela Mistral Museum gathers a wide array of artifacts from the writer's life, including handwritten letters, poems, and a signed copy of *Canto General* given to her by her compatriot and fellow Nobel Prize winner, Pablo Neruda. A pleasant garden behind the main salon pays tribute to Mistral's love of nature. ☒ *Gabriela Mistral 759, Vicuña* ☎ *51/241–1223* ⊕ *www.mgmistral.cl* ☒ *Free* ☾ *Closed Mon.*

Observatorio Cerro Mamalluca
OBSERVATORY | The most welcoming of the Elqui Valley observatories and the one that attracts the most visitors, Mamalluca

is 9 km (6 miles) north of Vicuña. On the Basic Astronomy tour, visitors are given an introductory talk before stargazing on the terrace and taking turns looking through a 12-inch digital telescope at sights including the moons of Jupiter and the rings of Saturn. Another tour focuses more on the Andean interpretation of the constellations. Tours should be booked at least a month in advance during spring and summer. You can either make your own way to the observatory or contract transport from the tour office in Vicuña at 5,000 pesos per person. ✉ *Tour office, Gabriela Mistral 260, Vicuña* ☎ *51/267–0331* 🎟 *12000 pesos.*

★ Pangue Observatory

OBSERVATORY | One of the many tourist observatories to pop up across the region catering to the growing numbers of visitors keen to catch their own glimpse of the mysteries of the universe, Pangue—17 km (11 miles) south of Vicuña—boasts more firepower than most, with arguably the most powerful telescope in the region. Through the 16- and 25-inch telescopes, you can view solar systems, planets, galaxies, and nebulae. The standard tour allows enough time to see eight to 10 such phenomena, while budding stargazers are welcome to bring their own list, and tour guides can help you find them. Tours can be organized from the tour office at San Martín 233 in Vicuña and are available in English, French, and Spanish. Note that tours do not run for the week around each full moon. ✉ *17 km north of Vicuña, Ruta Antakari D445, Vicuña* ☎ *51/241–2584* 🌐 *observatoriodelpangue.blogspot.com* 🎟 *From 24000 pesos* ⏲ *Closed July and Aug.*

Pisquera Aba

DISTILLERY | This small, family-run distillery is known for producing several premium piscos that are consistently winning awards and international accolades. The free 40-minute tour includes a tasting; make sure you try the variety made with maqui, a berry native to the southern forests of Chile and Argentina. The distillery is located just off the road between Vicuña and Pisco Elqui. ✉ *Fundo San Juan, sector El Arenal, Km 66 Ruta 41, Vicuña* ☎ *51/241–1039* 🌐 *www.pisquera-aba.cl* 🎟 *Free.*

Viña Cavas del Valle

WINERY | A pleasant stop along the drive between Vicuña and Pisco Elqui, this family-owned boutique vineyard uses natural processes to produce several much-praised wines. Production is limited, and the wine is sold only here at the vineyard. Tours by the affable staff include a visit of the original ancestral home, which now houses the wine cellar. Tours are free but purchase of the wine tasting glass is necessary and not included in the cost. ✉ *Ruta R-485, at Km 14.5; 1 km (1/2 mile) before Montegrande from Vicuña, Vicuña* ☎ *56/9–7476–8200* 🌐 *www.cavasdelvalle.cl* 🎟 *Free.*

🍴 Restaurants

Delicias del Sol

$$ | **CHILEAN** | Just outside of Vicuña is the small settlement of Villa Seca that has attracted attention in Chile due to their use of solar-powered ovens. Delicias del Sol is one such restaurant serving Chilean-style lunches and desserts all cooked outside beneath the sun's rays. **Known for:** unique, eco-friendly dining experience; ice-cold papaya juices; sun-baked fudge brownies. [$] *Average main: pesos7000* ✉ *Chiloe 164, Villa Seca, Vicuña* ☎ *51/198–2184, 9/32303382.*

🛏 Hotels

★ Hostal Valle Hermoso

$ | **B&B/INN** | Set in a beautiful turn-of-the-century house that seeps history and has some of the most reasonable rates in town, it's no wonder that Hostal Valle Hermoso has become a favorite with visitors. **Pros:** near major museums; beautiful building; great value. **Cons:** no pool or cable television; Wi-Fi signal can be patchy in rooms; no garden. $ *Rooms from: pesos24000* ✉ *Gabriela Mistral 706, Vicuña* 🕿 *51/241–1206* ⌨ *hostal-vallehermoso@gmail.com* 🛏 *8 rooms* ⧉ *Free Breakfast.*

Hotel Halley

$ | **B&B/INN** | In a pretty colonial house with wood trim and white walls, this is the ideal place to relax if you've had a long journey to Vicuña. **Pros:** central location; great for families; pool, cable, and Wi-Fi. **Cons:** rooms a little musty; average breakfast; pool is small. $ *Rooms from: pesos45000* ✉ *Gabriela Mistral 542, Vicuña* 🕿 *9/6339–5132* ⊕ *www.turismo-halley.cl* 🛏 *12 rooms* ⧉ *Free Breakfast.*

Nightlife

Antawara Restobar

CAFÉS | While it admittedly has little competition, Antawara has cemented its position as Vicuña's principal spot for evening entertainment. Traditional Chilean fare is on the menu, while regular live music and a wide selection of locally produced piscos keep things lively in the only real nightlife spot in this otherwise permanently sleepy town. ✉ *Gabriela Mistral 107, Vicuña* 🕿 *9/3291–1380.*

Pisco Elqui

43 km (27 miles) east of Vicuña.

This idyllic village of fewer than 600 residents has two pisco plants. Once known as La Unión, the town, perched on a sun-drenched hillside, received its current moniker in 1939. Gabriel González Videla, at that time the president of Chile, renamed the village in a shrewd maneuver to ensure that Peru would not gain exclusive rights over the term "pisco." It's also a popular place for backpackers, so expect the usual run of hippie stores and plenty of hostels. Sunsets here are particularly beautiful.

GETTING HERE AND AROUND

From Vicuña, take Ruta 41 east to the turn for Paihuano (Ruta D-485). Follow this serpentine, narrow road south about 12 km (7½ miles) into Pisco Elqui. Buses and colectivos run with frequency between La Serena, Vicuña, and Pisco Elqui. A bus or colectivo between Vicuña and Pisco Elqui costs about 1,500 pesos. The small bus lines Via Elqui and Sol de Elqui make the 30-minute trip between La Serena and Pisco Elqui with 20-passenger buses.

BUS CONTACTS Valle de Elqui Colectivos. ✉ *Pisco Elqui* 🕿 *51/222–0665.* **Via Elqui.** 🕿 *51/231–2422.*

TOURS

Turismo Dagaz

GUIDED TOURS | With a wide range of specialized tours around Pisco Elqui, Turismo Dagaz is part of the town's booming tourism sector. Visits to Elqui Valley and the high Andean scenery of Agua Negra, close to the Argentine border, round out stargazing evenings and trekking activities. ✉ *Arturo Prat s/n, Pisco Elqui* 🕿 *9/7399–4105* ⊕ *www.turismodagaz.com* 🛏 *From 15000 pesos.*

★ Turismo Migrantes

GUIDED TOURS | Trekking, bicycle hire, horseback riding, and astronomical tours are organized by this well-regarded operator, based close to Pisco Elqui's central plaza. ✉ *Av. Libertador Bernardo O'Higgins s/n, Pisco Elqui* 🕿 *51/245–1917* ⊕ *www.turismomigrantes.cl* 🛏 *From 15000 pesos.*

Sights

Casa Escuela

NOTABLE BUILDING | On the way to Pisco Elqui is the tiny village of Montegrande, where Gabriela Mistral grew up and considered her hometown. Her family lived in the schoolhouse where her elder sister taught. This was later turned into a museum and now displays some relics from the poet's life. Visitors can also visit

The pisco sour, Chile's national drink, is sometimes topped with whipped egg white.

the Nobel Prize–winning poet's tomb on a nearby hillside. ⊠ *Central Plaza, Gabriela Mistral 759, Monte Grande* 🖼 *500 pesos* ⊘ *Closed Mon.*

Destilería Mistral

DISTILLERY | In the older section of this pisco plant, maintained strictly for show, you can see the antiquated copper cauldrons and wooden barrels formerly used to distill the famous brand. The distillery arranges daily tours, followed by tastings of pisco sours. There is also an on-site restaurant. ⊠ *Av. Libertador Bernardo O'Higgins 746, Pisco Elqui* 🖼 *9/3416–6049 for WhatsApp or text only* ⊕ *www.destileriapiscomistral.cl/home* 🖼 *Tours 6500 pesos.*

★ Fundo Los Nichos

DISTILLERY | About 4 km (3 miles) past Pisco Elqui lies this operational pisco distillery. Guided tours show you around its workings and culminate in the basement, where the original owner and his partners would raid the stock for prolonged, secretive drinking sessions. More clearheaded visitors should note that he

and his friends also found time to amass a rather morbid collection of epithets, now displayed on the walls. If you want to get to the dregs of this valley's historic distillery story, this is the site to visit. ⊠ *Camino Público Pisco Elqui Horcón, at Km 3.5, Pisco Elqui* 🖼 *51/245–1085* ⊕ *www.fundolosnichos.cl* 🖼 *3000 pesos (includes tour and tasting).*

★ Viñedos de Alcohuaz

WINERY | Ancient viticulture meets avant garde techniques at this unimposing but extraordinary vineyard near the head of the Elqui Valley. Their two-hour tour begins with a drive through an eclectic mix of vines such as Carménère, Petit Verdot, Carignan, and Touriga Nacional. Next, see the barn housing maceration pools where, during harvest season, tourists can still help trample barefoot on the grapes. Finally, travel underground into a James Bond–esque room where giant concrete vats ferment the wine. After the tour, try three wines with a selection of cheese and dry fruit. If you visit one vineyard in Chile, make it this one.

Chile's National Drink

Distilled from muscat grapes grown in the sunbaked river valleys of El Norte Chico, pisco is indisputably Chile's national drink. This fruity, aromatic brandy is enjoyed here in large quantities—most commonly in a delightful elixir known as a pisco sour, which consists of pisco, lemon juice, and sugar. A few drops of bitters on top is optional. Some bars step it up a notch by adding whipped egg white to give the drink a frothy head. Another concoction made with the brandy is piscola—the choice of many late-night revelers—which is simply pisco mixed with cola (often more pisco than cola). Tea with a shot of pisco is the Chilean answer to the common cold, and it may just do the trick to relieve a headache and stuffy nose. Whichever way you choose to take your pisco, expect a pleasant, smooth drink.

Chileans have enjoyed pisco, which takes its name from *pisku*, the Quechuan word for "flying bird," for more than 400 years. The drink likely originated in Peru—a source of enmity between the two nations. In 1939, Chilean President Gabriel González Videla went so far as to change the name of the town of La Unión to Pisco Elqui in an attempt to gain exclusive rights over the name pisco, but Peru already had its own town south of Lima named Pisco. The situation is currently at a standoff, with both countries claiming they have the better product.

The primary spots for pisco distillation in Chile are the Elqui and Limari valleys, which are particularly renowned for the quality of their grapes. The 300 days of sunshine per year here make it perfect for cultivating the muscat varietals. The distillation process has changed little over the past four centuries. The fermented wine is boiled in copper stills, and the vapors are then condensed and aged in oak barrels for three to six months—pisco makers call the aging process "resting." The result is a fruity but potent brandy with between 30% and 50% alcohol.

✉ Alcohuaz, Pisco Elqui ☎ 9/7476–8200 ⊕ vdalcohuaz.cl 🍴 30000 pesos ☞ Tasting before midday, when the palette is most sensitive, is recommended.

Restaurants

El Durmiente Elquino

$$$ | **CHILEAN** | Just off the main square is this popular restaurant that serves delicious lunches and early evening meals, including meat entrées, pizzas, and vegetarian options. Be sure to try the *costillar de cerdo al horno* (pork ribs), and if you can, nab a table in the pleasant courtyard with its excellent view of the surrounding hills. **Known for:** friendly staff;

alfresco dining in a spectacular setting; impressive wine list. **$** *Average main: pesos12000* ✉ *Las Carreras s/n, Pisco Elqui* ☎ *9/8906–2754* ⊗ *Closed Mon. from Mar.–Dec.*

Hotels

★ Elqui Domos

$$$$ | **HOTEL** | Though the walls of these modern pods are made from heavy, translucent material, this is far from camping; each dome has a skylight so you can gaze at the stars from the comfort of your bed on the loftlike second floor. **Pros:** luxurious rooms; stargazing seclusion in a unique setting; unbeatable valley views. **Cons:** no wheelchair access;

very secluded; public transport required if you don't arrive by car. [$] *Rooms from: pesos120000* ✉ *Camino Público Pisco Elqui Horcón, at Km 3.5, Pisco Elqui* ☎ *9/7709–2879* ⊕ *www.elquidomos.cl* ⤳ *7 domes, 4 cabins* ⦿❘ *Free Breakfast.*

El Tesoro de Elqui

$$$ | **B&B/INN** | Beautiful gardens with flowers of every imaginable shape and size surround this hotel's cabañas, which have gleaming pine floors and furniture and adobe walls. **Pros:** pretty garden; rooms with views of the stars; quiet. **Cons:** not the most comfortable beds; unreliable Wi-Fi; hard to navigate paths at night to reach rooms. [$] *Rooms from: pesos88000* ✉ *Arturo Prat s/n, Pisco Elqui* ☎ *9/7979–0833* ⊕ *www. eltesorodeelqui.cl* ⤳ *15 rooms* ⦿❘ *Free Breakfast.*

Refugio Misterios de Elqui

$$$ | **RESORT** | The mountainside slopes up sharply immediately behind these cabañas, affording stunning views. **Pros:** on-site restaurant with extensive menu; a great spot to unwind; minigolfing green. **Cons:** no Wi-Fi in rooms; footpaths a bit steep; only some rooms have fridges. [$] *Rooms from: pesos90000* ✉ *Arturo Prat s/n, Pisco Elqui* ☎ *51/245–1126* ⊕ *www.misteriosdeelqui.cl* ⤳ *6 cabañas, 1 suite* ⦿❘ *Free Breakfast.*

Nightlife

La Escuela

CAFÉS | At nighttime, La Escuela (located between all the hotels on Arturo Prat) is a comfy joint, playing jazz and American pop tunes. During the day, it's a decent restaurant serving Chilean meals. ✉ *Arturo Prat s/n, Pisco Elqui* ✛ *At Baquedano* ☎ *51/266–3290.*

Shopping

Frutos de Elqui

Fresh fruit marmalade, jam, and preserves are sold at Frutos del Elqui, just off the town's main plaza. It's been a local institution for over 18 years. ✉ *Av. Libertador Bernardo O'Higgins, Local 1, Pisco Elqui* ☎ *9/9011–9192.*

Ovalle

88 km (55 miles) south of La Serena via Ruta 43.

The gateway to the Limarí Valley, Ovalle is an overlooked town surrounded by acres of vineyards. Seventy-five percent of the the nation's pisco comes from this important valley, despite the Elqui Valley taking much of the credit. It is a great base for launching an off-road adventure to Vicuña, taking in the entire Limarí Valley along the way (note: a good driver and a quality 4x4 are essential.) It's also ideally located for visiting the petroglyphs of Valle del Encanto.

GETTING HERE AND AROUND

Ovalle is about an hour from La Serena via Ruta 43. A 15-minute drive on Ruta 45 out of Ovalle takes you to Valle del Encanto; just beyond that to the west, it intersects with the Pan-American Highway (Ruta 5). Many buses make daily trips between Ovalle and Santiago (five hours) or La Serena (one hour).

BUS CONTACTS Medialuna Terminal.

✉ *Ariztía 769, Ovalle.*

Sights

Iglesia San Vicente Ferrer

CHURCH | On the Plaza de Armas, this church, constructed in 1849, is worth a visit if religious tourism is your thing. Its bells were made in the Chilean port town of Valparaíso in 1877, and although damaged by an earthquake in 1997, the church was completely restored in 2002 and remains open. ✉ *Libertad 260, Ovalle.*

The Elqui Valley and The Limarí Valley

Monumento Natural Pichasca

CAVE | Heading along the Hurtado River in the spectacular Limari Valley, you come across this nature reserve covered with a forest of petrified tree trunks imprinted with dozens of leaf and animal fossils. Nearby is a cave beneath a stone overhang that housed indigenous peoples thousands of years ago, and where cave paintings by the Molle people are still visible. This archaeological site was also the discovery site of the Antarctosaurus dinosaur. ✉ 50 km (31 miles) northeast of Ovalle on Camino Ovalle–Río Hurtado, Ovalle ☎ 9/8923–0010, 51/224–4769 CONAF office ⊕ www.conaf.cl/parques/ monumento-natural-pichasca ✉ 7400 pesos ⊗ Closed Mon., Tues., and Wed. in high season.

Plaza de Armas

PLAZA/SQUARE | The town's shady central plaza is a pleasant place to pass an afternoon. ✉ Bordered by Libertad, Miguel Aguirre, Av. Benjamín Vicuña Mackenna, and Victoria, Ovalle.

Termas de Socos

HOT SPRING | A tourist complex cut from the rough land, this hot spring is said to have waters with incredible healing powers, spouting from the earth at 26°C (79°F) but heated to 37°C (99°F) for bathing purposes. Curative or not, a thermal bath here is extremely relaxing, even if the experience is the same as being in the tub in your bathroom at home (you sit in a bathtub in a private room indoors). Massages, sauna, and use of the Jacuzzis are also available at an extra cost. ✉ Pan-American Highway at Km 370; 24 km (15 miles) west of Ovalle on Ruta 45,

Ovalle ☎ 53/198–2505 🌐 www.termasocos.cl 🎟 7000 pesos for ½ hr.

★ Valle del Encanto

RUINS | One of the more intriguing spots in all of Norte Chico, this isolated and sprawling protected wilderness area is crisscrossed by unexplained holes in the stone floor, made most likely by the Molle and Diaguita cultures. Also dotted all around the park are rock carvings known as petroglyphs and pictographs, which date back from about 4,000 years and feature everything from a (supposed) alien to people with elaborate headdresses. Wildlife roams everywhere here, so keep an eye out for the *liebre* (hare), *loica* (long-tailed meadowlark), and the *degu*, a native rodent.

Sometimes a guide waits near the petroglyphs and can show you the best of the carvings for a small fee. To reach the site, take Ruta 45 west from Ovalle. About 19 km (12 miles) out of town, head south for 5 km (3 miles) on a rough, dry road. *✉ 24 km (15 miles) west of Ovalle, Ovalle ☎ 53/266–1237 🎟 2500 pesos ⏲ Closed Mon. and Tues.*

★ Viña Tabalí

WINERY | This small-scale winemaker is a Limari Valley pioneer, known for producing premium quality wines that highlight the character of each of their vineyards. The winery can be found on the same unpaved road that leads to the Valle del Encanto and makes a perfect place to relax after exploring the petroglyphs. Tours, which must be reserved at least one day in advance, include a tasting session in the impressive underground cellar. It's open only on weekends for appointments made in advance. *✉ Hacienda Santa Rosa de Tabalí s/n, Camino Monumento Histórico de Valle del Encanto; about 2 km (1 mile) after turnoff from Ruta 45, on right, Ovalle ☎ 2/2352–6800 🌐 www.tabali.com 🎟 12000 pesos, includes tasting.*

🍴 Restaurants

★ Fuente Toscana

$$$ | **MEDITERRANEAN** | One of the most exciting gastronomic opportunities anywhere between Santiago and Lima, Fuente Toscana has quickly established itself as one of Chile's best restaurants. Offering Mediterranean foods made with local products, the family-run restaurant serves affordable and delicious dishes such as gnocchi with pesto; only here, it's made with local almonds instead of pine nuts and local cilantro instead of basil. **Known for:** alfresco dining; Italian recipes with Chilean ingredients; wine from nearby vineyards. *[$] Average main: pesos12000 ✉ Independencia 146, Ovalle ☎ 9/3411–0588 🌐 www.fuentetoscana.cl ⏲ Closed Mon.*

🛏 Hotels

★ Hacienda Santa Cristina

$$ | **B&B/INN** | One of the Limarí Valley's best-kept secrets, this homestead is a rural oasis just a few kilometers from the Pan-American Highway as it heads north from Ovalle toward La Serena. **Pros:** delicious food in a restaurant that serves only local wines; personalized attention with English spoken; beautiful, tranquil location. **Cons:** away from anything else; can get noisy; access by unpaved road (look out for the sign!). *[$] Rooms from: pesos74000 ✉ Ruta D-505, Quebrada Seca-Ovalle, at Km 4, Ovalle ☎ 53/262–2335, 53/242–2270 🌐 www.haciendasantacristina.cl 🛏 12 rooms 🍴 Free Breakfast.*

★ Hostal Ovalle Suite Boutique

$ | **HOTEL** | Set inside a revamped colonial building, this charming small hotel has big bedrooms with quality bedding, soft mattresses, and amenities such as Wi-Fi and on-site parking. **Pros:** suites have small terraces; Wi-Fi in every room; amazing showers. **Cons:** cramped bathrooms; no wheelchair access; staff not always at reception. *[$] Rooms from: pesos40000*

Parque Nacional Bosques de Fray Jorge is a lush, foggy cloud forest.

✉ *Carmen 176, Ovalle* ☎ *53/262–7202* 🌐 *www.ovallesuite.cl* 🛏 *8 rooms* 🍴 *Free Breakfast.*

Hotel Limarí

$$ | HOTEL | This ranch-style hotel with only two floors opened at the forefront of a renewed effort to attract tourists to the area. **Pros:** attractive outdoor pool; a wide range of programs and activities to get to know the region better; great restaurant. **Cons:** rooms can get chilly; underwhelming free breakfast; outside town center. [$] *Rooms from: pesos75300* ✉ *Camino Sotaqui at Km 5, Ovalle* ☎ *53/266–1400* 🌐 *www.hotellimari.cl* 🛏 *40 rooms* 🍴 *Free Breakfast.*

Nightlife

Kata Bar & Resto

BARS | A sprawling family-friendly restaurant by day and lively bar by (late) night, this is the most happening place in Ovalle. While large, the place is divided into cozy sections marked by a wood motif; there are wooden benches and wooden crates on the walls and ceiling. Lots of natural light fills the room. The food is an eclectic mix of shawarma sandwiches, pizzas, and empanadas. On Friday and Saturday, it transforms into a karaoke bar. ✉ *Vicuña Mackenna 376, Ovalle* ☎ *9/5964–7019, 53/262–8952.*

Parque Nacional Bosques de Fray Jorge

110 km (68 miles) south of La Serena.

Seemingly defying the logic of El Norte Chico's otherwise barren landscapes, Parque Nacional Fray Jorge is a lush cloud forest formed by a unique microclimate. Where cliffs emerge from the Pacific Ocean, air condenses and forms clouds that nourish the forest. Calling this semidesert oasis home are the *chungungo* (South American sea otter), Humboldt penguins, and the Andean fox, as well as almost 300 endemic plant species.

Penguins are the star attraction at Reserva Nacional Pingüino de Humboldt.

GETTING HERE AND AROUND
From the Pan-American Highway at km 387, turn off onto an unpaved road and follow the signs to the park, which is 27 km (11 miles) west. Public transport to the park is not available.

 Sights

Parque Nacional Fray Jorge
NATIONAL PARK | A patch of land so rich in vegetation and animal life in the heart of El Norte Chico's dry, desolate landscape defies logic. But Parque Nacional Fray Jorge has been a UNESCO world biosphere reserve since 1977, with a small cloud forest similar to those found in Chile's damp southern regions. The forest, perched 600 meters (1,968 feet) above sea level, receives its life-giving nourishment from the *camanchaca* (fog) that constantly envelops it. Within this forest, you will come across ferns and trees found nowhere else in the region as

you maneuver a slightly slippery boardwalk on a 20-minute tour. Although Fray Jorge will not take a lot of time to see, it makes a pretty spot to stop, and there is a picnic table from where you can watch the fog drift over the Pacific Ocean below. ⊠ *Pan-American Hwy. at Km 387* ✛ *Do not take route D560 as this is now closed* ☎ *51/224–4769* ⊕ *www.conaf.cl* ⊠ *6000 pesos* ⊘ *Closed Dec. 25 and Jan. 1; Mon., Tues., Wed. in low season.*

Reserva Nacional Pingüino de Humboldt

123 km (76 miles) north of La Serena.

One of the top attractions in northern Chile, this national reserve comprises more than 2,000 acres spread across several islands, providing a home for a dazzling array of species, including sea otters, sea lions, birds, and the occasional whale and dolphin. But the star of the wildlife show is the Humboldt penguin, an endangered breed that mates only off the coasts of Chile and Peru, and which has suffered due to guano exploitation, overfishing, and habitat destruction.

GETTING HERE AND AROUND

Boat trips launch from Punta de Choros, a cold and dusty town with little else to recommend it, or you can visit as part of a tour from La Serena. If you come with your own wheels, keep an eye out as you drive down the dirt road from the highway, as wild guanacos are often spotted. Be sure to take advantage of the olive oil for sale, as it is some of the best in Chile.

■ TIP➔ **The Chilean navy, which has a base in Punta de Choros, carefully monitors the boat trips, as weather can be volatile. High winds often prevent trips between September and October, so plan accordingly. Also be sure to bring cash as there are no ATM machines in the town and credit cards are not accepted at most establishments.**

TOURS

Turismo Punta de Choros

BOAT TOURS | Fishermen turned tour guides lead groups out to sea, passing by Isla Choros to spot the penguins and finishing with a visit to Isla Damas, the largest of the islands and home to gorgeous white-sand beaches. Tours last around three hours, and a separate fee of 3,500 pesos is needed to visit the penguin reserve. Only 30 boat trips are permitted per day in the reserve. In high season, you will need to arrive by 9 am to secure a trip. Boats go to sea in waves of up to 9 ft, which can induce seasickness. ✉ *Caleta San Agustin, La Higuera* ☎ *9/3101–5528, 9/9076–5078, 9/8515–3961* ⊕ *www.turismopuntadechoros.cl* 💰 *From 15000 pesos.*

Parque Nacional Llanos de Challe

264 km (164 miles) north of La Serena.

The *desierto florido,* or flowering desert, is a jaw-droppingly vivid array of flowers that mysteriously bloom in the otherwise arid landscape of the Atacama Desert. More than 200 species have been recorded blossoming in the area, predominately in the Parque Nacional Llano de Challe, including the pink *pata de guanaco* (guanaco hoof) and the native red *garra de león* (lion's claw). The stunning display is produced thanks to El Niño phenomenon, which brings increased rainfall into the area most years, and occurs between late July and September. Locals are the best source to find out where the most spectacular spots are within the park, although most tour operators from Copiapó and La Serena will offer the trip when it is available. Even if you don't get to the park, patches of the desierto florido can be seen from the highway north of Vallenar most years, while the semi-arid land around Punta de Choros can also be spectacularly covered with plant life.

GETTING HERE AND AROUND

The best way to get to the park is with your own set of wheels. From Huasco, take the coastal highway C-360 40 km (25 miles) until you reach the CONAF (the national parks service) guard site at Los Pozos. From Vallenar, you can drive on C-440. Either route takes around 1½ hours on decent roads. There is also a bus that leaves from the front of the Estadio Techado in Vallenar every Friday. Another alternative is a guided tour from La Serena or Copiapó.

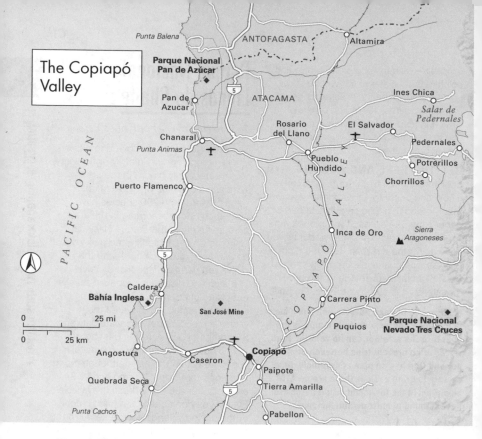

The Copiapó Valley

Sights

Parque Nacional Llanos de Challe

NATIONAL PARK | This coastal national park is home to 206 native plant species (14 of those are found only in the Atacama) and is famed primarily for its proliferation of flowers during the wetter months (a rarity in this part of the world). It's also home to various cacti species, foxes, peregrine falcons, and the guanaco, the largest of the wild South American camelids. There is one campsite in the park, with minimal facilities, so you should come prepared with what you may need for an overnight stay. No buses run to the park, although it is possible to visit via tour groups from Copiapó or by private vehicle; it's accessible from either Huasco heading north or from the Pan-American Highway north of Vallenar. ✉ *Parque Nacional Llanos de Challe,*

Copiapó ☎ *51/261–1555* ⊕ *www.conaf.cl/ parques/parque-nacional-llanos-de-challe* 🎫 *7200 pesos.*

Copiapó

145 km (90 miles) north of Vallenar.

Copiapó was officially founded in 1744 by Don Francisco Cortés, who called it Villa San Francisco de La Selva. Originally a *tambo,* or resting place, it was also the spot where Diego de Almagro recuperated after his grueling journey south from Peru in 1535. In the 19th-century silver strikes solidified Copiapó's status as an important city in the region, and today most residents make their living from copper mining. The city itself is modern and prosperous, with a lovely central park lined with 100-year-old pepper trees and plenty of flower-filled avenues. You can also see the site of South America's first train station, built in 1852, which once ran to the coastal port of Caldera.

GETTING HERE AND AROUND

Copiapó's Desierto de Atacama Airport (DAT) is a bit more than one hour's flying time from Santiago and connects to other points in El Norte Chico and El Norte Grande via Sky and LAN airlines. The DAT is about an hour from Copiapó but more like 30 minutes from Caldera—think of it as a big triangle. Several car rental companies have branches at DAT airport. Copiapó's bus terminal is serviced by all major bus lines. To the north (about 45 minutes via Ruta 5) lie the beaches of Caldera and Bahía Inglesa.

AIR CONTACTS Desierto de Atacama Airport. ⊠ *Ruta 5 Norte, KM 863, Caldera* ☎ *52/252–3600* ⊕ *www.aeropuertodecaldera.cl/index.html.*

ESSENTIALS

BUS CONTACTS Copiapó Bus Station. ⊠ *Chañarcillo 680, Copiapó* ☎.

TAXI CONTACTS Radio Taxi San Francisco. ⊠ *Santiago Watt 856, Copiapó* ☎ *52/221–8788.*

VISITOR INFORMATION Sernatur. ⊠ *Los Carrera 691, Copiapó* ☎ *51/221–2838* ⊕ *www.sernatur.cl/region-de-atacama.*

Sights

Iglesia Catedral Nuestra Señora del Rosario

CHURCH | English architect William Rogers built this neoclassical church facing the central square in the middle of the 19th century. Check out the silver tabernacle and image of the Virgen del Rosario at the altar. ⊠ *Chacabuco at Av. Libertador Bernardo O'Higgins, Copiapó* ☎.

Iglesia San Francisco

CHURCH | This red-and-white candy cane of a church was built in 1872, and although it looks as if it's made of cement, it's actually constructed of

Oregon pine. The adjacent Plaza Godoy has a statue of woodcutter Juan Godoy, who accidentally discovered huge silver deposits in nearby Chañarcillo in 1832, prompting thousands of people to move to the region to ignite the great silver boom of the day. ⊠ *Juan Godoy 65, Copiapó* ☎.

★ Museo Mineralógico

SCIENCE MUSEUM | This museum offers a geological history of the region and the country's best collection of rocks and minerals. There are close to 2,500 samples, including some found only in the Atacama Desert. The museum even displays a few meteorites that fell in the area. ⊠ *Colipí 333, At Manuel Rodriguez, Copiapó* ⊕ *www.geologia.uda.cl* ☒ *Free* ☉ *Closed weekends* ☞ *Open 10–1 and 3–6.*

Museo Regional de Atacama

HISTORY MUSEUM | A historic home that once belonged to the wealthy Matta family now houses this museum. The house, built by mining engineer Felipe Santiago Matta between 1840 and 1850, shows the history of the region through its reconstructions of 19th-century rooms. The exhibits themselves are dedicated to mining and archaeology. ⊠ *Atacama 98, Copiapó* ☎ *52/221–2313* ⊕ *www.museodeatacama.cl* ☉ *Closed Mon.*

San José Mine

MINE | If you have your own car, you can make a road trip to this mine which made worldwide headlines in 2010, as the site where 33 miners were trapped underground and then rescued after a grueling 69 days. From the highway, the drive is a dusty one beside a stunning desert landscape until you reach the lookout, where there is an audiovisual guide and the rescue pod used to pull the miners out. One of the 33 is often on-site to speak to visitors (in Spanish only, however); although site visits are free, it is recommended to leave a tip. ⊠ *Copiapó* ✢ *Turn at Copec on Ruta 5 Norte toward San Jose* ☒ *Tips encouraged* ☉ *Closed Mon.–Wed.*

🍴 Restaurants

Drive In

$$$ | **CHILEAN** | Located inside a former gas station, this restaurant has seafood, Chilean classics, and pizza on the menu. While the overall experience here can be hit-or-miss, Drive In remains one of the more popular lunch and dinner spots for Copiapó locals. **Known for:** former gas station location; local hangout; big pizzas. [$] *Average main: pesos10000* ✉ *Near exit ramp from highway, Pan America Norte 107–115, Copiapó* ☎ *52/221-1535.*

Rukalaf

$ | **VEGETARIAN** | This eatery is a vegan-friendly oasis in the Atacama Desert. Open only for lunch, it serves unpretentious, hearty food like Indian-style rice, dahl, and vegetable dishes or a classic Chilean empanada made from soya. **Known for:** great homemade bread; family-friendly atmosphere; Indian flavors. [$] *Average main: pesos5000* ✉ *Colipi 262, Copiapó* ☎ *51/222–4289* 🌐 *instagram.com/rukalaf_veg* 💳 *No credit cards* 🕓 *Closed Sat. and Sun., no dinner.*

🛏 Hotels

Hotel Chagall

$$ | **HOTEL** | Located half a block from the Copiapó's central plaza, this well-equipped business hotel has clean, modern, and spacious rooms, with colorful woven comforters in local designs. **Pros:** large rooms with comfortable beds; located right in the center of the city; nice furnishings. **Cons:** poorly lit bedrooms; no Wi-Fi in rooms; some rooms on street side may be noisy. [$] *Rooms from: pesos79000* ✉ *Av. Bernardo O'Higgins 760, Copiapó* ☎ *52/235–2900* 🌐 *www.chagall.cl* 🛏 *88 rooms* 🍽 *Free Breakfast.*

Hotel Diego de Almeida

$$$ | **HOTEL** | Enjoying a privileged spot on the city's main square, this hotel has comfortable and elegantly decorated rooms. **Pros:** helpful staff; excellent location; large bedrooms. **Cons:** decor is a bit run-down; parking is limited; can be noisy. [$] *Rooms from: pesos87000* ✉ *Av. Bernardo O'Higgins 640, Copiapó* ☎ *52/220–7700* 🌐 *www.dahoteles.com* 🛏 *136 rooms* 🍽 *Free Breakfast.*

🛍 Shopping

Casa de la Cultura

CRAFTS | The Casa de la Cultura has crafts workshops and a gallery displaying works by local artists. ✉ *Av. Bernardo O'Higgins 610, on Plaza Prat, Copiapó* ☎ *9/9415–4497* 🌐 *www.intipacha.cl.*

Fruit Market

MARKET | On Friday locals pack the normally tranquil Plaza Juan Godoy for its produce market. This is a great way to experience Copiapó life as the locals do, and also where you can snag some excellent deals. ✉ *Copiapó.*

Parque Nacional Nevado Tres Cruces

200 km (124 miles) northeast of Copiapó.

One of the most underrated and magical national parks in Chile, this spectacular high altitude wilderness area is home to the Coya people, as well as wildlife such as migratory flamingos and vicuña. It is also the gateway to climbing the highest volcano in the world, Ojos de Salado, which stands at 6,893 meters (22,615 feet).

To journey here is to venture into the Puna de Atacama, a high altitude Andean plateau where mountains emerge from 4,000-meter (13,000-foot) plains. "Puna" is also the local word used to describe the mountain sickness that can accompany foolhardy attempts to do too much too quickly in this breathless landscape.

Laguna Verde and Ojos del Salado are stunning landscapes in Parque Nacional Nevado Tres Cruces.

A classic road trip through Parque Nacional Nevado Tres Cruces known as the Circuito de los Seis Miles (the Circuit of the 6,000-Meter Peaks) is ideally done in two days, with time taken at the outset of the first day to acclimatize at sites of interest at lower altitude. Principal attractions include Laguna Santa Rosa, Salar Santa Rosa, Ojos del Salado viewpoint, and Laguna Verde's thermal pools. Much of the journey is above 4,000 meters (13,100 feet) of altitude, so preacclimatization on lower trekking peaks (potentially when passing through Santiago) is advisable.

The roads are wild and remote, which means there are serious consequences for breakdowns if you're unprepared. A dedicated 4x4 is essential.

TOURS
★ Turismo Alma Atacama
ADVENTURE TOURS | This outfit run by Vanessa Orrego offers one- or two-day tours of Parque Nacional Nevado Tres Cruces leaving from Copiapó. Used to driving three-story mining vehicles,

Orrego switched to tourism services several years ago and knows these mountain roads better than almost anyone. She is also an accomplished mountaineer and takes care to allow appropriate acclimatization. (Be sure to ask her about her experiences on Ojos del Salado.) Tours include all meals as well as 4x4 transport and can be adapted to your interests. An accompanying Spanish-English translator can be arranged at an extra cost. ✉ *Copiapó* ☎ *9/9477–0777* 💻 *From 90000 pesos (per person for one day; minimum two guests).*

Hotels

★ Refugio Maricunga
$ | HOTEL | At a dizzying altitude of 3,800 meters (12,500 feet) above sea level, this mountain lodge on the shore of Laguna Santa Rosa offers basic bunk beds or private rooms and the chance to watch flamingos fly onto the lagoon at twilight. **Pros:** Wi-Fi; spectacular views; good value for money. **Cons:** limited shade; no kitchen facilities; high altitude

Bahía Inglesa is known for its beautiful beaches with turquoise water.

can induce altitude sickness. $ *Rooms from: pesos20000* ✉ *Laguna Maricunga* ☎ *9/9051–3202* ⊕ *refugiomaricunga.com* ⇨ *4 rooms* ⦿ *No Meals.*

 ## Activities

Cerro Siete Hermanas

HIKING & WALKING | For well-experienced high-altitude hikers, the nontechnical peak Cerro Siete Hermanas (4,860 meters; 15,944 feet) is a realistic day hike from the backdoor of Refugio Maricunga. You'll need to be fit and very well acclimatized to hike the 1,000 meters (3,280 feet) to the summit. The trail is marked most of the way, but you will need topographical maps to be sure of the route, especially if setting off before first light. Starting early is highly advisable to avoid the powerful sun in the Puna de Atacama and to enjoy the sunrise as it casts the first light on the Laguna Santa Rosa and the Salar de Maricunga below. ✉ *Parque Nacional Nevado Tres Cruces.*

Bahía Inglesa

68 km (42 miles) northwest of Copiapó.

Some of the most beautiful beaches in El Norte Chico are at Bahía Inglesa, which was originally known as Puerto del Inglés because of the number of English buccaneers using the port as a hideaway. It's not just the beautiful white sand that sets these beaches apart, however: it's also the turquoise waters, fresh air, and fabulous weather. Combine all this with the fact that the town has yet to attract large-scale development and you can see why so many people flock here in summer. If you are fortunate enough to visit during the low season, you can experience a tranquility rarely felt in Chile's other coastal towns.

GETTING HERE AND AROUND

Follow the Pan-American Highway about one hour north until the small towns of Caldera and Bahía Inglesa come into view: you may smell the salty Pacific before you see the buildings. Buses big and small, as well as colectivo taxis, service Caldera, 5 km (3 miles) north of Bahía Inglesa. From Caldera it's a 10-minute cab ride to Bahía Inglesa. To the north lies Antofagasta, about six hours from both Caldera and Bahía Inglesa by car or bus on the Pan-American Highway.

Beaches

Playa La Piscina

BEACH | **FAMILY** | Stunningly pretty, impossibly calm, and perfect for swimming, Playa La Piscina is in many ways the ideal town beach. Bordering Bahía Inglesa's main drag, this beach—which translates as "the swimming pool"—enjoys perfect white sand and bright blue waters, all a short walk from most hotels and restaurants. Unsurprisingly, it gets very busy in the summer high season and suffers from quite a bit of littering. **Amenities:** food and drink; lifeguards (summer only); parking; toilets; water sports. **Best for:** swimming. ✉ *Bahía Inglesa.*

★ Playa Las Machas

BEACH | Stretching from the southernmost tip of Bahía Inglesa right around the bay, Playa Las Machas has escaped the attention of the majority of tourists and is a relaxing alternative to the more crowded beaches in the town proper. Whether you decide to explore the long shoreline on foot, taking in the dramatic scenery as you go, or find yourself a secluded spot for sunbathing and to get away from it all, this white-sand beach is a great place to while away a lazy afternoon. **Amenities:** none. **Best for:** solitude; sunset; surfing; walking. ✉ *Bahía Inglesa.*

Restaurants

Domo Lounge

$$$ | **EUROPEAN** | The most happening spot on the waterfront, this sprawling restaurant serves fresh seafood, pizzas, and shared plates of various European-inspired cuisine. It also transforms into a great spot to enjoy a few drinks, regular live music, and DJ events. **Known for:** delicious drinks and desserts; live music and late-night events; freshly caught seafood. [$] *Average main: pesos10000* ✉ *Av. El Morro 610, Bahía Inglesa* ☎ *9/6573–9100.*

El Plateao

$$$ | **ECLECTIC** | This bohemian bistro with ocean views is a must for anyone staying in the area. The innovative, contemporary menu lists such culinary non sequiturs as curry dishes and *tallarines con mariscos* (a pan-Asian noodle concoction served with shellfish and topped with cilantro). **Known for:** sunsets from the terrace; spicy, eclectic dishes; late-night events. [$] *Average main: pesos10000* ✉ *Av. El Morro 756, Bahía Inglesa* ☎ *9/6677–5174.*

Hotels

Apart Hotel Playa Blanca

$$ | **APARTMENT** | **FAMILY** | If you are tired of indistinguishable chain hotels, a condo at Playa Blanca, complete with comfortable living room and full kitchen, may just do the trick. **Pros:** excellent choice for families; super close to the water; fully equipped kitchens. **Cons:** rooms with basic furnishings; no website; location means a dark walk home from the action at night. [$] *Rooms from: pesos80000* ✉ *Camino de Martín 1300, Bahía Inglesa* ☎ *9/5011–1235* 💳 *No credit cards* 🛏 *10 condos, 1 apartment* 🍴 *No Meals.*

Hotel Rocas de Bahía

$$$ | **HOTEL** | This sprawling modern hotel has Southwest style rooms with large beds and huge windows facing the sea. **Pros:** free parking; rooftop pool; good location right on the bay. **Cons:** hit-and-miss service; poor breakfast; can get noisy. [$] *Rooms from: pesos100000* ✉ *Av. El Morro 888, Bahía Inglesa* ☎ *52/231–6005* 🌐 *www.rocasdebahia.cl* 🛏 *36 rooms* 🍴 *Free Breakfast.*

Nightlife

El Plateao

LIVE MUSIC | Head to funky El Plateao for hip-hop on weekends. ✉ *Av. El Morro 756, Bahía Inglesa* ☎ *9/6677–5174.*

Activities

WATER SPORTS

Oceano Aventura

SCUBA DIVING | Come here for scuba diving lessons and planned excursions to explore the stunning world beneath the waves. It's a great way to learn about the local flora and fauna as well as an excellent way to visit underwater statues. ✉ *Av. El Morro, Bahía Inglesa* ☎ *9/9546–9848* 🌐 *www.oceanoaventura.cl* 🎫 *From 40000 pesos.*

Parque Nacional Pan de Azúcar

175 km (109 miles) north of Copiapó.

Some of the best coastal scenery in the country can be found at Parque Nacional Pan de Azúcar. Imposing cliffs give way to deserted white-sand beaches in this captivating reserve, which stretches for 40 km (25 miles) along the coast and is home to dolphins, sea otters, and many types of endangered birds.

GETTING HERE AND AROUND

You can take Route C-120 north from Chañaral for 29 km (18 miles) directly into the park, or take the Pan-American Highway north of Chañaral to km marker 1,410, then cut toward the coast onto Route C-110 to the park.

Sights

★ **Parque Nacional Pan de Azúcar**

NATIONAL PARK | This national reserve stretching for 40 km (25 miles) along the coast north of the town of Chañaral has some of Chile's most spectacular coastal scenery. Steep cliffs fall into the crashing sea, their ominous presence broken occasionally by white-sand beaches made for picnics. Within the park is an incredible variety of flora and fauna, including sea lions, sea otters, foxes, and the very rare Peruvian diving petrel, as well as some 20 species of cacti, including the rare copiapoa, which resembles a little blue pin cushion. At the tiny fishing village of Caleta Pan de Azúcar, you can find several local guides who can take you on boat trips to see colonies of Humboldt penguins. ✉ *An unpaved but signposted road north of cemetery in Chañaral leads to park* ☎ *52/221–3404* 🌐 *www.conaf.cl* 🎫 *7200 pesos.*

Hotels

Lodge Pan de Azúcar

$$ | **HOTEL** | Surrounded by the imposing "Sugar Loaf" mountain range to the rear and the crashing waves of the Pacific in front, you'd be hard-pressed to find a more remote location to stay. **Pros:** environmentally friendly; gloriously remote; unbeatable views. **Cons:** hard to get to without your own car; few dining alternatives available in the only nearby village; no power other than lighting and kitchen. [$] *Rooms from: pesos55000* ✉ *Camino C-120, on left after passing park ranger's kiosk* ☎ *9/9844–7375* 🌐 *www.pandeazucarlodge.cl* 🛏 *5 cabañas* 🍴 *No Meals.*

EL NORTE GRANDE

Updated by
Matt Maynard

 Sights
★★★★★

 Restaurants
★★★★☆

 Hotels
★★★★☆

 Shopping
★★★★★

 Nightlife
★★★☆☆

WELCOME TO EL NORTE GRANDE

TOP REASONS TO GO

★ **San Pedro de Atacama:** This unassuming town in the middle of the desert is a world-class destination for the beautiful outdoor excursions nearby. Visit magical moonlike landscapes, large sand dunes, lush valleys filled with 900-year-old cactus plants, salt flats with blue lagoons, and surreal geysers with steam and bubbling water at sunrise.

★ **Flora and fauna:** Yes, the Atacama Desert is one of the driest places on earth. But head to the Chilean Altiplano, just a few hours east of Arica, and you'll find an abundance of fauna and, depending on the season, flora. Pink flamingos dot the edges of volcanic lakes like Lago Chungará on the Bolivian border, and slender brown vicuñas run in small herds through the sparse grasslands.

★ **Pristine beaches:** Pristine sands line the shore near Arica and Iquique. The beaches are packed during summer months, but in the off season you just might have the beach to yourself.

San Pedro de Atacama is one of the continent's gems, a hot spot for outdoor-sports enthusiasts, birdwatchers, and sandboarders. Resting between two giant branches of the Andean mountains is the *altiplano,* or high plains, where you'll see natural marvels such as crystalline salt flats, geysers, and volcanoes.

1 Antofagasta. Chile's wealthy and lively port city has all the modern conveniences.

2 Chacabuco. This ghost town is arguably the most important and fascinating site in the north of Chile for understanding the nation's history.

3 Calama. A transportation hub for reaching San Pedro.

4 San Pedro de Atacama. If you can't afford a space flight, the otherworldly landscapes of San Pedro are perhaps the next best thing for imagining life on Mars or beyond.

5 Geysers del Tatio. Venture into the desert to witness fantastic jets of steam erupt from the earth.

6 Reserva Nacional Los Flamencos. Glimpse flamingos at this reserve,

set on one of the world's largest salt flats with volcanoes in the background.

7 Iquique. This city has it all, including beautiful beaches, great food, and pulsing nightlife.

8 Mamiña. A remote hot spring set deep in the mountains.

9 Pica. If you really know your pisco sours, this is the essential stop-off to study the lemons that give it that special zing.

10 Reserva Nacional Pampa del Tamarugal. This forest oasis is famous for its ancient geoglyphs.

11 Gigante de Atacama. The world's largest humanlike geoglyph.

12 Arica. This energetic, modern town has year-round sunshine and beaches.

13 Parque Nacional Lauca. A spectacular riot of altiplano rock strata colors provides the backdrop to this land of volcanoes, flamingos, and Andean culture.

14 Reserva Nacional Las Vicuñas. This is the spot to see the cutest of the camelids, the very shy vicuña.

15 Salar de Surire. Flamingo spotters can spy the birds against a pristine salt flat here.

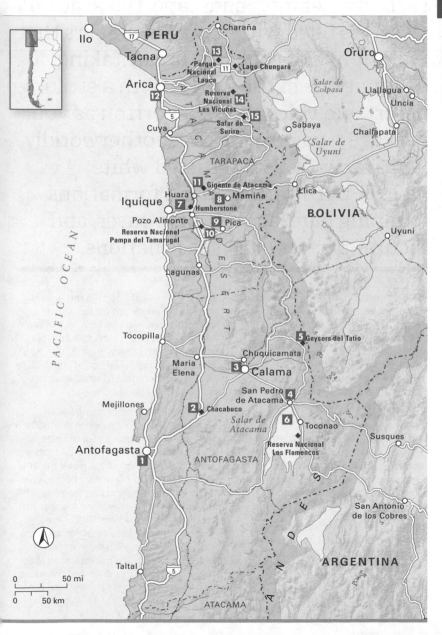

The Norte Grande is as vast as it is remote, but don't be fooled by this seemingly empty landscape: the Atacama Desert is filled with natural wonders that make it one of the most breathtaking destinations in the world. With a striking desert and volcano-lined horizon as your backdrop, you can discover otherworldly landscapes like salt-crusted white valleys, burnt-orange sand formations, stunning blue lagoons, lush oases, and picture-perfect beach destinations.

You are beginning a journey into Tawantinsuyu: the southern Incan Empire. Exhilarating hikes up volcanoes or through cactus-laden creeks and adrenaline-boosting bike rides attract outdoor sports enthusiasts, while relaxing thermal pools, a plethora of wildlife, calming beaches, and colorful native culture keep tamer travelers charmed.

Spanning some 1,930 km (1,200 miles), Chile's Great North stretches from the Río Copiapó to the borders of Peru and Bolivia. Here you will find the Atacama Desert, the driest place on Earth—so dry that in many parts no rain has ever been recorded.

Yet people have inhabited this desolate land since time immemorial. Indeed, the heart of El Norte Grande lies not in its geography but in its people. The indigenous Chinchorro people eked out a meager living from the sea more than 8,000 years ago, leaving behind the magnificent Chinchorro mummies, the oldest in the world. High in the Andes, the Atacameño tribes traded livestock with the Tijuanacota and the Inca. Many of these people still cling to their ways of life, though much of their culture was lost during the colonial period and, later, by the abandonment of small villages as mining in the region boomed.

When huge deposits of nitrates were found in the Atacama region in the 1800s, the "white gold" brought boom times to towns like Pisagua, Iquique, and Antofagasta. Because most of the mineral-rich region lay beyond its northern border, Chile declared war on neighboring Peru and Bolivia in 1878. Chile won the five-year battle and annexed the land north of Antofagasta, a continuing source of national pride for many Chileans. With the invention of synthetic nitrates, the market for these fertilizers dried up in the 1940s and the nitrate barons abandoned their opulent mansions and returned to Santiago. El Norte Grande was once again left on its own.

What you'll see today is a land of both decay and growth. The glory days of the nitrate era are gone, but copper has stepped in to help fill that gap while simultaneously creating strains on precious water supplies, local indigenous cultures, and the environment (the world's largest open-pit copper mine is here). Local lithium mining continues to show economic promise. El Norte Grande is still a land of opportunity for fortune seekers, as well as for tourists looking for a less traveled corner of the world. It is a place of beauty and dynamic isolation, a place where the past touches the present in a troubled yet majestic embrace.

MAJOR REGIONS

The Nitrate Pampa was previously home to the nitrate plants that made Chile a mining powerhouse in the mid-20th century. These days, towns like Antofagasta and Chacabuco are fading testaments to an old way of life, but copper mines are turning places like Calama into modern-day boomtowns. These cities make good stops as you journey north.

In **San Pedro and the Atacama Desert**, snowcapped volcanoes loom to the east, making mornings in this region especially memorable. Bird lovers will find the Reserva Nacional Los Flamencos well worth the high-altitude adjustment for a chance to see hundreds of pink flamingos wading in shimmering blue and green lakes. If you get beyond the hype, San Pedro is a great place. The range of outdoor activities and the breathtaking sights, including moonlike landscapes and Incan graveyards, make it a must-see stop in the north. Spend your mornings hiking, biking, and sandboarding, afternoons swimming, and nights beside a blazing outdoor fire in the patio of one of San Pedro's down-home but delicious eateries, gazing up at the star-filled heavens.

The port of **Iquique** is the world's largest exporter of fish meal, but its heyday was as a nitrate center in the 19th century. Fading mansions remain, and this regional capital is still a popular destination. From here you can do a day trip to the hot springs of Mamiña, also glimpsing the ghost town of Humberstone, while getting to the geoglyph Gigante de Atacama—Chile's largest—in time for the sunset.

Arica, at the intersection of Chile, Bolivia, and Peru, is part of the "land of eternal spring," and its pedestrian-mall eateries can ease even the most impatient traveler into a chair for a day. Sights include mummies dating to 6000 BC, Aymara markets, and national parks with alpine lakes and herds of vicuña.

Planning

When to Go

In the height of the Chilean summer, January and February, droves of Chileans and Argentines mob El Norte Grande's beaches. Although this is a fun time to visit, prices go up and finding a hotel can be difficult. Book your room a month or more in advance. The high season tapers off in March, an excellent time to visit if you're looking for a bit more tranquility. If you plan to visit the altiplano, bring the right clothing. Winter can be very cold, and summer sees a fair amount of rain. San Pedro is sunny year-round and pleasant to visit, but the best seasons are spring and fall when the crowds are gone and the days are not too hot, nor the nights too cold.

FESTIVALS

Every town in the region celebrates the day honoring its patron saint, Saint Peter, on June 29. Most are small gatherings attended largely by locals. One fiesta not to be missed takes place in La Tirana from July 12 to 18. During this time some 80,000 pilgrims converge on the town to honor the Virgen del Carmen with dancing in the streets.

Planning Your Time

You'll have to hustle to see much of El Norte Grande in less than a week. You should spend at least two days in San Pedro de Atacama, visiting the incredible sights such as the bizarre moonscape of the Valle de la Luna and the desolate salt flats of the Salar de Atacama. For half a day soak in the hot springs in the tiny town of Pica, then head to the nitrate ghost town of Humberstone. On the way to Iquique, take a side trip to the Gigante de Atacama, the world's largest human-like geoglyph. After a morning exploring Iquique, head up to Arica, the coastal town that bills itself as the "land of eternal spring." Be sure to visit the Museo Arqueológico de San Miguel de Azapa to see the Chinchorro mummies. Stop in Putre to catch your breath before taking in the flamingos at Parque Nacional Lauca or the vicuñas, llamas, and alpacas of Reserva Nacional Las Vicuñas.

Getting Here and Around

AIR

There are no international airports in El Norte Grande, but from Santiago you can transfer to a flight headed to Antofagasta, Calama, Iquique, or Arica. Round-trip flights start from 80,000 pesos, and can run up to 300,000 pesos in peak season. The cities within El Norte Grande are far apart, so while it can be useful to fly, you miss out on some of the magic of traveling by bus through Chile's remote areas in the Atacama and beyond.

AIR CONTACTS LAN. ☎ *600/526–2000* ⊕ *www.latam.com.* **Sky Airline.** ☎ *2/2353–2845* ⊕ *www.skyairline.cl.*

BUS

Bus travel is the most economic and efficient way to see El Norte Grande, and witnessing a desert sunset from a reclining "salon cama" sleeper bus seat is something quite special. It's also a great way to save a night's accommodation, with the bonus that you wake up 400 km (250 miles) farther down the road.

Travel between the larger towns and cities in El Norte Grande is easy, but there may be no bus service to some smaller villages or the more remote national parks. No bus company has a monopoly, so shop around for the best price and note there are often several bus stations in each city.

BUS CONTACTS Pullman. ⊠ *Latorre 2827, Antofagasta* ☎ *600/600–0018* ⊕ *www. pullman.cl.* **Turbus.** ⊠ *Latorre 2751, Antofagasta* ☎ *600/660–6600* ⊕ *www. turbus.cl.*

CAR

A car is another option for traveling through El Norte Grande. Driving in the cities can be a little hectic, but highway travel is usually smooth sailing and the roads are generally well maintained.

Ruta 5, more familiarly known as the Pan-American Highway, bisects all of northern Chile. Ruta 1, Chile's answer to California's Highway 101, is a beautiful coastal highway running between Antofagasta and Iquique. Avis, Budget, and Hertz all have car rental offices in the region.

Restaurants

The food of El Norte Grande is simple but quite good. Along the coast you can enjoy fresh seafood and shellfish, including *merluza* (hake), *corvina* (sea bass), *ostiones* (scallops), and *machas* (similar to razor clams but unique to Chile), to name just a few. Ceviche (a traditional dish made with raw fish marinated in lemon) is a Chilean (and Peruvian) specialty found in much of El Norte Grande, but make sure you sample it in a place where you are confident that the fish is fresh. Fish may be ordered *a la plancha* (grilled in butter and lemon) or accompanied by a sauce like *salsa margarita* (a butter-based sauce comprising almost every shellfish imaginable). As you enter the interior region you'll come across heartier meals such as *cazuela de vacuno* (beef stew served with corn on the cob and vegetables) and *chuleta con arroz* (pork chop with rice). In San Pedro, you'll find dishes that feature native meats like llama and vicuña.

People in the north generally eat a heavy lunch around 2 pm that can last two hours, followed by a light dinner around 10 pm. Reservations are seldom needed, except in the poshest of places. A 10% tip is expected and will be automatically added to your bill. Restaurant reviews have been shortened. For full information, visit Fodors.com.

Hotels

El Norte Grande has seen a boom in luxury accommodations in recent years. San Pedro, in particular, hosts more than half a dozen luxury lodgings that range from lavish desert resorts to tasteful boutiques. Luxury hotels usually are full board with activities included as well as transfers to the airports. If that's not your style, opt for one of the smaller hotels in town that offer lower prices. In San Pedro de Atacama, the gamut of hotels outside of town are less exciting, and be warned that some accommodation options bill themselves as "luxury" despite not having seen a lick of clean paint for years. In rural towns in El Norte Grande, accommodation is relatively inexpensive and hotels are few and far between, so you

might have to make do with guesthouses with basic rooms and shared bathrooms.

Hotel reviews have been shortened. For full information, visit Fodors.com.

What It Costs in Chilean Pesos (in Thousands)

	$	$$	$$$	$$$$
RESTAURANTS				
	Under 6	6–9	10–13	over 13
HOTELS				
	Under 51	51–85	86–115	over 115

Health and Safety

The main concern you should have in the North is the altitude. Gradual acclimatization over several days is essential for visiting high destinations, such as Parque Nacional Lauca and Lago Chungará, regardless of fitness level. The general rule is: if you feel unwell, descend as quickly as possible.

The sun should also be treated with respect; a hat and sunblock are always a good idea, and be sure to drink plenty of fluids during any outdoor activity.

Use common sense: don't be flashy with cash or expensive cameras. The North is relatively tranquil, but when venturing out from the center of any town into other neighborhoods, it's always safer to take a cab than to walk (ask an employee to call one for you). The main industry in El Norte Grande is mining, which means there is an inflated population of men and that foreign women often attract more than a few wandering gazes.

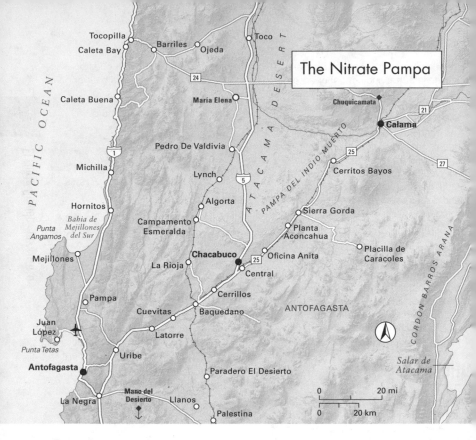

The Nitrate Pampa

Antofagasta

565 km (350 miles) north of Copiapó.

Antofagasta is the most important—and the richest—city in El Norte Grande. It was part of Bolivia until 1879, when it was annexed by Chile in the War of the Pacific. The port town became an economic powerhouse during the nitrate boom. With the rapid decline of nitrate production, copper mining stepped in to keep the city's coffers filled.

Many travelers end up spending a night in Antofagasta on their way to the more interesting destinations like San Pedro de Atacama, Iquique, and Arica, but a few sights here are worth a look. Around two in the afternoon the city shuts down most of the streets in the center of town, making for pleasant afternoon shopping

and strolling. Southeast of town on Rado-slav Razmilic is a sand dune world of burned-out desert race cars. Tracks from these cars lead up seemingly impossible orange waves of rock and sand, extending into the Atacama beyond.

GETTING HERE AND AROUND

Antofagasta's airport, 30 minutes from downtown, is a regular stop on Sky Airline's northern run, about a two-hour flight from Santiago. From Caldera in the south, it's a six- to seven-hour ride up the Pan-American Highway by bus or car, but at least on this stretch you'll see some of the ocean. The bus terminal on Latorre is just a short walk from downtown. Regular buses leave to Calama (3 hours), San Pedro (4½ hours), and Iquique (6 hours). The beaches of Juan Lopez are 45 minutes up the coast road, and the famous "La Portada" a mere 16 km (10 miles) from downtown—minibuses run there from Latorre 2723 frequently. The Turbus terminal, one of the bigger bus lines serving all of Chile, is just down the street on Latorre. Desertica Expediciones arranges trips into the interior, including excursions to Parque Nacional Pan de Azúcar in El Norte Chico.

AIR TRAVEL Cerro Moreno Airport (Antofagasta) (CNF). ☎ *55/225–4998* 🌐 *www.aeropuertoantofagasta.cl.*

ESSENTIALS

RENTAL CAR CONTACTS Avis. ✉ *Mario Silva Iriarte 560, Antofagasta* ☎ *22/795–3962, 600/368–2000* 🌐 *www.avis.com.* **Budget.** ✉ *Aeropuerto, Antofagasta* ☎ *600/441–0000* 🌐 *www.budget.cl.*

VISITOR INFORMATION Sernatur Antofagasta. ✉ *Prat 384, 1st fl., Antofagasta* ☎ *55/245–1818* 🌐 *www.sernatur.cl.*

👁 Sights

★ Mano del Desierto

PUBLIC ART | About 60 km (37 miles) southeast of Antofagasta via Ruta 5, this giant hand sculpture rises 36 feet tall from the Atacama Desert like a mirage. It was created in 1992 by famed sculptor Mario Irarrázabal, the same artist who created the Monumento al Ahogado hand sculpture in Punta del Este, Uruguay. It's best visited early in the morning or at sunset, when you can see the hand reaching out of the earth into the rays of the Andean sun. You can't miss the Mano from the highway, and a dirt trail leads off the main road toward it. Be sure to park at a respectful distance to ensure other visitors can also enjoy the sculpture. ✉ *Rte. 5, Antofagasta.*

Museo de Antofagasta

HISTORY MUSEUM | Inside the historic customs house, this museum is the town's oldest building, dating back to 1866. It displays clothing and other bric-a-brac from the nitrate era. ✉ *José Manuel Balmaceda 2786, Antofagasta* 🌐 *www.museodeantofagasta.cl* 🎟 *Free* 🕒 *Closed Mon.*

Torre Reloj

CLOCK | High above Plaza Colón is this clock tower whose face is a replica of London's Big Ben. It was erected by British residents in 1910. ✉ *Plaza Colón, Antofagasta.*

🍴 Restaurants

Amares Costafusion

$$$ | **CHILEAN** | This trendy bistro is a top spot for fusion food that mixes local seafood with different international cuisines. Try the crab lasagna, grilled octopus, Asian-style tuna, or tempura shrimp. **Known for:** tasty pisco sours; fusion seafood menu; great ceviche. [$] *Average main: pesos11000* ✉ *Antonino Toro 995, Antofagasta* ☎ *55/292–2376* 🌐 *www.amares.cl.*

Don Pollo

$ | **FAST FOOD** | **FAMILY** | This rotisserie restaurant prepares some of the best roasted chicken in Chile—a good thing, because it's the only item on the menu. The thatched-roof terrace is a great place to kick back after a long day of sightseeing. **Known for:** rotisserie chicken; fast service; relaxing terrace. [$] *Average main: pesos3000* ✉ *Ossa 2594, Antofagasta* ☎ *9/3457–7213 WhatsApp only* 🌐 *www.donpollodonlomo.cl* 💳 *No credit cards.*

★ El Nuevo Arriero

$$$$ | **CHILEAN** | Popular with locals, this unassuming restaurant may have simple decor, but the food is excellent. The serving staff bring out endless plates of steaming seafood and barbecue delights. **Known for:** fettuccini a la mancha; fair prices; grilled steak. [$] *Average main: pesos17000* ✉ *Filomena Valenzuela 270, Antofagasta* ☎ *57/243–0763* 🌐 *www.elnuevoarriero.cl* 🕒 *Closed after 7 pm on Sun.*

Hotels

Enjoy Hotel del Desierto
$$$ | **HOTEL** | If you need a break from footloose South American travels, this hotel is just the indulgent space, with a sprawling casino, spa, restaurant, and spacious rooms with big, comfortable beds. **Pros:** rooftop pool; relaxing space; modern amenities. **Cons:** can be noisy outside; a bit generic; slow service.
[$] *Rooms from: pesos82000* ✉ *Av. Angamos 01455, Antofagasta* ☎ *55/265–3000*
🌐 *https://www.enjoy.cl/#/antofagasta*
🛏 *100 rooms* 🍴 *Free Breakfast.*

Nightlife

Nightlife in El Norte Grande often means heading to the *schoperias,* beer halls where the almost entirely male clientele downs *schops* (draft beers). The drinking generally continues until everyone is reeling drunk, maybe dancing to the jukebox tunes. If this is your idea of fun, check out the myriad schoperias in the center of town around the Plaza Colón.

If you're not quite ready for the schoperia experience (and for many these are not the most pleasant places to spend an evening), don't worry: there are also a few bars around the city where you can have a quiet drink.

Shopping

You don't want to miss out on the people-watching or the shopping on the *plaza peotonal* (pedestrian mall) that runs for four blocks along Calle Arturo Prat. There are electronics shops, a Fallabella (Macy's-type national chain), cafés, jewelry shops, and sporting-goods stores for the outdoors enthusiast or collector of Chilean soccer jerseys.

On the corner of Manuel A. Matta and Maipú, you'll find the **Mercado Central,** a fruit and vegetable market with blue-and-yellow walls. Behind the market is the **Plaza del Mercado,** where artisans sell handmade jewelry and healing crystals, and where the occasional outdoor performance takes place.

Chacabuco

70 km (43 miles) northeast of Antofagasta.

There are many ghost towns left from the nitrate boom in the early 20th century, and Chacabuco is one of them, although this deserted town has a darker history than most. During his dictatorship, Augusto Pinochet used the abandoned town, originally founded in 1924 for saltpeter plain exploitations, as a concentration camp for almost 2,000 people between 1973 and 1974. The small town was surrounded by landmines to ensure no one attempted escape. Nowadays you can visit this unsettling place, one of the most fascinating attractions in the whole of Chile, learning about life in Chacabuco when it was a nitrate plant and about its days as a concentration camp. Do not walk around the walled town's exterior, as land mines from the Pinochet era could still be buried here.

GETTING HERE AND AROUND

To reach Chacabuco from Antofagasta, head east through the coastal range until you hit the Panamerican Highway (Ruta 5 Norte) and follow it northeast in the direction of Calama.

Sights

Chacabuco
GHOST TOWN | A mysterious dot on the desert landscape, the ghost town of Chacabuco is a decidedly eerie place. More than 7,000 employees and their families lived here when the Oficina Chacabuco (a company mining town that was made a national monument in 1971) was in operation between 1922 and 1944. It was the first nitrate mining office to pay

employees, unlike neighboring towns that only remunerated workers and their families with tokens that could be cashed in for food and services on-site. There was little justice, however, for Chacabuco's second wave of inhabitants.

During the first years of Augusto Pinochet's military regime, Chacabuco was used as a prison camp for political dissidents. In the office, you can still see a photograph of the emaciated men standing on parade. Prisoners were released in 1974, and democracy was restored in Chile in 1990.

If you are lucky, the encyclopedic guide Iván Pozo will be on shift during your visit. Be sure to ask him about his friendship with the ex-inmates and the tours they would give well into their 80s. ⊠ 70 km (43 miles) northeast of Antofagasta on Pan-American Hwy. 🕾 🖃 2500 pesos.

María Elena

FACTORY | Founded by a British company in 1926, María Elena is a dusty place that warrants a visit if you want to see a functioning nitrate town. It's home to the employees of the region's last two nitrate plants. The 5,000 people who live in María Elena are proud of their history—nearly every house has a picture of the town hanging inside. A tiny but informative museum in the town's main square houses many artifacts from the nitrate boom as well as a few from the pre-Columbian era. ⊠ 148 km (92 miles) north of Chacabuco.

Calama

215 km (133 miles) northeast of Antofagasta.

The discovery of vast deposits of copper in the area turned Calama into the quintessential mining town, and therein lies its interest. People from the length of Chile flock to this dusty spot on the map in hopes of striking it rich in "the land of sun and copper"—most likely working for Codelco, Chile's biggest company, which has three mines in the surrounding area. A modern-day version of the boomtowns of the 19th-century American West, Calama is rough around the edges, but it does possess a certain energy.

Founded as a tambo, or resting place, at the crossing of two Inca trails, Calama still serves as a stopover for people headed elsewhere. Some people traveling to San Pedro de Atacama end up spending the night here, and the town has a few attractions of its own.

GETTING HERE AND AROUND

Daily flights from Santiago via Sky, Air-Comet, and LAN arrive 20 minutes from downtown at Calama's El Loa Airport (CJC). Bus service to neighboring San Pedro is frequent and fast—it's about an hour between the two towns. To points north, you can fly to Iquique and Arica in an hour (if you can avoid the puddle-jumper service that adds a few stops), but a bus or car will take you seven and nine hours, respectively. Be very careful when passing the mining company trucks that may slow your journey. Mining companies own all the bright red pickups you'll no doubt notice around town.

ESSENTIALS

VISITOR INFORMATION Municipal Tourism Office. ⊠ Latorre 1689, Calama 🕾 55/253–1707 ⊕ www.calamacultural.cl.

◉ Sights

Catedral San Juan Bautista

CHURCH | The gleaming copper roof of this cathedral on Plaza 23 de Marzo, the city's main square, testifies to the importance of mining in this region. ⊠ Ramírez at Av. Granaderos., Calama.

Chuquicamata

MINE | The trucks never stop rolling and the machinery never stops grinding at Chuquicamata, the world's biggest open-pit mine, located just outside of

Calama. Nine-hundred workers split three eight-hour shifts, digging, transporting, and processing the metal on which Chile runs.

When visiting, you are dwarfed by the sheer scale of "Chuqui," as locals call it: it's 5 km (3 miles) long, 2 km (1 mile) wide, and 1 km (1/2 mile) deep. It takes any of the 96 trucks, some of which have beds 12 meters (39 feet) wide, a half hour to navigate the winding road to the bottom of the pit. The monstrous German-made trucks cost a pretty penny, about $4 million, and are refueled by pressure-hoses in the same way Formula One cars are gassed up. After all, a 4,000-liter (1,000-gallon) tank could take a while to fill the conventional way. Even the tires cost about $20,000 apiece. Because they run night and day, the trucks require constant maintenance and generally only about 80 are in operation at any one time. The most modern cranes can shovel out up to 50 tons of rock at a time and require a single operator, while in years gone by 20-ton cranes required a crew of 12.

Stare into the vast pit of Chuquicamata and you'll be convinced that Chile uncovered untold riches below the barren Atacama Desert. But after decades of mining, production has fallen sharply due to structural problems and lower copper content. As the mine becomes too deep to exploit profitably, the industry is looking into other reserves and resources, most especially lithium mines, of which Chile currently has the world's largest reserves.

There is a small museum at the mine's entrance where you can get a close-up view of the machinery used to make such big holes. Tours are in Spanish and English. Reserve in advance by phone or by email. It's about a 20-minute taxi ride (5,000 pesos) from downtown Calama. ✉ *16 km (10 miles) north of Calama, Calama* ☎ *55/232–2122* 🌐 *www.codelco.cl* 🎟 *By donation* 🕓 *No tours weekends.*

El Museo de Historia Natural y Cultural del Desierto de Atacama
HISTORY MUSEUM | This small museum in El Loa Park has artifacts from Calama's history and pre-Columbian times. ✉ *Parque El Loa (O'Higgins), Calama* ☎ *9/56573314* 🎟 *500 pesos.*

🍴 Restaurants

Patagonia
$$$ | **CHILEAN** | Decked with historic memorabilia, Patagonia is best known for its steak—large slices of steaming beef, cooked on the grill. Most people don't stray too far from the classics and it's probably best not to, as this is what Patagonia does best. **Known for:** nice wine and beer lists; huge, juicy steaks grilled to perfection; wooden decor. [$] *Average main: pesos12000* ✉ *Granaderos 2549, Calama* ☎ *55/234–1628* 🕓 *No dinner Sun.*

🛏 Hotels

Park Hotel Calama
$$ | **HOTEL** | It's easy to see why international mining consultants frequent this modern hotel. **Pros:** comfortable rooms and beds; nice swimming pool; relaxing lounge. **Cons:** no air-conditioning in rooms; some street noise; nothing within walking distance. [$] *Rooms from: pesos54900* ✉ *Alcalde Jose Lira 1392, Calama* ☎ *55/271–5800* 🌐 *www.parkcalama.cl* 🔑 *106 rooms* 🍽 *Free Breakfast.*

🍸 Nightlife

BARS

Calama is the land of the schoperia—locals say there are more schoperias than people. Come payday at the mine, these drinking halls fill up with beer-swilling workers. The schoperias near Plaza 23 de Marzo are less raucous than the ones farther from downtown.

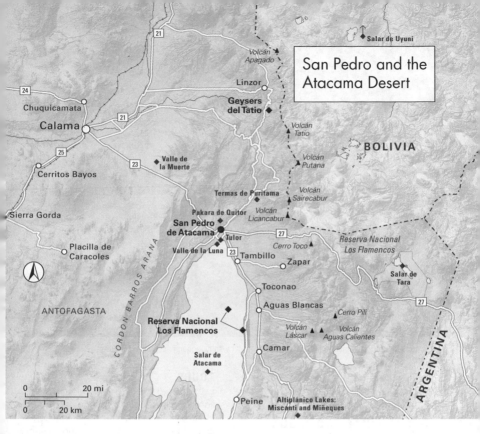

San Pedro and the Atacama Desert

Shopping

Locals sell clothing and jewelry at the covered markets off the pedestrian mall of Calle Ramírez. There are also markets on Calle Vargas between Latorre and Vivar. On Balmaceda, the road to the airport, the Calama Mall includes a movie theater screening the latest Hollywood releases.

San Pedro de Atacama

100 km (62 miles) southeast of Calama.

It is not an exaggeration to call San Pedro de Atacama a once-in-a-lifetime destination, as after all, there's nowhere else quite like the Atacama Desert in the entire world. The quiet town of San Pedro is an oasis in the desert in both

the literal and metaphorical sense: greenery, rushing irrigation channels, and striking white-washed adobe walls give life to this otherwise dusty town, and the intriguing community of travelers, artisans, and natives have created a stress-free paradise far removed from the burdens of normal life. Over the last decade San Pedro has exploded in tourism, now offering more than 100 accommodation options, three dozen restaurants, and more tourism operators than you'll care to count.

What is so attractive about San Pedro? For adventurists, it is the opportunity to do high-altitude climbing, sandboarding, and mountain biking. For sightseers, it is the volcano-lined horizon, the salt-encrusted valleys, the clear blue salt lakes dotted with flamingos, and the billowing geysers. And for pleasure seekers, it is

Laguna Chaxa, in the middle of Salar de Atacama, is a salty lagoon filled with flamingos.

simply soaking in the beautiful Atacama sun and landscapes while moving to the San Pedro pace: nice and slow.

GETTING HERE AND AROUND

San Pedro is an hour's bus or car ride from Calama. You can either take the private (50,000 pesos) or shared (12,000 pesos) shuttle services from the airport, or the cheaper option of a bus ride (1,500). There's no need to book in advance. You'll find four shuttle companies as you arrive at the baggage claim in the airport. If you want to take the public bus you'll need to travel into Calama bus station first. Turbus and a few other companies serve San Pedro, and the bus terminal is just a few blocks from downtown at the intersection of Lincacabur and Domingo Atienz. If planning other trips around Chile, there's a Turbus ticket window here.

ESSENTIALS

VISITOR INFORMATION Sernatur San Pedro de Atacama. ⊠ *Toconao at Gustavo LePaige, San Pedro de Atacama* ☏ *55/285–1420* ⊕ *www.chile.travel.*

TOURS

Every corner you turn in San Pedro, someone is offering a tour. Most of them offer the same classic routes—geysers, flamingos, Valle de la Luna—and all seem to have surprisingly low prices. But if it seems too good to be true, it probably is.

Make sure to ask how many people will be on the tour and how long you will spend at each place. Avoid unlicensed companies or agencies that sell into other company's tours. Try to stick with reputable companies that employ guides who have been in San Pedro long enough to know the best lookout points.

If you don't want to go with a group, hire a private driver and guide. A car and chauffeur should cost around 60,000 pesos per half-day, excluding gas. Ask the tourism office or your hotel for their recommendations.

Cosmo Andino Expediciones
Operating for more than 30 years, Cosmo is one of the most established and reliable tour operators. All guides and drivers

are contracted (not freelance) and the vehicles are their own. The classic tours are all covered, although Cosmo prides itself on beating the crowd with earlier start times and spending longer in each location than the other companies. They offer multiple hiking options, as well as a full-day Tara tour where you can enjoy volcanos, llamas, and spectacular views. ⊠ *Caracoles s/n, At Tocapilla, San Pedro de Atacama* ☎ *55/285–1069* ⊕ *www. cosmoandino.cl* ⊠ *From 16000 pesos.*

⊙ Sights

Iglesia San Pedro

CHURCH | To the west of the square is one of the altiplano's largest churches. It was miraculously constructed in 1744 without the use of a single nail—the builders used cactus sinews to tie the roof beams and door hinges. ⊠ *Gustavo Le Paige s/n, San Pedro de Atacama* ☎ .

Pukara de Quitor

RUINS | Just 3 km (2 miles) north of San Pedro lies this ancient fortress at the entrance to the Valle de Catarpe, which was built in the 12th century to protect the Atacameños from invading Incas. It wasn't the Incas but the Spanish who were the real threat, however. Spanish conquistador Pedro de Valdivia took the fortress by force in 1540. The crumbling buildings were carefully reconstructed in 1981 and declared a national monument in 1982. ⊠ *On road to Valle Catarpe, San Pedro de Atacama* ☎ ⊠ *3000 pesos.*

★ Salar de Atacama

NATURE SIGHT | About 10 km (6 miles) south of San Pedro you arrive at the edge of Chile's largest salt flat. The rugged crust measuring 3,000 square km (1,158 square miles) formed when salty water flowing down from the Andes evaporated in the stifling heat of the desert. Unlike other salt flats, which are smooth surfaces of crystalline salt, the Salar de Atacama is a jumble of jagged rocks that look rather like coral. **Laguna Chaxa**,

in the middle of Salar de Atacama, is a very salty lagoon that is home to three of the New World's four species of flamingos. The elegant pink-and-white birds are mirrored by the lake's glassy surface. Near Laguna Chaxa, beautiful plates of salt float on the calm surface of **Laguna Salada.** Visiting the salar is a half-day excursion from San Pedro and often better at sunset when the sky can paint pretty pink colors, reflected in the mirrorlike lagoons. Arrive early before the crowds scare off the birds, and bring your binoculars. ⊠ *Laguna Chaxa, San Pedro de Atacama.*

Salar de Tara

NATURE SIGHT | More than 14,000 feet high, Salar de Tara has some similarities to the Altiplánico Lakes, but what makes it unique is the unusual rock formations that appear like castles in the sky, surreal sculptures among the sand flats, and flamingo-spotted lagoons. It is a full day from San Pedro on the way to Bolivia, and involves a long and bumpy road both ways. ⊠ *Salar de Tara, San Pedro de Atacama.*

Salar de Uyuni

NATURE SIGHT | It's possible to take a three to five-day, four-wheel-drive organized tour from San Pedro into Bolivia's massive and mysterious salt flat, the largest in the world. Beware: the accommodations—usually clapboard lodgings in small oasis towns—are rustic to say the least, but speeding along the Salar de Uyuni, which is chalkboard flat, is a treat. Nearby are geysers, small Andean lagoons, and islands of cactus that stand in sharp contrast to the sealike salt flat.

Tulor

RUINS | This archaeological site, 9 km (6 miles) southwest of San Pedro, marks the remains of the oldest known civilization in the region. Built around 800 BC, the village of Tulor was home to the Linka Arti people, who lived in small mud huts resembling igloos. The site was uncovered only in the middle of the 20th century, when Jesuit missionary Gustavo Le Paige excavated it from a sand dune. Archaeologists hypothesize that the inhabitants left because of climatic changes and a possible sandstorm. Little more about the village's history is known, and only one of the huts has been completely excavated. As one of the well-informed guides will tell you, even this hut is sinking back into the obscurity of the Atacama sand. ⊠ *9 km (6 miles) southwest of San Pedro, then 3 km (2 miles) down road leading to Valle de la Luna, San Pedro de Atacama* 🕿 📧 *3000 pesos.*

★ Valle de la Luna

NATURE SIGHT | This surreal landscape of barren ridges, soaring cliffs, sand dunes, and pale valleys could be from a canvas by Salvador Dalí. Originally a small corner of a vast inland sea, the valley rose up with the Andes. The water slowly drained away, leaving deposits of salt and gypsum that were folded by the shifting of the Earth's crust and then worn away by wind and rain. The vastness and grandeur of some of the formations is quite breathtaking, and listening carefully to the cracking of the salt crystals as the sun warms up and cools down the surfaces is awe-inspiring. Visiting the Valle de la Luna is fabulous at sunset, although this is also when truckloads of tourists arrive. So if you want the valley to yourself, visit in the morning when there is barely a soul there. You can visit by car, bike (bring a big hat for shade!), or horseback. ⊠ *14 km (9 miles) west of San Pedro, San Pedro de Atacama* 📧 *3000 pesos.*

Valle de la Muerte

NATURE SIGHT | Not far from the Valle de la Luna, just on the other side of Ruta 98 leading to Calama, are the reddish rocks of the Valle de la Muerte (Death Valley). Jesuit missionary Gustavo Le Paige, who in the 1950s was the first archaeologist to explore this desolate area, discovered many human skeletons. These bones

are from the Indigenous Atacameño people, who lived here before the arrival of the Spanish. He hypothesized that the sick and the elderly may have come to this place to die. The name of the valley comes from its red Mars-like appearance and was originally called Valle de Martes (Mars Valley), but Gustavo's foreign pronunciation of Martes (Mars) was heard as Muerte (dead). ⊠ *San Pedro de Atacama* 📧 *3000 pesos.*

🍴 Restaurants

Café Adobe Restaurante

$$$ | **LATIN AMERICAN** | One of the most popular restaurants in San Pedro, Adobe gets extra points for its atmospheric fire pit and local Andean band. The food reflects international and local tastes with quesadillas, salads, and pizzas, alongside the calorific Chilean favorite of steak *a la pobre* (topped with fried egg, onions, and fries). **Known for:** pisco sours with local ingredients; cozy outdoor fireplace; Atacama-fusion dishes like roast lamb kofte. $ *Average main: pesos13000* ⊠ *Carcoles 211, San Pedro de Atacama* 🕿 *9/5028–1158* ⊕ *cafeadobe. cl* ⊗ *No lunch Wed.*

Charrua

$$ | **PIZZA** | While you may not have come to San Pedro to eat pizza, this busy joint serves respectable thin-crust pies. The restaurant itself is not classy, but if you're looking for a bit of home comfort or take-out for your hotel patio, Charrua is the place. **Known for:** small setting; decent pizza; quick meals. $ *Average main: pesos8000* ⊠ *Tocopilla 442, San Pedro de Atacama* 🕿 *55/285–1443.*

Delicias de Carmen

$$ | **CHILEAN** | Owner Carmen has managed to attract locals and tourists alike with her immensely popular restaurant that serves affordable, typically Chilean home-style dishes, ranging from soups and stews to roast meats and fish. Warm bread is served with a killer *pebre*

The cliffs and sand dunes of Valle de la Luna are otherworldly.

(spicy salsa), and the lunch specials are the best value in San Pedro. **Known for:** affordable lunches; Chilean comfort food; local favorite. $ *Average main: pesos7000* ⊠ *Calama 360, San Pedro de Atacama* ☎ *9/089–5673.*

Kunza

$$ | **CHILEAN** | This might be a bit out of town, but the volcanic views and delicious Chilean cuisine are worth the trip. Part of the Cumbres Hotel, Kunza is open every day so you can enjoy interesting dishes like guanaco carpaccio, llama jerky, and fish cooked in Atacama salt served with a traditional corn tamale. **Known for:** outdoor fire pits great for star-gazing; local cuisine that takes risks; tasty pisco sours. $ *Average main: pesos9000* ⊠ *Cumbres, Las Chilcas s/n, San Pedro de Atacama* ☎ *55/285–2136* ⊕ *www.cumbressanpedro.com.*

Coffee and Quick Bites

Babalu Heladeria

$ | **CAFÉ** | **FAMILY** | The altiplano sun burns bright and hot in San Pedro, so stop in at Babalu Heladeria to sample one of 52 flavors of ice cream. **Known for:** refreshing pick-me-up; 52 flavors; quick stop. $ *Average main: pesos3000* ⊠ *Caracoles 160, San Pedro de Atacama* ☎ *9/9943–2271* ⊟ *No credit cards.*

🛏 Hotels

★ Alto Atacama Desert Lodge & Spa

$$$$ | **RESORT** | No other hotel makes you feel quite as part of the Atacama Desert landscape as Alto; set in the middle of the Salt Mountains Range (Cordillera de la Sal), this 42-room luxury retreat is a surprising oasis in a desert that seems to extend endlessly in every direction. **Pros:** fantastic restaurant and service; one-of-a-kind desert escape; excellent facilities. **Cons:** weak Wi-Fi in rooms; far from town; expensive. $ *Rooms from: pesos780000* ⊠ *Camino Pukará, Sector Suchor, San*

Pedro de Atacama ☎ *2/2912–3900 in Chile, 844/865–2002 in U.S.* 🌐 *www.altoatacama.com* 🛏 *42 rooms* 🍴 *Free Breakfast.*

Cumbres San Pedro de Atacama
$$$$ | **RESORT** | Atacama's largest resort features 60 large and comfortable rooms spread over the vast property, offering peace and privacy, with each room having its own patio looking onto native flora and an indoor/outdoor shower. **Pros:** private and peaceful rooms; gorgeous facilities including spa and pools; plenty of excursions offered. **Cons:** busy meal times; slow service; spa can get full. [$] *Rooms from: pesos250000* ✉ *Av. Las Chilcas s/n Lote 10, Parcela 2, San Pedro de Atacama* ☎ *55/285–2160* 🌐 *www.cumbressanpedro.com* 🛏 *60 rooms* 🍴 *Free Breakfast.*

Explora Atacama
$$$$ | **HOTEL** | This all-inclusive hotel looks more like an estancia or even a stable from the outside, but inside spacious rooms and airy interiors look out onto the volcanoes in the distance and the friendly staff is there to help you plan your excursions in the altiplano and desert. **Pros:** great social scene in bar area; excellent excursions; great pool area. **Cons:** restaurant disappointing for price; no Wi-Fi in rooms; expensive. [$] *Rooms from: pesos2632520* ✉ *Domingo Atienza s/n, Ayllu de Larache, San Pedro de Atacama* ☎ *2/2395–2800 in Chile* 🌐 *www.explora.com/explora-atacama* 🛏 *50 rooms* 🍴 *All-Inclusive* ☞ *Rate reflects three-day minimum.*

Hotel Altiplánico
$$$$ | **HOTEL** | **FAMILY** | Outside the center of San Pedro, this hotel village has the look and feel of a pueblo: a labyrinth of walkways leads you from room to room, which are each constructed with typical mud-color adobe and adorned with private terraces and often outdoor showers. **Pros:** great stargazing at night; refreshing pool; plenty of privacy. **Cons:** noise travels between rooms; rooms quite dark; long walk from town (no provided transfers). [$] *Rooms from: pesos155000* ✉ *Domingo Atienza 282, San Pedro de Atacama* ☎ *55/285–1212* 🌐 *www.altiplanico.cl* 🛏 *32 rooms* 🍴 *Free Breakfast.*

Hotel Kimal
$$ | **RESORT** | This adobe-walled dwelling has comfortable rooms and a cheery central courtyard dotted with islands of desert shrubbery. **Pros:** friendly staff; close to center of town; good price. **Cons:** simple facilities; no air-conditioning; pool is on small side. [$] *Rooms from: pesos82700* ✉ *Domingo Atienza 452, San Pedro de Atacama* ☎ *55/285–1152* 🛏 *40 rooms* 🍴 *Free Breakfast.*

Lodge Andino Terrantai
$$$$ | **HOTEL** | Right behind the main plaza, Terrantai is a real gem combining the historical and modern; the historical part is a 200-year-old colonial house with high cane ceilings supported by entire tree trunks, and the modern part (constructed in 1996) opens out into a maze of river-stone walls with hidden fountains and gardens. **Pros:** plenty of homey touches; unique design; great location for walking to the plaza. **Cons:** slow Wi-Fi; rooms are basic for price; noise travels. [$] *Rooms from: pesos230000* ✉ *Tocopilla 411, San Pedro de Atacama* ☎ *9/4495–0131, 9/8818–6114* 🌐 *www.terrantai.com* 🛏 *21 rooms* 🍴 *Free Breakfast.*

Tierra Atacama
$$$$ | **RESORT** | This stylish hotel has an imaginative take on design, services, and excursions to give it a touch of luxury and originality without losing that *atacameño* feel, or respect for local places, people, and traditions. **Pros:** great tours; down-to-earth luxury; excellent spa. **Cons:** communal areas not very inviting; expensive; small bathrooms. [$] *Rooms from: pesos2000000* ✉ *Calle Séquitor s/n, Ayllú de Yaye, San Pedro de Atacama* ☎ *800/914–249 in Chile, 800/910–0865 in U.S.* 🌐 *www.tierrahotels.com* 🛏 *32 suites* 🍴 *All-Inclusive* ☞ *Rate reflects two-day minimum.*

Nightlife

The bohemian side of San Pedro gets going after dinner and generally ends around midnight. Afterward, locals move to the outskirts for clandestine raves. There is an increasing problem with trafficked cocaine from Bolivia through San Pedro, so be careful if anyone tries to offer you some. Back in the legal sphere, most of the bars and small cafés are on Caracoles, and it is all pretty mellow. Your choices are pretty much limited to whether you want to sit outside by a fire or inside where it's a bit warmer.

Cervecería St. Peter

BARS | If drinking artisanal beers around a warm fire sounds like your ideal night, then head to Cervecería St. Peter, where you can try microbrews created using native plants including rica rica and algarrobo. ⊠ *Toconao 479, San Pedro de Atacama* ☎ *9/4287–9893.*

Chela Cabur

BARS | Yes, you can find a true pub even in the desert. At Chelacabur, football shirts hang from the mud walls, sports constantly play on the television, and lots of cheap beers are on tap. This place fills up fast on the weekends, so be sure to get there early if you want a seat. There's no food on-site, but they let you bring in pizza from the place next door. ⊠ *Caracoles 212, San Pedro de Atacama* ☎ *9/9489–8191.*

La Estaka

BARS | A hippie bar with funky decor, La Estaka has a true local feel. Reggae music rules, and the international food isn't half bad either. ⊠ *Caracoles 259B, San Pedro de Atacama* ☎ *55/285–1047* ⊕ *www.laestakarestaurant.cl.*

🛍 Shopping

Just about the entire village of San Pedro is an open-air market. Shopping here is fun, but prices are probably about 20% to 30% higher than in neighboring areas, and you'll find many of the same products: the traditional altiplano ponchos (aka *serapes*), jewelry, and even musical instruments. If you are taking a tour out to some of the smaller villages, you might find the same products being sold at a much lower price. Most upscale hotels also have a small shop with high-quality goods, often at an even higher price.

Feria Artesanal

CRAFTS | Just off the Plaza de Armas, the Feria Artesanal is bursting at the seams with artisan goods. Here, you can buy high-quality knits from the altiplano, such as sweaters and other woolen items. ⊠ *Off plaza, San Pedro de Atacama.*

Galería Cultural de Pueblos Andinos

MARKET | This open-air market sells woolen goods and crafts. ⊠ *Caracoles s/n, east of town, San Pedro de Atacama* ☎.

★ Libreria del Desierto

BOOKS | For a unique literary experience, head out to this eclectic bookshop and library in the small *ayllu* (village) of Solor. It's an hour walk or 20-minute bike ride out of town, but you'll be rewarded with an impressive collection of books in multiple languages, eco-friendly architecture, stunning volcano views, and philosophical conversation with the passionate and intellectual owner, Diego. The bookshop also operates as a publishing house, producing original works about the local culture. ⊠ *Calle Volcan Lascar 67, Solor Ayllu, San Pedro de Atacama* ☎ *9/7749–8473* ⊕ *www.libreriadeldesierto.cl.*

Activities

San Pedro is an outdoors lover's dream. There are great places for biking, hiking, and horseback riding in every direction. Extreme-sports enthusiasts can try their hand at sandboarding on the dunes of the Valle de la Muerte. Climbers can take on the nearby volcanoes, which provide an exhilarating high-altitude ascent; the only trouble can be the crowds. At the

Valle de la Luna, for example, sunset at the large dune is somewhat spoiled by the large tourist vans that dump a couple hundred sightseers there for the renowned sundown. The number of tour agencies and outfitters in San Pedro can be a bit overwhelming: shop around, pick a company you feel comfortable with, ask questions, and make sure the company is willing to cater to your needs.

Whatever your sport, keep in mind that San Pedro lies at 2,400 meters (7,900 feet) above sea level. If you're not acclimated to the high altitude, you'll feel tired much sooner than you might expect, so save excursions to the altiplánico or geysers until your last days. Also, remember to slather on the sunscreen and drink plenty of water.

BIKING

An afternoon ride to the Valle de la Luna is unforgettable, as is a quick trip to the ruins of Tulor, or the Laguna Cejar. Bike rentals can be arranged at most hotels and tour agencies. A bike can be rented for a half day for 5,000 pesos and for an entire day for upward of 10,000 pesos. There are also several bike rentals on offer in the city center (look around Caracoles and Toconao streets). You can go ride on your own to the local sites (Valle de la Luna, Valley de la Muerte, Tulor, Pukara de Quitor, and Laguna Chaxa), or you can book a bike tour with most of the local tourism agencies. La Bicicleta Verde (⊕ www.labicicletaverde.com) offers tours to different local villages. Don't forget sunscreen, sunglasses, a scarf for the dust and wind, and plenty of water.

HIKING

There is fantastic hiking throughout San Pedro, whether you want to spend a half-day trekking the Valle de Luna, an afternoon in the Cactus Valley, or a full day hiking up a volcano.

Lascar Volcano

HIKING & WALKING | There are several volcano ascents you can attempt in San Pedro de Atacama, but Lascar is one of the more accessible and rewarding hikes. You'll need about a week of gradual acclimation to higher altitudes to safely reach the 18,346 foot summit, but the hike itself isn't particularly rigorous if the weather is on your side. It's always advisable to summit with a group, and most tours will drive you out to just before the start of the summit. This leaves you with a couple hours to reach the summit, where you can peer into the belly of one of northern Chile's most active volcanoes. ⊠ *San Pedro de Atacama*.

Quebrada de Guatin

HIKING & WALKING | Informally known as Cactus Valley, the Quebrada de Guatin is a steep gorge where you can follow the Puritama River through the stunning rocky landscape where century-old cacti loom overhead. Don't let the small waterfalls and eagle nests distract you too much; this is a tricky walk with curves, turns, and a couple of jumps between rocks. The most rewarding route is heading uphill and finishing in the Puritama Hot Springs. It takes about three hours (over 3 miles) from the road. ⊠ *San Pedro de Atacama.*

Valle de la Luna and Valle de la Muerte

HIKING & WALKING | **FAMILY** | This is a popular afternoon and sunset walking spot for when the heat dies down and the colors of the landscape change. Although you have to stick to the paths, there are numerous different tracks through the valleys that will take you away from the busloads of tourists and into complete isolation staring up, or down, at the Cordillera de la Sal (Salt Mountains). You can make this a quick trek or spend a few hours exploring the valleys. ⊠ *San Pedro de Atacama* ⊠ *3000 pesos.*

HORSEBACK RIDING
Atacama Horse

HORSEBACK RIDING | San Pedro has the feeling of a Wild West town, so why not hitch up your horse and head out on an adventure? Atacama Horse offers an immersive desert exploration experience and a unique vantage on San Pedro de Atacama and its surroundings. You can do day rides or multiday rides and crossings. On the multiday trips, you ride with provisions, make camp, and cook around a fire when the sun sets. ⊠ *Tocopilla 406, San Pedro de Atacama* ☎ *9/9084–5518* ⊕ *www.atacamahorseadventure.com* ✉ *From 23000 pesos per person.*

SANDBOARDING

Sandboarding in the Atacama is surprisingly popular among backpackers, despite the occasional heat rash and painful abrasions. Many agencies offer a three-hour sandboarding excursion into the Valle de la Muerte from 4 pm to 9 pm—the intelligent way to beat the desert heat. These tours run about 15,000 pesos and include an instructor. If you're brave and have your own transportation, you can rent just the board for 7,000 pesos. There are several combination tours with Valle de la Luna. Since a fall on the sand can be hard, you should wear a helmet and board with caution.

STARGAZING

The Atacama Desert is one of the best places for stargazing in the world due to its clear skies, high altitude, and isolation from light pollution. So good is the stargazing here that San Pedro de Atacama is home to one of the world's biggest space ventures, the international ALMA observatory.

While the naked eye is perfectly good for spotting constellations, planets, and shooting stars (there's an average visibility of four every hour here), you shouldn't miss out on an opportunity to look through one of the many powerful telescopes while in San Pedro. Luxury hotels sometimes have their own telescopes and outdoor observatories.

ALMA

STARGAZING | The biggest astronomic observatory in the world, ALMA (Atacama Large Millimeter Aray) has 66 antennas that produce imagery of the coldest, most hidden parts of the sky. The public can visit on weekends and see the back-of-house operations in this international observatory, but you must reserve in advance. ⊠ *ALMA, San Pedro de Atacama* ☎ *2/2467–6100* ⊕ *www.alma.cl* ✉ *Free.*

SPACE

STARGAZING | SPACE (San Pedro de Atacama Celestial Explorations) offers one of the best astronomical tours in San Pedro. The complete darkness allows you to observe the night sky with the naked eye and through a dozen powerful telescopes. The tour finishes with an astronomy chat over hot chocolate. Popular with backpackers, tours are nightly (weather depending) and depart from the city center with native English-speaking specialist guides. ⊠ *166 Caracoles, San Pedro de Atacama* ☎ ⊕ *www.spaceobs.com* ✉ *From 25000 pesos (includes transport).*

Geysers del Tatio

95 km (59 miles) north of San Pedro.

Witnessing the fumaroles at daybreak here is one of the best experiences Chile has to offer. The geysers pump out boiling water throughout the day, and seeing the steam rise against the stark landscapes is breathtaking.

GETTING HERE AND AROUND

El Tatio is open all day for visits, but nearly everyone arrives just before sunrise, when the cold night air gives the steaming geysers an imposing presence. Tour groups depart San Pedro around 4 or 5 am, depending on the time of year.

The Geysers del Tatio erupt into jets of steam, but be careful; the water is boiling hot.

Most tours start with a walk through the geyser field and end with a simple breakfast. Tours usually return to San Pedro at midday.

 Sights

★ Geysers del Tatio

NATURE SIGHT | The world's highest geothermal field, the Geysers del Tatio is a breathtaking natural phenomenon. The sight of dozens of geysers throwing columns of steam into the air is unforgettable. A trip to El Tatio usually begins at 4 or 5 am, on a guided tour, when San Pedro is still cold and dark (any of the tour agencies in San Pedro can arrange this trip). After a two-hour bus ride on a relentlessly bumpy road, you reach the high plateau around daybreak. (The entrance fee is covered if you are on a tour, otherwise it is 15,000 pesos.) The jets of steam are already shooting into the air as the sun slowly peeks over the adjacent cordillera. The rays of light illuminate the steam in a kaleidoscope of chartreuses, violets, reds, oranges, and blues. The vapor then silently falls onto the sulfur-stained crust of the geyser field. As the sun heats the cold, barren land, the visibility and force of the geysers gradually diminish, allowing you to explore the mud pots and craters formed by the escaping steam. Be careful, though—the crust is thin in places and people have died falling into the boiling-hot water. ⊠ *Geysers El Tatio, San Pedro de Atacama* 🖃 *15000 pesos.*

Termas de Puritama

HOT SPRING | On your way back to San Pedro, you may want to stop at the Termas de Puritama hot springs. A hot soak may be just the thing to shake off that early morning chill. A relaxing day trip in itself, the hot springs are a series of eight pools, each one connected by wooden platforms and surrounded by foliage in the middle of a natural valley that is also a popular hiking area. If you don't have your own transport, you can book a transfer or group tour from many agencies in San Pedro. If you're staying at Hotel Explora, you'll have exclusive access to the first (and warmest) spring.

⊠ Termas de Puritama, San Pedro de Atacama ⊕ www.termasdepuritama.cl/en/ ⊠ 15000 pesos (discounted after 2 pm).

Reserva Nacional Los Flamencos

10 km (6 miles) south and east of San Pedro.

In the middle of one of the largest salt flats in the world, crowds of pink flamingos flock to a couple of pretty lagoons. While the flamingos often get the most attention, the whole setting is stunning, with volcanoes in the backdrop and vast, white stretches of land that paint a beautiful picture at sunset.

GETTING HERE AND AROUND

Nearly all San Pedro tour companies take you to the Reserva, but if you're in your own vehicle, take the road toward Toconao for 33 km (21 miles) to the park entrance.

ESSENTIALS

CONAF

VISITOR CENTER | You can get information about the Reserva Nacional Los Flamencos at the station run by CONAF, the Chilean forestry service. *⊠ CONAF station near Laguna Chaxa ☎ ⊕ www.conaf.cl ⊠ 2500 pesos.*

Sights

Altiplánico Lakes: Miscanti and Miñeques

BODY OF WATER | At more than 13,000 feet above sea level, these lakes are in a completely different climate than San Pedro below. The altiplánico has much more moisture in the air and while that means you are likely to experience rain and snow in certain seasons, it also means the area is alive with color and wildlife. The pastel-color backdrop is picture-perfect with the large blue lagoons and volcanoes in the distance. The largest of the lagoons is Miscanti,

at 4,350-meter-high (14,270-foot-high), which merits a few moments of contemplation and is one of the prettiest spots in Atacama (on a sunny day). The smaller lake, Miñeques, is equally spectacular and is home to wildlife like vicuña and huge flocks of flamingos. The altiplánico lakes are usually a full-day excursion from San Pedro. *⊠ Laguna Miscanti, San Pedro de Atacama.*

★ Reserva Nacional Los Flamencos

NATURE PRESERVE | Many of the most astounding sights in El Norte Grande lie within the boundaries of the protected Reserva Nacional Los Flamencos. This sprawling national reserve to the south and east of San Pedro encompasses a wide variety of geographical features, including alpine lakes, salt flats, and volcanoes. And of course, here is where you will find the most stunning collection of pink flamingos on the planet.

Iquique

390 km (242 miles) northwest of Calama.

Iquique is the capital of Chile's northernmost region, but it wasn't always so important. For hundreds of years it was a tiny fishing community. After the arrival of the Spanish, the village grew slowly into a port. The population, however, never totaled more than 100. It was not until the great nitrate boom of the 19th century that Iquique became a major port. Many of those who grew rich on nitrate moved to the city and built opulent mansions, almost all of which still stand today. Many of the old mansions are badly in need of repair, however, giving the city a rather worn-down look. The boom went bust, and those who remained turned again to the sea to make a living. Today Iquique is the world's largest exporter of fish meal.

At the base of a coastal mountain range, Iquique is blessed with year-round good weather. This may explain why it's

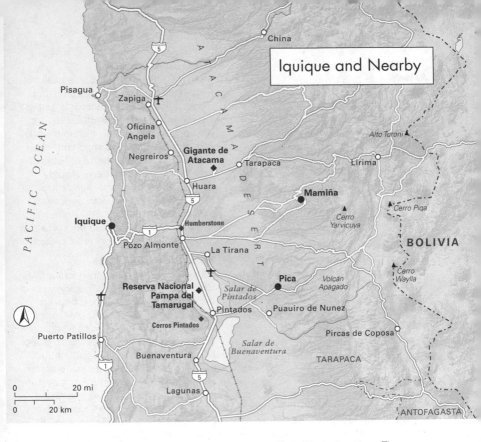

popular with vacationing Chilean families, who come for the long stretches of white beaches as well as the *zona franca* (duty-free zone).

GETTING HERE AND AROUND

Iquique's Diego Aracena airport (IQQ) is about 45 minutes from downtown proper (35 km [22 miles]; 17,000 pesos in taxi fare) and is served by the country's two major airlines: Sky and LATAM. Iquique is about seven hours via bus or car from Calama (400 km [249 miles]); once you've turned off the Pan-American Highway it's a narrow, serpentine road down to the town, so don't try passing any of the big trucks or other vehicles that may be slowing you down.

The tourist sights of Mamiña, Pica, and the Gigante de Atacama can all be done in one day's driving, and if you don't want to drive yourself, tour companies in town offer all-inclusive tours. There are two official taxi stands, one on Plaza Prat and one on the pedestrian street of Baquedano. Both will quote you rates to and from the airport, as well as day tours to nearby sites like the Gigante de Atacama, Humberstone, and Mamiña. To get to Pica, La Tirana, and the surrounding sights from Iquique, head south on Ruta 5 (Pan-American Highway) to Km 1,800 (Cruce Sara). Then head east on Ruta 685. As for rental cars, the best deals are in Iquique, but cars rented here can't be taken out of the area.

AIR TRAVEL Diego Aracena Airport (IQQ).
✉ 1, Iquique ☎ 57/247–3473.

ESSENTIALS
VISITOR INFORMATION Sernatur Iquique.
✉ Arturo prat 384 piso 1, Iquique
☎ 55/245–1818 ⊕ www.sernatur.cl.

TOURS
Avitours
ADVENTURE TOURS | Offering full or multi-day tours to local attractions like Parque Nacional Isluga Volcano, the Pampa Calichera, and Humberstone, Avitours can also organize paragliding over Iquique. ☒ *Rancagua 3444, Iquique* ☎ *9/7861–6806* ⊕ *www.avitours.cl* 🖼 *40000 pesos.*

Desierto Verde Expediciones
GUIDED TOURS | This tour operator provides excursions throughout the region, picking you up from a central hotel in Iquique and transporting you to sights including the Nitrate ghost towns, the Pintados geoglyphs, Lauca National Park, Isluga Volcano National Park, and more. ☒ *Av. Salvador Allende N° 450, Iquique* ☎ *9/9885–0310* ⊕ *desiertoverdexpediciones.cl* 🖼 *From 55000 pesos.*

 ## Sights

Calle Baquedano
PEDESTRIAN MALL | Leading out from Plaza Prat is this pedestrian mall with wooden sidewalks. This is a great place for an afternoon stroll past some of Iquique's *salitrera*-era mansions or for a leisurely cappuccino in one of the many sidewalk cafés. An antique trolley runs the length of the mall. ☒ *Iquique.*

★ Humberstone
GHOST TOWN | One of the last nitrate plants in the region, Humberstone closed in 1960 after operating for nearly 100 years. Now it's a ghost town where ancient machines creak and groan in the wind. You can wander through the central square and along the streets of the company town, where almost all of the original buildings survive. The theater, with its rows of empty seats, is particularly eerie. Take the time to explore beyond the residential area, heading out into the desert where the machines lie rusting in the wind. ☒ *45 km (28 miles) east of Iquique on the Pan-American Hwy., Iquique* 🖼 *4000 pesos.*

Museo Corbeta Esmeralda
HISTORY MUSEUM | Located on a beautifully maintained historical naval ship, this museum is a highlight in Iquique as the long lines will tell you. Professional and passionate guides detail the inner workings of the ship and its important role in Chile's history and the 1879 battle of the War of the Pacific. ☒ *Av. Arturo Prat Chacón, Paseo Almirante Lynch, Iquique* ☎ *57/253–0812* ⊕ *www.museoesmeralda.cl* 🖼 *2500 pesos (3500 if group is larger than 12 or if booked through a tour operator)* ⊗ *Closed Mon. in Mar.–Dec.*

Museo Regional de Iquique
HISTORY MUSEUM | Along the historic Calle Baquedano is this natural history museum of the Tarapacá region. It displays paleontological collections, pre-Columbian cultures, and archaeological artifacts such as arrowheads, as well as an eclectic collection from the region's nitrate heyday. Also on display are war artifacts from the Pacific and Aymara ethnographic collections from the Isluga territory. Every month the museum has exhibits of modern local art. ☒ *Baquedano 951, Iquique* ☎ *57/252–3653* ⊕ *www.registromuseoschile.cl* 🖼 *Free* ⊗ *Closed Sun.*

Palacio Astoreca
HISTORIC HOME | For a tantalizing view into the opulence of the nitrate era, visit this Georgian-style palace. Built in 1903, it includes highlights such as the likeness of Dionysus, the Greek god of revelry; a giant billiard table; and a beautiful skylight over the central hall. An art- and natural-history museum on the upper level houses rotating exhibitions by Chilean artists and artifacts such as pottery and textiles. ☒ *Av. Bernardo O'Higgins 350, Iquique* ☎ *2/2937–5100* ⊕ *www.patrimonio.bienes.cl/patrimonio/palacio-astoreca* 🖼 *Free* ⊗ *Closed Mon.*

Plaza Prat
PLAZA/SQUARE | Life in the city revolves around this plaza, where children ride bicycles along the sidewalks and adults chat on nearly every park bench. The

1877 **Torre Reloj,** with its gleaming white clock tower and Moorish arches, stands in the center of the plaza. ✉ *Iquique.*

Teatro Municipal

PERFORMANCE VENUE | Unlike most cities, Iquique does not have a cathedral on the main plaza. Instead, you'll find the sumptuous Teatro Municipal, built in 1890 as an opera house. The lovely statues on the Corinthian-columned facade represent the four seasons. ✉ *Plaza Prat, Iquique* ☎ *57/241–1292* 🎫 *Free.*

Beaches

Playa Blanca

BEACH | Thirteen km (8 miles) south of the city center on Avenida Balmaceda, Playa Blanca is a sandy spot that you can often have all to yourself and enjoy the active sealife. **Amenities:** food and drink; parking. **Best for:** snorkeling; swimming. ✉ *Iquique.*

Playa Brava

BEACH | If you crave privacy, head south on Avenida Balmaceda to Playa Brava, a pretty beach that's often deserted except for young people lighting bonfires in the evening. The currents here are quite strong, so swimming is not recommended. **Amenities:** food and drink; parking; toilets. **Best for:** sunset; surfing. ✉ *Iquique.*

★Playa Cavancha

BEACH | **FAMILY** | Just south of the city center on Avenida Balmaceda is Playa Cavancha, a long stretch of white, sandy beach that's great for families and often crowded. You can stroll along the boardwalk and touch the llamas and alpacas at the petting zoo. There's also a walk-through aquarium housing a group of *yacares,* small crocodiles that inhabit the rivers of Bolivia, Argentina, and Uruguay. **Amenities:** food and drink; showers; toilets. **Best for:** partiers; surfing; swimming. ✉ *Iquique.*

Restaurants

Club Nautico Cavancha

$$$ | **SEAFOOD** | Located away from the center of the city, this seafood restaurant treats you to views of Playa Cavancha. Try the sole in Cleopatra sauce, with shrimp, capers, and olive oil; the Thai-style sautéed shrimp; or the paella for two, served by friendly bow-tied waiters. **Known for:** hearty stews; great views; local seafood. [$] *Average main: pesos12000* ✉ *Los Rieles 110, Iquique* ☎ *57/243–6015.*

★La Mulata

$$ | **PERUVIAN** | This hip eatery creatively combines Peruvian, Japanese, and Chilean flavors in dishes served straight on the waterfront. You can expect Chilean classics like ceviche and empanadas as well as Peruvian and Nikkea staples of *lomo saltado* and rich seafood broth. **Known for:** top-notch cocktails; Asian and Southern American fusion dishes; sunset views. [$] *Average main: pesos9000* ✉ *Av. Arturo Prat Chacon 902, Iquique* ☎ *57/247–3727* 🌐 *www.lamulata.cl* 🕒 *No lunch Sun.*

Hotels

Hotel Terrado Arturo Prat

$ | **HOTEL** | In the heart of Iquique's historic district, the highlight of this modern hotel is a very pleasant rooftop pool area decorated with white umbrellas and navy-blue sails. **Pros:** lovely pool area; central location; friendly staff. **Cons:** small gym; some rooms nicer than others; noise from plaza travels. [$] *Rooms from: pesos58000* ✉ *Anibal Pinto 695, Iquique* ☎ *57/236–3134* 🌐 *www.terrado.cl* 🛏 *175 rooms* 🍴 *Free Breakfast.*

Terrado Suites

$$$ | **HOTEL** | A skyscraper at the southern end of Playa Cavancha, the Terrado is in a great location for Iquique. **Pros:** good breakfast; everything you'd need in one place; on the beach with pool. **Cons:** a bit run-down; pricey restaurant; poor Wi-Fi. [$] *Rooms from: pesos88500* ✉ *Los*

Rieles 126, Iquique ☎ *600/582–0500* ⊕ *www.terrado.cl* ⤢ *98 rooms* ¶ *Free Breakfast.*

Nightlife

Iquique really gets going after dark. Young vacationers stay out all night and then spend the next day lazing around on the beach.

BARS
Bar Sovia
BARS | This bar is popular with a wide range of ages thanks to live music, dancing, and lots of different beers on tap. ✉ *Vivar 1406, Iquique* ☎ *57/242–1373.*

DANCE CLUBS
At about 2 am, the beachfront discos start filling with a young, energetic crowd. Check out the dance clubs along Playa Brava and just south of town.

Shopping

Zona Franca
MALL | Many Chileans come to Iquique with one thing on their minds—shopping. About 3 km (2 miles) north of the city center is the Zona Franca—known to locals as the Zofri—the only duty-free zone in the country's northern tip. This big, unattractive mall is stocked with cheap cigarettes, alcohol, and electronic goods. Remember that large purchases, such as personal computers, are taxable upon leaving the country. ✉ *Av. Salitrera Victoria, Iquique* ☎ *57/515–100* ⊕ *www. zofri.cl.*

Mamiña

125 km (78 miles) east of Iquique.

An oasis cut from the brown desert, the tiny village of Mamiña has hundreds of hot springs. Renowned throughout Chile for their curative powers, these springs draw people from around the region. Every hotel in town has the thermal water pumped into its rooms, so you can enjoy a soak in the privacy of your own *tina,* or bathtub. The valley also has several public pools fed by thermal springs. The town itself is perched on a rocky cliff above a terraced green valley where locals grow alfalfa.

GETTING HERE AND AROUND
Mamiña is 125 km (78 miles) from Iquique proper: go back to Ruta 5, and head south briefly before taking Ruta A-65 directly east into Mamiña. If you'd also like to see Tambillo (a resting spot on the Inca trail), take the turnoff for Ruta A-651. There are also (admittedly uncomfortable) minivans that head to Mamiña from Iquique.

Sights

Most directions in town are given in relation to the Mamiña bottling plant, which produces the popular mineral drinking water sold in many Chilean shops.

Pukara del Cerro Inca
RUINS | A two-hour hike from Mamiña will bring you here, a great place to watch the sunset. You'll find interesting petroglyphs left by the Incas and an excellent view of the valley. To find it, head west on the trail a block west of the bottler. ✉ *Mamiña.*

Termas Mamiña
HOT SPRING | Ipla is the hottest of the *termas* (thermal baths) with a direct channel of thermal water practically going straight to the large public baths. The Barros El Chino is where you can relax covered in therapeutic mud, bake it off on the drying rack, and then wash clean in the plunge pools. There are basic changing facilities, showers, and a snack bar. ✉ *Near Mamiña bottler, Mamiña* 🖭 *2000 pesos.*

Vertiente del Radium
FOUNTAIN | This fountain near the Baños Ipla has slightly radioactive spring water (because it occurs naturally, it's fine to bathe in but not drink), which is said to cure every type of eye malady. ✉ *Mamiña.*

Pica

114 km (71 miles) southeast of Iquique.

From a distance, Pica appears to be a mirage. This oasis cut from the gray and brown sand of the Atacama Desert is known for its fruit—the limes used to make pisco sours are grown here. A hint of citrus hangs in the air because the town's chief pleasure is sitting in the Plaza de Armas and sipping a *jugo natural,* fresh-squeezed juice of almost any fruit imaginable, including mangoes, oranges, and passion fruit. You can buy a bag of them from a vendor for the bus trip back to Iquique. Be sure to try the mango sour (a variation of the traditional pisco sour) made from Chile's pastilla mangos.

Sights

Cocha Resbaladero

HOT SPRING | Most people come to Pica not for the town itself but for the incredible hot springs at Cocha Resbaladero. Tropical green foliage surrounds this lagoonlike pool cut out of the rock, and nearby caves beckon to be explored. It is quite a walk, about 2 km (1 mile) north of town, but well worth the effort. You can also drive here or catch a bus from town. ✉ *Gen. Ibañez, Pica* ☎ 🎟 *3000 pesos* 🕒 *Closed Wed.*

Restaurants

El Pomelo

$ | **CHILEAN** | You'll find simple, homemade food at good prices here at El Pomelo. The fresh juices are particularly worth trying. **Known for:** large portions; tasty fresh juices; good value Chilean food. [$] *Average main: pesos5000* ✉ *Maipu, at Bolivar, Pica* ☎ *9/9894–3134.*

Yatiri

$$ | **CHILEAN** | Abundant dishes of northern Chilean cuisine at Yatiri make for a great and affordable meal in Pica. Expect roast meats, colorful salads, and fresh seafood. **Known for:** friendly service; standard northern Chilean cuisine; rich stews. [$] *Average main: pesos6000* ✉ *Balmaceda 319, Pica* ☎ *9/743–0097.*

Reserva Nacional Pampa del Tamarugal

96 km (60 miles) southeast of Iquique.

This large forest in the middle of the desert is a unique sight. One of the highlights of the Reserva is the enormous geoglyphs that were created 500–1,500 years ago in the Cerros Pintados.

GETTING HERE AND AROUND

From Iquique, drive to the Pan-American Highway and head south. The entrance, which is 2 km east of the highway, lies 24 km (15 miles) south of Pozo Almonte. There is a CONAF kiosk on a dirt road 2 km (1 mile) west of the Pan-American Highway.

Sights

★ **Cerros Pintados** (*Painted Hills*)

RUINS | The amazing Cerros Pintados, the largest group of geoglyphs in the world, within the Reserva Nacional Pampa del Tamarugal are well worth a detour. These figures, which scientists believe helped ancient peoples navigate the desert, date from AD 500 to 1400. They are also quite enormous—some of the figures are decipherable only from the air. Drawings of men wearing ponchos were probably intended to point out the route to the coast to the llama caravans coming from the Andes. More than 400 figures of birds, animals, and geometric patterns adorn this 4-km (3-mile) stretch of desert. ✉ *45 km (28 miles) south of Pozo Almonte* ☎ *57/275–1055* 🎟 *4000 pesos.*

Reserva Nacional Pampa del Tamarugal

NATURE PRESERVE | The tamarugo tree is an anomaly in the almost lifeless desert. These bushlike plants survive where

Geoglyphs of the Atacama Desert

In addition to the Gigante de Atacama, the world's largest anthropomorphic geoglyph at 86 meters (282 feet) high, there are geoglyphs throughout El Norte Grande. The rock art at Cerros Pintados comprises the largest collection of geoglyphs in South America. Geoglyphs are man-made designs, in which the *addition* of materials arrange patterns, shapes, animals, or people. Petroglyphs are designs made by *elimination*of materials, most commonly rock carvings.

At the Reserva Nacional Pampa del Tamarugal, more than 400 images adorn the hillside. Figures representing birds, animals, people, and geometric patterns appear to dance along the mountain slope. Farther north, Tiliviche geoglyphs decorate a hill sitting not far from the modern-day marvel of the Pan-American Highway. These geoglyphs, most likely constructed between AD 1000 and 1400 during the Inca reign, depict a large caravan of llamas. All of these llamas are headed in the same direction—toward the sea—a testament, perhaps, to the geoglyphs' navigational use during the age when llama trains brought silver down to the coast in exchange for fish.

most would wither because they are especially adapted to the saline soil of the Atacama. Over time they developed extensive root systems that search for water deep beneath the almost impregnable surface. Reserva Nacional Pampa del Tamarugal has dense groves of tamarugos, which were almost wiped out during the nitrate era when they were felled for firewood. ⊠ *24 km (15 miles) south of Pozo Almonte on Pan-American Hwy* ☎ *57/275–1055* 🖦 *Free.*

Gigante de Atacama

84 km (52 miles) northeast of Iquique.

Although there are more than 5,000 geoglyphs in the Atacama, this one is the most iconic. The Gigante de Atacama is an 86-meter depiction of a giant man (or perhaps Pachamama, otherwise known as Mother Earth) that looks like a computer-game character from the 1980s. Of course, this geoglyph is far older—most likely dating back to AD 900—and was created by the area's Indigenous peoples.

GETTING HERE AND AROUND
To get here from Iquique, head north on Ruta 5, take Ruta A-483 toward Chusmiza (east), then turn west at Huara, and travel for 14 km (8 miles).

Sights

★ **Gigante de Atacama**

RUINS | The world's largest anthropomorphic geoglyph, the Gigante de Atacama, measures an incredible 86 meters (282 feet). The Giant of the Atacama is a depiction of a giant man, perhaps an Incan chief or shaman, that with his square head looks a bit like a video game space alien. It is adorned with a walking staff, a cat mask, and a feathered headdress that resembles rays of light bursting from his head. The exact age of the figure is unknown, but it certainly hails from before the arrival of the Spanish, perhaps around AD 900. The geoglyph, which is on a hill, is best viewed just before dusk, when the long shadows make the outline clearer. ⊠ *Cerro Unita, 14 km (8 miles) west of turnoff to Chusmiza* ☎ 🖦 *Free.*

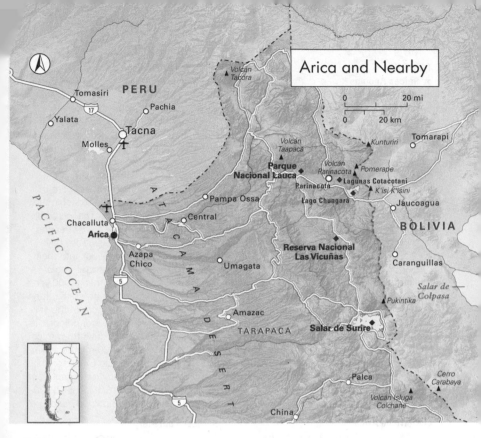

Arica

301 km (187 miles) north of Iquique.

Arica boasts that it is "the land of the eternal spring," but its temperate climate and beaches are not the only reason to visit this small city. Relax for an hour or two on the Plaza 21 de Mayo. Walk to the pier and watch the pelicans and sea lions trail the fishing boats as the afternoon's catch comes in. Walk to the top of the Morro and imagine battles of days gone by, or wonder at the magnitude of modern shipping as Chilean goods leave the port below by container ship.

GETTING HERE AND AROUND

Arica is a true international crossroads: planes arrive daily from Santiago (via Sky and LATAM airlines), buses pull in from La Paz, and colectivos laden with four passengers head in both directions for Tacna and the Peruvian border. The airport is about 15 minutes north of town (a taxi fare is about 7,000 pesos). The bus terminal is a quick five-minute taxi ride to downtown. Vans leave in the morning from Patricio Lynch if you want a local's experience of getting to Putre; you can also take colectivos there for a bargain rate (about US$1) to the museum out in Azapa Valley (a 15- to 20-minute ride). Arica is about four or five hours north of Iquique by car or bus (300 km [187 miles]) and the journey through the canyon lands is spectacular.

AIR Arica Chacalluta Airport (ARI). ✉ *Ruta 12 3150, Arica* ☎ *58/221–2773.*

ESSENTIALS

VISITOR INFORMATION Sernatur, Chilean Tourism. ✉ *San Marcos 101, Arica* ☎ *58/225–2054.*

TOURS

★ Raíces Andinas

DRIVING TOURS | This excellent family-run business is a reliable, professional choice for trips at high altitude, including Parque Nacional Lauca. Trips range from single-day to 15-day expeditions and most include lunch and a guide. Multiday trips often begin with a sensory trip to the market Terminal Agropecuario Arica to sample and select provisions. ✉ *Héroes del Morro 632, Arica* ⊕ *raicesandinas. com/en* 🖃 *From 40000 pesos.*

Sights

Aduana de Arica

NOTABLE BUILDING | Across from the Parque General Baquedano, the Aduana de Arica, the city's former customs house, is one of Alexandre Gustave Eiffel's creations. It currently contains the town's cultural center, where you can find exhibits about northern Chile, old photographs of Arica, and works by local painters and sculptors. ✉ *Arica* 🏛 🖃 *Free.*

El Morro de Arica

MILITARY SIGHT | Hanging over the town, this fortress is impossible to ignore. This former Peruvian stronghold was the site of one of the key battles in the War of the Pacific. The fortress now houses the **Museo de las Armas**, which commemorates that battle. As you listen to the proud drum roll of military marches, you can wander among the uniforms and weapons of past wars. ✉ *Reached by footpath from Calle Colón, Arica* 🖃 *600 pesos.*

Iglesia de San Marcos

CHURCH | Located on the Plaza Colón, the Iglesia de San Marcos was erected in 1876 and constructed entirely from iron. Alexandre Gustave Eiffel, designer of that famed eponymous Parisian tower, had the individual pieces cast in France before bringing them to Arica. ✉ *Arica.*

★ Museo Arqueológico de San Miguel de Azapa

HISTORY MUSEUM | A visit here is a must for anyone who travels to El Norte Grande. In an 18th-century olive oil refinery, this museum houses an impressive collection of artifacts from the cultures of the Chinchorros (a coastal people) and Tijuanacotas (a group that lived in the antiplano). Of particular interest are the Chinchorro mummies, the oldest in the world, dating to 6000 BC. The incredibly well-preserved mummies are arranged on beds behind thick glass. They have a great presence, and to look into their expressive faces is to glimpse into a history that spans more than 8,000 years. The tour ends at an olive press that functioned until 1956, a reminder of the still thriving industry in the surrounding valley. The museum is a short drive from Arica. You can also make the 20-minute journey by colectivo from Patricio Lynch for about 1,200 pesos. ✉ *12 km (7 miles) south of town en route to Putre, Arica* ☎ *58/220– 5555* ⊕ *masma.uta.cl* 🖃 *2000 pesos.*

★ Museo del Mar

OTHER MUSEUM | This museum houses a well-maintained and colorful collection of more than 1,000 seashells and oceanic oddities from around the world. The owner has traveled the globe for more than 30 years to bolster his collection, which includes specimens from Africa, Asia, and you guessed it—Arica. ✉ *Pasaje Sangra 315, Arica* ⊕ *www.museodelmardearica.cl* 🖃 *3000 pesos* ☾ *Closed Sun.*

Beaches

Part of the reason people flock to Arica is the beaches. The surf can be quite rough in some spots, so look for—and heed— signs that say "no apta para bañarse" ("no swimming").

Playa Brava

BEACH | The long stretch of Playa Brava is renowned for its consistent waves (which are too strong for swimming) and beautiful sunsets. **Amenities:** parking. **Best for:** solitude; sunset; surfing. ⊠ *Arica.*

Playa Chinchorro

BEACH | **FAMILY** | The white sands of Playa Chinchorro, 2 km (1 mile) north of the city are popular with families and swimmers. You can also rent Jet Skis in high season. **Amenities:** food and drink; parking; toilets. **Best for:** swimming. ⊠ *Arica.*

Playa El Laucho

BEACH | **FAMILY** | South of El Morro, Playa El Laucho is the closest to the city, and thus the most crowded. It's also a bit rocky at the bottom, but waters are calm and inviting. **Amenities:** food and drink; lifeguards; parking; showers; toilets. **Best for:** swimming. ⊠ *Arica.*

🍴 Restaurants

El Rey de Mariscos

$$ | **SEAFOOD** | Locals love this seafood restaurant, and for good reason. The *corvina con salsa margarita* (sea bass in a seafood-based sauce) is a winner, as is the *paila marina*, a hearty soup stocked with all manner of fish. **Known for:** great ceviche; affordable seafood dishes; down-to-earth ambience. $ *Average main: pesos8500* ⊠ *Colon 565, 2nd fl., Arica* ☎ *58/229–4315* ⊕ *facebook.com/mariscosarica.*

★ Maracuyá

$$$$ | **SEAFOOD** | Wicker furniture enhances the cool South Pacific atmosphere of this pleasant, open-air restaurant that literally sits above the water on stilts. The seafood, lauded by locals, is always fresh; ask the waiter what the fishing boats brought in that day. **Known for:** sea bass with pineapple; seaside views; international cuisine with a focus on seafood. $ *Average main: pesos15000* ⊠ *Av. Comandante San Martin 0321, Arica* ☎ *58/222–7600.*

Hotels

Hotel Arica

$$ | **HOTEL** | **FAMILY** | Sitting on the ocean between Playa El Laucho and Playa Las Liseras, this hotel has a sense of somewhat faded grandeur with elegant but dated rooms, although the views of the ocean are top-notch and the staff are courteous and attentive. **Pros:** good breakfast; beautiful setting; nice restaurant. **Cons:** a bit worn and scruffy; far from downtown; somewhat dated. $ *Rooms from: pesos75000* ⊠ *Av. Comandante San Martin 599, Arica* ☎ *58/225–4540* ⊕ *www.panamericanahoteles.cl* ⇨ *148 rooms* ⊠ *Free Breakfast.*

Hotel Aruma

$$$ | **HOTEL** | This modern boutique hotel is located in the city center and has minimalist furnishings with a splash of color in the comfortable communal spaces and outdoor sun terrace and pool. **Pros:** comfy beds; central location; modern amenities and decor. **Cons:** small closet space; no elevator; rooms are a little small. $ *Rooms from: pesos88000* ⊠ *Calle Patricio Lynch 530, Arica* ☎ *58/225–0000* ⊕ *www.aruma.cl* ⇨ *16 rooms* ⊠ *Free Breakfast.*

🍸 Nightlife

You can join the locals for a beer at one of the cafés lining the pedestrian mall of 21 de Mayo. These low-key establishments, many with outdoor seating, are great places to spend afternoons watching the passing crowds.

Discoteca SoHo

DANCE CLUBS | Located near Playa Chinchorro, Discoteca SoHo livens things up on weekends with the sounds of pop and cumbia. ⊠ *Buenos Aires 209, Arica* ☎ *9/8905–1806.*

Lago Chungará is surrounded by mountains, lush vegetation, and alpacas.

Shopping

Calle Bolognesi
CRAFTS | This street is crowded with artisan stalls that sell handmade goods. ✉ *Bolognesi, Arica.*

Calle Chacabuco
MARKET | The length of Calle Chacabuco is closed to traffic on Sunday for a market featuring everything from soccer jerseys to crafts. ✉ *Chacabuco, Arica.*

Calle 21 de Mayo
NEIGHBORHOODS | This is a good street for window-shopping. ✉ *21 de Mayo, Arica.*

Feria Internacional
MIXED CLOTHING | This shop on Calle Máximo Lira sells everything from bowler hats (worn by Aymara women) to blankets to batteries. The Terminal Pesquero next door offers an interesting view of fishing, El Norte Grande's predominant industry. ✉ *Maximo Lira, Arica.*

Poblado Artesenal
CRAFTS | Located outside the city in the Azapa Valley, the Poblado Artesenal is an artisan cooperative designed to resemble an altiplano community. This is a good place to pick up traditionally styled ceramics and leather. ✉ *Hualles, Arica.*

Parque Nacional Lauca

47 km (29 miles) southeast of Putre.

The Parque Nacional Lauca offers dramatic landscapes and eye-catching wildlife. Stunning volcanic landscapes and colorful desert scrubland are dotted with llamas, flamingos, and all sorts of flora.

GETTING HERE AND AROUND
Follow the CH-11 International Highway out of Arica toward Bolivia. Just after the town of Putre, take the right-hand turn toward Palca. The park entrance lies 47 km (29 miles) southeast of Putre.

⊙ Sights

★ Lago Chungará

BODY OF WATER | A contender for the best viewpoint in Chile, this roadside lake sits on the Bolivian border at an amazing altitude of 4,600 m (15,100 feet) above sea level. Volcán Parinacota, at 6,330 m (20,889 feet), casts its shadow onto the lake's glassy surface. Hundreds of flamingos make their home here. There is a CONAF-run office at Lago Chungará on the highway just before the lake. ⊠ *From Ruta 11, turn north on Ruta A-123* 🖅 ⊕ *www.conaf.cl* ✉ *Free.*

★ Lagunas Cotacotani

BODY OF WATER | About 8 km (5 miles) east of Parinacota is the beautiful Laguna Cotacotani, which means "land of many lakes" in the Quechua language. This string of ponds—surrounded by a desolate moonscape formed by volcanic eruptions—attracts many species of bird, including Andean geese.

★ Parinacota

TOWN | Within the park, off Ruta 11, is the altiplano village of Parinacota, one of the most beautiful in all of Chile. In the center of the village, among houses made of adobe with thatched roofs, sits the white-washed Iglesia Parinacota, dating from 1789. Inside are murals depicting sinners and saints and a mysterious "walking table," which parishioners have chained to the wall for fear that it will steal away in the night. An interesting Aymara cultural commentary can be found in the Stations of the Cross, which depict Christ's tormenters not as Roman soldiers, but as Spanish conquistadors. Opposite the church you'll find crafts stalls run by Aymara women in the colorful shawls and bowler hats worn by many altiplano women. Only 18 people live in the village, but many more make a pilgrimage here for annual festivals such as the Fiesta de las Cruces, held on May 3, and the Fiesta de la Virgen de la Canderlaria, a three-day romp that begins on February 2.

★ Parque Nacional Lauca

NATIONAL PARK | On a plateau more than 4,000 meters (13,120 feet) above sea level, the magnificent Parque Nacional Lauca shelters flora and fauna found in few other places in the world, and rivals even Torres del Paine for its beauty. Cacti, grasses, and a brilliant emerald-green moss called *llareta* dot the landscape. Playful *vizcacha*—rabbitlike rodents with long tails—laze in the sun, and llamas, graceful vicuñas, and alpacas make their home here as well. About 10 km (6 miles) into the park is a CONAF station with informative brochures. ⊠ *Off Ruta 11* 🖅 *58/220–1201 in Arica* ⊕ *www.conaf. cl* ✉ *Free.*

Reserva Nacional Las Vicuñas

121 km (75 miles) southeast of Putre.

This 100-km (62-mile) reserve is filled with vicuñas that graze in the high plains near the blue alpine lakes. There are also volcanoes in the distance and salt flats in the forefront.

GETTING HERE AND AROUND

From the town of Putre, follow the international highway to Bolivia for a few kilometers, then take the turn southeast on an unpaved road that leads to the Lauca National Park. The entrance to the Las Vicuñas National Reserve lies 121 km (75 miles) past Putre.

⊙ Sights

★ Reserva Nacional Las Vicuñas

NATURE PRESERVE | Although it attracts far fewer visitors than neighboring Parque Nacional Lauca, Reserva Nacional Las Vicuñas contains some incredible sights—salt flats, high plains, and alpine lakes. And you can enjoy the vistas without running into buses full of tourists. The reserve, which stretches some 100 km (62 miles), has a huge herd of graceful vicuñas. Although quite similar to their larger cousins, llamas and alpacas, vicuñas have not been domesticated. Their incredibly soft wool, among the most prized in the world, led to so much hunting that these creatures were threatened with extinction, and today it is illegal to kill a vicuña. Getting to this reserve, unfortunately, is quite a challenge. There is no public transportation, and the roads are passable only in four-wheel-drive vehicles. Many people choose to take a tour out of Arica. ✉ *From Ruta 11, take Ruta A-21 south to park headquarters* ⊕ *www.conaf.cl.*

Salar de Surire

126 km (78 miles) southeast of Putre.

From a distance, Surire looks like a giant white lake, but as you approach you'll see the small white crystals of salt that define this intriguing nature spot.

Sights

Salar de Surire

NATURE SIGHT | After passing through the high plains, where you'll spot vicuña, alpaca, and the occasional desert fox, you'll catch your first glimpse of the sparkling Salar de Surire. Seen from a distance, the salt flat appears to be a giant white lake. Unlike its southern neighbor, the Salar de Atacama, it's completely flat. Three of the four New World flamingos (Andean, Chilean, and James's) live in the nearby lakes. ✉ *South from Reserva Nacional Las Vicuñas on Ruta A-235* ⊕ *www.conaf.cl* 🎫 *Free.*

Chapter 7

THE CENTRAL VALLEY

7

Updated by
Mark Johanson

⊙ Sights	🍴 Restaurants	🛏 Hotels	💼 Shopping	🍸 Nightlife
★★★★☆	★★★★☆	★★★★☆	★★☆☆☆	★★☆☆☆

WELCOME TO THE CENTRAL VALLEY

TOP REASONS TO GO

★ **Wine tasting:** The Central Valley is the heart of Chile's wine country. Vineyards for both table and wine grapes cover the landscape—in fact, the Pan-American Highway runs through some of the longest continuous vineyards in the world. There is ample opportunity to taste Chile's most famous export, too, from full-bodied reds that pair great with an *asado* (cookout) to crisp whites sipped right by the hotel pool.

★ **Rowdy rodeos:** The Central Valley is also home to the *huaso,* a cousin of the Argentine gaucho. Huasos, in their typical flat-topped, wide-brimmed hats, are a common sight around Rancagua, where they flock to the national Medialuna (rodeo arena) for their favorite sport.

★ **Scenic countryside:** The Central Valley is not limited to vineyards. Rivers and lakes lie between hillsides dotted with cactus and fruit trees. East in the Andean countryside, dirt roads weave the high mountaintops, passing gem-colored waterfalls and refreshing swimming holes.

Geographically speaking, the Central Valley isn't really a valley at all, but rather an "Intermediate Depression" between two mountain ranges—the Andes to the east, and the Coastal Range to the west. The two run parallel through much of Chile but create a particularly fertile flatland south of Santiago that runs all the way to the Bío Bío.

The large Central Valley is divided into the four subregions: the Maipo Valley (Santiago sits in its center), the Rapel Valley (divided into Cachapoal and Colchagua), the Curicó Valley (around the city of Curicó), and the Maule Valley (south from Talca).

1 Rancagua. Historic and commercial center that is ground zero for Chile's rodeo culture.

2 San Fernando and Nearby. Gateway to the Colchagua Valley surrounded by popular wineries and natural attractions.

3 Santa Cruz. Chic destination with luxury lodgings and top Colchagua Valley wineries.

4 Curicó. The city's charming plaza fills with excitement and grape stomping each April for one of the country's most traditional wine fests. If wine's not your thing, try camping at Radal Siete Tazas National Park.

5 Lago Vichuquén. Popular kayaking and paddleboarding destination with upscale resorts.

6 Talca. The capital of Maule, Chile's largest wine valley. Its O'Higginiano Museum and the Villa Huilquilemu beautifully portray the area's cultural heritage.

Quillota

Valparaíso

Quilpué

VALPARAÍSO

57

5

Colina

Algarrobo

Isla Negra

Maipo Valley

68

SANTIAGO

San Antonio

Talagante

San Bernardo

Melipilla

78

Puente Alto

Buin

REGIÓN METROPOLITANA
DE SANTIAGO

Rancagua

1

Pichilemu

Peumo

5

Rapel Valley

LIBERTADOR GENERAL
BERNARDO O'HIGGINS

2

San
Fernando

Santa Cruz

3

Lago Vichuquén
(Vichuquén Lake)

5

Curicó Valley

Curicó

Hualañé

4

PACIFIC OCEAN

Constitución

6

Talca

Radal Siete Tazas
National Park

Malargüe

MAULE
Maule Valley

0   50 mi

0   50 km

Cauquenes

Linares

5

Quirihue

Talcahuano

Chillán

San Pedro
de la Paz

Concepción

Chiguayante

BÍO-BÍO

ARGENTINA

Coronel

Lota

Curanilahue

Chos Malal

Lebu

Los Ángeles

Santa Barbara

Angol

5

Collipulli

ANDES

Victoria

ARAUCANÍA

Lonquimay

Las Lajas

40

40

The Central Valley is the most abundant valley in Chile, not just for fruit and grape production, but also for its wealth of opportunities for adventure: hiking the Andes, steaming in thermal pools, scaling rocks, or heli-skiing down snowy slopes. At the coast, you can tan on the lovely beaches, surf world-class waves, and nosh on outstanding seafood. In between, indulge in some of the finest wines South America has to offer while enjoying the laid-back charm of rural life.

Above all else, this is Chile's agricultural heartland. The rich soil benefits from ample spring melt-water for irrigation and long, warm, and dry summers. Grapes especially thrive, and wine has been an important product in much of the Central Valley for the past four centuries.

The Central Valley is a straight shot down the Pan-American Highway between the volcanic cones of the Andes on the east and the lower Coastal Mountains to the west. As you head south, the arid foliage of short, scrubby native bushes gives way to verdant pastures and thick pine and eucalyptus forests.

It's about a five-hour drive straight south from Santiago to Chillán and nearly another hour west to Concepción, but plan to stop and explore along the way. Most valleys have Wine Route (Ruta del Vino) associations, which are happy to help visitors plan tours of the wineries, as are most hotels.

MAJOR REGIONS

The Rapel Valley may be wine country, but it's also rodeo country, home of the Chilean huasos, known for their wide-brimmed hats and jaunty smiles. You'll see them riding horses on the country roads that lead to Chile's top wineries. The valley is divided into two wine appellations, Cachapoal and Rancagua to the north and Santa Cruz and Colchagua to the south.

The Curicó Valley may play second fiddle to Colchagua in terms of glamour, but it is a sizable region with both natural and vinous delights ready to be discovered between the mountains and coast. With several Andean parks and reserves, plus the serene Lago Vichuquén, there are plenty of outdoor sports to keep the adrenaline flowing between a few glasses of the region's famed Cabernet Sauvignon.

Dozens of wineries are scattered throughout Chile's largest wine region, **Maule Valley**, which begins north of Talca in San Rafael and extends south to the regional border at the Perquilauquén River, just south of Parral. Most are roughly grouped into two areas: east of the highway around San Clemente, or slightly west of the highway around San Javier and Villa Alegre. Long ignored as backward, Maule is now an up-and-coming region, as insightful winemakers have discovered its value in producing excellent red wines with some of the oldest vines in the Americas. Scratch any surface in this subregion and find plenty of rural tradition and natural beauty.

Planning

When to Go

Timing your visit to the Central Valley really depends on what you want to do. January and February are peak summer vacation months in Chile, so parks are open and beaches are full. The weather is clear and sunny—cool on the mountains and coast, and quite hot in between—making this the best time for many outdoor activities. If winter sports are on the bucket list, it's best to come from June to September, although climate change is making the season more variable.

If wineries draw you to the Central Valley, consider that grapes are picked from late February through early April, depending on the varietal and area. This is certainly the best time to visit vineyards, since you can see everything from crushing to bottling. Visit on a weekend, and there's a good chance of joining one of the many harvest festivals that take place throughout the region at this time of year. But don't overlook a visit outside of harvest season, as wineries offer tastings and fun activities year-round.

FESTIVALS

The harvest season is the most important time of the year in wine country. Most of Chile's wine-producing regions mark the moment with a *Fiesta de la Vendimia*, or harvest festival, which take place in March and April. The biggest and most spectacular events are held in Colchagua and Curicó, including grape-stomping competitions and harvest-queen contests. Maule kicks off the season with its Carménère Festival in January, in honor of Chile's signature red wine grape.

Not every fiesta is wine related, of course. Catholic roots run deep here, and many traditional religious festivals remain, such as those in honor of San Pedro and San Pablo, the patron saints of fishermen (on June 29 in fishing villages all along the coast). San Sebastian, the much persecuted, arrow-pierced saint, draws thousands of devotees to Yumbel (68 km [42 miles] from Concepción) on January 20. And during the fiesta de San Francisco, held October 4 in the small colonial-era village of Huerta de Maule, 60 km (37 miles) southwest of Talca, more than 200 huasos gather from all over Chile for a day of horseback events, including races around the central square. Fiestas Patrias, Chile's independence day (September 18), spills into a week of festivities all over the country.

Getting Here and Around

BUS

The two big bus companies in the region, Pullman Bus and Turbus, offer regular departures that leave precisely on time from Santiago's Alameda Terminal bound for Rancagua, Talca, Curicó, Chillán, and Concepción. One-way fare from Santiago to Chillán runs about 10,000 pesos.

BUS CONTACTS Pullman del Sur. ⊠ *Camilo Henríquez 281, Curicó* ☎ *75/231–0387* ⊕ *www.pdelsur.cl.* **Turbus.** ⊠ *O'Carrol 1175, Rancagua* ☎ *72/224–1117* ⊕ *www. turbus.cl.*

CAR

Traveling by car is often the most convenient way to see the region. The Central Valley is sliced in half by Chile's main artery, the Pan-American Highway, also called Ruta 5, which passes through all of the major towns in the region. Be sure to have local cash on hand for the frequent tolls, which are rather high and increase on weekends and holidays.

TRAIN

The train remains an excellent way to travel through the Central Valley. Express trains from Estación Central in Santiago to the cities of Rancagua, Curicó, Talca, Chillán, and (occasionally) Concepción are comfortable and faster than taking the bus or driving. Keep in mind, however, that these cities are generally jumping-off points for attractions farther afield that will require either a car, taxi, or onward bus.

Restaurants

No matter where or when you eat in the Central Valley, a good bottle of local wine is likely to be on the table, so a couple of wine-related words will come in handy. *Vino* is the Spanish word for wine; red is *tinto* (never *rojo*) and white is *blanco*. Drink them by the *copa,* or wine glass, or take part in a more formal wine tasting, called *desgustación* or *cata.*

Central Valley cuisine consists of hearty fare based on locally raised beef and pork, served with local vegetables and followed by fruit-based desserts. These are always accompanied by regional—usually red—wine. Most Chileans eat a big lunch around 1 pm and have a light dinner late in the evening. If you want to try real, home-style Chilean cooking, your best bet is to follow suit and look for lunch at the same time. Afterward you may need to adopt the local siesta habit as well.

In the summer, look for popular favorites such as *porotos granados* (fresh cranberry beans with corn, squash, and basil), *humitas* (Chilean tamales) with fresh-sliced tomatoes, or *pastel de choclo* (a savory ground-beef base served in a clay bowl, sometimes with a piece of chicken, and always generously slathered with a rich grated corn topping). Desserts are often simply fresh fruits served in their own juice. Do watch for the refreshing *mote con huesillo* served cold as a drink or dessert. Begin by eating the *mote,* a type of wheat hominy; then slurp up the juice from the *huesillo,* a large dried peach, which serves as the final act of this three-course treat.

Restaurant reviews have been shortened. For full information, visit Fodors.com.

Hotels

Accommodation ranges from homey bed-and-breakfasts to beautiful old estancias, rustic-chic mountain lodges, and basic city hotels. While in wine country, you might want to opt for lodgings at the wineries themselves, whether in resorts, guesthouses, or boutique hotels.

Hotel reviews have been shortened. For full information, visit Fodors.com.

What It Costs in Chilean Pesos (in Thousands)			
$	$$	$$$	$$$$
RESTAURANTS			
Under 6	6–9	10–13	over 13
HOTELS			
Under 51	51–85	86–115	over 115

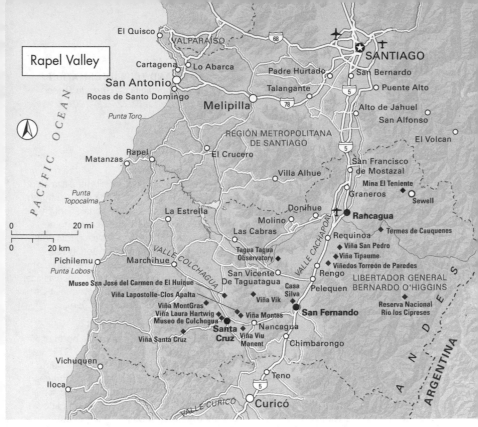

Tours

Most wineries in the Central Valley allow you to make your own direct booking, and the relatively easy-to-navigate road network makes renting a car a good option for you to get around. However, Chile has a zero tolerance law for drinking and driving, so booking a taxi for the day is often preferable, and safer. Alternatively, each of the agencies below organizes private and group tours to the different wine regions.

★ Wines and Barrels Travel

FOOD AND DRINK TOURS | Whether you want to visit the big players in Chilean wine or have an intimate experience with more boutique producers, this company has inside access to some of the most unique food and wine experts in the country. Most itineraries are day trips from Santiago and include a mix of wineries grouped around a common theme, though the team can also build multiday experiences across the Central Valley. ☎ *9/9018–3654* ⊕ *www.winesandbarrels. com* ✉ *Tours from US$150–300.*

Upscape

GUIDED TOURS | This tourism outfitter organizes wine tours from Santiago to the different wine routes either in full-day or multiday trips, the latter of which might be combined with skiing or cycling. Visits usually come with premium wine pours, your own bilingual guide, private transfer, and pickup from your hotel doorstep. ✉ *Tegualda 1352, Providencia* ☎ *2/2244–2750* ⊕ *www.upscapetravel. com* ✉ *From 193000 pesos.*

Rancagua

87 km (54 miles) south of Santiago along Pan-American Hwy.

In 1814, the hills around Rancagua were the site of a battle in the War of Independence known as the *Desastre de Rancagua* (Disaster of Rancagua). Chilean independence fighters, including Chile's independence leader Bernardo O'Higgins, held off the powerful Spanish army for two days before surrendering, but escaping to fight another day. In the resulting blaze, much of the town was destroyed.

Despite its historical significance and current importance as a regional commercial center, the city has relatively little to offer in terms of tourism. By all means, visit the historic area around the central plaza or take in a rodeo in the national *Medialuna,* or rodeo arena, but otherwise skip the city and head straight for one of the more interesting attractions outside of town such as a copper mine, hot spring, nature reserve, or winery.

GETTING HERE AND AROUND

Rancagua is a one-hour hop due south from Santiago by car or bus. It's a bit faster by train, and there are no options to fly (it's much too close anyway). Wheeled transport takes the Pan-American Highway, while rail options go beside it. Traffic heading out of Santiago is often sluggish, and delays due to roadwork are frequent, but the highway is generally in good condition and allows for speeds of 120 kph (75 mph) for most of the route.

BUS CONTACTS Terminal O'Higgins. ✉ *Libertador Bernardo O'Higgins 0484, Rancagua* ☎ *72/222–5425* ⊕ *www. terminalohiggins.cl.* **Terminal Rancagua.** ✉ *O'Carrol 1175, Rancagua* ☎ *72/224–1117.*

ESSENTIALS

VISITOR AND TOUR INFORMATION

Sernatur Rancagua. ✉ *German Riesco 350, Rancagua* ☎ *72/222–7261* ⊕ *www. sernatur.cl.*

 Sights

Iglesia de la Merced

CHURCH | A block north of the plaza along Calle Estado is this 18th-century church that was declared a national monument for its beauty and significance in the city's fateful history. It was in this bell tower that O'Higgins waited in vain for reinforcements during the Battle of Independence. The somber, neoclassical twin spires are a fitting memorial. ✉ *At Cuevas and Estado, Rancagua.*

Mina El Teniente and Sewell

MINE | High in the mountains north of Termas de Cauquenes, 60 km (37 miles) northeast of Rancagua, the El Teniente Mine is the world's largest subterranean copper mine, in operation since colonial times. In 1905 the city of Sewell, known as the "City of Stairs," was constructed at 2,130 meters (6,988 feet) above sea level to house miners. Abandoned in the early 1970s, Sewell was declared a UNESCO World Heritage site in 2006. Rancagua tour operator VTS offers guided tours of both the mine and the city every day (except Monday), with transport from Santiago or Rancagua. ✉ *Millán 1020, Rancagua* ☎ *72/295–2692 VTS* ⊕ *www.vts.cl* 💷 *From 44000 pesos.*

Museo Regional de Rancagua

HISTORY MUSEUM | This three-room museum re-creates a typical 18th-century home, complete with period furniture and religious artifacts. A small collection of 19th-century weaponry is the type that would have been used in the momentous Battle of Rancagua. Dioramas illustrate this dramatic moment in the country's quest for independence. The white-washed colonial building is a few blocks south of Plaza de los Héroes. ✉ *Estado*

Reserva Nacional Río los Cipreses has thick forests of cypress trees and views of the Andes.

685, at Ibieta, Rancagua ☎ *72/222–1524* 🌐 *www.museorancagua.gob.cl* ✉ *Free.*

Plaza de los Héroes

PLAZA/SQUARE | Today's Rancagüinos enjoy relaxing in the city's central square, the Plaza de los Héroes. A statue of the valiant war hero and future first president Bernardo O'Higgins on horseback stands proudly in the center of the plaza. Although each side of the statue base contains one of his famous sayings, curiously enough, there is nothing to indicate to visitors and newcomers that it is a statue of O'Higgins. ✉ *Plaza de los Heroes, Rancagua.*

Reserva Nacional Río los Cipreses

NATURE PRESERVE | Numerous short and moderate trails lead through thick forests of cypress trees at this 92,000-acre national reserve 50 km (31 miles) east of Rancagua. Some of the trails come to clearings where you are treated to spectacular views of the Andes above. CONAF, the national parks service, has an office here with informative displays and maps. Hiking, swimming, and horseback riding are all available, and you can camp overnight at well-run grounds. Just south of the park is the spot where a plane carrying Uruguayan university students crashed in 1972. The story of the group, some of whom survived three months in a harsh winter by resorting to cannibalism, was told in the book and film *Alive.* ✉ *Carretera del Cobre s/n, Rancagua* ☎ *72/220–4610* 🌐 *www.conaf. cl* ✉ *6200 pesos.*

Termas de Cauquenes

HOT SPRING | On the southern banks of the Río Cachapoal about 34 km (21 miles) east of Rancagua, the Termas de Cauquenes spout mineral-rich water that has been revered for its medicinal properties since colonial days. The Spanish discovered the 48°C (118°F) springs in the late 1500s, and basic visitor facilities have existed since the 1700s. José de San Martín, who masterminded the defeat of Spanish forces in Chile, is said to have relaxed here before beginning his campaign. Naturalist Charles Darwin, who visited in 1834, wrote that the springs were situated in "a quiet, solitary spot, with a good deal of wild beauty." Nowadays though, the Gothic-style bathhouse and accommodation are a little run-down and the view is interrupted by pipelines and a road mainly used by trucks heading to the nearby mine. To reach the springs, take Ruta 29 from Rancagua to Coya and then head south for 5 km (3 miles). ✉ *Termas de Cauquenes s/n, Machalí* ☎ *9/4246–1350* 🌐 *www.htdc.cl* 🎟 *Individual bath: 10,000 pesos, Individual whirlpool: 15,000, Jacuzzi (double) 25,000.*

Viña San Pedro

WINERY | One of Chile's most important wine exporters with bottles in 80 countries, Viña San Pedro makes its range of five fine wines (Altair, Cabo de Hornos, Sideral, Kankana del Elqui, and Tierras Moradas) at this striking gravity-flow facility 30 km (19 miles) south of Rancagua. Expect sweeping Andes views as you tour the property by foot or on a cycle through the vines. Both picnic lunches and full-on Chilean feasts are available with advanced reservation. ✉ *Fundo Totihue, Camino Pimpinela s/n, Rancagua* ☎ *2/2477–5300* 🌐 *www.sanpedro.cl* 🎟 *From 22,000 pesos* ✍ *Reservations essential.*

★Viña Tipaume

WINERY | A great counterpoint to the huge wine exporters is this small, biodynamic winery 34 km (21 miles) south of Rancagua. It's run by a lovely French-Chilean couple who were regional pioneers in aging wines in clay amphoras. Intimate tours end with a tasting in the subterranean wine cave. You can also sleep on-site at the small B&B (from US$80 per room) to wake up ensconced in the wild organically grown vines. ✉ *Cerrillo Bajo s/n, Rancagua* ☎ *9/6208–8347* 🌐 *www.tipaume.cl* 🎟 *Tours US$45* ✍ *Reservations required.*

Viñedos Torreón de Paredes

WINERY | Off-the-beaten-path Viñedos Torreón de Paredes has the soul of a small winery with the ambition of its larger counterparts up and down the Central Valley. Named for the 300-year-old adobe tower at its heart, the winery's tours take in the historic grounds and end with a tasting of either reserve or premium wines, most of which are made only for export. ✉ *Fundo Santa Teresa, Camino Las Nieves s/n, Rancagua* ☎ *9/9274–2137* 🌐 *www.torreon.cl* 🎟 *Tours from 18000* 🕒 *Closed Sun.* ✍ *Advanced reservations only.*

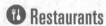

🍴 Restaurants

Juan y Medio

$$ | **CHILEAN** | **FAMILY** | On the north-bound side of the Pan-American Highway, between the towns of Requinoa and Rosario, this well-loved Chilean diner caters to hearty appetites. It began as a humble truck stop in 1946 and established a tremendous reputation for its trucker-size portions of Chilean favorites—whopping steaks and ribs grilled over a wood fire, slow-cooked *cazuelas,* and stews that leave you wanting nothing more than a hammock and a long nap. **Known for:** family-friendly atmosphere; large portions; Chilean dishes. [$] *Average main: pesos8000* ✉ *Ruta 5, Km 109, Rengo* ☎ *72/252–1726* 🌐 *www.juanymedio.cl.*

🛏 Hotels

Hotel Termas de Cauquenes

$$$$ | **HOTEL** | The main attractions of this hillside hotel are the mineral baths, the thermal swimming pool, and the peace and quiet. **Pros:** pleasant restaurant; thermal waters; peace and quiet. **Cons:** outdated hotel facilities; hard to access without car; simple rooms for the price. [$] *Rooms from: pesos200000* ✉ *Termas de Cauquenes s/n, Machalí* ☎ *9/4246–1351* 🌐 *www.htdc.cl* ⇆ *53 rooms* 🍴 *All-Inclusive.*

Noi Puma Lodge

$$$$ | **HOTEL** | This large mountain lodge set right in the middle of the Andes offers heli-skiing in winter and mountain treks in the summer. **Pros:** outdoor pool; peaceful location; valley views. **Cons:** poor road access; expensive; remote location requires 4x4 in winter. [$] *Rooms from: pesos175000* ✉ *Reserva Nacional Rio Los Cipreses, Fundo Sierra Nevada, Km 22, Rancagua* ☎ *2/2432–6800* 🌐 *www.noihotels.com* 🛏 *26 rooms* 🍴 *Free Breakfast.*

Activities

RODEO

National Rodeo Arena

RODEO | One of the great highlights of life in Rancagua includes excursions to the National Rodeo Arena: the *Medialuna Monumental,* especially in April, when it hosts the national championship. This is a great opportunity to glimpse huaso tradition in its full glory: horsemanship, riding, and cow-herding skills, traditional foods, crafts, music, and dance. ✉ *Av. German Ibarra 950, Rancagua* ☎ *2/2671–1501* 🌐 *www.caballoyrodeo.cl.*

San Fernando and Nearby

152 km (94 miles) south of Santiago.

San Fernando is surrounded by popular wineries, handsome hotels, colonial estancias, and beautiful nature spots. It makes a convenient stopping point alongside Ruta 5 with streets lined with fruit stands selling eye-catching citrus, melons, and ripe avocados. The gateway to Colchagua Valley, San Fernando has an attractive plaza and all the necessary conveniences, although the main attractions lie in the rural areas beyond city limits. West of San Fernando is where the wine route to Santa Cruz begins, but there is much to discover toward the Andes, too.

GETTING HERE AND AROUND

From Santiago, San Fernando is almost two hours by car, more than two hours by bus, and a bit faster by train. If you are moving farther south by public transport, you may have to stop off in San Fernando first to change buses at the terminal.

BUS CONTACTS San Fernando Terminal de Buses. ✉ *Manso de Velasco, (corner of Rancagua), San Fernando* ☎ *72/271–3912.*

Sights

Casa Silva

WINERY | The Silva family is a true wine dynasty of Chile, and the family vineyard, just five minutes off the Pan-American Highway, is one of the most convenient in the area to visit. The atmospheric wine cellar is one of the oldest in Colchagua, and the colonial architecture has been tastefully refurbished throughout the winery and production rooms, where a tour shows you the main facilities as well as the family's collection of classic cars. Finish up with a tasting in the modern wine shop, or cycle, drive, or walk through the vineyards to the excellent restaurant overlooking the polo fields. ✉ *Hijuela Norte, (El Tambo exit from Ruta 5), San Fernando* ☎ *72/271–6519* 🌐 *www.casasilva.cl* 🎫 *Tours from 16000 pesos.*

Tagua Tagua Observatory

OBSERVATORY | **FAMILY** | On a clear night, the Colchagua Valley can be excellent for stargazing. Eccentric expat Ian Hutcheon runs an observatory just outside of Tagua Tagua, where events begin with a welcome glass of wine (made with meteorites in the barrel), after which there is entertaining discussion, presentation, and observation through advanced telescopes. During the day, Hutcheon leads nature hikes in the area with a buried treasure surprise. ✉ *Observatorio Tagua Tagua, Tunca Arriba s/n, San Vicente de Tagua Tagua* ☎ *9/9228–5005* 🌐 *www.taguatagua.com* 🎫 *12000 pesos.*

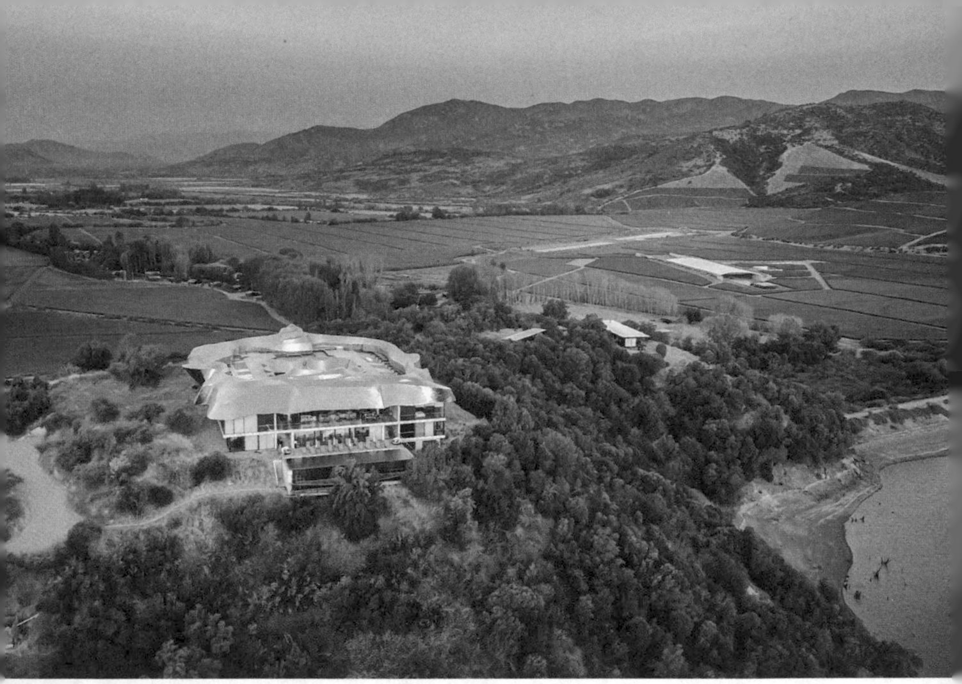

One of the area's best wineries, Viña Vik, is located on a private 11,000-acre estate.

Viña Vik

WINERY | Jaw-dropping architecture and stunning views over the valley make this one of Chile's most extravagant wineries. Nestled in a private 11,000-acre estate, the VIK winery is pure luxury, and the Norwegian-American couple who owns it don't do anything by half measures. A visit includes a barrel tasting of the individual components before a taste of the final blend. Make a day of it with horseback riding in the stunning estate and lunch in the hotel restaurant, one of Chile's best. ✉ *Millahue s/n, San Vincente de Tagua Tagua, San Fernando* ☎ *9/6193–1754* 🌐 *www.vikwine.com* 🎫 *From 40000 pesos.*

🍴 Restaurants

★ Casa Silva Restaurant

$$$$ | **CHILEAN** | This sun-drenched restaurant overlooking the vineyards and polo field serves local delicacies including fresh ceviche, Chilean *asado* (barbecued meats), seafood salads, beef jerky empanadas, an eclectic mix of tapas, and indulgent Chilean desserts. The wine list is all from the Casa Silva winery, of course, but it's an enormous portfolio and the prices carry attractive discounts. **Known for:** chic polo club aesthetic; modern Chilean cuisine; wines from the surrounding vines. [$] *Average main: pesos15000* ✉ *Hijuelas Norte, San Fernando* ☎ *9/6847–5786* 🌐 *www.casasilva.cl.*

Hydro Restobar

$$ | **INTERNATIONAL** | If you're looking for new flavor combinations, this fusion sushi bar is a great spot for creative cuisine and craft beers. A range of fresh ceviches, delicious octopus tacos, imaginative sushi rolls, and skyscraper burgers are just some of the regular menu items. **Known for:** craft beer; creative sushi; flavorful ceviche. [$] *Average main: pesos6000* ✉ *Av. Bernardo O'Higgins Sur 0280, San Fernando* ☎ *2/2983–4063* 🌐 *www.hydrorestobar.cl* ⏲ *Closed Sun.*

Milla Milla

$$$$ | **CHILEAN** | It takes quite a drive to get here, but Milla Milla—the restaurant at VIK Hotel—is worth the trip. Fabulous valley views and monumental artworks are the only things pulling your eyes away from the colorful plates of contemporary Chilean cuisine. **Known for:** fine dining; beautiful presentation; locally sourced organic ingredients. [$] *Average main: pesos25000* ✉ *Viña Vik, Millahue s/n, San Vicente de Tagua Tagua* 🌐 *www.millamilla.cl.*

Hotels

Hacienda Los Lingues

$$$$ | **HOTEL** | This tastefully restored 17th-century hacienda is one of the oldest in Chile, and its sweeping 20,000-acre estate exudes an old-world charm. **Pros:** Wi-Fi in bedrooms; history handsomely restored; beautiful estate. **Cons:** lacks some mod cons; some facilities a bit tired; service can be stuffy. [$] *Rooms from: pesos170000* ✉ *Ruta 5 S, Km 124.5 s/n, San Fernando* ☎ *72/297–7080* 🌐 *www.loslingues.com* 🛏 *16 rooms* 🍴 *Free Breakfast.*

Tumunan Lodge

$$$ | **B&B/INN** | Set high in the mountains, this peaceful family-run lodge is surrounded by a private estate of woodland, trout-filled rivers; waterfalls; and swimming holes. **Pros:** nice hot tub; tranquil location; homey atmosphere. **Cons:** close quarters with other guests; hard to reach without private transport; far from any services. [$] *Rooms from: pesos120000* ✉ *I-325 s/n, Las Penas, San Fernando* ☎ *9/9630–1152* 🌐 *www.tumunan.com* 🛏 *4 rooms* 🍴 *No Meals* ☞ *Rates include wine tasting and hot tub.*

★ **Viña Vik Hotel**

$$$$ | **HOTEL** | With a grand, swooping titanium roof and rooms that are individually decorated by different artists, this statement hotel is one of Chile's most luxurious. **Pros:** excellent restaurant and food; stunning valley views; quirky art design. **Cons:** far from other wineries; impersonal reception; expensive. [$] *Rooms from: pesos400000* ✉ *Millahue s/n, San Vincente de Tagua Tagua, San Fernando* ☎ *9/6193–1754 cell phone* 🌐 *www.vikwine.com* 🛏 *22 suites, 7 glass bungalows* 🍴 *Free Breakfast.*

Santa Cruz

180 km (112 miles) southwest of Santiago; 104 km (65 miles) southwest of Rancagua via the Pan-American Hwy. to San Fernando, then southwest on I–50.

This once sleepy village has become the height of rural chic in recent years due, in large part, to the booming Colchagua Valley wine industry, which produces many of Chile's award-winning reds. It has an attractive central plaza surrounded by a mix of modern and traditional architecture, including the town hall, the Colchagua Museum, the Wine Route office, and the grand Hotel Santa Cruz. The church still stands on the plaza although little of the 19th-century building survived the 2010 earthquake; it has been completely refurbished and rebuilt since.

This is farm country par excellence, and huasos in their wide-brimmed, flat-topped chupalla hats are as common behind the wheel of a pickup truck as they are on horseback. They take pride in their traditional dress and often seek out formal occasions to don their short-cropped black or white jackets, pin-striped black pants, colorful woven sash-belts, and short black boots, to which they strap jangling silver spurs and knee-high black spats. You'll probably see the *cueca,* Chile's national dance, performed at some point during your visit to Colchagua.

Santa Cruz is the perfect home base for visiting the Colchagua wineries that extend out to the east and west, mostly along Route I–50.

History of Chilean Wine

The birth of Chilean wine can be traced to missionaries who arrived here in the 16th century. Spanish priests, who needed wine to celebrate the Catholic Mass, planted the country's first vineyards from Copiapó in the north to Concepción in the south. Of course, not all the wine was intended for religious purposes, and vines were quickly planted in the Maipo Valley around Santiago to fill the "spiritual void" experienced by the early Spanish settlers—many of whom were soldiers and sailors.

With the rise of cross-Atlantic travel and trade that began in the 19th century, some Chileans made fortunes in the mining industry. They returned from Europe with newfound appreciation for French food, dress, architecture, and lifestyles. Many began building their own Chilean-style chateaux, particularly on the outskirts of Santiago. French varietals such as Cabernet Sauvignon, Malbec, and Carménère (known as "Chilean Merlot" until 1994) thrived in the Central Valley's rich soils and the near-perfect climate, and thus Chile's second "wine boom" was launched.

Chilean wineries did not keep pace with the rest of the world and stagnated throughout much of the 20th century. However, the introduction of modern equipment such as stainless steel tanks in the late 1980s caught the country some global attention. Fresh national and international investment in the industry made Chilean wine a tasty and affordable option. Continued advances in growing techniques and wine-making methods throughout the 1990s and into the early 21st century have resulted in the production of exceedingly excellent wines of premium and ultrapremium quality, with increasingly hefty price tags. Wine exports increase annually, and Chile is now one of the top five wine exporters worldwide, shipping its wine to more than 150 countries around the globe.

GETTING HERE AND AROUND

Getting to Santa Cruz is easiest by car. After reaching San Fernando on Ruta 5, you need to pass the first exit north of the city and continue another 2 km (1 mile) to the exit marked "Santa Cruz, Carretera del Vino, Pichilemu." This is I–50, the "Wine Highway," which takes you west through wine country along the coast to Pichilemu, surf capital of Chile. It is very easy to visit most of the valley's wineries by car; in fact, you see a number of them along the way on this aptly named route.

If using public transportation, buses depart from Santiago's Terminal Sur for Santa Cruz every hour. The journey takes about three hours and costs about 6,000 pesos.

BUS CONTACTS Santa Cruz Terminal.
✉ *Rafael Casanova 480, Santa Cruz* ☎ *72/282–2191.*

Sights

Iglesia Parroquial

CHURCH | Facing the central square is this imposing, fortress-like, white stucco structure. Originally built in 1817, the church has had numerous refurbishments following major earthquakes. ✉ *Plaza de Armas 306, Santa Cruz* ⊕ *www.parroquialasantacruz.cl.*

★ Museo de Colchagua

HISTORY MUSEUM | One of the best museums in Chile, this attractive, colonial-style, 20th-century building houses exhibitions on the history of the region. It's the largest private natural-history collection in the country and second only in size to Santiago's Museo Nacional de Historia Natural. Exhibits include pre-Columbian mummies, extinct insects set in amber viewed through special lenses, the world's largest collection of silver work by the indigenous Mapuche, and the only known original copy of Chile's proclamation of independence. A few early vehicles and wine-making implements surround the building. The museum is the creation of Santa Cruz native and wealthy businessman Carlos Cardoen. His foundation, Fundación Cardoen, runs three additional museums in greater Santa Cruz, which are dedicated to wine, antique cars, and indigenous arts and crafts. Purchase a Route of the Museums pass if you want to visit two or more. ⊠ *Av. Errázuriz 145, Santa Cruz* ☏ *72/282–1050* ⊕ *www.museocolchagua.cl* ☞ *7000 pesos.*

Museo San José del Carmen de El Huique
HISTORIC HOME | Here you can look into the lifestyle of Chile's 19th-century rich and famous. Construction began on the current house in 1829 and was completed with the inauguration of the chapel in 1852. The Errázuriz family, who can trace the 2,600-acre estate back through family lines to 1756, donated it to the Chilean Army in 1975. It was reopened as a museum in the 1990s and is now the only remaining preserved, intact estate of its kind in Chile open to the public. Inside, sumptuous suites are filled with opal glass, lead crystal, bone china, antique furniture, and family portraits evoking Chile's aristocratic past. Servants' quarters are also part of the tour, as are the kitchens and 16 working patios, each dedicated to a specific household chore, such as laundry, butchering, or cheese-making. Guides are knowledgeable and have tales to tell, as many grew up hearing family stories about working at the estate. The tour ends with a visit to the chapel, which has

Venetian blown-glass balustrades around the altar and the choir loft. Visits are by prior reservation only, and English-speaking guides are available with sufficient notice. ⊠ *26 km (16 miles) north of Santa Cruz to Palmilla, turn left to Estación Colchagua, then turn right and follow signs to museum, Santa Cruz* ☏ *9/9733–1105 cell phone* ⊕ *www.museoelhuique.cl* ☞ *3000 pesos.*

Plaza de Armas
PLAZA/SQUARE | FAMILY | In the center of the palm-lined Plaza de Armas is a colonial-style bell tower with a carillon that chimes every 15 minutes. Inside the tower is a tourism kiosk with information leaflets. ⊠ *Plaza de Armas, Santa Cruz.*

Ruta del Vino de Colchagua
VISITOR CENTER | Right on the main square, the Ruta del Vino office organizes tours and tastings at 21 of Colchagua's best-known wineries. Prices start at 12,000 pesos per person and rise up to almost 200,000, depending on the complexity of the tour. Some options include traditional meals or hikes amid the vines. The harvest season—March and April— kicks off with the *Fiesta de la Vendimia* (Grape Harvest Festival) and is always a great time to visit.

■TIP→ **Though most wineries have their own guides, few speak English, and some wineries accept visits arranged only by Ruta del Vino.** ⊠ *Plaza de Armas 298, Santa Cruz* ☏ *72/282–4339* ⊕ *www. colchaguavalley.cl.*

Viña Lapostolle-Clos Apalta
WINERY | Lapostolle's showcase winery rises impressively from the vineyards in a wooden nest formation, offering a memorable view from both inside and out. The prized grapes are picked from the biodynamic vineyards and taken to the top floor, where they are separated by hand, dropped into tanks on the floor below, then racked to barrels on the floor below that, and so on until the grapes are six floors down into the hillside, where

Clos Apalta is known for its biodynamic vineyards and upscale wine residence.

they are finally trucked out and shipped around the world. Join one of the daily tours with tastings, or stay for a fabulous lunch at the Clos Apalta Residence with a fresh and organic menu picked straight from the on-site garden. ⊠ *Apalta, Km 5, Santa Cruz* ☎ *72/295–3360* ⊕ *www. closapalta.com* ✉ *From 20000 pesos* ⚠ *Reservations essential.*

Viña Laura Hartwig

WINERY | This small winery, which rests on lands where grapes have been grown for more than a century, is one of the few places in the area where you can simply show up unannounced and sip some vino. As you sample the red wines, including Chile's unique Carménère variety, a tasty Petit Verdot, juicy Malbec, and rich Cabernet Sauvignon, you'll notice that the likeness of Laura Hartwig, the elegant owner of the estate, has been beautifully drawn on the labels by the famous Chilean artist Claudio Bravo. ⊠ *Camino Barreales s/n, Santa Cruz* ☎ *9/8533–2787* ⊕ *www.laurahartwig.cl* ✉ *Tastings from 2500 pesos.*

Viña Montes

WINERY | Montes is one of most recognized wine brands in Chile today, but it started with humble roots in 1987 in the Curicó Valley with a group of young entrepreneurs. Today it is in the heart of Apalta, Colchagua, where the second generation of the Montes family helps run this feng shui–designed winery and restaurant. Deep, rich, and concentrated red wines and bright whites showcase a diverse portfolio of vineyards from around Chile. Enjoy the wines with food at Fuegos de Apalta with its show-stopping fire-themed menu from star Argentine chef Francis Mallmann. The regular tour takes you through the winery processes and finishes with a wine tasting inside, or there is also a more active wine tour that involves a mountain hike followed by a picnic and wine tasting at the summit. ⊠ *Parcela 15, Millahue de Apalta, Santa Cruz* ☎ *72/281–7815* ⊕ *www.monteswines.com* ✉ *Tours from 18000 pesos* ⚠ *Reservations essential.*

★ Viña MontGras

WINERY | Despite dripping with charm and class, MontGras is one of the friendliest and most approachable vineyards in the valley, with excellent English-language tours of the property as well as the option to just taste wines by the glass. Creative tour options include a blind tasting, an open-air barbecue, or a "Winemaker for the Day" class where you can create your own blend. If your visit coincides with harvest (February-April), you can also do a "My Harvest" tour to pick grapes and then foot-tread them in a traditional way. ✉ *Camino Isla de Yáquil s/n, Santa Cruz* ☎ *72/282–2845* 🌐 *www.montgras.cl* 🎫 *Tours from 18000 pesos* 🕒 *Closed Sun. and Mon.* ✍ *Reservations recommended.*

Viña Santa Cruz

WINERY | **FAMILY** | In the lesser-visited Lolol region, this winery is owned by the same businessman who has the Santa Cruz Hotel and Museum. Something of a Disney World for wine lovers, it's one of the most kid-friendly options in the area with an antique car museum, wagon rides, bike rentals, and a cable car ride to a hilltop lookout. Adult tours finish, of course, with plenty of wine tasting.

■ **TIP→ Visit at night and you can stargaze from the observatory (open all year, depending on weather).** ✉ *Carretera I–72, Km 25, Lolol* ☎ *9/7218–8755* 🌐 *www.vinasantacruz.cl* 🎫 *Tours from 15000 pesos* ✍ *Reservations essential* ☞ *Astronomy tour Fri. and Sat. at 8 pm.*

Viña Viu Manent

WINERY | What better way to visit the vineyards at Viu Manent than via a horse-drawn carriage ride? The stylish equestrian entrance is part of the tour package, which also includes a wine tasting in the beautiful colonial-style house. Focusing mainly on red wines from the Colchagua Valley, including Malbec, Viu Manet also pours a couple of coastal wines from Casablanca. Pick bottles to taste after the tour or over lunch at the excellent Rayuela restaurant, which keeps live oysters in freezing-cold Jacuzzis out back. ✉ *Carretera del Vino, Km 37, Santa Cruz* ☎ *72/285–8350 general, 2/2840–3181 tours and wine shop* 🌐 *www.viumanent.cl* 🎫 *Tours from 17000 pesos; tastings from 14000 pesos* ☞ *Tours: 10:30, 12, 3, and 4:30 year-round.*

🍴 Restaurants

Casa Colchagua

$$$$ | **CHILEAN** | Surrounded by vineyards, this ever-popular restaurant is a countryside culinary experience serving contemporary Chilean cuisine that celebrates native ingredients: seaweed ceviche, scallop and quinoa risotto, and *carne mechada* (pulled beef) among them. There's inside seating in a cozy country home, but most diners choose to take advantage of the clement Colchagua weather and the vineyard view from the garden. **Known for:** intimate setting; modern Chilean dining; local ingredients. [$] *Average main: pesos14000* ✉ *Camino a los Boldos* ☎ *9/9424–5007* 🌐 *www.casacolchagua.cl* 🕒 *Closed Mon. and Tues.*

Club Social de Santa Cruz

$$ | **CHILEAN** | One of the most traditional restaurants in town, the social club specializes in simple, hearty Chilean fare like *conejo guisada* (rabbit stew) and *arrollado* (rolled roast pork). In summer, the courtyard fills with locals lunching under the shady pergola. **Known for:** old-school service; local flavor; hearty dishes. [$] *Average main: pesos7000* ✉ *Plaza de Armas 178, Santa Cruz* ☎ *72/282–2529.*

Los Varietales

$$ | **CHILEAN** | Offering Chilean à la carte and large lunch buffets, this hotel restaurant is an institution in Santa Cruz. The menu features typical Chilean dishes using local ingredients and producers, and boasts an extensive list of Colchagua Valley wines available by glass or bottle. **Known for:** big breakfast buffet; Chilean classics; large parties. [$] *Average main:*

pesos7000 ✉ Plaza de Armas 286, Santa Cruz ☎ 72/220–9600 🌐 www.hotelsantacruzplaza.cl.

★ Ristorante Vino Bello

$$$ | **ITALIAN** | This stylish restaurant—one of the best in Santa Cruz—features an eclectic range of clay oven–cooked pizzas, as well as scratch-made pastas, salads, and fish and meat dishes, alongside local wines and don't-miss cocktail offerings (try the chili-laced version of a pisco sour). Smooth music, attractive surroundings, and some nice twists on the classics make Vino Bello a taste of *la dolce vita* in Colchagua. **Known for:** romantic atmosphere amid the vines; creative pizza toppings; wicked pisco sours. [$] *Average main: pesos11000 ✉ Barreales s/n, Santa Cruz ☎ 72/282–2755 🌐 www.ristorantevinobello.com.*

Hotels

★ Clos Apalta Residence

$$$$ | **RESORT** | Overlooking the stunning Apalta Valley and Lapostolle winery, the Clos Apalta Residence is one of South America's most upscale wine residences, where fresh, made-to-order cuisine is prepared daily in a four-course, wine-paired menu for breakfast, lunch, and dinner. **Pros:** fantastic service; excellent homegrown food; beautiful valley. **Cons:** late check-in; limited activities; extremely expensive. [$] *Rooms from: pesos1415000 ✉ Camino Apalta, Km 5, Santa Cruz ☎ 72/295–3360 🌐 www.closapalta.com ⏲ Closed Aug. 🛏 4 rooms 🍴 All-Inclusive.*

Hotel Santa Cruz

$$$$ | **HOTEL** | Right on the Plaza de Armas, this beautiful, colonial-style hotel is certainly Santa Cruz's most central, but it isn't the most historical. **Pros:** handsome decor; central location; quirky museum displays. **Cons:** labyrinthine layout makes some rooms hard to find; some street noise in back rooms; rooms can be small. [$] *Rooms from: pesos115000 ✉ Plaza de Armas 286, Santa Cruz ☎ 72/220–9600 🌐 www.hotelsantacruzplaza.cl 🛏 116 rooms 🍴 Free Breakfast.*

Hotel TerraViña

$$$$ | **HOTEL** | This pretty Spanish-style boutique hotel is only minutes outside of Santa Cruz, yet it's peacefully surrounded by its own vineyards and gardens. **Pros:** convenient location; buffet breakfast; late check-out. **Cons:** some beds could do with replacing; noise travels between rooms; small bathrooms. [$] *Rooms from: pesos130000 ✉ Camino Los Boldos s/n, Barreales, Santa Cruz ☎ 72/282–1284 🌐 www.hotelterravina.cl 🛏 19 rooms 🍴 Free Breakfast.*

Hotel Vendimia Parador

$$ | **B&B/INN** | This countryside B&B is in a charming family house with six en suite bedrooms comfortably decorated in a homey style with hand-painted wash basins. **Pros:** big lawn and pool; convenient location; homey atmosphere. **Cons:** few mod cons; some road noise in bedrooms; a bit worn in places. [$] *Rooms from: pesos73000 ✉ Camino a Los Boldos s/n, Santa Cruz ☎ 9/6839–1678 🌐 www.hotelvendimiaparador.cl 🛏 6 rooms 🍴 Free Breakfast.*

Hotel Viña La Playa

$$$ | **HOTEL** | **FAMILY** | This large, Spanish-style villa boasts vineyards, green lawns, a big garden with fragrant orange trees, pool, and tennis court to keep you amused when you aren't winery hopping in nearby Santa Cruz. **Pros:** lots of activities for children; on-site winery; spacious suites. **Cons:** kid-friendly, so can be noisy for couples; will need private transportation; a bit far from Santa Cruz. [$] *Rooms from: pesos100000 ✉ Fundo San Jorge, Peralillo, Santa Cruz ☎ 72/290–1638 🌐 www.hotelvinalaplaya.cl 🛏 11 rooms 🍴 Free Breakfast.*

Posada Colchagua
$$$ | **B&B/INN** | **FAMILY** | With a large, sunny garden, a pool, and a fountain, this cheerful family posada in the rural Isla de Yaquil area provides both good value and a peaceful stay in the Colchagua Valley. **Pros:** experience of rural Chile; good value; kind hospitality. **Cons:** far from restaurants; limited mod cons; car required. [$] *Rooms from: pesos90000* ✉ *Isla de Yaquil, Santa Cruz* ☎ *9/9223–2196* 🌐 *www.posadacolchagua.com* 🛏 *10 rooms* 🍴 *Free Breakfast.*

Solaz Bella Vista De Colchagua
$$ | **B&B/INN** | In the wine region of Lolol, this peaceful countryside getaway has value, comfort, and warm hospitality that begins with a welcome glass of wine. **Pros:** charming hospitality; countryside location; you can reserve a massage. **Cons:** far from restaurants; breakfast is simple (but you can get eggs to order); car required for remote location. [$] *Rooms from: pesos75000* ✉ *San Pedro de Callihue Lote 5 J* ☎ *9/7808–3785* 🌐 *www.solazbellavistadecolchagua.cl* 🛏 *9 rooms* 🍴 *Free Breakfast.*

Shopping

La Lajuela
SOUVENIRS | For a souvenir you can't find elsewhere, head to La Lajuela, a hamlet 8 km (5 miles) southwest of Santa Cruz. Residents here weave chupallas , straw hats made from a fiber called *teatina* that is cut, dyed, dried, and braided by hand. ✉ *La Lajuela, Santa Cruz.*

Outlet de Vinos Colchagua
WINE/SPIRITS | Do you like your fine wines at outlet store prices? This excellent shop on the road into Santa Cruz has knowledgeable staff who can help you stock up on bottles, direct you to nearby wineries, or provide you with a card that will let you uncork your purchases free of charge at some of the valley's top restaurants. There are often wine tastings here, too. ✉ *Ruta 90, 1 km from Santa Cruz, Santa Cruz* 🌐 *www.outletdevinos.cl.*

Tienda Ecobazar Santa Cruz
CRAFTS | From ceramics and textiles to soaps, jams and scented oils, this small artist-run store offers only products that have been made by hand in the region. You can pick up supplies for your charcuterie board as well as one-of-a-kind gifts to take back home. ✉ *Av. Rafael Casanova 572, Santa Cruz* ☎ *9/4482–1281.*

Curicó

60 km (37 miles) south of San Fernando along the Pan-American Hwy.

Founded in 1743, Curicó means "Black Water" in Mapudungún, the language of the Mapuche. Today this agroindustrial center is the provincial capital and the gateway to the Curicó wine valley. The Plaza de Armas is one of the most attractive in the Central Valley; it is a center of activity year-round but fills to capacity for the Fiesta de la Vendimia (Wine Harvest Festival) each March. Most of the wineries are south of the city and easily reached from the Pan-American Highway. Other points of interest are found toward the Andes or on the coast.

GETTING HERE AND AROUND

From Santa Cruz, you can either head back to San Fernando and hop on the Pan-American Highway or take country roads south for about 58 km (36 miles) to reach Curicó. Those using public transportation can take an interurban bus to Curicó. Once you're in town, you can get around by local bus, taxi, or colectivo. If you're visiting wineries, be sure to contact the Ruta del Vino de Curicó, which can help make arrangements for visits and transport to other sights, such as Radal Siete Tazas or Vichuquén.

BUS CONTACTS Curicó Terminal. ✉ *Arturo Prat 780, Curicó* ☎ *75/255–8118.*

ESSENTIALS

VISITOR INFORMATION Curicó Tourism Office. ⊠ *Manso de Velasco 449, Curicó* ☎ *75/254–7690* ⊕ *www.curico.cl.*

 Sights

Parque Nacional Radal Siete Tazas

NATIONAL PARK | This 10,000-acre national reserve, 70 km (43 miles) southeast of Curicó, is famous for the unusual "Seven Teacups," a series of pools created by waterfalls along the Río Claro (although it is more accurately five teacups since the 2010 earthquake displaced two). The falls are a short hike from the park entrance, where you'll find a CONAF station. Farther along the trail are two other impressive cascades: the *Salto Velo de la Novia* (Bridal Veil Falls) and *Salto de la Leona* (Lioness Falls). Black woodpeckers, hawks, and eagles are common throughout the park, and condors nest in the highest areas. If you're lucky, you might glimpse the scarce *loro tricahue*, an endangered species that is Chile's largest and most colorful parrot. Camping is permitted in the park, which is snowed over in winter. October–March is the best time to visit. ⊠ *Camino Molina–Parque Inglés, Curicó* ☎ *75/222–4461 CONAF* ⊕ *www.conaf.cl* ☑ *6200 pesos.*

Plaza de Armas

PLAZA/SQUARE | The lovely Plaza de Armas has a pretty fountain ringed by statues of dancing nymphs. Nearby is an elaborate bandstand constructed in New Orleans in 1904. ⊠ *Plaza de Armas, Curicó.*

Ruta del Vino

VISITOR CENTER | The local Ruta del Vino office provides basic information and a variety of tours that range from simple half-day visits to a single winery to combination packages that include hiking, biking, and rafting. It is a useful place to visit as Curicó Valley vineyards are not as focused on tourism as other regions. English-speaking guides are available. ⊠ *Carmen 727, Curicó* ☎ *75/232–8972* ⊕ *www.rutadelvinocurico.cl* ☑ *From 60000 pesos (2 wineries, lunch, transport).*

Viña Miguel Torres

WINERY | Curicó's star winery is owned by the Spanish wine mogul Miguel Torres, who hasn't spared a peso in building this large facility just south of town (and immediately off the Pan-American Highway). There are tastings that pair wine with either chocolate or cheese, plus a handful of unique tours—from a classic winery tour to a bike tour to one with a sparkling wine focus—and in each you'll get a glimpse into the pioneering nature of Torres, who was the first in Chile to use a stainless-steel tank (now de rigueur). He also brought another tradition from his native Iberia: the annual Wine Harvest Festival that takes place in Curicó's main plaza.

■**TIP**➔ **Be sure to visit the restaurant, definitely one of the finest in the area.** ⊠ *Ruta 5 S, Km 195, Curicó* ☎ *75/256–4100* ⊕ *www.migueltorres.cl* ☑ *Tours from 18000 pesos* ⚠ *Reservations recommended.*

Lago Vichuquén

112 km (70 miles) west of Curicó.

At a little under two hours' drive from Curicó, this lake is a popular place for water sports such as boating, kayaking, and paddleboarding. The town itself, about 8 km (5 miles) away, is worth a visit for its museum but has little to offer in terms of dining or lodging. Black-necked swans are a common sight on meandering Lago Vichuquén and nearby Laguna Torca, which is a protected reserve ideal for bird-watching.

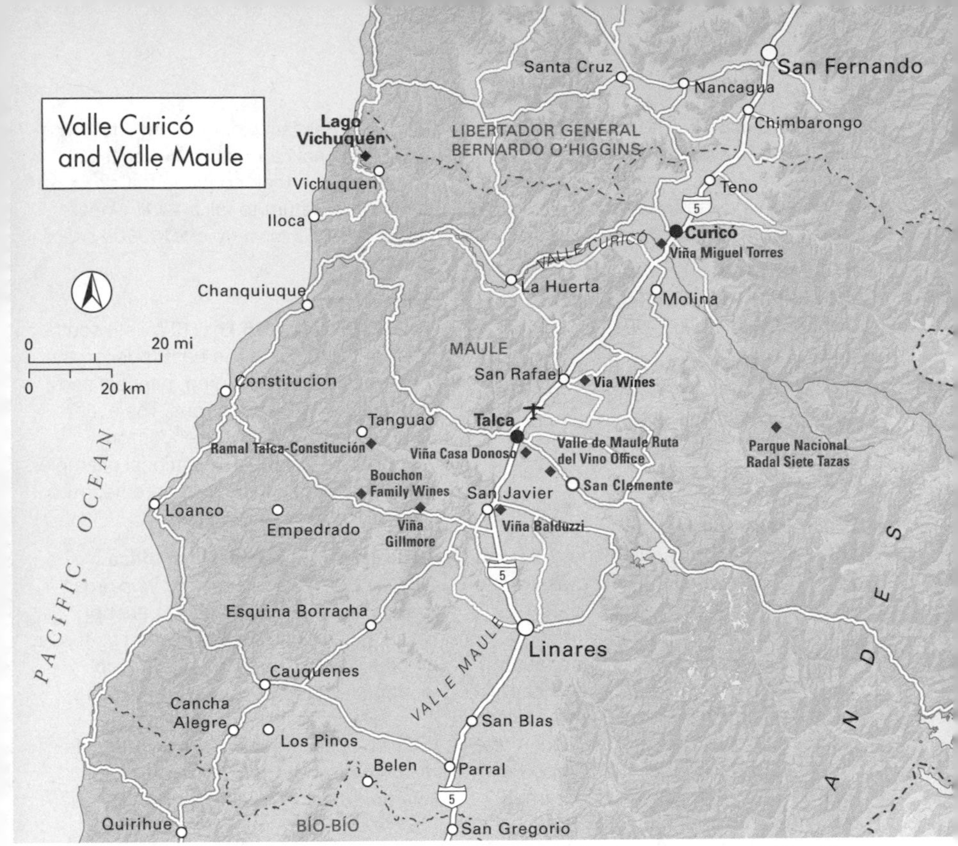

Sights

Museo Colonial de Vichuquén

HISTORY MUSEUM | Ceramics, stone tools, and other artifacts collected from pre-Columbian peoples are on display at this small outpost from Fundación Cardoen, which operates four other museums near Santa Cruz. ✉ *Av. Manuel Rodríguez 332, Vichuquén* ☎ *9/8292–8991* 🌐 *www.fundacioncardoen.cl* 🎟 *2000 pesos.*

Hotels

Marina Vichuquén

$$$ | **HOTEL** | The comfortable Marina Vichuquén has an enviable location right on the shore and makes use of it with its own marina, where there are plenty of opportunities for water sports. **Pros:** good restaurant; plenty to do here; well kept. **Cons:** some tired facilities; no beach; somewhat remote location. [$] *Rooms from: pesos100000* ✉ *Sector Aquelarre, Lago Vichuquén, Vichuquén* ☎ *9/3202–8229* 🛏 *18 rooms* 🍴 *Free Breakfast.*

Talca

65 km (40 miles) south of Curicó on Ruta 5.

Situated at the confluence of the Río Claro and Rio Lircay, Talca is not only Maule's most important industrial center; it is also one of the most appealing towns in the Central Valley. It was founded in 1692 and intelligently designed on a regimented grid pattern divided into quadrants—*poniente* means west, *oriente* east, *sur* south, and *norte* north—centered around the pretty Plaza de Armas. Be sure to take some time to check out its native and exotic trees.

GETTING HERE AND AROUND

No surprises here; once again it's back to the Ruta 5 (Pan-American Highway) for an easy ride to Talca, about 65 km (40 miles) south of Curicó.

ESSENTIALS

BUS CONTACTS Talca Terminal. ⊠ *2 Sur 1920, Talca* ☎ *71/231–0815.*

RENTAL CAR CONTACTS Rosselot. ⊠ *Av. San Miguel 2710, Cruce Varoli, Talca* ☎ *71/224–7979* ⊕ *www.rosselot.cl.*

Sights

Bouchon Family Wines

WINERY | Bouchon Family Wines' historic Mingre Estate, about 10 minutes west of Viña Gillmore on the road to Constitución, is a wild and atmospheric setting for an afternoon of wine tasting. Tours start in the wine cellar and barrel room, and end in tastings of three wines, including two unique interpretations of the rustic and long maligned grape País (one of which is made from extremely old vines). The attached Casa Bouchon hotel is one of the region's most luxurious stays. ⊠ *Fundo Mingre, Viña Bouchon, Km 30, Camino a Constitución, San Javier* ☎ *9/7477–4879* ⊕ *www.casabouchon.com* ⊠ *Tours from 15000 pesos* ⌁ *Reservations essential.*

Cerro la Virgen

VIEWPOINT | You can make out the city's orderly design from this hill that affords a panoramic view of Talca and the vineyards in the distance. ⊠ *Talca.*

Ramal Talca-Constitución

TRAIN/TRAIN STATION | **FAMILY** | There may be no better way to get to know the Central Valley than by taking a ride on one of Chile's few remaining narrow-gauge *buscarril* lines, which runs from Talca to the wine region of Gonzalez Bastias and on to the coastal port of Constitución. It departs from Talca's Estación de Tren three times daily. A good option is to stop at the Estación González Bastías and visit

Gonzalez Bastias winery to get a tasting and traditional *campestre* (countryside) lunch. You can then continue to Constitución or return to Talca. ⊠ *11 Oriente 1000, Talca* ⊕ *www.efe.cl* ⊠ *10000 pesos return.*

San Clemente

TOWN | This town 16 km (10 miles) southeast of Talca, hosts the best rodeo in the region, with riding, roping, dances, and beauty-queen competitions. The events take place 11–6 on weekends from September to April. The national championship selections are held here near the end of the season. ⊠ *Talca.*

Valle del Maule Ruta del Vino Office

VISITOR CENTER | This *ruta del vino* organization, an information center east of Talca, is not quite as established as those in other valleys but can usually help arrange visits to its 18 partner wineries. This may include transportation and an English-speaking guide, which simplifies and enriches the trip. ⊠ *Camino a San Clemente, Km 11, Talca* ⊕ *www.valledelmaule.cl.*

Viña Balduzzi

WINERY | Albano Balduzzi, descended from 200 years of Italian winemakers, built this 1235-acre estate in San Javier in 1900; today it is run by his great-grandson and produces more than 7 million liters a year. One of the most tourist-friendly wineries in the region, it does not require any advanced reservations for tastings or tours, the latter of which include a peek at the cellars that stretch underneath the property. Within the estate is a small wine museum and a beautiful expanse of oak and cedar trees perfect for a picnic; lunches can be organized on request. ⊠ *Av. Balmaceda 1189, San Javier* ☎ *73/232–2138* ⊕ *www.balduzzi.com* ⊠ *Tours from 9000 pesos.*

Viña Casa Donoso

WINERY | Ten minutes east of Talca along a dirt road are the massive iron gates that mark the entrance to this historic hacienda with barrel-tile roof. The estate was once called Domain Oriental because it is east of the city, but today it bears the name of the family who owned it for generations before it was purchased by four Frenchmen in 1989 (it's been back in Chilean hands since 2010). The vineyards themselves climb up into the Andean foothills, while the grounds are ideal for a leisurely picnic (which can be booked in advance). ✉ *Fundo La Oriental, Camino a Palmira, Km 3.5, Talca* ☎ *71/234–1400* 🌐 *www.casadonoso.cl* 🎫 *Tour from 15000 pesos* ✍ *Reservations essential.*

★ Viña Gillmore

WINERY | The Gillmores, who own this winery, were instrumental in creating the VIGNO label, a type of appellation of origin for Maule Valley Carignan whereby wines must be made from at least 65% old-vine, dry-farmed grapes. This experimental vineyard has also raised the profile of Chile's long neglected País grape, which was previously used only for bulk wines. Try both, as well as the lush red blends, on a tour or tasting. In addition to making fine red wines, the Gillmores have created a fun place to stop and spend a couple of hours or stay on for a night or two. Take the Pan-American Highway to the "Camino a Constitución" turnoff, south of San Javier. Head west over the Loncomilla River and through the rolling hills of the Coastal Mountains for 20 km (13 miles); Viña Gillmore is on the right. ✉ *Camino a Constitución, Km 20, San Javier* ☎ *9/9645–0851* 🌐 *www.gillmorewines.cl* 🎫 *Tours from 6000 pesos* ✍ *Reservations recommended.*

🍴 Restaurants

Ryoshi Sushi Bar Marisqueria

$$$ | **SUSHI** | In southern Chile, where fresh fish and seafood come in daily from the port, Ryoshi puts a contemporary twist on Chilean seafood classics, including scallop sashimi, flame-grilled octopus maki, tuna ceviche, and a truly Chilean delicacy—fresh sea urchin. **Known for:** good soups; fresh seafood; Chilean-style sushi. [$] *Average main: pesos12000* ✉ *Av. Isidoro del Solar 260, Talca* ☎ *71/268–2018* 🕒 *Closed Sun.*

🛏 Hotels

★ Casa Bouchon

$$$$ | **HOTEL** | Tucked into a 19th-century hacienda at Bouchon Family Wines' Mingre Estate is this intimate boutique hotel, which oozes historic charm. **Pros:** free bikes to explore the property; romantic winery setting; fine dining at the on-site restaurant. **Cons:** remote location; no phone or TV in rooms; full-board meals don't include wine. [$] *Rooms from: pesos282000* ✉ *Fundo Mingre, Viña Bouchon, Km 30, Camino a Constitución, San Javier* ☎ *9/7477–4878* 🌐 *www.casabouchon.com* 🛏 *5 rooms* 🍴 *All-Inclusive.*

Hostal del Puente

$ | **HOTEL** | This quiet, family-run hotel, at the end of a dusty street two blocks west of the Plaza de Armas, is quite a bargain. **Pros:** clean and tidy rooms; good budget option; centrally located. **Cons:** weak Wi-Fi; simple breakfast; no frills. [$] *Rooms from: pesos33000* ✉ *1 Sur 407, Talca* ☎ *41/213–1091* 🌐 *www.hostaldelpuente.cl* 💳 *No credit cards* 🛏 *18 rooms* 🍴 *Free Breakfast.*

Hotel Casino Talca

$$ | **HOTEL** | This modern hotel offers one of the more comfortable stays in downtown Talca and is right in the heart of the city's main shopping area with bars and restaurants nearby. **Pros:** good breakfast (for Chile); inviting pool; modern furnishings. **Cons:** no elevator from car park; no personal heating; can be noisy. [$] *Rooms from: pesos80000* ✉ *Av. Circunvalacion Oriente 1055, Talca* ☎ *71/252–7000* 🌐 *www.casinotalca.cl* 🛏 *48 rooms* 🍴 *Free Breakfast.*

Did You Know?

Herding sheep is big in the town of San Clemente, known for hosting the best rodeo in the region.

Tabonko

$$$$ | HOTEL | Designed to look like two large wine barrels, this boutique hotel right in the Gillmore vineyard is owned and run by the Gillmore family, who have created a warm space with plenty of personal touches. **Pros:** garden and pool; personally attended by the owners; vineyard setting. **Cons:** weak Wi-Fi; a bit remote; closed in winter. [$] *Rooms from: pesos215000* ✉ *Camino a Constitución, Km 20, San Javier* ☎ *9/9645–0851* 🌐 *www.tabonko.cl* 🕒 *Closed Apr.–Oct.* 🛏 *15 rooms* 🍴 *Free Breakfast.*

🍸 Nightlife

Casa Alameda

BARS | This busy resto-bar is a popular spot for late-night mojitos and beer on the outdoor patio; frequently in the evenings there's live music. Supplement your liquid indulgences with the stream of sushi and burgers from the kitchen. ✉ *4 Norte 1065, Talca* ☎ *2/2419–0910* 🌐 *www.pizzaestado.cl* 🕒 *Closed Sun.*

🛍 Shopping

Mercado Central

CRAFTS | This central market has stands filled with ceramics, copperware, baskets, and other handicrafts. ✉ *1 Sur, between 4 and 5 Oriente, Talca* ☎ .

🏃 Activities

HORSEBACK RIDING

Rutas de Achibueno

HORSEBACK RIDING | With horseback expeditions that run from a full day to a week, Rutas de Achibueno lead you through the Andes, passing waterfalls, hot springs, and mountain lakes. Trekking and camping are also possible in the Cajón del Río Achibueno, which is often referred to as the Patagonia of the Central Valley. ✉ *Cajón del Río Achibueno, Sector Los Canelos, Linares* ☎ *9/9983–8275* 🌐 *www.rutasdelachibueno.cl.*

Chapter 8

THE LAKE DISTRICT

8

Updated by
Jimmy Langman

⊙ **Sights**
★★★★★

🍴 **Restaurants**
★★★★☆

🛏 **Hotels**
★★★★☆

⊖ **Shopping**
★★☆☆☆

🍸 **Nightlife**
★★☆☆☆

WELCOME TO THE LAKE DISTRICT

TOP REASONS TO GO

★ **Volcanoes:** Volcán Villarrica and Volcán Osorno are the conical, iconic symbols of the Lake District, but some 50 other volcanoes loom and fume in this region. Not to worry; eruptions are rare.

★ **Stunning summer nights:** Southern Chile's austral summer doesn't get more glorious than January and February, when sunsets don't fade until well after 10 pm and everyone is out dining, shopping, and enjoying the outdoors.

★ **Lakes and rivers:** The region may sport a long Pacific coastline, but everyone flocks to the inland lakes to swim, sunbathe, kayak, sail, and more. The region also hosts numerous wild rivers that are, among other things, excellent for fly-fishing.

★ **Soothing hot springs:** Chile counts some 280 thermal springs, and a good many of the well-operated ones are in the Lake District, the perfect place to pamper yourself after a day of outdoor adventure and sightseeing.

1 Temuco. The northern gateway to the Lake District is a mix of modern architecture and indigenous markets.

2 Parque Nacional Conguillío. One of Chile's best national parks is home to a volcano and unique araucaria trees.

3 Curacautín and Nearby. Hot springs, parks, a towering volcano, and wild nature grace this indigenous homeland.

4 Villarrica. Tranquil lakeside town with volcano views and Mapuche culture.

5 Pucón. Lake Villarrica's tourism hot spot has good lodging options.

6 Parque Nacional Huerquehue. Just outside of Pucón, it is home to hiking trails featuring blue lagoons and forest.

7 Parque Nacional Villarrica. Villarrica Volcano looms over this park, perfect for outdoor adventures.

8 Lican Ray. Off-the-beaten-path town on the shores of Lake Calafquén.

9 Valdivia. Los Ríos region's capital and most scenic city is traversed by rivers and wetlands.

10 Huilo Huilo. Private nature reserve with evergreen forests, a volcano, and wildlife.

11 Lago Ranco and Nearby. The stunning Lake Ranco is surrounded by rain forest, mountains, and rivers.

12 Osorno. Convenient base for exploring nearby national parks.

13 Parque Nacional Puyehue. National park home to popular hot springs and nature trails.

14 Puerto Octay. Small, picturesque town on the northern tip of the Lake Llanquihue area.

15 Frutillar. Lakeside town known for its theater, volcano views, and German influence.

16 Puerto Varas. Fast-growing hub for adventure tourism with volcano views on Lake Llanquihue.

17 Ensenada. Next door to Osorno Volcano, it's the heart of Chile's murta (berry)-growing country.

18 Parque Nacional Vicente Pérez Rosales. Chile's oldest national park and a treasure for hiking and fly-fishing.

19 Puerto Montt. The biggest city in southern Chile and a port for ships.

20 Cochamó. Vast natural wonderland with lush forests and high mountains.

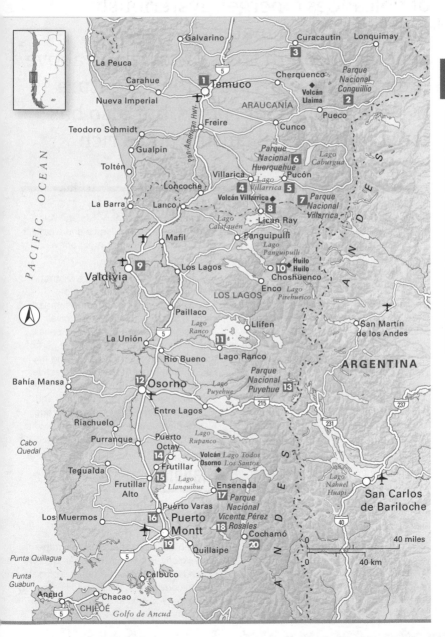

As you travel the winding roads of the Lake District, the snowcapped shoulders of volcanoes emerge, mysteriously disappear, then materialize again, peeping through trees or towering above broad valleys. It's great for adventure travel and outdoor sports, but also has outstanding local cuisine and a rich cultural past.

With densely forested national parks, a dozen large lakes, vastly improved hotels and restaurants, and easy access to roads and public transportation, Chile's Lake District has come pretty close to perfecting tourism.

The Lake District is the historic homeland of Chile's indigenous Mapuche people, who revolted against the early Spanish colonists in 1598, driving them from the region. The Mapuche kept foreigners away for nearly three centuries. Though small pockets of the Lake District were controlled by Chile after it won its independence in 1818, most viewed the forbidding region south of the Río Bío Bío as a separate country.

Eventually, an 1881 treaty ended the Mapuche control over the territory, and in the middle of the 18th century Santiago began to recruit waves of German, Austrian, and Swiss immigrants to settle the so-called empty territory. The Lake District quickly took on the Bavarian-Tyrolean sheen that is still evident today.

MAJOR REGIONS
La Araucanía is the historic home of the Mapuche indigenous people and today contains some of Chile's most spectacular lake scenery. Several volcanoes, among them Villarrica and Llaima, two of South America's most active, loom over the region.

The southern half of the Lake District, **Los Lagos and Los Ríos,** is a land of snowcapped volcanoes, rolling farmland, and the shimmering lakes that give the region its name. This landscape is literally a work in progress, as it's part of the so-called Ring of Fire encircling the Pacific Rim. Most of the region's active volcanoes are here. There's a distinctly Germanic flair in this part of Chile, and you might swear you've taken a wrong turn to Bavaria when you pull into towns like Frutillar or Puerto Octay.

Planning

When to Go

Most Chileans head here during southern Chile's glorious summer, between December and March. For fishermen, the official season commences the second Friday of November and runs through the first Sunday of May. Visiting during the off-season is no hardship, though, and lodging prices drop dramatically. An increasing number of Santiaguinos flee the capital in winter to enjoy the Lake District's brisk, clear air or to ski and snowboard down volcanoes and Andean hills.

FESTIVALS AND EVENTS

Summer means festival season in the Lake District. Communities across the region hold their own festivals in January and February, but the Festival Costumbrista in Castro, Chiloé, held the third week of February, is the can't-miss event. In late January and early February, Semanas Musicales de Frutillar brings together the best in classical music. Verano en Valdivia is a two-month-long celebration centered on the February 9 anniversary of the founding of Valdivia. During the second week of October, Valdivia also hosts a nationally acclaimed international film festival. February in Puerto Varas is filled with concerts, beer fests, and other special events.

Getting Here and Around

AIR

None of the Lake District's airports— Osorno, Puerto Montt, Temuco, and Valdivia—receives international flights; flying here from another country means connecting in Santiago. Of the five cities, Puerto Montt has the greatest frequency of domestic flights.

BUS

There's no shortage of bus companies traveling the Pan-American Highway (Ruta 5) from Santiago south to the Lake District. The buses, which are very comfortable, have assigned seating and aren't too crowded. Tickets may be purchased in advance. If you are traveling overnight, consider spending extra dough on a "cama" bus; the seats are wider, fold back like a bed, and therefore are much more comfortable.

BUS CONTACTS Buses JAC. ⊠ Balmaceda 1005, Temuco ☎ 45/299–3117 ⊕ www. jac.cl. **Cruz del Sur.** ⊠ Bus Terminal, Av. Vicente Pérez Rosales 1609, Temuco ☎ 45/273–0310 ⊕ www.busescruzdelsur. cl. **Turbus.** ⊠ Bus Terminal, Vicente Pérez Rosales 1609, Of. 6A, Temuco ☎ 45/220– 1521 ⊕ www.turbus.cl.

CAR

It's easier to see more of the Lake District if you have your own vehicle. The Pan-American Highway through the region is a well-maintained four-lane toll highway. Bring plenty of small bills for the frequent toll booths.

RENTAL CAR CONTACTS Econorent. ⊠ Blanco Encalada 838, Temuco ☎ 45/221–5997 ⊕ www.econorent. cl. **Europcar.** ⊠ Panamericana Sur 4750, Padre Las Casas, Temuco ☎ 45/291–8940 ⊕ www.europcar.cl. **Mitta.** ⊠ Aeropuerto Internacional La Araucanía, Temuco ☎ 45/254–4548 ⊕ www.mitta.cl.

Restaurants

Meat and potatoes are popular in the cuisine of southern Chile. The omnipresent *cazuela* (a plate of rice and potatoes with beef or chicken) and *pastel de choclo* (a corn, meat, and vegetable casserole) are solid, hearty meals. But it is the seafood that most sets this region apart from other places. In Puerto Montt, tourists regularly fall in love with the local shellfish offerings, especially when served in traditional plates like *curanto* (cooked by hot stones) and *paila marina* (seafood stew).

Among the greatest gifts from the waves of German immigrants were their tasty *küchen,* rich fruit-filled pastries (raspberry and local *murta* berries are a special favorite here). Sample them during the late-afternoon *onces,* the coffee breaks locals take to tide them over until dinner. The Germans also brought their beer-making prowess to the New World;

Valdivia, in particular, is where the popular Kunstmann brand got its start.

Restaurant reviews have been shortened. For full information, visit Fodors.com.

Hotels

Many hotels, even the newly built ones, are constructed in Bavarian-chalet style echoing the region's Germanic heritage. Central heating is a much-appreciated feature whenever it's available in lodgings here in winter and on brisk summer evenings. If not, you grow to appreciate the wood-heated stoves that abound all over the region. Air-conditioning is uncommon, but it's rarely necessary this far south. Rates usually include a continental breakfast of coffee, cheese, bread, and jam. Although most of the places listed here stay open all year, call ahead to make sure the owners haven't decided to take a well-deserved vacation during the April–October off-season.

Hotels reviews have been shortened. For full information, visit Fodors.com.

What It Costs in Chilean Pesos (in Thousands)

$	$$	$$$	$$$$
RESTAURANTS			
Under 6	6–8	9–11	over 11
HOTELS			
Under 46	46–75	76–105	over 105

Tours

Awash in rivers, mountains, forests, gorges, and its namesake lakes, this part of the country is one of Chile's outdoors capitals. Outfitters traditionally are concentrated in the northern resort town of Pucón and the southern Puerto Varas, but companies up and down this 400-km-long (240-mile-long) swath of Chile can rent you equipment or guide your excursions.

The increasing popularity of such excursions means that everybody wants a slice of the adventure pie. Quality varies widely, especially in everybody's-an-outfitter destinations such as Pucón or Puerto Varas. Ask questions about safety and guide-to-client ratios. (A few unscrupulous businesses might take 20 climbers up the Villarrica Volcano with a single guide.) Also, be brutally frank with yourself about your own capabilities: Are you really in shape for rappelling? Or is bird-watching more your style? This is nature at its best and sometimes most powerful.

Temuco

675 km (405 miles) south of Santiago.

This northern gateway to the Lake District acquired a bit of pop-culture cachet as the setting for a scene in *The Motorcycle Diaries*, a film depicting Che Guevara's prerevolutionary travels through South America in the early 1950s. But with its office towers and shopping malls, today's Temuco would hardly be recognizable to Guevara. The city has a more Latin flavor than the communities farther south (it could be the warmer weather and the palm trees swaying in the pleasant central park). It's also an odd juxtaposition of modern architecture and indigenous markets, with traditionally clad Mapuche women darting across the street and business executives talking on cell phones, but oddly enough it all works. It warrants a day in town if you have the time.

GETTING HERE AND AROUND

At least a dozen bus lines serve Temuco; it's an obligatory stop on the long haul between Santiago and Puerto Montt. The city also hosts Manquehue Airport, 6 km (4 miles) southwest of town,

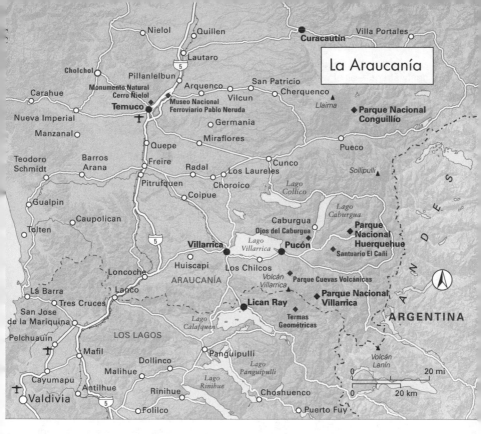

La Araucanía

which has daily connections to Santiago and other Chilean cities. At the airport, in addition to taxis, there are several transfer services that can take you into town. If going to Villarrica or Pucón, you probably come through here as well. The Pan-American Highway, Ruta 5, runs through the city and is paved, but several of the outlying roads connecting Temuco to smaller, rural towns are two-lanes and unpaved. Be careful on such roads, as the Chilean auto accident rate due to passing cars is high.

ESSENTIALS

VISITOR INFORMATION Sernatur. ✉ *Manuel Bulnes 590, Temuco* ☎ *600/600–6066* ⊕ *www.sernatur.cl.*

Sights

Catedral de Temuco

CHURCH | The city's modern cathedral sits on the northwest corner of the central square, flanked by an office tower emblazoned with a cross. ✉ *Temuco.*

Cholchol

TOWN | The experience of visiting this small village 29 km (18 miles) northwest of Temuco begins the moment you board the bus. Expect to share space with Mapuche vendors and their enormous sacks and baskets of fruits and vegetables, all returning from market. A trip in your own vehicle is much less wearing but infinitely less colorful. Regardless of your chosen mode of transport, you arrive in Cholchol to the sight of *rucas*, traditional indigenous thatch huts, plus claptrap wooden houses, horse-drawn carts, and artisan vendors lining the dusty streets—all of whom sell their wares from 9 until about 6. Photo opportunities are plentiful, but be unobtrusive and courteous with your camera. Locals dislike being treated as merely part of the scenery. ✉ *Temuco.*

Galería de Arte

ART GALLERY | The small subterranean gallery displays rotating exhibits by Chilean artists. ✉ *Plaza Aníbal Pinto, Temuco* ☎ *45/223–6785* 💲 *Free.*

★ Monumento Natural Cerro Ñielol

HISTORIC SIGHT | **FAMILY** | This imposing hillside site is where the 1881 treaty between the Mapuche and the Chilean army was signed, allowing the city of Temuco to be established. It's a great spot for a short day hike or picnic, with nice views of the city. Trails bloom with bright red *copihues* (a bell-like flower with lush green foliage), Chile's national flower, in autumn (March–May). The monument, not far from downtown, is part of Chile's national park system. ✉ *Av. Arturo Prat, 5 blocks north of Plaza Teodoro Schmidt, Temuco* ☎ *45/229–8222* ⊕ *www.conaf.cl* 💲 *3000 pesos* ⊙ *Closed Mon.*

Museo Mapuche de Cholchol

HISTORY MUSEUM | This small museum in Temuco exhibits a collection of animal-shaped ceramics and textiles with bold rhomboid and zigzag designs—both are distinctively Mapuche specialties—as well as old black-and-white photographs. A *fogón*, the traditional cooking pit, graces the center of the museum. ✉ *Balmaceda s/n, Temuco* ☎ *45/273–4200* 💲 *500 pesos.*

Museo Nacional Ferroviario Pablo Neruda

HISTORY MUSEUM | Author Pablo Neruda was Chile's most famous train buff; he spent his childhood in Temuco, and his father was a rail worker. Accordingly, the city has transformed its old rail yard into this well-laid-out museum documenting Chile's rail history and dedicated it to the author's memory. Thirteen locomotives (one diesel and 12 steam) and nine train carriages are housed in the round engine building. Scattered among the exhibits are snippets from Neruda's writings: "Trains were dreaming in the station, defenseless, sleeping, without locomotives," reads one. Exhibits are labeled in Spanish, but an English-speaking guide is on hand if you need translation. The museum lies a bit off the beaten path, but if trains fascinate you, as they did Neruda, it's worth the short taxi ride from downtown. ✉ *Av. Barros Arana 0565, Temuco* ☎ *45/297–3940* 💲 *1000 pesos* ⊙ *Closed Mon.*

Museo Regional de la Araucanía

HISTORY MUSEUM | **FAMILY** | Housed in a 1924 mansion, this small museum covers the history of the area. It has an eclectic collection of artifacts and relics, including musical instruments, utensils, and the country's best collection of indigenous jewelry. Upstairs, exhibits document the Mapuche people's three-century struggle to keep control of their land. The presentation could be more evenhanded: the rhetoric glorifies the Central European colonization of this area as the *pacificación de la Araucanía* (taming of the Araucanía territories). But the museum gives you a reasonably good Spanish-language introduction to Mapuche history, art, and culture. ✉ *Av. Alemania 84, Temuco* ☎ *45/289–6784* ⊕ *www.museoregionalaraucania.cl* 💲 *Free* ⊙ *Closed Mon.*

Plaza Aníbal Pinto

PLAZA/SQUARE | Temuco's bustling central square is ringed with imported palm trees—a rarity in this part of the country. A monument to the 300-year struggle between the Mapuche and the Spaniards sits in the center. ✉ *Temuco.*

The Mapuche People

The Mapuche profoundly affected the history of southern Chile. For almost 300 years this indigenous group fought to keep colonial, then Chilean, powers out of their land. The Spanish referred to these people as the Araucanos, from a word in the Quechua language meaning "brave and valiant warriors." In their own Mapudungun language, today spoken by some 270,000 people, the word *mapuche* means "people of the land." In colonial times only the Spanish missionaries, who were in close contact with the Mapuche, seemed to grasp what this meant. "There are no people in the world," one of them wrote, "who so love and value the land where they were born."

Chilean schoolchildren learning about the Mapuche are likely to read about Lautaro, a feared and respected young chief whose military tactics were instrumental in driving out the Spanish. He cunningly adopted a know-thy-enemy strategy that proved tremendously successful in fending off the colonists. Students are less likely to hear about the tightly knit family structure or nomadic lifestyle of the Mapuche. Even the region's two museums dedicated to Mapuche culture, in Temuco and Valdivia, traditionally focused on the three-century war with the Spaniards. They toss around terms like *pacificación* (meaning "to pacify" or "to tame") to describe the waves of European immigrants who settled in the Lake District at the end of the 1800s, the beginning of the end of Mapuche dominance in the region.

Life has been difficult for the Mapuche since the signing of a peace treaty in 1881. Their land was slowly usurped by the Chilean government. Some 200,000 Mapuche today are living on small settlements known as *reducciones* (literally meaning "reductions"). Other Mapuche have migrated to the cities, in particular fast-growing Temuco, in search of employment. Many have lost their identity in the urban landscape, assimilating to the popular Chilean way of life.

A resurgence in Mapuche pride these days takes several forms, some peaceful, some militant. Mapuche demonstrations in Temuco are now commonplace, many calling attention to deplorable living conditions. Some are seeking the return of their land, while others are fighting against the encroachment of power companies damming the rivers and logging interests cutting down the forests. News reports occasionally recount attacks and counterattacks between indigenous groups and police in remote rural areas far off the beaten tourist path. The courts have become the newest battleground as the Mapuche seek legal redress for land they feel was wrongfully taken.

Awareness of Mapuche history is increasing. (Latest census figures show that about 1.4 million of Chile's population of 19 million can claim some Mapuche ancestry.) There is also a newfound interest in the Mapuche language and its seven dialects. Mapudungun poetry movingly describes the sadness and dilemma of integration into modern life and of becoming lost in the anonymity of urban life. Never before really understood by others who shared their land, the Mapuche have finally begun to make their cause known.

🍴 Restaurants

Imperio Del Inca

$$$$ | **PERUVIAN** | Serving excellent Peruvian food, this restaurant founded by the Valerio family has become so popular that they've opened five locations in Temuco. Try the pisco sour with a ceviche or *lomo saltado como Dios manda* ("stir-fried beef as God intended") . **Known for:** ceviche; Peruvian-style pisco sour; good service. $ *Average main: pesos15500* ⊠ *Senador Estébanez 598, Temuco* ☎ *45/224–8386* ⊕ *www.grupoimperio.cl* ⊘ *No dinner Sun.*

La Pampa

$$$$ | **STEAKHOUSE** | Popular with wealthy professionals, this upscale modern steak house is known for its huge, delicious cuts of beef, abundant salads, and the best *papas fritas* (French fries) in Temuco. Although most Chilean restaurants douse any kind of meat with a creamy sauce, this is one of the few exceptions; the entrées are served without anything but the simplest of seasonings. **Known for:** friendly service; huge bife de chorizo steaks; excellent salads. $ *Average main: pesos14500* ⊠ *San Martin 135, Temuco* ☎ *45/232–9999* ⊕ *www.lapampa.cl* ⊘ *Closed Mon.*

Las Muñecas del Ñielol

$$ | **CHILEAN** | This place has been an institution in Temuco since 1975, attaining legendary status for its homemade food. The kitchen puts its own tasty spin on traditional Chilean dishes like *guatitas a la española,* a stew of cow's stomach, bacon, sausage, and tomato cooked in wine. **Known for:** friendly service; simple setting where authentic dishes shine; great prices. $ *Average main: pesos6500* ⊠ *Caupolicán 1347, Temuco* ☎ *45/223–7368* ⊘ *Closed Sat. and Sun.*

★ Mercato

$$$$ | **ITALIAN** | With its extensive Italian menu and lively atmosphere, this is a place not to be missed when in Temuco. The pizza and pasta are spectacular, but do try their desserts as well (churro with manjar and nutella is heavenly). **Known for:** big crowds on the weekends so reserve ahead; great traditional pizza and pastas; fresh juices. $ *Average main: pesos12990* ⊠ *Hochstetter 425, Temuco* ☎ *45/248–2617* ⊕ *www.mercato.cl* ⊘ *Closed Mon.*

Toro Bravo

$$$ | **SPANISH** | At this eclectic-looking restaurant steaks are huge and delicious, and there's also a variety of seafood and pasta dishes on the menu. Upon arrival, be sure to start it all off with a pisco sour. **Known for:** best to make reservations; diverse menu; eclectic decor. $ *Average main: pesos9500* ⊠ *San Martín 0468, Temuco* ☎ *9/6356–2650* ⊘ *No dinner Sun.*

☕ Coffee and Quick Bites

Confitería Central

$$ | **CAFÉ** | **FAMILY** | Coffee and homemade pastries are the specialties of this café, but old-school (and big) sandwiches, excellent hot dogs, ice cream, and other simple dishes are also available. A classic stop in Temuco since the 1940s, it seems the whole town stops by for a quick lunch during the week, among the clattering of dishes and the army of waitstaff maneuvering their way around the tables. **Known for:** plenty of Temuco history; great coffee; classic Chilean pastries. $ *Average main: pesos6000* ⊠ *Manuel Bulnes 442, Temuco* ☎ *45/210–083* ⊕ *www.confiteriacentral.cl.*

🛏 Hotels

Holiday Inn Express Temuco

$$ | **HOTEL** | Near the highway, the hotel is convenient for travelers driving through the Lake District and has clean, spacious rooms. **Pros:** spacious rooms; close to highway; pool during summer. **Cons:** restaurant food could be better; not much local character; 15-minute drive to downtown. $ *Rooms from: pesos70000* ⊠ *Ave. Ortega 01800, Temuco*

☎ *45/222–3300* 🌐 *www.holidayinnex-press.cl* 🛏 *62 rooms* 🍴 *Free Breakfast.*

Hotel Don Eduardo

$ | **HOTEL** | Close to the city center, this orange, classic nine-story hotel has simple rooms that are clean, pleasant, and mostly spacious. **Pros:** parking available; central location; very clean. **Cons:** can be noisy due to thin walls; restaurant closed on weekends; no gym. [$] *Rooms from: pesos58000* ✉ *Andres Bello 755, Temuco* ☎ *45/221–4133* 🌐 *www.hoteldoneduardo.cl* 🛏 *46 rooms* 🍴 *Free Breakfast.*

Hotel Frontera

$$ | **HOTEL** | This lovely old hotel is really two in one, with *nuevo* (new) and *clásico* (classic) wings facing each other across Avenida Bulnes in the city center. **Pros:** comfortable rooms; centrally located; good service. **Cons:** parking is limited; not all rooms are the same quality; old wing does not have A/C. [$] *Rooms from: pesos70000* ✉ *Av. Bulnes 733–726, Temuco* ☎ *45/220–0506* 🌐 *www.hotelfrontera.cl* 🛏 *91 rooms* 🍴 *Free Breakfast.*

Hotel RP

$$ | **HOTEL** | **FAMILY** | In a central location, this hotel has fine rooms, attentive service, and secure parking on-site. **Pros:** more amenities than other hotels in the area; comfortable, ample rooms; central location. **Cons:** basic breakfast with few options; no room service; street noise. [$] *Rooms from: pesos69000* ✉ *Diego Portales 779, Temuco* ☎ *45/297–7777* 🌐 *www.hotelrp.cl* 🛏 *24 rooms* 🍴 *Free Breakfast.*

Posada Selva Negra

$ | **B&B/INN** | This B&B run by a German-Chilean couple is a good option; it's not in the center of the city but plenty close to shopping (including Mall Portal) and restaurants. **Pros:** comfy beds; super affordable; great breakfast. **Cons:** small rooms; not much privacy; pretty far from the city center. [$] *Rooms from: pesos45000* ✉ *Tirzano 110, Temuco* ☎ *45/223–6913* 🌐 *www.hospedajeselvanegra.cl* 💳 *No credit cards* 🛏 *8 rooms* 🍴 *Free Breakfast.*

Small Hotel Goblin's House

$ | **B&B/INN** | Well located in a major shopping district of Temuco, this solar-powered boutique hotel has simple, brightly colored rooms with all the amenities, many with their own outdoor terraces. **Pros:** great location; attentive service; colorful rooms. **Cons:** rooms book up fast; no breakfast; no gym or other services. [$] *Rooms from: pesos49000* ✉ *Pirineos 0841, Temuco* ☎ *45/232–0044* 🌐 *www.hotelgoblin.cl* 🛏 *11 rooms* 🍴 *No Meals.*

🍸 Nightlife

Caravan Resto Beer

BREWPUBS | This bar has more than 50 beers available and excellent sandwiches. It's also open for lunch. ✉ *Alemania 0740, Temuco* ☎ *45/224–0666* 🌐 *caravantemuco.cl.*

Casa Birra Temuco

BEER GARDENS | A great spot to sample Chilean microbrews, Casa Birra Temuco also has good food and, on the weekends, live music of the local rock, blues, or funk variety. ✉ *Alemania 0425, Temuco* ☎ *9/8760–9206* 🕒 *Closed Sun.*

🛍 Shopping

Temuco is ground central for the Mapuche Nation. Here you will find the gamut of Mapuche handicrafts, from carpets to sweaters to sculpture.

Farmacia Mapuche Lawen Kiyen

OTHER HEALTH & BEAUTY | This shop sells ancestral Mapuche remedies for everything from simple head colds to cancers and improving sexual performance. ✉ *Aldunate 245, Temuco* ☎ *9/6125–0961* 🕒 *Closed Sun.*

Llaima Volcano rises into the clouds over Parque Nacional Conguillío.

Feria Libre

MARKET | At the Feria Libre, you can bargain hard with the Mapuche vendors, who sell their crafts and produce in the blocks surrounding the railroad station and bus terminal. Leave the camera behind, as the vendors aren't happy about being photographed. ⊠ *Barros Arana at Miraflores, Temuco.*

★ Fundación Chol-Chol

CRAFTS | This nonprofit promotes the fair trade of Mapuche handicrafts; the quality of their handwoven, colorful wool rugs, blankets, pillows, scarves, gloves, and other textiles are spectacular. They also have a stunning selection of jewelry and ceramics. ⊠ *Alemania 084, (Inside Tienda Museo), Temuco* ☎ *9/9903–1499* ⊕ *www.cholchol.org* ✆ *Closed Mon.*

Padre Las Casas

CRAFTS | Across the Río Cautín from Temuco is the suburb of Padre Las Casas, a Mapuche community whose center is populated by artisan vendors selling locally crafted woodwork, textiles, and pottery under the auspices of the town's rural development program. You can purchase crafts here weekdays 9 to 5. ⊠ *2 km (1 mile) southeast of Temuco, Temuco.*

Parque Nacional Conguillío

126 km (78 miles) northeast of Temuco.

One of southern Chile's most beautiful and oldest tree species, the araucaria tree thrives in the native forest that blankets one of Chile's best national parks. This natural paradise is a wonderful place for hiking, with lakes surrounded by forest and steep mountains. It's also home base for Llaima Volcano, one of Chile's most active volcanoes.

GETTING HERE AND AROUND

About 126 km (78 miles) northeast of Temuco, the roads are paved until the town of Curacautín; from there it's 40 km (25 miles) on gravel and dirt roads, marked with signs, to the park.

ESSENTIALS
CONAF

Chile's national parks are administered by CONAF, which provides maps and other information about them. In summer the organization arranges hikes in Parque Nacional Conguillío. The agency is strict about permits to ascend the nearby volcanoes, so expect to show evidence of your climbing ability and experience. ⊠ *Bilbao 931, Temuco* ☎ *45/229–8114.*

Sights

★ Parque Nacional Conguillío

NATIONAL PARK | Volcán Llaima, which has shown constant but not dangerous levels of activity since 2002, is the brooding centerpiece of Parque Nacional Conguillío. One of Chile's most active volcanoes, the 3,125-meter (10,200-foot) monster has created the moonscape of hardened lava flow that characterizes the park's southern portion. In the 610-square-km (235-square-mile) northern sector, there are thousands of umbrella-like araucaria pines, also known as monkey puzzle trees. The Sierra Nevada Trail is the most popular for short hikes. The three-hour trek begins at park headquarters on Laguna Conguillío and continues northeast to Laguna Captrén. Heavy snow can cut off the area in winter, so November to May is the best time to visit the park's eastern sector. Conguillío's western sector, Los Paraguas, comes into its own in winter because of a small ski center.

The main entrance to the park is in the Melipeuco sector, which is reached from Temuco via a paved road that passes through the towns of Cunco and Melipeuco before becoming a gravel road over its final section. In Melipeuco, a private company, Sendas Conguillío, administers excellent cabins and camping facilities. ⊠ *Parque Nacional Conguillío, Melipeuco* ☎ *45/229–8114* 🖭 *9300 pesos* 🕙 *Closed Mon.*

Hotels

Sendas Conguillío

$$$$ | **B&B/INN** | The official lodging concession at the park, Sendas Conguillío rents 11 rustic but comfortable cabins in the spectacular Araucaria forest. **Pros:** cabins are well equipped; quality cabins in the middle of stunning nature; outdoor hot tubs for each cabin. **Cons:** hot tubs available only if climatic conditions are not a fire risk; you need a vehicle and patience to arrive; service is slow at times. 🖭 *Rooms from: pesos107,000* ⊠ *Parque Nacional Conguillío, Melipeuco* ☎ *9/7656–8198* ⊕ *www.sendasconguillio. cl* 🛏 *11 cabins* ⧄ *Free Breakfast.*

Curacautín and Nearby

90 km (56 miles) northeast of Temuco.

The ancient homeland of the proud indigenous Pehuenche people, Curacautín province is one of the most spectacular places in southern Chile for adventuring into wild nature, with the ever-present Llaima and Lonquimay volcanoes towering over the landscape. Here you will find several reserves and parks, hot springs, and increasing tourism activities, which are beginning to rival the more well-known area to the south around Villarrica and Pucón.

GETTING HERE AND AROUND

You can get to Curacautín via Temuco, going north from Temuco on Ruta 5 for about 30 km (18 miles) until you reach the Lautaro exit. From there it's about 60 km (37 miles) on a paved road through hilly, scenic countryside landscape before arriving in the small town of Curacautín, the starting point for adventures at the many nature parks and reserves in the zone.

Hotels

★ Endemiko

$$$$ | **B&B/INN** | The cabins at Endemiko are quite plush, with all the creature comforts you'd expect yet fresh, minimalist, and attractive in their design. **Pros:** personalized service; attractive design; cabins have top-quality comfort. **Cons:** no pool; expensive; no Wi-Fi in cabins. $ *Rooms from: pesos173000* ⊠ *Ruta Internacional 181, Km 89, Malalcahuello* ☎ *9/9825–2577* ⊕ *www.endemiko.cl* ⇗ *5 cabins* ⦿*Free Breakfast.*

La Baita Conguillío

$$$$ | **B&B/INN** | Located in the heart of Conguillío National Park, this rustic eco-lodge is powered almost entirely by renewable energy. **Pros:** excellent food and service; proximity to nature trails; eco-friendly facilities. **Cons:** no Internet or television; strict energy diet means some luxuries are sacrificed; difficult and dirt roads. $ *Rooms from: pesos120000* ⊠ *Camino Laguna Verde, Km 18, Melipeuco* ☎ *45/258–1073* ⊕ *www.labaitaconguillio.com* ⊗ *Closed June* ⇗ *17 rooms* ⦿*Free Breakfast.*

Lodge Nevados de Sollipulli

$$$$ | **RESORT** | This extraordinary lodge at the base of Sollipulli Volcano, whose crater is filled with a massive glacier, is located 130 km (81 miles) from Temuco inside Reserva Nacional Villarrica. **Pros:** diverse trails and excursions; surrounded by nature; new cabins. **Cons:** no Wi-Fi; road is unpaved; remote location. $ *Rooms from: pesos130000* ⊠ *Fundo el Carmen, Sector Laguna Carilafquen, Melipeuco* ☎ *9/8729–8490* ⊕ *www.sollipulli.cl* ⊟ *No credit cards* ⇗ *9 rooms* ⦿*No Meals.*

Los Pioneros

$$ | **HOTEL** | The Llaima Volcano at the nearby Conguillío National Park looms over this rustic hotel from a distance, a constant reminder of the fabulous nature that awaits you. **Pros:** relaxed environment; close access to nature areas;

comfortable. **Cons:** rooms are simple; thin walls; infrastructure is old. $ *Rooms from: pesos55,000* ⊠ *Ruta S-61, km 1, Camino Internacional Icalma, Melipeuco* ☎ *9/6848–3775* ⊕ *www.lospioneros.cl* ⇗ *15 rooms* ⦿*Free Breakfast.*

Valle Corralco Hotel & Spa

$$$$ | **RESORT** | This modern, spiffy hotel and spa is situated in a wonderful mountain setting. **Pros:** modern facilities; great skiing; spa with all the amenities. **Cons:** prices higher in ski season; restaurant menu is limited; Internet connection is weak. $ *Rooms from: pesos180000* ⊠ *Reserva Nacional Forestal Malalcahuello, Malalcahuello* ☎ *2/2206–0741* ⊕ *www.corralco.com* ⇗ *54 rooms* ⦿*Free Breakfast.*

Villarrica

87 km (52 miles) southeast of Temuco.

Villarrica was founded in 1552, but the Mapuche wars prevented extensive settlement of the area until the early 20th century. Founded by the Spanish conqueror Pedro de Valdivia, it was a Spanish fortress built primarily to serve as a base for gold mining in the area. The fortress's mission succeeded until 1599, when the Mapuche staged an uprising and destroyed the original town. On December 31, 1882, a historic meeting between more than 300 Mapuche chiefs and the Chilean government was held in Putue, a few kilometers outside of the town. The next day, the town was refounded.

Today this pleasant town is home to about 55,000 people. Situated on the lake of the same name, it is one of the loveliest locations in the southern Andes and has nice views of the Villarrica and Llaima volcanoes. To Villarrica's eternal chagrin, it lives in the shadow of Pucón, a flashier neighbor several miles down the road. Many travelers drive through without giving Villarrica a glance, but it has worthy hotels that are less likely to give

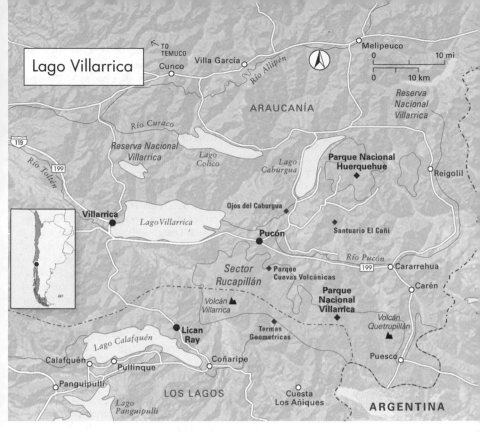

Lago Villarrica

TO TEMUCO • Cunco • Villa García • Río Allipén • ARAUCANÍA • Melipeuco

Río Curaco

119 • Reserva Nacional Villarrica • Río Toltén • 199 • Lago Colico • Lago Caburgua • Parque Nacional Huerquehue • Reigolil

Reserva Nacional Villarrica

Villarrica • Lago Villarrica • Ojos del Caburgua • Pucón • Santuario El Cañi

Sector Rucapillán • Parque Cuevas Volcánicas • Río Pucón • 199 • Cararrehua • Carén

Volcán Villarrica • Parque Nacional Villarrica • Volcán Quetrupillán

Lican Ray • Termas Geométricas • Puesco

Lago Calafquén • Calafquén • Pullinque • Coñaripe

Panguipulli • LOS LAGOS • Cuesta Los Añiques • ARGENTINA

Lago Panguipulli

0 — 10 mi / 0 — 10 km

you a case of high-season sticker shock. Well-maintained roads and convenient public transportation make the town a good base for exploring the area.

GETTING HERE AND AROUND

Located southeast of Temuco, Villarrica can be reached by a paved, two-lane road, from the town of Freire, or farther to the south, from Loncoche. Several bus lines serve the town. Buses leave every hour from the Temuco bus terminal and arrive in Villarrica about one hour later, at a cost of about 3,000 pesos.

ESSENTIALS

VISITOR INFORMATION Villarrica Tourist Office. ✉ *Pedro de Valdivia 1070, Villarrica* ☎ *9/6837–1604* ⊕ *www.visitvillarrica.cl.*

TOURS

Agencia de Turismo Campesino

CULTURAL TOURS | This company offers cultural tours, including half-day visits to farms in the countryside around Villarrica and learning about the way of life of local Mapuche people. ✉ *Villarrica* ☎ *9/9544–4873* ⊕ *www.turismocampesino.cl.*

 Sights

Museo Histórico y Arqueológico de Villarrica

HISTORY MUSEUM | The municipal museum displays an impressive collection of Mapuche ceramics, masks, leather, and jewelry. A replica of a *ruca* hut graces the front yard. It's made of thatch so tightly entwined that it's impermeable to rain. ✉ *Pedro de Valdivia 1050, Villarrica* ☎ *45/241–5706* ✉ Free ⊗ *Closed weekends.*

🍴 Restaurants

Café 2001

$$ | **CAFÉ** | For a filling sandwich, a homemade *küchen* cake, and an espresso or cappuccino brewed from freshly ground beans, this longtime staple is the place to stop in Villarrica. Pull up around a table in front or slip into one of the quieter booths by the fireplace in the back. **Known for:** quaint setting; one of the best lomito completo sandwiches in southern Chile; great coffee. [$] *Average main: pesos6200* ✉ *Valentín Letelier 650, Villarrica* ☎ *45/241–1470* 🌐 *cafebar2001.cl.*

★ Fuego Patagon

$$$$ | **BARBECUE** | **FAMILY** | On the outskirts of town near the lake, this stellar restaurant serves exceptional steaks. The menu has good and generous barbecue plates (including wild boar, goat, and lamb); there is a nice variety of seafood and pasta dishes, too. **Known for:** tasty tiramisu; friendly owner; great barbecue and steaks. [$] *Average main: pesos12400* ✉ *Pedro Montt 40, Villarrica* ☎ *45/241–2207* 🌐 *www.fuegopatagon.cl* 🕒 *No dinner Sun.*

Mesa del Mar

$$$$ | **SEAFOOD** | **FAMILY** | The menu at this local favorite has diverse offerings, but it is the colorful, exquisitely prepared fish and shellfish that deserve your close attention. They also have a special kids' menu. **Known for:** gourmet seafood; grilled conger eel or sea bass; great choices for kids. [$] *Average main: pesos12900* ✉ *Las Industrias 1228, Villarrica* ☎ *45/241–9515* 🌐 *www.mesadelmar.cl* 🕒 *No dinner Sun.*

🛏 Hotels

Hostal y Cabañas Don Juan

$ | **B&B/INN** | This is an inexpensive option in the center of Villarrica that gives you all you need; rooms are simply furnished but clean, with Wi-Fi, cable, and parking on-site. **Pros:** affordable; central location; helpful staff. **Cons:** thin walls; light breakfast; rooms are simple. [$] *Rooms from: pesos44000* ✉ *General Korner 770, Villarrica* ☎ *45/241–1833* 🌐 *www.hostaldonjuan.cl* 🔑 *23 rooms* 🍴 *No Meals.*

Hotel Casa Marron

$$ | **HOTEL** | Just minutes from the center of town, this charming, quiet hotel is a highly regarded lodging option in Villarrica, complete with ample green space and a pool. **Pros:** relatively new; close to city center; second-floor rooms have lake views. **Cons:** first-floor guests may hear noise from above; no lunch or dinner; not many common areas. [$] *Rooms from: pesos60000* ✉ *Clemente Félix 134, Villarrica* ☎ *45/275–8019* 🌐 *www.hotelcasamarron.cl* 🔑 *6 rooms* 🍴 *Free Breakfast.*

Hotel El Ciervo

$$$ | **B&B/INN** | Villarrica's oldest hotel is an unimposing house on a quiet street, but inside are elegant details such as wrought-iron fixtures and wood-burning fireplaces. **Pros:** excellent views all over; friendly, attentive service; great food. **Cons:** thin walls; furnishings are dated; some rooms are small. [$] *Rooms from: pesos95000* ✉ *General Körner 241, Villarrica* ☎ *45/241–1215* 🌐 *www.hotelelciervo.cl* 🔑 *13 rooms* 🍴 *Free Breakfast.*

Hotel Terraza Suite

$$$$ | **HOTEL** | If you want to stay right in town, Hotel Terraza Suite may be the best choice; the views across the lake are tremendous, and the pool is a great refuge on a hot summer day. **Pros:** walking distance to restaurants and shopping; lakefront; nice views. **Cons:** service is sometimes slow; basic breakfasts; unstable Internet connection. [$] *Rooms from: pesos110000* ✉ *Julio Zegers 351, Villarrica* ☎ *45/241–4508* 🌐 *www.hotelterrazasuite.cl* 🔑 *16 rooms* 🍴 *Free Breakfast.*

☻ Nightlife

The Travellers Resto Bar

BARS | Part bar, part restaurant, Travellers offers a wide array of international cuisine, serving one or two dishes from Germany, Thailand, China, Italy, Mexico, and many countries in between. While you chow down on an enchilada, your companions might be having spaghetti with meatballs or sweet-and-sour pork. The restaurant is open only in the evenings from 5:30 pm. On summer nights, sit on the front lawn under the umbrella-covered tables when the Travellers also turns into a bar playing retro dance music. ⊠ *Valentín Letelier 753, Villarrica* ☎ *45/241–3617* ☉ *Closed Sun.*

● Shopping

Feria Huimpay

MARKET | This market features some of the area's best crafts from local artisans, especially Mapuche sweaters, ponchos, and wooden figurines. ⊠ *At Pedro de Valdivia and Julio Zegers, Villarrica.*

Activities

★ Aurora Austral

SNOW SPORTS | Spectacular dog-sledding trips pulled by huskies that regularly win mushing tournaments in the region are run by this tour agency, from one-day dog sledding below Villarrica Volcano to seven days crossing the Andes from Chile to Argentina. In summer, the dogs pull carriages. ⊠ *Novena Region Husky Farm Patagonia, 19 km (12 miles) from Villarrica on road to Lican Ray, Villarrica* ☎ ✉ *info@auroraaustral.com* ⊕ *www.auroraaustral.com.*

Pucón

25 km (15 miles) east of Villarrica.

The resort town of Pucón, on the southern shore of Lago Villarrica, attracts Chileans young and old. By day, there are loads of outdoor activities in the area. The beach on Lago Villarrica feels like one of Chile's popular coastal beach havens near Viña del Mar. By night, young people flock to the many night spots and party until dawn, while the older crowd has a large array of fine restaurants and trendy shops to visit. Pucón has many fans, though some lament the town's meteoric rise to fame. Be warned that accommodations are hard to come by in February, which is easily the busiest month. Outside of summer, some stores, restaurants, and pubs here close down.

With Volcán Villarrica looming south of town, a color-coded alert system on the Municipalidad (city hall) on Avenida Bernardo O'Higgins signals volcanic activity, and signs around town explain the colors' meanings: green—that's where the light almost always remains—signifies "normal activity," indicating steam being let off from the summit with sulfuric odors and constant, low-level rumblings; yellow and red indicate more dangerous levels of activity. But remember that the volcano sits a good 15 km (9 miles) away, and you are scarcely aware of any activity. Indeed, ascending the volcano is the area's most popular excursion.

GETTING HERE AND AROUND

Pucón has only a small air strip 2 km (1 mile) outside of town for private planes, but national airlines such as LATAM and Sky fly regularly to Temuco. From Temuco, Buses JAC has frequent service to Pucón. Roads that connect Pucón to Ruta 5, the Pan-American Highway, are paved from Loncoche and Freire. In Pucón, there are several taxis that can move you about, but the town itself is small and in most cases you just need your two feet.

ESSENTIALS

BUS CONTACTS Buses JAC. ⊠ *Uruguay 505, Pucón* ☎ *45/299–3182* ⊕ *www.jac. cl.* **Pullman Bus.** ⊠ *Palguín 555, Pucón* ☎ *45/244–3331* ⊕ *www.pullman.cl.* **Turbus.** ⊠ *Av. Bernardo O'Higgins 910, Pucón* ☎ *45/268–6101* ⊕ *www.turbus.cl.*

VISITOR INFORMATION Pucón Tourist Office. ⊠ *Av. Bernardo O'Higgins 483, Pucón* ☎ *45/288–8001* ⊕ *www.puconchile.travel.*

Sights

Ojos del Caburgua

WATERFALL | This series of four small waterfalls surrounded by Valdivian rain forest is a classic day trip from Pucón, just 11 mi (18 km) away. The water cascades into natural pools that are a mesmerizing shade of blue. In summer, it's an especially popular spot for swimming, picnics, and camping. A great way to arrive is by bike, which allows you to see the southern Chilean countryside up close. ⊠ *Camino Internacional 2045, Pucón* ☎ *9/6471–7884* 🖅 *2000 pesos.*

Parque Cuevas Volcánicas

CAVE | Halfway up Volcán Villarrica, you find this cave right next to a very basic visitor center. It first opened up in 1968 for spelunkers to explore, but eventually tourism proved more lucrative. A short tour takes you deep into the electrically illuminated cave via wooden walkways that bring you close to the crystallized basalt formations. Your tour guide may make occasional hokey references to witches and pumas hiding in the rocks, but it's definitely worth a visit—especially if uncooperative weather prevents you from partaking of the region's other attractions and activities. ⊠ *Volcán Villarrica National Park, Camino al Volcán Km 14.5, Pucón* ☎ *45/321–1000* ⊕ *www. cuevasvolcanicas.cl* 🖅 *18000 pesos.*

★ Termas Geométricas

HOT SPRING | Chile's volcanoes have endowed the area around Pucón with numerous natural hot springs. About a two-hour drive from Pucón, this is one of the best and most beautiful. Seventeen natural hot-spring pools, many of them secluded, dot the dense native forest. Each thermal bath has its own private bathrooms, lockers, and deck. ⊠ *3 km (2 miles) south of Villarrica National Park, Pucón* ☎ *9/7477–1708* ⊕ *www.termasgeometricas.cl* 🖅 *35000 pesos.*

 Restaurants

Cassis

$$$$ | **CAFÉ** | This wonderful café and restaurant is dessert heaven, with assorted pastries baked fresh every day, chocolates galore, and an excellent selection of ice cream. The restaurant also has a varied menu of sandwiches, pizza, and more, and an extensive wine list. **Known for:** big sandwiches; some of the best desserts in the area; sidewalk seating. Ⓢ *Average main: pesos12000* ⊠ *Fresia 223, Pucón* ☎ *45/244–9088* ⊕ *www.chocolatescassis.com.*

El Camino

$$ | **BURGER** | The place to get comfort food, this lively restaurant has outdoor seating and is open from 1 pm until late in the evening. Rock music blares; the stars shine above; and the steak sandwiches, hamburgers, burritos, and quesadillas hit the spot. **Known for:** late-night spot; great sandwiches; vegetarian options. Ⓢ *Average main: pesos7500* ⊠ *Ansorena 191, Local 3, Pucón* ☎ *45/244–4078* ⊕ *www.elcaminopucon.com.*

La Maga

$$$$ | **STEAKHOUSE** | Argentina claims to prepare the best *parrillada,* or grilled beef, but here's evidence that Uruguayans are no second best. Watch the beef cuts turn slowly over the wood fire at the entrance. **Known for:** huge portions; traditional

Termas Geométricas' hot springs are tucked into the forest of Panguipulli, Chile.

parrillada with a Uruguayan flair; great chimichurri sauce. $ *Average main: pesos24000* ✉ *Gerónimo de Alderete 276, Pucón* ☎ *45/244–4277.*

★ Luthier Bistro

$$$$ | **MEDITERRANEAN** | You may not want to eat anywhere else in Pucón after sampling the varied, well-prepared dishes at this centrally located cafe. The fresh pasta, made in-house, is rich and soft; the pizzas are out of this world. **Known for:** homemade pizza and pasta; local ingredients; one of Pucón's top dining spots. $ *Average main: pesos14000* ✉ *Fresia 124, Pucón* ☎ *45/244–3214.*

Pizza Cala

$$$$ | **PIZZA** | The excellent pizza here is cooked in a wood-fired oven, making for exquisite crust. A host of great toppings is exactly the way Italy meant a pizza to be. **Known for:** outdoor seating; classic pizza; craft beers. $ *Average main: pesos15000* ✉ *Lincoyan 361, Pucón* ☎ *45/265–6458.*

★ Trawen Restaurant

$$$$ | **CONTEMPORARY** | This solar-powered, creative restaurant features fresh and organic ingredients. Breakfasts include homemade yogurt, free-range eggs, and Italian coffee, while lunch and dinner present everything from oversize empanadas and sandwiches to meat, fish, and pasta. **Known for:** vegetarian and vegan options; eco-friendly ethos; diverse menu. $ *Average main: pesos12000* ✉ *Bernardo O'Higgins 311, Pucón* ☎ *45/244–2024* ⊕ *www.trawen.cl.*

Viva Perú

$$$$ | **PERUVIAN** | As befits the name, Peruvian cuisine reigns supreme at this restaurant with rustic wooden tables. Try the *ají de gallina* (hen stew with cheese, milk, and peppers), ceviche, or the splendid *saltado nikkei*, a Japanese-style dish of fish, shrimp, squid, and stir-fried vegetables. **Known for:** two-for-one pisco sours; classic Peruvian dishes; lovely porch dining. $ *Average main: pesos14800* ✉ *Lincoyan 372, Pucón* ☎ *45/244–4025.*

🛏 Hotels

★ &Beyond Vira Vira
$$$$ | ALL-INCLUSIVE | Located on the forested banks of the Liucura River, this all-inclusive luxury lodge is just 20 minutes from downtown Pucón but feels far, far away from everything. **Pros:** outdoor hot tubs; beautifully designed with floor-to-ceiling windows and in-room fireplaces; excursions and gourmet meals included in rate. **Cons:** remote; restaurant service is sometimes slow; expensive. [$] *Rooms from: pesos692,000* ✉ *Parcela 19-22A Quetroleufu, Pucón* ☎ *45/237–4000* 🌐 *www.andbeyond.com* 🕒 *Closed May and June* 🛏 *23 rooms* 🍴 *All-Inclusive.*

Hosteria ¡école!
$ | B&B/INN | This eco-conscious hostel has several shared rooms, but opt for one of the excellent private rooms and stay in good style. **Pros:** staff helps you organize expeditions; great food in restaurant; easy to meet other travelers. **Cons:** breakfast not included in room rate; hostel environment not for everyone; some rooms are noisy. [$] *Rooms from: pesos39000* ✉ *General Urrutia 592, Pucón* ☎ *45/244–1675* 🌐 *www.ecole.cl* 🛏 *22 rooms* 🍴 *No Meals.*

Hotel Antumalal
$$$$ | B&B/INN | A young Queen Elizabeth stayed here in the 1950s, as did actor Jimmy Stewart—and the Antumalal hasn't changed much since then. **Pros:** lots of history; secluded location and views; fireplace in room. **Cons:** no refrigerator in rooms; hotel restaurant closes early; some rooms are small. [$] *Rooms from: pesos350000* ✉ *Km 2, Camino Pucon-Villarrica, Pucón* ☎ *45/244–1011* 🌐 *www.antumalal.com* 🛏 *19 units* 🍴 *Free Breakfast.*

Hotel CasaEstablo
$$$ | B&B/INN | A boutique hotel with just 10 rooms, the CasaEstablo provides service above and beyond. **Pros:** lake views; friendly hosts; spacious rooms. **Cons:** dogs on-site not great for those with allergies; extra fee to use the wood-fired hot tub; road to hotel is very steep (don't go here without your own vehicle). [$] *Rooms from: pesos94000* ✉ *Camino Villarrica, Km 20, Pucón* ☎ *45/244–3084* 🌐 *www.casaestablo.com* 🛏 *10 rooms* 🍴 *Free Breakfast.*

Hotel Del Volcán
$$$$ | HOTEL | This chalet-style hotel looks like it comes straight from Germany; inside, the hotel has nondescript decor but it maximizes comfort with amenities not so common in southern Chilean hotels, including smart televisions, refrigerators, and air-conditioning. **Pros:** large suites; daily breakfast in the room; central location. **Cons:** no common areas; street noise in summer; no restaurant. [$] *Rooms from: pesos115000* ✉ *Fresia 420, Pucón* ☎ *45/244–2055* 🌐 *www.hoteldelvolcan.com* 🛏 *17 rooms* 🍴 *Free Breakfast.*

Hotel Gerónimo
$$$ | HOTEL | A solid choice and well located, this older hotel is an easy walk to everything yet is on a quiet street. **Pros:** A/C; central location; some rooms have a terrace with volcano views. **Cons:** hotel is old; rates have increased; small rooms. [$] *Rooms from: pesos95000* ✉ *Gerónimo Alderete 665, Pucón* ☎ *45/244–3762* 🌐 *www.hotelgeronimo.com* 🛏 *27 rooms* 🍴 *Free Breakfast.*

Hotel Posada del Río
$$$$ | B&B/INN | FAMILY | This hotel has good quality rooms and cabins on its beautiful, 4-hectare (10-acre) private park, Metreñehue, which is covered with native forest and skirts along the Trancura River. **Pros:** spacious cabins; good facilities; secluded riverside location near Pucón. **Cons:** road to hotel needs better signage; Wi-Fi and cell phone service is weak here; no air-conditioning. [$] *Rooms from: pesos130000* ✉ *Km 11, Camino Pucon-Calburga, Pucón* ☎ *9/5821–5306* 🌐 *www.parquemetrenehue.com* 🛏 *6 rooms* 🍴 *Free Breakfast.*

Mirador los Volcanes

$$$$ | B&B/INN | In a gorgeous, rural setting, complete with sheep outside your spacious cabin, this is an idyllic spot to relax and stay close to several of the best sights in the Pucón area, like Lake Caburga, Huerquehue National Park, and numerous natural hot springs. **Pros:** great pools; tranquil, beautiful countryside setting; nearby lake and park. **Cons:** Wi-Fi doesn't always work; some furnishings need upgrade; 18 km (11 miles) from Pucón. $ *Rooms from: pesos151000* ⊠ *Km 15.5, Camino Pucon-Caburgua, Pucón* 🕾 *9/8189–8801* ⊕ *www.mirador-losvolcanes.com* 🍽️ *10 rooms* 🍴 *Free Breakfast.*

Peumayen Lodge & Termas Boutique

$$$ | B&B/INN | This hotel is set on a stunning, 48-hectare (119-acre) property dominated by native forests and biking and hiking trails. **Pros:** close to nature parks; a great place to relax; award-winning restaurant. **Cons:** some plumbing issues; 30 minutes from Pucón; hot springs are small. $ *Rooms from: pesos103000* ⊠ *Camino Pucón Huife, Km 28, Pucón* 🕾 *45/197–0060* ⊕ *www.termaspeumayen.cl* 🌙 *Closed Apr. to Sept.* 🍽️ *12 rooms* 🍴 *Free Breakfast.*

Nightlife

Beanies & Bikinis

BEER GARDENS | A fun local hangout, this is where the drinks flow, the music blares, and soccer games are always on the televisions. ⊠ *Fresia 477, Pucón* 🕾 *45/244–1109.*

Kamikaze

DANCE CLUBS | This is one of Pucón's great discos to party the night away. Summer brings big crowds and often special promotions on drinks. ⊠ *Camino Internacional 5, Pucón* ✛ *Sector El Claro* 🕾 *9/7138–5721.*

Mamas & Tapas

BARS | A local favorite is the friendly Mamas & Tapas, which is de rigueur among the expat crowd. Light Mexican dining morphs into DJ sets or live music at night, which lasts into the wee hours. ⊠ *Av. Bernardo O'Higgins 597, Pucón* 🕾 *45/244–9002.*

Sala Murano

DANCE CLUBS | This discotheque chain in Chile has one of the liveliest party centers in Pucón, with fiestas and drink specials throughout the year. ⊠ *Pasaje Las Rosas 175, Pucón* 🕾 *9/8799–8865.*

Activities

Just 20 minutes from the 2,847-meter-high (9,341-foot) Villarrica Volcano, Pucón is one of Chile's top spots for adventure travel. The active volcano has itself become an obligatory climb for the many nature- and adventure-seeking tourists who come to Chile. In winter, the volcano is a favorite spot for skiing and snowboarding. Nearby Trancura River is a rafting, kayaking, and fishing paradise. Villarrica and Caburgua lakes are outstanding for fishing, swimming, kayaking, and water-skiing. There are several worthy nature hikes close to Pucón, featuring some of the most beautiful forests in Chile, including the El Cani Sanctuary and Huerquehue National Park.

At first glance Pucón's myriad outfitters look the same and sell the same slate of activities and rentals; quality varies, however. The firms we recommend get high marks for safety, professionalism, and friendly service. Although a given outfitter might have a specialty, it usually offers other activities as well. Pucón is the center for rafting expeditions in the northern Lake District, with Río Trancura 15 minutes away, making for easy half-day excursions on Class III–V rapids.

FLY-FISHING

Chilepescamosca

FISHING | For more than 20 years, Juanjo Ortiz has been leading fishing excursions across the Lake District; he also runs a fishing store in Pucón. From September to early May, full-day (225,000 pesos) or half-day (125,000 pesos) fishing trips are on offer to any of the five rivers and 21 lakes that can be reached within 1½ hours driving from Pucón. Standout spots for both trout and salmon are the Trancura and Liucura rivers. ⊠ *Avenida O'Higgins 717, Local 8, Pucón* ☎ *9/8709–4440* ⊕ *www.chilepescamosca.com.*

HORSEBACK RIDING

★ Campo Antilco

HORSEBACK RIDING | Beautiful Criollo Chileno horses, descendants of the Iberian horses that Spanish conquistadors introduced to Chile centuries ago, take you on amazing rides for a half day (35,000 pesos), full day (80,000 pesos), or two days (185,000 pesos) along the Trancura or Liucura river valleys, crossing through Mapuche lands. They also offer extended expeditions of up to 11 days that cross the Andes into Argentina. ⊠ *Carhuello, Km 7, Pucón* ☎ *9/9713–9758* ⊕ *www. antilco.com.*

MULTISPORT OPERATORS

Aguaventura

HIKING & WALKING | Friendly, French-owned Aguaventura outfits for rafting, as well as canyoning, kayaking, snowshoeing, and snowboarding. They specialize in trekking up Volcán Villarrica, including some trips combined with a ski descent, although you should be an expert skier if you want to join them. ⊠ *Palguín 336, Pucón* ☎ *45/244–4246* ⊕ *www.aguaventura.com* ✉ *From 22000.*

Captura Chile

SKIING & SNOWBOARDING | This tour operator specializes in heli-skiing and heli-fishing, but also provides individuals and private groups with flight tours of the Pucón area via small plane or helicopter. ⊠ *Pucón* ☎ *9/699–3686* ⊕ *www.captura.cl.*

Politur

HIKING & WALKING | This tour operator can take you rafting or ziplining at the Río Trancura, trekking in nearby Parque Nacional Huerquehue, and hiking up Volcán Villarrica, not to mention skiing and skydiving. They also offer a laid-back tour of the natural attractions in the Pucón area that includes a dip in a local hot spring. ⊠ *Av. Bernardo O'Higgins 635, Pucón* ☎ *9/6846–0264* ⊕ *www.politur. com* ✉ *From 28000 pesos.*

Sol y Nieve

HIKING & WALKING | For rafting trips, canyoning, hiking, and skiing expeditions, sign up with this longtime tour operator. Their specialty is taking groups up Villarrica Volcano. ⊠ *Lincoyan 361 B, Pucón* ☎ *9/9531–4549* ⊕ *www.solynievepucon. cl* ✉ *From 15000 pesos.*

Summit Chile

MOUNTAIN CLIMBING | The bilingual, certified mountain guides at Summit Chile lead treks to the Villarrica Volcano summit; they also offer other outdoor adventures, including sport rock-climbing, about 20 minutes from town at El Cerduo. ⊠ *General Urrutia 585, Pucón* ☎ *9/9277–4424* ⊕ *www.summitchile.org* ✉ *From 100,000 pesos.*

Parque Nacional Huerquehue

35 km (21 miles) northeast of Pucón.

Behold the region's magical native forests, lakes and lagoons, and mountain vistas at this 12,500-hectare (30,888-acre) national park; it's a great place for a day hike. One popular route is the Los Lagos trail, which begins at the ranger station near the park entrance. You head up into the Andes through groves of araucaria trees, eventually reaching three startlingly blue lagoons with panoramic views of the whole area, including distant Villarrica Volcano. A slightly longer route

Skiing is a top winter activity near Villarrica Volcano.

includes two other lakes, Los Patos and Huerquehue. Plan on a six- to eight-hour round-trip hike, depending on which route you take.

GETTING HERE AND AROUND

Take the Caburgua road from Pucón, following the signs to Huerquehue, which is about 22 km (14 miles) northeast of Pucón.

Hotels

Termas de Huife

$$$$ | **B&B/INN** | About 20 minutes from Parque Nacional Huerquehue, this resort lets you relax in three steaming pools set beside an icy mountain stream. **Pros:** comfy beds; access to hot springs and park; large pools. **Cons:** no transfer service from Pucón; Wi-Fi signal is weak; price is steep. [$] *Rooms from: pesos250000* ✉ *33 km (20 miles) from Pucón on road to Calburga, Pucón* ☎ *9/7548–2529* 🌐 *www.termashuife.com* 🛏 *12 units* 🍴 *Free Breakfast.*

Parque Nacional Villarrica

15 km (9 miles) south of Pucón.

Dominated by Villarrica Volcano, this park is on the outskirts of Pucón and has become Chile's most popular place to climb a volcano, as well as a great destination for skiing, treks, and other outdoor adventures.

Sights

★ **Parque Nacional Villarrica**

VOLCANO | The main draw of this popular 610-square-km (235-square-mile) national park, which has skiing, hiking, and many other outdoor activities, is the volcano. Happily, you don't need to have any climbing experience to reach the 3,116-meter (9,350-foot) summit, but a guide is a good idea. The volcano sits in the park's Sector Rucapillán, a Mapuche word meaning "house of the devil." That name is apt, as the perpetually smoldering volcano is one of South America's most active. CONAF closes off access to the trails at the slightest hint of volcanic activity deemed out of the ordinary. It's a steep uphill walk to the snow line, but doable any time of year. All equipment is supplied by any of the Pucón outfitters that organize daylong excursions for about 100,000 pesos per person. Your reward for the six-hour climb is the rare sight of an active crater, which continues to release clouds of sulfur gases and explosions of lava. You're also treated to superb views of the nearby volcanoes, the less visited Quetrupillán and Lanín. ☎ 45/244–3781 ⊕ www.conaf.cl ✉ 7200 pesos.

★ **Santuario El Cañi**

NATURE PRESERVE | Chile's first private nature preserve, this park hosts one of the last remaining, extensive araucaria forests, a magnificent tree species that can live up to 2,000 years and that is oft nicknamed "monkey puzzle" because of its tangled branches that swirl around its treetop. With about 500 hectares (1,235 acres) altogether, this is simply one of the best treks in southern Chile. The hike to El Cañi's highest ground (1,600 meters), called Mirador Melidekiñ, is a three- to four-hour steep climb but rewards you with an awesome view of four volcanoes. Guides are not necessary for the trails, and there are camping sites and a *refugio* for overnight stays (4,000 pesos). Located about 20 km (12 miles) east of Pucón, the park is accessible via the road to Lago Caburgua (take the turnoff at Km 14). Then turn on the paved road with the sign "Termas Huife" and drive until you reach El Cañi. It is also possible to arrive by bus. ✉ *Camino Pucón Huife, Km 21, Pucón* ☎ *9/9837–3928, 9/897–38147* ⊕ *www.santuariocani.cl* ✉ *4000 pesos.*

 Activities

SKIING
Ski Pucón

SKIING & SNOWBOARDING | This popular ski resort, in the lap of Volcán Villarrica, has 20 runs of varying levels of expertise, but they're mostly for beginners and intermediate skiers. There are six ski lifts, but note that these lifts are quite slow-going. There's also equipment rental and good snowboarding too. The ski season usually begins early July and often runs through mid-October. High-season rates are 39,500 pesos per day. There is also a restaurant, coffee shop, and boutique for skiing accessories, as well as skiing and snowboarding classes. ✉ *Parque Nacional Villarrica, Pucón* ☎ *45/244–1901.*

TREKKING
Patagonia Experience

HIKING & WALKING | Pucón-based tour operator Patagonia Experience has a park concession to guide one of Chile's best hikes, the Villarrica Traverse. The three- to six-day hike around Parque Nacional Villarrica, mostly above the treeline, follows a difficult trail but provides stunning views. You'll move along calderas, alpine tarns, and lava flows into lenga and monkey-puzzle forests. It's best to go in summer when the streams are flowing, but be warned that it can get very hot this time of year. The route begins at either Refugio Villarrica or Termas de Palguin and ends in Puesco. The trail is for experienced hikers only, and going with a knowledgeable guide is highly recommended. ✉ *Pucón* ☎ *9/7891–8247* ⊕ *patagoniaexperience.cl* ✉ *60,000 pesos for guided one-day hike.*

Lican Ray

30 km (18 miles) south of Villarrica.

In the Mapuche language, Lican Ray means "flower among the stones." This pleasant, unhurried little resort town of 3,342 inhabitants is on Lago Calafquén, the first of a chain of seven lakes that spills over into Argentina. You can rent rowboats and sailboats along the shore, which is also a fine spot to soak up sun.

GETTING HERE AND AROUND

You can reach Lican Ray via the paved Ruta 199 from Temuco and Villarrica. From Valdivia and points south, take Ruta 203 to Panguipulli, then travel on dirt and gravel roads north to Lican Ray. There is daily and frequent bus service to the town from nearby locales such as Villarrica.

ESSENTIALS

VISITOR INFORMATION Lican Ray Tourist Office. ✉ *Plaza Lican Ray, Lican Ray* ☎ *45/243–1516.*

Beaches

The peninsula on which Lican Ray sits has two gray-sand beaches.

Playa Chica
BEACH | This smaller of the beaches near Lican Ray is south of town and a good place to go with kids. There's space for sunbathing on the beach and parking for boats. **Amenities:** food and drink; lifeguards; parking (free); toilets; water sports. **Best for:** sunrise; sunset; swimming; walking ✉ *Lican Ray.*

Playa Grande
BEACH | This beach stretches a few blocks on the west side of Lican Ray and is the place to go for swimming and soaking up the sun. **Amenities:** food and drink; lifeguards; parking (free); toilets; water sports. **Best for:** sunrise; sunset; swimming; walking ✉ *Lican Ray.*

Restaurants

Cábala Restaurant
$$ | ITALIAN | Impeccable service is the hallmark of this Italian-style restaurant on Lican Ray's main street. The brick-and-log building has indoor and outdoor seating, perfect to watch the summer crowds stroll by as you enjoy pizza and pasta. **Known for:** friendly service; classic Italian dishes; nice outdoor seating. [$] *Average main: pesos7000* ✉ *General Urrutia 201, Lican Ray* ☎ *9/2251–8503* 💳 *No credit cards* ⏲ *Closed Apr.–Nov.*

Restaurant Mi Fundo
$$$ | CHILEAN | FAMILY | Showcasing southern Chilean hospitality at its finest, this restaurant was actually constructed using wood from trees taken from the bottom of Lake Calafquén. The gregarious owners are on-site serving up stories and exquisite food, from diverse dishes using local trout and salmon to roast beef covered with a delicious mushroom sauce. **Known for:** ice-cream cake for dessert; friendly and proudly local service; tasty trout dishes. [$] *Average main: pesos10000* ✉ *Lican Conaripe, Km 1, Lican Ray* ☎ *9/9450–3948.*

Hotels

Hostal Hofmann
$$ | B&B/INN | The bright, airy rooms at this house just outside town are built for extra comfort with lots of pillows and thick, colorful quilts on the beds. **Pros:** nice sitting area; comfortable rooms; friendly owner. **Cons:** Wi-Fi comes and goes; breakfasts could be improved; no restaurant. [$] *Rooms from: pesos50000* ✉ *Camino a Coñaripe 100, Lican Ray* ☎ *45/243–1109* 🛏 *10 rooms* 🍴 *Free Breakfast.*

Hotel Lican Ray
$$$ | HOTEL | You will sleep well in this boutique hotel, which is the best lodging option in town, by far. **Pros:** cafe and bar on-site; modern infrastructure; centrally

Los Lagos and Los Ríos

located. **Cons:** Wi-Fi connection only in common areas; some rooms have only a skylight, no window; double standard rooms are on the small side. ⓢ *Rooms from: pesos82000* ✉ *General Urrutia 585, Lican Ray* ☎ *2/2947–9338* ⊕ *www.hotellicanray.cl* ⤳ *27 rooms* ⦿ *Free Breakfast.*

 Activities

FISHING
Azul Errante

FISHING | Juan Suarez is the man to talk to for guided fishing trips on Lake Calafquén. ✉ *Av. Cacique Punulef, Playa Grande Licán Ray, Lican Ray* ☎ *9/8451–3499.*

Valdivia

120 km (72 miles) southwest of Villarrica.

One of Chile's most scenic cities, Valdivia gracefully combines Chilean wood-shingle construction with the architectural style of the well-to-do German settlers who colonized the area in the mid-1800s. The historic appearance is a bit of an illusion, as the 1960 earthquake destroyed all but a few old riverfront structures. The city painstakingly rebuilt its downtown area, seamlessly mixing old and new buildings. Today you can enjoy evening strolls through its quaint streets and along two rivers, the Valdivia and the Calle-Calle.

Various tour boats leave from the docks at Muelle Schuster along the Río Valdivia for a one-hour tour around nearby Isla

Teja (about 3,000 pesos). Another option, cheaper and perhaps better, is to take the bright yellow, solar-powered public water taxis, the Transporte Fluvial Sustentables, from the dock behind the submarine museum for just 1,600 pesos round-trip. It's a delightful 40-minute ride each way, and because the boats are energized by the sun, they are very quiet. They sail along the Calle-Calle and Valdivia rivers to the historic Collico sector before returning.

If you have more time, the big tour boats at the docks offer a five-hour excursion that takes you to Niebla near the coast for a visit to the colonial-era forts. There's also a four-hour tour north that transports you to Punucapa, the site of a 16th-century Jesuit church and a nature sanctuary at San Luis de Alba de Cruces. Most companies charge around 29,000 pesos for either of these longer tours (depending on whether the tour includes a meal). These excursions run daily during the December–March high season, and you can always sign on to one at the last minute. Most will not operate tours for fewer than 15 passengers, however, which makes things a bit iffy during the rest of the year.

GETTING HERE AND AROUND

Like most other major cities in the Lake District, Valdivia is served by Ruta 5, the Pan-American Highway. The city also has an airport with frequent flights by national airlines such as LATAM, and the nation's bus lines regularly stop here as well. Valdivia's bus terminal is by the river at the cross section of Muñoz and Prat. Some outlying towns and sites around Valdivia you may want to visit, however, are connected only by dirt roads.

ESSENTIALS

BUS CONTACTS Buses JAC. ✉ Anfión Muñoz 360, Of. 159, Valdivia ☎ 63/233–3343 ⊕ www.jac.cl. **Cruz del Sur.** ✉ Anfión Muñoz 360, Of. 146, Valdivia ☎ 63/221–3840 ⊕ www.busescruzdelsur.cl. **TurBus.** ✉ Anfión Muñoz 360, Of. 123-145, Valdivia ☎ 63/226–8402 ⊕ www.turbus.cl.

RENTAL CAR CONTACTS Assef y Méndez. ✉ General Lagos 1335, Valdivia ☎ 63/221–3205 ⊕ www.assefymendez. cl. **Autoval.** ✉ Vicente Pérez Rosales 660, Valdivia ☎ 63/221–2786 ⊕ www.autovalrentacar.cl.

VISITOR INFORMATION Sernatur. ✉ Pedro de Valdivia 260, Valdivia ☎ 63/223–9060 ⊕ www.descubrelosrios.cl.

Sights

Castillo San Sebastián de la Cruz

MILITARY SIGHT | Across the estuary from the Fuerte de Niebla is this large and well-preserved fort from 1645. In the January through February summer season, historic reenactments of Spanish military maneuvers take place daily at 4 and 6. To get there, you need to rent a small boat, which costs only about 1,000 pesos at the marina near Fuerte de Niebla. ✉ 1 km (½ mile) north of Corral, Valdivia ☎ 63/247–1824 ☒ 1000 pesos.

Catedral de Nuestra Señora del Rosario

CHURCH | Valdivia's imposing modern cathedral faces the west side of the central plaza. A small museum inside documents the evangelization of the region's indigenous peoples from the 16th through 19th centuries. ✉ Independencia 514, Valdivia ☎ 63/223–3663 ⊕ www.obispadodevaldivia.cl ☒ Free ⊙ Closed Sat. afternoon and Sun.

Centro Cultural El Austral

HISTORIC HOME | A walk south of downtown on Yungay and General Lagos takes you through a neighborhood of late-19th- and early-20th-century houses that were spared the ravages of the 1960 earthquake. One of these houses dates to 1870 and accommodates the Centro Cultural El Austral. It's worth the stop if you have an interest in period furnishings. ✉ Yungay 733, Valdivia ☎ 63/213–6588 ⊕ www.cculturalvaldivia.cl ☒ Free ⊙ Closed Sun. and Mon.

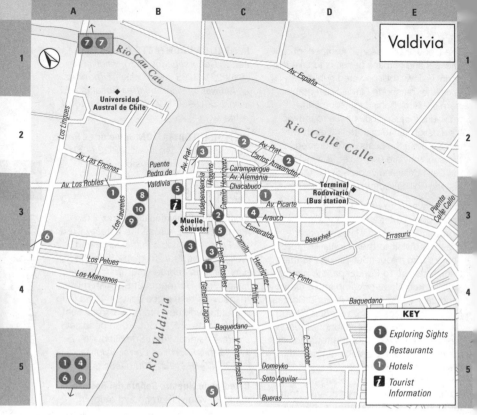

Valdivia

Sights ▼

1 Castillo San Sebastián
   de la Cruz **A5**

2 Catedral de Nuestra
   Señora del Rosario **C3**

3 Centro Cultural
   El Austral **B3**

4 Cervecería
   Kunstmann **A5**

5 Feria Fluvial.............. **B3**

6 Fuerte de Niebla **A5**

7 Jardín Botánico......... **A1**

8 Museo de Arte
   Contemporáneo......... **B3**

9 Museo de la Exploración
   Rudolph Amandus
   Philippi **B3**

10 Museo Histórico y
   Antropológico Maurice
   van de Maele............ **B3**

11 Torreón de los
   Canelos **C4**

Restaurants ▼

1 Café Haussmann **A3**

2 La Parrilla de Thor **D2**

3 La Ultima Frontera **C3**

4 New Orleans **C3**

5 Salón de
   Té Entrelagos............ **C3**

Hotels ▼

1 Aires Buenos Hostel **C3**

2 Hotel Diego de
   Almagro Valdivia......... **C2**

3 Hotel Dreams
   Pedro de Valdivia **B2**

4 Hotel El Castillo
   de Niebla **A5**

5 Hotel Naguilán **C5**

6 Hotel Puerta del Sur ... **A3**

7 Pilolcura Lodge **A1**

Cervecería Kunstmann

BREWERY | Valdivia has a long history of producing beer, and this brewery brews the country's beloved lager. The Anwandter family emigrated from Germany a century-and-a-half ago, bringing along their beer-making know-how. The *cervecería* (brewery), on the road to Niebla, hosts interesting guided tours by prior arrangement. There's also a small museum and a souvenir shop where you can buy the requisite caps, mugs, and T-shirts, plus a pricey restaurant serving German fare. ⊠ *Ruta 350 No. 950, Valdivia* ☎ *63/229–2969* ⊕ *www.cerveza-kunstmann.cl* 🌐 *Free.*

Feria Fluvial

MARKET | This awning-covered market in the southern shadow of the bridge leading to Isla Teja is a perfect place to soak up the atmosphere of a real fish market. Vendors set up early in the morning; you hear the thwack of fresh trout and the clatter of oyster shells as they're piled on the side of the market's boardwalk fronting the river. If the sights, sounds, and smells are too much for you, fruit and vegetable vendors line the other side of the walkway opposite the river. ⊠ *Av. Arturo Prat at Libertad, Valdivia* ☎ *63/222–4776.*

Fuerte de Niebla

MILITARY SIGHT | To protect the all-important city of Valdivia, the Spanish constructed a series of strategic fortresses at Niebla, where the Valdivia and Tornagaleones rivers meet. Portions of the 1671 Fuerte de Niebla and its 18 cannons have been restored. The ground on which the cannons sit is unstable; you can view them from the ramparts above. The old commander's house serves as a small museum documenting the era's military history. ⊠ *1 km (½ mile) west of entrance to Niebla, Valdivia* ☎ *63/233–6182* ⊕ *www.museodeniebla.cl* 🌐 *Free* 🕑 *Closed Sun. and Mon.*

Jardín Botánico

GARDEN | North and west of the Universidad Austral campus, this garden is awash with 1,000 species of flowers and plants native to Chile. It's a lovely place to wander among the alerce, cypress, and laurel trees whatever the season. If you can't make it to Conguillío National Park to see the monkey puzzle trees, this is the place to see them. It's particularly enjoyable in spring and summer. ⊠ *Isla Teja, Valdivia* ☎ *63/222–1344* ⊕ *www.jardinbotanicouach.cl* 🌐 *Free.*

Museo de Arte Contemporáneo

ART MUSEUM | Fondly known around town as the "MAC," this is one of Chile's foremost modern-art museums. The complex on Isla Teja was built on the site of the old Anwandter brewery destroyed in the 1960 earthquake. The minimalist interior, formerly the brewery's warehouses, contrasts sharply with a modern glass wall fronting the Río Valdivia, completed for Chile's bicentennial. The museum has no permanent collection; it's a rotating series of temporary exhibits by contemporary Chilean artists. ⊠ *Los Laureles, Valdivia* ✛ *Isla Teja* ☎ *63/222–1968* ⊕ *www.macvaldivia.cl* 🌐 *1500 pesos* 🕑 *Closed on Mon. in Mar.–Dec.*

Museo de la Exploración Rudolph Amandus Philippi

SCIENCE MUSEUM | FAMILY | This museum is dedicated to the life and work of Rudolph Amandus Philippi, a 19th-century German-Chilean naturalist. The museum's collection explores the botanical studies of Philippi and is housed in the historic Schüller house, built in 1914. The exhibits include watercolors, drawings, photographs, and other objects that belonged to Philippi and tools, furniture, and other scientific objects from the 1800s. ⊠ *Los Laureles s/n, Valdivia* ☎ *63/221–2872* ⊕ *www.museosaustral.cl* 🌐 *1500 pesos* 🕑 *Closed Mon. in Mar.–Dec.*

Museo Histórico y Antropológico Maurice van de Maele
HISTORY MUSEUM | For a historic overview of the region, visit this museum on neighboring Isla Teja. The collection focuses on the city's colonial period, during which time it was settled by the Spanish, burned by the Mapuche, and invaded by Dutch corsairs. Downstairs, rooms re-create the interior of the late-19th-century Anwandter mansion that belonged to one of Valdivia's first immigrant families; the upper floor delves into Mapuche art and culture. ✉ *Los Laureles, Isla Teja, Valdivia* ☎ *63/221–2872* 🌐 *www.museosaustral.cl* 🎟 *1500 pesos* 🕓 *Closed Mon. in Mar.–Dec.*

Torreón Los Canelos
MILITARY SIGHT | Just south of the Centro Cultural El Austral lies one of two fortress towers constructed in 1774 to defend Valdivia from constant attacks by the Mapuche. Both towers—the other sits on Avenida Picarte between the bus terminal and the bridge entering the city over the Río Calle-Calle—were built in the style of those that guarded the coasts of Andalusia, in southern Spain. A wall and moat connected the two Valdivia towers in the colonial era, effectively turning the city into an island. ✉ *General Lagos 801, Valdivia.*

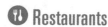

🍴 Restaurants

Café Haussmann
$$$ | **GERMAN** | The excellent *crudos* (steak tartare), German-style sandwiches, and delicious *küchen* cakes here are testament to the fact that Valdivia was once a mecca for German immigrants. The restaurant's newer, bigger location is spacious and has relaxing outdoor seating, the perfect spot to down crudos with local beer. **Known for:** outdoor seating; German-style dining; excellent steak tartare. [$] *Average main: pesos8550* ✉ *Av. Los Robles 202, Isla Teja, Valdivia* ☎ *63/222–2100* 🌐 *www.cafehaussmann.cl.*

★ La Parrilla de Thor
$$$$ | **STEAKHOUSE** | This riverfront institution is constantly packed with locals, which is always a good sign that you've come to the right restaurant. The Argentine owner Teodoro Poulsen serves beef and chicken in delicious Argentine *parrilla* style. **Known for:** great wine list; one of the best steakhouses in Chile; river views. [$] *Average main: pesos12000* ✉ *Arturo Prat 653, Costanera, Valdivia* ☎ *63/227–0767.*

La Ultima Frontera
$$ | **CAFÉ** | The creative and wide variety of sandwiches in this bohemian café have made it legendary. On first glance, La Ultima Frontera appears to be nothing more than a college hangout or a trendy place for the artsy crowd, but the abundant and delicious food attracts young and old. **Known for:** locally brewed beers on tap; creative sandwiches; artsy, youthful ambience. [$] *Average main: pesos7000* ✉ *Vicente Perez Rosales 787, Valdivia* ☎ *63/223–5363* 🌐 *www.laultimafrontera.cl* 🕓 *Closed Sun.*

New Orleans
$$$$ | **AMERICAN** | **FAMILY** | Louisiana Cajun cooking in southern Chile is far from common, but this place pulls it off and has become a must-stop on the tourist trail. Excellent meats and seafood with a spicy, Cajun twist populate the extensive menu, like *filete Mardi Gras* or red curry shrimp. **Known for:** Mardi Gras–inspired ambience; Cajun cuisine; seafood straight from a NOLA menu. [$] *Average main: pesos12000* ✉ *Esmeralda 682, Valdivia* ☎ *63/221–8771* 🌐 *www.neworleans.cl* 🕓 *Closed Sun. and Mon.*

Salón de Té Entrelagos
$$$ | **CAFÉ** | This swanky café caters to Valdivian business executives who come here to make deals over sandwiches, decadent crepes, and desserts. In the evenings, the atmosphere feels less formal—the menu is exactly the same—as the Entrelagos becomes a place to meet friends who converse well into the

night. **Known for:** business lunches; Isla Teja sandwich with grilled chicken and vegetables; chocolate shop next door. [$] *Average main: pesos10000* ✉ *Vicente Pérez Rosales 640, Valdivia* ☎ *63/221–2047* 🌐 *www.entrelagos.cl.*

Hotels

Aires Buenos Hostel

$ | **HOTEL** | Well situated near Valdivia's downtown, this renovated, strikingly handsome house is clean and charges reasonable rates for its basic but comfortable private rooms. **Pros:** eco-conscious; just a few blocks from downtown; reasonable rates. **Cons:** no parking; basic furnishings; no elevator to private rooms on 4th floor. [$] *Rooms from: pesos39,000* ✉ *Garcia Reyes 550, Valdivia* ☎ *2/222–202* 🌐 *www.airesbuenos.cl* 💳 *No credit cards* 🛏 *9 rooms* 🍴 *Free Breakfast.*

Hotel Diego de Almagro Valdivia

$$$ | **HOTEL** | A good choice based on the location alone, this hotel has a superb address on the riverfront, close to the city center. **Pros:** nice views; near the city center; good breakfast. **Cons:** no local character; gym is small; interior decor is old-fashioned. [$] *Rooms from: pesos86000* ✉ *Arturo Prat 433, Costanera, Valdivia* ☎ *2/235–59250* 🌐 *www.dahoteles.com* 🛏 *105 rooms* 🍴 *Free Breakfast.*

★ **Hotel Dreams Pedro de Valdivia**

$$$$ | **HOTEL** | This swanky hotel is the tallest in Valdivia and thus has tremendous views no matter the vantage point. **Pros:** near the action; rooms with a view; modern comforts. **Cons:** service could be more attentive; no privacy between balconies; noisy casino. [$] *Rooms from: pesos121000* ✉ *Carampangue 190, Valdivia* ☎ *600/424–0000* 🌐 *valdivia.dreams.cl/hotel-y-spa* 🛏 *104 rooms* 🍴 *Free Breakfast.*

Hotel El Castillo de Niebla

$$ | **B&B/INN** | This grand 1920s German-style house sits at Niebla's main intersection near the picturesque coastline and has been converted into a lovely bed-and-breakfast with lots of knickknacks, antiques, and cuckoo clocks in the common areas. **Pros:** good value; nice ambience; lovely views from rooms. **Cons:** barking dogs at night; basic breakfast; no restaurant. [$] *Rooms from: pesos46000* ✉ *Antonio Ducce 750, Valdivia* ☎ *63/228–2061* 🌐 *www.hotelycabanaselcastillo.com* 🛏 *13 rooms* 🍴 *Free Breakfast.*

Hotel Naguilán

$$$ | **HOTEL** | Located on the banks of the Río Valdivia, this is an entertaining and pretty spot, and the hotel itself is overall one of good quality. **Pros:** outdoor pool in summer; attentive service; river location. **Cons:** traffic noise in rooms facing main road; outdated furnishings in older wing; 15-minute walk to downtown. [$] *Rooms from: pesos102000* ✉ *General Lagos 1927, Valdivia* ☎ *63/221–2851* 🌐 *www.hotelnaguilan.com* 🛏 *36 rooms* 🍴 *Free Breakfast.*

Hotel Puerta del Sur

$$$ | **HOTEL** | In a near-perfect location, on a secluded spot on Isla Teja yet only eight blocks from downtown Valdivia, this highly regarded lodging has spacious, pleasant rooms decorated in soft lavender tones and views of the river. **Pros:** lots of activity options; central location; great service. **Cons:** no gym; thin walls; maintenance issues due to advancing age of property. [$] *Rooms from: pesos89000* ✉ *Los Lingues 950, Isla Teja, Isla Teja* ☎ *63/222–4500* ✎ *recepcion@hotelpuertadelsur.com* 🛏 *40 rooms* 🍴 *Free Breakfast.*

Pilolcura Lodge

$$$ | **B&B/INN** | Just 25 km (15 miles) from Valdivia, Pilolcura Lodge comes with a tremendous beachside location and five immaculate rooms facing the ocean. **Pros:** clean and relaxing rooms; location

on a quiet, lovely beach; easy access to world-class mountain biking. **Cons:** Wi-Fi only in common area; no TV; road to lodge is in poor condition. [$] *Rooms from: pesos80000* ✉ *Playa Pilolcura* ☎ *9/6472–9876* 🛏 *5 rooms* 🍴 *Free Breakfast.*

Nightlife

The hometown of Austral University of Valdivia, a major Chilean university, the nightlife is lively and fun, particularly in and around the downtown area known as Calle Esmeralda. Bars, discos, and pubs are not just student-oriented, though; there are also many establishments in Esmeralda and elsewhere in the city that cater to older folks.

★ El Growler

BREWPUBS | Opened by an ex-pat from Oregon, this microbrew pub has taken Valdivia by storm and brushed to the side the old traditional German beers the area had previously been known for. The Growler's own IPA beer is offered in-house only, and is a bar highlight. They also have a plethora of other beers, and good pub food like fish-and-chips. ✉ *Saelzer 41, Valdivia* ☎ *63/222–9545* 🌐 *www.elgrowler.cl.*

Gazgaz Club Valdivia

LIVE MUSIC | National and local bands of diverse musical styles, from jazz to rock, supply the live music at this club and bar. There are two main rooms, one of which features a DJ that spins electronic dance music. The bar is always filled with a festive crowd. ✉ *Camilo Henriquez 436, Valdivia* ☎ *9/9088–8598* 🕒 *Closed Sun. and Mon.*

Rio Musicbar

LIVE MUSIC | This vibrant bar is popular with the twenty-something crowd, thanks to the live music, DJ, and good food. ✉ *Alemania 290, Valdivia* ☎ *63/221–1229* 🕒 *Closed Sun.*

Shopping

Entrelagos

CHOCOLATE | Affiliated with the restaurant of the same name next door, Entrelagos has been whipping up sinfully rich chocolates for decades and arranging them with great care in the storefront display windows. Most of what is sold here is actually made at Entrelagos's factory outside town, but a small army of chocolate makers is on-site to let you see, on a smaller scale, how it's done, and to carefully package your purchases for your plane ride home. ✉ *Vicente Pérez Rosales 622, Valdivia* ☎ *63/221–2047* 🌐 *www.entrelagos.cl.*

Mercado Municipal

MARKET | The city's 1918 Mercado Municipal barely survived the 1960 earthquake intact, but it thrives again after extensive remodeling and reinforcement as a shopping-dining complex. A few restaurants, mostly hole-in-the-wall seafood joints (but some quite nice) share the three-story building with artisan and souvenir vendors. ✉ *Block bordered by Av. Arturo Prat, Chacabuco, Yungay, and Libertad, Valdivia.*

Activities

A complex network of 14 rivers cuts through the landscape in and around this southern Chilean city, forming dozens of small islands. About 160 km (99 miles) of the river system are navigable in waters ranging from 5 to 20 meters (16½ to 66 feet) deep. That makes ideal territory for kayaking, canoeing, and sailing, among other water sports. Valdivia is also near the Pacific coast. Curiñanco beach, 25 km (16 miles) from Valdivia, is a valued spot for fishing. Then there are the intact coastal temperate rain forests on the outskirts of town, secluded areas with beautiful scenery for long hikes and camping trips. At the private Oncol Park, 22 km (14 miles) from Valdivia, are hiking trails and an 870-meter (2,854-foot) tree-top canopy course.

Bird-watching is a joy here, particularly when you witness the rare black-necked swans, one of the world's smallest, which have made the Valdivia area their main habitat despite past pollution problems from a nearby pulp mill.

Alerce Outdoor

HIKING & WALKING | Treks into ancient coastal alerce forest at Parque Nacional Alerce Costero, a mountain bike tour of the evergreen forests at Futangue Park near Lago Ranco, trekking on the Mocho Choshuenco Glacier, and skiing at Cordon Caulle are just a few of the noteworthy trips offered by this outdoor education and tour operator. ✉ *Los Laureles 075, Piso 2, Valdivia* ☎ *63/269–4287* ⊕ *www. turismoalerce.cl* ▣ *From 50,000 pesos.*

Panchito El Lobo Marino

ECOTOURISM | A young, local veterinarian founded this unique eco-tourism company that aims to show and explain the region's wildlife species and natural ecosystems through photo safaris, as well as mountain bike and kayaking tours. ✉ *Ramón Picarte 1778, Valdivia* ☎ *9/7296–0188* ⊕ *www.panchitoellobom-arino.com.*

★ Pueblito Expediciones

KAYAKING | This highly regarded Valdivia-based tour operator organizes kayaking trips at rivers and lakes in the city and surrounding region. They also offer several kayaking courses. ✉ *San Carlos 188, Valdivia* ☎ *9/4130–1264* ⊕ *www.pueblito-expediciones.cl* ▣ *From 29000 pesos.*

Turismo Hua Hum

SPECIAL-INTEREST TOURS | This veteran tour operator runs excellent city tours daily, as well as hiking excursions to the nearby private nature preserve Parque Oncol and day-long tours of the spectacular Lago Ranco watershed. ✉ *Carelmapu 2133, Valdivia* ☎ *9/9771–5083* ⊕ *www.huahum. cl* ▣ *From 45000 pesos.*

Huilo Huilo

165 km east of Valdivia.

At this private nature reserve, which spans nearly 120,000 hectares (300,000 acres), you find some of the last and best stands of Chile's native evergreen forest, a temperate rain-forest ecosystem rich in plants and unique wildlife like the world's smallest deer, the pudu, and the *monito del monte,* the only surviving member of an otherwise extinct marsupial order. In addition, Huilo Huilo has undergone an ambitious project to restore the endangered huemul deer to the landscape. The reserve is home to rivers ideal for rafting and fishing, plus the spectacular Lake Pirihueico, which can be crossed by ferry to get to Argentina's tourist resort San Martín de Los Andes. Snow at the top of the park's Mocho Volcano is year-round, making it one of the country's best destinations for snowboarding. In the nearby town of Neltume and at the park store, you can purchase unique local handicrafts based on forest mythological characters known as *duendes* and *hadas.*

GETTING HERE AND AROUND

Travel east from Valdivia by car, pass by picturesque country farms along Ruta 5, going through Lanco until you reach the town of Panguipulli. From there, pick up the Panguipulli–Puerto Fuy International Highway, which becomes gravelly and narrow, with wicked curves, over the last stretch of 10 km (6 miles) leading into Huilo Huilo.

Hotels

★ Huilo Huilo

$$$$ | **RESORT** | **FAMILY** | This massive eco-tourism complex boasts five hotels, numerous cabins, and several camping sites amid the beautiful temperate forest, rivers, and lakes at the Huilo Huilo Biological Reserve. **Pros:** amazing views; close access to nature; unique architecture. **Cons:** a long drive to get there; customer service is inconsistent; no Wi-Fi in rooms. $ Rooms from: pesos200,700 ⊠ Camino Internacional, Huilo Huilo, between Netulme and Puerto Fuy ☎ 2/2887–3536 ⊕ www.huilohuilo.com ⤵ 118 rooms ‖◎‖ Free Breakfast.

Lago Ranco and Nearby

104 km (65 miles) south of Valdivia.

Situated among mountains, spectacular waterfalls, and dense temperate rain forests, the Lago Ranco province is home to the fourth-largest lake (442 km²) in Chile and is a popular destination for trekking, biking, fishing, sailing, and other outdoor sports. In summer, the beaches along Lake Ranco fill up with tourists. Most of the better options for lodging around the lake are usually independent *cabañas* (cabins). During the second week of February, there is a popular outdoor blues festival at the small town of Lago Ranco, located on the southern shores of the lake of the same name.

The name Ranco means "rough water" in the language of the Huilliche, an indigenous community that is prevalent throughout this area. In addition to tourism, agriculture and forestry are the main economic sectors here. The provincial capital is the town of Futrono, population 15,261, which is located on the northern banks of the lake.

There are several towns in the province, but Futrono is the main launching off point for outdoor excursions in the zone. You can get there from Valdivia by traveling on a scenic road through the countryside about 75 km (47 miles) on Route 206 southeast before taking a slight right on to T-55 for the final stretch of 18 km (11 miles) of gravel road to Futrono.

 Restaurants

★ Kume Yeal

$$$ | CHILEAN | About 20 minutes south of Futrono in the small town of Llifén, this may be the best place in Chile to sample Mapuche gastronomy. Everything cooked here by owner Margarita Leiva comes from organic gardens that she and her family maintain behind the restaurant. **Known for:** Mapuche food; organic ingredients; large portions. $ *Average main: pesos10,000 ⊠ Llifén ☎ 9/6691–8677 ⊕ www.facebook.com/kumeyeal.llifen ☉ Closed Mon.*

Restaurante De Pellin y Coigüe

$$$$ | BARBECUE | If you love a great steak house, and even if you don't (they also have fish and vegetarian options), this is the place to go in Futrono. In addition to the good food, there's a wide, impressive view of the lake and mountains: reserve a table on their terrace to appreciate it even further. **Known for:** terrace dining; great lake views; excellent steak house. $ *Average main: pesos14,500 ⊠ Condominio San Andrés, Km. 45, Futrono ☎ 9/9641–3004 ⊕ www.pellinycoigue.cl ☉ Closed Mon.*

Hotels

Bahía Coique

$$$$ | APARTMENT | Upscale apartments and cabins at Bahía Coique are a reasonable rate considering their high quality and lakefront location. **Pros:** great for longer stays; pool, tennis courts, and restaurant on-site; located on the lake with access to outdoor activities. **Cons:** a car is needed to fully take advantage; no meals included; in summer, you can rent for only one week at a time. $ *Rooms from: pesos140,000 ⊠ Playa Coique, Futrono ☎ 63/248–1264 ⊕ www.bahiacoique.cl ⤵ 40 units ‖◎‖ No Meals.*

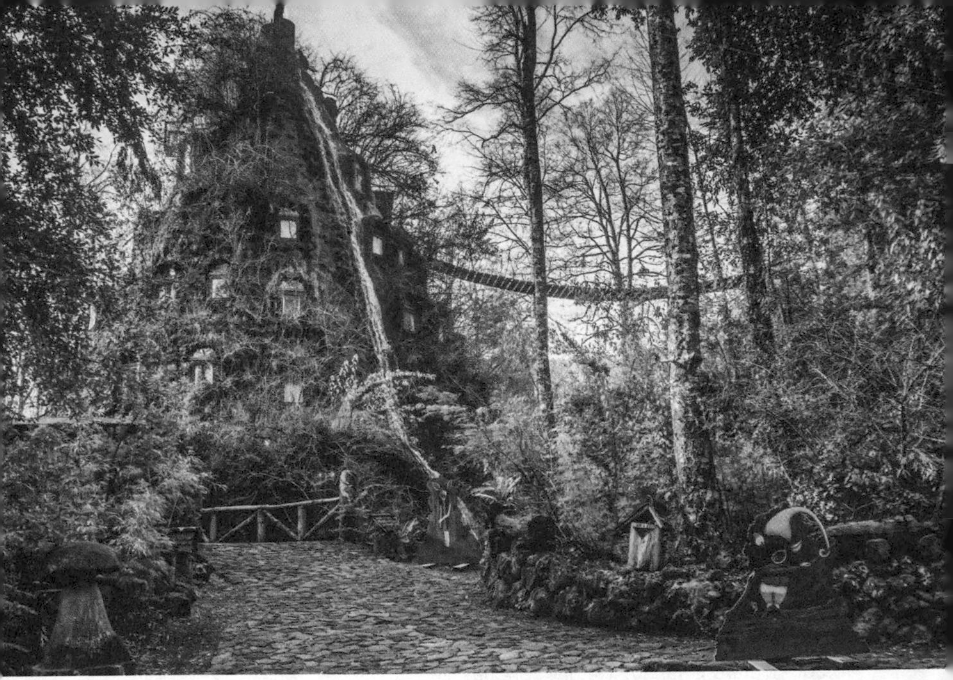

At the private nature reserve Huilo Huilo, the lodges blend into the rain forest.

Cabañas Ranco Lodge
$$$ | **APARTMENT** | These cozy, well-equipped cabins with kitchens have direct access to a lakeside beach, plus hot tubs and a sauna that are made private by forest but have an amazing view of the river. **Pros:** friendly and family-run; lake views; good location. **Cons:** three-night minimum; no meals; no TV. [$] *Rooms from: pesos80000* ✉ *T-777, Calle Viña del Mar 219, Lago Ranco* ☎ *9/8230–3056* 🌐 *www.rancolodge.cl* 🛏 *7 cabins* 🍴 *No Meals.*

Fundo Chollinco Lodge
$$$$ | **B&B/INN** | Located in perhaps the most beautiful part of Lago Ranco, Fundo Chollinco Lodge is a slice of paradise with five rustic, relaxing cabins, and tremendous views. **Pros:** great service; a place to disconnect; top fly-fishing spot. **Cons:** you'll need a car to get there; meals cost extra; some of the cabins need updating. [$] *Rooms from: pesos125,000* ✉ *Km 3, Camino Llifén* ☎ *63/197–1979, 9/8816–3256* 🌐 *www.lodgechollinco.cl* 🛏 *5 cabins* 🍴 *Free Breakfast.*

Hostal Mi Casa
$$ | **B&B/INN** | One of the oldest bed and breakfasts in Futrono, Hostal Mi Casa has comfortable rooms with all the amenities (cable TV, Wi-Fi, and a bathroom in each room), and it is close to the center of town. **Pros:** central; quiet; reasonable rates. **Cons:** books up fast in high season; no laundry service; no restaurant. [$] *Rooms from: pesos55000* ✉ *O'Higgins 259, Futrono* ☎ *63/248–2566* 🌐 *www.hostalmicasa.cl* 🛏 *16 rooms* 🍴 *Free Breakfast.*

Activities

Aventura Sport
ADVENTURE TOURS | This local travel agency can set up all kinds of outdoor trips around Lago Ranco, including horseback riding, trekking, fishing, and kayaking. ✉ *Balmaceda 910, Futrono* ☎ *9/5049–7302* 🌐 *www.aventurasport.cl* 🎫 *From 40,000 pesos.*

Isla Huapi

INDIGENOUS SIGHT | Some 20% of Chile's 1.4 million indigenous Mapuche live on *reducciones*, or reservations. One of the most welcoming communities is this settlement of Mapuche and Huilliches on Isla Huapi, a leafy island in the middle of deep-blue Lago Ranco. A boat departs from Futrono, on the northern shore of the lake, at 7:30 am every day except Thursday, returning at 4 pm. The pastoral quiet of Isla Huapi is broken once a year in January or February with the convening of the island council, in conjunction with the Lepún harvest festival. You are welcome during the festival, but be courteous and unobtrusive with your camera.

★Parque Futangue

NATURE PRESERVE | A private nature preserve about 40 km from Futrono, the 13,500-hectare Futangue Nature Park has a fantastic variety of outdoor recreational activities to offer. There is a network of more than 100 km of trails for hiking and mountain biking through lush, Valdivian temperate rain forest. The scenery is breathtaking, and always unique: sometimes you are deep in virgin forest then occasionally find yourself among rock formations so visually unusual as to seem extraterrestrial. Views of mountains and volcanoes peak around the corner. Hike about three to four hours in and there are natural hot springs. Kayakers and fly fishermen can spend countless hours on one of the several lakes or rivers. There are also opportunities for horseback riding. From May to October you must reserve your park entrance ticket ahead of time on their website, where you can also book a variety of excursions with bilingual guides. There is no camping permitted, but they have a highly regarded upscale lodge with 16 rooms, fine dining restaurant, pool and sauna room (two-night minimum, 550,000 pesos). ☒ *Ruta T-85, Km 22, Riñinahue, Lago Ranco* ☎ *9/5197–0972* ⊕ *www.parquefutangue. com* ✉ *12,000 pesos.*

Osorno

107 km (65 miles) southeast of Valdivia, via Ruta 5, Pan-American Hwy.

Although the least visited of the Lake District's four major cities, Osorno is one of the oldest in Chile. Originally founded in 1558, the town suffered a major earthquake in 1575 followed by conflicts with the Mapuche, keeping Spanish colonizers out until 1796. Like other communities in the region, it bears the imprint of the German settlers who came here later, in the 1880s. The 1960 earthquake left Osorno with little historic architecture, but a row of 19th-century houses miraculously survived on Juan Mackenna between Lord Cochrane and Freire. Their distinctively sloped roofs, which allow adequate drainage of rain and snow, are replicated in many of Osorno's newer houses. Situated in a bend of the Río Rahue, the city makes a convenient base for exploring the nearby national parks.

GETTING HERE AND AROUND

Osorno is about a 1½-hour flight from Santiago. By car, Osorno is reached by the paved Ruta 5, or Pan-American Highway. All the main bus lines serve Osorno on a frequent basis. If you plan to cross the border to reach the resort town of Bariloche in Argentine Patagonia, this is the closest Chilean city.

ESSENTIALS

BUS CONTACTS Buses Cruz del Sur. ☒ *Errázuriz 1400, Of. 9, Osorno* ☎ *64/223–2778* ⊕ *www.busescruzdelsur. cl.* **Turbus.** ☒ *Errázuriz 1400, Of. 5-A, Osorno* ☎ *64/220–1526* ⊕ *www.turbus.cl.*

VISITOR INFORMATION Sernatur. ☒ *Av. Bernardo O'Higgins 667, Osorno* ☎ *64/223–4104* ⊕ *www.sernatur.cl.*

Sights

Auto Museum Moncopulli

OTHER MUSEUM | An Osorno business executive's love for tailfins and V-8 engines led him to establish this auto museum in 1995. His particular passion is the little-respected Studebaker, which accounts for about half of the 140 vehicles on display. Elvis and Buddy Holly bop in the background. ✉ *Ruta 215, 25 km (16 miles) east of Osorno, Puyehue* ☎ *9/6918–5258* 🌐 *www.moncopulli.cl* 🎟 *4500 pesos* 🕒 *Closed Mon.*

Catedral de San Mateo Apostol

CHURCH | This modern cathedral fronts the Plaza de Armas and is topped with a tower resembling a bishop's mitre. "Turn off your cell phone," the sign at the door admonishes those who enter. "You don't need it to communicate with God." ✉ *Plaza de Armas, Osorno* ☎.

Museo Municipal Osorno

HISTORY MUSEUM | This museum contains a decent collection of Mapuche artifacts, Chilean and Spanish firearms, and exhibits devoted to the German settlement of Osorno. Housed in a pink neoclassical building dating from 1929, this is one of the few older structures in the city center. ✉ *Manuel Antonio Matta 809, Osorno* ☎ *64/223–8615* 🎟 *Free* 🕒 *Closed Sun.*

Parque Cuarto Centenario

CITY PARK | **FAMILY** | Close to the city center, Cuarto Centenario Park was established in 1958 to celebrate the city's 400th anniversary. A popular picnic and recreation spot, the park is about 67,000 square meters in size and has bicycle paths, playgrounds, and lots of green space to escape the urban jungle. Among the more than 20 species in the small forest of the park are younger specimens of the ancient Sequoia trees native to California. ✉ *Manuel Antonio Matta 336, Osorno.*

Restaurants

Café Central

$$ | **CAFÉ** | **FAMILY** | You can dig into a hearty American-style breakfast in the morning and burgers, sandwiches, and ice cream the rest of the day at this diner on the Plaza de Armas. It's most famous around town for its *completos*—Chilean hot dogs topped with gobs of mayo, guacamole, and whatever else you desire. **Known for:** ice cream; big breakfasts; famous Chilean hot dogs. [$] *Average main: pesos6000* ✉ *Av. Bernardo O'Higgins 610, Osorno* ☎ *64/225–7711* 🕒 *Closed Sun.*

★ El Galpón

$$$$ | **BARBECUE** | This is a good place to eat barbecue, steaks, and chicken (and just that, as it's meat-only here). The design intrigues as well, resembling a *galpón,* which means "barn" in English. **Known for:** fun, rustic ambience; best dining option in Osorno; meat-centric menu. [$] *Average main: pesos12500* ✉ *Lord Cochrane 816, Osorno* ☎ *64/223–4098* 🕒 *Closed Sun.*

Gallardia

$$ | **BURGER** | This place seeks mastery over the art of sandwich-making. Not to be missed is the Abuela Lucy, a juicy hamburger with onions and cilantro, a thick layer of soft cheese, roasted peppers, a grilled egg, and French fries. **Known for:** outdoor seating; gourmet sandwiches; 70 beers on tap. [$] *Average main: pesos7000* ✉ *Av. Bernardo O'Higgins 1236, Osorno* ☎ *64/222–1011* 🕒 *Closed Sun. and Mon.*

Gustoso Pizza

$$$$ | **ITALIAN** | Good, quality pizza is the specialty at Gustoso. You must pay more for premium styles, but if you appreciate a slowly fermented, thin-crust pizza with quality Italian cheese, extra virgin olive oil, and all manner of healthy toppings like arugula, then you'll leave happy. **Known for:** homemade pastas; premium pizza; thin crust. [$] *Average main: pesos12000* ✉ *Casanova 944, Osorno* ☎ *64/224–8186* 🕒 *Closed Mon. and Tues.*

Hotels

Conrado Hotel Osorno

$$ | HOTEL | The modern and spotless hotel facilities at the Conrado are welcome among Osorno's old and tired hotel offerings. **Pros:** fast Internet connection; great value; walkable to downtown. **Cons:** no gym; simple breakfasts; no restaurant. $ *Rooms from: pesos62000* ✉ *Conrado Amthauer 1153, Osorno* ☎ *64/221-8550* ☞ *30 rooms* ◉ *Free Breakfast.*

Hotel Diego de Almagro Osorno

$$$ | HOTEL | Catering primarily to business travelers, this relatively new hotel—part of a national chain—is a fine choice for your stay in Osorno. **Pros:** pool and sauna on-site; clean, spacious rooms; excellent service. **Cons:** plain decor; restaurant is subpar; bathrooms are small. $ *Rooms from: pesos90000* ✉ *Av. Alcalde Alberto Fuschlocher 1236, Osorno* ☎ *64/241-3000* ⊕ *www.dahotelesosorno.com* ☞ *123 rooms* ◉ *Free Breakfast.*

Mapa Hostel Boutique

$$ | B&B/INN | FAMILY | Each of the four rooms here is large and private with a high quality bed and linens, but the real bonus is the hostel's helpful owner, who gives you tips on all the hidden gems around town. **Pros:** tour guides available; located in one of Osorno's oldest and best neighborhoods; wood-fired hot tub. **Cons:** few rooms; no TVs; rooms do not have private bathrooms. $ *Rooms from: pesos65000* ✉ *Hermanos Phillipi 1351, Osorno* ☎ *9/8182-1078* ⊕ *www.mapahostel.cl* ☞ *4 rooms* ◉ *Free Breakfast.*

★ Sonesta Hotel Osorno

$$$$ | HOTEL | Part of the upscale, international hotel chain of the same name, this modern, high-quality hotel overlooks the Rahue River and is adjacent to Plaza de Los Lagos, a shopping center with a large casino. **Pros:** next to casino and shops; spacious rooms; high-quality facilities. **Cons:** thin walls; location is not near city center; service is sometimes slow. $ *Rooms from: pesos111500* ✉ *Ejercito 395, Osorno* ☎ *64/255-5000* ⊕ *www.sonesta.com/osorno* ☞ *106 rooms* ◉ *Free Breakfast.*

 ## Shopping

Centro de Artesanía Local

CRAFTS | Osorno's city government operates this complex of 46 artisan vendors' stands built with steeply sloped roofs. Woodwork, leather, and woolens abound. Prices are fixed but fair. ✉ *Juan MacKenna at Ramón Freire, Osorno.*

 ## Activities

No outdoor wonder, this city is within an hour's drive of Puyehue National Park, one of Chile's best hiking areas, and several lakes for fishing and boating, such as Rupanco. To the west, there is horseback riding, fishing, and hiking along the Pacific coast and at the indigenous network of parks, Mapu Lahual, which is managed by Huilliche native communities.

★ Mapu Lahual

NATURE PRESERVE | On the Pacific coast, about a three-hour drive from Osorno, is a network of indigenous parks spread over nine Huilliche communities amid 50,000 hectares (124,000 acres) of pristine temperate rain forest. Overnight trips include a sail up the coast to visit a Huilliche settlement and the beautiful, white sand and turquoise waters of Condor Beach (www.caletacondorexpediciones.cl). The eight-person boat leaves from Bahía Mansa, but keep an eye on the weather as the boat won't run if it's really windy. Exploring the indigenous parks by land is a more intrepid trip. The Agencia de Turismo Mapu Lahual, which represents the Huilliche communities, offers three- to six-day programs that include trekking, horseback rides, and homestays (simple, basic accommodations) with descendants of the Huilliche. Nature lovers will appreciate the native alerce forest as you cross the Chilean

An adventurous soul hikes up Volcán Puyehue.

Coastal Range, home to 30 different bird species and an equal number of mammals, including the Molina's hog-nosed skunk, mountain monkeys, and pumas. ⊠ *Osorno* ✢ *Maicolpué* ☎ *9/9053–4372* ⊕ *www.mapulahual.com.*

Parque Nacional Puyehue

81 km (49 miles) east of Osorno, via Ruta 215.

One of Chile's most popular national parks, Parque Nacional Puyehue draws crowds who come to bask in its famed hot springs. Most never venture beyond them, and that's a shame. A dozen miles east of the Aguas Calientes sector lies a network of short trails leading to spectacular moonlike volcanic landscapes and evergreen forests with dramatic waterfalls.

GETTING HERE AND AROUND
From Osorno, the park is about 80 km (50 miles) to the east off Highway 215. There are also several buses and travel agencies in Osorno that can help with transport to the park.

Sights

Volcán Puyehue
VOLCANO | Truly adventurous types attempt the five-hour hike to the summit of 2,240-meter (7,350-foot) Volcán Puyehue. As with most climbs in this region, CONAF rangers insist on ample documentation of experience before allowing you to set out. Access to the 1,070-square-km (413-square-mile) park is easy; head east from Osorno on the highway leading to Argentina. ⊠ *Ruta 215* ☎ *64/222–1304* ⊕ *www.conaf.cl* ⌦ *Free.*

Hotels

★ Lodge El Taique

$$ | B&B/INN | This B&B run by a friendly French couple is situated in a charming country setting with tremendous lake and volcano views. **Pros:** good value rooms; excellent French cuisine; gorgeous views. **Cons:** no television; no guides for outdoor activities; located 8 km (5 miles) from the main road. $ *Rooms from: pesos66000* ⊠ *Sector El Taique, Km 4, Puyehue* 🕿 *9/9213–8105* ⊕ *www.lodgeeltaique.cl* ⇆ *10 rooms* ⦿ *Free Breakfast.*

Termas Aguas Calientes

$$$$ | RESORT | FAMILY | Now under the same management as the bigger Puyehue spa just down the road, this hotel's triangular-shaped cabins were recently remodeled and have seen a corresponding price hike; the well-equipped accommodations include kitchens, Internet, cable TV, and phones. **Pros:** good option for families or groups; thermal pools; kitchen in cabins. **Cons:** hot springs get crowded; Wi-Fi signal is weak; lack of privacy. $ *Rooms from: pesos125000* ⊠ *Camino Antillanca, Km 4, Puyehue National Park* 🕿 *64/233–1700* ⊕ *www.termasaguascalientes.cl* ⇆ *26 cabins* ⦿ *Free Breakfast.*

Termas Puyehue Wellness and Spa Resort

$$$$ | RESORT | FAMILY | This grandiose stone-and-wood hot springs resort sits on the edge of Parque Nacional Puyehue. **Pros:** all-inclusive benefits; restaurants, bars, and activities on-site; thermal pools. **Cons:** rates substantially higher in summer; pools can get crowded; some of the older rooms are in need of updates. $ *Rooms from: pesos300000* ⊠ *Ruta 215, Km 76, Puyehue* 🕿 *600/293–6000 in Chile, 2/2293–6000 from abroad* ⊕ *www.puyehue.cl* ⇆ *112 rooms* ⦿ *Free Breakfast.*

Puerto Octay

50 km (30 miles) southeast of Osorno, via Ruta 5, Pan-American Hwy.

The story goes that a German merchant named Ochs set up shop in this tidy community on the northern tip of Lago Llanquihue. A phrase uttered by customers looking for a particular item, "*¿Ochs, hay…?*" ("Ochs, do you have…?"), gradually became "Octay." With spectacular views of the Osorno and Calbuco volcanoes, the town was a pioneer in Lake District tourism. A wealthy Santiago businessman constructed a mansion outside the town in 1913 (it would become a hotel in 1942), using it as a vacation home to host his friends.

GETTING HERE AND AROUND
Puerto Octay is easily accessible on paved roads from Ruta 5, the Pan-American Highway. It's about an hour north of Puerto Montt.

 Restaurants

★ Rancho Espantapajaros

$$$$ | CHILEAN | FAMILY | Midway between Puerto Octay and Frutillar, this countryside restaurant next to the lake has an all-you-can-eat buffet, with dishes that combine German and local Chiloé gastronomy. One of the most noteworthy options on the menu is *carne de jabalí*, or wild boar meat. **Known for:** reservations recommended on weekends; extensive all-you-can-eat buffet; wild boar meat. $ *Average main: pesos16000* ⊠ *Quilanto, Km 6, Puerto Octay* 🕿 *9/3228–1683* ⊕ *www.espantapajaros.cl* ⦵ *Closed Mon. and Tues.*

Hotels

Los Lingues Lodge

$$$$ | B&B/INN | FAMILY | Offering much more than just four spacious, well-equipped cabins, Los Lingues Lodge also comes with a southern Chilean breakfast delivered right to your door and a full-on outdoor adventure in a beautiful setting. **Pros:** beautiful natural setting; well-equipped cabins; outdoor adventure options on-site. **Cons:** other meals not included; Internet connection is not always the best; long road to the lodge. [$] *Rooms from: pesos120000* ✉ *Rte. U-55-V, Km 27.5, Cruce El Escudo, Puerto Octay* ☎ *9/9642–8604* 🌐 *www.loslingueslodge.com* 🛏 *4 cabins* 🍴 *Free Breakfast.*

★Zapato Amarillo

$$ | B&B/INN | This modern alerce-shingled house and accompanying cabins with grassy roofs give a drop-dead gorgeous view of Volcán Osorno outside town. **Pros:** kitchen available for use; amazing breakfast; fantastic views. **Cons:** located about 20 minutes from town; cash only; neighbor noise through thin walls. [$] *Rooms from: pesos50000* ✉ *Ruta U-55, Km 2.5, Puerto Octay* ☎ *64/221–0787* 🌐 *www.zapatoamarillo.cl* 💳 *No credit cards* 🛏 *5 rooms* 🍴 *Free Breakfast.*

Frutillar

30 km (18 miles) southwest of Puerto Octay.

Halfway down the western edge of Lago Llanquihue lies the picturesque town of Frutillar, a destination for European immigrants in the late 19th century and, today, increasingly a destination for Chileans resettling in the south. The 20,000-person town—actually two adjacent hamlets, Frutillar Alto and Frutillar Bajo—is known for its perfectly preserved German architecture. Don't be disappointed if your first sight of the town is the nondescript neighborhood (the Alto) on the top of the hill; head down to the charming streets of Frutillar Bajo that face the lake, with their picture-perfect view of Volcán Osorno. The town has a well-developed touristic infrastructure, and it is worth a stop.

GETTING HERE AND AROUND

The town is about 45 minutes north of Puerto Montt, on Ruta 5, the Pan-American Highway. Several bus lines make stops here on Santiago–Puerto Montt routes.

ESSENTIALS

VISITOR AND TOUR INFORMATION

Información Turística. ✉ *Costanera Philippi in front of boat dock, Frutillar* ☎ *65/246–7450.* **Secretaria Municipal de Turismo.** ✉ *Av. Philippi 753, Frutillar* ☎ *65/242–1685.*

Sights

★Museo Colonial Alemán

HISTORY MUSEUM | Step into the past at one of southern Chile's best museums. Besides displays of 19th-century agricultural and household implements, this open-air museum has full-scale reconstructions of buildings—a smithy and barn, among others—used by the original German settlers. Exhibits at this complex administered by Chile's Universidad Austral are labeled in Spanish and German, but there are also a few signs in English. A short walk from the lake up Avenida Arturo Prat, the museum also has beautifully landscaped grounds and great views of Volcan Osorno. ✉ *Av. Vicente Pérez Rosales at Av. Arturo Prat, Frutillar* ☎ *65/242–1142* 🎫 *2500 pesos.*

Beaches

Playa Frutillar

BEACH | Packed with crowds in summer, the gray-sand Playa Frutillar stretches for 15 blocks along Avenida Philippi. From this point along Lago Llanquihue you have a spectacular view due east of the conical Volcán Osorno, as well as the lopsided Volcán Puntiagudo. **Amenities:** food and drink; lifeguards; parking (fee); toilets; water sports. **Best for:** sunrise; sunset; swimming; walking ✉ *Frutillar.*

 Restaurants

Club Alemán

$$$$ | **GERMAN** | One of the German clubs that dot the Lake District, Alemán serves up ample portions alongside prompt service. This is the perfect spot to try Germanic pork and sauerkraut dishes. **Known for:** tasty küchen cake for dessert; traditional German cuisine; rotating prix-fixe menus. $ *Average main: pesos13000* ⊠ *Philippi 747, Frutillar* ☎ *65/242–1249* ⊕ *www.cartafrutillar.cl.*

Restaurante Cocina Frau Holle

$$$$ | **BARBECUE** | **FAMILY** | Get a table with an incredible view of the lake during the day if you can, and prepare to enjoy mouthwatering homemade bread and a delicious pisco sour. Then, go for one of their huge steaks, pork chops, or short ribs, along with the homemade French fries. **Known for:** lake views; succulent steaks; tasty homemade bread and awesome desserts. $ *Average main: pesos15000* ⊠ *Antonio Varas 54, Frutillar* ☎ *65/242–1345.*

★ Se Cocina

$$$$ | **CONTEMPORARY** | The gourmet meals at Se Cocina, made with fresh local ingredients from the organic garden on-site, are excellent, but it's worth coming here for the experience alone. The food is prepared right in front of you at the open kitchen, which is next to the dining room tables. **Known for:** microbrews made on-site; local organic ingredients and open kitchen; lake views. $ *Average main: pesos13500* ⊠ *Camino a Tortal Km 2, sector Quebrada Honda, Frutillar* ☎ *9/8972–8195* ⊙ *Closed Mon.*

Hotels

Hosteria Winkler

$$ | **B&B/INN** | Steps away from the Teatro del Lago on the costanera, this small B&B is a great find if there's a room available. **Pros:** relatively low price; central location; best bakery in town is on the first floor.

Cons: classic furniture may not suit all tastes; walking noises can be heard; old house. $ *Rooms from: pesos65,000* ⊠ *Av. Philippi 1155, Frutillar* ☎ *65/242–1388* ⚲ *6 rooms* ¶○¶ *Free Breakfast.*

★ Hotel Ayacara

$$$ | **B&B/INN** | This attractive yellow-and-green house built at the turn of the 19th century has tasteful design and beautiful views of the lake and Osorno Volcano. **Pros:** good food; historic, remodeled home; great views. **Cons:** lots of stairs; can hear noise from other rooms; limited parking. $ *Rooms from: pesos100000* ⊠ *Philippi 1215, Frutillar* ☎ *65/242–1550* ⊕ *www.hotelayacara.cl* ⚲ *8 rooms* ¶○¶ *Free Breakfast.*

Hotel Elun

$$$$ | **B&B/INN** | From just about every vantage point at this hillside lodging just south of town—the lobby, the library, and, of course, the guest rooms—you have a spectacular view of Lago Llanquihue. **Pros:** good common areas; great views; attentive service. **Cons:** on outskirts of town; noise from neighbors; some rooms are small. $ *Rooms from: pesos116000* ⊠ *Camino Punta Largo, Km 0.2, Frutillar* ☎ *65/242–0055* ⊕ *www.hotelelun.cl* ⚲ *14 rooms* ¶○¶ *Free Breakfast.*

Hotel Frutillar

$$$ | **HOTEL** | **FAMILY** | This centrally located hotel is the perfect place to base an extended trip in the area, offering both comfortable rooms and private apartments with a kitchen. **Pros:** lovely decor; centrally located; friendly service. **Cons:** not much in the way of amenities; thin walls; limited parking. $ *Rooms from: pesos102500* ⊠ *Vicente Pérez Rosales 673, Frutillar* ☎ *65/242–1413* ⊕ *www.hotelfrutillar.cl* ⚲ *16 rooms* ¶○¶ *Free Breakfast.*

Hotel Serenade de Franz Schubert

$$$ | **B&B/INN** | The names of the guest rooms in this old, classic Frutillar home reflect musical compositions—like Fantasia and Wedding March—and each door is painted with the first few sheet-music bars of the work it's named for. **Pros:** lovely flower garden; central, lakeside location; good breakfasts. **Cons:** no television in rooms; lacking in services; rooms have an old, formal decor. [$] *Rooms from: pesos102000* ✉ *Pedro Aguirre Cerda 50, Frutillar* ☎ *65/242–0332* ✉ *aledoepking@yahoo.com* 🛏 *6 rooms* 🍴 *Free Breakfast.*

Playa Maqui Lodge
$$$ | **B&B/INN** | In the countryside, this excellent lodging combines quiet nights, great views, and private access to a lakeside beach. **Pros:** great service; secluded location with private lakefront; rural ambience. **Cons:** old house with thin walls; you may feel isolated without your own vehicle; off-the-beaten-track vibe not for everyone. [$] *Rooms from: pesos85000* ✉ *Km 6, Ruta V155, Frutillar* ☎ *9/9567–8446* 🌐 *www.playamaqui.cl* ⏲ *Closed Mar. and Apr.* 🛏 *10 rooms* 🍴 *Free Breakfast.*

Performing Arts

Semanas Musicales de Frutillar
CONCERTS | Each year, in late January and early February, the town hosts an excellent series of mostly classical concerts (and a little jazz) at Teatro del Lago and the lakeside Centro de Conciertos y Eventos, a semi-outdoor venue. Ticket prices for their midday concerts are 12,000 pesos. ✉ *Av. Philippi 777, Frutillar* ☎ *65/242–1386* 🌐 *www.semanasmusicales.cl.*

★ **Teatro del Lago**
PERFORMANCE VENUE | Culture in Frutillar, and the southern Lake District in general, nowadays follows the lead of Teatro del Lago, which hosts a year-round schedule of concerts, art shows, and film. Events take place every week, and the state-of-the-art building is considered one of the finest of its kind in the world. Even if you can't attend an event, it's worth a look when walking along the lakefront in Frutillar. ✉ *Av. Philippi 1000, Frutillar* ☎ *65/242–2900* 🌐 *www.teatrodellago.cl.*

Puerto Varas

27 km (16 miles) south of Frutillar via Ruta 5, Pan-American Hwy.

One of the fastest-growing cities in Chile, Puerto Varas is located on the shores of Lake Llanquihue and is renowned for its views of both the Osorno and Calbuco volcanoes. Stunning rose arbors and Germanic-style architecture grace many of the centuries-old houses and churches that dot the town. Well situated, it's close to Puerto Montt and its regional airport. It's also within a few hours driving to regional hot spots like Chiloé, Vicente Pérez Rosales National Park, Cochamó, and Puelo. With dozens of big hotels and smaller B&Bs added in recent years, as well as numerous cafés and trendy restaurants, a modern casino, lots of tour operators, and an interesting bar scene, it now rivals Pucón as the tourism capital of the Lake District.

GETTING HERE AND AROUND

Puerto Varas is only about a 20-minute drive from the center of nearby Puerto Montt. You can get to the Puerto Montt airport via a 25-minute drive on Camino Las Lomas just north of the town. Most of the bus lines that serve Puerto Montt make obligatory stops in Puerto Varas on their way north or south. Around town, there are numerous taxis and several minivan buses, which make several stops, the most prominent being on Avenida Salvador near the corner of Santa Rosa. Both taxis and buses can take you to countryside locations such as Ensenada and Puerto Montt for a minimal cost. You can cross to Argentina via bus or boat.

ESSENTIALS

BUS CONTACTS Buses ETM. ✉ *Ramón Ricardo Rosas 1017, Puerto Varas* ☎ *65/223–0830* 🌐 *www.busesetm.cl.*

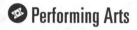

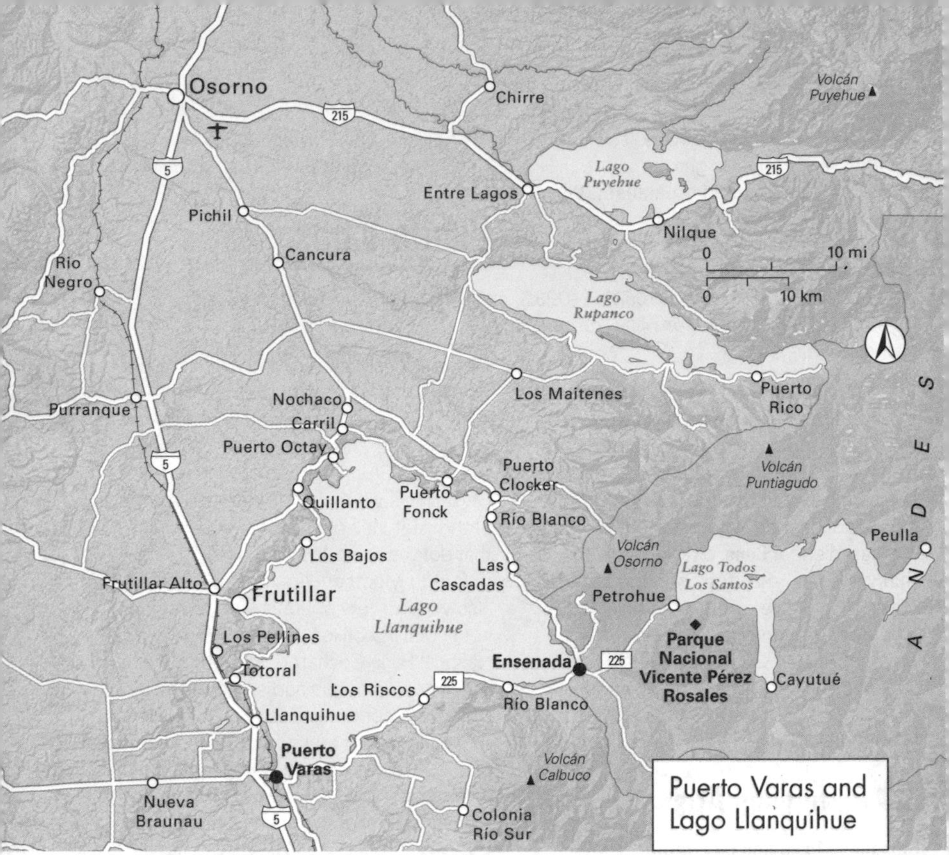

Puerto Varas and Lago Llanquihue

Turbus. ✉ *Del Salvador 1093, Puerto Varas* ☎ *65/223–3787* 🌐 *www.turbus.cl.*

RENTAL CAR CONTACTS Sur Rent a Car. ✉ *Av. Gramado 544, Puerto Varas* ☎ *9/7306–3545* 🌐 *www.surentacar.cl.* **Dobe Rent A Car.** ✉ *Quintanilla 950, Puerto Varas* ☎ *9/9548–4204.*

VISITOR AND TOUR INFORMATION Casa del Turista. ✉ *Piedra Plen, in front of Plaza de Armas, Puerto Varas* ☎ *65/223–7956.* **Oficina de Turismo.** ✉ *Del Salvador 320, Puerto Varas* ☎ *65/236–1175.*

🍴 Restaurants

★ Casa Valdes

$$$ | SEAFOOD | Start your dinner off right with a cool pisco sour at this fine dining, lakeside restaurant with great views. The cooking style is influenced in part by Basque cuisine, with its fish and other plates often accompanied by peppers, beans, and potatoes. **Known for:** crowds at dinnertime; Basque-inspired seafood; lake views. [$] *Average main: pesos10000* ✉ *Santa Rosa 040, Puerto Varas* ☎ *9/9079–3938* 🌐 *www.restaurant-casavaldes.cl.*

El Patio de Mi Casa

$$$ | CHILEAN | A small wooden sign on the front lawn of a local home invites visitors to the residents' very own terrace and restaurant. Past the modest exterior a world of authentic Chilean culinary delights awaits. **Known for:** intimate atmosphere; grilled merluza with pastel de choclo; hot brownie for dessert. [$] *Average main: pesos10,000* ✉ *Decher 830, Puerto Varas* ☎ *65/223–1507* 🕒 *Closed Sun. and Mon.*

La Marca

$$$$ | STEAKHOUSE | For quality steaks, this is the top spot in town. Start it all off with a pisco sour and sopaipillas, a sort of sweet fried bread, before moving on to the *bife chorizo* or *lomo vetado*—both are tasty cuts of meat. **Known for:** attentive service; parrilla-style grilled meats; great pisco sour menu. $ *Average main: pesos13900* ⊠ *Camino a Ensenada, Km 1,5, Puerto Varas* ☎ *65/223–2026* ⊕ *www.lamarca.cl* ⊗ *Closed Sun. and Mon.*

La Olla

$$$ | SEAFOOD | This Puerto Varas institution is well-known for its great fish plates, but they also serve a variety of seafood plates, empanadas, and Chilean-style beef dishes. The restaurant, located just past Puerto Chico at the beginning of the Camino Ensenada road, is big, with two dining rooms. **Known for:** big crowds on weekends, so book ahead; excellent fish dishes; tasty empanadas. $ *Average main: pesos10000* ⊠ *R-225, Km 1 (Camino a Ensenada), Puerto Varas* ☎ *65/223–3540, 9/7629–0668* ⊕ *www.laolla.cl.*

Mesa Tropera

$$$ | PIZZA | Situated on a lone pier jutting out into the lake, Mesa Tropera offers Italian-Patagonian cuisine that features a wide array of creative toppings on their thin crust pizzas, inventive pasta dishes, and abundant salads. Mesa Tropera is also a connoisseur of fine beer, brewing their own flavors as well as keeping a selection of microbrews in stock from others in the region. **Known for:** large crowds and no reservations; creative pizzas with a Patagonian flair; great microbrew menu. $ *Average main: pesos9000* ⊠ *Santa Rosa 161, Puerto Varas* ☎ *65/223–7973* ⊕ *www.mesatropera.cl* ⊗ *Closed Sun.*

Pataliebre

$$$ | SANDWICHES | Located near the center of town, Pataliebre has all manner of gourmet sandwiches, including hamburgers, chicken or steak sandwiches, and vegetarian options, all made with fresh, organic ingredients. If you're hankering for a hamburger from back home, this will hit the spot. **Known for:** central location; burgers and cocktails; outdoor seating. $ *Average main: pesos9000* ⊠ *Diego Portales 318, Puerto Varas* ☎ *65/223–7196* ⊕ *www.pataliebre.cl.*

 Hotels

Casa Kalfu

$$$ | B&B/INN | This bright-blue cozy B&B is in one of the many distinctive, old-style German homes found throughout the older sections of Puerto Varas. **Pros:** bilingual staff; good service; comfortable rooms. **Cons:** some rooms are small; limited parking; soundproofing issues. $ *Rooms from: pesos85000* ⊠ *Tronador 1134, Puerto Varas* ☎ *65/275–1261* ⊕ *www.casakalfu.cl* ⇥ *19 rooms* ⦿| *Free Breakfast.*

Casa Molino

$$$$ | B&B/INN | Located in a secluded spot about 15 minutes north of Puerto Varas, Casa Molino is a B&B at its best. **Pros:** great views of the lake and volcanoes; home environment; private access to a lakeside beach. **Cons:** gravel road to hotel; no air-conditioning; 15 minutes from Puerto Varas. $ *Rooms from: pesos245,000* ⊠ *Parcela 8, Costanera Viento Norte, Llanquihue, Puerto Varas* ☎ *65/223–2142, 9/9039–8343* ⊕ *www.casamolino.cl* ⇥ *10 rooms* ⦿| *Free Breakfast.*

Enjoy Puerto Varas Hotel

$$$$ | HOTEL | FAMILY | This upscale hotel on a lovely residential street just minutes to downtown has spacious rooms, some of them with commanding views of the lake and volcanoes. **Pros:** diverse on-site services; spacious rooms; tranquil location. **Cons:** frequent events at the hotel draw crowds; hotel needs some upkeep; spa and pool not always working. $ *Rooms from: pesos142800* ⊠ *Klenner 349, Puerto Varas* ☎ *65/220–1000* ⊕ *www.enjoy.cl* ⇥ *91 rooms* ⦿| *Free Breakfast.*

Gracias a la Vida Lodge

$$$ | **B&B/INN** | **FAMILY** | In addition to five new suites, the lodge's three plush, beautiful cabins are located on stilts on the banks of Lago Pichilaguna, complete with a dramatic view of Osorno Volcano and all the peace and tranquility one could desire. **Pros:** bird-watching and other excursions offered; beautiful lake setting; spacious cabins and new suites. **Cons:** sauna costs extra; no TV; really best if you have your own car. [$] *Rooms from: pesos90000* ✉ *Fundo Pichilaguna Parcela 44, Puerto Varas* ☎ *9/9826–1268, 9/9292–1521* 🌐 *www.graciasalavidalodge.com* 🛏 *8 units* 🍴 *Free Breakfast.*

Hotel Cabaña del Lago

$$$ | **HOTEL** | **FAMILY** | Encompassing a large swath of the western end of the Puerto Varas waterfront, the biggest hotel in the city has a full slate of services, including a spa, pool, gym, children's playroom, and outdoor hot tubs. **Pros:** restaurant and bar on-site; all rooms have lake views; walking distance to downtown. **Cons:** basic breakfasts; noise issues, can hear neighbors; limited parking spots. [$] *Rooms from: pesos105000* ✉ *Luis Wellmann 195, Puerto Varas* ☎ *65/220–0100* 🌐 *www.hotelcabanadellago.cl* 🛏 *157 rooms* 🍴 *Free Breakfast.*

Hotel Cumbres Puerto Varas

$$$$ | **HOTEL** | A towering hotel on a hill overlooking the lake, Cumbres Puerto Varas is part of a leading hotel chain in Chile that has gained a sterling reputation for their impeccable customer service. **Pros:** modern infrastructure; service is exemplary; impressive views of lake. **Cons:** lacks unique character; restaurant is average; pool is small. [$] *Rooms from: pesos147206* ✉ *Imperial 0565, Puerto Varas* ☎ *2/222–2000* 🌐 *www.cumbrespuertovaras.cl* 🛏 *90 rooms* 🍴 *Free Breakfast.*

Hotel Dreams Los Volcanes

$$$$ | **HOTEL** | In the center of town next to the casino, this hotel has exceptional rooms with excellent views, and many have their own private terrace overlooking the lake. **Pros:** downtown location; lake views; spa and pool. **Cons:** restaurant needs more variety; limited parking; casino environment not for everyone. [$] *Rooms from: pesos110000* ✉ *Del Salvador 21, Puerto Varas* ☎ *65/249–2000* 🌐 *puerto-varas.dreams.cl* 🛏 *50 rooms* 🍴 *Free Breakfast.*

Hotel Puelche

$$$ | **HOTEL** | The exterior of this quiet, laid-back hotel resembles a mix of hotel and mountain lodge, which is apt because Puelche combines a large hotel's amenities and services with the more intimate feel and personalized attention seen in a mountain lodge. **Pros:** quiet; lake views from rooms; personalized service. **Cons:** limited parking; breakfast is basic; no gym. [$] *Rooms from: pesos99000* ✉ *Imperial 695, Puerto Varas* ☎ *65/223–3600* 🌐 *www.hotelpuelche.com* 🛏 *21 rooms* 🍴 *Free Breakfast.*

★ **Los Caiquenes Hotel Boutique**

$$$$ | **B&B/INN** | This tranquil, high-end boutique hotel on the shore of Lake Llanquihue is just outside of Puerto Varas. **Pros:** lakeside location; maximum comfort; big, luxurious rooms. **Cons:** small staff; lacks extra amenities of the bigger hotels; hotel is on the outskirts of town. [$] *Rooms from: pesos215,000* ✉ *Camino Ensenada, Km 9.5, Puerto Varas* ☎ *9/8159–0489, 9/9741–1781* 🌐 *www.hotelloscaiquenes.cl* 🛏 *8 rooms* 🍴 *Free Breakfast.*

Radisson Hotel Puerto Varas

$$$$ | **HOTEL** | Located at the edge of downtown, facing the lake and across the street from the casino, this well-situated, modern hotel has the high-quality rooms and amenities you come to expect from a brand like the Radisson. **Pros:** good service; central location; views from the balcony. **Cons:** the regular rooms are small; gym is subpar; small spa. [$] *Rooms from: pesos175000* ✉ *Del Salvador 24, Puerto Varas* ☎ *65/223–1100* 🌐 *www.radissonhotelsamericas.com* 🛏 *98 rooms* 🍴 *Free Breakfast.*

ⓨ Nightlife

Bravo Cabrera

BARS | This lively bar-restaurant packs a nice local crowd most nights, with music getting louder as the night goes on. But do not underestimate the excellent restaurant here as well. The pizzas are the most popular choice by the locals, but the menu also includes soups, salads, sandwiches, ribs, pasta, and more—all for a reasonable price. ⊠ *Vicente Perez Rosales 1071, Puerto Varas* ☎ *65/223–3441* ⊕ *www.bravocabrera.cl.*

★ Casino Dreams Puerto Varas

THEMED ENTERTAINMENT | The flashy Casino Dreams Puerto Varas has the most prestigious address in town, facing the center of the waterfront. For a small-town casino, it's actually a modern, well-done place, with all the Vegas-style trappings, from slot machines to roulette, along with a restaurant, bar, and frequent music, comedy, and other entertainment. ⊠ *Del Salvador 21, Puerto Varas* ☎ *65/249–2000.*

Club Orquidea

BARS | Near the center of town, this is the most popular nightlife spot in Puerto Varas, with drinks constantly flowing at the long bar, two outdoor seating areas for smokers, karaoke or live music on some evenings, and good pizza and bar food. ⊠ *San Pedro 537, Puerto Varas* ☎ *9/6141–2648* ⓥ *Closed Mon.*

🏃 Activities

Puerto Varas has a plethora of outdoor options, including mountain biking, canyoning, wind surfing, sailing, hiking in nearby Vicente Pérez Rosales Park, or just enjoying the lake by kayak. You can also hike up the Osorno or Calbuco volcanoes. Fly-fishing is prominent in the area, with many rivers and the huge Lago Llanquihue making appealing targets. With so much attractive nature in its backyard, it's no wonder

Puerto Varas has become a global destination for outdoor-adventure enthusiasts.

The lake itself frequently boasts strong winds suitable for first-class windsurfing and sailing. At Canopy Lodge of Cascadas, the largest canopy area in Chile, not far from Puerto Varas, you can zipline 70 meters (230 feet) above canyons and forest. The Petrohué River offers the opportunity for rafting, and along with numerous other rivers in the area, great fishing. Biking alongside the lake is a popular trip, too. Vicente Pérez Rosales Park and Alerce Andino Park have good trails for hiking and camping, while Osorno Volcano excels for treks, skiing, and snowboarding. Some two hours from Puerto Varas is Cochamó Valley, a fantastic spot that has drawn comparisons to Yosemite Park in California for its high granite mountain cliffs, waterfalls, and overall landscape. This is a rock climber's paradise and a hiker's dream, with exceptional horseback-riding trails as well. Just south from Cochamó is Puelo, a river valley in the shadow of the Andes Mountains. It's the launching point for some of Chile's best fly-fishing, in addition to great hiking and other outdoor action.

BIRD-WATCHING
BirdsChile

BIRD WATCHING | This group leads three-day overnight treks to the park, hiking on trails to the El Amarillo Glacier, Chaitén Volcano, and Escondidas Waterfall. The tour group flies on a small plane from Puerto Varas and returns by boat through the fjords. ⊠ *Pasaje Ricke 108, Puerto Varas* ☎ *9/9269–2606, 9/9235–4818* ⊕ *www.birdschile.com* 🎫 *From 25000 pesos.*

FLY-FISHING
Tafkahr

FISHING | A fishing store that sells a diverse selection of gear and clothing, Tafkahr also offers fishing tours to nearby lakes and rivers. ⊠ *Centro Comercial Doña Ema, Local 68, Puerto Varas* ☎ *9/6602–0657* ⊕ *www.tafkarh.com.*

Tres Piedras

FISHING | This longtime fly-fishing agency in Puerto Varas organizes day- and multiday trips at nearby lakes and rivers. ✉ *Puerto Varas* ☎ *9/7618–7826* ➔ *australwaters@gmail.com* ⊕ *www.trespiedras.cl* 💰 *From 150000 pesos.*

HORSEBACK RIDING

Alanca

HORSEBACK RIDING | This company offers half-day horseback trips through native forest, wetlands, and on the lake shore in a rural park just 15 minutes from Puerto Varas. They also lead trips along the Pacific coast at Reloncaví Sound, just south of Puerto Montt. ✉ *Puerto Varas* ☎ *9/6496–5291* ⊕ *www.alancachile.com* 💰 *From 55000 pesos.*

MULTISPORT OPERATORS

Al Sur Expediciones

HIKING & WALKING | This operator runs a variety of excursions in Puerto Varas and the Lake District, including sea kayaking, trekking, and rafting. ✉ *Aconcagua 8, Puerto Varas* ☎ *65/223–2300* ⊕ *www.alsurexpeditions.com* 💰 *From 32000 pesos.*

Jass Puerto Varas

HIKING & WALKING | Trekking and kayaking tours in the region are offered by Jass, from half-day to multiday trips. Their guides provide special expertise in nearby areas such as Cochamo, Puelo, Volcán Osorno, and Alerce Andino Park. ✉ *San Jose 192, Office 203, Puerto Varas* ☎ *9/6590–6458* ⊕ *www.jasspuertovaras.com* 💰 *From 65000 pesos.*

★ Ko'Kayak

KAYAKING | This longtime tour operator in Puerto Varas offers sea and river kayaking, as well as white-water rafting trips, from half-day excursions to multiday trips. Ko'Kayak specializes in excursions on the Petrohue River, but they also do longer trips to other places in the region, like Pumalín National Park. ✉ *Ruta 225, Km 40, Puerto Varas* ☎ *9/9310—5272* ⊕ *www.kokayak.cl* 💰 *From 35000 pesos.*

Saltos del Maullín

BOATING | Go exclusive fly-fishing on the Maullin River, located about 24 km (15 miles) outside of Puerto Varas. Take lessons, go boating on the river, take a guided hike in the nearby forest, and enjoy a Patagonian barbecue. ✉ *Fundo la Isla, Río Maullin, Nueva Braunau* ☎ *9/9325–9490* ⊕ *www.saltosdelmaullin.cl.*

TREKKING

★ Huella Andina Expeditions

MOUNTAIN CLIMBING | These experts guide excursions to the major volcanoes of southern Chile, including trekking to the summit of Osorno Volcano. ✉ *Camino Volcán Calbuco, Km 3.9, Puerto Varas* ☎ ➔ *info@huellandina.com* ⊕ *www.huellandina.com* 💰 *From 120000 pesos.*

Ensenada

47 km (28 miles) east of Puerto Varas.

A drive along the southern shore of Lago Llanquihue to Ensenada takes you through the heart of Chile's murta-growing country. Queen Victoria is said to have developed a fondness for these tart red berries, and today you find them used as ingredients in syrups, jams, and küchen. Frutillar, Puerto Varas, and Puerto Octay might all boast about their views of Volcán Osorno, but you can really feel up close and personal with the volcano when you arrive in the town of Ensenada, which also neighbors the jagged Volcán Calbuca. The lake drive to Ensenada is also without doubt one of the prettiest in southern Chile.

GETTING HERE AND AROUND

By car, it's a beautiful scenic ride about 48 km (30 miles) east of Puerto Varas on the Camino Ensenada. In Puerto Varas, a regular, hourly minibus (until 9 pm) also provides transport to Ensenada.

☕ Coffee and Quick Bites

Onces Bellavista

$$$$ | CAFÉ | If traveling by car near Ensenada, make sure to swing by this classic stop between 4 pm to 8 pm, when they serve *onces*, a sort of Chilean teatime. For 14,000 pesos, you're served great küchen, cake, bread, cheese, salami, Nescafe coffee, tea, hot chocolate, and more. **Known for:** Chilean teatime; panoramic view of the volcanoes and lake; cabins if you want to spend the night. $ *Average main: pesos 14000* ✉ *Km 34, Camino Ensenada, La Ensenada* ☎ *9/8880–6181* ⊕ *www.oncesbellavista.cl.*

🛏 Hotels

★ Cabañas Ensenada

$$ | HOTEL | Surrounded by a native forest of Arrayan trees, this eco-conscious hotel is a great value. **Pros:** cool geodesic dome lodging; hot tub and hammocks for relaxing; quiet forest oasis. **Cons:** close proximity to neighboring guests; hot tub costs extra; no meals included. $ *Rooms from: pesos 60,000* ✉ *Km 42, Camino Ensenada, La Ensenada* ☎ *9/6238–1395, 65/235–7243* ⊕ *www.ensenadabosquenativo.cl* ⇥ *6 rooms* ⦿ *No Meals.*

Casa Pumahue

$$ | B&B/INN | With a bird's-eye view of Osorno Volcano from their countryside perch, Casa Pumahue is an excellent accommodation with friendly, attentive service by Rodolfo, the owner. **Pros:** helpful owner; great view; comfortable lodging. **Cons:** the room in a geodesic dome is small; best to go here by car; not all rooms have TV. $ *Rooms from: pesos 70,000* ✉ *Ruta 225, Km 37, La Ensenada* ☎ *9/7398–4624* ⊕ *www.casapumahue.com* ⇥ *4 units* ⦿ *No Meals.*

Hotel AWA

$$$$ | HOTEL | An attentive staff, great food, a variety of services that cater to each guest's interest, and comfortable rooms make this a good choice for those exploring Ensenada or even Puerto Varas, which is only about half an hour or so away. **Pros:** creative design of rooms; gourmet dining; floor-to-ceiling views of the lake and volcano. **Cons:** small gym; limited menu in restaurant; 30-minute drive to Puerto Varas. $ *Rooms from: pesos 192,000* ✉ *Km 27, Camino Ensenada, La Ensenada* ⬦ *Sector Los Riscos* ☎ *9/5397–0740* ⊕ *www.hotelawa.info* ⇥ *31 rooms* ⦿ *Free Breakfast.*

Yan Kee Way Lodge

$$$ | HOTEL | FAMILY | This venerable lodge is tucked up close to Lake Llanquihue and Osorno Volcano. **Pros:** near volcano and park; excellent restaurant; spacious suites. **Cons:** Wi-Fi and cell phone connection is unstable; bungalows are expensive; an hour drive from Puerto Varas. $ *Rooms from: pesos 95000* ✉ *Km 42, Camino Ensenada, La Ensenada* ☎ *9/4554–1660* ⊕ *www.southernchilexp.com* ⇥ *19 rooms* ⦿ *Free Breakfast.*

Parque Nacional Vicente Pérez Rosales

3 km (2 miles) east of Ensenada.

Chile's oldest national park, with its spectacular Lago Todos los Santos, forests, and Andean mountain backdrop, Vicente Pérez Rosales is a real treasure for hiking, fly-fishing, and more.

GETTING HERE AND AROUND

Take a one-hour drive along Ruta 224, Camino a Ensenada, from Puerto Varas. Several agencies in Puerto Varas run guided trips and transport to the park.

◉ Sights

Parque Nacional Vicente Pérez Rosales

NATIONAL PARK | Chile's oldest national park was established in 1926. South of Parque Nacional Puyehue, this vast 2,538-square-km (980-square-mile) preserve includes the Osorno and lesser-known Puntiagudo volcanoes, as well as the deep-blue Lago Todos los Santos. The Volcán Osorno appears in your car window soon after you drive south from Osorno and doesn't disappear until shortly before your arrival in Puerto Montt. There is a visitor center opposite the Hotel Petrohué that can provide info on several hikes, such as the Rincón del Osorno trail that hugs the lake and the Saltos de Petrohué trail, which runs parallel to the river of the same name. ☎ *65/248–6115* 🌐 *www.conaf.cl* 🎟 *6400 pesos.*

Hotels

Petrohué Lodge

$$$$ | **B&B/INN** | The common areas in this rustic orange chalet have vaulted ceilings and huge fireplaces. **Pros:** attentive service; inside Vicente Pérez Rosales Park; very good breakfast. **Cons:** no television in rooms; Wi-Fi unstable; no elevator to upper floors. [$] *Rooms from: pesos180000* ✉ *Parque Nacional Vicente Perez Rosales, Ruta 225, Km 60, Petrohué* ☎ *9/8464–4870* 🌐 *www.petrohue.com* 🕒 *Closed May and June* 🛏 *20 rooms* 🍴 *Free Breakfast.*

Activities

Canopy Chile

ZIP LINING | Make like Tarzan and swing through the treetops in the shadow of Volcán Osorno with Canopy Chile. A helmet, a very secure harness, 2 km (1 mile) of zipline strung out over 11 platforms (the second-longest in South America), and experienced guides give you a bird's-eye view of the forest below. ✉ *Ruta U99-V, Camino Cascadas Km 60, Puerto Varas* ☎ *9/5666–1305* 🌐 *www.canopychile.cl* 🎟 *From 27000 pesos.*

Cruce Andino

BOAT TOURS | This all-day crossing of the spectacular Andean mountain lakes between Puerto Varas and Bariloche is the classic trip of the area and worth doing. It leaves out of Lake Todos los Santos in Vicente Pérez Rosales National Park at 8 am every day. There is a stop for lunch at an island called Peulla before eventually arriving in Bariloche at around 8 pm. The operator can also pick you up at your hotel if in Puerto Varas or Bariloche. ✉ *Del Salvador 72, Puerto Varas* ☎ *9/3406–2885* 🌐 *www.cruceandino.com* 🎟 *From 250000 pesos.*

Kotaix Bike Park

BIKING | The first paved pump track in South America, this 270-meter bike track is surrounded by forest in the shadow of the ever-present Osorno Volcano. There's a small café on-site that serves drinks and snacks. ✉ *Camino Volcan Osorno, Km 3, La Ensenada* ☎ *9/5617–5334* 🌐 *www.kotaixbikepark.cl* 🎟 *From 7,000 pesos* 🕒 *Closed Mon. and Tues.*

★ Ski & Outdoor Volcán Osorno

SKIING & SNOWBOARDING | About 60 kilometers (37 miles) from Puerto Varas, Volcán Osorno is the setting for entertaining skiing with breathtaking vistas of the Lake District. The Ski & Outdoor Center on the volcano has two ski lifts, 11 ski trails with varied levels of difficulty, and a store that rents equipment and provides ski and snowboard lessons. The Mirador restaurant has hot lunch and coffee. Daily ski passes are 30,000 pesos. In summer, the volcano is a great spot for hiking and mountain biking. ✉ *Camino Volcán Osorno, Km 14,2, Puerto Varas* ☎ *9/9158–7337* 🌐 *www.volcanosorno.com.*

Puerto Montt

20 km (12 miles) south of Puerto Varas via Ruta 5, Pan-American Hwy.

For most of its history, windy Puerto Montt was the end of the line for just about everyone traveling in the Lake District. Now the Carretera Austral carries on southward, but for all intents and purposes Puerto Montt remains the region's last significant outpost, a provincial city that is a hub for the

Fishing boats are docked in the water of Puerto Montt.

nation's salmon farming industry as well as local fishing, farming, and forestry.

Today, the city center is full of malls, condos, and office towers, but away from downtown, Puerto Montt consists mainly of low clapboard houses perched above its bay, the Seno de Reloncaví. If it's a sunny day, head east to Playa Pelluco or one of the city's other beaches. If you're more interested in exploring the countryside, drive along the shore toward Chinquihue for a good view of the surrounding hills.

GETTING HERE AND AROUND
Puerto Montt is a main transit hub in the region. Buses from Santiago and all points in southern Chile ramble through here at some point, while many cruise ships dock at the port. Puerto Montt's El Tepual Airport has daily air traffic from all the major airlines that serve Chile. The Pan-American Highway also stops here, while the mostly unpaved Carretera Austral, which winds its way through Chilean Patagonia, begins south of the city. To cross over into Argentina, buses leave from here and from Puerto Varas. There is

also regular ferry service to Chaitén from the port. Chiloé Island is less than two hours' drive from Puerto Montt. Take the last part of Ruta 5, or the Pan-American Highway, to Pargua, where two ferries cross the Chacao Channel every hour.

CRUISE TRAVEL TO PUERTO MONTT
The many large cruise ships that arrive to the public port of Puerto Montt, the most important in southern Chile, must anchor offshore and use smaller tender boats to carry passengers to the dock. The port is located at the western end of the city near Caleta Angelmo, which conveniently for travelers is also the best place to shop for local handicrafts and try local seafood in numerous small restaurants at the tail end of the waterfront.

Downtown Puerto Montt, where all the malls, office buildings, and hubbub are located, is about nine blocks, or 1 mile away. You can walk there in about 20 minutes or so, but buses or cheap taxis (usually about 1,500 pesos per person) are prevalent near the port and can whisk you to the city center within minutes. Moreover, many of the taxis and local tour operators are often waiting at the port to offer you deals on day trips in the city or nearby tourism destinations like Puerto Varas, Volcán Osorno, and Frutillar.

ESSENTIALS

BUS CONTACTS Buses JAC. ⊠ *Av. Diego Portales 1001, Puerto Montt* ☎ *65/238–4600* ⊕ *www.jac.cl.* **Cruz del Sur.** ⊠ *Av. Diego Portales 1001, Puerto Montt* ☎ *65/225–4731* ⊕ *www.busescruzdelsur. cl.* **Turbus.** ⊠ *Av. Diego Portales 1001, Puerto Montt* ☎ *65/249–3402* ⊕ *www. turbus.cl.*

RENTAL CAR CONTACTS Rent a Car ZKAR. ⊠ *Santa Teresa 655, Puerto Montt* ☎ *9/4980–5923* ⊕ *www.zkar.cl.*

VISITOR AND TOUR INFORMATION Puerto Montt Tourist Office. ⊠ *Plaza de Armas, Antonio Varas 415, Puerto Montt* ☎ *65/222–3016* ⊕ *puertomontt.travel.*

Sights

★ Caleta Angelmó

MARINA/PIER | About 3 km (2 miles) west of downtown along the coastal road lies Puerto Montt's fishing cove. This busy port serves small fishing boats, large ferries, and cruisers carrying travelers and cargo southward through the straits and fjords that form much of Chile's shoreline. On weekdays, small launches from Isla Tenglo and other outlying islands arrive early in the morning and leave late in the afternoon. There are dozens of stalls selling local handicrafts, and the fish market here has one of the most varied seafood selections in all of Chile. ⊠ *Puerto Montt.*

Catedral de Puerto Montt

CHURCH | Latin America's ornate church architecture is nowhere to be found in the Lake District. More typical of the region is Puerto Montt's stark 1856 Catedral. The alerce-wood structure, modeled on the Pantheon in Paris, is the city's oldest surviving building. ⊠ *Plaza de Armas, Puerto Montt.*

Museo Historico de Puerto Montt

HISTORY MUSEUM | This museum, east of the city's bus terminal, has a collection of crafts and relics from the nearby archipelago of Chiloé. Historical photos of Puerto Montt give a sense of the area's slow and often difficult growth, plus the impact of the 1960 earthquake, which virtually destroyed the port. Pope John Paul II celebrated Mass on the grounds during his 1987 visit; one exhibit documents the event. ⊠ *Av. Diego Portales 997, Puerto Montt* ☎ *65/222–3029* ⊠ *Free* ⊙ *Closed Sat. and Sun.*

Parque Nacional Alerce Andino

NATIONAL PARK | Close to Puerto Montt, the mountainous 398-square-km (154-square-mile) Parque Nacional Alerce Andino, with more than 40 small lakes, was primarily established to protect the endangered alerce trees that are spread out upon some 20,000-hectares (49,421 acres) of the park. Comparable to California's redwood trees, alerce grow to average heights of 50 meters (165 feet) and can reach 5 meters (16 feet) in diameter. Immensely popular as building material for houses and furniture in southern Chile, they have been nearly wiped out from the landscape. They are also the world's second-oldest living tree species, many living up to 4,000 years. ⊠ *Carretera Austral, 35 km (21 miles) east of Puerto Montt, Puerto Montt* ☎ *65/248–6115* ⊕ *www.conaf.cl* ⊠ *5200 pesos.*

⊕ Beaches

Beaches at Maullín

BEACH | About 70 km (43 miles) southwest of Puerto Montt, at this small town near Pargua—the ferry crossing to Chiloé—the Maullín River merges with the Pacific Ocean in spectacular fashion. Be sure to visit the expansive Pangal Beach, with large sand dunes teeming with birds. If staying overnight, there are cabins and a campground. ⊠ *Ruta 5 south from Puerto Montt, about a 1-hr drive, Puerto Montt.*

🍴 Restaurants

Azzurro

$$$ | **ITALIAN** | This Italian restaurant has good pizza, but they're best known for their creative pastas. The restaurant is housed in a modest blue building, with a rustic wooden interior and informal atmosphere. **Known for:** casual ambience; simple, classic Italian dishes; excellent pasta. [$] *Average main: pesos11000* ✉ *Liborio Guerrero 1769, Puerto Montt* ☎ *65/231–8989* 🌐 *www.azzurro.cl.*

Caleta Angelmó

$$ | **SEAFOOD** | More than a dozen small kitchens and eateries at this enclosed market 3 km (2 miles) west of Puerto Montt along the coast road prepare southern Chilean seafood favorites like *curanto,* a potpourri of shellfish, meat, and potatoes, and *paila marina,* a hearty seafood stew with mainly shellfish. Each kitchen has separate tables and counters. **Known for:** fish market and handicraft stores also on-site; food stalls serving Chilean specialities; no set hours but usually open for lunch and dinner in high season. [$] *Average main: pesos6500* ✉ *Caleta Angelmó, Puerto Montt* ☎ 💳 *No credit cards.*

Chile Picante

$$$$ | **CHILEAN** | Nestled on a steep hill in a nondescript neighborhood, the decor here is no frills, but the view of the city is spectacular and the food is some of the best in Puerto Montt. They offer daily set menus for 12,000 pesos, including an appetizer, drink, and dessert. **Known for:** good value; awesome views; regularly changing menu of spicy Chilean classics. [$] *Average main: pesos12000* ✉ *Vicente Perez Rosales 567, Puerto Montt* ☎ *9/8454–8923* 💳 *No credit cards* 🕒 *Closed Sun.*

★ Cotelé

$$$ | **STEAKHOUSE** | The older of Cotelé's two locations in the city (the other is at Rengifo 867), this restaurant has the look and feel of a typical *quincho* (barbecue), with wooden walls and tables with the grill in the middle. Here, it is strictly about meticulously preparing the best possible steaks. **Known for:** nice selection of wines and pisco sours; one of the top-rated steak houses in Chile; selection of prime meats you can then watch be grilled in front of you. [$] *Average main: pesos11000* ✉ *Juan Soler Manfredini 1661, Puerto Montt* ☎ *65/227–8000* 🌐 *www.coteleres-taurante.cl* 🕒 *No dinner Sun.*

El Fogón de Pepe

$$$$ | **STEAKHOUSE** | If you need a change of pace from the ubiquitous seafood in Puerto Montt, this is a great option. Roast-beef plates, roasted ribs, chicken, and steaks are all great. **Known for:** big weekend crowds; excellent meats; friendly service. [$] *Average main: pesos12000* ✉ *Rengifo 845, Puerto Montt* ☎ *9/7979–7056, 65/239–6386* 🕒 *Closed Sun. and Mon.*

★ Restaurant Kiel

$$$ | **SEAFOOD** | Founded in 1973, this Chilean-German seafood restaurant is located on the coast about 15 minutes west of Puerto Montt and is considered an institution in the area. The interesting decor and sea views are nice, but it's the beautifully prepared seafood and, in particular, the curanto that draws crowds. **Known for:** reservations necessary in summer; great seafood curanto; fresh produce from on-site garden. [$] *Average main: pesos9200* ✉ *Camino Chinquihue, Km 8, Chinquihue* ☎ *65/225–5010* 🌐 *www.kiel.cl.*

Restaurante Nana Bahamonde

$$$$ | **CHILEAN** | A mom and pop–type restaurant you won't soon forget, this simply adorned restaurant makes you feel right at home. Seemingly everything on their varied, unique Chilean menu, from seafood to beef to chicken, looks and tastes delicious. **Known for:** excellent service; memorable seafood; large portions. [$] *Average main: pesos13000* ✉ *Rengifo 917, Puerto Montt* ☎ *9/9005–1936.*

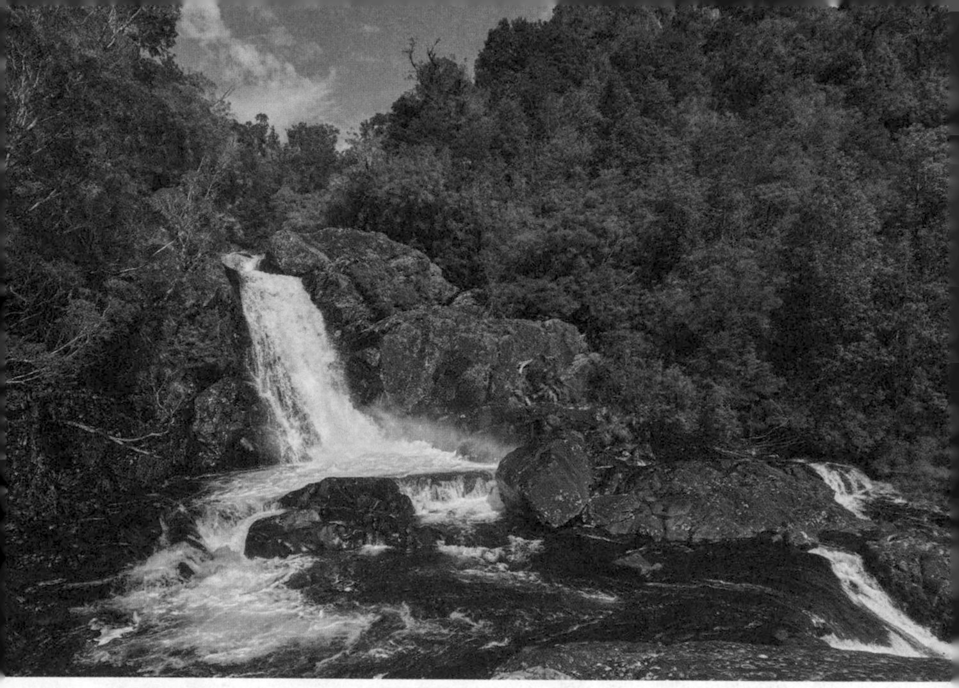

Waterfalls and lakes dot Parque Nacional Alerce Andino, which protects the endangered alerce tree.

🛏 Hotels

abba Presidente Suites Puerto Montt

$$ | **HOTEL** | Although this classic hotel is starting to show its age, the comfortable rooms have beautiful sea views, it is centrally located near downtown shopping, and the heated pool is a plus. **Pros:** views and location; good value option; helpful service. **Cons:** limited breakfast options; older hotel; thin walls. [$] *Rooms from: pesos69,000* ✉ *Diego Portales 664, Puerto Montt* ☎ *65/225–1666* 🌐 *www.abbahoteles.com* 🛏 *47 rooms* 🍴 *Free Breakfast.*

Hostal Pacífico

$$ | **B&B/INN** | European travelers favor this solid budget option up the hill from the bus station. **Pros:** near bus station; friendly staff; affordable. **Cons:** street noise; lots of stairs; small rooms. [$] *Rooms from: pesos60000* ✉ *Juan J. Mira 1088, Puerto Montt* ☎ *65/225–6229* 🌐 *www.hostalpacifico.cl* 🛏 *13 rooms* 🍴 *Free Breakfast.*

Hotel Central

$$ | **HOTEL** | Close to the bus station, this is a decent, low-price option for a night or two in Puerto Montt. **Pros:** near the bus station; attentive service; inexpensive. **Cons:** simple breakfast; neighborhood is not the best; decor is old-fashioned. [$] *Rooms from: pesos55000* ✉ *Juan José Mira 1092, Puerto Montt* ☎ *65/225–7516* 🛏 *29 rooms* 🍴 *Free Breakfast.*

Hotel Don Luis

$$ | **HOTEL** | In an excellent location down the street from the cathedral and city plaza, this hotel has rooms with panoramic vistas of Reloncaví Sound. **Pros:** great views from the seventh and eighth floors; central; good breakfast. **Cons:** some rooms are small; parking is two blocks away; noisy part of town. [$] *Rooms from: pesos69000* ✉ *Quillota 146, Puerto Montt* ☎ *65/220–0300* 🌐 *www.hoteldonluis.cl* 🛏 *65 rooms* 🍴 *Free Breakfast.*

Hotel Gran Pacífico

$$ | **HOTEL** | Thanks to an ideal location just steps away from downtown, Hotel Gran Pacífico is a great choice in Puerto Montt, especially with its awesome views of the bay. **Pros:** centrally located; nice

views; good restaurant on top floor. **Cons:** decor is nothing special; spa and gym are small; Wi-Fi sometimes unstable. $ *Rooms from: pesos72000* ⊠ *Urmeneta 719, Puerto Montt* ☎ *65/248–2100* ⊕ *www.hotelgranpacifico.cl* ⇌ *48 rooms* ⍁ *Free Breakfast.*

Manquehue Hotel Puerto Montt
$$ | **HOTEL** | The premier business hotel in Puerto Montt, this hotel goes above and beyond by offering travelers good value and comfort. **Pros:** safer part of town; good business hotel; heated pool. **Cons:** hard to find if arriving by car; slow elevators; outside of the city center. $ *Rooms from: pesos77000* ⊠ *Seminario 252, Puerto Montt* ☎ *65/233–1000* ⇌ *142 rooms* ⍁ *Free Breakfast.*

Nightlife

Baradero
LIVE MUSIC | The best place to catch live music in the city, Baradero is known for its diverse music styles and a large selection of microbrews at the bar, along with the occasional DJ or karaoke night. ⊠ *Rengifo 964, Puerto Montt* ☎ *9/4294–0230.*

Boulebar
BARS | This is a fun bar in the city center for music, tapas, and drinks. There's a second, more modern branch at Rengifo 920. ⊠ *Benavente 435, 2nd fl., Puerto Montt* ☎ *9/5800–4442* ⊗ *Closed Sun.*

Taytao
DANCE CLUBS | A lively night spot, this longtime bar and disco at Pelluco beach has two dance floors, six rooms, karaoke, a restaurant, and live music. ⊠ *Juan Soler Manfredini 1881, Puerto Montt* ☎ *9/3933–3764* ⊗ *Closed Sun. and Mon.*

 Performing Arts

Casa del Arte Diego Rivera
ARTS CENTERS | A gift of the government of Mexico, this art center commemorates the famed muralist of the same name. It hosts art exhibitions in the gallery, as well as evening theater productions and occasional music and film festivals. ⊠ *Quillota 116, Puerto Montt* ☎ *65/226–1836* ⊕ *www.culturapuertomontt.cl.*

Shopping

Feria Artesanal Angelmó
CRAFTS | An excellent selection of handicrafts is sold at the best prices in the country at the Feria Artesanal Angelmó, on the coastal road near Caleta Angelmó. Chileans know there's a better selection of crafts from Chiloé for sale here than in Chiloé itself. Baskets, ponchos, figures woven from different kinds of grasses and straw, and warm sweaters of raw, hand-spun, and hand-dyed wool are all for sale. Much of the merchandise is geared toward tourists, so look carefully for more authentic offerings. Haggling is expected. It's open daily from 9 am to dusk. ⊠ *Puerto Montt.*

Cochamó

94 km (59 miles) southwest of Puerto Varas.

The small fishing villages of Cochamó are blessed with friendly people but little infrastructure. Only a few farms dot the countryside. In short, nature with a capital "N" is the real reason to come here. Civilization has barely touched these great, vast nature areas, some of Chile's (and the world's) last. Think of Yosemite National Park in California without the crowds. Granite walls and domes are prevalent throughout the valley. At Río Puelo, the emerald-blue water seems like a dream amid the Valdivian temperate rain forests and Andean mountain scenery. An old frontier cattle trail in Cochamó Valley, once used as a hideout by Butch Cassidy and the Sundance Kid, reminds travelers that the only way through this natural wonderland is by foot or horse. You don't find any cars or roads here.

GETTING HERE AND AROUND

There are few cars in Cochamó, and even fewer gas stations (though you can get gas by the container). Walking or biking is probably the most efficient way to get around. Nearby Puelo is even smaller than Cochamó. If you must, rent a car in Puerto Montt or Puerto Varas. Roads in the region are mostly gravel and dirt, so four-wheel drive would be preferable. Buses do service these towns, however. If you take the bus, arrange with a travel agency or outfitter beforehand to help with transport to the nature areas on your wish list.

ESSENTIALS

VISITOR INFORMATION Cochamó Oficina de Turismo. ✉ *Casa del Turista, Plaza de Puelo, Cochamó* ☎ *9/9963–1246.*

Hotels

Mítico Puelo Lodge

$$$$ | HOTEL | FAMILY | Built in 1991 as a private getaway for fly-fishing enthusiasts on the shores of Lake Tagua Tagua, this lodge is reached by boat or plane (the hotel has its own motorboat, and transfers are included in rates) and also offers activities like biking, horseback riding, trekking, and kayaking. **Pros:** great for families; facilitates trips to nearby Tagua Tagua Park; quiet and remote. **Cons:** Wi-Fi is slow; only satellite phone service (extra charge); two hours from closest airport. [$] *Rooms from: pesos219000* ✉ *Lago Tagua Tagua, Cochamó* ☎ *9/8184–0544* 🌐 *www.miticopuelo.com* 🛏 *21 rooms* 🍴 *All-Inclusive.*

Posada Puelo Lodge

$$$$ | B&B/INN | This cozy fly-fishing lodge is on the banks of the beautiful Puelo River. **Pros:** great fly-fishing; excellent service; beautiful surroundings. **Cons:** can get windy and rainy in the area; geared primarily to fly fishermen; three-hour drive from airport on difficult roads. [$] *Rooms from: pesos233000* ✉ *Río Puelo, Cochamó* ☎ *9/9265–0665* 🌐 *www.posadapuelo.cl* 🕒 *Closed June–Aug.* 🛏 *5 rooms* 🍴 *All-Inclusive.*

Activities

Cochamó and Río Puelo's vast forests, fast-flowing rivers, and mountains are an outdoors lover's mecca. Before you pursue any of the myriad activities available, though, be sure to get your bearings. Unlike national parks, these areas are not formally protected and maintained, and therefore often lack well-marked trails. Check with a local outfitter or travel agency to get more information on where to go and how. Because of growing tourism in the Cochamó nature area, any potential campers must first reserve campsites ahead of time online (www.reservasvallecochamo.org).

Mahuida Patagonia

HIKING & WALKING | In summer, this reputable local tour operator can take you on multiday treks to the Cochamó Valley or Tagua Tagua Park, and fly-fishing on the Puelo River. ✉ *Cochamó* 🌐 *www.mahuidapatagonia.com.*

Southern Trips

HIKING & WALKING | Run by Cochamó locals, this outfitter is often cited as the best and most experienced guiding company for horseback rides and treks throughout the Cochamó Valley nature area. ✉ *Cochamó* ☎ *9/8407–2559* 🌐 *www.southern-trips.cl.*

Trekka

MOUNTAIN CLIMBING | Led by an accomplished local mountaineer, Trekka can take you on multiday backpacking trips through the incredible landscapes of Cochamó and Puelo as well as rock climbing to the summit of Cochamó's fabled granite peaks. ✉ *Puerto Montt* ☎ *9/989–40820* 🌐 *www.trekka.cl.*

Chapter 9

CHILOÉ

Updated by
Jimmy Langman

⊙ **Sights** 🍴 **Restaurants** 🛏 **Hotels** 👜 **Shopping** 🍸 **Nightlife**
★★★★☆ ★★★★☆ ★★★★☆ ★★★☆☆ ★★☆☆☆

WELCOME TO CHILOÉ

TOP REASONS TO GO

★ **Charming churches:** Within Chile, Chiloé is known for the centuries-old, wooden churches that dot Isla Grande. Almost all are open to the public, and a visit is essential.

★ **Traditional crafts:** Chiloé's sweaters, ponchos, blankets, and rugs are a defining feature of the island. There's nothing warmer, woollier, or more wonderful anywhere else in Chile.

★ **Nature:** Chiloé's close proximity to breeding grounds for blue whales, a globally endangered species, makes it one of the planet's top destinations for whale-watching. Many other animals call Chiloé home, too; there's wildlife like the Pudu, the world's smallest deer, and spectacular bird-watching, including penguin colonies and rare birds like the Chucao Tapaculo.

★ **Fantastic folklore:** Spirits of all stripes haunt Chiloé—or at least populate its colorful folklore, which is full of trolls, witches, mermaids, and ghost ships.

Most people explore Chiloé by car. Major towns and landmarks are no more than an hour or two apart. The Pan-American Highway (Ruta 5) that meanders through northern Chile ends at the Golfo de Ancud and continues again on Isla Grande. It connects the cities of Ancud, Castro, and Chonchi before ending in Quellón. Paved roads connect the Pan-American to Quemchi and Dalcahue, and Achao on Isla Quinchao. The coastal route connecting the village of San Antonio de Chacao with Dalcahue is also mostly paved. A more scenic route leads from Chacao to Caulín and Ancud, via Huicha. The scenic, curvy road west from Ancud is now paved all the way to the lighthouse at Corona Point.

1 Ancud. Although it's the second-largest city in Chiloé, Ancud feels like a small town. With its hills, irregular streets, and commanding ocean views, it gets rave reviews for its quiet charm.

2 Quemchi. Small, tranquil fishing village.

3 Quicaví. Fog- and folklore-steeped town and the center of magic and mysticism in Chiloé.

4 Dalcahue. Stop here for the artisan market and to catch a ferry to Isla Quinchao.

5 Isla Quinchao. When you venture to this island, stop in Achao, a busy fishing town.

6 Castro. The capital of the island province, this is Chiloé's largest city and, with good dining options, it's a fine base for your travels.

7 Chonchi. South of Castro, Chonchi's colorful wooden houses climb the hillside.

8 Parque Nacional Chiloé. One of the island's main attractions, it boasts a wild beach with many sand dunes and excellent hiking in coastal forest.

9 Queilén. Beach town named for the red cypress trees that dot the area.

10 Quellón. Chiloé's southernmost city, it's a good stopover for those headed to hiker heaven at nearby Parque Tantauco or to catch a ferry and continue your journey on to Chaitén and the southern coast.

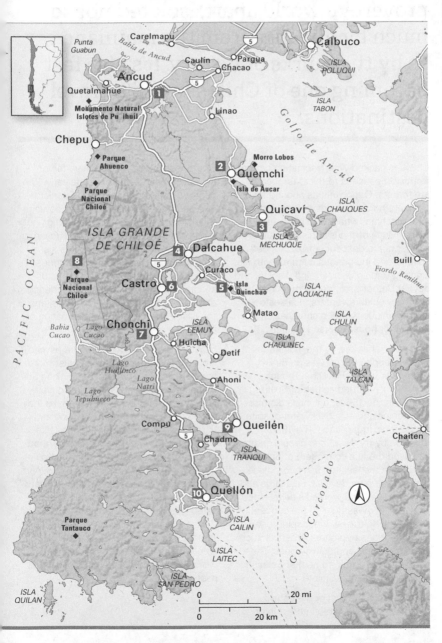

Punta Guabun

Carelmapu

Bahía de Ancud

Caulín

Calbuco

ISLA POLUQUI

Ancud

Chacao

Pargua

Quetalmahue

Monumento Natural Islotes de Pu ihuil

Linao

ISLA TABON

Golfo de Ancud

Chepu

Parque Ahuenco

Morro Lobos

Quemchi

Isla de Aucar

Parque Nacional Chiloé

Quicaví

ISLA CHAUQUES

ISLA GRANDE DE CHILOÉ

Dalcahue

ISLA MECHUQUE

Buill

Fiordo Reñihue

Parque Nacional Chiloé

Castro

Curaco

Isla Quinchao

ISLA CAQUACHE

ISLA CHULIN

Chonchi

Matao

ISLA LEMUY

Huicha

ISLA CHAULINEC

ISLA TALCAN

Bahía Cucao

Lago Cucao

Detif

PACIFIC OCEAN

Lago Huillinco

Lago Natri

Ahoni

Lago Tepuhueco

Compu

Queilén

Chaitén

Parque Tantauco

Chadmo

ISLA TRANQUI

Quellón

Golfo Corcovado

ISLA CAILIN

ISLA LAITEC

ISLA QUILAN

ISLA SAN PEDRO

0   20 mi

0   20 km

Steeped in magic, shrouded in mist, the 41-island archipelago of Chiloé is that proverbial world apart, isolated not so much by distance from the mainland as by the quirks of history. It's also fast becoming one of Chile's favorite travel destinations.

Chiloé is packed with fascinating nature, from wild beaches to thick, temperate forests. Opportunities abound for trekking, horseback riding, kayaking, bird-watching, whale-watching, and more. Much of the island's 200,000 residents are descendants of blended colonial and indigenous cultures with fascinating traditions in farming, fishing, and devout Catholicism, not to mention finely crafted woolen sweaters, rich seafood stews, unique wooden churches, and *palafito*, or houses poised on stilts.

Originally inhabited by the indigenous Chono people, Chiloé was gradually taken over by the Huilliche. Though Chiloé was claimed as part of Spain's empire in the 1550s, colonists dismissed the archipelago as a backwater despite its strategic importance. The 1598 rebellion by the Mapuche people on the mainland drove a contingent of Spanish settlers to the isolated safety of Chiloé. Left to their own devices, Spaniards and Huilliche lived and worked side by side. Their society was built on the concept of *minga*, a help-thy-neighbor spirit resembling traditions of pioneer America, such as barn raisings and quilting bees. The outcome was a culture neither Spanish nor indigenous, but Chilote.

Isolated from the rest of the continent, islanders had little interest in or awareness of the revolutionary fervor sweeping Latin America in the early 19th century. In fact, the mainland Spaniards recruited the Chilote to help put down rebellions in the region. When things got too hot in Santiago, the Spanish governor took refuge on the island, just as his predecessors had done two centuries earlier. Finally defeated, the Spaniards abandoned Chiloé in 1826, surrendering their last outpost in South America, and the island soon joined the new nation of Chile.

Nowadays, the isolation is more psychological than physical. Chiloé is just more than 2 km (1 mile) from the mainland at its nearest point, and dozens of buses and frequent ferries every day make the half-hour crossing between Chiloé and Pargua, near Puerto Montt in the Lake District on the mainland. As well, a modern airport was inaugurated in Castro in 2013. In recent years, the island's tourism offerings have taken a giant leap forward with several luxury hotels and sophisticated gourmet restaurants opening in the Castro area and the massive private park Tantauco drawing droves of trekkers near Quellón. Today, Chiloé is embracing the world while firmly preserving its cultural past.

MAJOR REGIONS

Your ferry may arrive on Chiloé at Chacao, but **Ancud** is the area's main transportation hub and the island's second-largest city. Explore here the penguins of Puñihuil, the fog- and folklore-steeped towns of Quemchi and Quicaví, and northeastern Chiloé's famous churches. If you venture to Isla Quinchao, stop in Achao, a busy fishing town.

Castro is the capital and the larger, more cosmopolitan answer to Ancud. You can see a lot near here, including Chonchi's brightly painted houses and the Parque Nacional Chiloé. Other small towns dot the east coast down to Quellón, home to nearby Parque Tantauco and where you can take ferries to Chaitén and the mainland.

Planning

When to Go

Chiloé is increasingly a year-round destination, but like the rest of southern Chile, the ideal time to go is during the summer months, from December to March. Summer is sunnier and the prime time for cultural festivals all over the island. Although Chiloé is known to be rainy—some parts receive more than 150 inches annually—periods of sunshine regularly break the spells. Year-round, however, mist and fog prevail and deepen the mystery of the islands, while the crisp, breezy air is refreshing.

FESTIVALS AND EVENTS

Like elsewhere in southern Chile, most of Chiloé's festivals take place in summer. Fiestas Costumbristas, which celebrate Chilote customs and folklore, take place over several weekends between December and February in Ancud, Castro, and other towns. There are still other special events, such as a biodiversity fair in Castro the third week of February and a small open-air film festival in Ancud during the first few days of February.

Planning Your Time

After crossing the Golfo de Ancud on the morning ferry on your first day, drive south to Ancud. Soak up the port town's atmosphere, but do try to visit the colony of penguins at nearby Puñihuil. Head to Dalcahue the next day, and have lunch at the colorful artisans' market. Then, take the short ferry ride to Isla Quinchao and visit the colorful church of Santa María de Loreto. Back on Isla Grande, proceed to Castro. Spend the next day relaxing, shopping, or visiting the capital's museums and the lovely church, then head south to tour Chonchi, known to locals as the "City of Three Stories." From there it's just a one-hour drive to the Pacific coast to visit the Parque Nacional Chiloé, where you can enjoy a hike through the forest and go horseback riding on the beach. If you have another day or two, consider going to Parque Tantauco near Chiloé's southernmost town, Quellón.

Getting Here and Around

AIR

Chiloé's modern Mocopulli Airport near Castro connects the island with national and international flights four times a week via Aeropuerto El Tepual in Puerto Montt. Chiloé also has several small airports for regional flights and private planes.

BOAT AND FERRY

Since Chiloé is an archipelago, the only way to arrive by car is to take one of the frequent ferries across the eastern end of the Chacao Channel. Both Cruz del Sur and Transmarchilay operate the frequent ferry service that connects mainland Pargua with Chacao.

FERRY SERVICE Cruz del Sur. ✉ *Los Carrera 850, Ancud* ☎ *65/262–2249* ⊕ *www.busescruzdelsur.cl.*

BUS

Cruz del Sur and its subsidiary Transchiloé operate some 30 buses per day between Ancud and the mainland, usually terminating in Puerto Montt. Many routes continue north to Temuco, and a few travel all the way to Santiago. Buses arriving from the mainland provide local service once they reach the island, making frequent stops.

BUS CONTACTS Cruz del Sur. ✉ *San Martín 486, Castro* ☎ *65/263–5152* ⊕ *www.busescruzdelsur.cl.* **ETM.** ✉ *Bus terminal, Aníbal Pinto 1200, Of. 4, Ancud* ☎ *65/262–0997* ⊕ *www.etm.cl.* **Queilén Bus.** ✉ *San Martín 667, Of. 2 and 3, Castro* ☎ *65/263–2173* ⊕ *www.queilenbus.cl.*

CAR

Rather than terminating in Puerto Montt, the Pan-American Highway skips over the Golfo de Ancud and continues through Ancud, Castro, and Chonchi before stopping in Quellón. Paved roads also lead to Quemchi, Dalcahue, and Achao on Isla Quinchao. There are rental car agencies in Castro and Ancud.

RENTAL CAR CONTACTS Rent a Car Chiloé. ✉ *Calle Dieciocho 182, Ancud* ☎ *9/9069–9675.* **SalfaSur.** ✉ *Ruta 5 Sur 2843, Castro* ☎ *65/263–0422, 9/8188–2503* ⊕ *www.salfasur.cl.*

Restaurants

As befits an island culture, seafood reigns in Chiloé. The signature Chilote dish is the *curanto,* a hearty stew of shellfish, chicken, sausages, and smoked pork ribs. It's served with plenty of potato-and-flour patties, known as *milcao* and *chapaleles. Salmón ahumado* (smoked salmon) is another favorite, though salmon is not native to this area. Avoid any uncooked shellfish unless you're certain you can trust the chef.

Breakfast here is often a humble menu of instant Nescafe coffee with warm bread, rolls, jam, and butter. Like the rest of Chile, most residents take their lunch between 1 pm and 3 during the week and often do so with gusto. In addition to seafood, Chilotes enjoy empanadas— baked or fried bread stuffed with meat, chicken, seafood, and other fillings. Roasted lamb is another favorite, with sheep raising still a common livelihood throughout the island.

The archipelago is also known for its tasty fruit liqueurs, usually from the central Chiloé town of Chonchi. Islanders take berries and apples and turn them into the *licor de oro* that often awaits you at your hotel.

Restaurant reviews have been shortened. For full information, visit Fodors.com.

Hotels

Over the past five years, Chiloé's hotel offerings have taken a quantum leap, with world-class luxury lodgings beginning to appear on the mainland. But the islands are still mostly dominated by smaller, more reasonably priced hotels. Castro and Ancud have the most choices; Chonchi, Achao, and Quellón less so. Central heating and a light breakfast are standard in better hostelries. Not all places, especially in rural towns, take credit cards, but ATMs are more readily available than you might expect.

Outside the major cities, *hospedaje* (lodgings) are few and far between. But in summer, they seem to sprout in front of every other house in Castro and Ancud, as homeowners rent rooms to visitors. Quality varies, so inspect the premises before agreeing to take a room from someone who greets you at the bus station.

Hotel reviews have been shortened. For full information, visit Fodors.com.

What it Costs in Chilean Pesos (in Thousands)			
$	$$	$$$	$$$$
RESTAURANTS			
Under 6	6–8	9–11	over 11
HOTELS			
Under 46	46–75	76–105	over 105

Ancud

90 km (54 miles) southwest of Puerto Montt.

The village of Chacao (where your ferry arrives) was actually the site of one of the first Spanish shipyards in the Americas, but it was moved in 1769 to Ancud, which was deemed a more defensible location. Ancud was repeatedly attacked during Chile's war for independence and remained the last stronghold of the Spaniards in the Americas—as well as the seat of their government-in-exile after they fled from Santiago, until 1826—when the island was finally annexed by Chile.

GETTING HERE AND AROUND

Boats leave Pargua, on the mainland, every 15 minutes from 7 am until late in the evening. Trips take about 30 minutes. An additional 30 minutes down the road from Chacao, Ancud is the first real stop on Chiloé Island for most visitors. Roads from Chacao to Ancud are paved, and most roads are now paved if you venture north or west of town to visit attractions such as the lighthouse at Faro Corona or the penguin colony at Puñihuil. There are several bus lines that serve Chiloé cities, particularly Ancud and Castro. Most visitors board buses in Puerto Montt, which is about 2½ hours from Ancud. Add another hour to get to Castro. The main bus line serving Chiloé, Cruz del Sur, has frequent service throughout the island, including Chonchi and Quellón.

ESSENTIALS

VISITOR INFORMATION Sernatur. ⊠ *Libertad 665, Ancud* ☎ *65/262–2800* ⊕ *www. sernatur.cl.*

⦿ Sights

Fuerte de San Antonio

MILITARY SIGHT | Northwest of downtown Ancud, the 16 cannon emplacements of this fort are nearly all that remain of Spain's last outpost in the New World. Constructed in 1786, the fort was a key component in the defense of the Canal de Chacao, especially after the Spanish colonial government fled to Chiloé during Chile's war for independence. ⊠ *Lord Cohrane at San Antonio, Ancud* ☎ ⊠ *Free.*

★ Monumento Natural Islotes de Puñihuil

WILDLIFE REFUGE | **FAMILY** | One of the best nature excursions on Chiloé is to Monumento Natural Islotes de Puñihuil. Located 29 km (18 miles) southwest of Ancud, the three small islets here are home to an abundant colony of Humboldt and Magellanic penguins, along with a variety of other birds and marine otters. From September to March, a local tour operator, Ecomarine Puñihuil (www.pinguineraschiloe.cl), for 8,000 pesos, offers 30-minute boat excursions to view the penguins up close. From December to March, they can take up to eight people in the mornings for longer voyages farther out at sea to search for blue whales, which have been extensively tracked in the area by scientists. ⊠ *Ruta W-20, Ancud* ☎ *9/8317–4302 mobile* ⊕ *www. pinguineraschiloe.cl.*

Museo Regional de Ancud

HISTORY MUSEUM | Statues of mythical Chilote figures, such as the Pincoya and Trauco, greet you on the terrace of this fortresslike museum, just uphill from the Plaza de Armas. The replica of the schooner *La Goleta Ancud* is the museum's centerpiece; the ship carried Chilean settlers to the Strait of Magellan

Penguins roam around Monumento Natural Islotes de Puñihuil.

in 1843. Inside is a collection of island handicrafts. ✉ *Libertad 370, Ancud* ☎ *65/250–4780* 🌐 *www.museoancud.cl* 🕒 *Closed Mon.*

🍴 Restaurants

★ Café Amaranthine

$$ | CAFÉ | FAMILY | The tasty vegetarian fare made with fresh, locally grown organic ingredients at this cozy restaurant with an ocean view will impress even meat eaters. Creative dishes include the *papas rellenas,* the island's famed potatoes stuffed with sautéed veggies, quinoa, cheese, and a special pesto sauce. **Known for:** mouthwatering desserts; delicious vegetarian food; ocean views. [$] *Average main: pesos6000* ✉ *Lord Cochrane 412, Ancud* ☎ *65/262–7448* 🌐 *www.amaranthine-chiloe.com* 🕒 *Closed Sun.*

Kuranton

$$$ | CHILEAN | This intimate establishment specializes in *curanto* (a Chilean feast cooked in the ground), available at both dinner and lunch (most restaurants have it only for lunch). A variety of other dishes fill out the menu, from *paila marina* (seafood stew) to pizza, beef, chicken, and sandwiches. **Known for:** cozy spot; curanto; Chiloé memorabilia. [$] *Average main: pesos10000* ✉ *94 Arturo Prat, Ancud* ☎ *65/262–3090* 🕒 *Closed Mon.*

Ostras Caulin

$$$$ | SEAFOOD | Just 12 miles outside of Ancud, this classic spot is the place to crack open some of the world's best oysters, taken each day from the coast in front of the small wooden restaurant. Oysters come in multiple forms: fried, poached, creamed, and raw. **Known for:** good spot for bird-watching; fresh oysters; wine. [$] *Average main: pesos15000* ✉ *Caulin (9 km from Chacao), Ancud* ☎ *9/9643–7005* 🌐 *www.ostrascaulin.cl* 🕒 *No dinner. Closed Tues.*

Hotels

Cabañas y Hostel Isla Mágica
$$ | **B&B/INN** | **FAMILY** | Located near the town center with excellent views, Isla Mágica's cozy cabins and apartments are each warmed by their own wood stoves and decorated with local crafts and flair. **Pros:** full kitchens; wood stoves; centrally located with parking. **Cons:** no breakfast; Wi-Fi is slow; showers are small. [$] *Rooms from: pesos55000* ✉ *Bellavista 438, Ancud* ☎ *65/262–1326* 🌐 *www.islamagica.cl* 🛏 *30 rooms* 🍴 *No Meals.*

Faros del Sur
$$ | **HOTEL** | This rustic wooden hotel that bills itself as a "boutique hostel" is a worthy choice for the views alone. **Pros:** tranquil location; ocean views; family atmosphere. **Cons:** hard to get to without a car; bathrooms could use a face-lift; no elevator. [$] *Rooms from: pesos49000* ✉ *Costanera Norte 320, Ancud* ☎ *65/262–5799* 🌐 *www.farosdelsur.cl* 🛏 *18* 🍴 *Free Breakfast.*

Hostal Mundo Nuevo
$$ | **HOTEL** | This Swiss-run lodging is more upscale hostel than hotel, but it is a good choice if you're after a nice view, parking, and a clean, spacious room. **Pros:** parking; clean and spacious rooms; good location with a view. **Cons:** simple breakfast; rooms are basic; can get noisy. [$] *Rooms from: pesos63000* ✉ *Av. Salvador Allende 748, Ancud* ☎ *65/262–8383* 🌐 *www.mundonuevohostal.com* 🛏 *12 rooms* 🍴 *Free Breakfast* ☞ *Book well in advance.*

Hotel Balai
$ | **B&B/INN** | Facing the town plaza, this hotel has an ideal location in the center of town. **Pros:** friendly service; good location; well-maintained rooms. **Cons:** small bathrooms; parking is two blocks away; paper-thin walls. [$] *Rooms from: pesos43000* ✉ *Pudeto 169, Ancud* ☎ *65/262–2541* 🌐 *www.hotelbalai.cl* ⏲ *Closed on some holidays* 🛏 *12 rooms* 🍴 *Free Breakfast.*

Panamericana Hotel Ancud
$$$ | **HOTEL** | A solid choice for your stay, the venerable Panamericana Hotel Ancud has long been one of Chiloé's top hotels. **Pros:** excellent service; privileged views of Ancud Bay; good restaurant. **Cons:** not much storage space for luggage; hotel is older; rooms are on the small side. [$] *Rooms from: pesos95000* ✉ *San Antonio 30, Ancud* ☎ *65/262–2340* 🌐 *www.panamericanahoteles.cl* 🛏 *24 rooms* 🍴 *Free Breakfast.*

Nightlife

L'Chinchel Bar and Cafe
BARS | This friendly, laid-back bar has great local beers on tap, tasty bar food, and trendy tunes in the background as it fills up. ✉ *Eleuterio Ramirez 317, Ancud* ☎ *65/262–4749* ☞ *Closed Sun.*

Q'ilú Restobar
BARS | A good spot for a beer and meal near the town plaza, Q'ilú Restobar has a relaxed atmosphere and a big-screen TV for watching sports. ✉ *Eleuterio Ramirez, 278, Ancud* ☎ *65/262–0658* ⏲ *Closed Sun.*

Shopping

Feria Municipal Rural y Artesanal
OTHER SPECIALTY STORE | Shopping in Ancud is nothing extraordinary, though there's a fine artisans' market just below the town plaza and a few blocks up from the waterfront. There you'll find woolen blankets, sweaters, dolls, wooden figurines, and other items by Chiloé artisans. ✉ *At Libertad and Dieciocho, Ancud.*

Activities

Water sports such as sailing or sea kayaking are popular in the Ancud area. There are several fishing and trekking possibilities as well. Along the coastline you may see dolphins, penguins, and sometimes even whales from the area's picturesque beaches.

MULTISPORT OPERATORS

Austral Adventures

KAYAKING | Austral Adventures arranges bilingual, tailor-made kayaking, trekking, and bird-watching trips. ⊠ *Ave. Salvador Allende 904, Ancud* ☎ *65/262–5977* ⊕ *www.austral-adventures.com.*

★ Chiloé Natural

HIKING & WALKING | This sustainable tour operator offers a diverse array of excursions, from kayaking and trekking to tours of the island's historic churches, and does so with creativity, insight, and authenticity. ⊠ *Auquilda rural s/n, Castro* ☎ *9/631–97388* ⊕ *www.chiloenatural. com.*

Turismo Pehuén

HIKING & WALKING | A pioneer on the island, the leading tourism operator on Chiloé has long been Turismo Pehuén. It runs a variety of top-notch nature and culture excursions of Castro, Ancud, and the surrounding region. ⊠ *Chacabuco 498, Castro* ☎ *9/757–31901* ⊕ *turismopehuen.cl.*

Quemchi

62 km (37 miles) southeast of Ancud.

On the protected interior of the Golfo de Ancud, Quemchi is a small, tranquil fishing village that makes for a good stopover when visiting churches and other tourist sites in northeastern Chiloé. There are several historic churches and scenic islands nearby.

GETTING HERE AND AROUND

You can reach Quemchi via paved roads from Ancud in less than an hour by car. To get to nearby tourist sites, be prepared for gravelly, dusty country roads that require careful driving, preferably in a four-wheel-drive vehicle. Additionally, there are a few small islands nearby worth seeing. You can hire a boat at the town port, where there is usually a handful of captains on hand ready to negotiate a fee for the service.

◉ Sights

Isla de Aucar

ISLAND | This tiny forested islet 6 km (4 miles) south of Quemchi is reached by walking across a stunning wooden bridge some 510 meters (1,673 feet) long. Black-necked swans and other birds frequent the area. The island hosts a botanical garden and Jesuit chapel and cemetery that date to 1761. ⊠ *Isla de Aucar, Quemchi.*

Morro Lobos

ISLAND | Reached by a 45-minute boat ride from the port of Quemchi, this immense rock outcrop juts out of the sea off the coast of Caucahue Island. Hundreds of sea lions and marine birds call it home. Boats at the port can be hired for about 12,000 pesos. ⊠ *Quemchi.*

Parque Ahuenco

NATURE PRESERVE | This 1,120-hectare (2,768-acre) private reserve is a magic landscape with windswept, old-growth temperate rain forest bumping up to a coastline that attracts a Humboldt and Magellanic penguin colony from September to February. A unique conservation initiative involving 46 different private owners, the park hosts the majority of the flora and fauna found on the big island of Chiloé, including the endangered Darwin's fox and the tiny pudú deer. Get here by taking a 30-minute boat ride from the Club de Pesca y Caza in Chepu, then once you reach the mouth of the river it's a three-hour hike into the park. ⊠ *Chepu* ✉ *info@ahuenco.cl* ⊕ *www.ahuenco.cl.*

🍴 Restaurants

El Chejo

$$ | **CHILEAN** | This waterfront restaurant is the place to eat in Quemchi. They have an ample menu, but it's the dozen types of empanadas—filled with beef, cheese, clams, salmon, or crab meat, to name a few—that impress most. **Known for:** waterfront dining; empanadas; local seafood dishes. $ *Average main: pesos7000* ⊠ *Diego Bahmonde 251, Quemchi* ☎ *9/9997-6318* ⊟ *No credit cards.*

Quicaví

25 km (15 miles) southeast of Quemchi.

The center of all that is magical and mystical about Chiloé, Quicaví sits forlornly on the eastern coast of Isla Grande. Superstitious locals strongly advise against going anywhere near the coast to the south of town, where miles of caves extend to the village of Tenaún. They believe that witches, and evil ones at that, inhabit them. On the beaches, local lore says, are mermaids that lure fishermen to their deaths. (These are not the beautiful and benevolent Pincoya, a legendary kelp-covered mermaid. A glimpse of her is thought to portend good fishing for the day.) Many Quicaví denizens claim to have glimpsed Chiloé's notorious ghost ship, the *Caleuche,* roaming the waters on foggy nights, searching for its doomed passengers. Of course, a brief glimpse of the ship is all anyone dares admit, as legend holds that a longer gaze could spell death.

GETTING HERE AND AROUND
From Ancud, Quicaví is reached by going first to Quemchi, then driving south along a two-lane dirt road through the Chiloé countryside for about 40 minutes.

 Sights

Iglesia de San Pedro
CHURCH | In an effort to win converts, the Jesuits constructed this enormous church on the Plaza de Armas. The original structure survives from colonial times, though it underwent extensive remodeling in the early 20th century. It's open for services on the first Sunday of every month at 11 am, which is your best bet for getting a look inside. ⊠ *Quicaví.*

Iglesia de Tenaún
CHURCH | The small fishing village of Tenaún, 7 km (4 miles) south of Quicaví, is notable for its 1845 neoclassical Iglesia de Tenaún, which replaced the original 1734 structure built by the Jesuits. The style differs markedly from that of other Chilote churches, as the two towers flanking the usual hexagonal central bell tower are painted a striking deep blue. You can see the interior during services on Sunday at 9:30 am and the rest of the week at 5 pm. ⊠ *Plaza de Armas, Tenaún.*

Dalcahue

44 km (27 miles) southwest of Quicaví; 74 km (44 miles) southeast of Ancud; 20 km (12 miles) northeast of Castro.

Many travelers in the laid-back port town of Dalcahue stop only long enough to board the ferry that deposits them 15 minutes later on Isla Quinchao. But the artisan market here is a worthy destination in itself, if only to sample the local food. Dalcahue is a pleasant coastal town—one that deserves a longer visit.

GETTING HERE AND AROUND
Dalcahue is about an hour from Ancud along paved roads. There is also frequent bus service, particularly from Castro, which is about a 15-minute drive from Dalcahue. Dalcahue Expreso buses can be caught at Castro's bus terminal (at the corner of Freire and O'Higgins) or at several bus stops along the road between Dalcahue and Ancud.

 Sights

Iglesia de Nuestra Señora de los Dolores
CHURCH | This 1850 church, modeled on the churches constructed during the Jesuit era, sits in the main square (Plaza de Armas). A portico with nine arches, an unusually high number for a Chilote

Boats float off the coast of Dalcahue.

church, fronts the structure. The church holds a small museum with historic town and church documents and old church ornaments. ⊠ *Dalcahue* 🖼 *Free.*

Museo Histórico Etnográfico de Dalcahue
HISTORY MUSEUM | A *fogón*—a traditional indigenous cooking pit—sits in the center of the small *palafito* (a shingled house built on stilts and hanging over the water) housing this museum that displays historical exhibits about the indigenous peoples of Chiloé—the Chonos and Huilliche. ⊠ *Pedro Montt 40, Dalcahue* 🕾 *65/264–2379* 🖼 *Free* ⊗ *Closed Sat. and Sun. from Mar. to Dec.*

 ## Hotels

Hotel Mawün
$$ | B&B/INN | A friendly attitude greets you at this recently renovated, wood-shingled hotel with a cozy sitting room and a big fireplace off the lobby. **Pros:** centrally located; comfortable; friendly service. **Cons:** street noise; not on the waterfront; staff does not speak

English. ⓢ *Rooms from: pesos60000* ⊠ *Elías Navarro 420, Dalcahue* 🕾 *9/9092– 0672* ⊕ *www.hotelmawun.com* 🛏 *20 rooms* ⏹ *Free Breakfast.*

★ Refugio de Navegantes
$$$ | B&B/INN | Close to both the historic church and the waterfront, this boutique hotel has just five rooms and is run with a very personal touch by its owners. **Pros:** excellent café; contemporary decor; near the town plaza. **Cons:** lacks local Chilote character; limited café menu; Wi-Fi sometimes falters. ⓢ *Rooms from: pesos97000* ⊠ *San Martín 165, Dalcahue* 🕾 *65/264–1128* ⊕ *www.refugiodenave- gantes.cl* 🛏 *5 rooms* ⏹ *Free Breakfast.*

 ## Shopping

Feria Artesanal in Dalcahue
MARKET | Dalcahue's crafts market, near the waterfront municipal building, draws crowds who come to shop for Chilote handicrafts, woolens, baskets, and woven mythical figures. It's open every day, but the best time to go is on Sunday

mornings as more vendors travel from surrounding areas to sell their wares. Don't miss the lively food stalls at the Cocinería behind the market. Bargaining is expected, though the prices are already quite reasonable. ✉ *Av. Pedro Montt, Dalcahue.*

Isla Quinchao

1 km (½ mile) southeast of Dalcahue.

For many visitors, the elongated Isla Quinchao, the easiest to reach of the islands in the eastern archipelago, defines Chiloé. Populated by hardworking farmers and fisherfolk, Isla Quinchao provides a glimpse into the region's past. Head to Achao, Quinchao's largest community, to see the alerce-shingle (a wood native to Chile) houses, busy fishing pier, and colonial church. And if you have more time, visit one of the nine outlying islands near Quinchao.

GETTING HERE AND AROUND

The roads from Dalcahue, and the main road through Isla Quinchao, are paved. About two hours from Ancud, Achao is a 30-minute journey from Dalcahue, the town from which you catch the ferry to cross Ayacara Bay. The ride is a mere five minutes, and there are frequent departures from 7 am to midnight. It's free for pedestrians and 2,500 pesos each way for cars. Once on the island, the road to Achao winds its way through verdant countryside, often with tremendous views of the surrounding sea.

👁 Sights

Iglesia de Nuestra Señora de Gracia

CHURCH | About 10 km (6 miles) south of Achao is the archipelago's largest church. As with many other Chilote churches, the 200-foot structure sits in solitude near the coast. The church has no tours but may be visited from 11 am to 3:30 pm during the summer months and the rest of the year when they celebrate Sunday Mass at 11 am. ✉ *7 km (4 miles) north of Castro, Nercon.*

★ Iglesia de Santa María de Loreto

CHURCH | Achao's centerpiece is this 1730 church, the oldest house of worship in Chile. In addition to the alerce wood so commonly used to construct buildings in the region, the church also uses cypress and *mañío* trees. Its typically unadorned exterior contrasts with the deep-blue ceiling embellished with gold stars and rich Baroque carvings on the altar inside. Mass is celebrated Sunday at 11 am and Tuesday at 7 pm, but docents give guided tours when the church is open during the day. An informative Spanish-language museum behind the altar is dedicated to the period of Chiloé's Jesuit missions. ✉ *Plaza de Armas, Delicias at Amunategui, Achao* 🎫 *Free* 🕒 *Closed Mon. Mar.–Nov.*

🍴 Restaurants

Hostería la Nave

$$$ | **CHILEAN** | Inside this rambling beachfront building that arches over the street, this restaurant serves seafood, beef, and other dishes. Try the oysters or *merluza margarita,* hake fish in a shellfish sauce. **Known for:** basic hotel upstairs; merluza margarita; beachfront location. [$] *Average main: pesos11000* ✉ *Arturo Prat at Sargento Aldea, Achao* ☎ *9/9945–8817.*

Mar y Velas

$$$ | **SEAFOOD** | Scrumptious oysters and a panoply of other gifts from the sea are served on the top floor of this big wooden house at the foot of Achao's dock (accessible via a side stairway). Open late and serving generous portions, many in town maintain the food here is the best around. **Known for:** local favorite; fresh seafood; late dining. [$] *Average main: pesos10000* ✉ *Serrano 2, Achao* ☎ *65/266–1375.*

Chile's oldest house of worship is the wooden Iglesia de Santa María de Loreto, built in 1730.

Hotels

Hotel Boutique Antukenu
$$$ | HOTEL | Great views abound at this friendly, warm boutique hotel in a quiet spot on the edge of town. **Pros:** warm rooms; tremendous views; attentive service. **Cons:** no TV in rooms; creaky pipes; thin walls between rooms. [$] *Rooms from: pesos78000* ✉ *Alto La Paloma s/n, Achao* ☎ *9/7151–4608* 🌐 *www.antukenu.cl* 🛏 *10 rooms* 🍴 *Free Breakfast.*

Castro

45 km (28 miles) west of Achao; 88 km (55 miles) south of Ancud.

Founded in 1567, Castro is Chile's third-oldest city. Its history has been one of destruction, with three fires and three earthquakes laying waste to the city over four centuries. The most recent disaster was in 1960, when a tidal wave caused by an earthquake on the mainland engulfed the city.

Castro's future as Isla Grande's governmental and commercial center looked promising after the 1598 Mapuche rebellion on the mainland drove the Spaniards to Chiloé, but then Dutch pirates sacked the city in 1600. Many of Castro's residents fled to the safety of more isolated parts of the island. It wasn't until 1982 that the city finally became Chiloé's administrative capital.

Next to its wooden churches, *palafitos,* shingled houses on stilts in the water along the coast, are the best-known architectural symbol of Chiloé. Avenida Pedro Montt, which becomes a coastal highway as it leads out of town, is the best place to see palafitos in Castro. Many of these ramshackle structures have been transformed into restaurants, boutique hotels, and artisan markets.

GETTING HERE AND AROUND

In the center of the Isla Grande de Chiloé, Castro is only about a one-hour drive from Ancud along Ruta 5, the Pan-American Highway. For a more interesting journey, consider the mostly

Chiloé's Chapels

More than 150 wooden churches are scattered across the eastern half of Chiloé's main island and the smaller islands nearby. Jesuit missionaries came to the archipelago after the 1598 Mapuche rebellion on the mainland, and the chapels they built were an integral part of the effort to convert the indigenous peoples. Pairs of missionaries traveled the region by boat, making sure to celebrate Mass in each community at least once a year. Franciscan missionaries continued the tradition after Spain expelled the Jesuits from its New World colonies in 1767.

The architectural style of the churches calls to mind those in rural Germany, the home of many of the missionaries.

The complete lack of ornamentation is offset only by a steep roof covered with wooden shingles called *tejuelas* and a three-tier hexagonal bell tower. An arched portico fronts most of the churches. Getting to see more than the outside of many of the churches can be a challenge. Many stand seemingly forlorn in their solitude on the coast and remain locked most of the year; others are open only for Sunday services. There are two main exceptions: Castro's orange-and-lavender Iglesia de San Francisco, dating from 1906—it's technically not one of the Jesuit churches but built in the same style—opens its doors to visitors; and Achao's Iglesia de Santa María de Loreto gives daily guided Spanish-language tours.

unpaved coastal road to Castro via Quemchi, which takes twice as long but passes numerous historic churches and other tourist sites.

Castro's Mocupulli Airport receives commercial flights from the mainland four days a week. There is also regular and frequent bus service from the terminal in Puerto Montt to Castro, which takes almost four hours. Buses Queilén and Gallardo operate on Chiloé Island only. Various buses go to Dalcahue from the Castro bus terminal. ETM buses can take you to the main cities of Chiloé and several cities in Chile. Cruz del Sur has routes nationwide and even into Argentina. Reserve ahead for buses.

ESSENTIALS

BOAT CONTACTS Ferry dock. ⊠ *Pedro Montt 48, Castro* ☎.

VISITOR INFORMATION Tourism Office of the Castro Municipality. ⊠ *Plaza de Armas, Castro* ☎ *65/253–8054.*

◉ Sights

★ Iglesia de San Francisco

CHURCH | Any tour of Castro begins with this much-photographed 1906 church, constructed in the style of the archipelago's wooden churches, only bigger and grander. Depending on your perspective, terms like "pretty" or "garish" describe the orange-and-lavender exterior colors chosen when the structure was spruced up before Pope John Paul II's 1987 visit. It's infinitely more reserved on the inside. The dark-wood interior's centerpiece is the monumental carved crucifix hanging from the ceiling. In the evening, a soft, energy-efficient external illumination system makes the church one of Chiloé's most impressive sights. ⊠ *Plaza de Armas, corner of Freire and Caupolicán, Castro* ☎ *65/253–8000.*

Museo de Arte Moderno de Chiloé

ART MUSEUM | Housed in five refurbished barns in a city park northwest of downtown, this modern-art complex—referred to locally as the MAM—exhibits works by Chilean artists. The museum opens to the public only when there are exhibitions or special events. ✉ *Pasaje Díaz 181, Castro* ☎ *9/881–89401* 🌐 *www.mamchiloe.cl* 🎟 *Free* 🕒 *Closed Mon.*

Museo Municipal de Castro

HISTORY MUSEUM | This museum, one block from the Plaza de Armas, gives a good (Spanish-only) introduction to the region's history and culture. Packed into a fairly small space are artifacts from the Huilliche era (primarily farming and fishing implements) through the 19th century (looms, spinning wheels, and plows). One exhibit displays the history of the archipelago's wooden churches; another shows black-and-white photographs of the damage caused by the 1960 earthquake that rocked southern Chile. The museum has a collection of quotations about Chiloé culture by outsiders. "The Chilote talks little, but thinks a lot. He is rarely spontaneous with outsiders, and even with his own countrymen he isn't too communicative," wrote one ethnographer. ✉ *Esmeralda 255, Castro* ☎ *65/263–5967* 🌐 *www.museodecastro.cl* 🎟 *Free* 🕒 *Closed Sun., Mar.–Dec.*

Plazuela del Tren

PLAZA/SQUARE | All that remains of Chiloé's once-thriving Castro–Ancud rail service is the locomotive and a few old photographs displayed outdoors on this plaza down on the waterfront road. Nobel laureate Pablo Neruda called the narrow-gauge rail service "a slow, rainy train, a slim, damp mushroom." Service ended with the 1960 earthquake. ✉ *Av. Pedro Montt s/n, Castro.*

🍴 Restaurants

★ El Mercadito

$$$ | **CONTEMPORARY** | With a fresh, creative approach to traditional Chilote cuisine, this restaurant is a nice change of pace in the island's restaurant scene—and, most importantly, it serves up really good food. El Mercadito is in a restored house overlooking the waterfront in the historic Pedro Montt barrio. **Known for:** tradition with a twist; spicy conger eel stew; waterfront setting. [$] *Average main: pesos11000* ✉ *Pedro Montt 210, Castro* ☎ *9/8313–9887* 🌐 *www.elmercaditodechiloe.cl.*

Rucalaf Putemun

$$$$ | **CONTEMPORARY** | A blend of traditional Chiloé and international cuisine, this restaurant serves a tasty take on local food, such as the unique *chochoca rellena,* which is shellfish in a sort of potato-bread wrapping. The owner and chef is from Chiloé and studied and worked for several years at restaurants in Germany. **Known for:** must-stop on the way to the Rilan Peninsula; excellent fish; flavors from the Chiloé countryside. [$] *Average main: pesos12000* ✉ *Km 3.6, Ruta Rilan (W-55), Castro* ☎ *9/9579–7571.*

Sacho Restaurant

$$ | **SEAFOOD** | Going strong since the late 1970s, Sacho features the favorite seafood plates Chiloé is known for, cooked in the traditional style, from fish and curanto to *chupe de jaiba* (crab stew). Service is friendly and mostly prompt, even when it fills up at lunchtime with locals. **Known for:** popular lunch spot; local institution; traditional seafood. [$] *Average main: pesos8000* ✉ *Thomson 213, Castro* ☎ *65/263–2079* 🌐 *www.sachorestaurant.cl* 🕒 *Closed Sun.*

★ Travesia

$$$$ | **CHILEAN** | Co-owned by the authors of an award-winning cookbook about Chiloé cuisine, Travesia is a wonderful way to experience Chiloé dishes that are prepared with inventive, modern twists by a young team of chefs. A favorite is the out-of-this-world *chancho ahumado* (smoked pork), which is served with a delightful sauce made of local murta berries together with potatoes (a star ingredient here—Chiloé hosts 90% of the world's known potato varieties). **Known for:** cookbook owners; creative Chilote food; hancho ahumado (smoked pork).

Average main: pesos 13000 ⌧ *Eusebio Lillo 188, Castro* 📞 *65/263–0137* ⊕ *www. restaurantravesia.wordpress.com* ☾ *Closed Sun.*

 Coffee and Quick Bites
===

Palafito Patagonia
$$ | CAFÉ | For coffee fanatics in need of a good cup of joe in southern Chile, Palafito Patagonia is the answer. Situated in a refurbished palafito on Ten Ten Bay, it offers nice views from the refreshing outdoor terrace; inside smooth tunes play while you kick back with a selection of gourmet coffee imported from around the world. **Known for:** cool ambience; gourmet coffee; delicious cakes. *$ Average main: pesos 6500* ⌧ *Pedro Montt 651, Castro* 📞 *9/5618–8933* ⊕ *www. facebook.com/palafitopatagonia.*

 Hotels
===

Hotel de Castro
$$$ | HOTEL | Looming over downtown near the estuary, this hotel has a sloped chalet-style roof with a long skylight, which makes the interior seem bright and airy even on a cloudy day. **Pros:** spa; central location; bay views. **Cons:** limited parking space; weak Wi-Fi signal on some floors; older building is dated. *$ Rooms from: pesos 79000* ⌧ *Chacabuco 202, Castro* 📞 *65/263–2301* ⊕ *www. hoteldecastro.cl* 🛏 *49 rooms* ⼁⊙⼁ *Free Breakfast.*

Hotel de la Isla Enjoy Chiloé
$$$$ | HOTEL | This five-star hotel, part of Chile's Enjoy casino chain, rents a mix of rooms and self-catering apartments that tastefully blend into the landscape. **Pros:** updated, comfortable rooms; bay views; amenities and entertainment on-site. **Cons:** not near the city center; casino attracts large crowds; lacking authentic, local feel. *$ Rooms from: pesos 135000* ⌧ *Ruta 5 Sur 2053, Castro* 📞 *65/258–4500* 🛏 *76 rooms* ⼁⊙⼁ *Free Breakfast.*

Hotel Parque Quilquico
$$$$ | HOTEL | Across the Dalcahue Channel at Rilan Peninsula, Hotel Parque Quilquico incorporates the colorful style of Chiloé architecture into a hotel with a green conscience. **Pros:** all rooms have terraces; indoor pool and outdoor hot tubs; private trail. **Cons:** no TVs; some rooms are small; spotty Wi-Fi connection. *$ Rooms from: pesos 132300* ⌧ *Quilquico Rural s/n, Castro* 📞 *65/297–1000* ⊕ *www.hpq.cl* 🛏 *23 rooms* ⼁⊙⼁ *Free Breakfast.*

★ Ocio Territorial Hotel
$$$$ | B&B/INN | A tremendous place to relax while exploring Chiloé, this beautiful, countryside hotel rents various types of lodging; there are three large and stunning independent suites/cabins, assorted rooms in a renovated Chilote farmhouse, two spacious rooms in the main lodge, and a row of connected apartments in the upper area of the property. **Pros:** hot tubs; privacy; stunning view of the city and estuary. **Cons:** restaurant is in a separate building; hard to get here; Wi-Fi only in common area. *$ Rooms from: pesos 250000* ⌧ *Península de Rilán, Castro* 📞 *9/7300–7056* ⊕ *www. ocioterritorial.com* 🛏 *18 rooms.*

Palafito 1326 Hotel Boutique
$$$ | B&B/INN | A renovated *palafito* (traditional stilt house) in the Gambo neighborhood, this hotel inside Castro is a small, quiet alternative to the bigger, luxury options in the area. **Pros:** excellent breakfasts; views from the terrace; central heating. **Cons:** street noise; no TV in rooms; often sold out. *$ Rooms from: pesos 89000* ⌧ *Ernesto Riquelme 1326, Castro* 📞 *65/253–0053* ⊕ *www.palafito1326.cl* 🛏 *12 rooms* ⼁⊙⼁ *Free Breakfast.*

★ Refugio Pullao
$$$$ | B&B/INN | This beautifully designed hotel on the Pullao Bay is a haven for bird lovers, with a rooftop observation deck surrounded by twigs, branches, and a roof that literally blooms during summer, allowing the birds to come right to you. **Pros:** peace and quiet; extraordinary

bird-watching; stupendous views. **Cons:** no TV in rooms; hot tub use is an extra charge; difficult to access by road. [$] *Rooms from: pesos169000* ✉ *Quilquico Bajo s/n, Castro* ⊕ *Península de Rilán* ☎ *9/6149–6883, 9/9895–7911* 🌐 *www.refugiopullao.cl* 🛏 *6 rooms* 🍴 *Free Breakfast.*

★ Tierra Chiloé

$$$$ | HOTEL | Tranquility and absorbing views of verdant farmland and Chiloé coastline make this truly upscale home-away-from-home quite intimate, as does the reading room, fireplace lounge, and dining area in the main lodge. **Pros:** indoor-outdoor spa; impressive architecture; beautiful setting and views. **Cons:** can be difficult to find; most of the excursions are group trips; occasional salmon farming pens amid the sea views. [$] *Rooms from: pesos240000* ✉ *San José Playa, Castro, Casilla, Castro* ☎ *800/914–249* 🌐 *www.tierrachiloe.com* 🛏 *24 rooms* 🍴 *All-Inclusive.*

Shopping

Feria Artesanal Castro

MARKET | The city's Feria Artesanal, a lively, often chaotic crafts market, is regarded by most as the best place on the island to pick up the woolen sweaters, woven baskets, and straw figures for which Chiloé is known. Prices are already quite reasonable, but vendors expect some bargaining. The stalls share the place with several food vendors. It's open daily 9 to dusk though the best time to come is Saturday morning, when artisans from all over the island come to sell their wares. ✉ *Eusebio Lillo s/n, Castro.*

Activities

Sea kayaking around the outlying islands near Castro has become one of Chiloé's main draws. There are also interesting options for fishing, horseback riding, and hiking in the surrounding countryside, particularly in and around Chiloé National Park.

Altue Sea Kayaking

KAYAKING | Altue Sea Kayaking is one of Chile's oldest adventure travel operators. From December to April, the outfitter leads five-day/four-night trips around the Chiloé archipelago, departing from its sea-kayaking center near Dalcahue. ✉ *Dalcahue* ☎ *9/419–6809* 🌐 *www.seakayakchile.com.*

Cabalgatas Chiloé

HORSEBACK RIDING | The gorgeous, wooded San Pedro Valley, just a short drive from Castro, is full of flowing rivers, dense forests, and picturesque Chilote houses. It's prime territory for horseback riding, which you can arrange with Cabalgatas Chiloé. They also offer kayak excursions. ✉ *Castro* ⊕ *San Pedro* ☎ *9/9079–0722* 🌐 *www.cabalgataschiloe.cl.*

Chonchi

23 km (14 miles) south of Castro.

The colorful wooden houses of Chonchi are on a hillside so steep that it's known in Spanish as the Ciudad de los Tres Pisos (City of Three Stories). The town's name means "slippery earth" in the Huilliche language, and if you tromp up the town's steep streets on a rainy day you can understand why. Arranged around a scenic harbor, Chonchi wins raves as one of Chiloé's most picturesque towns.

GETTING HERE AND AROUND

Chonchi is 15 minutes south of Castro via the Pan-American Highway, Ruta 5.

Sights

Iglesia de San Carlos

CHURCH | The town's centerpiece, this church on the Plaza de Armas was started by the Jesuits in 1754 but left unfinished until 1859. Rebuilt in the neoclassical style, the church is now a national monument. An unusually ornate arcade with five arches fronts the church, and inside are an intricately carved altar and wooden

Chonchi is known for its pretty harbor and colorful wooden houses.

columns. The church contains Chonchi's most prized relic, a statue of the Virgen de la Candelaria. According to tradition, this image of the Virgin Mary protected the town from the Dutch pirates who destroyed neighboring Castro in 1600. Townspeople celebrate the event every February 2 with fireworks and gunpowder symbolizing the pirate attack. The building is open daily; mass takes place every Sunday at 11 am. ✉ *Plaza de Armas, at Centenario and Francisco Corral, Chonchi.*

Museo de las Tradiciones Chonchinas
HISTORY MUSEUM | This small but interesting museum documents early life in Chonchi through furnishings and photos in a 19th-century house. ✉ *Centenario 116, Chonchi* ☎ *65/267–2802* 🎟 *1000 pesos.*

🍴 Restaurants

Mercado Chonchi
$ | **SEAFOOD** | In a tidy building, this market with four restaurants is a great spot for an informal lunch or dinner. The restaurants, in a food court overlooking the water, mainly serve standard Chiloé fare such as curanto and assorted seafood. **Known for:** convenient to stores selling local crafts; classic Chiloé fare; casual vibe. [$] *Average main: pesos5000* ✉ *Irarrázabal 47, Chonchi* 💳 *No credit cards.*

🛏 Hotels

Cabañas Treng Treng
$$$ | **APARTMENT** | This is a very comfortable option if you need a rest stop when traveling by car to Quellón or to Chiloé National Park; the six cabins have fully equipped kitchens, satellite TV, high speed Wi-Fi, and fantastic views of the sea. **Pros:** great views; full kitchens; close

Chilean countryside meets the sea at Parque Nacional Chiloé.

to town. **Cons:** price increases for more than two people; best suited to travelers by car; no meals included. [$] *Rooms from: pesos80000* ✉ *José Pinto Perez 420, Chonchi* ☎ *65/267–2532, 9/9817–6094* 🌐 *www.trengtreng.cl* 🛏 *6 cabins.*

Huillin Lodge

$$$$ | **B&B/INN** | For the perfect escape from the town of Castro, head to this rural lodge, whose six separate rooms overlook the tranquil Huillinco Lake. **Pros:** just 14 miles from Chiloé National Park; good service; great views. **Cons:** hot tub costs extra; difficult access to parking; off the beaten track. [$] *Rooms from: pesos107000* ✉ *Lago Huillinco Km 9.5, Chonchi* ☎ *9/9825–4463* 🌐 *www.huillinlodge.cl* 🛏 *6 suites* 🍴 *Free Breakfast.*

Parque Nacional Chiloé

35 km (21 miles) west of Chonchi.

The Parque Nacional Chiloé comprises a huge swath of Chiloé's Pacific coast. It's a wonderful mix of broad beaches, rolling sand dunes, lush temperate rain forest, and, to the north, extensive wetlands, that come together to form one of the country's most visually compelling parks. It's a draw for eco-tourists. Even though the climate is often windy and rainy, this is also just a spectacular place to roam the beautiful beach.

GETTING HERE AND AROUND

To get to Chiloé National Park, take the Pan-American Highway, or Ruta 5, south from Ancud or Castro. A paved side road from the highway leading to the park is found at Notuco, near the town of Chonchi, which is only 22½ km (14 miles) south of Castro.

Sights

★ Parque Nacional Chiloé

NATIONAL PARK | This 430-square-km (166-square-mile) park hugs Isla Grande's sparsely populated Pacific coast. The park's two sectors differ dramatically. Heavily forested with evergreens, Sector Anay, to the south, is most easily entered from the coastal village of Cucao. A road heads west to the park from the Pan-American Highway at Notuco, just south of Chonchi. Popular among backpackers is its short woody Tepual Trail, which begins at the Chanquín Visitor Center, 1 km (1 mile) north of the park entrance and winds through a rare, intact forest of tepu trees (*Tepualia stipularis*), whose large, twisted trunks are visible above and below your walking path. Along the path as well are signs explaining the significance of the forest and what it holds. The longer Dunas Trail leads through the forest to the beach dunes near Cacao. Keep an eye out for the Chiloé fox, native to Isla Grande; more reclusive is the pudú, a miniature deer. Some 3 km (2 miles) north of the Cucao entrance is a Huilliche community on the shore of Lago Huelde. Unobtrusive visitors are welcome. At the southern end of the park is one of Chile's best beaches, Cucao Beach, where dunes extend along the unusually wide sand. Camping is permitted. The northern Sector Chepu contains primarily wetlands and a large bird population (most notably penguins) and sea lion colony. Get there via Ruta 5, but take the crossroad toward Río Chepu, then continue west on a gravel road until Puerto Anguay. ✉ *North of Cucao and south of Chepu, Parque Nacional Chiloe* ☎ *65/253–2502* 🌐 *www.conaf.cl* 🎫 *5200 pesos.*

Hotels

El Fogon de Cucao

$ | **B&B/INN** | Founded in 1997 by a former newspaper reporter in Chile, El Fogon de Cucao has a friendly atmosphere with rustic decor and big beds. **Pros:** good food; excellent service; lakeside. **Cons:** reservations only by telephone; no Wi-Fi; few rooms so bookings must be made in advance. [$] *Rooms from: pesos35000* ✉ *Within Chiloé National Park, near Cucao entrance at southern end of park, Chiloé National Park* ☎ *9/9946–5685* 💳 *No credit cards* 🛏 *9 rooms* 🍴 *Free Breakfast.*

Palafito Cucao Lodge

$$$ | **B&B/INN** | With 13 rooms, each with private bathroom and a view of Cucao Lake, this is an excellent option for overnight visits to Chiloé National Park. **Pros:** well designed; lake views; good place to meet people. **Cons:** Wi-Fi is slow; heating system erratic; neighbor noise. [$] *Rooms from: pesos85000* ✉ *Chiloé National Park, Cucao* ☎ *65/297–1164, 9/8403–4728* 🌐 *www.palafitocucaolodge.com* 🛏 *13 rooms* 🍴 *Free Breakfast.*

Queilén

47 km (29 miles) southeast of Chonchi.

This town named for the red cypress trees that dot the area sits on an elongated peninsula and, as such, is the only town on Isla Grande with two seafronts. Though Chiloé's windy, rainy, and cold climate is mostly unfavorable for typical beach activities, the beauty of the unspoiled seaside is unquestionable. Two of Isla Grande's best beaches are the **Playa de Queilén,** in the center of town, and the **Playa Lelbun,** 15 km (9 miles) northwest of the city.

GETTING HERE AND AROUND

From Castro, go south on Ruta 5 until you get to the Chonchi exit; from Chonchi a gravel road heads southeast to Queilén.

Sights

Mirador

VIEWPOINT | Uphill on Calle Presidente Kennedy, this scenic overlook has stupendous views of the Golfo de Ancud, the smaller islands in the archipelago, and, on a clear day, the Volcán Corcovado on the mainland. ✉ *Calle Presidente Kennedy, Queilén.*

Refugio de Navegantes

HISTORY MUSEUM | The town's cultural center contains a small museum with artifacts and old black-and-white photographs. Nothing is very colorful here—the muted tones of the pottery, fabrics, and farm implements reflect the stark life of colonial Chiloé. ✉ *Av. Alessandri s/n, Queilén* ☎ 🎟 *Free.*

Hotels

El Coo Lodge

$$$$ | **B&B/INN** | If your lodging criteria includes peace, empty beaches, abundant nature, and magical views, this small but stylish hotel is the perfect escape. **Pros:** peace and quiet; magnificent views; private beach. **Cons:** just three rooms; few services; only breakfast is offered. [$] *Rooms from: pesos115000* ✉ *Sector Rural ñida, Queilén* ✣ *2 km from center of Queilen* ☎ *9/6867–8334* 🌐 *www.elcoolodge.com* 🛏 *3 rooms* 🍴 *Free Breakfast.*

Quellón

99 km (60 miles) south of Castro.

The Pan-American Highway, which begins in Alaska and stretches for most of the length of North and South America, ends without fanfare here in Quellón, Chiloé's southernmost city. Quellón was the famed "end of Christendom" described by Charles Darwin during his 19th-century visit. Just a few years earlier it had been the southernmost outpost of Spain's empire in the New World. For most visitors today, Quellón is also the end of the line. But for hikers and nature lovers, there's plenty to explore along the coast and Parque Tantauco nearby. It's also the starting point for ferries that head to the Southern Coast.

GETTING HERE AND AROUND

Quellón is about a one-hour drive south of Castro, on the paved Ruta 5. From Quellón, you can also catch a ferry with Naviera Austral to Chaitén (Thursday), Puerto Cisnes (Tuesday), or Chacabuco (Wednesday and Saturday) along the Carretera Austral.

ESSENTIALS

FERRY INFORMATION Ferry dock. ✉ *Pedro Montt 48, Quellón* ☎ *65/268–2207.*

Sights

★ Parque Tantauco

NATIONAL PARK | This vast, 118,000-hectare (300,000-acre) park founded by former Chile President Sebastián Piñera has added an attractive guesthouse, campground with modern bathrooms, and a series of hiking trails and overnight shelters for those who wind their way through the park's thick Valdivian temperate rain forests and rocky coastline. Serious hiking and camping enthusiasts should consider the five-day, 32-mile Transversal Trail from Chaiguata (also reachable by bus from Quellón) to Caleta Inío, the park headquarters, where you can get a boat back to Quellón. En route, you can sleep at four simple shelters, complete with bunks, cooking facilities, and latrines. Park entrance for adults costs 5,000 pesos and children 1,000 pesos. Trekking shelters run 15,000 pesos per night, while Caleta Ines Guesthouse has rooms for 60,000 pesos per night. There are also six geothermal domes for overnight stays at Lake Chaiguata that have central heating, from four to eight beds, and include access to a restaurant and hot tubs on-site (from 90,000 pesos). You can also rent tents and kayaks and take guided, multiday tours from the park. ✉ *Ruta 5 camino a Quellón, Quellón* ☎ *65/253–2696* 🌐 *www.parquetantauco.cl* 🎫 *5000 pesos park entrance; 60000 pesos per night rooms at Caleta Ines Guesthouse* ☞ *Information office in Castro (Pasaje las Delicias 270).*

🍴 Restaurants

El Chico Leo
$$ | **CHILEAN** | Standard Chilean fish and seafood plates are the main dishes to try at this favorite stop for travelers going through Quellón. The service is friendly; plus, getting here includes a nice walk along the waterfront. **Known for:** friendly service; clam chowder; draft beer. [$] *Average main: pesos8900* ✉ *Pedro Montt 325, Quellón* ☎ *652/268–1567* 🕒 *Closed Sun.*

Sandwichería Mitos
$$ | **FAST FOOD** | The giant sandwiches here have attained mythical status in these parts. The restaurant also has an extensive daily menu featuring a variety of traditional Chilean dishes like cazuela, roasted chicken, *lentejas* (lentils), and more. **Known for:** fun atmosphere; giant sandwiches; traditional Chilean cuisine. [$] *Average main: pesos6500* ✉ *Jorge Vivar 235, Quellón* ☎ *65/268–0798* 🌐 *www.mitoschiloe.cl.*

🛏 Hotels

Cabañas San Pedro
$ | **HOTEL** | In front of the port on the coastal road in town, this hotel has four independent cabins with kitchens, cable TV, wood stove, and parking. **Pros:** personal kitchens; quiet; independent. **Cons:** basic; modest furnishings; managing the wood stove for heating. [$] *Rooms from: pesos40000* ✉ *Pedro Montt 457, Quellón* ☎ *9/9877–8581* 🌐 *www.cabañassanpedro.cl* 💳 *No credit cards* 🛏 *4 cabins* 🍴 *No Meals.*

Hotel El Chico Leo
$ | **B&B/INN** | This nice waterfront hotel has an especially popular restaurant serving *curanto* and other seafood dishes. **Pros:** clean; good location; electric heating. **Cons:** some rooms have no windows; no frills; small rooms. [$] *Rooms from: pesos35000* ✉ *Pedro Montt 325, Quellón* ☎ *65/268–1567* 🛏 *23 rooms* 🍴 *Free Breakfast.*

Hotel Patagonia Insular
$$ | **HOTEL** | Owner Anita Azocar has transformed this somewhat plain hotel into a warm and inviting space, and the most modern lodging in Quellón. **Pros:** friendly owner; Quellón Bay views; good food. **Cons:** plain rooms; unstable Wi-Fi signal; no gym or spa. [$] *Rooms from: pesos75000* ✉ *Av. Juan Ladrilleros 1737, Quellón* ☎ *65/268–1610* 🌐 *www.hotelpatagoniainsular.cl* 🛏 *34 rooms* 🍴 *Free Breakfast.*

Hotel Tierra del Fuego
$ | **B&B/INN** | This rambling alerce-shingle house, dating from the 1920s, is on Quellón's waterfront. **Pros:** inexpensive; great location; recent updates to the decor. **Cons:** hot water is sometimes an issue; old facilities; rooms vary in quality. [$] *Rooms from: pesos35000* ✉ *Av. Pedro Montt 445, Quellón* ☎ *65/268–2079* 🛏 *37 rooms* 🍴 *Free Breakfast.*

320

Shopping

Feria Artesanal Llauquil

MARKET | Quellón's market doesn't have
the hustle and bustle of similar ones in
Castro and Dalcahue, but there are some
good buys on woolens and straw folkloric
figures. Don't bother to bargain; the
prices are already extremely reasonable.
⊠ *Av. Gómez García, Quellón* ⊙ *Closed
Sun. Mar.–Nov.*

Activities

Orígenes Tour

ECOTOURISM | This trusty tour operator
offers sailing trips, scuba diving, hiking at
nearby parks (including Parque Tantauco), and photographic tours of the town
and countryside. ⊠ *Santos Vargas 348,
Quellón* ☎ *9/5798-3922* ⊕ *www.origenes-
tour.com.*

Sendero Antüpani

HIKING & WALKING | About 20 miles outside
of Quellón, in Compu, join Huilliche guide
Sandra Antipani on a two-hour native
forest trek as she explains her family's
indigenous traditions and the diverse
native flora and fauna of the Fundo Cohu-
in private nature reserve. The trek can be
followed by a grand *curanto* lunch, a visit
to the first indigenous church in Chiloé,
and kayaking. ⊠ *Ruta 5, Sector Compu,
Quellón* ☎ *9/8900–8841* ✎ *antipani.s@
gmail.com* ⊕ *www.facebook.com/
turismocompu.*

Chapter 10

THE SOUTHERN COAST

Updated by
Jimmy Langman

⊙ **Sights**
★★★★★

🍴 **Restaurants**
★★★☆☆

🛏 **Hotels**
★★★☆☆

🛍 **Shopping**
★★☆☆☆

🍸 **Nightlife**
★☆☆☆☆

WELCOME TO
THE SOUTHERN COAST

TOP REASONS
TO GO

★ **Scenery:** The Carretera Austral, a dusty dirt road that was blazed through southern Chile in the 1970s and '80s, has opened up one of the most beautiful places in the world to tourists.

★ **Glaciers:** There's a world-class network of national parks with amazing attractions, such as the breathtaking mountainscapes of Cerro Castillo National Park, the wildlife and spectacular ecology of Patagonia National Park, and the glaciers merging with the sea at Laguna San Rafael National Park.

★ **Fishing:** Fly-fishing fanatics were among the first to explore this area thoroughly. At any number of lodges, you can step right outside your door for great fishing or take a short boat trip to more isolated spots.

★ **Rafting and kayaking:** The Futaleufú River is beautiful, turquoise blue, and Class V-plus (that's raft speak for very fast-moving water). The surrounding countryside is a magnificent setting for it.

The Southern Coast is a tranquil, expansive region covered with pristine nature, much of it protected in national parks and reserves. By and large, this is territory for people who love the outdoors and rural tourism.

1 Chaitén. The beginning point for most journeys down the Carretera Austral and a good base to explore the coast or Pumalín National Park.

2 Parque Nacional Pumalín Douglas Tompkins. The national park is home to rivers, lakes, volcanoes, mountains, rain forests, and more.

3 Futaleufú. Located next to a world-class river for rafting, kayaking, and fishing, this spectacular mountain valley is so beautiful locals sometimes say "it must have been painted by God."

4 La Junta. Home to several lakes and rivers that are among the best anywhere for fishing.

5 Puerto Puyuhuapi. A scenic Patagonian town near the hot springs and hanging glaciers of Queulat National Park.

6 Parque Nacional Queulat. Camp and hike among the underrated park's rain forests, waterfalls, lakes, and mountains.

7 Coyhaique. Where Río Simpson and Río Coyhaique come together, Coyhaique is by far the largest settlement on the Carretera Austral. The capital city of the Aysén Region, Coyhaique has some 60,000 residents—more than half of the region's population.

8 Puerto Chacabuco and Puerto Aysén. The town of Puerto Aysén and its port, Chacabuco, are home to beautiful farmland and natural wonders.

9 Parque Nacional Laguna San Rafael. Encompassing the length of Chile's vast northern Patagonia ice fields, this park is home to the San Rafael glacier.

10 Lago General Carrera. A gorgeous, almost surreal blue lake, the biggest in Chile (and the second-largest in South America, after Lake Titicaca).

11 Parque Nacional Patagonia. A range of ecosystems from meadows and mountains to forests and wetlands have brought back healthy populations of species like guanaco, puma, condors, and more.

Chonchi

Caleta Gonzalo ◆ **2**
Parque Nacional
Pumalín Douglas Tompkins

ISLA
GRANDE
DE CHILOÉ · Compu

1 ◦ Chaitén

Esquel ◦ ✝

Termas de Amarillo

Quellón

Puerto
Cardenas ◦ Futaleufú

CHILOÉ

Volcán
Corcovado

Lago
Yelcho **3**

Estancia
La Mimosa

Parque
Nacional
Corcovado

LOS
LAGOS

40

ISLA
GUAFO

ISLA GRAN
GUAITECA

Volcán
Melimoyu ▲ La Junta ◦ **4**

Parque
Nacional
Palena

Lago
General
Vintter

0   50 Mi
0   50 km

Puerto
Puyuhuapi ◦ **5**

Parque
Nacional
Queulat **6** ◆ Puerto
Las Juntas ◦

ARGENTINA

Río Cisnes

Parque
Nacional
Isla Guamblín

ISLA
MAGDALENA

Volcán
Mentolat

Puerto
Cisnes ◦

Seccíon
Tapera ◦

ISLA
GUAMBLÍN

AISÉN DEL
GENERAL CARLOS
IBÁÑEZ DEL CAMPO

Volcán
Co Maca

Lago
Yulton

Alto Río
Sanguer ◦

Casa de
Richards

PACIFIC OCEAN

Puerto Aysén

Puerto
Chacabuco ◦ **8**

7

Coyhaique

ARCHIPIÉLAGO DE LOS CHONOS

Kolovrat ✝

Cerro Castillo National Park ◆

7

Volcán
Hudson ▲

Bahía
Murta ◦

Puerto
Avellanos ◦

Lago
Buenos Aires

40

Puerto Tranquilo ◦

10

Lago General
Carrera

Los Antiguos ◦

Perito
Moreno ◦

Golfo de Penas

9 ◆
Parque Nacional
Laguna San Rafael

Puerto
Bertrand ◦

11 ◆
Parque Nacional
Patagonia

PATAGONIA

Cochrane ◦

La Colonia ◦

Bajo de
Los Caracoles ◦

El Salto ◦

40

Puerto
Bajo Pisagua 7

The sliver of land known as the Southern Coast stretches for more than 1,000 km (620 miles), from the southernmost part of the Lakes District through southernmost Aysén. For travelers driving along the Carretera Austral, or Southern Highway, it's like a seemingly boundless tour through a natural playground. Many of its wondrous places are preserved in numerous national parks and reserves, making the region a growing global hot spot for outdoors sports and ecotourism.

In the Southern Coast, also known as the Aysén region, thick green forested mountains dominate, some of which rise dramatically from the shores of shimmering lakes. Slender waterfalls and nearly vertical streams, often seeming to emerge from the rock itself, tumble and slide from neck-craning heights. Some dissipate into misty nothingness before touching the ground, while others flow into innumerable rivers—large and small, wild and gentle—heading westward to the sea.

With the expansion of the Carretera Austral, migration has jumped to the region and land speculation is on the rise. Still, this is one of the least-populated areas in South America, with a population density said to be lower than the Sahara Desert. The infrequent hamlets scattered along the low-lying areas of this rugged region subsist mainly from fishing or farming, but increasingly cater to tourism. Coyhaique, the only town here of any size, has lots of dining and lodging options. Several intrepid entrepreneurs have also established excellent accommodations in remote locations throughout the region, frequently near spectacular rivers, mountain peaks, lakes, volcanoes, and glaciers.

Planning a visit to the region's widely separated points of interest can be challenging, as the distance from place to place can take considerable time and the climate is ever-changing. Creating a logical itinerary in southern Chilean Patagonia is as much about choosing how to get here as it is about choosing where you want to go. A rewarding mode of transport through this area is a combination of boat and plane, with an occasional car rental if you want to journey a little deeper into the hinterlands.

Planning

When to Go

Late spring through summer—mid-November to mid-March—is considered high season in this part of southern Chile. It's highly recommended that you make advance reservations if your intention is to stay at high-end hotels or resorts during this time. Although the weather is cooler and likely rainier in the spring (September into November) and fall (March to May), the change in seasons is quite beautiful, making both great times to visit.

Planning Your Time

Upon arrival to Chaitén, if you have time to spare, perhaps spend a day or two exploring Parque Nacional Pumalín, but then head straight to Futaleufú, home to one of the world's fastest and most spectacular rivers and situated among breathtaking Patagonian mountain valleys. After a few nights there, spend a day going down the Carretera Austral, or Southern Highway, to Puerto Puyuhuapi, preferably in a rented, four-wheel-drive truck or jeep to give you more flexibility. A stay at Puyuhuapi Lodge & Spa, a resort accessible only by boat, is a great way to relax and recharge for the next phase of your journey. While in Puyuhuapi, consider spending an extra day there to visit the "hanging glacier" at Parque Nacional Queulat. Afterward, go to Coyhaique, located about five hours south. The largest city in the region, Coyhaique will be a good place for shopping and eating a nice meal before heading south to Lake General Carrera and Patagonia National Park, or to nearby Puerto Chacabuco, where you can board a boat bound for the unforgettable glaciers at Laguna San Rafael National Park. Consider returning to Puerto Montt via a ferry boat that departs from Puerto Chacabuco.

Getting Here and Around

AIR

LATAM has flights to the region from Santiago, Puerto Montt, and Punta Arenas. They arrive at the Southern Coast's only major airport, 55 km (34 miles) south of Coyhaique, in the town of Balmaceda. Other carriers serving southern Chile include Sky Airlines, Jetsmart, DAP, Aerocord, and Pewen.

BOAT AND FERRY

Be warned that ferries in southern Chile can be slow and sometimes suffer delays, but they are reliable. If you're touring the region by car, the ferry is a good choice. The main companies serving this area are Navimag, Naviera Austral, and Transmarchilay.

BUS

Service between Puerto Montt and Coyhaique is by private operators such as TransAustral and Becker. A nearly 48-hour journey including fjord crossings via ferry, it is a long haul but very scenic; you *must* overnight in the town of Chaitén before heading south to Coyhaique. Another option to get to Coyhaique are buses departing from Bariloche, Argentina.

BUS CONTACTS Buses Becker. ✉ *General Parra 335, Coyhaique* ☎ *67/223–2167* ⊕ *www.busesbecker.com.* **Don Carlos.** ✉ *Subteniente Cruz 63, Coyhaique* ☎ *67/223–1981* ✎ *trplecltda14@gmail. com.* **Suray.** ✉ *Arturo Prat 265, Coyhaique* ☎ *67/223–8387* ⊕ *www.suray.cl.*

CAR

In Chile, the northern part of the Southern Coast must be done with the aid of a ferry, which departs from Puerto Montt, Hornopiren, or Quellón, Chiloé. Another route is to loop through Argentine Patagonia, crossing back into Chile near Futaleufú. This Argentine route takes you to Bariloche, crossing over the Argentina border near Osorno and Puyehue, just north of Puerto Montt.

The Carretera Austral, the road that runs through the southern coast, is partly a dirt and gravel road and during rainy periods requires especially careful driving. The road cuts through awesome virgin nature though, connecting tiny fishing towns and quaint villages all the way from Puerto Montt to Villa O'Higgins.

Navigating the Carretera Austral requires some planning, as communities along the way are sometimes few and far between. Some parts of the highway, especially in the southernmost reaches, are deserted. Check out your car thoroughly, especially the air in the spare tire. Make sure you have a jack and jumper cables. Plan your refueling stops ahead of time and bring along food in case you find yourself stuck far from the nearest restaurant.

RENTAL CAR CONTACTS Europcar.
✉ *Aeropuerto Balmaceda and Errázuriz 454, Coyhaique* ☎ *67/267–8640* ⊕ *www. europcar.cl.* **Varona.** ✉ *Riquelme 438, Coyhaique* ☎ *9/3221–6745* ⊕ *www. rentacarvarona.cl.*

Restaurants

All manner of fish, lamb, beef, and chicken dishes are available in the Southern Coast. By and large, entrées are simple and hearty. Given the area's great distance from Chile's Central Valley, where the majority of Chile's fruits and vegetables are grown, most things that appear on your plate probably grew somewhere nearby. Many dishes are prepared from scratch when you order.

Restaurant reviews have been shortened. For full information, visit Fodors. com.

Hotels

This region offers a surprisingly wide choice of accommodations. What you don't find is the blandness of chain hotels. Most of the region's establishments reflect the distinct personalities and idiosyncrasies of their owners.

Some of the most humble homes in villages along the Carretera Austral are supplementing their family income by becoming bed-and-breakfasts. A stay in one of these *hospedajes* is an ideal way to meet the people and experience the culture. These accommodations are not regulated, so inquire about the availability of hot water and confirm that breakfast is included. Don't hesitate to ask to see the room—you may even get a choice.

What It Costs in Chilean Pesos (in Thousands)

	$	$$	$$$	$$$$
RESTAURANTS				
	Under 6	6–8	9–11	over 11
HOTELS				
	Under 46	46–75	76–105	over 105

Chaitén

201 km (125 miles) south of Puerto Montt.

If you are traveling by ferry to and from Chiloé or Puerto Montt, you will likely pass through Chaitén. In May 2008, a volcano erupted near the town, forcing its residents to evacuate. Today, however, Chaitén has sprung back to life, with the remnants of the disaster a tourist attraction in its own right. It's an interesting and pleasant place to stay for a night or two. You can also buy food and other supplies in town before your southbound journey.

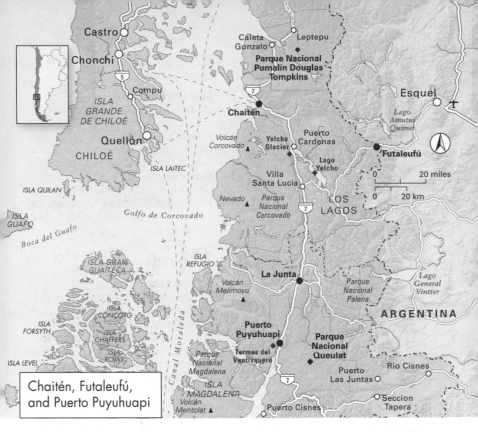

Chaitén, Futaleufú,
and Puerto Puyuhuapi

GETTING HERE AND AROUND

Six days a week (Monday through Saturday), Naviera Austral operates a ferry service between Chaitén and Puerto Montt in the Lake District and Quellón on Chiloé.

It's also possible to drive to Chaitén from Puerto Montt via the "Ruta Bimodal," a 10-hour, scenic journey along the Carretera Austral in which you utilize ferries to cross an estuary and two fjords. The ferry ship that crosses the fjords is operated by Somarco and leaves out of Hornopiren; you must reserve your ticket ahead of time through their website (www.barcazas.cl) or a travel agency.

Flying is also an option; small airlines like Aerocord and Pewen Servicios Aéreos run flights between Chaitén and Puerto Montt.

TOURS

Chaitur Excursions

GUIDED TOURS | Vermont native Nicholas La Penna is a pioneer in the tourist trade on the Carretera Austral, leading tours and providing transport on the mostly dirt roads of northern Patagonia for well more than two decades. His office doubles as the Chaitén bus station, making him an especially rich source for tips on the region. Among his destinations in the Chaitén area are Pumalín National Park, Futaleufú River, the Yelcho and Michimahuida glaciers, and still-smoking Chaitén Volcano. Tour prices start from 30,000 pesos. ⊠ *Av. Bernardo O'Higgins 67, Chaitén* ☎ *65/273–1429, 9/7468–5608* ⊕ *www.chaitur.com.*

Puma Fishing

SPECIAL-INTEREST TOURS | Just 15 minutes from Chaitén, the Yelcho lake and river is a fishermen's paradise. Veterinarian Steve Selway, who, in the off-season, takes care of Thoroughbred race horses in Kentucky, is a master guide who has caught world record–size coho and Chinook salmon here. Their lodge can hold up to eight persons in two cabins and two suites. They also have a "floating lodge," a 60-foot yacht that holds six people in two cabins that they take out on extended fishing trips in the lake. ✉ *Sector Rio Yelcho/ Puerto Cardenas Hijuela 51 Rural, Chaitén* ☎ *954/922–5389* 🌐 *www.pumafishing.com* 🎫 *Rates start at US$950 per day.*

Sights

Lago Yelcho

BODY OF WATER | One of the best places in the region to fish, this lake is constantly packed with brown trout. It runs along the Carretera Austral south of Chaitén, and there are several lodges nearby catering to anglers. ✉ *Chaitén.*

Yelcho Glacier

NATURE SIGHT | Just 2 km (1 mile) past the village of Puerto Cárdenas is Puente Ventisquero Yelcho (Glacier Bridge), the beginning of a moderate three-hour round-trip hike to Ventisquero Cavi (Hanging Glacier). The trail is clearly marked, but Chaitur Excursions (*www.chaitur.com*) also organizes group treks to the glacier. ✉ *Carretera Austral, Chaitén.*

Restaurants

Cabañas Tranqueras del Monte

$$$ | **CHILEAN** | Here you can enjoy quality home-cooked meals prepared by the owners—such as incredible steaks, crab stew, and freshly caught fish—as well as yummy pastries, including apple cinnamon rolls straight from the oven. **Known for:** friendly service; steaks; pastries. [$] *Average main: pesos10000* ✉ *Carretera Austral 178, Chaitén* ☎ *9/6406–4958.*

Donde Pizarrito

$$ | **CHILEAN** | Homemade sandwiches and pizza anchor the diverse menu at this favorite local hangout. Try the "El Gordito," an oversize steak sandwich with lettuce, guacamole, egg, and French fries. **Known for:** friendly service; homemade pizza; big steak sandwiches. [$] *Average main: pesos8000* ✉ *Av. Corcovado 466, Chaitén* ☎ *65/273–1451, 9/9093–1503* 🕒 *Closed Sun.*

Hotels

Cabañas Pudu

$$ | **APARTMENT** | Open year-round, this warm and inviting (but not fancy) place takes you in while you wait for the ferry boat out of Chaitén. **Pros:** independence; big and comfortable beds; friendly owners. **Cons:** located at the end of the waterfront; no breakfast included; often booked solid. [$] *Rooms from: pesos55000* ✉ *Corcovado 668, Chaitén* ☎ *9/8227–9602, 65/273–1336* ✉ *puduchaiten@hotmail.com* 🛏 *6 cabins, 1 apartment* 🍴 *No Meals.*

★ **Chucao Lodge**

$$$$ | **B&B/INN** | The all-inclusive Chucao Lodge is a high-end way to experience fly-fishing and more at Lago Yelcho and other top spots in the Palena area. **Pros:** great views; fishing at diverse spots; all-inclusive. **Cons:** Wi-Fi connection is unstable; mostly a destination for fly fishermen; a long journey to get here. [$] *Rooms from: pesos320000* ✉ *Lago Yelcho, Puerto Cárdenas* ☎ *9/6420–6416* 🌐 *www.chucaolodge.com* 💳 *No credit cards* 🕒 *Closed mid-Apr. through Oct.* 🛏 *6 rooms* 🍴 *All-Inclusive.*

Hotel Mi Casa

$$$ | **HOTEL** | The friendly owner, a former Olympic gymnast, makes you feel right at home at this simple rustic hotel, giving you access to bicycles for exploring and serving you pancakes for breakfast. **Pros:**

Carretera Austral: Chile's Road to Riches

The Pan-American Highway, which snakes its way through the northern half of Chile, never quite makes it to the Southern Coast. To connect this remote region with the rest of the country, former President Augusto Pinochet proposed a massive public works project to construct a highway called the Carretera Austral. But the $300 million venture had another purpose as well. Pinochet was afraid that without a strong military presence in the region, neighboring Argentina could begin chipping away at Chile's territory. The highway would allow the army easier access to an area that until then was accessible only by boat.

Ground was broken on the Carretera Austral in 1976, and in 1982 the first section, running from Chaitén to Coyhaique, opened to great fanfare. The only trouble was that you still couldn't get there from the mainland. It took another five years for the extension from Chaitén north to Puerto Montt to be completed. An extension from Coyhaique south to Cochrane was finished the following year.

The word *finished* is misleading, as construction continues to this day. Although the Carretera Austral is nicely paved near Puerto Montt, it soon reveals its true nature as a two-lane gravel surface that crawls inexorably southward for 1,156 km (718 miles) toward the outpost of Villa O'Higgins. Nor is the highway contiguous. In places the road ends abruptly at water's edge—ferries link these broken stretches of highway. The segment from Chaitén to Coyhaique is mostly gravel road, but every year the paved sections grow longer.

The Carretera Austral is lauded in tourism brochures as "a beautiful road studded with rivers, waterfalls, forests, lakes, glaciers, and the occasional hamlet." This description is accurate—you may live the rest of your life and never see anything half as beautiful as the scenery. However, the highway itself is far from perfect. The mostly unpaved road has dozens of single-lane, wide-board bridges over streams and rivers. Shoulders are nonexistent or made of soft, wheel-grabbing gravel.

What the Carretera Austral gives adventurous travelers is a chance to see a part of the world where relatively few have ventured. The views from the highway are truly amazing, from the conical top of Volcán Corcovado near Chaitén to the sprawling valleys around Coyhaique. Here you also find a spectacular network of national parks, such as Pumalin National Park and Patagonia National Park.

affable owner; town views; attention to detail. **Cons:** not a lot of storage space; some rooms are small; thin walls. $ Rooms from: pesos78000 ✉ Av. Norte 206, Chaitén ☎ 65/273–1285 ⊕ www.hotelmicasa.cl ⇄ 16 rooms ❍❘ Free Breakfast.

Posada de Expediciones Kahuel
$$ | **B&B/INN** | Located inside a forest and just steps from the seashore, this rustic B&B is a nice setting for a stay and yet it's just a five-minute drive from town. **Pros:** good food; big, comfortable rooms; steps away from the beach. **Cons:** facilities are very rustic; Wi-Fi connection is poor; cabins are basic. $ Rooms from:

pesos71000 ✉ *Km 4 Camino Chaitén-Sta. Bárbara, sector Fandango, Chaitén* ☎ *9/5629–2694* ⊕ *www.posadakahuel.cl* ⤵ *7 rooms* ❙❍❙ *Free Breakfast.*

Parque Nacional Pumalín Douglas Tompkins

56 km (35 miles) north of Chaitén.

One of Chile's true natural jewels, Pumalín Douglas Tompkins National Park was established in April 2019 after it was donated to the government by the late Douglas Tompkins and his wife, Kris, an American eco-philanthropist couple who have helped create seven national parks in Chile. Located in northern Chaitén, this 994,331-acre park hosts a magnificent landscape of mountains, temperate rain forests, volcanoes, lakes, and rivers. Kayaking around the park's coastal fjords is a popular activity, as is hiking through some of the country's last, large intact alerce forest (an ancient tree akin to the California redwood). The park also has excellent camping facilities, first-class cabins, and a superb café and restaurant at its headquarters in Caleta Gonzalo.

GETTING HERE AND AROUND

Caleta Gonzalo, headquarters of Pumalín Douglas Tompkins Park, is about 60 km (37 miles) north of Chaitén. The road from Chaitén to Caleta Gonzalo is well maintained but not paved. You can also reach Caleta Gonzalo by ferry. To venture to the northernmost areas of the park, such as Cahuelmo hot springs, you could rent a boat in Hornopirén, a small town about 110 km (68 miles) southeast of Puerto Montt.

TOURS

Alsur Expeditions

HIKING & WALKING | This longtime tour operator in Puerto Varas runs tours to the park, with all-inclusive tours including treks and sea kayaking of four days or more. ✉ *Aconcagua 8, Puerto Varas*

☎ *65/223–2300, 9/6619–7092* ⊕ *www.alsurexpeditions.cl* ✍ *From 1000 pesos.*

Chaitur

HIKING & WALKING | This agency in Chaitén knows the park better than almost anyone, outside of the park administrators. Tours include an inexpensive, one-day hike at three trails (Sendero los Alerces, Sendero Cascadas Escondidas, and Sendero el Volcán). ✉ *Av. Bernardo O´Higgins 67, Chaitén* ☎ *9/7468–5608* ⊕ *www.chaitur.com* ✍ *From 10000 pesos.*

BirdsChile

BIRD WATCHING | This group leads three-day overnight treks to the park, hiking on trails to the El Amarillo Glacier, Chaitén Volcano, and Escondidas Waterfall. The tour group flies on a small plane from Puerto Varas and returns by boat through the fjords. ✉ *Pasaje Ricke 108, Puerto Varas* ☎ *9/9269–2606, 9/9235–4818* ⊕ *www.birdschile.com* ✍ *From 25000 pesos.*

◉ Sights

★ Parque Nacional Pumalín Douglas Tompkins

NATIONAL PARK | Funded and organized by the late American conservationist Douglas Tompkins, this park covers 402,392 hectares (994,331 acres) and shelters the largest—and one of the few remaining—intact alerce forests in the world. Alerces, the world's second-longest-living tree species at up to 4,000 years, are often compared to the equally giant California redwood. Tompkins, who founded the clothing companies ESPRIT and The North Face, died in a kayaking accident in December 2015, and was posthumously lauded as an environmental hero in Chile and the world over. Pumalín Park represents the biggest parcel of altogether 1 million acres of land officially donated to Chile in March 2017 by Conservation Land Trust, the foundation set up to manage Tompkins's park projects in South America. Thanks in part to lands bought up and preserved by Tompkins, Pumalín became a

Did You Know?

Parque Nacional Pumalín Douglas Tompkins, which shelters the largest intact alerce forests in the world, became a national park in 2019. Here, you can hike trails that wind past lakes and stay in wooden cabins with the Chaitén Volcano looming in the distance.

full-fledged national park in April 2019. The Pan-American Highway, which trundles all the way north to Alaska, is interrupted at Pumalín, though the government plans to expand the highway through it. Meanwhile, there's a well-maintained road stretching 60 km (37 miles) from Chaitén to the northern entrance of the park at Caleta Gonzalo.

This park encompasses some of the most pristine landscape in the region, if not the world. There are a dozen trails that wind past lakes and waterfalls. Stay in excellent wooden cabins or at one of the 17 campsites, or put up your tent on one of the local farms scattered across the area that welcome travelers. After the Chaitén Volcano eruption here in 2008, the main entrance to the park was moved to El Amarillo, some 30 km (18 miles) south of Chaitén. But one can still arrive via the more developed Caleta Gonzalo entrance to the north, where a ferry from Hornopirén can drop you off and where the cabins and a park restaurant are located. ✉ *Conaf, Sector El Amarillo, Chaitén* ☎ *65/243–6337, 65/220–3107* 🎫 *Free.*

Hotels

Lodge Caleta Gonzalo
$$$$ | **B&B/INN** | Seven gray-shingled cabanas, each designed to be distinct from its neighbor, sit high on stilts against the backdrop of the misty mountains. **Pros:** ocean views; attractive design; close to nature. **Cons:** no kitchen; no Wi-Fi; often booked up. $ *Rooms from: pesos155000* ✉ *Caleta Gonzalo, Parque Pumalin* ☎ 📧 *reservas@lodgecaletagonzalo.cl* 🌐 *www.lodgecaletagonzalo.cl* 🛏 *7 cabins* 🍴 *Free Breakfast.*

Futaleufú

159 km (99 miles) east of Chaitén.

Near the town of Villa Lucia, Ruta 231 branches east from the Carretera Austral and winds around Lago Yelcho. About 159 km (99 miles) later, not far from the Argentine border, it reaches the tiny town of Futaleufú. Despite being barely five square blocks, Futaleufú is high on many global travelers' itineraries. World-class adventure sports await here, where the Río Espolón and the Río Futaleufú collide. It's the staging center for serious river kayaking and white-water rafting, as well as a glorious spot for mountain biking, fly-fishing, hiking, and horseback riding. The small community also has a growing number of lodging and dining options.

GETTING HERE AND AROUND

The road from Chaitén to Futaleufú, now partially paved, takes about three hours to drive. However, it's also possible to enter Futaleufú from Argentina, which is about 190 km (118 miles) southwest of Esquel. From Bariloche, Argentina, drive south for about five hours through pleasant Argentine tourist towns like El Bolsón and Esquel. After Esquel you come upon the road that leads to Futaleufú. The roads are paved throughout the Argentine portion of the trip, and a car rented in Puerto Montt costs less than 40,000 pesos per day, although better deals may be had in Santiago. Kemel Bus (65/225–6450, www.kemelbus.cl) offers service to Futaleufú from Puerto Montt. In Chaitén, Chaitur Excursions (9/7468–5608) runs minivan service to Futaleufú.

ESSENTIALS

VISITOR INFORMATION Tourist Office.
✉ *Av. Bernardo O'Higgins 596, Futaleufú* ☎ *65/272–1610.*

TOURS

Patagonia Elements

WATER SPORTS | Recognized for its experience and professionalism on the Futaleufú, this Chilean-owned outfitter offers rafting, fly-fishing, trekking, and kayaking excursions. Their rafting day trips are a relatively inexpensive way to experience the river. ✉ *Pedro Aguirre Cerda 537, Futaleufú* ☎ *9/7499–0296* 🌐 *www.patagoniaelements.com* 🎫 *From 60000 pesos.*

🍴 Restaurants

★ Martín Pescador

$$$$ | **CHILEAN** | The restaurant's fireplace and library supply ambience while you dine on some of the finest food on the Carretera Austral, such as Chilean and regional dishes like grilled trout and roasted lamb, which are prepared with style and organic, locally grown ingredients. An added benefit is that the restaurant is co-run by a longtime American rafting guide who can give inside info on outdoor activities in the area. **Known for:** meeting place; gourmet fare; organic ingredients. [$] *Average main: pesos12000* ✉ *Manuel Rodriguez 57, Futaleufú* ☎ *9/9558–2561* 🌐 *www.martinpescadorfutaleufu.cl.*

★ Pizzas de Fabio

$$$$ | **PIZZA** | Some swear Pizzas de Fabio has the best pizza in Patagonia, and that may well be. The Argentinean owner is a maestro with pizza cuisine, and he uses fresh ingredients from local organic growers. **Known for:** fun atmosphere; thin-crust pizza; fresh, local ingredients. [$] *Average main: pesos12000* ✉ *O'Higgins, corner of Isabel Riquelme, Futaleufú* ☎ *9/6485–1412.*

☕ Coffee and Quick Bites

Café Mandala

$ | **CAFÉ** | On a cold, rainy day nothing is finer than partaking of a rico coffee and *küchen* cake at Café Mandala in Futaleufú. Their calling card is their fine breakfasts, but don't miss out on their hot chocolate, delicious cakes, and homemade bread. **Known for:** homemade bread; coffee; pastries. [$] *Average main: pesos4500* ✉ *Pedro Aguirre Cerda 545, Futaleufú* ☎ *9/5108–2072* 💳 *No credit cards.*

🛏 Hotels

Hostal Las Natalias

$ | **HOTEL** | Part hostel, part B&B, this warm and welcoming place just outside of town is a good value option. **Pros:** spacious house; friendly owners; ample parking. **Cons:** communal living; a 10-minute hike to town; lacks the creature comforts. [$] *Rooms from: pesos40000* ✉ *Sector Noroeste s/n, Futaleufú* ☎ *9/9882–4637, 9/9631–1330* 🌐 *www.hostallasnatalias.info* 🕓 *Closed May–Oct.* 🔑 *9 rooms* 🍽 *Free Breakfast.*

Hostería Río Grande

$$ | **B&B/INN** | Guest rooms here are simply decorated with carpeting, wood-paneled walls, and big cozy beds, and lots of sunlight comes in through the windows. **Pros:** cozy fireplace; clean and simple; central location. **Cons:** noisy at times; no central heating; breakfast options could be better. [$] *Rooms from: pesos70000* ✉ *Av. Bernardo O'Higgins 397, Futaleufú* ☎ *65/272–1320* 🌐 *www.pachile.com* 🔑 *19 rooms* 🍽 *Free Breakfast.*

Hotel El Barranco

$$$$ | B&B/INN | FAMILY | This classic Futa-style boutique hotel is run by friendly owners and stands out for its first-class rooms and facilities, including a pool, gym, sauna, and bikes for guests. **Pros:** central location; good food; pool and sauna. **Cons:** simple breakfast; some rooms not well lit; Wi-Fi unstable. $ *Rooms from: pesos162000* ⊠ *Av. Bernardo O'Higgins 172, Futaleufú* ☎ *65/272–1314* ⊕ *www.elbarrancochile.cl* ⇌ *10 rooms* ¶⊙¶ *Free Breakfast.*

La Gringa Carioca

$$$ | B&B/INN | This small, rustic B&B within walking distance of the town plaza provides a countryside homey ambience with picturesque views of the surrounding mountains and Espolon River. **Pros:** service in three languages; patio with great views; homelike atmosphere. **Cons:** some bathrooms small; poor ventilation in some rooms; rooms get cold at night. $ *Rooms from: pesos101000* ⊠ *Sargento Aldea 498, Futaleufú* ☎ *65/272–1260* ✉ *lagringacarioca@gmail.com* ⊗ *Closed June–Aug.* ⇌ *5 rooms* ¶⊙¶ *Free Breakfast.*

Pata Lodge

$$$$ | B&B/INN | Located along the Futaleufú River, surrounded by granite cliffs and a 250-acre sustainable farming project called Fundo Las Escalas, this is an eco-lodge in the truest sense: they practice organic and regenerative agriculture, generate their own power, and recycle and treat their own waste. **Pros:** beautiful setting; environmentally conscious; breakfast and dinner included. **Cons:** no TV; high cost; isolated. $ *Rooms from: pesos350000* ⊠ *Futaleufú* ☎ *9/7955–9817* ⊕ *www.pata.cl* ⇌ *6 cabins* ¶⊙¶ *Free Breakfast.*

⚑ Activities

The main reason to visit Futaleufú is to partake in the plethora of sports and outdoor options in the area.

Bio Bio Expeditions

KAYAKING | With offices in California and Chile, Bio Bio Expeditions runs nine-day outings based out of its excellent riverside lodge facilities in the Futaleufú countryside. The trip can include rafting, kayaking, fly-fishing, trekking, horseback riding, yoga, and mountain biking. ⊠ *Futaleufú* ☎ *800/246–7238* ⊕ *www.bbxrafting.com* ▣ *Rates from US$4,500.*

Earth River Expeditions

KAYAKING | This popular eco-conscious river outfitter offers nine-day rafting trips down the Futaleufú. Earth River owns four "wilderness camps" along the river, each decked out with hot tubs and access to a variety of other sports in addition to the rafting. ⊠ *Futaleufú* ☎ *800/643–2784* ⊕ *www.earthriver.com* ▣ *From US$4,900.*

★ Expediciones Chile

KAYAKING | Founded by former Olympic kayaker Chris Spelius, who was one of the first ever to kayak the entire river, this outfitter offers rafting itineraries ranging from three days to two weeks. Mountain-biking and horseback-riding trips are available, too. ⊠ *Gabriela Mistral 296, Futaleufú* ☎ *208/629–5032* ⊕ *www.exchile.com.*

Matapiojo Anglers

FISHING | Francisco Rivera and his guides prepare you for world-class fishing at lakes, rivers, and lagoons outside of their small fishing lodge about 20 miles outside of Futaleufú. Their clients can also stay at the lodge's luxurious glamping tents—with all the comforts—right alongside the river. ⊠ *Futaleufú* ☎ *9/8929–3015* ⊕ *www.matapiojoanglers.com* ▣ *From 250000 pesos per day* ⊗ *Closed May–Oct.*

La Junta

150 km (93 miles) south of Chaitén.

If you're traveling by car or jeep down Carretera Austral, this small town of approximately 1,200 residents is a good place to stop for gas, meals, or an overnight rest. The town is also within close proximity to top fishing and ecotourism spots, such as the Palena River and the 12,725-hectare (31,444-acre) Reserva Nacional Lago Rosselot.

GETTING HERE AND AROUND

There is only one road in and out of La Junta, the Carretera Austral. There are several minibus transport options to La Junta, leaving from Chaitén and Coyhaique.

Hotels

★ Espacio y Tiempo Hotel de Montaña
$$$$ | B&B/INN | A great find after a long day driving down the Carretera Austral, this hotel has comfortable and modern rooms complete with cable TV and telephone, and the in-house restaurant serves excellent meals and generous breakfasts. **Pros:** excellent in-house restaurant; telephone service in rooms; modern comforts. **Cons:** surrounding town has few touristic attractions; rooms on first floor are sometimes noisy; Internet connection can be slow. [$] *Rooms from: pesos114000* ✉ *Carretera Austral 399, La Junta* ☎ *67/231–4141* 🌐 *www.espacioytiempo.cl* 🛏 *9 rooms* 🍴 *Free Breakfast.*

Melimoyu Lodge
$$$$ | ALL-INCLUSIVE | Near the rarely explored Melimoyu Volcano, this lodge offers unique access to some of the most spectacular natural areas of southern Chile. **Pros:** free airport shuttle; access to virgin nature; fly-fishing program. **Cons:** guided activities are extra charge; no Internet; requires extensive travel to get there. [$] *Rooms from: pesos1300000* ✉ *Km 37, Camino La Junta a Puerto Raúl Marín Balmaceda, La Junta* ☎ *9/9609–5977* 🌐 *www.melimoyulodge.com* 🛏 *4 rooms* 🍴 *All-Inclusive.*

Terrazas del Palena
$$ | B&B/INN | This hotel and restaurant is likely your first stop, 2 km (1 mile) north of La Junta, after leaving Chaitén by car on the Carretera Austral. **Pros:** views of the Palena Valley; spacious, apartment-style accommodations; great pizza and sourdough bread at the restaurant. **Cons:** rooms get booked fast; prices increase for 2 or more people; Wi-Fi connection is unstable. [$] *Rooms from: pesos67000* ✉ *Carretera Austral, La Junta* ☎ *9/8549–3679* ✎ *terrazasdelpalena@gmail.com* 💳 *No credit cards* 🛏 *5 rooms* 🍴 *Free Breakfast.*

Activities

Austral Garden Route
CULTURAL TOURS | A collection of interesting tours and workshops provides a great glimpse of the way of life in these parts. Tours include visits to organic farms, hikes in forests, hunting for mushrooms, workshops on permaculture, and making sourdough bread. ✉ *La Junta* ☎ *9/3442–5514* 🌐 *www.australgardenroute.com* 🎫 *15,000 pesos.*

Puerto Puyuhuapi

196 km (123 miles) south of Chaitén.

This mossy fishing village of about 900 residents is one of the oldest along the Carretera Austral. It was founded in 1935 by German immigrants fleeing the economic ravages of post–World War I Europe. As in much of Patagonia, Chile offered free land to settlers with the idea of making annexation by Argentina more difficult. Those early immigrants ventured into the wilderness to clear the forests and make way for farms.

Puerto Puyuhuapi is a sleepy town near Queulat National Park and Termas de Puyuhuapi.

Today this sleepy town near Queulat National Park and Termas de Puyuhuapi is a convenient stopover for those headed farther south in the region. It has a few modest guesthouses and restaurants, as well as some markets and a gas station.

GETTING HERE AND AROUND

The mostly unpaved 210-km (130-mile) drive from Coyhaique to Puerto Puyuhuapi along the Carretera Austral can be undertaken by car or bus. A small landing strip nearby serves private planes only.

🍴 Restaurants

Mi Sur

$$ | CHILEAN | With quick and pleasant service and a diverse daily menu, Mi Sur has become an obligatory stop for hungry travelers who regularly drive the Carretera Austral. The meals are prepared with great care and are colorful, abundant, and well presented. **Known for:** solid choice on the Carretera Austral; fish stew; friendly service. [$] *Average main: pesos8000* ✉ *Otto Uebel 36, Puyuhuapi* ☎ *9/7550–7656.*

🛏 Hotels

Comuy-Huapi

$$ | B&B/INN | At this friendly hostel on the waterfront, rooms are basic but clean and comfortable, each with a private bath and hot showers. **Pros:** Wi-Fi; good restaurant; near the water. **Cons:** no TV; no parking; no central heating. [$] *Rooms from: pesos47000* ✉ *Pedro Llautureo 143, Puyuhuapi* ☎ *9/7766-1984, 9/5741-6146* 🌐 *www.comuyhuapi.cl* 🕓 *Closed in June* 🛏 *7 rooms* 🍽 *Free Breakfast.*

El Pangue Lodge

$$$$ | ALL-INCLUSIVE | Located 18 km (11 miles) north of Puyuhuapi, on the shores of Lake Risopatrón, this is a fun stop along the Carretera Austral; in addition to the dozen independent, fully equipped cabins (including Wi-Fi, kitchen, phones, and more) the lodge provides great views, a pool, sauna, hot tub, easy access to the lake, and great hiking trails

amid the Patagonian Andes. **Pros:** fishing and hiking; lake setting; independent cabins. **Cons:** heating issues; bathrooms are small; Wi-Fi is hit-and-miss. $ *Rooms from: pesos136577* ⊠ *Carretera Austral Km 240, Puyuhuapi* ☎ *67/252–6906* ⊕ *www.elpangue.com* ☾ *Closed June and July* ⤳ *12 rooms.*

Hostal Aonikenk-Puyuhuapi

$$ | **B&B/INN** | Providing green spaces, excellent facilities, and a comfortable place to sleep, this accommodation option also has a great on-site café that offers a healthy, hearty breakfast with homemade bread. **Pros:** barbecue available; friendly service; good location. **Cons:** simple rooms without TV; kerosene heaters are problematic; cabins don't have kitchens. $ *Rooms from: pesos54000* ⊠ *Hamburgo 16, Puyuhuapi* ☎ *67/232–5208, 9/8200–3154* ✍ *aonikenkturismo@yahoo.com* ⊕ *www.aonikenkpuyuhuapi.cl* ▤ *No credit cards* ☾ *Closed May–Aug.* ⤳ *13 rooms* ⊙| *Free Breakfast.*

Hostería Alemana

$ | **B&B/INN** | The home of Ursula Flack, the last of the town's original German settlers, is a great choice for travelers. **Pros:** cozy atmosphere; friendly host; good breakfast. **Cons:** rooms are basic; thin walls; located just outside of town. $ *Rooms from: pesos45000* ⊠ *Otto Uebel 450, Puyuhuapi* ☎ *67/232–5118, 9/9881–3164* ⊕ *www.hosteriaalemana.cl* ⤳ *8 rooms, 2 cabins* ⊙| *Free Breakfast.*

Puyuhuapi Lodge & Spa

$$$$ | **RESORT** | Located 13 km (8 miles) south of Puerto Puyuhuapi, this first-class lodge takes care of your every need, whether you're in the mood for hiking and kayaking, excursions to glaciers at nearby Queulat National Park, or just relaxing with a massage and splashing in one of three indoor and outdoor hot-spring pools. **Pros:** views of the bay and mountains; quality spa treatments; three pools. **Cons:** food menu is limited; well-ness facilities cost extra; no Wi-Fi or TV. $ *Rooms·from: pesos242000* ⊠ *Bahia*

Dorita s/n, Puyuhuapi ☎ *67/245–0305, 2/2225–6489 in Santiago* ⊕ *www.puyu-huapilodge.com* ⤳ *30 rooms* ⊙| *Free Breakfast.*

Activities

More than 50 rivers are within easy driving distance of Puerto Puyuhuapi, making this a cherished destination among fishing enthusiasts. Poles reel in rainbow and brown trout, silver and steelhead salmon, and local species such as the *robalo*. The average size is about six pounds, but it's not rare to catch some twice that size. Daily trips are organized by the staff at Puyuhuapi Lodge & Spa (67/325–103, 2/225–6489 in Santiago, www.puyuhuapi-lodge.com). It's also possible to organize boating trips into the fjord with local guides; inquire at the waterfront.

Termas del Ventisquero

HOT SPRING | About 15 minutes from Puyuhuapi, this facility provides an inexpensive option for enjoying the area's natural hot springs. It's open daily, and the entrance fee affords you three hours in the four pools of varying sizes, either from 10 am to 1 pm, or 2 pm to 5 pm. The grounds are well organized, with bathrooms, indoor and outdoor showers, and a small café on-site that serves coffee, cake, pizza, and sandwiches. ⊠ *Puyuhuapi* ☎ *9/6860–3454* ▤ *20,000 pesos.*

Parque Nacional Queulat

175 km (109 miles) south of Chaitén.

Many tourists mistakenly neglect to stop at this vastly underrated park, yet it is a good place to camp and hike. If you do make time for a visit, you can experience rich temperate rain forest, hidden lakes, huge waterfalls, white-water rivers, and high mountains. The highlight is Ventisquero Colgante, or Hanging Glacier, which is among Chile's most memorable sights. Although camping is a fun way to visit the park, there are also some good lodging options within a short drive.

Sights

★ Parque Nacional Queulat

NATIONAL PARK | The rugged 154,000-hectare (380,000-acre) Parque Nacional Queulat begins to rise and roll to either side of the Carretera Austral some 20 km (12 miles) south of Puyuhuapi. The rivers and streams crisscross dense virgin forests. At the higher altitudes, brilliant blue glaciers can be found in the valleys between snowcapped peaks. If you're lucky, you'll spot a *pudú,* one of the diminutive deer that make their home in the forest. Less than 1 km (about a half mile) off the east side of the Carretera Austral, you are treated to a close-up view of the hanging glacier, Ventisquero Colgante, which slides a sheet of ice between a pair of gentle rock faces. Several waterfalls cascade down the cliffs to either side of the glacier's foot. There is an easy 15-minute walk leading to one side of the lake below the glacier, which is not visible from the overlook. A short drive farther south, where the Carretera Austral makes sharp switchback turns as it climbs higher, a small sign indicates the trailhead for the Salto Padre García. There is no parking area, but you can leave your car on the shoulder. This short hike through dense forest is worth attempting for a close-up view of this waterfall of striking proportions. There are three CONAF stations (the national forestry service), and an informative Environmental Information Center at the parking lot for the Ventisquero Colgante overlook and the southern and northern entrances to the park. ✉ *Parque Nacional Quelat, Puyuhuapi* ☎ *67/221–2225* 🌐 *www.conaf.cl* 🎫 *8,200 pesos.*

Hotels

★ Posada Queulat

$$$$ | **B&B/INN** | **FAMILY** | Inside Queulat National Park, about 20 miles south of Puyuhuapi, Posada Queulat is what you might imagine a Patagonian lodge to be: tucked inside a temperate rain forest, the ecotourism complex of six rustic cabins and big clubhouse sits in an idyllic spot along the Queulat River close to the mouth of the Queulat Fjord. **Pros:** cozy cabins; great base for exploring Queulat Park; good food. **Cons:** 2-night minimum stay required; excursions cost extra; no Wi-Fi. [$] *Rooms from: pesos160000* ✉ *Carretera Austral, Km 192* ☎ *9/9919–3520* 🌐 *www.posadaqueulat.cl* 🛏 *6 cabins* 🍴 *All-Inclusive.*

Coyhaique

224 km (140 miles) south of Puerto Puyuhuapi.

The hub of the Aysén region in Patagonia, this is a city in contrast, with modernity mixing with a traditionally slower rhythm in the shadow of the Andes. Within minutes of departing Coyhaique, you can be fly-fishing on the Simpson River or trekking and horseback riding amid magnificent countryside scenery. The town itself is constantly improving its shopping and cultural offerings for tourists. Throughout the year there are regular cultural festivals of all kinds, outdoor sports competitions, and surprisingly lively night spots on weekends.

GETTING HERE AND AROUND

There are regular domestic flights every day to the Southern Coast's only major airport, 55 km (34 miles) south of Coyhaique in the town of Balmaceda. Ferry lines operating in southern Chile sail the interwoven fjords, rivers, and lakes of the region. Navimag (www.navimag.com) operates a cargo and passenger fleet throughout the region. Naviera Austral (www.navieraustral.cl) also operates a cargo and passenger ferry fleet, with ships starting in Puerto Montt and sailing to nearby Puerto Chacabuco. Tour companies often have more luxurious boats that include stops in Chacabuco.

Renting a car, although expensive, is a worthwhile option for getting around. At Balmaceda airport there are several rental agencies. Make sure you understand the extent of your liability for any damage to the vehicle, including routine events such as a chipped or cracked windshield. As well, plan ahead for fueling stops, which are few and far between on the Carretera Austral. If you want to visit one of the more popular parks, check out tour prices. They may prove far cheaper than driving yourself. A number of bus companies with offices in Coyhaique serve most destinations in the area.

ESSENTIALS

MEDICAL ASSISTANCE Hospital Regional Coyhaique. ⊠ *Dr. Jorge Ibar 068, Coyhaique* ☎ *67/226–2079* ⊕ *www.hospitalcoyhaique.cl.*

POST OFFICE Correos. ⊠ *Lord Cochrane 226, Coyhaique* ☎ *600/950–2020.*

VISITOR INFORMATION Sernatur. ⊠ *Bulnes 35, Coyhaique* ☎ *67/224–0290, 67/224–0299* ⊕ *www.sernatur.cl.*

TOURS

Aysén Somos
ADVENTURE TOURS | Horseback riding, rock climbing, trekking, backcountry skiing, and viewing Andean condors are among the many excursions this tour operator can offer. ⊠ *Coyhaique* ☎ *9/7660–2609* ⊕ *www.aysensomos.cl.*

★ ChileTrout
FISHING | ChileTrout runs fishing trips from its boutique lodge located on the shores of Lago Frio, about a 20-minute drive from Coyhaique. Run by Karina and Pancho, the lodge caters to up to eight anglers; they have a smaller cabin in the more remote Nirehuao Valley.

They can also design custom trips to fish other rivers and lakes in the Coyhaique area, such as Río Simpson, Río Coyhaique, Lago Ardillas, Lago Paloma, and others. ⊠ *Lago Frio, Coyhaique* ✐ *info@chiletrout.com* ⊕ *www.chiletrout.com* ✉ *All-inclusive; 1-week packages start at US $5,400.*

Patagonia Bikers
BICYCLE TOURS | Founded by Gabriel Benoit, one of Chile's top pro bikers, they offer several types of multiday mountain bike excursions, including enduro, trail riding, family trips, e-bike trips, and journeys along the Carretera Austral. They also rent bikes. ⊠ *Camino a Puerto Aysén, Km, 2,, Coyhaique* ☎ *9/8159–3383* ⊕ *www.patagoniabikers.cl* ⊗ *Closed May to Oct.*

★ Patagona Excursiones
ADVENTURE TOURS | **FAMILY** | This local tour operator is run by Marcela Rios, who knows virtually every nook and corner of Aysén and can help you explore them through rafting, trekking, kayaking, horseback riding, skiing, boating, fossil hunting, and more. Of particular expertise is the Lago General Carrera–Cochrane area; trips go to the Capillas de Marmol, Valle de Exploradors, Laguna San Rafael, Baker River, and Mount San Lorenzo, among others. ⊠ *Paseo Horn 48, Interior, Coyhaique* ☎ *9/5626–9633* ⊕ *www.patagonaexcursiones.com.*

◉ Sights

★ Cerro Castillo National Park
NATIONAL PARK | Just 64 km (40 miles) south of Coyhaique, this national park is home to one of the most beautiful mountain chains in the region, crowned majestically by the rugged Cerro Castillo. Glacier runoff fills the lakes below the mountain, and the reserve is also home to several species of deer, puma, and guanaco. Cerro Castillo could be called one of the best hikes in Patagonia, but it gets only a tiny percent of visitors

Did You Know?

Queulat National Park provides some stunning views, including those of Cascada Ventisquero Colgante (Hanging Glacier Falls).

compared with its more popular counterpart to the south, Torres del Paine. One excellent hiking route begins at Las Horquetas Grandes, 8 km (5 miles) south of the park entrance. From there, go along La Lima River until Laguna Cerro Castillo, where you can begin your walk around the peak, and then head toward the nearby village of Villa Cerro Castillo. There is bus service from Coyhaique, but it's better to come here in your own rented vehicle. It's also preferable to hike with a guide, as trails are not always clearly marked. Senderos Patagonia (aysensenderospatagonia.com, 9/6224–4725) offers several options for both day hikes and multiday expeditions, as well as horseback rides through the park. ⊠ *Parque Nacional Cerro Castillo, Villa Cerro Castillo* ☎ *67/221–2225* ⊕ *www. conaf.cl* 🎟 *18,000 pesos.*

Monumento al Ovejero

MONUMENT | The Carretera Austral leads to this monument in the northeastern corner of town. On the broad median of the Avenida General Baquedano, a solitary shepherd with his horse and his dog lean motionless into the wind behind a plodding flock of sheep. ⊠ *Av. General Baquedano, Coyhaique.*

Museo Regional de Aysén

HISTORY MUSEUM | This award-winning museum, which recently moved to a larger space, has a collection of black-and-white photos of early 20th-century pioneering in this region, as well as sections devoted to archaeology and geology of Aysén. One of the most fascinating collections features Father Antonio Ronchi, an Italian Catholic missionary who assisted communities throughout the region during the 1960s. ⊠ *Km. 3, Camino a Coyhaique Alto, Coyhaique* ☎ *67/257–6800, 9/4526–7721* ⊕ *www. museoregionalaysen.cl* 🎟 *Free* ⊗ *Closed Sun. and Mon.*

Plaza de Armas

PLAZA/SQUARE | This is the center of town and the nexus for its attractions, including the town's cathedral and government building. ⊠ *Coyhaique.*

Reserva Nacional Coyhaique

NATURE PRESERVE | The 2,150-hectare (5,313-acre) Reserva Nacional Coyhaique, about 4 km (2½ miles) north of Coyhaique, provides hikers with some stunning views when the weather cooperates. If it's raining you can drive a 9-km (5½-mile) circuit through the park. ⊠ *Reserva Nacional Coyhaique, Coyhaique* ☎ *67/221–2225* ⊕ *www.conaf.cl* 🎟 *6,200 pesos.*

Reserva Nacional Río Simpson

NATURE PRESERVE | This classic fishing spot in Aysén is dotted with waterfalls tumbling down steep canyon walls. A lovely waterfall called the Cascada de la Virgen is a 1-km (about a mile) hike from the information center, and another called the Velo de la Novia is 8 km (5 miles) farther. About 1 km from Coyhaique, along the banks of the Simpson River, you can also see the Piedra del Indio, a rock shaped in the profile of an indigenous individual. Get to the park via the highway that connects Coyhaique with Puerto Aysén; the park entrance is 32 km (20 miles) northeast of Coyhaique. ⊠ *Reserva Nacional Rio Simpson, Coyhaique* ☎ *67/233–2743, 9/9946–8566* ⊕ *www.conaf.cl* 🎟 *8,200 pesos* ⊗ *Closed Mon.*

🍽 Restaurants

DaGus Restaurant

$$$ | **FUSION** | Organic, fresh, regional produce stars in the indulgent Chilean-international fusion dishes at DaGus Restaurant. The menu is constantly changing, but standouts include pasta dishes and sandwiches like the "Terrible Pollo," a large grilled chicken affair with pesto,

The Carretera Austral winds its way past Cerro Castillo National Park.

tomato, arugula, olives, and melted cheese. **Known for:** pleasant ambience; gourmet sandwiches; organic ingredients. $ *Average main: pesos10000* ✉ *Latauro 82, Coyhaique* ☎ *9/7498–4204* ⊕ *www.dagus-restaurant.negocio.site* ☉ *Closed Sun.*

La Casona

$$$ | **CHILEAN** | This restaurant is run by the González family—the mother cooks, her husband and son serve—and they all exude a genuine warmth to everyone who walks in the door. There's plenty of traditional Chilean fare on the menu, including Patagonian cordero (roasted lamb), their standout *centolla* (king crab) and *langostino* (lobster), and the hearty *filete casona*—roast beef with bacon, mushrooms, and potatoes. **Known for:** prompt service; regional dishes; Patagonian lamb. $ *Average main: pesos11000* ✉ *Baquedano 11, Coyhaique* ☎ *67/223–8894* ⊕ *www.lacasonarestaurantcoyhaique.negocio.site.*

★ Mamma Gaucha

$$$ | **PIZZA** | This "Italo-Patagon" pizzeria in the heart of Patagonia mixes the best of Italian cuisine with local ingredients and cooking methods. There is the excellent clay-oven-baked pizza (the one with cordero meat is a running favorite), heaping salads, and inventive plates like grilled Camembert smothered in *calafate* (a local berry) sauce and homemade panzotti pasta stuffed with crab. **Known for:** craft beer; pizza; big salads. $ *Average main: pesos10000* ✉ *Paseo Horn 47-D, Coyhaique* ☎ *9/6409–7808* ⊕ *www.mammagaucha.cl* ☉ *Closed Sun.*

Hotels

Austral Patagonian Lodge

$$$$ | **B&B/INN** | Located at the foot of the imposing Cerro Mackay, a rocky massif about 1,200 meters (3,937 feet) high, this new lodge has stylish decor and tremendous views of the Patagonian countryside yet is just a 10-minute ride from the center of town. **Pros:** short distance to Coyhaique; stunning views;

quiet place to disconnect. **Cons:** no frills; no TV; not a lot of amenities. $ *Rooms from: pesos168000* ⊠ *Recta Foitzick, Km 5, Coyhaique* ☎ *9/9229–4170* ✉ *oscaraguilargallardo@gmail.com* 🍴 *8 rooms* 🍽 *Free Breakfast.*

El Reloj
$$$ | B&B/INN | Rooms at this hotel along the river (yet just four blocks from the town center) are simple, clean, and paneled in wood, while the salon is warmly decorated with Patagonian flair, with local antiques and a cozy, large fireplace. **Pros:** comfortable; on the river; good food. **Cons:** restaurant closed on Sun.; parking is limited; no frills. $ *Rooms from: pesos85000* ⊠ *Av. General Baquedano 828, Coyhaique* ☎ *67/223–1108* ⊕ *www.elrelojhotel.cl* 🍴 *20 rooms* 🍽 *Free Breakfast.*

Hostal Belisario Jara
$$$ | B&B/INN | You realize how much attention has been paid to detail in this quaint lodging when the proprietor points out that the weather vane on the peak of the single turret is a copy of one at Chilean poet Pablo Neruda's home in Isla Negra. **Pros:** excellent service; good parking; central location. **Cons:** small breakfast area; mornings sometimes are noisy; some rooms are small. $ *Rooms from: pesos90000* ⊠ *Francisco Bilbao 662, Coyhaique* ☎ *67/223–4150* ⊕ *www.belisariojara.cl* 🍴 *8 rooms* 🍽 *Free Breakfast.*

Nomades Hotel Boutique
$$$$ | B&B/INN | The rooms in this small, boutique hotel are spacious, with river views. **Pros:** quiet; 10 minutes from the center of town; beautiful decor. **Cons:** restaurant serves only dinner and closes on Sun.; service is sometimes lacking in friendliness; no gym or spa. $ *Rooms from: pesos145000* ⊠ *Baquedano 84, Coyhaique* ☎ *67/223–7777* ⊕ *www.nomadeshotel.com* 🍴 *8 rooms* 🍽 *Free Breakfast.*

Raices Bed and Breakfast
$$$$ | B&B/INN | FAMILY | This B&B with a thick Patagonian accent is not just warm because of its big, open fireplace but because of its service: the friendly owner and her staff help you with whatever you need. **Pros:** local flair; just a five-minute walk from town center; big breakfast. **Cons:** expensive; street noise at front of hotel; no parking on-site. $ *Rooms from: pesos125000* ⊠ *Baquedano 444, Coyhaique* ☎ *9/9619–5672* ⊕ *www.raicesbedandbreakfast.com* 🍴 *12 rooms* 🍽 *Free Breakfast.*

 Nightlife

Café Peña Quilantal
LIVE MUSIC | For music and dancing to the tunes and traditions of down-home Aysén Patagonia, try Café Peña Quilantal. Admission includes a sit-down dinner and dancing all night to the varied tunes of the Quilantal band. ⊠ *Baquedano 791, Coyhaique* ☎ *9/8156–1051.*

Casino Dreams Coyhaique
THEMED ENTERTAINMENT | Gambling has arrived in Patagonia at this sleek, modern—but small—casino. It also has a popular bar and regular entertainment on most weekends, especially music, which attracts audiences of all ages. Admission is 3,000 pesos. ⊠ *Magallanes 131, Coyhaique* ☎ *67/226–4700.*

 Shopping

Coyhaique is no shopping mecca, but as it's the largest settlement around, you should stock up on general supplies here if you're heading off on a long exploring expedition.

Feria Artesanal
CRAFTS | This market hosts several stalls selling unique woolen clothing, small leather items, and pottery, making it a good place to search for gifts. ⊠ *Plaza de Armas between Dussen and Horn, Coyhaique.*

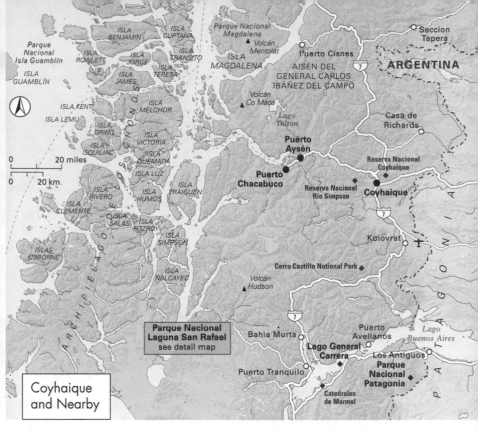

Parque
Nacional
Isla Guamblín

ISLA BENJAMÍN

ISLA ROWLETT

ISLA CUPTANA

ISLA JORGE

ISLA TRANSITO

Parque Nacional
Magdalena

▲ Volcán
Mentolát

ISLA
MAGDALENA

AISÉN DEL
GENERAL CARLOS
IBÁÑEZ DEL CAMPO

Puerto Cisnes

Sección
Tapera

ARGENTINA

ISLA
GUAMBLÍN

ISLA
JAMES

ISLA
TERESA

Volcán
▲ Co Maca

Casa de
Richards

ISLA KENT

ISLA LEMU

ISLA
MELCHOR

Lago
Yulton

Reserva Nacional
Coyhaique

ISLA
DRING

ISLA
VICTORIA

Puerto
Aysén

ISLA
ISQUILIAC

ISLA
QUEMADA

Puerto
Chacabuco

Reserva Nacional
Río Simpson

Coyhaique

ISLA LUZ

0   20 miles

0   20 km.

ISLA
RIVERO

ISLA
HUMOS

ISLA
TRAIGUEN

Kolovrat

ISLA
CLEMENTE

ISLA
SALAS

ISLA
FITZROY

ISLA
SIMPSON

ISLAS
USBORNE

ISLA
NALCAYEC

Cerro Castillo National Park

Volcán
▲ Hudson

Parque Nacional
Laguna San Rafael
see detail map

Bahía Murta

Lago General
Carrera

Puerto
Avellanos

Lago
Buenos Aires

Los Antiguos

Parque
Nacional
Patagonia

Puerto Tranquilo

Catedrales
de Marmol

Coyhaique
and Nearby

Activities

SKIING
El Fraile Ski Center

SKIING & SNOWBOARDING | The only ski center in the Aysén region is located on Camino Lago Pollux, about 29 km (18 miles) outside of Coyhaique. There are two lifts for five slopes surrounded by native forest on the 1,600-meter (5,250-foot) Cerro Fraile. This small, government-run ski center has equipment available for rent, and there is a ski school. There are no accommodations, but there is a cafeteria on-site for meals. The season runs June through September. ⊠ *Cerro Fraile, Coyhaique* ☎ *67/221–3187.*

Puerto Chacabuco and Puerto Aysén

68 km (43 miles) northwest of Coyhaique.

The drive from Coyhaique to the town of Puerto Aysén and its port, Chacabuco, is beautiful. The mist hangs low over farmland, adding a dripping somnolence to the scenery. Dozens of waterfalls and rivers wend their way through mountain formations. Yellow poplars surround charming rustic lodges, and sheep and cattle graze on mossy, vibrant fields. The picture of serenity terminates at the sea, where the nondescript town of Puerto Aysén and its port Chacabuco—Coyhaique's link to the ocean—sits. This harbor ringed by snowcapped mountains is where you board the ferries that head north to Puerto Montt in the Lake District and Quellón on Chiloé, as well as boats going south to the spectacular Laguna San Rafael.

GETTING HERE AND AROUND

Puerto Chacabuco is less than an hour's drive from Coyhaique, and about 10 minutes from nearby Puerto Aysén. Several bus lines in Coyhaique serve Chacabuco. The town is also the jumping-off point for Laguna San Rafael, although the boats going to the park are almost all luxury tour vessels, which you need to contract in Coyhaique or in Santiago. Consult a travel agent beforehand if you plan to use one of these.

Sights

Puerto Aysén

TOWN | A hanging bridge leads from Chacabuco to Puerto Aysén, founded in 1928 to serve the region's burgeoning cattle ranches. Devastating forest fires that swept through the interior in 1955 filled the once-deep harbor with silt, making it all but useless for transoceanic vessels. Nowadays, fishing and salmon farming are the leading economic activities. The town gained some fame in February 2012, when protests here sparked a region-wide revolt over an array of social issues. The busy main street is a good place to stock up on supplies for boat trips to the nearby national parks. ✉ *Puerto Aisén.*

Hotels

Hotel Aysén Patagonia

$$ | **HOTEL** | The best option in town, this hotel has small rooms and basic furnishings, but the service is friendly and your cable TV will help overcome any discomforts. **Pros:** central heating; central location; good food. **Cons:** thin walls mean you may hear the neighbors; Wi-Fi connection is hit and miss; rooms are small. [$] *Rooms from: pesos69000* ✉ *Sargento Aldea 560, Puerto Aisén* ☎ *67/233–0928* 🌐 *www.hotel-aysenpatagonia.cl* 🛏 *14 rooms* 🍴 *Free Breakfast.*

Hotel Loberías del Sur

$$$$ | **HOTEL** | On a hill overlooking the modest port, this hotel came into being because the owner, who runs a catamaran service to Parque Nacional Laguna San Rafael, needed a place to pamper vacationers for the night. **Pros:** good restaurant; well-equipped spa; boat tours to Laguna San Rafael Park. **Cons:** meals cost extra; pool is small; nothing to do in the port itself. [$] *Rooms from: pesos203000* ✉ *Carrera 50, Puerto Chacabuco* ☎ *67/235–1112* 🌐 *www.loberiasdelsur.cl* 🛏 *60 rooms* 🍴 *Free Breakfast* ☞ *2-night minimum.*

Activities

The principal reason to come here for most travelers is to board a boat bound for the spectacular glaciers and ice at Laguna San Rafael Park. To do so, you must arrange with a tour operator or organize your own private boat. The area around Puerto Aysén is nature-rich and also well worth checking out. Nearby, for example, is Parque Aiken del Sur, a small private park on the banks of Lake Riesco with trails through native flora. For fly fishermen, this area is bountiful in prime fishing spots at the numerous rivers and lakes.

Aysén Rivers Outfitter

FISHING | Proving that a good guide can make all the difference in fishing trips, veteran guide Carlos Dinamarca and his team are well equipped to take you to the many fishing spots in the area. ✉ *Paseo Horn 47, Coyhaique* ☎ *9/8724–9914* 🌐 *www.aysenrivers.com.*

Catamaranes del Sur

BOATING | This agency can arrange day trips (168,000 pesos) by boat to Laguna San Rafael, or an all-inclusive package deal including a three-night stay (811,000 pesos) at its Loberías del Sur Hotel in Puerto Chacabuco. They also offer a

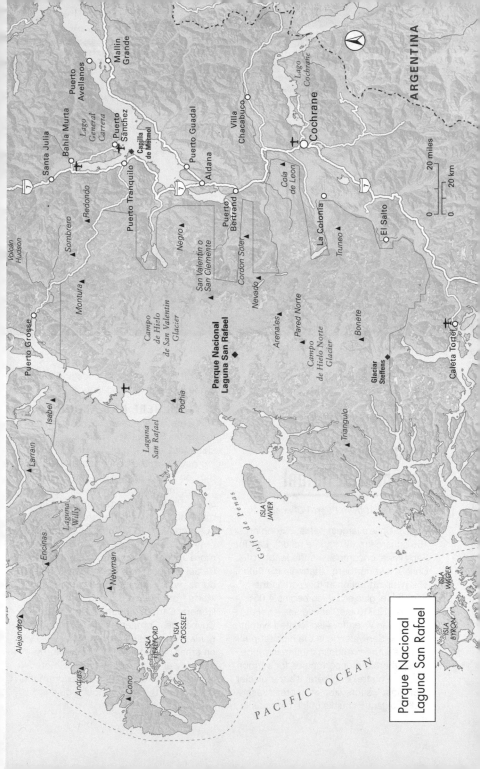

Parque Nacional
Laguna San Rafael

A boat tour passes an iceberg near San Rafael glacier.

half-day hike at nearby Aiken del Sur park. ⊠ *Carrera 50, Puerto Chacabuco* ☏ *67/235-1112, 2/2231-1902 in Santiago* ⊕ *www.catamaranesdelsur.cl.*

Parque Nacional Laguna San Rafael

5 hrs by boat from Puerto Chacabuco.

One of Chile's largest parks, extending 168 square km (65 square miles), Laguna San Rafael encompasses the length of Chile's vast northern Patagonia ice fields. The main attraction at this park is the San Rafael glacier, which begins 4,056 meters (13,310 feet) above sea level at Monte San Valentín. Also located within the park, San Valentín is the highest peak in the southern Andean mountain range. While there are opportunities for serious hikers to go trekking here, it's the glacier that most visitors stop at to breathlessly watch gigantic chunks of ice continually split off its brilliant blue sides and thunderously crash into the lagoon.

GETTING HERE AND AROUND
There are several ways to make the trip to Laguna San Rafael. There are luxury ships that leave out of Puerto Montt and journey down the coast before toasting the San Rafael glacier, like the six-night cruises that Skorpios (www.skorpios. cl) do. There are catamarans that make a much shorter trip via Puerto Chacabuco in Aysén, such as Catamaranes del Sur (www.catamaranesdelsur.cl). Perhaps a more adventurous route to Laguna San Rafael is a boat ride from Bahía Exploradores, which is connected by a road that starts from Puerto Río Tranquilo on Lake General Carrera, about 220 km south of Coyhaique. Companies like Destino Patagonia (www.destinopatagonia.cl) take you on small boats for 10 to 12 people. They have fewer amenities, but it is a more intimate experience. It's not recommended to make this trip without a guide.

Sights

Parque Nacional Laguna San Rafael
NATIONAL PARK | Nearly all of the 1,742,000-hectare (3,832,400-acre) Parque Nacional Laguna San Rafael is inaccessible fields of ice, and only a handful of the people have ever set foot on land. Most travel by boat from Puerto Chacabuco or Puerto Montt through the maze of fjords along the coast to the expansive San Rafael Lagoon. Floating on the surface of the brilliant blue water are scores of icebergs that rock from side to side as boats pass. Most surprising is the variety of forms and colors in each iceberg, including a shimmering, translucent cobalt blue. The massive Ventisquero San Rafael glacier measures 4 km (3 miles) from end to end but is receding about 182 meters (600 feet) a year. Paint on a bordering mountain marks the location of the glacier in past years. It's a noisy beast, roaring like thunder as the sheets of ice shift. If you're lucky, you can see huge pieces of ice calve off, causing violent waves that should make you glad your boat is at a safe distance.

Wildlife lovers can glimpse black-browed albatross and elegant black-necked swans here, as well as sea lions, dolphins, elephant seals, and *chungungos*—the Chilean version of the sea otter. ⊠ *Parque Nacional Laguna San Rafael* ☎ *67/221–2109* ⊠ *7,000 pesos.*

Activities

★ **Destino Patagonia**
BOAT TOURS | This tour operator based in tranquil Puerto Río Tranquilo offers a faster way to experience Laguna San Rafael than the bigger, slow catamarans that take dozens of tourists to the area. They have quicker, smaller (and comfortable) boats that get there with time to spare and more time to enjoy nature. There are two options: a day trip (155,000 pesos) or an overnight adventure with a hike and stay in a *refugio* (240,000 pesos). They

also offer a special three-day trip that includes camping at the wildly beautiful beaches of Istmo de Ofqui (380,000 pesos). ⊠ *Gilberta Flores 208, Puerto Río Tranquilo* ☎ *9/8822–9491* ⊕ *www.destinopatagonia.cl.*

Lago General Carrera and Nearby

280 km (174 miles) southeast of Coyhaique.

It takes a 280-km (174-mile) drive from Coyhaique along the rutted, mostly unpaved Carretera Austral to reach Lago General Carrera—a beautiful, almost surreally blue lake, the biggest in Chile (and the second largest in South America, after Lake Titicaca). This spectacular place is more than worth the trip. Every year, more and more travelers have been making the pilgrimage to fish, hike, and gasp at the mountains, glaciers, and waterfalls that dot the landscape.

TOURS

Patagonia Adventure Expeditions
HIKING & WALKING | Founded and led by American Jonathan Leidich, Patagonia Adventure Expeditions has been guiding in Patagonia for more than two decades, specializing in glacier excursions on the dramatic and highly beautiful Aysén Glacier Trail and raft trips down the Baker River. ⊠ *Cochrane* ☎ *9/8182–0608* ⊕ *www.adventurepatagonia.com.*

Sights

Catedrales de Marmol
NATURE SIGHT | The Catedrales de Marmol ("Marble Cathedrals") are impressive rock formations of calcium carbonate formed over 6,200 years on the western shores of Lake General Carrerra. Over time, they have been worn away by the water, creating a maze of caves, tunnels, and huge columns of multicolored pure

marble. This popular spot on the tourist trail is possible to reach by boat or kayak. There are small boat tours on offer near the site, which is on the Carretera Austral about 218 km (135 miles) south of Coyhaique near the small town of Puerto Río Tranquilo. ✉ *Carretera Austral, Puerto Rio Tranquilo* 🎟 *15,000 pesos per person.*

Hotels

★ El Mirador de Guadal

$$$$ | **B&B/INN** | With spacious rooms and a spectacular location on the south end of Lake General Carrera, this hotel is a great place to relax, reflect, or honeymoon. **Pros:** spacious cabins; personalized service; the view. **Cons:** Internet is slow; low water pressure in shower; unstable Wi-Fi connection. [$] *Rooms from: pesos125000* ✉ *Km 2, Camino a Chile Chico, Puerto Guadal* ☎ *9/9234–9130* 🌐 *www.elmiradordeguadal.com* 🕒 *Closed May–Sept.* 🛏 *10 rooms, 2 suites* 🍴 *Free Breakfast.*

★ Entre Hielos Lodge

$$$$ | **B&B/INN** | Halfway up a hill in the center of Caleta Tortel in southern Aysén, Entre Hielos is the best option for your stay in this roadless (but charming) village, where residents move about on cypress walkways. **Pros:** best quality lodging in town; great views; managed directly by the owner. **Cons:** if you have trouble walking, don't go here; uphill climb to the lodge; town has infrastructure problems. [$] *Rooms from: pesos119000* ✉ *Sector Centro s/n, Caleta Tortel* ☎ *9/9579–3779, 9/9599–5730* 🌐 *www.entrehielostortel.cl* 🛏 *5 rooms* 🍴 *Free Breakfast.*

Mallin Colorado Ecolodge

$$$$ | **B&B/INN** | Rustic, native wood cabins with tremendous views of Lake General Carrera highlight this tranquil spot to relax when you're not on your Patagonia adventures. **Pros:** views from cabins; comfortable beds; personalized service. **Cons:** remote location; thin walls between rooms; no Internet. [$] *Rooms from: pesos130000* ✉ *Carretera Austral, Km 273* ☎ *2/2263–2370* 🌐 *www.mallincolorado.cl* 🕒 *Closed June and July* 🛏 *10 rooms* 🍴 *Free Breakfast.*

Rumbo Sur Deep Patagonia

$$$$ | **B&B/INN** | At the southernmost end of the Carretera Austral, or Southern Highway, this is the modern hotel in town. **Pros:** clean; modern facilities; pleasant decor. **Cons:** weak Internet connection; no excursions offered; no frills. [$] *Rooms from: pesos113000* ✉ *Carretera Austral, Km 1240, Villa O'Higgins* ☎ *9/4217–7577* 🌐 *www.rumbosurdeeppatagonia.com* 🛏 *12 rooms* 🍴 *Free Breakfast.*

Terra Luna Lodge

$$$ | **B&B/INN** | Occupying 15 peaceful acres at the southeastern edge of the Lake General Carrera, this property boasts charming but basic redwood cabins, grazing horses, and a beautiful main lodge, where all meals are served. **Pros:** offer several excursions in the area; good value; location is ideal. **Cons:** temperatures chilly in the mornings; Wi-Fi in main lodge only; room quality varies. [$] *Rooms from: pesos93000* ✉ *Hijuelas 10, Puerto Guadal* ✥ *Camino a Mallín Grande* ☎ *9/8449–1092 bookings, 9/3456–5287 lodge* 🌐 *www.terraluna.cl* 🛏 *20 cabins* 🍴 *Free Breakfast.*

Parque Nacional Patagonia

57 km (36 miles) north of Cochrane.

This world-class park runs from east to west between the grasslands of the Argentine Patagonian steppes and the *coigüe* and *ñire* forests of Chile; it encompasses a diverse range of ecosystems and is home to a wide array of wildlife. Travelers here can hike one of the many trails, go bird-watching at the several lagoons, drive the scenic

Route X-83 toward Roballos Pass, kayak or raft the Cochrane River, or visit the spectacular confluence of the Baker and the Chacabuco rivers. Designed by the legendary American conservationist Douglas Tompkins, the park has well-done camping facilities and an excellent restaurant and lodge now managed by Chile's five-star Explora hotel chain.

Sights

Parque Nacional Patagonia

NATIONAL PARK | In 2019, this formerly private park became a national park and, moreover, merged territory with the Jeinimeni National Reserve (to the north) and the Tamango National Reserve (to the south) to form a much larger conservation preserve encompassing 304,527 hectares (752,503 acres). It was a major achievement for Kris Tompkins McDivitt, a former CEO of outdoor clothing company Patagonia and wife of the late nature philanthropist Doug Tompkins. With a landscape reminiscent of the American Southwest, this park includes semiarid steppe, temperate beech forests, grasslands, wetlands, and high mountains. The park includes unique fauna such as *huemul,* an endangered Chilean deer species; pumas; the hairy armadillo; and numerous birds species such as the Andean condor and pygmy owl. Guanacos especially abound here. Like other parks created by the Tompkins clan in the region, the trails and infrastructure here have set not just a national standard but a global one. Don't miss the excellent Patagonia Park Museum, which, through interactive exhibits, tells the natural and cultural history of the Chacabuco Valley, as well as the importance of national parks in ecological recovery. ✉ *Valle Chacabuco* ☎ *65/225–0079* 🌐 *www.conaf.cl* 🎟 *4,200 pesos* ☞ *For reservations at Lodge Valle Chacabuco, contact: reserve@explora.com.*

Hotels

Bahia Catalina

$$$ | B&B/INN | Located about one hour from the remote Parque Nacional Patagonia, Bahia Catalina makes for a good, affordable base if you prefer to forego camping; its cozy, rustic cabins have wood stoves to keep you warm, and the glamping tents are decked out with all the creature comforts. **Pros:** organic, fresh food; comfortable rooms; friendly hosts. **Cons:** poor Wi-Fi connection; no frills; remote. [$] *Rooms from: pesos110,000* ✉ *Carretera Austral Sur km 265* ☎ *9/8248–7037* 🌐 *www.bahiacatalina.com* 🛏 *7 rooms* 🍴 *Free Breakfast.*

BordeBaker Lodge

$$$$ | B&B/INN | With magnificent views of the mighty Baker River—one of Chile's best destinations for fly-fishing and rafting—this lodge earns much praise for its great service and attention to detail. **Pros:** good service; nice facilities; great view. **Cons:** small space for showers; limited restaurant menu; Wi-Fi signal is weak. [$] *Rooms from: pesos190000* ✉ *Carretera Austral, 8 km south of Puerto Bertrand, Puerto Bertrand* ☎ *2/2585–8464* ✉ *contacto@bordebaker.cl* 🌐 *www.bordebaker.cl* 🛏 *7 rooms* 🍴 *Free Breakfast.*

★ Lodge Valle Chacabuco

$$$$ | B&B/INN | Located within Parque Nacional Patagonia, this stately, stone-and-wood lodge was patterned after the Ahwahnee Lodge in Yosemite National Park. **Pros:** views of nearby Mount Tamanguito; luxurious stay inside the park; great food. **Cons:** no TV; excursions cost extra; unstable Wi-Fi. [$] *Rooms from: pesos1252000* ✉ *Avenida Américo Vespucio Sur 80, Piso 5, Santiago* ☎ *2/2395–2800* 🌐 *www.explora.com* 🛏 *6 rooms* 🍴 *Free Breakfast.*

⚘ Activities

Chulengo Expeditions

GUIDED TOURS | From December through April, this American-owned tour operator offers eight-day backpacking expeditions in the Parque Nacional Patagonia. Founded by a former park employee, Nadine Lehner, Chulengo offers pioneering knowledge that will lead you to the park's best hiking spots. ⊠ *Puerto Guadal* ⊕ *www.chulengo.org.*

★ Patagonia Big Five

ECOTOURISM | With tours led by some of the top wildlife experts in the region, Patagonia Big Five offers a great opportunity to see some of the beautiful, charismatic fauna that inhabits Patagonia National Park and its environs. The photosafari and bird-watching tours go in search of species like the huemul deer, Darwin's rhea, guanaco, puma, and the majestic Andean Condor while taking you around one of the world's most admired conservation areas. They can also custom-design wildlife observation trips. ⊠ *Camino a Coyhaique Alto, Km 6.5, Coyhaique* ☎ *9/9499–7678* ⊕ *www. patagoniabigfive.com.*

Patagonia Huts

GUIDED TOURS | Trek deep into the backcountry on an old trail that traverses Patagonia Park with well-trained mountain guides and utilize a network of comfortable huts at the overnight base camps during this company's five-day journey into remote sections of the park. ⊠ *O'Higgins, #750, Chile Chico* ☎ *9/6779–3390* ⊕ *www.patagoniahuts. com* ⊠ *From $1,200.*

Chapter 11

SOUTHERN CHILEAN PATAGONIA AND TIERRA DEL FUEGO

Updated by
Jimmy Langman

⊙ Sights | 🍴 Restaurants | 🛏 Hotels | 🛍 Shopping | 🍸 Nightlife
★★★★★ | ★★★★☆ | ★★★★☆ | ★★☆☆☆ | ★★☆☆☆

WELCOME TO SOUTHERN CHILEAN PATAGONIA AND TIERRA DEL FUEGO

TOP REASONS TO GO

★ **Natural wonders:** With jaw-dropping mountains, awesome glaciers, turquoise-blue lakes, and dark, deep forests, there's no end to Patagonia's wonders. Be prepared to feel astounded.

★ **Gaucho culture:** A rich Patagonian cowboy culture thrives at the many sheep ranches dotting the region. Go horseback riding on a visit to one of these classic *estancias*, and end the day with a traditional *asado*.

★ **Glaciers:** This region is like an Alaska South, with massive glaciers amid a wild landscape. Hike around, observe, or even trek on top of one of these massive walls of ice, contemplating the blue-green-turquoise spectrum trapped within.

★ **Penguins:** Humboldt, Rockhopper, and Magellanic penguins congregate around the southern Patagonian coast—at the noisy, malodorous colony of Isla Magdalena you'll find an old lighthouse and more than 80,000 of our waddling friends.

1 Puerto Natales. Puerto Natales serves as the last stop before Torres del Paine. This small port side city has an array of fine eateries and lodging choices.

2 Parque Nacional Torres del Paine. Known for its stunning glaciers, mountains, and abundant wildlife, this is the crown jewel of the national parks of South America.

3 Punta Arenas. Lord Byron's legendary mariner grandfather gave Chile's southernmost city its name. Situated next to the Strait of Magellan, the windy, monument-laden Punta Arenas is the capital of the Magallanes region and faces the big island of Tierra del Fuego, where the Atlantic and Pacific oceans merge.

4 Puerto Hambre. "Port Famine" commemorates an ill-fated historic settlement where most settlers starved to death amid the unforgiving terrain.

5 El Calafate and Parque Nacional Los Glaciares, Argentina. The dramatic wall of ice at Glacier Perito Moreno and the exquisite turquoise surface of Lago Argentino are the major attractions around the touristic town of El Calafate, a great place to look for souvenirs and sample the legendary Argentine steak.

6 El Chaltén, Argentina. This small town is a good base for accessing the iconic Mount Fitzroy and Cerro Torre at Parque Nacional Los Glaciares.

7 Ushuaia, Argentina. Argentina's southernmost city has beautiful vistas of the sea and mountains, and is a primary launching-off point for cruises to Antarctica and excursions around Tierra del Fuego.

8 Tierra del Fuego. Part-Chilean, part-Argentinean, this archipelago is dominated by its biggest island, Isla Grande. It is where the world's longest mountain chain peters out to become *el fin del mundo* (the end of the world) and is synonymous with seclusion and natural beauty.

9 Puerto Williams. The world's southernmost city, this port on the Beagle Channel is the gateway to spectacular trekking and fly-fishing on Chile's Navarino Island.

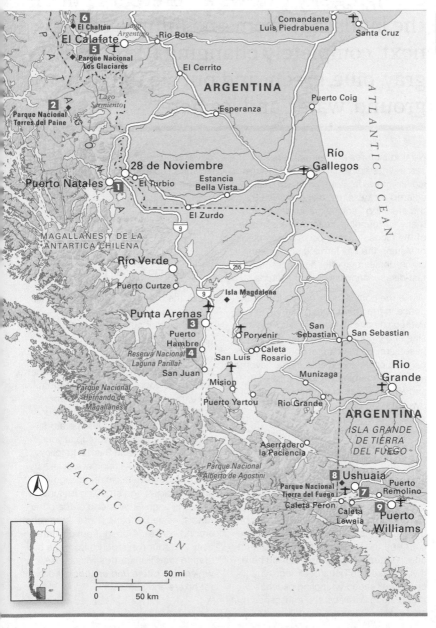

6 El Chaltén
Lago
Argentino
El Calafate
5
Parque Nacional
Los Glaciares

Río Bote

Comandante
Luis Piedrabuena

Santa Cruz

El Cerrito

ARGENTINA

Lago
Sarmiento

2

Parque Nacional
Torres del Paine

Esperanza

Puerto Coig

A T L A N T I C   O C E A N

28 de Noviembre

Río
Gallegos

Puerto Natales   1   El Turbio

Estancia
Bella Vista

MAGALLANES Y DE LA
ANTARTICA CHILENA

El Zurdo

9

Río Verde

255

Puerto Curtze

9   Isla Magdalena

Punta Arenas

3

San
Sebastián   San Sebastián

Puerto
Hambre   Porvenir

Reserva Nacional   4
Laguna Parilla

Caleta
Rosario

San Luis

San Juan

Misión   Munizaga

Parque Nacional
Hernando de
Magallanes

Puerto Yartou   Río Grande

Río
Grande

ARGENTINA

ISLA GRANDE
DE TIERRA
DEL FUEGO

Aserradero
la Paciencia

Parque Nacional
Alberto de Agostini

8   Ushuaia

Parque Nacional
Tierra del Fuego   Puerto
Remolino

7

Caleta Perón   9

Caleta
Lewaia   Puerto
Williams

P A C I F I C   O C E A N

0   50 mi

0   50 km

There's no doubt about it that Patagonia is striking in its beauty—the constantly changing sky throws a different light on the landscape from one minute to the next, completely changing the hues of gray, blue, green, and purple found in the ground, water, and ice here.

No two pictures of Patagonia are ever the same, whether you're looking onto the iconic Torres del Paine and their multi-colored rocky spires; being wowed by the stunning Perito Moreno glacier and many surrounding ice formations in one of the biggest glacier parks on the planet; or visiting the tiny farming and fishing communities that offer a glimpse into a fast-disappearing lifestyle of solitude.

While the population is one of the least dense in the world, those that inhabit Patagonia have introduced exquisite cuisine and world-class activities. Cuisine is based around the natural bounty in these parts: succulent king crab; richly flavored and freely roaming Patagonian lamb; and a host of native vegetation and sea dwellers. Outdoor activities involve the sea and land, too: from trekking through deep forests, rivers, and mountain ranges, to sea-kayaking past icebergs and along fjords, to spotting wildlife like penguins and puma.

Southern Chilean Patagonia is at the extreme edge of South America, and Tierra del Fuego is physically cut off from the rest of the continent by two vast ice caps and the Strait of Magellan, but that doesn't stop visitors from flocking here. If you make it to Tierra del Fuego, you'll encounter sheep-wrangling gauchos there, along with austere landscapes that never fail to captivate and remote islands inhabited solely by elephant seals and penguin colonies.

MAJOR REGIONS

Serious hikers often come to **Torres del Paine** and use **Puerto Natales** as their base for hiking the classic "W" or circuit treks in Torres del Paine, which take between four days and a week to complete. You can camp within Torres del Paine, or break the trip up into daily hikes while staying in more luxurious accommodations inside or outside the park.

If you have less time, however, it's possible to spend just one day touring the park, as many people do, with Puerto Natales as your starting point. In that case, rather than drive, you'll want to book a one-day Torres del Paine tour with one of the many tour operators here. Most tours pick you up at your hotel between 8 and 9 am and follow the same route, visiting several lakes and mountain vistas, seeing Lago Grey and its glacier, and stopping for lunch in Hostería Lago Grey or one of the other hotels inside the park. These tours return around sunset. A budget option is the daily bus tour (year-round) from the bus station with Transportes María José, which also offers hop-on, hop-off options for hikers and campers.

While visiting Torres del Paine remains the most popular excursion, nearby Parque Nacional Bernardo O'Higgins is also ripe for exploration with popular boat tours to glaciers with companies like Turismo 21 de Mayo (year-round) and Agunsa (September through April).

As the transportation hub of southern Patagonia, **Punta Arenas** is within reach of Chile's Parque Nacional Torres del Paine (a four-hour drive) and Argentina's Parque Nacional Los Glaciares. It's also a good base for penguin-watchers and a key embarkation point for boat travel to Ushuaia and Antarctica.

The Hielo Continental (Continental Ice Cap) spreads its icy mantle from the Pacific Ocean across Chile and the Andes into Argentina, covering an area of 21,700 square km (8,400 square miles). Approximately 1.5 million acres of it are contained within **Parque Nacional Los Glaciares** (Glaciers National Park), a UNESCO World Heritage Site. The park extends along the Chilean border for 350 km (217 miles), and 40% of it is covered by ice fields that branch off into 47 glaciers feeding two enormous lakes—the 15,000-year-old Lago Argentino (Lake Argentino, the largest body of water in Argentina and the third largest in South America) at the park's southern end, and Lago Viedma (Lake Viedma) at the northern end near Monte Fitzroy, which rises 3,395 meters (11,138 feet).

Plan on a minimum of two to three days to see the glaciers and enjoy **El Calafate**—more if you plan to visit **El Chaltén** or any of the other lakes. Entrance to the southern section of the park, which includes Perito Moreno Glacier, costs around US$25 for non-Argentineans.

Tierra del Fuego, a more or less triangular island separated from the southernmost tip of the South American mainland by the twists and bends of the Estrecho de Magallanes, is indeed a world unto itself. The vast plains on its northern reaches are dotted with trees bent low by the savage winds that frequently lash the coast. The mountains that rise in the south are equally forbidding, traversed by huge glaciers slowly making their way to the sea.

Tierra del Fuego is split in half. The island's northernmost tip, well within Chilean territory, is its closest point to the continent. The only town of any size here is Porvenir. Its southern extremity, part of Argentina, points out into the Atlantic toward the Falkland Islands. Here you'll find **Ushuaia**, the main destination, on the shores of the Beagle Channel. Farther south is Cape Horn, the southernmost point of land before Antarctica (still a good 500 miles across the brutal Drake Passage).

Cruising and Land Tour Company Profiles

As beautiful as it is vast, it's practically impossible to see everything Patagonia has to offer in one visit. It's not surprising that there are hundreds of companies out there that offer various ways to explore, be it land-based touring, sea-cruising, or a combination of both.

Boutique Cruise and Land Combo Tours

Boutique tour operators often offer what the major cruise lines cannot: personalized service and attention. At sea you might end up seeing or doing similar things as you would during a sailing on a big cruise. But during the land portion of these trips you'll have more chances to explore the region doing the activities you really like—be it mountain biking, horseback riding, or relaxing at a family-run estancia or lodge.

Adventure Life

BOAT TOURS | This company specializes in small-group tours that have a positive impact on the local culture and environment. Their Patagonia options are as varied as the terrain: you can secure crampons and trek a glacier, board a motor yacht and explore the fjords, or grab your packs and head for the towering spires of Chile's Torres del Paine. **Who it's for:** Eco-conscious travelers who enjoy camping and eating under the stars as much as a three-course meal at a local restaurant. **Highlights:** A picnic lunch sitting on the lateral moraine of Perito Moreno Glacier listening to its thunderous concerto of groaning and cracking ice dropping into the lake below. **Departs:** Buenos Aires, Argentina. **Ships:** M/V *Ventus Australis* accommodates 210 passengers. **Route(s):** The trip begins by boarding the expedition ship *Ventus Australis* in Ushuaia for a sea journey through the Strait of Magellan. After docking in Punta Arenas, three nights at Eco Camp in Torres del Paine to hike or horseback ride in the park. Then overland to Argentina for two nights in El Calafate and Los Glaciares National Park at a historic hacienda. Starting from $5,853 for 12 days. ☎ *406/541–2677* ⊕ *www. adventure-life.com.*

Comapa

GUIDED TOURS | One of the most trusted tour operators in Punta Arenas, Comapa has provided a diverse array of quality tours in and around the city for more than 40 years. Among their offerings are several land and sea combo programs, including a rapid tour spanning four days and three nights, combining a visit to Torres del Paine with a day-long sail from Puerto Natales to the Balmaceda and Serrano glacier. Along the way, guests have the chance to view dolphins, sea lions, and more. **Who it's for:** For those on a time crunch, this is a quick and relatively inexpensive way to see both Torres del Paine and Patagonia's fjords and glaciers. **Highlights:** Touring the mountains, waterfalls, and glaciers of Torres del Paine and viewing wildlife and glaciers on a sail through a Patagonian fjord are top experiences. **Departs:** Punta Arenas airport. **Ships:** The *21 de Mayo* and *Alberto De Agostini* ships. **Route(s):** Punta Arenas airport, Puerto Natales, Torres del Paine, Last Hope Sound, Serrano and Balmaceda glaciers, Puerto Natales, Punta Arenas airport. Starting from $390 for four days. ☎ *9/9183–2787* ⊕ *www. comapa.com.*

★ Cruceros Australis

BOAT TOURS | This Chilean expedition cruise company sails on its fleet of luxury ships through the Strait of Magellan and Beagle Channel. They offer programs for four or five nights from September to April. **Who it's for:** Travelers who prefer to explore the region while sailing. **Highlights:** Navigate through Beagle Channel to disembark near the Pia Glacier; penguin excursions; Cape Horn visit. **Departs:** Punta Arenas, Chile, and Ushuaia, Argentina. **Ships:** *Ventus Australis* and *Stella Australis.* **Route(s):** Punta Arenas, Ainsworth Bay and Tucker Islet, Pia Glacier and Glacier Alley, Cape Horn, Wulaia Bay, Ushuaia. Starting from $1,590 for four nights. ☎ *800/743–0119, 2/2797–1000 Chile* ⊕ *www.australis.com.*

G Adventures

ADVENTURE TOURS | Specializing in small-group outdoor adventure travel, this outfitter takes you off the beaten track to the heart of the destination. Expect anywhere from 12 to 15 travelers on the three-week Discover Patagonia adventure with National Geographic Journeys, exploring the Lake District of Chile and Argentina, hiking near glaciers in Patagonia and sailing the Beagle Channel. **Who it's for:** Budget-conscious and adventurous spirits who prefer to experience a destination at a grass-roots level. **Highlights:** Doing the W trek and exploring glaciers. **Departs:** Buenos Aires, Argentina. **Ships:** Ferry cruise ship. **Route(s):** Buenos Aires, Bariloche, Puerto Varas,

Torres del Paine, El Calafate, Perito Moreno, Ushuaia, Buenos Aires. Starting from
$6,399 for 14 days. ☎ 211/9629–4006
⊕ www.gadventures.com.

Knowmad Adventures

GUIDED TOURS | This award-winning tour
operator based in Minnesota has extensive experience in Chilean Patagonia
with knowledgeable guides. **Who it's
for:** Travelers who want both the best of
city life and adventures in the outdoors.
Highlights: Travelers get to know Buenos
Aires, cruise through remote Patagonia
fjords, hike in Torres del Paine, and visit
Chilean wineries. **Departs:** Ship off from
Buenos Aires, Argentina, in a luxury
cruise liner. **Route(s):** Buenos Aires, Ushuaia, Tierra del Fuego, Cape Horn, Strait
of Magellan, Torres del Paine, Valparaíso
and Wine Country, Santiago. Starting
from $7,750 for 15 days. ☎ 612/315–2894
⊕ www.knowmadadventures.com.

MT Sobek

ADVENTURE TOURS | MT Sobek was the
first-ever adventure travel company,
founded in 1969; they have since set the
standard in the industry, putting together
itineraries with experienced guides,
great food, and accommodations full of
character for small groups of fewer than
10 people. **Who it's for:** Those who crave
adventure on day trips yet want to enjoy
upscale lodging at night. **Highlights:** Rare
access to remote Chilean fjords and
sailing around Cape Horn, hiking in Torres
del Paine National Park, and visiting
the breathtaking Perito Moreno Glacier.
Departs: Punta Arenas, Chile. **Ships:** The
Ventus Australis, a 210-passenger expedition vessel. **Route(s):** Punta Arenas, Torres
del Paine, El Calafate, Perito Moreno
Glacier, Ushuaia, Cape Horn, Alberto de
Agostini National Park, Tierra del Fuego,
Magdalena Island, Punta Arenas. Starting
from $10,595 for 13 days. ☎ 800/974–
0300 ⊕ www.mtsobek.com.

Quark Expeditions

ADVENTURE TOURS | Quark Expeditions
is one of the leading operators of polar
expedition cruises aboard comfortable
but powerful Russian polar icebreakers.
Who it's for: They offer three ways to
travel: Icebreaker Adventures take you to
regions inaccessible to traditional expedition vessels, with aerial sightseeing by
onboard helicopters; Active Adventures
offer landings for camping, cross-country
skiing, kayaking, overnight kayaking and
mountaineering; and leisure travelers can
opt for Adventures in Comfort, which
explores the region at a more relaxed
pace. **Highlights:** The Icebreaker Adventure takes you to an emperor penguin
rookery while the chicks are very young.
Departs: Ushuaia, Argentina. **Ships:**
The Icebreaker *Kapitan Khlebnikov* is
equipped with helicopters and Zodiacs
for shore landings. Their newest vessel,
the *Ultramarine*, is also decked out with
two helicopters and 20 Zodiacs, along
with spacious suites for guests. **Route(s):**
The 10- to 12-day Classic Antarctica itinerary sails from Ushuaia through the Drake
Passage to the Antarctic Peninsula and
South Shetland Islands before returning
to Ushuaia. Starting from $6,925 for 10
days. ☎ 888/979–4073, 802/490–1843
⊕ www.quarkexpeditions.com.

Swoop Patagonia

SPECIAL-INTEREST TOURS | This British
tour operator is perhaps the world's
leading travel specialist for tours of all
types in Patagonia. Among their best
trips is Pumas, Penguins & Whales
Wildlife Tour. **Who it's for:** The traveler
who prioritizes wildlife viewing can
combine whale-watching tours with
land excursions. **Highlights:** Tracking the
impressive pumas in Torres del Paine,
watching humpback whales in the fjords
of the Strait of Magellan, and visiting a
king penguin colony are top experiences.
Departs: Torres del Paine National Park.
Ships: The motor yacht *Esturion* and

11

Southern Chilean Patagonia and Tierra del Fuego CRUISING AND LAND TOUR COMPANY PROFILES

Zodiac boats. **Route(s):** Torres del Paine, Punta Arenas, Tierra del Fuego, Punta Arenas, Strait of Magellan, Carlos III Island, Punta Arenas. Starting from $6,498 for 11 days. ☎ *855/369–7866* ⊕ *www.swoop-patagonia.com.*

★ Wilderness Travel

SPECIAL-INTEREST TOURS | This Berkeley, California–based tour operator has been leading the way in ecotourism and adventure travel around the world for more than 40 years. They put together exciting, unique itineraries with excellent trip leaders. **Who it's for:** Nature enthusiasts who want to explore the wildlife of Patagonia in depth will like this tour. **Highlights:** Puma tracking in Torres del Paine, visiting a king penguin colony in Tierra del Fuego, and searching for wildlife in parks and remote islands can't be beat. **Departs:** Ushuaia, Argentina. **Ships:** The 65-foot *Alakush*is their motor vessel with five double cabins and a Zodiac for shore landings. **Route(s):** Ushuaia, Beagle Channel, Karukinka Nature Park, Tierra del Fuego, Strait of Magellan, Torres del Paine, Punta Arenas. Starting from $11,495 for 14 days. ☎ *800/368–2794* ⊕ *www.wildernesstravel.com.*

Boutique Land Tours

Andes Adventures

GUIDED TOURS | Led by local bilingual guides with in-depth knowledge of the culture and history of the region, this company features all-inclusive trips for 12 to 20 participants. The Patagonia Hiking Adventure explores the three national parks in the region (Torres del Paine, Los Glaciares, and Tierra del Fuego) with hikes to the base of the Towers of Paine, Cerro Torre, and Fitzroy. During the trip you'll tour Punta Arenas, Ushuaia, and Buenos Aires, and spot penguins, guanacos, flamingos, and other wildlife. You'll like these trips if your days at hostels may be over but you still enjoy traveling in a group, eating simple but hearty meals,

and staying in rustic mountain lodgings with shared bathrooms. ✉ *info@andesadventures.com* ⊕ *www.andesadventures.com.*

BlueGreen Adventures

SPECIAL-INTEREST TOURS | Based in Puerto Natales, this longtime Chilean-British travel agency offers a variety of excursions in Patagonia, and in particular, Torres del Paine Park. One unique trip involves horseback riding to Patagonian *estancias* (ranches) in both Chile and Argentina, staying overnight in several of them along the route. ☎ *61/241–1800* ⊕ *www.bluegreenadventures.com.*

Butterfield & Robinson

GUIDED TOURS | Well-heeled travelers with B&R trade in their Chanel coats for North Face fleece jackets, hike between wine tastings and meals at Michelin-starred restaurants, and rest their weary heads at superluxe hotels. During their bespoke Patagonia Walking tour, guests check out the rare and unusual trees of the Bosque de Arrayanes, strap on crampons for an ice climb in Perito Moreno Glacier, hike in Torres del Paine, and enjoy a glass of great local wine while taking in spectacular glacier views from a hotel room in Los Glaciares National Park. ☎ *866/551–9090* ⊕ *www.butterfield.com.*

★ Chile Nativo

SPECIAL-INTEREST TOURS | For more than 20 years, Chile Nativo has offered diverse trips all over Patagonia, with a particular focus on Torres del Paine. They offer horseback rides as well as multisport trips, kayaking, trekking, biking, and bird-watching excursions. Groups are small (maximum eight people) and leave from Puerto Natales. One of their most noteworthy excursions is the Fast Track W, a three-day trek in Torres del Paine that packs in the park's major highlights and is based each night out of their riverside camp in the Rio Serrano sector of the park. ☎ *800/649–8776, 61/269–1391* ⊕ *www.chilenativo.travel.*

Focus Tours
GUIDED TOURS | English-speaking naturalists guide all of this company's birding tours. They also carry the equipment: a spotting telescope, tape recorder and microphone to bring rare animals into view, and a powerful spotlight for night viewing. A checklist of the birds, mammals, reptiles, and amphibians of each area they tour, with common English and Latin names, helps participants keep track and learn the animals they see. They offer custom tours to Peninsula Valdés, El Calafate, Tierra del Fuego, Bariloche, Torres del Paine, and Chile's Lake District. ☎ *505/216–9696* ⊕ *www. focustours.com.*

Geographic Expeditions
GUIDED TOURS | Expect accommodations in superb hotels and estancias, small group sizes, and leaders intimate with the corners of Patagonia. Travelers hike among the astounding granite monoliths, forests, and blue lakes of the Torres del Paine and Fitzroy. Tours farther afield go to the Aysén Glacier region in Chile, kayaking in the Pumalín Reserve, and fishing in Lago Yungue in Bariloche. ☎ *888/570– 7108* ⊕ *www.geoex.com.*

Inca
GUIDED TOURS | This outfitter offers custom-made Patagonia itineraries designed to fit your budget and time constraints. They also have a 10-day Wild South trip that includes a stay at the exclusive Tierra Patagonia lodge inside Torres del Paine National Park and a cruise through the Strait of Magellan aboard the *Stella Australis* to see elephant seals, penguins, seabirds, and glaciers. ☎ *510/420–1550* ⊕ *www.inca1.com.*

Journeys International
GUIDED TOURS | Trips, which may be combined with Antarctic cruises, offer opportunities to hike, kayak, climb on a glacier, and get up close to penguins.

In Chile, they offer an 11-day Torres del Paine trek suitable for active travelers able to make demanding hikes of five to six hours per day. In Argentina, they offer a two-week Patagonia Nature Safari that begins in Buenos Aires and travels along the Atlantic coast to Bahia Bustamente, for bird-watching, sailing, trekking, and mountain biking. Guests venture to Gaiman, a traditional Welsh village, the Valdés Peninsula, Tierra del Fuego National Park, and Los Glaciares National Park, including a trek on Perito Moreno Glacier. ☎ *800/255–8735* ⊕ *www.journeysinternational.com.*

Ladatco Tours
GUIDED TOURS | This company has been planning and operating tours in South America since 1966. In Patagonia they offer eight different programs, which vary from a two-day journey crossing the Lake District, from Puerto Montt to Bariloche, and exploring the Inland Fjords of Chile, known for pristine forests, lakes, and national parks, to exploring Tierra del Fuego and Los Glaciares National Park in Argentina. They can tailor a trip that follows your wish list. ☎ *305/854–8422, 800/327–6162* ⊕ *www.ladatco.com.*

Offtrail Patagonia
ADVENTURE TOURS | This Puerto Natales–based tour operator specializes in guiding six- to eight-day backpacking expeditions on the Dientes de Navarino circuit on Navarino Island or at Torres del Paine National Park. This is a good choice if you're in good physical condition and like to really immerse yourself in nature, hiking the trails with a backpack and camping under the stars each night. ☎ *9/9522–7851* ⊕ *www.offtrailpatagonia. cl.*

Planning

When to Go

In each season Patagonia has its own magic. December to February—summer in the Southern Hemisphere—is considered high season in Patagonia, when temperatures rise and provide for some stunning days (that is, when the cloudy skies open up). Demand for accommodations is highest in January and February, so advance reservations are vital. The weather in Patagonia can change in an instant no matter the season, so always bring layers. Summer weather in these latitudes swings between warm and pleasantly cool, although strong winds and rains are common, and on or near Antarctic waters, the breezes can be quite biting.

In spring (September to November) and fall (March to May) the weather is usually delightfully mild, but can also be downright cold, depending on clouds and the wind. These seasons do, however, bring wonderful colors to the landscape, and the population shrinks by more than half. The winter months of June, July, and August are blissfully free of tourists, although many attractions and hotels near the parks go into hibernation.

Getting Here and Around

If you want to begin your trip in Chile, you could fly into Punta Arenas, the region's principal city, and from there arrange for travel to several points throughout the region, including a bus to Puerto Natales, the jumping-off point for exploring Parque Nacional Torres del Paine. If you prefer to go directly to Torres del Paine, the small airport at Puerto Natales receives direct LATAM and Sky Airline flights from Santiago during the high season. If you've been visiting El Calafate, it's just a 3½-hour drive to Puerto Natales and

Torres del Paine. If you'd like to travel to or from Ushuaia, there are many flights or cruises between Punta Arenas and Ushuaia. Remote spots, such as Isla Magdalena or Puerto Williams, can be reached by boat or airplane.

AIR

LATAM (www.latam.com) operates flights daily between Punta Arenas and Santiago, Coyhaique, and Puerto Montt. Sky Airline (www.skyairline.com) also has competitive fares on flights from Santiago to Punta Arenas and to Puerto Natales in summer. Aerovías DAP (www.dapairline.com) has regularly scheduled flights exclusively in Patagonia, between Punta Arenas, Porvenir, and Puerto Williams. Aerolíneas Argentinas (www.aerolineas.com.ar) has service between Buenos Aires, El Calafate, and Ushuaia, Argentina.

BOAT

Boat tours are a great way to see otherwise inaccessible parts of Patagonia and Tierra del Fuego. **Cruceros Australis** (www.australis.com) runs four or five-night luxury cruises between Punta Arenas and Ushuaia, Argentina, with stops in Tierra del Fuego, Cape Horn National Park, Isla Magdalena, and other destinations. **Navimag** (www.navimag.cl) runs a popular, more affordable service between Puerto Natales and Puerto Montt to the north. In Punta Arenas, **Transbordadora Austral Broom** (www.tabsa.cl) offers daily crossings to Porvenir (two to three hours) and crossings to Puerto Williams.

BUS

The four-hour trip between Punta Arenas and Puerto Natales is serviced several times a day by small private companies. The best is Buses Fernández. To travel the longer haul between Punta Arenas, Río Gallegos, and Ushuaia, Argentina, your best bet is Tecni-Austral, based in Argentina and the only regular bus service that crosses the Magellan Strait. Book your ticket in advance.

BUS CONTACTS Buses Fernández. ✉ *Eleuterio Ramirez 399, Puerto Natales* ☎ *9/9438–5125* ⊕ *www.busesfernandez. com.* **Transportes María José.** ✉ *Av. España 1455, Puerto Natales* ☎ *61/241–0951, 9/9321–1378* ⊕ *www.busesmariajose. com.* **TecniAustral.** ✉ *Av. Colón 568, Punta Arenas* ☎ *9/5970–4649* ⊕ *www.tecniaustral.com.*

CAR

If you truly enjoy the call of the open road, there are few places that can rival the vast emptiness and spellbinding beauty of Patagonia. Be prepared for miles and miles of possibly inclement weather and semidesert steppes with no gas stations, towns, or even restrooms. Always carry plenty of water, snacks, a jack, and tire-changing tools, with at least one spare. Take extra care when driving on *ripio* (gravel roads); it's easy to flip small cars at speeds over 80 kmh (55 mph). Fill your tank at every opportunity. If you're not driving, consider simply paying for a *remis* (car with driver) for day excursions.

RENTAL CARS Avis (Emsa). ✉ *Barros Arana 118, Puerto Natales* ☎ *61/261–4388* ⊕ *www.emsarentacar.com.*

CRUISE

Cruising is a leisurely and comfortable way to take in the rugged marvels of Patagonia and the southernmost region of the world. Sailing through remote channels and reaching islands virtually untouched by man, you'll witness fjords, snowcapped mountains, granite peaks, and their reflections dominating the glacial lakes. You'll get a close look at elephant seals and colonies of Magellanic penguins and cormorants from the comfort of your vessel and during shore excursions taken in Zodiacs (small motorized boats) led by naturalist guides.

Most short cruises depart from Ushuaia, Argentina, or Punta Arenas, Chile, while longer and more luxurious itineraries typically depart from either Buenos Aires

or Santiago. The majority of cruisers plan their trips four to six months ahead of time. Book a year ahead if you're planning to sail on a small adventure vessel, as popular itineraries may be full six to eight months ahead. Cruise Lines International Association (www.cruising.org) lists recognized agents throughout the United States.

Ever since Lars-Eric Lindblad operated the first cruise to the "White Continent" in 1966, Antarctica has exerted an almost magnetic pull for serious travelers. From Ushuaia, the world's southernmost city, you'll sail for two (often rough) days through the Drake Passage. Most visits are to the Antarctic Peninsula, the continent's most accessible region. Accompanied by naturalists, you'll travel ashore in motorized rubber craft called Zodiacs to view penguins and nesting seabirds. More adventurous cruisers can kayak between icebergs and walk, or even camp, on the ice. Founded to promote environmentally responsible travel to Antarctica, the International Association of Antarctica Tour Operators (401/841–9700; iaato.org) is a good source of information and includes suggested readings. Most companies operating Antarctica trips are, members of this organization and display its logo in their brochures.

Cruising the southern tip of South America and along Chile's western coast north to the Lake District reveals fjords, glaciers, lagoons, lakes, narrow channels, waterfalls, forested shorelines, fishing villages, and wildlife. Boarding your vessel in Punta Arenas, Chile, or Ushuaia, Argentina, you'll cruise the Strait of Magellan and the Beagle Channel, visiting glaciers, penguin rookeries, and seal colonies before heading north along the fjords of Chile's western coast.

Some ships set sail in the Caribbean and stop at one or two islands before heading south; a few transit the Panama Canal en route. West Coast (U.S.) departures might include one or more Mexican

11

Southern Chilean Patagonia and Tierra del Fuego PLANNING ports before reaching South America. Fourteen- to 21-day cruises are the norm. Vessels vary in the degree of comfort or luxury as well as in what is or isn't included in the price.

Celebrity Cruises: Fjords, glaciers, and emerald lakes are the highlight of a cruise down the west coast of Chile and back up the Atlantic Coast to Buenos Aires. ☎ 305/262–6677.

Oceania Cruises: Patagonia voyages with Oceania are as relaxed and elegant as a private country club—mahogany decor, plush carpeting, and grand, sweeping staircases. ☎ 800/383–8114.

Princess Cruises: Trips (in January and February) on this cruise line include eight ports of call in the Argentine and Chilean Patagonia region. ☎ 800/774–6237.

Seabourn Cruise Line: Patagonia cruises with Seabourn include visits to the Beagle Channel and the Chilean fjords. ☎ 800/442-4448.

Silversea Cruises: Voyages with Silversea dock in Uruguay, the Falkland Islands, and Ushuaia, among others. ☎ 954/522-2299.

Restaurants

Menus tend to be extensive, although two items in particular are considered regional specialties: *centolla* (king crab) and moist, tender *cordero magallánico* (Magellanic lamb). You should also try *ostiones del sur* (southern oysters), typically served with Parmesan cheese. If you hop the border into Argentina, the dining options are cheaper and similar. You'll find the same fire-roasted cordero (in Argentina it's *cordero a la cruz* or *al asador*), but you'll also get a chance to try the famous Argentine *parrillas* (grilled-meat restaurants). Many restaurants close for several hours in the afternoon and early evening (3–8).

Huge numbers of foreign visitors mean that vegetarian options are getting better; *woks de verdura* (vegetable stir-fries) are a newly ubiquitous option. Most cafés and bars serve quick bites known as *minutas*. The region is also famous for its stone fruits, which are used in various jams, preserves, sweets, and *alfajores* (a chocolate-covered sandwich of two cookies with jam in the middle). When in El Calafate, be sure to nibble on some calafate berries (or drink them in cocktails like the Calafate sour)—legend has it if you eat them in El Calafate you are destined to return one day soon.

Restaurant reviews have been shortened. For full information, visit Fodors.com.

Hotels

Punta Arenas is a pleasant place to spend a night or two; there's an abundance of quality hotels, and many are housed in historic buildings. In Puerto Natales, there are accommodations of all kinds, including high-end luxury options in and around Torres del Paine National Park.

There aren't a lot of budget options in this part of Chile. The luxury market, on the other hand, is booming. Patagonia is a "once-in-a-lifetime" destination that many people are happy to splurge on, and the increasing cruise culture doesn't ease accommodation prices. The inaccessible nature of Patagonia also means that all-inclusive packages (which usually include food, excursions, and transfers) may be a preferable choice, if you can afford them. In most cities and towns you'll find a mix of big, expensive hotels with comfortable resorts, local flavor estancias, and small B&B-style *hosterías*.

The terms *hospedaje* and *hostal* are used interchangeably in the region, so don't make assumptions based on the name. Many *hostals* are fine hotels—not youth hostels with multiple beds—just very small. By contrast, some *hospedajes* are little more than a spare room in someone's home.

Hotel reviews have been shortened. For full information, visit Fodors.com.

What It Costs in Chilean Pesos (in thousands)			
$	$$	$$$	$$$$
RESTAURANTS			
Under 6	6–9	10–13	over 13
HOTELS			
Under 51	51–85	86–115	over 115

Health and Safety

Emergency services and hospitals are widely available in the cities. At Torres del Paine, there is an emergency clinic during the summer at the National Park administration office. The closest hospital is in Puerto Natales. Additionally, every park guide is trained in first aid.

Most mountains are not high enough to induce altitude sickness, but the weather can turn nasty quickly. Sunglasses and sunscreen are essential. Tap water is safe to drink throughout the region, although bottled water is also widely available. Do not approach or let your children approach sea lions, penguins, or any other animals, no matter how docile or curious they might seem.

Visitor Information

Sernatur, Chile's national tourism agency, has offices in Punta Arenas and in Puerto Natales (www.sernatur.cl). You can also try the helpful folks at the Punta Arenas City Tourism Office, in an attractive wooden kiosk in the main square. Sometimes they offer last-minute specials to fill remaining seats on popular tours. Ask for complete printouts of transportation timetables; information sometimes changes on short notice.

Puerto Natales

242 km (150 miles) northwest of Punta Arenas.

Considered the gateway to Parque Nacional Torres del Paine and Parque Nacional Bernardo O'Higgins, the town of Puerto Natales has grown leaps and bounds over the past decade. The surge of boutique hotels and hip eateries that have opened here to cater to tourists bound for the parks and beyond has transformed what was once a sleepy fishing village. The city, population 19,116, has impressive views of mountains in the distance and of Seno Última Esperanza, or Last Hope Sound, so named by Spanish navigator Juan Ladrillero in the 16th century, as it was his last hope to reach the Strait of Magellan.

GETTING HERE AND AROUND

Since the opening of the small Teniente Julio Gallardo Airport in Puerto Natales, the town has become a major hub for exploring Patagonia. All of Chile's national airlines now fly direct here from Santiago and Puerto Montt. LATAM has flights year-round and two cheaper alternatives, JetSmart and Sky Airline, provide service during the high season. Some flights also connect the town to El Calafate, Argentina.

Most travelers, however, fly to Punta Arenas because more flights are available. From there, three inexpensive bus lines (7,400 pesos) provide daily service for the four-hour journey, about 247 km (153 miles) on Ruta 9, a paved road that follows mostly through a flat, Patagonian steppe landscape. Buses depart from the terminal in the city center or directly from the Punta Arenas airport. Many tour companies and hotels also provide their

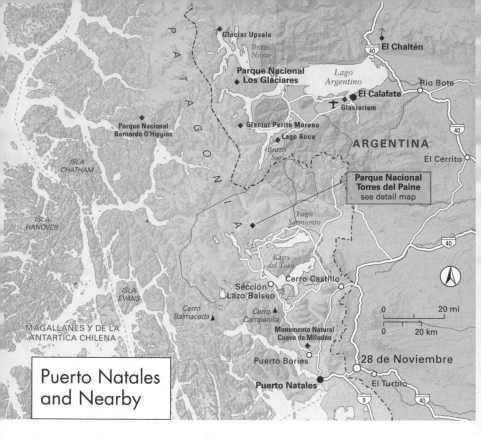

Puerto Natales and Nearby

own private transportation service for guests arriving in Punta Arenas.

If you're traveling overland from El Calafate across the Argentina border, this route extends 115 km (71 miles), but the gravel roads and passport checkpoints make it a 5½-hour trip. It is a scenic trip though, with color-washed Patagonian landscapes and picturesque sheep and cattle estancias along the way. Several bus lines (about 20,000 pesos) make the journey each day. Private transfers are also an option for a much higher price.

Puerto Natales has a mostly grid layout, with everything centered around the Plaza de Armas, a lovely, well-landscaped sanctuary. A few blocks west of the plaza on Avenida Bulnes, you'll find the small Museo Histórico Municipal. On a clear day, an early-morning walk along Avenida Pedro Montt, which follows the shoreline of the Seno Última Esperanza (or Canal Señoret, as it's called on some maps), can be a soul-cleansing experience. The rising sun gradually casts a glow on the mountain peaks to the west.

ESSENTIALS

RENTAL CARS Avis (Emsa). ⊠ *Barros Arana 118, Puerto Natales* ☎ *61/261–4388* ⊕ *www.emsarentacar.com.*

VISITOR AND TOUR INFORMATION

Sernatur Puerto Natales. ⊠ *Av. Pedro Montt 199, Puerto Natales* ☎ *61/241–2125* ⊕ *www.patagonia-chile.com.*

◉ Sights

Estancia Bahía Esperanza

FARM/RANCH | Just outside of Puerto Natales is a new, private nature park on former ranch lands called Estancia Bahía Esperanza. The park makes for a great day trip for biking, hiking, and bird-watching along the seven short and mostly easy trails covering more than 20 kilometers of peatlands, forests, lagunas, hills, and coastline. Some of the trails offer panoramic views of the fjords and bays in the area. Accessible only by boat, for 35,000 pesos you get access to the park and a round-trip ticket on a short, 15-minute ride on a speedboat that departs from Muelle Natalis (Natales Pier) at Puerto Bories, located 7 km (4 miles) from Puerto Natales. The park also offers guided excursions (including e-bikes and horseback rides) for a special rate and has a café that offers lunch, snacks, and drinks. ⊠ *Península Antonio Varas, Puerto Natales* ⊕ *www.estancia-bahiaesperanza.com* ⊠ *35,000 pesos.*

Iglesia Parroquial

CHURCH | Across from the Plaza de Armas is the squat, little Iglesia Parroquial. The ornate altarpiece in this church depicts the town's founders, Indigenous peoples, and the Virgin Mary all in front of the Torres del Paine. ⊠ *Arturo Prat and Eberhard, Puerto Natales.*

Monumento Natural Cueva de Milodón

CAVE | In 1896, Hermann Eberhard stumbled upon a gaping cave that extended 200 meters (650 feet) into the earth. Venturing inside, he discovered the bones and dried pieces of hide (with deep red fur) of an animal he could not identify. It was later determined that what Eberhard had discovered were the extraordinarily well-preserved remains of a prehistoric herbivorous mammal, *mylodon darwini,* about twice the height of a man, which they called a *milodón.* The discovery of a stone wall in the cave, and of neatly cut grass stalks in the animal's feces led researchers to conclude that 15,000 years ago the extinct beast inhabited this place and that an ancient tribe of Tehuelches likely captured the animal there. The cave at the Monumento Natural Cueva de Milodón is an impressive, cathedral-size space carved

out of a solid rock wall by rising waters. It makes for an interesting stop for anyone fascinated by paleontology, or for fans of Bruce Chatwin's legendary travel book, *In Patagonia,* which centers in part on Chatwin's quest to find the origins of the remnant of mylodon skin he saw in his grandmother's home as a boy that she had told him came from a "brontosaurus."⊠ *5 km (3 miles) off Ruta 9 signpost, 28 km (17 miles) northwest of Puerto Natales, Puerto Natales* ☎ *61/241–1438, 61/236–0485* ⊕ *www.cuevadelmilodon.cl* ⊠ *8400 pesos.*

Museo Histórico Municipal

HISTORY MUSEUM | A highlight in the small but interesting Museo Historico Municipal is a room filled with antique prints of Aonikenk and Kawéskar peoples. Another room is devoted to the exploits of Hermann Eberhard, a German explorer considered the region's first settler. Check out his celebrated collapsible boat. In an adjacent room you will find some vestiges of the old Bories sheep plant, which processed the meat and wool of more than 300,000 sheep a year. ⊠ *Av. Bulnes 285, Puerto Natales* ☎ *61/220–9534* ⊠ *1000 pesos* ⊘ *Closed Sun.*

Plaza de Armas

PLAZA/SQUARE | A few blocks east of the waterfront overlooking Seno Última Esperanza is the Plaza de Armas. This well-manicured, open square with gardens and a fountain is one of the town's pride and joys. An old church and several shops and restaurants surround the plaza, making it a pleasant spot to spend some time. ⊠ *Arturo Prat at Eberhard, Puerto Natales.*

🍴 Restaurants

★ Afrigonia

$$$$ | **INTERNATIONAL** | The idea of a "taste of Africa in Patagonia" might sound unusual, but the fusion menu here is well rehearsed and flavor combinations are well-tuned and tasty. With bamboo shoots adorning the walls, you might forget you are in Puerto Natales, but then you'll see the local seafood, Patagonian lamb, and king crab on the menu, presented with enticing ingredients like masala curry, mango, and coconut cream. **Known for:** dressed up Patagonian dishes; spicy flavors; friendly service. [$] *Average main: pesos14000* ✉ *Magallanes 247, Puerto Natales* ☎ *61/241–2877* 🕒 *Closed May–Aug.*

Asador Patagónico
$$$ | **CHILEAN** | This restaurant is zealous about meat; so zealous, in fact, that there's no seafood on the menu. Great care is taken with the excellent *lomo* and other grilled steaks, and the room is filled with the smell of roasting meat. **Known for:** hard to get a table; mouthwatering meats; cozy open fire. [$] *Average main: pesos13000* ✉ *Prat 158, Puerto Natales* ☎ *61/241–3553* 🕒 *Closed June.*

Cangrejo Rojo
$$ | **SEAFOOD** | A bit off-the-beaten path, but only about a 10-minute walk from the center of town, this is an excellent nautical-chic café. The tasty, feel-good food prepared lovingly by the marine biologist owners, Francisco and Nuriys, is well worth the effort to get there. **Known for:** organic wine menu; excellent king crab; homemade waffles. [$] *Average main: pesos8500* ✉ *Santiago Bueras Av. 782, Puerto Natales* ☎ *61/241–2436* 🕒 *Closed Sun.*

Espacio Ñandu
$$ | **CHILEAN** | **FAMILY** | Right on the corner of the plaza, this superb souvenir and bookshop doubles as a restaurant, bar, café, post office, and the best Wi-Fi spot in town, where you can surf on your own computer or rent one of theirs. With empanadas, tacos, seafood, and salads, you've got all bases covered for breakfast, lunch, dinner, or just coffee and a snack. **Known for:** local beers; quick bites; souvenir shopping over lunch. [$] *Average main: pesos7500* ✉ *Eberhard and Arturo Prat, Puerto Natales* ☎ *61/241–5660.*

Kosten
$$$ | **CONTEMPORARY** | You'll watch the wind whip the Seno Última Esperanza from a comfortable lounge in front of the fireplace at this modern bar and café in the hotel NOI Indigo Patagonia. It is a nice spot for a Calafate sour, and when you're ready, just amble downstairs to the small restaurant where they have an excellent menu with a little bit of everything, including organic salads made with veggies from their very own *huerto* (garden). **Known for:** organic salads; good views; fun cocktail list. [$] *Average main: pesos11900* ✉ *NOI Indigo Hotel, Ladrilleros 105, Puerto Natales* ☎ *61/261–3450* 🌐 *www.noihotels.com.*

Last Hope Distillery
$$ | **ECLECTIC** | After falling in love with Patagonia while doing the famed W trail, Australian tourists Keira and Matt decided to stay, and opened the world's southernmost distillery and whisky and gin bar. Local cheese platters and home-smoked jerky mean you can spend most of the evening here imbibing. **Known for:** good bar food; creative cocktails with Patagonian spirits; great selection of world gins and whiskey. [$] *Average main: pesos6000* ✉ *Esmeralda 882, Puerto Natales* ☎ *9/7201–8585* 🌐 *www.lasthope-distillery.com* 🕒 *Closed Mon. and Tues.*

Mesita Grande
$$$ | **PIZZA** | It's not a backpacker town without a great pizza joint, and this one is Puerto Natales's, located on the Plaza de Armas. Diners eat together at long, open tables on classic pies and more creative offerings heaped with *cordero* (Patagonian lamb), *merkén* (a spice similar to smoked paprika), or local smoked salmon. **Known for:** locally sourced pizza toppings; communal seating; central location. [$] *Average main: pesos10000* ✉ *Calle Arturo Prat 196, Puerto Natales* ☎ *61/241–1571* 🌐 *www.mesitagrande.cl.*

Restaurant Última Esperanza

$$$ | CHILEAN | Named for the strait on which Puerto Natales is located, Restaurant Última Esperanza is perhaps your last chance to try Patagonian seafood classics in a town being overrun by hip eateries. This traditional restaurant is well known for attentive, if formal, service, and top-quality, typical dishes. **Known for:** old-school service; classic king crab stew; poached conger eel in shellfish sauce. $ *Average main: pesos10000* ✉ *Av. Eberhard 354, Puerto Natales* ☎ *61/241–1391* ⊕ *www.restaurantultimaesperanza.com* ⊘ *Closed July.*

★ Santolla

$$$$ | SEAFOOD | This trendy restaurant inside a funky shipping container is almost always packed, and for good reason. Their menu is an ode to the *centolla* (king crab), the rare, highly prized crustacean which is caught in the frigid, turbulent waters of the region's fjords. **Known for:** king crab legs in white wine; beautiful presentation; cool, intimate setting. $ *Average main: pesos18,900* ✉ *Calle Magallanes 73 B, Puerto Natales* ☎ *61/241–3493* ⊕ *www.santollarestaurant.com* ⊘ *Closed Sun.*

★ The Singular

$$$$ | CHILEAN | An evening dining at the Singular is a quintessential Puerto Natales experience where old-world charm meets modern Chilean cuisine in a stylish and historical setting. Smartly dressed and attentive waiters welcome you with a long list of aperitifs and hand you fur-bound menus that list exquisitely original Patagonian dishes like ceviche of fresh king crab and seafood; guanaco steak with native cracked wheat; and locally caught rabbit with homemade pickles. **Known for:** exceptional overall dining experience; unforgettable food; stylish setting. $ *Average main: pesos15000* ✉ *Puerto Bories s/n, Puerto Natales* ☎ *61/272–2030* ⊕ *www.thesingular.com* ⊘ *Closed May–Sept.*

Wine & Market Patagonia

$$ | WINE BAR | If wine tasting at the end of the world is what you are after, this smart wine bar and shop offers personal wine tastings to get to know all the main valleys and varieties of Chile. Select a bottle from the excellent range of Chilean wines and brews, and enjoy it at the informal bar with some of the local delicacies and nibbles on sale in the shop. **Known for:** artisan beers; best wine selection in Puerto Natales; local cheeses and cold cuts. $ *Average main: pesos6000* ✉ *Magallanes, at Senoret, Puerto Natales* ☎ *61/269–1138* ⊕ *www.wmpatagonia.cl* ⊘ *Closed Sun.*

Coffee and Quick Bites

The Coffee Maker

$$ | CAFÉ | This coffee bar is the best spot for a steaming cup of joe in Puerto Natales, thanks to its well-sourced beans, expert baristas, and some of the best views in town. The Coffee Maker also sells sandwiches, salads, vegetarian options, delicious cakes, and has a daily set menu. **Known for:** great views; the best coffee in town; unique pisco sours. $ *Average main: pesos8000* ✉ *Kau, Pedro Montt 161, Puerto Natales* ☎ *61/241–4611.*

🛏 Hotels

Hostal Francis Drake

$$ | B&B/INN | Toss a coin in the wishing well out front before you enter this half-timbered house near the center of town; inside, the proprietor is a delightful European who dotes on her guests and carefully maintains cleanliness. **Pros:** central location; among the better of Natales's budget options; clean and well cared for. **Cons:** basic rooms; all the wind off the lake, but no views; the beds are not the most comfortable. $ *Rooms from: pesos52000* ✉ *Philippi 383, Puerto Natales* ☎ *61/241–1553* ⊕ *www.hostalfrancisdrake.com* 🛏 *12 rooms* ⫶⦿⫶ *Free Breakfast.*

Hotel CostAustralis

$$$ | **HOTEL** | This old grande dame of Puerto Natales has been somewhat superseded by more modern, eye-catching hotels, but its peaked, turreted roof and distinctive architecture still dominate the waterfront. **Pros:** startlingly low off-season rates; great views from bay-facing rooms; courteous and professional staff. **Cons:** wind and street noise; endless corridors a little impersonal; rooms are somewhat bland. [$] *Rooms from: pesos113000* ✉ *Av. Pedro Montt 262, at Av. Bulnes, Puerto Natales* ☎ *61/271–5037* ⊕ *www.hotelcostaustralis.com* ⤳ *110 rooms* ⊚ *Free Breakfast.*

Hotel Lady Florence Dixie

$$ | **B&B/INN** | Named after an aristocratic English immigrant and tireless traveler, this long-established hotel with an alpine-inspired facade is on the town's main street; its bright, spacious upstairs lounge is a good people-watching perch. **Pros:** relaxed atmosphere; convenient location; good value. **Cons:** basic breakfast; dowdy rooms; simple amenities. [$] *Rooms from: pesos81000* ✉ *Av. Bulnes 655, Puerto Natales* ☎ *61/241–1158* ⊕ *www.hotelflorencedixie.cl* ⤳ *19 rooms* ⊚ *Free Breakfast.*

Hotel Martín Gusinde

$$$$ | **HOTEL** | Don't let the dowdy exterior put you off—inside is a modern hotel with a good downtown location and simple but well-equipped rooms. **Pros:** central location; urbane atmosphere; comfortable beds. **Cons:** noise travels; simple breakfast; weak Wi-Fi. [$] *Rooms from: pesos123000* ✉ *Carlos Bories 278, Puerto Natales* ☎ *61/271–2100* ⊕ *www.martingusinde.com* ⤳ *28 rooms* ⊚ *Free Breakfast.*

Kau Lodge

$$$ | **B&B/INN** | This waterfront B&B comes with excellent views of the fjord, comfy and large beds draped in wool throws, and insider touring tips from the mountain-guide owner. **Pros:** fantastic coffee; cozy rooms; good location. **Cons:** small showers; basic breakfast; wind can be noisy on windows. [$] *Rooms from: pesos88500* ✉ *Pedro Montt 161, Puerto Natales* ☎ *61/241–4611* ⊕ *www.kaulodge.com* ⤳ *9 rooms* ⊚ *Free Breakfast.*

NOI Indigo Patagonia

$$$$ | **HOTEL** | Chilean architect Sebastian Irarrazabel was given free rein to redesign this building along a nautical theme; inside, a maze of gangplanks, ramps, and staircases shoot out across cavernous open spaces, minimalist wood panels line walls and ceilings, and water burbles down a waterfall that borders the central walkway. **Pros:** good location; some rooms have great views of the fjord; nice on-site restaurant. **Cons:** no parking; standard rooms are smallish; restaurant open only for dinner. [$] *Rooms from: pesos164000* ✉ *Ladrilleros 105, Puerto Natales* ☎ *61/274–0670* ⊕ *www.noihotels.com* ⤳ *41 rooms* ⊚ *Free Breakfast.*

OUTSIDE PUERTO NATALES

Several lodges have been constructed on a bluff overlooking the Seno Última Esperanza, about a mile outside of town. The views at these hotels are spectacular, with broad panoramas and unforgettable sunsets. While some might complain about the 10- to 30-minute trek into town, it is an easy walk along the seafront. A taxi will set you back around 2,000–4,000 Chilean pesos.

Altiplánico Sur

$$$$ | **HOTEL** | This is the Patagonian representative of the Altiplánico line of thoughtfully designed eco-hotels, and nature takes center stage: the hotel blends so seamlessly with its surroundings, it's almost subterranean. **Pros:** quiet location; eco-friendly; stellar views. **Cons:** patchy Wi-Fi; few technological amenities, including television; slow service. [$] *Rooms from: pesos149000* ✉ *Ruta 9 Norte, Km 1.5, Huerto 282, Puerto Natales* ☎ *61/241–2525* ⊕ *www.altiplanico.cl* ⊘ *Closed May–Sept.* ⤳ *22 rooms* ⊚ *Free Breakfast.*

Parque Nacional Torres del Paine is full of stunning glaciers, mountains, and turquoise lakes.

★ Remota

$$$$ | **HOTEL** | The eye-catching architecture of Remota competes with stunning views over the Última Esperanza for your attention, especially at night when the soft orange lighting beckons. **Pros:** inspiring design; great spa area; restaurant menu of delicious, native ingredients. **Cons:** expensive; unstable Wi-Fi in rooms; wind noises can be wild in the common areas. $ *Rooms from: pesos218000* ✉ *Ruta 9 Norte, Km 1.5, Huerto 279, Puerto Natales* ☎ *61/241-4040* ⊕ *www.remotahotel.com* ⇲ *72 rooms.*

★ The Singular Patagonia

$$$$ | **HOTEL** | Inhabiting the former Bories Cold-Storage Plant, which used to process and export more than 250,000 sheep a year and practically built Puerto Natales as a town, the Singular may well be Puerto Natales's most luxurious and tasteful hotel. **Pros:** fantastic restaurant; one-of-a-kind historic setting; expeditions and tours for all levels of fitness. **Cons:** breakfast can get busy; super pricey; taxi ride from town. $ *Rooms from: pesos300000* ✉ *Y-300 Rd., toward Torres del Paine National Park, Puerto Bories* ☎ *61/272–2030* ⊕ *www.thesingular.com* ⇲ *57 rooms.*

Weskar Patagonian Lodge

$$$$ | **HOTEL** | Weskar stands for "hill" in the language of the Kawéskar, to whom owner Juan José Pantoja, a marine biologist, pays homage in creating and maintaining this cozy lodge, which is high on a ridge overlooking the Última Esperanza fjord. **Pros:** rustic and cozy design; great views from your room; cozy log-cabin decor. **Cons:** poor temperature regulation; Wi-Fi and TV only in common areas; less luxurious than neighbors. $ *Rooms from: pesos128000* ✉ *Ruta 9 Norte, Km 1/Puerto Natales, Puerto Natales* ☎ *61/224–0494, 61/241–4168* ⊕ *www.weskar.cl* ⇲ *31 rooms* ⦿ *Free Breakfast.*

Parque Nacional Torres del Paine

80 km (50 miles) northwest of Puerto Natales.

A top global destination for hikers and nature lovers, Torres del Paine National Park is, quite simply, outstanding. With breathtaking mountains, glaciers, and lakes, along with wildlife like guanacos, rheas, foxes, and pumas, the park offers plenty of picture-perfect moments. Frequently changeable Patagonian weather is the only potential drawback at this UNESCO World Heritage site, which attracts more than 300,000 visitors a year.

ESSENTIALS
VISITOR INFORMATION CONAF. ✉ *CONAF station in southern section of the park past Hotel Explora* ☎ *61/269–1931* ⊕ *www.conaf.cl.*

Sights

★ Parque Nacional Torres del Paine
NATIONAL PARK | About 12 million years ago, lava flows pushed up through the thick sedimentary crust that covered the southwestern coast of South America, cooling to form a granite mass. Glaciers then swept through the region, grinding away all but the twisted ash-gray spire, the "towers" of Paine (pronounced "pie-nay"; it's the old Tehuelche word for "blue"), which rise over the landscape to create one of the world's most beautiful natural phenomena, now the Parque Nacional Torres del Paine. The park was established in 1959. Rock formations, windswept trees, and waterfalls dazzle at every turn of road, and the sunset views are spectacular. The 2,420-square-km (934-square-mile) park's most astonishing attractions are its lakes of turquoise, aquamarine, and emerald waters; its magnificent Grey Glacier; and the Cuernos del Paine ("Paine Horns"), the geological showpiece of the immense granite massif.

Another draw is the park's wildlife; creatures like the guanaco and the ñandú abound. They are acclimated to visitors and don't seem to be bothered by approaching cars and people with cameras. Predators like the gray fox make less frequent appearances. You may also spot the dramatic aerobatics of falcons and the graceful soaring of endangered condors. The beautiful puma, the apex predator of the ecosystem here, is an especially elusive cat, but sightings have grown more common.

The vast majority of visitors come during the summer months of January and February, which means the trails can get congested. Early spring, when wildflowers add flashes of color to the meadows, can be an ideal time to visit because the crowds have not yet arrived. In summer, the winds can be incredibly fierce, but the days are also incredibly longer (in December, there's light for almost 20 hours). During the wintertime of June to September, the days are sunnier yet colder (averaging around freezing) and shorter, but the winds all but disappear and wildlife sightings become more frequent. The park is open all year, but some trails are not accessible in winter. Storms can hit without warning, so be prepared for sudden rain at any time of year. The sight of the Paine peaks in clear weather is stunning; if you have any flexibility in your itinerary, visit the park on the first clear day. ⊕ *conaf.cl/parques/parque-nacional-torres-del-paine* 🎫 *21000 pesos.*

Parque Nacional Bernardo O'Higgins
NATIONAL PARK | Bordering the Parque Nacional Torres del Paine on the southwest, Parque Nacional Bernardo O'Higgins marks the southern tip of the vast Campo de Hielo Sur (Southern Ice Field). As it is inaccessible by land, the only way to visit the park is to take a boat up the Seno Última Esperanza. The Navimag boat passes through on the way to Puerto Montt, but only the Puerto Natales–based, family-run outfit Turismo

21 de Mayo operates boats that actually stop here—the *21 de Mayo* and the *Alberto de Agostini*. (Several operators run trips to just the Balmaceda Glacier.) These well-equipped boating day trips are a good option, especially if for some reason you don't have the time to make it to Torres del Paine. On your way to the park you approach a cormorant colony with nests clinging to sheer cliff walls, venture to a glacier at the foot of Mt. Balmaceda, and finally dock at Puerto Toro for a 1-km (½-mile) hike to the foot of the Serrano Glacier. Congratulations, you made it to the least-visited national park in all of Chile. In recognition of the feat, on the trip back to Puerto Natales the crew treats you to a *pisco sour* (brandy mixed with lemon, egg whites, and sugar) served over a chunk of glacier ice. As with many full-day tours, you must bring your own lunch. Warm clothing, including gloves, is recommended year-round, particularly if there's even the slightest breeze. ⊕ *conaf.cl/parques/ parque-nacional-bernardo-ohiggins*.

 ## Hotels

EcoCamp Patagonia
$$$$ | B&B/INN | These unique geodesic domes are comfy and well situated for trekkers headed to the famed towers of Torres del Paine. **Pros:** dining and bar on-site; great location; tranquil atmosphere. **Cons:** no Wi-Fi; shared bathrooms for standard domes; standard domes have no heating. $ *Rooms from: pesos250000* ⊠ *Estancia Cerro Paine, Parque Nacional Torres Del Paine* ☎ *2/2923–5950 Santiago office* ⊕ *www. ecocamp.travel* ۞ *Closed mid-May to Sept.* ⇨ *33 rooms* ۠◉۠ *No Meals.*

Hosteria Pehoé
$$$ | B&B/INN | Cross a 100-foot footbridge to get to this hotel on its own island with a volcanic black-sand beach in the middle of glistening Lake Pehoé, across from the beautiful Torres del Paine mountain peaks. **Pros:** friendly staff; views are jaw-dropping; great location. **Cons:** Wi-Fi signal is faint; rooms are rundown; outdated facilities. $ *Rooms from: pesos100500* ⊠ *Lago Pehoé* ☎ *9/3400– 5950* ⊕ *www.hosteriapehoe.cl* ⇨ *40 rooms* ۠◉۠ *Free Breakfast.*

★ Hotel Explora
$$$$ | HOTEL | There's no better location in the park than Hotel Explora: on top of a gently babbling waterfall on the southeast corner of Lago Pehoé with a shimmering lake offset by tiny rocky islets and a perfect view of Torres del Paine. **Pros:** adventurous park excursions; the grande dame of Patagonian hospitality; heart-stopping views from the center of the national park. **Cons:** 4-night minimum; poor Wi-Fi and no TV in rooms; a bank breaker. $ *Rooms from: pesos2610000* ⊠ *Lago Pehoé, Parque Nacional Torres Del Paine* ☎ *2/2395–2800 in Santiago* ⊕ *www.explora.com* ⇨ *49 rooms* ۠◉۠ *All-Inclusive.*

Hotel Lago Grey
$$$$ | HOTEL | The panoramic view from the restaurant and bar, past the lake dappled with floating icebergs to the glacier beyond, is worth the somewhat difficult journey here. **Pros:** heated bathroom floors; great views in communal areas; excellent location. **Cons:** standard rooms are basic; Wi-Fi is weak; gravel road to hotel is a rocky ride. $ *Rooms from: pesos160000* ⊠ *Lago Grey* ☎ *61/271– 2100* ⊕ *www.lagogrey.com* ⇨ *60 rooms* ۠◉۠ *Free Breakfast.*

★ Hotel Río Serrano
$$$$ | HOTEL | A good value option among the pricey in-park lodgings, this grand hotel has great service and magnificent views of the entire Torres del Paine mountain range, with the Serrano River and windswept forest in the foreground. **Pros:** great indoor pool and spa; stunning location and all-encompassing views; comfortable rooms. **Cons:** no TV in standard rooms; Wi-Fi is unstable; limited menu for lunch and dinner. $ *Rooms from: pesos268000* ⊠ *Lago Toro, Torres*

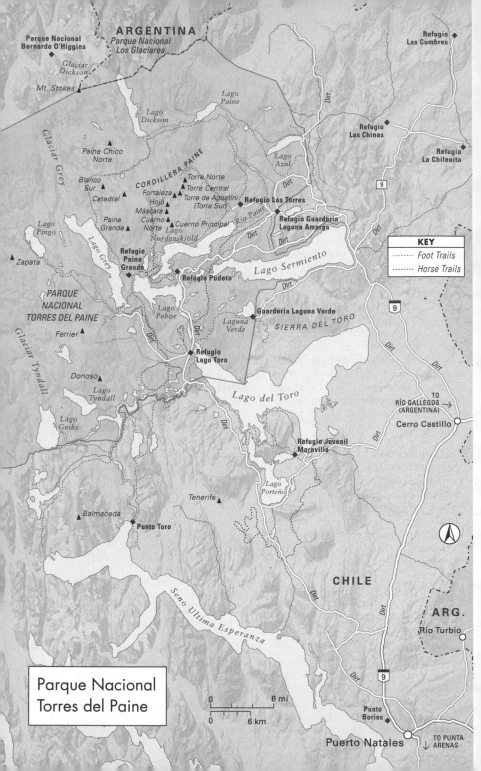

Parque Nacional Torres del Paine

There are three entrances to the park: Laguna Amarga (all bus arrivals), Lago Sarmiento, and Laguna Azul. You are required to sign in when you arrive and pay your entrance fee (US$34 in high season for three consecutive days). *Guardaparques* (park rangers) staff six stations around the reserve and can provide a map and up-to-the-day information about the state of various trails. A regular minivan service connects Laguna Amarga with the Hostería Las Torres, 7 km (4 miles) to the west.

If you intend to stay overnight at campsites and mountain cabins along the trails, you must reserve your spot in advance. CONAF manages the several free campsites inside the park; go to www.parquetorresdelpaine. cl to make reservations. Cozy cabins and more elaborate campsites—with hot showers, electricity, even cooking facilities—can be booked at www. verticepatagonia.cl and www.fantasticosur.com

Although considerable walking is necessary to take full advantage of Parque Nacional Torres del Paine, you need not be a hard-core trekker. Many people choose to hike the W route, which takes four days, but others prefer to stay in one of the comfortable lodges and hit the trails in the morning or afternoon. Glaciar Grey, with its fragmented icebergs, makes a rewarding and easy hike; equally rewarding is the spectacular boat or kayak ride across the lake, past icebergs, and up to the glacier, which leaves from Hostería Lago Grey. Another great excursion is the 900-meter (3,000-foot) ascent to the sensational views from Mirador Las Torres, four hours one way from Las Torres Patagonia.

If you do the W, you'll begin (or end, if you reverse the route) at Laguna Amarga and continue to Mirador Las Torres and Los Cuernos, then continue along a breathtaking path up Valle Frances to its awe-inspiring and fiendishly windy lookout (hold on to your hat!) and finally Lago Grey. The W runs for 100 kilometers (62 miles) but always follows clearly marked paths, with gradual climbs and descents at relatively low altitude. The challenge comes from the weather. Winds whip up to 90 mph, and a clear sky can suddenly darken with storm clouds, producing rain, hail, or snow in a matter of minutes. An even more ambitious route is the Circuito, which essentially leads around the entire park and takes from a week to 10 days. Along the way some people sleep at the dozen or so humble *refugios* (shelters) evenly spaced along the trail, and many others bring their own tents.

Driving is an easy way to enjoy the park; one road cuts the distance to Puerto Natales from a meandering 140 km (87 miles) to a more direct 80 km (50 miles). Inside the national park more than 100 km (62 miles) of roads leading to the most popular sites are safe and well maintained, though unpaved.

You can also hire horses from Hotel Las Torres and trek to the Torres, the Cuernos, or along the shore of Lago Nordenskjold. Water transport is also available, with numerous tour operators offering sailboat, kayak, and inflatable Zodiac speedboat options along the Río Serrano.

del Paine ☎ *9/3255–3915* 🌐 *www.rios-errano.com* ⏲ *Closed May–Oct.* 🛏 *106 rooms* 🍴 *Free Breakfast.*

Las Torres Patagonia

$$$$ | **HOTEL** | Owned by one of the earliest families to settle in what eventually became the park, Las Torres has a long history and is the closest hotel to the main trails into the heart of the Torres del Paine itself. **Pros:** close access to top trail in the park; friendly and efficient; homey atmosphere. **Cons:** noisy bar; poor Wi-Fi; not cheap and prices keep rising. [$] *Rooms from: pesos300000* ✉ *Lago Amarga* ☎ *2/2898–6043, 9/5358–0026* 🌐 *www.lastorres.com* ⏲ *Closed May to Sept.* 🛏 *74 rooms* 🍴 *Free Breakfast.*

★ **Patagonia Camp**

$$$$ | **RESORT** | These luxury yurts fully immerse you in the romance and wilderness of the Patagonian landscape; enjoy the sounds of the whistling winds and patter of rain, gaze onto the expanse of stars on a peaceful night, and awake to a spectacular sunrise over the blue glacial waters of Lake Del Toro, all from the comfort of your king-size bed in a heated yurt with a full tub and rain shower. **Pros:** great restaurant; beautiful location and stunning views; immersive nature experience. **Cons:** expensive (and some tours cost extra); weak Wi-Fi; more than an hour to park activities. [$] *Rooms from: pesos765000* ✉ *Camino al Milodón, Km 74, Parque Nacional Torres Del Paine* ☎ *2/2594–0591 hotel, 61/241–5149 reservations* 🌐 *www.patagoniacamp.com* ⏲ *Closed May–Aug.* 🛏 *20 rooms* 🍴 *Free Breakfast* ☞ *Inclusive rates available.*

Tierra Patagonia

$$$$ | **RESORT** | With stunning views of Lago Sarmiento and the Torres del Paine range from the huge interior windows, this luxurious hotel and spa keeps nature directly in the foreground at all times. **Pros:** fabulous views; gorgeous architecture and design; excellent spa. **Cons:** food a bit bland; transfers in/out are limited; expensive. [$] *Rooms from: pesos535000* ✉ *Lago Sarmiento, Ruta Y, Parque Nacional Torres Del Paine* ☎ *2/3705–301* 🌐 *www.tierrapatagonia.com* ⏲ *Closed May–Sept.* 🛏 *43 rooms* 🍴 *Free Breakfast.*

Punta Arenas, Chile

Founded in 1848, Punta Arenas was Chile's first permanent settlement in Patagonia. Great developments in cattle-keeping, mining, and wood production led to an economic and social boom at the end of the 19th century; today, though the port is no longer an important stop on trade routes, it exudes an aura of faded grandeur. Plaza Muñoz Gamero, the central square (also known as the Plaza de Armas), is surrounded by evidence of its early prosperity: buildings whose then-opulent brick exteriors recall a time when this was one of Chile's wealthiest cities.

The newer houses here have colorful tin roofs, best appreciated when seen from a high vantage point such as the Mirador Cerro la Cruz. The city is a relaxed and pleasant place to stroll, with interesting details if you have a keen eye: the pink-and-white house on a corner, the bay window full of potted plants, and schoolchildren in identical naval pea coats reminding you how the city's identity is tied to the sea.

Although Punta Arenas is 3,141 km (1,960 miles) from Santiago, daily flights from the capital make it an easy journey. As the transportation hub of southern Patagonia, Punta Arenas is within reach of Chile's Parque Nacional Torres del Paine (a four-hour drive) and Argentina's Parque Nacional Los Glaciares. It's also a good base for penguin-watchers and a key embarkation point for boat travel to Tierra del Fuego and Antarctica and connecting flights to the Falkland Islands.

The sights of Punta Arenas can be done in a day or two. The city is mainly a jumping-off point for cruises that operate from here, and while tours to Torres del Paine do operate from here, a visit to Chilean Patagonia's main attraction is much more pleasantly done from the town of Puerto Natales, which is close to the park and has greatly improved its touristic services in recent years.

GETTING HERE AND AROUND

Most travelers will arrive at Aeropuerto Presidente Carlos Ibañez del Campo, a modern terminal approximately 12 miles from town. On a clear day you'll get a memorable fly-by view of Torres del Paine. To get to the city, there are some private transfers by small companies running minivans out of the airport, a shared service costing around 5,000 pesos per person. A quicker, more comfortable option is a taxi, which costs 10,000 pesos.

Set on a windy bank of the Magellan Strait, eastward-facing Punta Arenas has four main thoroughfares that were originally planned wide enough to accommodate flocks of sheep. Bustling with pedestrians, Avenida Bories is the main drag for shopping, and O'Higgins for dining. Overall, the city is quite compact, and navigating its central grid of streets is fairly straightforward.

CRUISE

Arturo Prat Port is not far from the main drag of town. You can either walk five minutes from the pier or take a taxi for around 3,000 or 4,000 pesos. Stroll along the portside a few minutes until you reach Calle O'Higgins, where you'll find many bars and restaurants, and then head up Calle Roca or Pedro Montt to the main plaza.

The small town center is easy to walk around, although you'll want to bring layers with you, as you never know when the wind might pick up. Also remember to bring a warm jacket for the evening, as nighttime temperatures are cold year-round.

ESSENTIALS

BUS CONTACTS Buses Fernández.
✉ *Armando Sanhueza 745, Punta Arenas* ☎ *61/2242–313* ⊕ *www.busesfernandez. com.* **Bus-Sur.** ✉ *Av. Colón 842, Punta Arenas* ☎ *61/261–4224* ⊕ *www.bussur. com.*

VISITOR AND TOUR INFORMATION

Punta Arenas City Tourism. ✉ *Plaza Muñoz Gamero, Punta Arenas* ☎ *61/220–0350* ⊕ *www.puntaarenas.cl.* **Sernatur Punta Arenas.** ✉ *Monseñor José Fagnano 643, Punta Arenas* ☎ *61/224–1330* ⊕ *www. sernatur.cl.*

Sights

★ Cementerio Municipal
(*Municipal Cemetery*)
CEMETERY | The fascinating history of this region is chiseled into stone at what may well be one of the world's most beautiful cemeteries. Set among a labyrinth of paths lined with immaculately sculpted cypress trees, the elaborate mausoleums and tombstones honor the original families who built Punta Arenas. In an effort to recognize the region's indigenous past, there's a shrine in the northern part of the cemetery to the Selk'nam tribe (look for the copper dome), the target of an ethnic genocide at Tierra del Fuego in the 19th century. Local legend says that rubbing the statue's left knee brings good luck. ✉ *Av. Bulnes 949, Punta Arenas* ☎ 🎟 *Free.*

Mirador Cerro la Cruz
VIEWPOINT | The white cross that gives this hill its name marks a pretty good vantage point over the city, but it's not the best; to get to the best spot, climb down the stairs to the road just in front on the cross and turn right, until you reach a novelty road sign showing the distance to far-flung points of the globe. You'll have a panoramic view of the city's colorful corrugated rooftops and across the Strait of Magellan. Stand with the amorous local couples gazing out toward the flat expanse of Tierra del Fuego in the

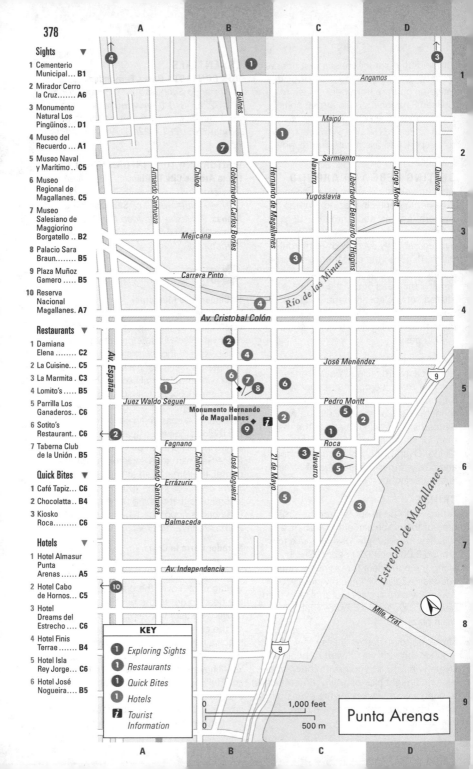

378

Sights ▼

1 Cementerio Municipal... **B1**
2 Mirador Cerro la Cruz....... **A6**
3 Monumento Natural Los Pingüinos... **D1**
4 Museo del Recuerdo... **A1**
5 Museo Naval y Marítimo.. **C5**
6 Museo Regional de Magallanes. **C5**
7 Museo Salesiano de Maggiorino Borgatello.. **B2**
8 Palacio Sara Braun........ **B5**
9 Plaza Muñoz Gamero..... **B5**
10 Reserva Nacional Magallanes. **A7**

Restaurants ▼

1 Damiana Elena **C2**
2 La Cuisine... **C5**
3 La Marmita. **C3**
4 Lomito's **B5**
5 Parrilla Los Ganaderos.. **C6**
6 Sotito's Restaurant.. **C6**
7 Taberna Club de la Unión . **B5**

Quick Bites ▼

1 Café Tapiz... **C6**
2 Chocolatta.. **B4**
3 Kiosko Roca......... **C6**

Hotels ▼

1 Hotel Almasur Punta Arenas **A5**
2 Hotel Cabo de Hornos... **C5**
3 Hotel Dreams del Estrecho **C6**
4 Hotel Finis Terrae **B4**
5 Hotel Isla Rey Jorge... **C6**
6 Hotel José Nogueira.... **B5**

KEY

- Exploring Sights
- Restaurants
- Quick Bites
- Hotels
- Tourist Information

0 — 1,000 feet
0 — 500 m

Punta Arenas

distance. ⊠ *Fagnano at Señoret, Punta Arenas* ☜ *Free.*

★ Monumento Natural Los Pingüinos
(*Penguin Natural Monument*)

ISLAND | Punta Arenas is the launching point for a boat trip to see the more than 80,000 Magellanic penguins at the Monumento Natural Los Pingüinos on Isla Magdalena. Visitors walk a single trail, marked off by rope, and penguins are everywhere—wandering across your path, sitting in burrows, skipping along just off the shore, strutting around in packs. The trip to the island, in the middle of the Estrecho de Magallanes, takes about two hours. To get here, you must take a tour boat. If you haven't booked in advance, you can stop at any of the local travel agencies and try to get on a trip at the last minute, which is often possible. You can go only from November to the end of March; the penguin population peaks in January and February. Almost all cruise ships that stop at Punta Arenas visit the colony. However you get here, bring warm clothing, even in summer; the island can be chilly, and it's definitely windy, which helps with the occasional penguin odor. ⊠ *Punta Arenas* ☎ ☜ *8000 pesos.*

Museo del Recuerdo
HISTORY MUSEUM | In the gardens of the Instituto de la Patagonia, part of the Universidad de Magallanes, the Museum of Memory is an enviable collection of machinery and heavy equipment used during the late-19th- and early-20th-century pioneering era. There are exhibits of rural employment, such as a carpenter's workshop, and displays of typical home life. ⊠ *Av. Bulnes 01890, Punta Arenas* ☎ *61/2207–051* ☜ *3000 pesos* ⊙ *Closed Sun.*

Museo Naval y Marítimo (*The Naval and Maritime Museum*)
HISTORY MUSEUM | This museum extols Chile's high-seas prowess, particularly where Antarctica is concerned. In fact, a large chunk of ice from the great white continent is kept just below freezing in a

glass case. The exhibits are worth a visit by anyone with an interest in merchant or military ships and sailing, but the real highlight is in the screening room, where you can watch Irving Johnson's incredible film *Around Cape Horn*—his account of the hardship faced by crews in frigid southern waters in the early 20th century. His astounding black-and-white footage of daredevil crew members and mountainous seas is accompanied by a gruff and often hilarious voice-over. ⊠ *Av. Pedro Montt 981, Punta Arenas* ☎ *9/4138–0335* ☜ *2000 pesos* ⊙ *Closed Sun. and Mon.*

★ Museo Regional de Magallanes
(*Regional Museum of Magallanes*)

HISTORY MUSEUM | Housed in what was once the mansion of the powerful Braun-Menéndez family, the Regional Museum of Magallanes is an intriguing glimpse into the daily life of a wealthy provincial family in the early 1900s. Lavish Carrara marble hearths, English bath fixtures, a billiard room that was a social hub in the city's glory days, and cordovan leather walls are all kept in immaculate condition, helped by the sockettes you wear over your shoes. The museum has an excellent group of displays depicting Punta Arenas's past, from prehistoric animals to European contact to its decline with the opening of the Panama Canal. The museum is half a block north of the main square. ⊠ *Av. Magallanes 949, Punta Arenas* ☎ *61/224–4216* ⊕ *www. museodemagallanes.cl* ☜ *Free* ⊙ *Closed Tues., Sat. and Sun.*

Museo Salesiano de Maggiorino Borgatello
HISTORY MUSEUM | Commonly referred to simply as El Salesiano, this museum is operated by Italian missionaries whose order arrived in Punta Arenas in the 19th century. The Salesians, most of whom spoke no Spanish, proved to be daring explorers. Traveling throughout the region, they collected the artifacts made by indigenous tribes that are currently on display. They also relocated

many of the indigenous people to nearby Dawson Island, where they died by the hundreds (from diseases like influenza and pneumonia). The museum contains an extraordinary collection of everything from skulls and native crafts to stuffed animals. ✉ *Av. Bulnes 336, Punta Arenas* ☎ *61/222–1001* 🌐 *www.museomaggiorinoborgatello.cl* 🎫 *3000 pesos* 🕒 *Closed Sun. and Mon.*

Palacio Sara Braun

HISTORIC HOME | This resplendent 1895 mansion, a national landmark and architectural showpiece of southern Patagonia, was designed by French architect Numa Meyer at the behest of Sara Braun (the wealthy widow of wool baron José Nogueira). Materials and craftsmen were imported from Europe during the home's four years of construction. The city's central plaza and surrounding buildings soon followed, ushering in the region's golden era. The Club de la Unión, a social organization that now owns the building, opens its doors to nonmembers for tours of some of the rooms and salons, which have magnificent parquet floors, marble fireplaces, and hand-painted ceilings. After touring the rooms, head to the cellar tavern for a drink or snack. ✉ *Plaza Muñoz Gamero 716, Punta Arenas* ☎ *61/224–2049* 🎫 *2000 pesos* 🕒 *Closed Sun. and Tues.*

Plaza Muñoz Gamero

PLAZA/SQUARE | A canopy of pine trees shades this grandiose main square, which is surrounded by splendid baroque-style mansions from the 19th century. The heart of the city gives perhaps the strongest impression of Punta Arenas at its peak of wealth and power. A grandiose bronze sculpture commemorating the voyage of Hernando de Magallanes dominates the center of the plaza. Local lore has it that a kiss on the shiny toe of Calafate, one of the Fuegian statues at the base of the monument, will one day bring you back to Punta Arenas. ✉ *José Nogueira at 21 de Mayo, Punta Arenas.*

Reserva Nacional Magallanes

NATURE PRESERVE | **FAMILY** | Only about 10 minutes west of Punta Arenas, this national reserve has some excellent hiking trails that weave through native forests and provide views over the city and the Strait of Magellan. All ages can enjoy the trails, which take about three to four hours to complete at an easy walking pace. ✉ *7 km west of Punta Arenas, Punta Arenas* ☎ *61/223–8554* 🌐 *www.conaf.cl/parques/reserva-nacional-magallanes* 🎫 *5400 pesos* 🕒 *Closed Mon.*

🍴 Restaurants

★ Damiana Elena

$$$$ | **CONTEMPORARY** | Named for the grandmother of the chef, who was said to have cooked like a goddess, Damiana Elena is a culinary experience you won't soon forget. Housed in a cozy Victorian home with high ceilings, the restaurant has no fixed menu; instead, the chef cooks eight different dishes each night, and the waiter explains them at your table. **Known for:** enormous portions; bespoke culinary adventures; ever-changing menu. [$] *Average main: pesos25000* ✉ *Hernando de Magallanes 341, Punta Arenas* ☎ *61/222–2818* 🕒 *Closed Sun. and Mon.*

★ La Cuisine

$$$ | **FRENCH** | This place became one of the most popular restaurants in Punta Arenas by adding a French and European twist to typical Chilean seafood and meat dishes. Layered king crab lasagna and guanaco with calafate berry reduction are house favorites, as well as their signature pâté. **Known for:** reservations necessary in summer; creative dishes like three-flavor crème brûlée; intimate atmosphere. [$] *Average main: pesos13000* ✉ *Av. Bernardo O'Higgins 1037, Punta Arenas* ☎ *61/222–8641* 🕒 *Closed Mon; no dinner Sun.*

★ La Marmita

$$$ | **CHILEAN** | Just a short distance from downtown, the popular La Marmita is warm and inviting, charmingly decorated with an old kitchen stove, spatulas, whisks, and wooden children's toys from yesteryear. There's often live jazz music, which seems to make menu standouts like *charquicán de cochayuyo* (pumpkin stew) and guanaco steak even more delicious. To warm the cold Magellanic afternoon, try their legendary *caldillo de congrio* (conger chowder). **Known for:** reservations recommended; cozy and rustic atmosphere; legendary conger chowder. [$] *Average main: pesos11000* ✉ *Francisco Sampaio 678, Punta Arenas* ☎ *9/7657–0361* 💳 *No credit cards* 🕒 *Closed Sun.*

Lomito's

$ | **AMERICAN** | A fast-moving but friendly staff serves Chilean-style blue-plate specials at this bustling deli. In addition to traditional hamburgers, you can try the ubiquitous *completos*: hot dogs buried under mounds of your choice of toppings, from spicy mayonnaise to an intense guacamole—they're among the best hot dogs in southern Chile. **Known for:** fast food; quick service; cheap eats. [$] *Average main: pesos4500* ✉ *José Menéndez 722, between Bories and Av. Magallanes, Punta Arenas* ☎ *61/224–3399* 💳 *No credit cards* 🕒 *Closed Sun.*

Parrilla Los Ganaderos

$$$$ | **CHILEAN** | **FAMILY** | This bright restaurant resembles a rural *estancia*, with retro decor and waiters dressed in gaucho costumes serving up spectacular *cordero al ruedo* (spit-roasted lamb) cooked over a big fire in the dining room. A lamb serving comes with three different cuts of meat, or you can pick your way through other barbecue dishes. **Known for:** extensive Chilean wine list; traditional ranch-inspired decor and menu; spectacular roast lamb. [$] *Average main: pesos20000* ✉ *Av. Bernardo O'Higgins 1166, Punta Arenas* ☎ *61/222–5103.*

Sotito's Restaurant

$$$ | **SEAFOOD** | An institution in Punta Arenas, Sotito's is old school. Attentive, bow-tied waiters serve large grilled meat dishes and mouthwatering plates of *centolla* (king crab). **Known for:** hearty portions; waterfront location; king crab entrées. [$] *Average main: pesos11000* ✉ *Av. Bernardo O'Higgins 1138, Punta Arenas* ☎ *61/224–3565* 🕒 *Closed Sun. and Tues.*

Taberna Club de la Unión

$$ | **CAFÉ** | A jovial, publike atmosphere prevails in this wonderful, labyrinthine cellar down the side stairway of Sara Braun's old mansion on the main plaza. Patagonian beers like Austral are served cold in frosted mugs while you eat tapas-style meat, cheese, and seafood appetizers. **Known for:** traditional decor; excellent drinks; historical setting. [$] *Average main: pesos9000* ✉ *Plaza Muñoz Gamero 716, Punta Arenas* ☎ *9/5974–6467, 61/222–2777* 🌐 *www.tabernabar.cl* 🕒 *Closed Sun. No lunch.*

☕ Coffee and Quick Bites

Café Tapiz

$$ | **CAFÉ** | This colorful and cozy café has a warm, inviting atmosphere, aided by the steaming hot chocolates and coffee on offer, alongside sweet treats and Chilean sandwiches. You can buy local handicrafts here as well and take advantage of the Wi-Fi. **Known for:** nice spot for Chilean teatime; tasty warm beverages; hip ambience. [$] *Average main: pesos8900* ✉ *Roca 912, Punta Arenas* ☎ *9/6565–5294* 🕒 *Closed Sat. and Sun.*

Chocolatta

$$ | **CAFÉ** | **FAMILY** | At once a tea and coffeehouse, chocolate shop, and bakery, Chocolatta is the perfect refueling stop during a day of wandering in Punta Arenas. The interior is warm and cozy, and the staff is efficient and friendly. **Known for:** cozy atmosphere; chocolate shop; coffee hangout. [$] *Average main:*

pesos7000 ✉ *Bories 852, Punta Arenas* ☎ *61/224–8150* 🌐 *www.chocolatta.cl* 🕓 *Closed Sun.*

Kiosko Roca

$ | **SANDWICHES** | This little bar is always packed with locals who come here for their specialty: a small sandwich with chorizo paste and béchamel sauce, and a banana milkshake. It might not seem like much, but Kiosko Roca is an institution in Punta Arenas. **Known for:** quick snack; local flavor; amazing banana milkshakes. [$] *Average main: pesos1300* ✉ *Roca 875, Punta Arenas* ☎ 🌐 *www.kioskoroca.cl* 🕓 *Closed Sun.*

Hotels

Hotel Almasur Punta Arenas

$$$ | **HOTEL** | With modern, comfortable rooms; a reasonably priced restaurant; and a convenient location, this is one of the better hotels in Punta Arenas. **Pros:** eco-conscious policies; good value; quiet surroundings. **Cons:** service could be friendlier; uninspiring views; limited parking. [$] *Rooms from: pesos100000* ✉ *Armando Sanhueza 965, Punta Arenas* ☎ *61/229–5000* 🌐 *www.almasurhoteles.cl* 🛏 *115 rooms* 🍴 *Free Breakfast.*

★ Hotel Cabo de Hornos

$$$$ | **HOTEL** | This hotel towers impressively over the main plaza, but unlike the bland sameness many large hotels fall into, there's a quirk around every corner here—from the dramatic slate-walled lobby with tube lighting to the open-plan bar/lounge with cowhide high-backed chairs and the blackened wreck of an old skiff. **Pros:** central location; friendly, professional service; spacious, comfortable rooms. **Cons:** rooms have basic amenities; can be noisy; standard rooms don't match the brave design choices downstairs. [$] *Rooms from: pesos154000* ✉ *Plaza Muñoz Gamero 1025, Punta Arenas* ☎ *61/271–5000* 🌐 *www.hotelcabodehornos.com* 🛏 *110 rooms* 🍴 *Free Breakfast.*

Hotel Dreams del Estrecho

$$$$ | **HOTEL** | Equipped with a big casino, convention center, and disco, Hotel Dreams is one of the flashiest hotels in Punta Arenas. **Pros:** sea views; great location and amenities; modern. **Cons:** restaurant is a bit mediocre; noise from the casino crowds; can fill up with cruise passengers. [$] *Rooms from: pesos150000* ✉ *Av. O'Higgins 1235, Punta Arenas* ☎ *600/424–0000* 🌐 *www.punta-arenas.dreams.cl* 🛏 *104 rooms* 🍴 *Free Breakfast.*

Hotel Finis Terrae

$$$ | **HOTEL** | This classic Punta Arenas hotel is a few blocks from the main square but offers panoramic views from its rooftop living area and restaurant. **Pros:** staff friendly and professional; central location; sensational views from sixth-floor restaurant. **Cons:** simple breakfast; old hotel infrastructure; standard rooms are small. [$] *Rooms from: pesos91000* ✉ *Av. Colón 766, Punta Arenas* ☎ *61/2209–100* 🌐 *www.hotelfinisterrae.com* 🛏 *64 rooms* 🍴 *Free Breakfast.*

Hotel Isla Rey Jorge

$$ | **HOTEL** | Though it's an older hotel, Hotel Isla Rey Jorge is just one block from Plaza Muñoz Gamero, and its clean comfortable rooms come at a nice price. **Pros:** centrally located; staff is friendly and efficient; inviting interior in old mansion. **Cons:** simple breakfasts; traffic noise; bathrooms need updating. [$] *Rooms from: pesos77000* ✉ *21 de Mayo 1243, Punta Arenas* ☎ *61/222–2681* 🌐 *www.islareyjorge.com* 🛏 *25 rooms* 🍴 *Free Breakfast.*

Hotel José Nogueira

$$$$ | **HOTEL** | Originally the home of Sara Braun, this opulent 19th-century mansion has a superior location—just steps off the main plaza. **Pros:** ample breakfast buffet; central location; historic. **Cons:** uncomfortable mattresses; can have street noise; small rooms. [$] *Rooms from: pesos160000* ✉ *Bories 967, Punta Arenas*

☎ *61/271–1000* ⊕ *www.hotelnogueira. com* ➪ *22 rooms* ⧉ *Free Breakfast.*

Nightlife

Jekus Restobar
BARS | This gastro pub is a popular night-spot, where locals come for beer on the tap, live music, and karaoke at the weekends. They have a menu of local cuisine for when you get a bit peckish, too. ⊠ *Av. Bernardo O'Higgins 1021, Punta Arenas* ☎ *61/224–5851.*

La Taberna Club de la Unión
BARS | The city's classic speakeasy, La Taberna Club de la Unión, hops into the wee hours with a healthy mix of younger and older patrons. It is also open for an early evening drink if you just want an aperitif before dinner. ⊠ *Plaza de Armas, Punta Arenas* ☎ *9/5974–6467, 61/222–2777* ⊕ *www.tabernabar.cl* ⊙ *Closed Sun.*

Performing Arts

FILM
Sala Estrella
FILM | In the early evening take in a movie at the only cinema in town. The charming Sala Estrella runs an eclectic mix of Hollywood and art-house films in an old-style, one-screen theater. ⊠ *Mejicana 777, Punta Arenas* ☎ *99/6150–7643* ⊕ *www. cinesalaestrella.com.*

Shopping

You don't have to go far to find local handicrafts, pricey souvenirs, wool clothing, hiking gear, postcards, custom chocolates, or semiprecious stones like lapis lazuli. You will see penguins of every variety, from keychain size to larger than life. Warm wool clothing is for sale in almost every shop, but it isn't cheap. One advantage to shopping in Punta Arenas is that it has a duty free zone, the *Zona Franca*, with more than 80 stores offering goods at bargain prices.

Plaza de Armas
MARKET | The pretty Plaza de Armas in the center of town has a dozen small artisan kiosks that offer a wide range of tourist trinkets and souvenirs. ⊠ *Plaza de Armas, Punta Arenas* ☎.

Quilpué
SOUVENIRS | This downtown shop sells traditional Chilean clothing, handicrafts and souvenirs, and *huaso* (cowboy) supplies such as bridles, bits, and spurs. Pick up some boots for folk dancing. ⊠ *José Nogueira 1256, Punta Arenas* ☎ *9/8418–7482.*

Zona Franca
SHOPPING CENTER | You can find real bargains on electronic goods, from digital cameras and laptops to thumb drives and USB devices, at the Zona Franca, a free-trade zone about 5 km (3 miles) out of town along Bulnes. ⊠ *Punta Arenas* ☎ *61/236–2000* ⊕ *www.zonaustral.cl/en/ zona-franca.*

Puerto Hambre

50 km (31 miles) south of Punta Arenas.

In an attempt to gain a foothold in the region, Spain founded Ciudad Rey Don Felipe in 1584. Pedro Sarmiento de Gamboa constructed a church and homes for more than 100 settlers. But just three years later, British navigator Thomas Cavendish came ashore to find that almost all had died of hunger, which some might say is a natural result of founding a town where there isn't any fresh water. He renamed the town Port Famine. Today a tranquil fishing village, Puerto Hambre still has traces of the original settlement.

Sights

★ Fuerte Bulnes
MILITARY SIGHT | In the middle of a Chilean winter in 1843, a frigate under the command of Captain Juan Williams Rebolledo sailed southward from the island of

Chiloé carrying a ragtag contingent of 11 sailors and eight soldiers. Several months later, on a rocky promontory called Santa Ana overlooking the Strait of Magellan, they built a wooden fort, which they named Fuerte Bulnes, thereby founding the first Chilean settlement in the southern reaches of Patagonia. A replica of the fort, including a church, post office, and stable, was reconstructed on the site in 1944, and today it forms a key part of Parque del Estrecho de Magallanes, located 50 km (51 miles) south of Punta Arenas. The park has a state-of-the-art visitor center focused on the history of the Strait of Magellan, along with an elegant café and bookstore. There are also hiking trails with impressive views. ⊠ *5 km (3 miles) south of Puerto Hambre, Puerto Hambre* ⊕ *www.parquedelestrecho.cl* ⊠ *9000 pesos park entrance.*

Monolith

MONUMENT | About 2 km (1 mile) west of Puerto Hambre is a small white monolith that marks the geographical center of Chile, the midway point between northernmost Arica and the South Pole. ⊠ *Puerto Hambre.*

Reserva Nacional Laguna Parrillar

NATURE PRESERVE | The 47,000-acre Reserva Nacional Laguna Parrillar, west of Puerto Hambre, stretches around a shimmering lake in a valley flanked by hills. It's a great place for a picnic, if the weather cooperates. A number of well-marked paths lead to sweeping vistas over the Estrecho de Magallanes. ⊠ *Off Ruta 9, 52 km (32 miles) south of Punta Arenas, Puerto Hambre* ☎ *61/236–0488 No phone* ⊕ *www.conaf.cl* ⊠ *5400 pesos* ⊙ *Closed May–Sept.*

El Calafate and Parque Nacional los Glaciares, Argentina

320 km (225 miles) north of Río Gallegos; 253 km (157 miles) east of Río Turbio on Chilean border; 213 km (123 miles) south of El Chaltén.

Founded in 1927 as a frontier town, El Calafate is the base for excursions to the Parque Nacional Los Glaciares, which was created in 1937 as a showcase for one of South America's most spectacular sights, the Glaciar Perito Moreno. Because it's on the southern shore of Lago Argentino, the town enjoys a microclimate much milder than the rest of southern Patagonia.

To call El Calafate a boomtown would be a gross understatement. In the first two decades of this millennium the town's population has exploded from 4,000 to almost 30,000, and it shows no signs of slowing down. Tourism has been the principal motor behind the town's growth, and at seemingly every turn you'll see new construction cropping up. As a result, the downtown has a new sheen to it, although most buildings are constructed of wood, with a rustic aesthetic that respects the majestic natural environment. One exception is the casino in the heart of downtown, the facade of which seems to mock the face of the Glaciar Perito Moreno. Farther out of the city is another glacier lookalike, the Glaciarium Museum, architecturally modeled on Perito Moreno and with Argentina's only ice bar.

Now with a paved road between El Calafate and the glacier, the visitors continue to flock in to see the creaking ice sculptures. These visitors include luxury-package tourists bound for handsome estancias in the park surroundings, backpackers over from Chile's Parque

Nacional Torres del Paine, and *porteños* (from Buenos Aires) in town for a long weekend.

For a town that lives and dies on tourism, one of the most infuriating elements of the boom is the cash shortage that strikes El Calafate every weekend during high season. The four ATMs in town frequently run out of money starting as early as Friday evening, and there's often no respite until midday Monday. The shortage is compounded by tour companies who offer steep discounts for cash on combined glacier, ice-trekking, and estancia tours. Apart from stocking up during the week, the best plan to ensure that you won't run out is to bring all the cash you'll need for your stay here. If worse comes to worst, most hotels and many restaurants will accept credit cards, or exchange dollars.

GETTING HERE AND AROUND

Daily flights from Buenos Aires, Ushuaia, and Río Gallegos, and direct flights from Bariloche transport tourists to El Calafate's 21st-century glass-and-steel airport with the promise of adventure and discovery in distant mountains and glaciers. El Calafate is so popular that the flights sell out weeks in advance, so don't plan on booking at the last minute.

If you can't get on a flight or are looking for a cheaper option, there are daily buses between El Calafate, El Chaltén, Río Gallegos, Ushuaia, and Puerto Natales in Chile—all of which can be booked at the bus terminal. El Calafate is also the starting (or finishing) point for the legendary Ruta 40 journey to Bariloche. If you can bear the bus travel for a few days, you'll pass some exceptional scenery, and most operators allow you to hop on and hop off at canyons, lakes, and the famous handprint-covered caves en route.

Driving from Río Gallegos takes about four hours across desolate plains enlivened by occasional sightings of *ñandú* (rheas), shy llamalike guanacos,

silver-gray foxes, and fleet-footed hares the size of small deer. Esperanza is the only gas, food, and bathroom stop halfway between the two towns. Driving from Puerto Natales is similar, although snow-topped mountains line the distance; arriving by road from Ushuaia requires four border crossings and more than 18 hours.

A staircase ascends from the middle of Libertador to Avenida Julio Roca, where you'll find the bus terminal and a very busy Oficina de Turismo with a board listing available accommodations and campgrounds; you can also get brochures and maps, and there's a multilingual staff to help plan excursions. The tourism office has another location on the corner of Rosales and Libertador; both locations are open daily from 8 to 8 (during high season). The Oficina Parques Nacionales, open weekdays 8 to 4, has information on the Parque Nacional Los Glaciares, including the glaciers, area history, hiking trails, and flora and fauna.

BUS CONTACTS TAQSA. ✉ *Bus terminal, El Calafate* ☎ *2902/491–843* ⊕ *www. taqsa.com.ar.* **Turismo Zaahj.** ✉ *Terminal de Omnibus, Calle Antoine De Saint-Exupéry 87, El Calafate* ☎ *2902/491–631* ⊕ *www.turismozaahj.co.cl.*

RENTAL CARS ServiCar. ✉ *Av. Libertador 695, El Calafate* ☎ *2902/492–541* ⊕ *www.servicar4x4.com.ar.*

TAXIS Taxi Remis Calafate. ✉ *Av. Roca 1004, El Calafate* ☎ *2902/484–111* ⊕ *www.taxiremiscalafate.com.ar.*

TOURS

In El Calafate, each tour has to be approved by the local government and is assigned to one tour operator only. On the upside you'll never fall foul of a shady operator, but on the downside there is no competition to keep prices low. Whether you book a tour directly with the operator who leads it, with another operator, or through your hotel or other tour agency, the price should remain the same. Take note that most tour prices do not include the park entrance fee, an extra 2,520 pesos for foreigners.

ESSENTIALS

WHAT IT COSTS

$	$$	$$$	$$$$
RESTAURANTS			
Under 300 pesos	300– 500 pesos	501– 750 pesos	over 750 pesos
HOTELS IN USD			
Under $116	$116– $200	$201– $300	over $300

VISITOR AND TOUR INFORMATION Secretaría de Turismo El Calafate. ⊠ *Rosales at Libertador, El Calafate* ☎ *2902/491–090* ⊕ *www.elcalafate.gov.ar.* **Oficina Parques Nacionales.** ⊠ *Av. Libertador 1302, El Calafate* ☎ *2902/491–005* ⊕ *www.parquesnacionales.gob.ar.*

◉ Sights

Glaciarium
SCIENCE MUSEUM | About 10 km (6 miles) from town, this glacier museum gives you an educational walk through the formation and life of glaciers (particularly in Patagonia) and the effects of climate change, as well as temporary art exhibitions. A 3D film about the national park and plenty of brightly lit displays, along with the stark glacier-shape architecture, give it a modern appeal. Don't miss the Glaciobar—the first ice bar in Argentina—where you can don thermal suits, boots, and gloves, and where a whiskey on the rocks means 200-year-old glacier rocks from Perito Moreno. ⊠ *Ruta 11, Km 6, El Calafate* ⊹ *Arrive by taxi (200 pesos each way), 1 hr walking, or by free shuttle service from tourism office leaving every hr* ☎ *2902/497–912* ⊕ *www.glaciarium. com* 🎟 *1400 pesos.*

★ Glaciar Perito Moreno
NATURE SIGHT | Eighty km (50 miles) away on R11, the road to the Glaciar Perito Moreno has now been entirely paved. From the park entrance the road winds through hills and forests of lenga and ñire trees, until all at once the glacier comes into full view. Descending like a long white tongue through distant mountains, it ends abruptly in a translucent azure wall 5 km (3 miles) wide and 240 feet high at the edge of frosty green Lago Argentino.

Although it's possible to rent a car and go on your own (which can give you the advantage of avoiding large tourist groups), virtually everyone visits the park on a day trip booked through one of the many travel agents in El Calafate. The most basic tours start at 4,000 pesos for the round-trip (excluding entrance) and take you to see the glacier from a viewing area composed of a series of platforms wrapped around the point of the Península de Magallanes. The platforms, which offer perhaps the most impressive view of the glacier, allow you to wander back and forth, looking across the Canal de los Tempanos (Iceberg Channel). Here you listen and wait for nature's number-one ice show—first, a cracking sound, followed by tons of ice breaking away and falling with a thunderous crash into the lake. As the glacier creeps across this narrow channel and meets the land on the other side, an ice dam sometimes builds up between the inlet of Brazo Rico on the left and the rest of the lake on the right. As the pressure on the dam increases, everyone waits for the day it will rupture again.

In recent years the surge in the number of visitors to Glaciar Perito Moreno has created a crowded scene that is not always conducive to reflective encounters with nature's majesty. Although the glacier remains spectacular, savvy travelers would do well to minimize time at the madhouse that the viewing area

Perito Moreno glacier is the showstopper of El Calafate, Argentina.

becomes at midday in high season, and instead encounter the glacier by boat or on a mini-trekking excursion. Better yet, rent a car and get an early start to beat the tour buses, or visit Perito Moreno in the off-season when a spectacular rupture is just as likely as in midsummer, and you won't have to crane over other people's heads to see it. ⊠ *El Calafate* 🚉 *500 pesos park entrance.*

Glaciar Upsala

NATURE SIGHT | The largest glacier in South America, Glaciar Upsala is 55 km (35 miles) long and 10 km (6 miles) wide, and accessible only by boat. Daily cruises depart from Puerto Banderas (40 km [25 miles] west of El Calafate via R11) for the 2½-hour trip. Dodging floating icebergs (*tempanos*), some as large as a small island, the boats maneuver as close as they dare to the wall of ice that rises from the aqua-green water of Lago Argentino. The seven glaciers that feed the lake deposit their debris into the runoff, causing the water to cloud with minerals ground to fine powder by the

glacier's moraine (the accumulation of earth and stones left by the glacier). Condors and black-chested buzzard eagles build their nests in the rocky cliffs above the lake. When the boat stops for lunch at Onelli Bay, don't miss the walk behind the restaurant into a wild landscape of small glaciers and milky rivers carrying chunks of ice from four glaciers into Lago Onelli. Glaciar Upsala has diminished in size in recent years. ⊠ *El Calafate* 🚉 *Cruises start from 13500 pesos.*

Lago Roca

NATURE SIGHT | This little-visited lake is inside the national park just south of Brazo Rico, 46 km (29 miles) from El Calafate. The area receives about five times as much annual precipitation as El Calafate, creating a relatively lush climate of green meadows by the lakeshore, where locals come to picnic and cast for trophy rainbow and lake trout. Don't miss a hike into the hills behind the lake—the view of dark-blue Lago Roca backed by a pale-green inlet of Lago Argentino with the Perito Moreno glacier and jagged snowcapped peaks beyond is truly outstanding. ✉ *El Calafate.*

Laguna Nimez Reserva Natural

NATURE PRESERVE | A marshy area on the shore of Lago Argentino just a short walk from downtown El Calafate, the Laguna Nimez Reserva Natural is home to many species of waterfowl, including black-necked swans, buff-necked ibises, southern lapwings, and flamingos. Road construction along its edge and the rapidly advancing town threaten to stifle this avian oasis, but it's still a haven for bird-watchers and a relaxing walk in the early morning or late afternoon. Strolling along footpaths among grazing horses and flocks of birds may not be as intense an experience as, say, trekking on a glacier, but a trip to the lagoon provides a good sense of the local landscape. Don't forget your binoculars and a telephoto lens. ✉ *1 km (½ mile) north of downtown, just off Av. Alem, El Calafate* ☎ *2902/495–536* 🎫 *500 pesos.*

★ **Parque Nacional Los Glaciares** (*Los Glaciares National Park*)

NATIONAL PARK | As the name suggests, this national park is renowned for being the home of 47 glaciers, with almost a third of the entire park covered in ice. A giant ice cap located in the Andes Mountains, the world's largest outside of Antarctica and Greenland, feeds all 47 of the glaciers, which snake through the Patagonian steppe and sub-polar forests, eventually crumbling into milky blue glacial lakes. A UNESCO World Heritage site, it is also the largest national park in Argentina and spans over 2,500 square miles, encompassing the territories running from El Chaltén down to El Calafate, on the border of Chile's Torres del Paine. Spotting the glaciers is the highlight of any visit to the park, with the most accessible one being Perito Moreno, which can be reached by road. Visiting the Upsala and Spegazzini glaciers requires a boat journey, and the Viedma Glacier can be seen from hiking paths on the shore of Lake Viedma, a route that is particularly popular with trekkers and climbers who journey onward to Mount Fitzroy and Cerro Torre (which are also within the park limits). Lago del Desert and Lago Roca are the other two most visited sites in the park, but outside of these locations the majority of the park is left wonderfully unexplored and untouched. There are few places to stay in the park with the exception of a few estancias and campsites at Lago Roca and on the hiking routes of El Chaltén. Beyond the stunning landscapes, the park is the natural habitat of guanacos, ñandúes, cougars, and the South American gray fox, as well as more than 100 different species of birds. The park is open all year-round, although winter frequently sees snowfall as the temperature drops below freezing. ✉ *Los Glaciares National Park* ☎ *02902/491–005* 🌐 *www.losglaciares.com/en/parque* 🎫 *2520 pesos (buy tickets online at www.ventaweb.apn.gob.ar/reserva/parques).*

🍴 Restaurants

Casimiro Biguá

$$$$ | **ARGENTINE** | This restaurant and wine bar boasts a hipper-than-thou interior and modern menu serving such delights as Patagonian lamb with calafate sauce (calafate is a local wild berry). The Casimiro Biguá Parrilla, down the street from the main restaurant, has a similar trendy feel, but you can recognize the *parrilla* by the *cordero al asador* (spit-roasted lamb) displayed in the window. **Known for:** typical asado atmosphere; fantastic roast lamb; big portions. [$] *Average main: pesos2000* ✉ *Av. Libertador 963, El Calafate* ☎ *2902/492–590* 🌐 *www.casimirobigua.com.*

Isabel cocina al disco

$$$$ | **ARGENTINE** | It takes a lot of moxie to open a restaurant not serving *cordero,* barbecue, or pizza in Patagonia, and former "fancy" chefs José and Leandro show they have just that with their homey restaurant, which uses vintage plow wheels to cook a traditional and ultimately delicious stew-style dish known as *al disco*. The *al disco* menu offers all sorts of meats and veggies cooked in beer, red wine, or white wine; more creative and quasi-modern options like Bife al Napolitana; or you can create your own. And you've got to love a restaurant that tells you not to bother with starters but rather just dunk your bread in the disco sauce. **Known for:** massive portions; signature stew dish cooked several creative ways; charming and lively atmosphere. $ *Average main: pesos2500* ⊠ *Perito Moreno 95, El Calafate* ☎ *2902/489–000* ⊕ *www.isabelcocinaaldisco.com* ◔ *Closed Wed.*

La Lechuza

$$$$ | ARGENTINE | FAMILY | This bustling spot is where locals go for their pizza joint fix, thanks to the typical Argentine-style pizza of thick crust, and layered with stringy cheese. Their empanadas are just as good—pick up a few and you have the perfect pastry pick-me-up during a long day of exploring. **Known for:** crowds of locals; fantastic empanadas; classic Argentine pizza. $ *Average main: pesos950* ⊠ *Av. Libertador at 1 de Mayo, El Calafate* ☎ *2902/491–610.*

La Tablita

$$$$ | ARGENTINE | It's a couple of extra blocks from downtown and across a little white bridge, but this *parrilla* is where the locals go for a special night out to watch their food as it's cooking; Patagonian lamb and beef ribs roast gaucho-style on frames hanging over a circular asador, and an enormous grill along the back wall is full of steaks, chorizos, and *morcilla* (blood sausage). The whole place is filled with a warm glow despite the lackluster decor. **Known for:** big crowds on weekends; great traditional parrilla; tasty empanadas. $ *Average main: pesos800* ⊠ *Coronel Rosales 28, El Calafate* ☎ *2902/491–065* ⊕ *www.la-tablita.com.*

La Zaina

$$$$ | ARGENTINE | With a focus on modern and well-presented Patagonian cuisine, good cocktails, and a range of wines from Argentina, there's a lot to love at La Zaina. Hearty meats like Patagonian lamb and Argentine steak are served with a delicate touch. **Known for:** artfully presented dishes; modern and healthy Patagonian cuisine; nice wine list. $ *Average main: pesos1900* ⊠ *Gdor Gregores 1057, El Calafate* ☎ *2902/496–789* ◔ *Closed on Sun.*

Pura Vida

$$$$ | ARGENTINE | Bohemian music, homemade cooking, and colorful patchwork cushions set the tone for this unpretentious, friendly restaurant several blocks from downtown. You'll be surrounded by funky artwork, couples whispering under low-hung lights, and laid-back but efficient staff as you try to decide which big-enough-to-share dish you'll order while working your way through a great dome of steaming bread. **Known for:** fun and eclectic decor; lamb stew inside a pumpkin; great vegetarian options. $ *Average main: pesos850* ⊠ *Av. Libertador 1876, El Calafate* ☎ *2902/493–356* ⊕ *www.puravidaavlibertador1876. negocio.site/* ◔ *Closed Wed. No lunch.*

🛏 Hotels

★ Eolo

$$$$ | HOTEL | A luxury lodge on the road to Perito Moreno, Eolo offers full-board stays in handsome accommodations where you can take in the beauty of Patagonia's vast, empty lands and see Lago Argentino in the distance. **Pros:** endless acres of estate to explore; beautiful location; luxury service. **Cons:** far from town or any services; no drinks included in meal plans; expensive. $ *Rooms from: US$1,265* ⊠ *Ruta Provincial N 11, Km 23,000, El Calafate* ☎ *2902/492–042* ⊕ *www.eolo.com.ar* ◔ *Closed May–Sept.* ⇥ *17 rooms.*

★ Estancia Cristina
$$$ | **HOTEL** | Arriving at Estancia Cristina by catamaran on Lago Argentina past fields of ice and imposing mountains is just the beginning of a remarkable Patagonian adventure: on arrival you'll be treated to cozy accommodations, delicious cuisine, and unbeatable excursions to little-explored corners of the park. **Pros:** incredible views from well-appointed rooms; fantastic excursions; excellent restaurant. **Cons:** no alcoholic drinks included in price; expensive; patchy Wi-Fi. [$] *Rooms from: US$750* ✉ *Punta Bandera, El Calafate* ☎ *2902/491–133* 🌐 *www.estanciacristina.com* 🕒 *Closed mid-Apr.–mid-Oct.* 🛏 *20 rooms* 🍴 *All-Inclusive.*

Hotel Kau-Yatún
$$ | **HOTEL** | This converted ranch is nestled in a quiet tree-lined valley by a stream yet lies just six blocks from the main street and offers a full schedule of mountain biking, horseback riding, and four-wheel-drive expeditions in the 42,000-acre Estancia 25 de Mayo that lies just behind the hotel. **Pros:** central location; good value; nice details. **Cons:** Wi-Fi and modern amenities sparse; lost a bit of personality from chain takeover; water pressure is only adequate. [$] *Rooms from: US$124* ✉ *25 de Mayo, El Calafate* ☎ *2902/491–059* 🌐 *www.kauyatun.com* 🕒 *Closed Apr.–Sept.* 🛏 *44 rooms* 🍴 *Free Breakfast.*

Kosten Aike
$$ | **HOTEL** | Lined with wooden balconies, high-beamed ceilings, and a slate floor, this hotel is a paragon of Andean Patagonian architecture, while a sunny rooftop spa, gym, and spacious Jacuzzi offer great views over town to Lago Argentino. **Pros:** good value at this price point; large rooms and spa; central location. **Cons:** some rooms get outside noise; rooms are simply furnished; dining room decor is uninspired. [$] *Rooms from: US$145* ✉ *G. Moyano 1243, at 25 de Mayo, El Calafate* ☎ *2902/492–424* 🌐 *www.kostenaike.com.ar* 🕒 *Closed May–Sept.* 🛏 *80 rooms* 🍴 *Free Breakfast.*

Los Ponchos Apart Boutique
$$$ | **B&B/INN** | Cozy and handsomely designed two-floor apartments in this boutique complex have beautiful views over Lago Argentina and offer some independence and privacy with a self-catering kitchen and homey, gaucho-chic decoration. **Pros:** private; warm service; cozy atmosphere. **Cons:** pricey compared to local competition; street dogs noisy at night; a long walk from town. [$] *Rooms from: US$245* ✉ *Los Alamos 3321, El Calafate* ☎ *2902/496–330* 🌐 *www.losponchosapart.com.ar* 🕒 *Closed May–Sept.* 🛏 *11 units* 🍴 *Free Breakfast.*

Madre Tierra
$$ | **B&B/INN** | **FAMILY** | The friendly welcome from the owners makes staying at this B&B feel like visiting a friend's home (with great attention to detail in design and well-chosen furnishings). **Pros:** authentic; personalized and friendly service; central location. **Cons:** small rooms for price; expensive; walls are thin and noise travels. [$] *Rooms from: US$185* ✉ *9 de Julio 239, El Calafate* ☎ *2902/489–880* 🌐 *www.madretierrapatagonia.com* 🛏 *7 rooms* 🍴 *Free Breakfast.*

Mirador del Lago
$$ | **HOTEL** | Great views across the lake are the main selling point of this smartly kept hotel, where each lakeside vista has a seated window or armchair so you can watch the beautiful sunset colors dance across the sky. **Pros:** open all year; good value; modern. **Cons:** lots of steps; impersonal service; a bit of a walk from town. [$] *Rooms from: US$182* ✉ *Av. del Libertador 2047, El Calafate* ☎ *2902/493–213* 🌐 *www.miradordellago.com.ar* 🛏 *68 rooms* 🍴 *Free Breakfast.*

Nibepo Aike

$$$$ | ALL-INCLUSIVE | FAMILY | This lovely estancia is an hour and a half from El Calafate in a bucolic valley overlooking Lago Roca and backed by snowcapped mountain peaks; where sheep and horses graze, friendly gauchos give horse-racing and sheep-shearing demonstrations, and every evening a communal table is laid for a supper of spit-roasted locally reared lamb. **Pros:** friendly guides and excellent horseback riding; spectacular scenery; classic estancia experience. **Cons:** patchy Wi-Fi; restaurant has limited offerings; expensive for simple amenities. $ *Rooms from: US$375* ✉ *For reservations:, Av. Libertador 1215, El Calafate* ☎ *2902/492–797* ⊕ *www.nibepoaike.com.ar* ۞ *Closed May–Sept.* ⤢ *10 rooms* ⎮◎⎮ *Free Breakfast.*

Patagonia Queen

$$ | B&B/INN | An elegant, Patagonian-style home on a quiet street just two blocks from downtown, this hotel checks all the boxes: service is first-class; it's a good value for the price; accommodations are clean and comfortable, and little details like a Jacuzzi tub in the room make your stay a real pleasure. **Pros:** fun extras like Ping-Pong and pool tables; perfect location; excellent breakfast. **Cons:** some rooms don't have much of a view; gym is small; slow Wi-Fi. $ *Rooms from: US$120* ✉ *Av. Padre Agostini 49, El Calafate* ☎ *2902/496–701* ⊕ *www.patagoniaqueen.com* ⤢ *20 rooms* ⎮◎⎮ *Free Breakfast.*

Posada los Alamos

$$ | HOTEL | FAMILY | Surrounded by tall, leafy alamo trees, this enormous complex incorporates a country manor house, half a dozen convention rooms, a spa, and an indoor swimming pool, but for what it has in amenities Los Alamos lacks in service and attention. **Pros:** long breakfast hours; spa and gym; beautiful gardens. **Cons:** inattentive staff; small rooms; tired furnishings and decor. $ *Rooms from: US$175* ✉ *Guatti 1135,*

El Calafate ☎ *2902/491–144* ⊕ *www.posadalosalamos.com* ⤢ *144 rooms* ⎮◎⎮ *Free Breakfast.*

 ## Activities

BOAT TOURS

Glaciares Gourmet

BOATING | If fine dining and sipping wine while admiring the glaciers is your style, this is the no-effort-required cruise for you. With a maximum of 28 passengers, the deluxe cruise liner visits Spegazzini and Upsala glaciers and stops for a short leg-stretching walk at beauty spot Puesto de las Vacas before the six-course gourmet lunch with wine. If a full day isn't enough, you can opt for the two-night cruise option. ✉ *Cruceros Marpatag, 9 de Julio (Local 4, Galleria de los Pajaros), El Calafate* ☎ *2902/492–118* ⊕ *www.crucerosmarpatag.com* ▣ *From 15000 pesos.*

Safari Náutico

BOATING | Boats depart from a small port 7 km (4 miles) from Perito Moreno glacier and take tourists on an hour-long cruise around the glacier's south face for a closer inspection of the advancing glacier and floating icebergs. On a good day, you can stand on the deck for the best up-close photo opportunities. Tours happen all year and can be reserved at the port or in advance in the downtown office or other tour agencies. ✉ *Hielo y Aventura, Av. Libertador 935, El Calafate* ☎ *2902/492–205* ⊕ *www.hieloyaventura.com* ▣ *From 3000 pesos.*

Solo Patagonia

BOATING | With two different full-day boat excursions, Solo Patagonia has been navigating the milky waters for years. Their fleet of large cruisers offers access to some of the best views of the Perito Moreno, Upsala, and Spegazzini glaciers from October to March. ✉ *Av. Libertador 1265, El Calafate* ☎ *2902/491–155* ⊕ *www.solopatagonia.com* ▣ *From 13500 pesos.*

CAMPING
Camping Lago Roca
NATURE SIGHT | There are gorgeous campsites, simple cabins, fishing-tackle rentals, hot showers, and a basic restaurant at Camping Lago Roca. Make reservations in advance if visiting over the Christmas holidays; at other times the campground is seldom crowded. In high season Cal Tur offer shuttles from Lago Roca to Perito Moreno. For more comfortable accommodations, you can arrange to stay at the Nibepo Aike Estancia at the western end of Lago Roca, about 5 km (3 miles) past the campground. The national park entrance fee is collected only on the road to Perito Moreno Glacier or at Puerto Banderas, where cruises depart, so admission to the Lago Roca corner of the park is free. ⊠ *El Calafate* ☎ *2902/499–500* ☼ *Closed May–Sept.*

HIKING
Although it's possible to find trails along the shore of Lago Argentino and in the hills south and west of town, these hikes traverse a rather barren landscape and are not terribly interesting. The mountain peaks and forests are in the park, an hour by car from El Calafate. If you want to lace up your boots in your hotel, walk outside, and hit the trail, go to El Chaltén—it's a much better base than El Calafate for hikes in the national park. Good hiking trails are accessible from the camping areas and cabins by Lago Roca, 50 km (31 miles) from El Calafate.

HORSEBACK RIDING AND ESTANCIAS
Cabalgata en Patagonia
HORSEBACK RIDING | Anything from a short day ride along Lago Argentino to a weeklong camping excursion in and around the glaciers can be arranged in El Calafate. ⊠ *Av. Libertador 4315, El Calafate* ☎ *2902/493–278* ⊕ *www.cabalgataenpatagonia.com.ar.*

Estancia El Galpón del Glaciar
HORSEBACK RIDING | This estancia welcomes guests overnight or for the day—for a horseback ride, bird-watching, or an afternoon program that includes a demonstration of sheep dogs working, a walk to the lake with a naturalist, sheep-shearing, and dinner in the former sheep-shearing barn served right off the asador by knife-wielding gauchos. ⊠ *Ruta 11, Km 22, El Calafate* ☎ *11/5217–6720* ⊕ *www.elgalpondelglaciar.com.ar.*

Nibepo Aike
HORSEBACK RIDING | This pretty estancia an hour and a half from El Calafate offers a range of horseback experiences from hour-long excursions to full-day, nine-hour rides to view glaciers in the distance. It's possible to visit Nibepo Aike by booking a day trip at the office in downtown El Calafate, or you can stay overnight at the estancia. ⊠ *53 km (31 miles) from El Calafate near Lago Roca on Ruta 15, El Calafate* ☎ *2902/492–797* ⊕ *www.nibepoaike.com.ar.*

Provincial Tourist Office
HORSEBACK RIDING | *Estancias turísticas* (tourist ranches) are ideal for a combination of horseback riding, ranch activities, and local excursions. Information on all the estancias can be obtained from Estancias de Santa Cruz in Buenos Aires, or on the website. ⊠ *Reconquista 642* ☎ *11/5237–4043* ⊕ *www.estanciasdesantacruz.com.*

ICE TREKKING
Hielo y Aventura
HIKING & WALKING | For the most up-close-and-personal experience with Perito Moreno glacier, book yourself onto an ice trekking day where you'll don crampons and walk over the glacier studying crevasses and ice lakes before finishing with a whiskey on the rocks using ice from the glacier. The full day Mini Trekking excursion includes a 90-minute ice trek, a short trek in the forest, a 20-minute boat ride, and a transfer to the park from your hotel. You'll

have to pay your own park entrance, bring a packed lunch, and wear the right clothing (crampons are provided), but you also get over an hour to enjoy the view of Perito Moreno Glacier from the park. For a more in-depth and challenging ice day, opt for the Big Ice trek, which includes more time on the ice and ducking through bright-blue ice tunnels. ⊠ *Av. Libertador 935, El Calafate* ☎ *2902/492–205* ⊕ *www.hieloyaventura.com* ✉ *From 22500 pesos.*

KAYAKING
Mil Outdoor

KAYAKING | Those brave enough to get in the milky ice waters can get dropped off by a boat on the glacier's edge and take a two-hour guided kayaking excursion with this outfitter, weather permitting (not available in June and July). ⊠ *Av. Libertador 1037, El Calafate* ☎ *2902/491– 446* ⊕ *www.miloutdoor.com.ar* ✉ *From 15900 pesos.*

LAND ROVER EXCURSIONS
Mil Outdoor

FOUR-WHEELING | If pedaling uphill sounds like too much work, check out the Land Rover expeditions offered by Mil Outdoor October to April. These trips use large tour trucks to follow dirt tracks into the hills above town for stunning views of Lago Argentino. On a clear day, you can even see the peaks of Cerro Torre and Cerro Fitzroy on the horizon. During the winter, the same company (also known as Calafate Mountain Park) runs a children's snow park with sledding and snowmobiling. ⊠ *Av. Libertador 1037, El Calafate* ☎ *2902/491–446* ⊕ *www.miloutdoor.com.ar* ✉ *From 4800 pesos.*

MOUNTAIN BIKING
Bike Rental

BIKING | Mountain biking is popular along the dirt roads and mountain paths that lead to the lakes, glaciers, and ranches. There are several places to rent bikes in town; two options are **HLS Travesias** (Perito Moreno 95) and **E-Bike Calafate** (Av. Libertador 932). ⊠ *El Calafate.*

El Chaltén, Argentina

222 km (138 miles) north of El Calafate.

Founded in 1985, El Chaltén is Argentina's newest town, and it's growing at an astounding rate. Originally just a few shacks, lodges, and livestock ranches near the entrance to Parque Nacional Los Glaciares, the town has become a tourist center in its own right and is starting to fill a steep-walled valley near Cerro Torre and Cerro Fitzroy, two of the most impressive peaks in Patagonia.

Famous for the exploits of rock climbers who have been coming here since the 1950s to climb some of the most difficult rock walls in the world, the range is now drawing hikers whose more earthbound ambitions run to dazzling mountain scenery and unscripted encounters with wildlife including condors, Patagonian parrots, red-crested woodpeckers, and the *huemul,* an endangered deer species.

GETTING HERE AND AROUND
The three-hour car or bus trip to El Chaltén from El Calafate makes staying at least one night here a good idea. The only gas, food, and restroom facilities en route are at La Leona, a historically significant ranch 110 km (68 miles) from El Calafate where Butch Cassidy and the Sundance Kid once hid from the long arm of the law.

Before you cross the bridge into town over Río Fitzroy, stop at the Parque Nacional office. It's extremely well organized and staffed by bilingual rangers who can help you plan your mountain treks and point you to accommodations and restaurants in town. It's an essential stop; orientation talks are given in coordination with arriving buses, which automatically stop here before continuing on to the bus depot.

There's only one ATM in town (it's in the bus station), and it's in high demand; because of servicing schedules, on the weekend El Chaltén runs into the same cash availability problems that El Calafate does, though on a smaller scale.

■ TIP→ During the week, stockpile the cash you'll need for the weekend, or bring it with you if you're arriving between midday Friday and midday Monday.

ESSENTIALS

VISITOR INFORMATION Parque Nacional Office. ✉ *Av. M.M. de Güemes 21, El Chaltén* ☎ *2962/493–004.*

Sights

Cerro Torre and Cerro Fitzroy
TRAIL | You don't need a guide to do the classic treks to Cerro Torre and Cerro Fitzroy, each about six to eight hours round-trip out of El Chaltén. If your legs feel up to it the day you do the Fitzroy walk, tack on an hour of steep switchbacks to Mirador Tres Lagos, the lookout with the best views of Mt. Fitzroy and its glacial lakes. Both routes, plus the Mirador and various side trails, can be combined in a two- or three-day trip. ✉ *El Chaltén.*

Chorillo del Salta (*Trickling Falls*)
WATERFALL | Just 4 km (2.5 miles) north of town on the road to Lago del Desierto, the Chorillo del Salta waterfall is no Iguazú, but the area is extremely pleasant and sheltered from the wind. A short hike uphill leads to secluded river pools and sun-splashed rocks where locals enjoy picnics on their days off. If you don't feel up to a more ambitious hike, the short stroll to the falls is an excellent way to spend the better part of an afternoon. Pack a bottle of wine and a sandwich and enjoy the solitude. ✉ *El Chaltén.*

Laguna del Desierto (*Lake of the Desert*)
BODY OF WATER | A lovely lake surrounded by lush forest, complete with orchids and mossy trees, the Laguna del Desierto is 37 km (23 miles) north of El Chaltén on R23, a dirt road. Hotels in El Chaltén can arrange a trip for about $50 for the day. Locals recommend visiting Lago del Desierto on a rainy day, when more ambitious hikes are not an option and the dripping green misty forest is extra mysterious. ✉ *El Chaltén.*

Restaurants

Aonikenk
$$$$ | **ARGENTINE** | **FAMILY** | In a dark wooden dining hall you'll share hearty steaks, warming soups, and wine poured from penguin-shaped ceramic jugs in a family restaurant that includes a hostel upstairs. It's rustic, and the food is not spectacular, but you can't beat the friendly atmosphere in what is easily El Chaltén's largest and most popular restaurant. **Known for:** open hours even in the off-season; family-friendly atmosphere; standard Argentine cuisine. [$] *Average main: pesos950* ✉ *Av. M.M. de Güemes 23, El Chaltén* ☎ *2962/493–070* 💳 *No credit cards.*

★ La Cervecería Chaltén
$$$$ | **ARGENTINE** | This successful microbrewery is famous in the region for its brews and comfort food. Of course, it's not just the hops bringing in the crowds; they also cook up delicious soups, snacks, empanadas, and a great *locro* (hearty traditional northern Argentine stew). **Known for:** welcoming atmosphere; impressive craft beer; hearty comfort food. [$] *Average main: pesos550* ✉ *San Martín 320, El Chaltén* ☎ *2962/493–109* 🕒 *Closed June–Oct.*

Hotels

Aguas Arriba Lodge
$$$$ | **HOTEL** | Accessible only by boat or a three-hour trek, Aguas Arriba has a privileged location right on the Lago del Desierto, with a glimmer of Mt. Fitzroy in the distance. **Pros:** excellent excursions; fantastic location; attended by owners. **Cons:** no phone signal; private shuttle to lake required in addition to walk/boat; noise travels between rooms. [$] *Rooms*

Cerro Fitzroy can be spotted beyond the entrance to El Chaltén.

from: US$957 ✉ *Lago del Desierto, El Chaltén* ☎ *11/4152–5697 Buenos Aires* 🌐 *www.aguasarribalodge.com* 🕒 *Closed mid-Apr.–Sept.* 🛏 *6 rooms* 🍴 *Free Breakfast.*

★ Los Cerros

$$$$ | B&B/INN | The most upscale option in El Chaltén, this mountain lodge is a worthy upgrade if you are after more than just a comfortable bed, especially for the spa and restaurant with expansive views of the mountain valley. **Pros:** spa and restaurant on-site; great location; river and mountain views. **Cons:** no TV in rooms; you have to walk up a hill to get to the hotel; not all rooms have mountain views. [$] *Rooms from: US$460* ✉ *Av. San Martin 260, El Chaltén* ☎ *911/5460–0213 Whatsapp* 🌐 *www.loscerrosdelchalten.com.ar* 🕒 *Closed April–Oct.* 🛏 *44 rooms* 🍴 *Free Breakfast.*

Nothofagus

$ | B&B/INN | A simple B&B off the main road, Nothofagus is named after the southern beech tree, and the lodge has a rough-hewn, woodsy feel with exposed beams and leaves stamped into the lampshades. **Pros:** good value; great views; bright and sunny breakfast room. **Cons:** simple breakfast; spartan rooms and bathrooms, some of which are shared; staff energy too low for some. [$] *Rooms from: US$75* ✉ *Hensen, at Riquelme, El Chaltén* ☎ *2962/493–087* 🌐 *www.nothofagusbb.com.ar* 💳 *No credit cards* 🕒 *Closed May–Sept.* 🛏 *9 rooms* 🍴 *Free Breakfast.*

Posada Lunajuim

$ | HOTEL | A traditional A-frame roof keeps the lid on a funky, modern lodge filled with contemporary artwork, exposed brick masonry, and a spacious lounge and dining room complete with a roaring fireplace and a library stacked with an intriguing mix of travel books. **Pros:** awesome food and wine list; great lounge area; friendly staff. **Cons:** slow Wi-Fi; baths are quite small; not all rooms have views. [$] *Rooms from: US$115* ✉ *Trevisan 45, El Chaltén* ☎ *2962/493–047* 🌐 *www.lunajuim.com* 🛏 *26 rooms* 🍴 *Free Breakfast.*

Activities

El Chaltén owes its existence to those who wanted a base for trekking into this corner of Los Glaciares National Park, specifically Cerro Torre and Cerro Fitzroy. It's no surprise that nearly everyone who comes here considers hiking up to those two mountains to be the main event—though the *locro* (hearty stew) and micro-brews at the end of the day are a plus.

HIKING
Both long and short hikes on well-trodden trails lead to lakes, glaciers, and stunning viewpoints. There are two main hikes, one to the base of Cerro Fitzroy, the other to a windswept glacial lake at the base of Cerro Torre. Both hikes climb into the hills above town, and excellent views start after only about an hour on either trail. The six-hour round-trip hike to the base camp for Cerro Torre at Laguna Torre has (weather permitting) dramatic views of Torres Standhart, Adelas, Grande, and Solo.

Trails start in town and are very well marked, so if you stick to the main path there is little danger of getting lost. Just be careful of high winds and exposed rocks that can get slippery in bad weather. The eight-hour hike to the base camp for Cerro Fitzroy passes Laguna Capri and ends at Laguna de los Tres, where you can enjoy an utterly spectacular view of the granite tower. If you have time for only one ambitious hike, this is probably the best choice, though the last kilometer of trail is very steep. At campsites in the hills above town, hardy souls can pitch a tent for the night and enjoy sunset and dawn views of the mountain peaks. Ask about current camping regulations and advisories at the national park office before setting off with a tent in your rucksack. Finally, use latrines where provided, and under no circumstance should you ever think about starting a fire—a large section of forest near Cerro Torre was devastated several years ago when a foolish hiker tried to dispose of toilet paper with a match.

MOUNTAIN CLIMBING
Casa de Guias
MOUNTAIN CLIMBING | A guide is required if you want to enter the ice field or trek on any of the glaciers in Los Glaciares National Park. Casa de Guias is a group of professional, multilingual guides who offer fully equipped multiday treks covering all the classic routes in the national park, and longer trips exploring the ice field. They even offer a taste of big-wall climbing on one of the spires in the Fitzroy range. ✉ *Av. San Martín 310, El Chaltén* ☎ *2962/493–118* ⊕ *www. casadeguias.com.ar.*

El Chaltén Mountain Guides
MOUNTAIN CLIMBING | Five mountain guides offer expeditions in and around El Chaltén, as well as many other destinations in Argentina. One-day and multiday treks and ascents to rock and ice-climbing expeditions are available. In the winter they also offer backcountry skiing tours. ✉ *Rio de las Vueltas 212, El Chaltén* ☎ *2962/493–329* ⊕ *www.ecmg. com.ar.*

Ushuaia, Argentina

914 km (567 miles) south of El Calafate.

At 55 degrees latitude south, Ushuaia (pronounced oo-swy-ah) is closer to the South Pole than to Argentina's northern border with Bolivia. It is the capital and tourism base for Tierra del Fuego, the island at the southernmost tip of Argentina.

Although its stark physical beauty is striking, Tierra del Fuego's historical allure is based more on its mythical past than on rugged reality. The island was inhabited for 6,000 years by the Y·mana, Haush, Selk'nam, and Alakaluf peoples. But in 1902 Argentina, eager to populate Patagonia to bolster its territorial claims,

Just outside Ushuaia, the area surrounding Glaciar Martial is a popular place to hike.

moved to initiate an Ushuaian penal colony, establishing the permanent settlement of its most southern territories and, by implication, everything in between.

When the prison closed in 1947, Ushuaia had a population of about 3,000, made up mainly of former inmates and prison staff. Today the Indigenous peoples of Darwin's "missing link" theory are long gone—wiped out by diseases brought by settlers and by indifference to their plight—and the 75,000 residents of Ushuaia are hitching their star to tourism.

The city rightly (if perhaps too loudly) promotes itself as the southernmost city in the world (Puerto Williams, a few miles south on the Chilean side of the Beagle Channel, is closer in size to a small town). You can make your way to the tourism office to get your clichéd, but oh-so-necessary, "Southernmost City in the World" passport stamp. Ushuaia feels like a frontier boomtown, at heart still a rugged, weather-beaten fishing village, but exhibiting the frayed edges of a city that quadrupled in size in the

'70s and '80s and just keeps growing. Unpaved portions of Ruta 3, the last stretch of the Pan-American Highway, which connects Alaska to Tierra del Fuego, are finally being paved. The summer months (December through March) draw more than 300,000 visitors, and dozens of cruise ships. The city is trying to extend those visits with events like March's Marathon at the End of the World and by increasing the gamut of winter activities buoyed by the excellent snow conditions.

A terrific trail winds through the town up to the Martial Glacier, where a ski lift can help cut down a steep kilometer of your journey. The chaotic and contradictory urban landscape includes a handful of luxury hotels amid the concrete of public housing projects. Scores of "sled houses" (wooden shacks) sit precariously on upright piers, ready for speedy displacement to a different site. But there are also many small, picturesque homes with tiny, carefully tended gardens. Many of the newer homes are built in a

Swiss-chalet style, reinforcing the idea that this is a town into which tourism has breathed new life. At the same time, the weather-worn pastel colors that dominate the town's landscape remind you that Ushuaia was once just a tiny fishing village, snuggled at the end of the Earth.

As you stand on the banks of the Canal Beagle (Beagle Channel) near Ushuaia, the spirit of the farthest corner of the world takes hold. What stands out is the light: at sundown the landscape is cast in a subdued, sensual tone; everything feels closer, softer, and more human in dimension despite the vastness of the setting. The snowcapped mountains reflect the setting sun back onto a stream rolling into the channel, as nearby peaks echo their image—on a windless day—in the still waters.

Above the city rise the last mountains of the Andean Cordillera, and just south and west of Ushuaia they finally vanish into the often-stormy sea. Snow whitens the peaks well into summer. Nature is the principal attraction here, with trekking, fishing, horseback riding, wildlife spotting, and sailing among the most rewarding activities, especially in the Parque Nacional Tierra del Fuego (Tierra del Fuego National Park).

GETTING HERE AND AROUND

Arriving by air is the preferred option. Ushuaia's Aeropuerto Internacional Malvinas Argentinas (*Peninsula de Ushuaia 2901/431–232*) is 5 km (3 miles) from town and is served daily by flights to and from Buenos Aires, Río Gallegos, El Calafate, Trelew, and Comodoro Rivadavía. There are also flights to Santiago via Punta Arenas in Chile. A taxi into town costs about 250 pesos.

Arriving by road on the Ruta Nacional 3 involves Argentine and Chilean immigrations/customs, a ferry crossing, and a lot of time. Buses to and from Punta Arenas make the trip five days a week in summer, four in winter. Daily buses to Río Gallegos leave in the predawn hours, and multiple border crossings mean an all-day journey. Check prices on the 55-minute flight, which can be a much better value. There is no central bus terminal, just individual company locations.

There is no regular passenger transport (besides cruises) by sea.

BUS SERVICES Tecni-Austral. ✉ *Juana Genoveva Fadul 40, Ushuaia* ☏ *2901/608–088* ⊕ *www.tecniaustral. com.*

CRUISE TRAVEL TO USHUAIA

As you sail into Ushuaia, the captain almost always takes you around the picturesque lighthouse at the "end of the world": a beacon for the southernmost city perched on the edge of the Canal Beagle. The port is just two blocks from the main street, leaving you in a central location once you disembark.

Before undertaking the five-minute walk into town, stop at the tourism office (right in front of the port), where you can gather information and take advantage of the free Wi-Fi. Most city attractions can be reached on foot, although if you're spending the night here, you may need to take a taxi to your hotel. If you're in Ushuaia only for the day, lace on some good shoes, as the city is built on a hill and requires calves of steel.

ESSENTIALS

VISITOR INFORMATION Ushuaia Tourist Office. ✉ *Prefectura Naval 470, Ushuaia* ☏ *2901/437–666, 2901/432–001* ⊕ *www. turismoushuaia.com.*

 Sights

Antigua Casa Beban (*Old Beban House*)
HISTORIC HOME | One of Ushuaia's original houses, the Antigua Casa Beban long served as the city's social center. Built between 1911 and 1913 by Fortunato Beban, it's said he ordered the house through a Swiss catalog. In the 1980s the Beban family donated the house to the

Boats cruise to Canal Beagle from the harbor of Ushuaia.

city to avoid demolition. It was moved to its current location along the coast and restored, and is now a cultural center with art exhibits. ⊠ *Maipú at Pluschow, Ushuaia* ☎ *2901/431–386* ✉ *Free* ⊙ *Closed weekends.*

★ **Canal Beagle**

BODY OF WATER | Several tour operators run trips along the Canal Beagle, on which you can get a startling close-up view of sea mammals and birds on **Isla de los Lobos, Isla de los Pájaros,** and near **Les Eclaireurs Lighthouse.** Catamarans, motorboats, and sailboats usually leave from the tourist pier at 9:30, 10, 3, and 3:30 (trips depend on weather; few trips go in winter). Some trips include hikes on the islands. Check with the tourist office for the latest details; you can also book through any of the local travel agencies or scope out the offers yourself by walking around the kiosks on the tourist pier. ⊠ *Ushuaia* ✉ *From 6200 pesos.*

Canal Fun

SCENIC DRIVE | This unconventional tour goes to Monte Olivia, the tallest

mountain along the Canal Beagle, rising 1,358 meters (4,455 feet) above sea level. You also pass the Five Brothers Mountains and go through the Garibaldi Pass, which begins at the Rancho Hambre, climbs into the mountain range, and ends with a spectacular view of Lago Escondido. From here you continue on to Lago Fagnano through the countryside past sawmills and lumber yards. To do this tour in a four-wheel-drive truck with an excellent bilingual guide, contact Canal Fun; you'll drive *through* Lago Fagnano (about 3 feet of water at this point) to a secluded cabin on the shore and have a delicious asado, complete with wine and dessert. In winter they can also organize tailor-made dogsledding and cross-country-skiing trips. ⊠ *Roca 136, Ushuaia* ☎ *2901/435–777* ⊕ *www. canalfun.com.*

Estancia Harberton (*Harberton Ranch*)

FARM/RANCH | This property—50,000 acres of coastal marshland and wooded hillsides—was a late-19th-century gift from the Argentine government to

Reverend Thomas Bridges, who authored a Yamana–English dictionary and is considered the patriarch of Tierra del Fuego. His son Lucas wrote *The Uttermost Part of the Earth,* a memoir about his frontier childhood. Today the ranch is managed by Bridges's great-grandson, Thomas Goodall, and his American wife, Natalie, a scientist and author who has cooperated with the National Geographic Society on conservation projects and operates the impressive marine mammal museum, Museo Acatushun. Most people visit as part of organized tours, but you'll be welcome if you arrive alone. They serve up a tasty tea in their house, the oldest building on the island. For safety reasons, exploration of the ranch can be done only on guided tours (45–90 minutes). Lodging is available, either in the Old Shepherd's House or the Old Cook's House. Additionally, you can eat a three-course lunch at their Acawaia restaurant. Most tours reach the estancia by boat, offering a rare opportunity to explore the Isla Martillo penguin colony and a sea-lion refuge on Isla de los Lobos (Seal Island) along the way. ⊠ *85 km (53 miles) east of Ushuaia, Ushuaia ✍ info@estanciaharberton.com ⊕ www.estanciaharberton. com ☎ 2500 pesos ☉ Closed Tues.*

★ Glaciar Martial

NATURE SIGHT | It might pale in comparison to the glaciers in El Calafate, but a visit to the shrinking Glaciar Martial in the mountain range just above Ushuaia offers a nice walk. Named after Frenchman Luís F. Martial, a 19th-century scientist who wandered this way aboard the warship *Romanche* to observe the passing of the planet Venus, the glacier is reached via a panoramic *aerosilla* (ski lift) or by foot. Take the Camino al Glaciar (Glacier Road) 7 km (4.5 miles) out of town until it ends (this route is also served by the local tour companies). Stop off at one of the teahouses en route (at the foot of the ski lift, when it is functioning) because this is a steep, strenuous 90-minute hike to the top. You can cool your heels in one of the

many gurgling, icy rivulets that cascade down water-worn shale shoots or enjoy a picnic while you wait for sunset (you can walk all the way down if you want to linger until after the aerosilla closes). When the sun drops behind the glacier's jagged crown of peaks, brilliant rays beam over the mountain's crest, spilling a halo of gold-flecked light on the glacier, valley, and channel below. Moments like these are why this land is so magical. Note that temperatures drop dramatically after sunset, so come prepared with warm clothing. ⊠ *Glaciar Martial, Ushuaia.*

Lago Escondido (*Hidden Lake*)

BODY OF WATER | One good excursion in the area is to Lago Escondido and Lago Fagnano (Fagnano Lake). The Pan-American Highway out of Ushuaia goes through deciduous beech forests and past beavers' dams, peat bogs, and glaciers. The lakes have campsites and fishing and are good spots for a picnic or a hike. This can be done on your own or as a seven-hour trip, including lunch, booked through the local travel agencies (around 9,500 pesos with lunch and 4X4 transportation). ⊠ *Ushuaia.*

Museo del Fin del Mundo (*End of the World Museum*)

HISTORY MUSEUM | Here you can see a large taxidermied condor and other native birds, indigenous artifacts, maritime instruments, a reconstruction of an old Patagonian general store, and such seafaring-related objects as an impressive mermaid figurehead taken from the bowsprit of a galleon. There are also photographs and histories of El Presidio's original inmates, such as Simon Radowitzky, a Russian immigrant anarchist who received a life sentence for killing an Argentine police colonel. The museum is split across two buildings—the first, and original, is in the 1905 residence of a Fuegonian governor at Maipú 173. The newer museum building is farther down the road at Maipú 465, where you can see extended exhibitions of the same style. ⊠ *Maipú 173, at Rivadavía, Ushuaia* ☎ *2901/421–863* ⊕ *www.mfm.tierradel-fuego.gob.ar* ⊠ *500 pesos* ⏱ *Closed Sun.*

★ **Museo Marítimo** (*Maritime Museum*)
HISTORY MUSEUM | Part of the original penal colony, the Presidio building was built to hold political prisoners, murderous estancia owners, street orphans, and a variety of Buenos Aires' most violent criminals. Some even claim that singer Carlos Gardel landed in one of the cells for the petty crimes of his misspent youth. In its day it held 600 inmates in 380 cells. Today it's on the grounds of Ushuaia's naval base and holds the Museo Marítimo, which starts with exhibits on the canoe-making skills of the region's indigenous peoples, tracks the navigational history of Tierra del Fuego and Cape Horn and the Antarctic, and even has a display on other great jails of the world. You can enter cell blocks and read about the grisly crimes of the prisoners who lived in them and measure yourself against their eerie life-size plaster effigies. Of the five wings spreading out from the main guard house, one has been transformed into an art gallery and another has been kept untouched—and unheated. Bone-chattering cold and bleak, bare walls powerfully evoke the desolation of a long sentence at the tip of the continent. Well-presented tours (in Spanish only) are conducted at 11:30 am, 4:30 pm, and 6:30 pm daily. ⊠ *Gobernador Paz at Yaganes, Ushuaia* ☎ *2901/437–481* ⊕ *www.museomaritimo.com* ⊠ *3400 pesos (valid for 2 days).*

Tren del Fin del Mundo
(*End of the World Train*)
TRAIN/TRAIN STATION | Heavily promoted but a bit of a letdown, the Tren del Fin del Mundo purports to take you inside the Parque Nacional Tierra del Fuego, 12 km (8 miles) away from town, but you have to drive to get there, and it leaves visitors a long way short of the most spectacular scenery in the national park. The touristy 40-minute train ride's gimmick is a simulation of the trip El Presidio prisoners were forced to take into the forest to chop wood; but unlike them, you'll also get a good presentation of Ushuaia's history (in Spanish and English). The train departs daily at 9:30, noon, and 3 (only 10 and 3 in low season). One common way to do the trip is to hire a *remís* (taxi) that will drop you at the station for a one-way train ride and pick you up at the other end, then drive you around the Parque Nacional for two or three hours of sightseeing (which is far more scenic than the train ride itself). ⊠ *Ruta 3, Km 3042, Ushuaia* ☎ *2901/431–600* ⊕ *www.trendelfindel-mundo.com.ar* ⊠ *From 4900 pesos.*

Tres Marias Excursions
NAUTICAL SIGHT | Although there are a number of boat tours through the Canal Beagle or around the bays to Tierra del Fuego National Park, one offers an experience that will put you in the shoes of the earliest explorers to visit the far south. The operators of Tres Marias Excursions offer a half-day sailing trip to Island H, an outcrop in the middle of the channel, with cormorant colonies, families of snow geese, seaweed stands, and a weather station that records the howling winds blowing in from the misnamed Pacific Ocean. The guides are skillful sailors and storytellers. On a gusty day you'll marvel at the hardiness of the Yamana people, who survived frigid winters wearing little or no clothing by setting fires behind natural and manmade windbreaks. You'll find the same plant and moss species that grow in the high Andes; they thrive here at sea level because the conditions kill off less hardy, temperate species. On the way back you visit a sea lion colony, but won't soon forget arriving in Ushuaia under full sail as the late sun hits the mountains. It's only a little more expensive, and a lot more adventurous, than the motorized alternatives trawling for business at the dock. Tours only October to March. ⊠ *Port, Ushuaia* ☎ *2901/582–060* ✉ *tresmarias-mail@gmail.com* ⊠ *5600 pesos.*

 Restaurants

Bodegón Fueguino

$$$$ | ARGENTINE | A mustard-yellow pioneer house that lights up the main street, this traditional eatery is driven by its ebullient owner Sergio Otero, a constant presence bustling around the bench seating, making suggestions, and revving up his staff. Sample the *picada* plate (king crab rolls, Roma-style calamari, marinated rabbit) over an artisanal Beagle Beer—the dark version is the perfect balm on a cold windy day. **Known for:** no reservations but a quick wait; large and hearty portions; famous Patagonian lamb. $ *Average main: pesos900* ✉ *San Martín 859, Ushuaia* ☎ *2901/431–972* ⊕ *www. tierradehumos.com* ⊗ *Closed Mon.*

★ Chez Manu

$$$$ | SEAFOOD | *Herbes de provence* in the greeting room, a tank of lively king crabs in the dining room: French chef Manu Herbin gives local seafood a French touch and creates some of Ushuaia's most memorable meals with views to match. The first-rate wine list includes Patagonian selections, while all dishes are created entirely with ingredients from Tierra del Fuego. **Known for:** fantastic wine list; amazing views of Beagle Channel; excellent king crab gratin and other fresh seafood. $ *Average main: pesos1800* ✉ *Camino Luís Martial 2135, Ushuaia* ☎ *2901/432–253* ⊕ *www.chez-manu.com* ⊗ *Closed Mon.*

Kalma Resto

$$$$ | ARGENTINE | Beautiful dishes and a contemporary twist on traditional Patagonian flavors meet at this funky little restaurant at the end of the world. Owner and chef Jorge says that recipes are inspired by his grandma's classics, but there is also a hint of Peruvian and Mediterranean with signature dishes like octopus ceviche, centolla, Beagle Channel mussels, and paella. **Known for:** sophisticated service; creative cuisine with wines to match; fantastic tasting

menu. $ *Average main: pesos1440* ✉ *Gobernador Valdez 293, Ushuaia* ☎ *2901/425–786* ⊕ *www.kalmaresto. com.ar* ⊗ *Closed Sun.*

Kaupé

$$$$ | ARGENTINE | The white picket fence, manicured lawns, and planter boxes play up the fact that this out-of-the-way restaurant used to be a family home. Inside, the star ingredient is centolla, best presented as chowder with a hint of mustard. **Known for:** hard-to-find location; seafood served with elegance and sophistication; sunset views over the city. $ *Average main: pesos3200* ✉ *Roca 470, Ushuaia* ☎ *2901/422–704* ⊕ *www. kaupe.com.ar* ⊗ *Closed Sun.*

La Cabaña Casa de Té

$$$$ | ARGENTINE | This impeccably maintained riverside cottage is nestled in a verdant stand of lenga trees and overlooks the Beagle Channel and provides a warm, cozy spot for delicious loose-leaf tea or comforting snacks before or after a hike to the Martial Glacier (conveniently located at the end of the Martial road that leads up from Ushuaia). An afternoon tea with all the trimmings will satiate any peckish trekker, fondues are served at lunchtime, and at 8 pm in summer the menu shifts to pricier dinner fare with dishes like salmon in wine sauce (mainly for the guests at the adjoining cabin accommodation). **Known for:** lunchtime fondue; countryside setting and views; traditional afternoon tea menu. $ *Average main: pesos1000* ✉ *Camino Luís Martial 3560, Ushuaia* ☎ *2901/424–779* ⊕ *www.lacabania.com.ar* ⊗ *Closed Apr. and May.*

Ramos Generales

$$$$ | ARGENTINE | Entering this café on the waterfront puts you in mind of a general store from the earliest frontier years of Ushuaia, which is why locals call it the *viejo almacén* (old grocery store). Burgers and picada platters are uninspiring; choose fresh-baked bread or scrumptious lemon croissants instead, and try the

submarino—a mug of hot milk in which you plunge a bar of dark chocolate (goes well with a panini). **Known for:** good hot chocolate; old-school frontier vibe; sweet treats like lemon croissants. $ *Average main: pesos1200* ✉ *Maipú 749, Ushuaia* ☎ *2901/424–317* ⊘ *Closed 3 wks in May.*

Tía Elvira

$$$$ | **ARGENTINE** | On the street that runs right along the Beagle Channel, Tía Elvira is a good place to sample the local catch. Garlicky shellfish appetizers and centolla are delicious; even more memorable is the tender *merluza negra* (black sea bass). **Known for:** kitschy decor; good local seafood; attentive service. $ *Average main: pesos1150* ✉ *Maipú 349, Ushuaia* ☎ *2901/424–725* ⊘ *Closed Sun.*

Volver

$$$$ | **ARGENTINE** | A giant king crab sign beckons you into this red-tin-walled restaurant, where the maritime bric-a-brac hanging from the ceiling can be a little distracting. The name means "return," and it succeeds in getting repeat visits on the strength of its seafood; the culinary highlight is the centolla, which comes served with a choice of five different sauces. **Known for:** cozy maritime atmosphere; great place to try signature dish of Tierra del Fuego, centolla; waterfront views. $ *Average main: pesos1550* ✉ *Maipú 37, Ushuaia* ☎ *2901/423–977* ⊘ *No lunch Sun. Closed Mon.*

Hotels

Choosing a place to stay depends in part on whether you want to spend the night in town, several miles west toward the national park, or uphill in the hotels above town. The hotels with the best views all require a taxi ride or the various complimentary shuttle services to reach Ushuaia.

Arakur

$$$$ | **RESORT** | You can see this luxury hotel towering in the distance in front of Monte Olivia; it's one of the most extensive spa-and-resort complexes in Ushuaia and overlooks the entire bay and town from its own nature reserve out of town on the road to Cerro Castor. **Pros:** nature reserve at doorstep; modern design with luxury fittings; sweeping views. **Cons:** far from town; sterile atmosphere; expensive. $ *Rooms from: US$445* ✉ *Cerro Alarken, Access via Av. Héroes de Malvinas 2617, Ushuaia* ☎ *2901/442–900* ⊕ *www.arakur.com* 🛏 *131 rooms* ⍟ *Free Breakfast.*

Cumbres de Martial

$$$ | **B&B/INN** | This charming complex of cabins and bungalows, painted a deep berry purple, is high above Ushuaia in the woods at the base of the ski lift to the Martial Glacier; each spacious room has an extremely comfortable bed and a small wooden deck with terrific views down to the Beagle Channel. **Pros:** lovely spa; easy access to the glacier and nature trails; romantic cabins. **Cons:** slow service; few restaurant options or services within walking distance; you need to cab it to and from town. $ *Rooms from: US$290* ✉ *Camino Luís Martial 3560, Ushuaia* ☎ *2901/424–779* ⊕ *www.cumbresdelmartial.com.ar* ⊘ *Closed Apr. and May* 🛏 *10 units* ⍟ *Free Breakfast.*

Hostería Patagonia Jarké

$ | **B&B/INN** | Jarké means "spark" in a local native language, and this B&B is a bright, electric addition to Ushuaia; the three-story lodge cantilevers down a hillside on a dead-end street in the heart of town. **Pros:** friendly staff; warm, welcoming rooms with decent views; good price for Patagonia. **Cons:** noise travels through walls; can't compete with the views from the larger hotels farther uphill; steep walk home. $ *Rooms from: US$88* ✉ *Gobernador Paz 1305, Ushuaia* ☎ *11/6385–4226* ⊕ *www.patagoniajarke.com.ar* 🛏 *15 rooms* ⍟ *Free Breakfast.*

Hotel Fueguino

$$$ | **HOTEL** | In downtown Ushuaia, the Fueguino boasts all the modern amenities: a conference center; a gym; a spa;

shuttle service; outgoing, professional, multilingual staff; and one of the better Wi-Fi signals in town. **Pros:** on-site restaurant; blackout blinds; central location. **Cons:** mattresses may be too firm for some; small rooms; some street noise. [$] *Rooms from: US$208* ✉ *Gobernador Deloqui 1282, Ushuaia* ☎ *2901/424–894* 🌐 *www.fueguinohotel.com.ar* 🛏 *53 rooms* 🍴 *Free Breakfast.*

Hotel Los Yámanas
$$ | **HOTEL** | This cozy hotel 4 km (2.5 miles) from the center of town is named after the local tribe and offers a rustic mountain aesthetic. **Pros:** sauna is very nice; some stunning views from rooms; peaceful location. **Cons:** Wi-Fi not strong in rooms; questionable taste in decoration; far from town. [$] *Rooms from: US$173* ✉ *Costa de los Yámanas 2850, Km 4, Ushuaia* ☎ *2901/446–809* 🌐 *www.hotelyamanas.com.ar* ⏲ *Closed May* 🛏 *41 rooms* 🍴 *Free Breakfast.*

Hotel y Resort Las Hayas
$$$$ | **HOTEL** | In the wooded foothills of the Andes, Las Hayas is slightly dated in its facilities, but the views overlooking the town and channel below still make it worth the trip. **Pros:** relaxing spa; great views; delicious restaurant. **Cons:** rooms could use some revamping; facilities dated; decor doesn't suit everyone. [$] *Rooms from: US$315* ✉ *Camino Luís Martial 1650, Km 3, Ushuaia* ☎ *2901/442–000* 🌐 *www.lashayashotel.com* 🛏 *88 rooms* 🍴 *Free Breakfast.*

La Tierra de Leyendas
$$$ | **B&B/INN** | This adorable B&B is a honeymooners' delight, thanks to the multiple personal touches, from home-cooked cuisine to family photos on the walls. **Pros:** all seven rooms have views; tasty food in restaurant; enthusiastic, personal, and attentive service. **Cons:** closed during winter; immediate surroundings are a bit barren; the street name is no joke—it's insanely windy. [$] *Rooms from: US$280* ✉ *Tierra de Vientos 2448, Ushuaia* ☎ *2901/446–565* 🌐 *www.tierradeleyendas.com.ar* ⏲ *Closed mid-Apr.–mid-July* 🛏 *7 rooms* 🍴 *Free Breakfast.*

Los Acebos
$$ | **HOTEL** | **FAMILY** | From the owners of Las Hayas (just around the corner on the winding mountain road), Los Acebos is a modern hotel on a forested ridge with a commanding view over the Beagle Channel; spacious and superclean rooms feature the same iconoclastic decor as Las Hayas, including the trademark fabric-padded walls, only this time with a '60s-style color scheme. **Pros:** friendly staff; spacious rooms; expansive views of the channel. **Cons:** simple breakfast; no spa; out of town. [$] *Rooms from: US$195* ✉ *Luis F. Martial 1911, Ushuaia* ☎ *2901/442–200* 🌐 *www.losacebos.com.ar* 🛏 *60 rooms.*

★ Los Cauquenes Resort and Spa
$$$ | **HOTEL** | Right on the shore of the Beagle Channel about 8 km (5 miles) west of town, this resort is in a private community with privileged beach access and a nature hike that starts right outside your room. **Pros:** private boat excursions offered; luxurious spa offers comprehensive range of treatments and massages; free transfer into city. **Cons:** outside of town; thin walls can make for noisy nights; rooms can get uncomfortably hot. [$] *Rooms from: US$290* ✉ *De la Ermita 3462, Barrio Bahía Cauquén, Ushuaia* ☎ *2901/441–300* 🌐 *www.loscauquenes.com* 🛏 *54 rooms* 🍴 *Free Breakfast.*

Nightlife

Bar Ideal
BARS | This cozy and historic bar and café opens from 12:30 pm onward. ✉ *San Martín 393, at Roca, Ushuaia* ☎ *2901/437–860.*

El Náutico
DANCE CLUBS | The biggest and most popular pub in town, El Náutico attracts a young crowd with disco and techno music. ✉ *Belgrano 21, Ushuaia* ☎ *2901/61–8284.*

Tante Sara

BARS | This popular café-bar in the heart of town has a casual, old-world feel. Locals kick back with a book or a beer; they pour the local artisanal brews, too. During the day it's one of the few eateries to defy the 3–6 pm siesta and stays open late. Their other branch, at San Martín 175, closes at 8:30 pm. ⊠ *San Martín 701, Ushuaia* ☎ *2901/432–308* ⊕ *www.tantesara.com.*

Shopping

Boutique del Libro–Antartida y Patagonia

BOOKS | Part of a bookstore chain, this branch specializes in Patagonian and polar exploration. Along with dozens of maps and picture books, postcards, and posters, it offers adventure classics detailing every Southern expedition from Darwin's *Voyage of the Beagle* to Ernest Shackleton's incredible journeys of Antarctic survival. While books in English are hard to come by in the rest of Argentina, here you're spoiled for choice, and the Antarctica trip logbooks on sale at the counter might inspire you to extend your travel farther south. ⊠ *San Martín 1120, Ushuaia* ☎ *2901/4245–750* ⊘ *Closed Sun.*

Laguna Negra

CHOCOLATE | If you can't get to South America's chocolate capital Bariloche, pop into this chocolate boutique for planks of homemade chocolate and a selection of artisanal beers, chutneys, and spices. In the small coffee shop at the back, drop a glorious slab of dark chocolate into a mug of piping hot milk—one of the best *submarinos* in town. ⊠ *San Martín 513, Ushuaia* ☎ *2901/41–7597* ⊕ *www.lagunanegra.com.ar.*

Parque Nacional Tierra del Fuego, Argentina

21 km (13 miles) west of Ushuaia.

This park is one of the main reasons that travelers make a trip to the tip of Argentina. Its deep forests, glistening lakes, and wind-whipped trees will not disappoint. An easy day trip from Ushuaia, this 60,000-hectare park offers varied outdoor experiences and many wildlife-spotting opportunities.

Sights

★ Parque Nacional Tierra del Fuego

NATIONAL PARK | The pristine park offers a chance to wander through peat bogs, stumble upon hidden lakes, trek through native *canelo, lenga,* and wild cherry forests, and experience the wonders of wind-whipped Tierra del Fuego's rich flora and fauna. Everywhere, lichens line the trunks of the ubiquitous lenga trees, and "Chinese lantern" parasites hang from the branches.

Another thing you'll see everywhere are the results of government folly, in the form of *castoreros* (beaver dams) and lodges. Fifty beaver couples were first brought here from Canada in 1948 so that they would breed and create a fur industry. In the years since, without any predators, the beaver population has exploded to plague proportions (more than 100,000) and now represents a major threat to the forests, as the dams flood the roots of the trees; you can see their effects on parched dead trees on the lake's edge. Believe it or not, the government used to pay hunters a bounty for each beaver they killed (they had to show a tail and head as proof). To make matters worse, the government, after creating the beaver problem, introduced weasels to kill the beavers, but the

Detour: En Route

If you're in Ushuaia in the days leading up to New Year's Eve, drop in on **La Pista del Andino** campsite, on the edge of town. You'll be dwarfed by a mad mix of four-wheel-drive vehicles, enormous customized German trucks, and worn-out bicycles with beaten panniers. It's a tradition among overland explorers to spend Christmas and New Year's in the southernmost city in the world, and this turns out to be one of the most unusual "motorhog" celebrations around. Their routes zigzag across South America and are often painted on the sides of their vehicles—which have been known to be equipped with everything from rooftop tents to satellite dishes. Travelers share stories of crossing places like Siberia or northern Africa, and if you're lucky you'll encounter some who've ridden, driven, or pedaled the Pan-American Highway all the way from Alaska down to Ushuaia, a 17,000-mile journey that takes years to complete.

weasels killed birds instead; they then introduced foxes to kill the beavers and weasels, but they also killed the birds. With eradication efforts failing, some tour operators have accepted them as a permanent presence and now offer beaver-viewing trips.

Visits to the park, which is tucked up against the Chilean border, are commonly arranged through tour companies. Trips range from bus tours to horseback riding to more adventurous excursions, such as canoe trips across Lapataia Bay. Entrance to the park is 2,100 pesos.

Several private bus companies travel through the park making numerous stops; you can get off the bus, explore the park, and then wait for the next bus to come by or trek to the next stop (the service operates only in summer; check providers with the tourism office). Another option is to drive to the park on R3 (take it until it ends and you see the famous sign indicating the end of the Pan-American Highway, which starts 17,848 km [11,065 miles] away in Alaska, and ends here). If you don't have a car, you can hire a private *remís* (taxi) to spend a few hours driving through the park, including the Pan-American terminus, and perhaps combining the excursion with the Tren del Fin del Mundo. Trail and camping information is available at the park-entrance ranger station or at the Ushuaia tourist office. At the park entrance is a gleaming restaurant and teahouse set amid the hills, Patagonia Mia (*www.patagoniamia.com*); it's a great place to stop for tea or coffee, or a full meal of roast lamb or Fuegian seafood. A nice excursion in the park is by boat from lovely Bahía Ensenada to Isla Redonda, a wildlife refuge where you can follow a footpath to the western side and see a wonderful view of the Canal Beagle. This is included on some of the day tours; it's harder to arrange on your own, but you can contact the tourist office to try. While on Isla Redonda you can send a postcard and get your passport stamped at the world's southernmost post office. You can also see the Ensenada bay and island (from afar) from a point on the shore that is reachable by car.

Other highlights of the park include the spectacular mountain-ringed lake, Lago Roca, as well as Laguna Verde, a lagoon whose green color comes from algae at its bottom. Much of the park is closed

Parque Nacional Tierra del Fuego is a beautiful park with bogs, lakes, forests, and plenty of flora and fauna.

from roughly June through September, when the descent to Bahía Ensenada is blocked by up to 6 feet of snow. Even in May and October, chains for your car are a good idea. No hotels are within the park—the only one burned down in the 1980s, and you can see its carcass as you drive by—but there are three simple camping areas around Lago Roca. ☎ 2901/577-931 ⊕ www.parquesnacionales.gob.ar ☞ 2100 pesos.

Activities

FISHING

The rivers of Tierra del Fuego are home to trophy-size freshwater trout—including browns, rainbows, and brooks. Both fly- and spin-casting are available. The fishing season runs November through April; license fees range from $60 per week to $80 per season for nonresidents. Fishing expeditions are organized by the various local companies.

Asociación de Caza y Pesca

FISHING | Founded in 1959, the Asociación de Caza y Pesca is the principal hunting and fishing organization in the city. ⊠ Av. Maipú 822, Ushuaia ☎ 2901/423–168.

Rumbo Sur

FISHING | The city's oldest travel agency can assist in setting up fishing trips. ⊠ Av. San Martín 350 ☎ 2901/421–139 ⊕ www.rumbosur.com.ar.

Wind Fly

FISHING | In summer this outfitter is dedicated exclusively to fishing, and offers classes and arranges trips. ⊠ Av. los Nires 2466, Ushuaia ☎ 2901/515-158 ⊕ www.windflyushuaia.com.ar.

MOUNTAIN BIKING

A mountain bike is an excellent mode of transport in Ushuaia, giving you the freedom to roam without the rental car price tag. Good mountain bikes normally cost about $12 for a half day or $20 for a full day. Guided tours are about the same price.

All Patagonia

BIKING | Guided bicycle tours (including rides through the national park) are organized by All Patagonia. ⊠ *Juana Fadul 58, Ushuaia* ☏ *2901/401–603* ⊕ *www. allpatagonia.com.*

Rumbo Sur

BIKING | One of the city's biggest travel agencies, Rumbo Sur can arrange cycling trips. ⊠ *San Martín 350, Ushuaia* ☏ *2901/421–139* ⊕ *www.rumbosur.com. ar.*

Ushuaia Extreme

BIKING | You can rent bikes or do a tour with Ushuaia Extreme. ⊠ *San Martín 830, Ushuaia* ☏ *2901/434–373* ⊕ *www. ushuaiaextremo.com.*

SCENIC FLIGHTS

The gorgeous scenery and island topography of the area is readily appreciated on a Cessna tour.

Aeroclub Ushuaia

SKYDIVING | Half-hour- and hour-long trips are available through Aeroclub Ushuaia. The half-hour flight ($95 per passenger with a group; $125 for single passengers) with a local pilot takes you over Ushuaia, Tierra del Fuego National Park, and the Beagle Channel with views of area glaciers, waterfalls, and snowcapped islands south to Cape Horn. A 60-minute flight ($155 per passenger with a group; $205 for single passengers) crosses the Andes to Escondida and Fagnano lakes. ⊠ *Antiguo Aeropuerto, Luis Pedro Fique 151, Ushuaia* ☏ *2901/421–717* ⊕ *www. aeroclubushuaia.org.ar.*

Heli-Ushuaia

SKYDIVING | All sorts of helicopter trips are available from Heli-Ushuaia, beginning with a seven-minute spin at $99 per person. There are plenty of longer trips and excursions if you have money to burn. ⊠ *Luis Pedro Fique 119, Ushuaia* ☏ *2901/444–444* ⊕ *www.heliushuaia. com.ar.*

SKIING

Canopy Ushuaia

SNOW SPORTS | Located at the Martial Glaciar, Canopy Ushuaia offers skiing in winter and canopy lines in summer. ⊠ *Cerro Martial, Luis Fernando Martial 3551, Ushuaia* ☏ *2901/1550–3767* ⊕ *www.canopyushuaia.com.ar.*

★ Cerro Castor

SKIING & SNOWBOARDING | With off-piste and alpine skiing and almost guaranteed snow, this has become a popular ski haunt for European Olympic teams looking for summer snow. Pistes range from beginners to black-diamond runs with more than 33 trails and five high-speed lifts, with a vertical descent of 772 meters (2,533 feet). You can rent skis and snowboards and take ski lessons at this resort 26 km (17 miles) northeast of Ushuaia on R3. Day passes are 2,265 pesos in high season, and there are restaurants, bars, and a ski lodge on-site. This well-run, family-owned resort is open June to October, with guaranteed snow (they have artificial snow to make up for any deficit). It's worth coming here for the views alone; they're some of the best in South America. ⊠ *Ruta 3, Km 26, Ushuaia* ☏ *2901/499–301* ⊕ *www. cerrocastor.com.*

Club Andino

SKIING & SNOWBOARDING | Ushuaia is the cross-country skiing (*esqui de fondo* in Spanish) center of South America, thanks to enthusiastic Club Andino members who took to the sport in the 1980s and made the forested hills of a high valley about 20 minutes from town a favorite destination for skiers. It's a magnet for international ski teams who come from Europe to train in the northern summer. ⊠ *Alem 2873, Ushuaia* ☏ *2901/440–732* ⊕ *www.clubandinoushuaia.com.ar.*

Tierra Mayor

SKIING & SNOWBOARDING | Ushuaia's oldest ski resort is a fantastic place for backcountry skiing, ice skating when the lake is frozen, and snowshoeing and dog-sledding excursions. In summer, they offer horseback-riding excursions. The on-site restaurant, much beloved for its roasted lamb, is open for lunch only. ✉ *21 km northeast of Ushuaia, on Ruta 3, Ushuaia* ☎ *2901/619–245* ⊕ *www. tierramayor.com.ar.*

Puerto Williams, Chile

82 km (50 miles) southeast of Ushuaia, Argentina.

On Navarino Island, the town of Puerto Williams is the southernmost permanent settlement in the world (it's closer to the South Pole than to the northern border of Chile). Even though Ushuaia in Argentina often makes this claim, Ushuaia is in fact the southernmost *city,* although many here consider Puerto Williams to be a city, too. Originally called Puerto Luisa, it was renamed in 1956 in honor of the British-Chilean military officer who took possession of the Strait of Magellan for Chile in 1843, just after the country was founded. About half of the 2,000 residents are troops at the naval base. A tiny community of Yaghan peoples makes its home in the nearby Ukika village.

Puerto Williams is fast developing as a gateway for the increasing numbers of backpackers arriving to explore the Dientes de Navarino circuit, often called the southernmost trek in the world. In 2005, UNESCO created the Cape Horn Biosphere reserve to protect the unique ecosystems on Navarino Island. The 50 km (31 miles) of epic trail in the Dientes de Navarino circuit weave through a chain of mountain pinnacles and diverse landscapes of forests, rivers, swamps, and barren hillsides plundered by beavers.

GETTING HERE AND AROUND

Even though it's a short distance across the Canal Beagle from Ushuaia, there are no regular ferry services from Argentina to Puerto Williams. This is due in part to,

according to whom you talk to, the desire among tour operators in Ushuaia to restrict the smaller Chilean town's claims to the lucrative tourist market. For a hefty fee, Aeroclub Ushuaia can organize private flights to Puerto Williams. Ushuaia Boating (ushuaiaboating@argentina.com. ar) makes the crossing every day in about 30 minutes from December to February, weather permitting.

From Punta Arenas you have two options. By air you can take a 35-minute flight with DAP (dapairline.com). Book in advance as their small planes fill up quickly. It's also possible to take a ferry with Transbordadora Austral Broom (www.tabsa.cl), which takes around 30 hours to get to Puerto Williams, but is a beautiful journey through the Patagonian fjords and the Beagle Channel.

⦿ Sights

★ Museo Antropológico Martín Gusinde

HISTORY MUSEUM | Tierra del Fuego was inhabited for centuries by the indigenous Selk'nam, Yaganes, and Alacalufes, which were estimated to number between 10,000 and 12,000 people here before colonization in the 19th century. Founded in 1974, the Martin Gusinde Anthropological Museum is a very well-done introduction to these first inhabitants with archaeological, historical, and ethnographic collections about the cultural and natural heritage of the Tierra del Fuego archipelago and Cape Horn. It is a must-visit. ✉ *Aragay 1, Puerto Williams* ☎ *61/2621–043* ⊕ *www.museomartingusinde.cl* 🎟 *Free* ⊗ *Closed Sat., Sun., and Mon.*

Parque Etnobotánico Omora

NATURE PRESERVE | **FAMILY** | Five km (3 miles) west of Puerto Williams is Parque Etnobotánico Omora, a former ranch converted into a 1,000-hectare (2,471-acre) nature sanctuary in 2000 and now a biological research center for Chile's Magallanes University. On the park's interpretive trails, you can explore the various habitats of the Isla Navarino region: coastal coigue forests, lenga parks, nirre forests, sphagnum bogs, beaver wetlands, and alpine heath. A highlight is the Miniature Forests trail, where the park guide will give you a close-up view of the spectacularly diverse tiny plants in the park (on one tree, there could be more than 50 species of moss). You'll also spot the Robalo River run through the park, important because it provides potable water to the town. Call or email the park office to set up a guided tour; you must book 48 hours in advance. ⊠ *Puerto Williams* ☎ *61/262–1715* ⊕ *www.facebook.com/ParqueOmoraUM-AG* ⊙ *Closed Mon.*

Hotels

With the exception of Lakutaia Hotel and a few others, most of the lodging options in town are small, rustic *hospedajes* that also serve meals. Information on all the accommodations on offer can be had by visiting the tourism office located at Centro Comercial (tel. 9/6619–4121), which is across the street from the Navy hospital.

Errante Ecolodge
$$$ | B&B/INN | With its tremendous view of the Beagle Channel, the Errante Ecolodge is a beautiful place to relax when not out exploring. **Pros:** comfortable beds; great views from bar and dining room; excellent meals. **Cons:** Wi-Fi is unstable; rooms lack amenities; outside of town. $ *Rooms from: pesos115000* ⊠ *Ruta Y 905, km 5.5, Puerto Williams* ☎ *9/9368–9723* ⊕ *www.errantecolodge. com* ⟿ *11 rooms* ⦿ *Free Breakfast.*

★ Lakutaia Lodge
$$$$ | B&B/INN | The southernmost luxury lodge in the world packs in the adventures, offering excursions like trekking, biking, sailing, fly-fishing, and more. **Pros:** lovely decor; impressive range of activities; great restaurant. **Cons:** excursions are all weather-dependent; transfers are bumpy; comes with a high price tag. $ *Rooms from:*

pesos220000 ⊠ *Seno Lauta s/n, Puerto Williams* ☎ *61/2621–721* ⊕ *www.lakutaia. cl* ⟿ *24 rooms* ⦿ *Free Breakfast.*

Activities

Aerovís DAP
ADVENTURE TOURS | Weather permitting, Aerovís DAP offers charter flights over Cabo de Hornos, the southernmost tip of South America. Although the water looks placid from the air, strong westerly winds make navigating around Cape Horn treacherous. Over the last few centuries, hundreds of ships have met their doom here trying to sail to the Pacific. ⊠ *Av. Bernardo O'Higgins 891, Punta Arenas* ☎ *61/2616–100* ⊕ *www.dapairline.com.*

Cerro Bandera
HIKING & WALKING | A hike to the top of Cerro Bandera is well worth the effort if you have the stamina. The trail is well marked but very steep. The view from the top toward the south to the Cordón Dientes del Perro (Dog's Teeth Range) is impressive, but looking northward over the Beagle Channel to Argentina—with Puerto Williams nestled below and Ushuaia just visible to the west—is truly breathtaking. ⊠ *3 km (2 miles) west of Puerto Williams, Puerto Williams.*

Explora Isla Navarino
ADVENTURE TOURS | The largest tour operator on Isla Navarino, they offer a variety of excursions, including cultural tours and outdoor day trips for hiking, biking, kayaking, and stand-up paddleboarding. ⊠ *Centro Comercial 140B, Puerto Williams* ☎ *9/9185–0155* ⊕ *www.exploraislanavarino.com* ⊠ *From 48000 pesos.*

Chapter 12

EASTER ISLAND

Updated by
Sorrel Moseley-Williams

⊙ Sights	🍴 Restaurants	🛏 Hotels	🛍 Shopping	🍸 Nightlife
★★★★★	★★★☆☆	★★★★☆	★★☆☆☆	★★☆☆☆

WELCOME TO EASTER ISLAND

TOP REASONS TO GO

★ **Astounding archaeology:** Whether it's the ubiquitous moai statues, petroglyphs, or cave paintings, Easter Island is an open-air museum with a turbulent and mysterious past.

★ **Wonderful walking:** Easter Island's rolling hills, with the white-flecked ocean rarely out of sight, hold some glorious walking trails, especially along the north coast.

★ **Extraordinary diving:** Diving into the cobalt-blue waters is one of the most popular pastimes on Easter Island. Visibility is up to 120 feet, so you don't miss the bright tropical fish or the turtles. Coral formations like the Cavern of the Three Windows make for an unforgettable underwater experience.

★ **Souvenir shopping:** Locals have carved a living out of the stone and driftwood, making handicrafts like miniature moai, elaborate bowls, eerie masks, and shell jewelry.

It's nearly impossible to get lost on Easter Island. It's just 22 km (14 miles) from end to end and has only three roads that fan out from Hanga Roa: one crosses the island northeast to Anakena Beach; another curves along the southeastern coast before turning north and then west to Anakena; and the third snakes around Rano Kau volcano to the southwest.

1 Hanga Roa. Almost all hotels on Easter Island are in or near Hanga Roa, the only town, as are the offices of tour operators and car rental companies. Hanga Roa also has its own sights, including the Iglesia Hanga Roa, which has a magnificent view of the Pacific Ocean. Next door is the better of the town's two craft markets. A short walk along the coast to the north leads to the unique town cemetery, the Tahai moai statue, and the island's small but attractively didactic anthropology museum.

2 The Southeastern Circuit. Most of the archaeological sites on the island are along its southeastern coast. Lined with moai, including Ahu Tongariki with its 15 statues, re-erected after being toppled by a tidal wave, this road also leads to Ankena Beach and the so-called moai factory in the side of Rano Raraku volcano.

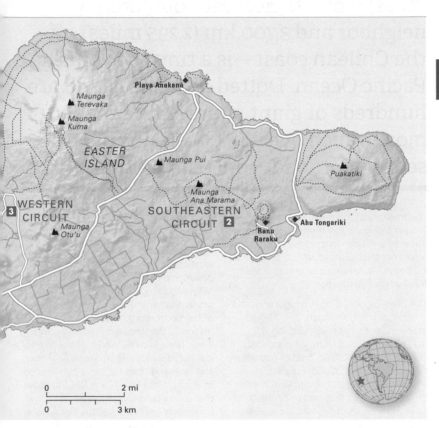

Maunga Terevaka

Maunga Kuma

Playa Anakena

EASTER ISLAND

Maunga Pui

Puakatiki

WESTERN CIRCUIT

3

Maunga Ana Marama

SOUTHEASTERN CIRCUIT

2

Maunga Otu'u

Rano Raraku

Ahu Tongariki

0   2 mi

0   3 km

3 The Western Circuit. A visit to the west of the island has really only one objective—to see the stone houses and petroglyphs in Orongo ceremonial village, the center of the island's birdman cult. On the way is the water-filled crater of the now-extinct Rano Kau volcano.

Easter Island, the most isolated inhabited island in the world—2,985 km (1,850 miles) from its nearest populated neighbor and 3,700 km (2,295 miles) off the Chilean coast—is a tiny speck in the Pacific Ocean. Dotted over the island are hundreds of giant stone statues called moai, which overlook the ruins of the settlements that constructed them.

The mystery of the moai, why the Rapa Nui (as the locals call themselves) constructed and later toppled them, plus the area's natural beauty, continue to attract explorers, archaeologists, and tourists to this far-flung destination.

The practice of carving, transporting, and erecting the large-headed, small-bodied stone moai, sometimes reaching 37 feet high, was central to the historical culture of Easter Island. Said to represent deceased leaders, the statues stand on an ahu, or burial platform, to watch over the communities they had once ruled. Several reconstructions and archaeological digs have confirmed the Rapa Nui had strong engineering skills, because the moai weigh many tons, and putting them in place using traditional materials and techniques must have been a tremendous strain on human and natural resources.

Various ahus and their moai have been reconstructed, inviting visitors to marvel at the enormous effort required to build them. Many travelers visit, or leave, with various questions: first, how did the Rapa Nui get here? Then, why did they build them? Then, why did they build

and how did they move the moai? Why were the moai later toppled?

Theories abound, and a combination of local oral history as well as European observations and guesswork tell the following story. King Hotu Matu'a and his family sailed here and landed on a beach at the north shore, which began the population of the land. Norwegian explorer Thor Heyerdahl believed that these original settlers came from South America, and he sailed from Peru in a balsa-wood boat called the Kon-Tiki in 1947 to prove that it was possible. However, it is now commonly believed that the Rapa Nui are of Polynesian descent, and indeed this influence is seen in the traditional dance, food names and preparation, and the greeting used all over the island: *iorana*.

Easter Island's peak population is estimated to have once been between 10,000 and 15,000 people, but from 1722 when the first European, Dutch explorer Jacob Roggeveen, set foot on the island to the 1774 arrival of British Captain James Cook, there was extreme population loss and many moai were toppled. Less than a hundred years later, 1,000 islanders were captured by Peruvian slave traders to work in guano mines. When they were eventually returned to the island, these freed slaves brought smallpox with them, further decimating the population down to just 110 people.

Chile claimed the island in 1888, and, with little regard for the inhabitants, leased it to a British sheep company, which corralled the Rapa Nui people into the village of Hanga Roa. The company departed in 1953, but it wasn't until 1967, when the airport was constructed, that the quality of life began to improve again for the people of Easter Island.

Today, geographical isolation and archaeological history are the two main draws for travelers. A visit to the quarry at Rano Raraku, where most moai were sourced and sculpted, is especially impressive, considering the engineering effort and know-how required. The Rapa Nui also had the only written language in Polynesia, called rongo rongo, which still hasn't been deciphered; petroglyphs can be seen at sites such as the ceremonial village of Orongo where the "birdman" culture thrived.

The culture of the Rapa Nui is another attraction to Easter Island, which despite its tumultuous history, continues to thrive, in language, cuisine, carving, dance, song, and the summer festival of Tapati, which takes place every February. There is also a special energy or mana (as it is locally called) at Te Pito o Te Henua (the navel of the world) that adds an intangible element to visits here, making a journey to Easter Island a once-in-a-lifetime trip that few get to share.

An adventurous spirit is a prerequisite for visiting Easter Island. Certainly, package tours are available and common, but they take you to only a handful of sights. Tour buses often fly past fascinating, off-the-beaten-path destinations or simply don't go to places that are harder to access with groups, like the west coast caves of Ana Kai Tangata (bring a flashlight or

headlamp). To fully experience the island, hire a private guide. Better yet, rent a four-wheel-drive vehicle, ATV, scooter, or mountain bike and head out on your own. Even in the height of the peak season you can find secluded spots if you time it well. A comprehensive guide to archaeological sites, including when to best find them empty is James Grant-Peterkin's *A Companion to Easter Island,* available on the island and in Santiago bookstores catering to tourists.

Planning
When to Go

Most people visit in summer, between December and March, often coinciding with Tapati Rapa Nui, a two-week celebration of music and dancing in the first two weeks of February. Temperatures can soar above 27°C (81°F) in summer. In winter, temperatures reach an average of 22°C (72°F), although brisk winds can often make it feel much cooler. Be sure to bring a light jacket. The wettest months are May and June.

FESTIVALS
The annual Tapati Rapa Nui festival, a two-week celebration of the island's heritage, takes place every year in February. The normally laid-back Hanga Roa bursts to life in a colorful music and dance festival. The Día de la Lengua (Language Day), which usually takes place in early November, celebrates the Rapa Nui language.

Planning Your Time

In a few days, you can visit the island's major sights. Spend one day in Hanga Roa, stopping by the Iglesia Hanga Roa, the cemetery, and the Museo Antropológico Padre Sebastián Englert. Finish the day soaking up the sunset at Tahai. On your second day, tour the coastal road, visiting the hundreds of moai in the quarry at Rano Raraku and the lineup of 15 at nearby Ahu Tongariki. On your last day, visit Rano Kau volcanic crater, where the ceremonial village of Orongo is. In the afternoon head inland to the small quarry of Puna Pau to see the seven statues of Ahu Akivi and where the red *pukao* (topknots) that crown some moai were crafted.

Almost all businesses close for a few hours in the afternoon. Most are open 9 to 1 and 4 to 8, but a few stay open late into the evening. Many are closed Sunday. Smaller restaurants and shops don't usually accept credit cards. Be aware that outside of Hanga Roa, the only place to buy anything to eat or drink is at Anakena, or at one of the more remote luxury hotels, which are quite off the beaten path.

Getting Here and Around

AIR

Easter Island's shoe-box-size Aeropuerto Internacional Mataveri is on the southern edge of Hanga Roa. LATAM Airlines operates all flights from Santiago to the east and Tahiti to the west. Eight flights a week arrive from Santiago throughout the year (twice on Monday and Thursday, none on Tuesday), and one from Tahiti. Planes are often full in January and February, so it's best to book well in advance.

Tickets to Easter Island are expensive—up to $1,000 for a round-trip flight from Santiago. There are better deals, however, if you buy your Santiago to Easter Island ticket as part of a multileg ticket that includes your flight from your city of departure to Santiago.

At the airport, the CONAF (national parks service) office outpost sells tickets for Rapa Nui National Park, which you need to get into all archaeological sites. As these tickets are sold in only two other places (Central Comunidad Indígena Ma'u Henua on Atamu Tekena Street and the CONAF office in the Mataveri neighborhood), it's usually best to pay the US$80 fee right at the airport.

CONTACTS LATAM. ✉ *Av. Atamu Tekena s/n, Hanga Roa, Hanga Roa* ☎ *32/2210– 0279* ⊕ *www.latam.com.*

CAR

To see Easter Island's less traveled areas, a four-wheel-drive vehicle is sometimes a necessity. There are three well-maintained, paved roads. The first traverses the island from Hanga Roa to Playa Anakena, the second goes to Ahu Akivi and forks off of the Anakena road, and the third runs along the southern coast. Other roads are loose gravel or packed dirt (or mud if it has rained recently), particularly those that take visitors to some of the most isolated spots. Though in some cases, there are no roads at all.

There are no international car rental chains with offices on Easter Island, but there are two reputable local agencies, Insular and Oceanic, which have vehicles for rent, as do the main tour operators. The minimum charge is about 55,000 pesos per day for a basic Jeep. Helmet use is mandatory on an ATV or scooter, which rent for 60,000 pesos and 40,000 pesos, respectively. If you plan on visiting during January and February, call a few days ahead to reserve a car.

You can also rent cars at many restaurants, souvenir shops, and guesthouses. If you ask around, you may find a significantly cheaper rate than what the rental companies charge. It is important to note that there is no vehicle insurance on Easter Island and any damage is charged to the client.

CONTACTS Aku Aku. ✉ *Av. Tu'u Koihu s/n, Hanga Roa, Hanga Roa* ☎ *3/2210–0770* ⊕ *www.akuakuturismo.cl.* **Insular.** ✉ *Av. Atamu Tekena s/n, Hanga Roa, Easter Island* ☎ *3/2100–0480* ⊕ *www. rentainsular.cl.* **Oceanic Rapa Nui.** ✉ *Av.*

Atamu Tekena s/n, Hanga Roa, Hanga Roa ☎ 3/2210–0985 Atamu Tekena, 3/2255–1392 Te Pito O Te Henua ⊕ www. rentacaroceanic.com.

TAXI

With no buses on Easter Island, taxis are a common form of transport, so it's never difficult to flag one down. Vehicles of the three main companies are identified by a yellow sign on the roof, but many local car owners also work as taxi drivers. They have a cardboard sign on the windscreen (and tend to be cheaper than radio taxis). Most trips to destinations in Hanga Roa should cost around 3,000 pesos (rates are lower for residents), but after 8 or 9 pm the price generally goes up to 5,000 or more depending on where you travel.

Restaurants

Compared to mainland Chile, Easter Island is expensive. Almost everything from petrol to vegetables has to be shipped or flown in, and you may sometimes feel you're not getting value for money. The upside to dining here is wonderful fresh fish and, in summer, mangoes and small, sweet pineapples. The guavas on the bushes are ripe (and plentiful) when yellow, and there are some other interesting island-only fruits around, which you can often try in the ice cream. Don't leave Easter Island without trying the local banana bread known as *poe* (best bought at the Riro bakery opposite the church), at 1,000 pesos per hearty square.

At restaurants, local fish such as kana kana and tuna are nearly always on the menu. The only restaurants are in Hanga Roa or at the luxury hotels. There are some simple snack bars at Playa Anakena, and a few other fast food places around town, serving sandwiches and empanadas. Most other restaurants serve fish, salads, ceviche, and international dishes like pasta; there are plenty of imported ingredients, such as shrimp, which tend to come from Ecuador.

Most restaurants are open for lunch and dinner, and a few scattered cafés open for breakfast. At restaurants, check your bill before leaving a tip; most places add a 10% service charge (which you are not legally obliged to pay).

Restaurant reviews have been shortened. For full information, visit Fodors. com.

Hotels

A key factor in where to stay is whether you're prepared to rent a car or bike or do quite a lot of walking. There are a few good hotels in the center of Hanga Roa, the only town, but most others are on the town's outskirts, a 15-minute walk or a 3,000-peso taxi ride away. Budget accommodation can be found at *residenciales*—often a few rooms attached to a private home—but standards vary enormously; rather than booking ahead, try to arrive on an early plane and talk to the representatives of the residenciales, or take a taxi into town and scout out the best bargains. Except in January and February, rooms are always available. The three main luxury hotels require a vehicle, though they, like most other hotels, provide transportation to and from the airport.

Most hotels take credit cards, but quite a few add a surcharge (as much as 10%). Ask ahead and, if there's a surcharge, consider getting money out of one of the two ATMs.

Hotel reviews have been shortened. For full information, visit Fodors.com.

What It Costs in Chilean Pesos (in Thousands)			
$	$$	$$$	$$$$
RESTAURANTS			
Under 6	6–9	10–13	over 13
HOTELS			
Under 75	75–140	141–220	over 221

Essentials

VISITOR INFORMATION Sernatur. ⊠ *Av. Policarpo Toro s/n, Hanga Roa, Hanga Roa* ☎ *3/2210–0255* ⊕ *www.sernatur.cl.*

Tours

There are several ways visitors arrange tours on Easter Island. Book ahead of time before setting foot on the island, which is recommended even for the plan-averse, especially for more strenuous, time-consuming hikes or horseback rides to the north coast and Poike. Fans of the all-inclusive experience can make the most of hotel-based tours, while more spontaneous travelers can arrange tours on-site with hotels and agencies, which can get you out the following, or even the same day, depending on the activity. Before visiting Rapa Nui National Park, make sure you purchase your national park ticket from CONAF, as agencies do not include them in packages.

Another option is to simply wander the streets of Hanga Roa, looking for storefronts that offer tours, which can also yield good results, but may not be the most time-efficient and keeps you away from some of the smaller, more innovative agencies. Sernatur, the local tourist office, has extensive knowledge of options and opportunities and can point you in the right direction.

Easter Island Travel

ADVENTURE TOURS | An unlikely transplant to Easter Island, Marcus Edensky, a Swedish man married to a Rapa Nui woman, runs some of the best-reviewed tours on the island. An outdoorsman, he leads multiday hiking tours, horseback riding, and spiritual tours, among others, often on the north coast. He speaks Swedish, Spanish, English, and Rapa Nui. Easter Island Travel specializes in small group tours, and the north coast tour ends (optionally) with *tunu ahi*, or food cooked directly on hot rocks. Private day-long hiking tours cost 120,000 pesos, and three-day adventure tours start at 915,000 pesos; both have a two-person minimum. ⊠ *Policarpo Toro, Hanga Roa* ☎ *9/7510–3841* ⊕ *www.easterisland. travel* ⊠ *From 65000 pesos.*

Kava Kava Tours

GUIDED TOURS | This local company runs small full- and half-day tours taking in major sights, including moai and caves. One half-day tour goes to Puna Pau, the quarry from which the red stone topknots that sat atop the moai were carved. Another day-long tour goes around the Poike Peninsula, the oldest part of the island, and one of two areas open to hikers or people on horseback with guides only and not accessible by vehicle. Prices are steep so team up with others to form a group of four and bring down costs. ⊠ *Av. Ana Tehe Tama, Hanga Roa* ☎ *9/7216–5015* ⊕ *www.kavakava-tours.com* ⊠ *From 193000 pesos.*

Hanga Roa

Hugging the coast on the northwest side is the island's capital of Hanga Roa. Of the almost 10,000 residents, about 3,000 are indigenous Rapa Nui and the rest are from continental Chile or abroad. Few people live outside Hanga Roa because the bulk of the island forms the Rapa Nui National Park or is state owned. The town's two main roads intersect a block from the ocean at a small plaza. Avenida Atamu Tekena, the road that runs the length of the village, is where to find most of the tourist-oriented businesses. Avenida Te Pito o Te Henua begins near the fishing pier and extends two blocks uphill to the church.

Buildings are not numbered and signs are nonexistent (street names are sometimes painted on curbstones), so finding a particular building can be frustrating at first. Locals give directions in terms of landmarks, so it's not a bad idea to take a walk around town as soon as you arrive to get your bearings. Important landmarks in town are the fishing cove and pier, the Catholic church, Cruz Verde pharmacy, and the LATAM (airline) office. A little farther away to the south and southeast, respectively, are Hanga Pika pier and the airport.

Sights

Caleta Hanga Roa
MARINA/PIER | Colorful fishing boats bob up and down in the water at Hanga Roa's tiny jetty. Here you may see fisherfolk hauling in the day's tuna catch, or a boatload of divers returning from a trip to neighboring islets. Nearby is Ahu Tautira, a ceremonial platform with a restored moai. ⊠ *Av. Policarpo Toro at Av. Te Pito o Te Henua, Hanga Roa.*

Cementerio
CEMETERY | Hanga Roa's colorful walled cemetery occupies a prime position overlooking the Pacific and is visually unlike most. With artificial flower arrangements, white tombstones, and even some replica moai, the cemetery has a cheerful feeling. The central cross is erected on a *pukao,* the reddish topknot or hat that likely topped a moai at some point. The cemetery keeps expanding toward the ocean, but by 2022, the newly deceased will have to be buried elsewhere, as it will likely be full. Some Rapa Nui bury family members around the island, such

as near Playa Ovahe, so be respectful should you come across burial sites. ⊠ *Av. Policarpo Toro at Petero Atamu, Hanga Roa.*

Iglesia Hanga Roa
CHURCH | Missionaries might have brought Christianity to Easter Island, but the Rapa Nui people brought their own beliefs to Christianity. Find the two intertwined in this white church on the hill overlooking Hanga Roa. The paintings of the Via Crucis on the walls are what you would find in any Catholic church, but the wood figures have a clear Rapa Nui flavor, and one of the altars rests on a block of local volcanic stone. At the first Mass on Sunday morning at 9 am, hymns are sung in Rapa Nui. ⊠ *Av. Te Pito o Te Henua s/n, Hanga Roa.*

★ MAPSE Museo Rapa Nui
HISTORY MUSEUM | **FAMILY** | This small museum, Museo Antropológico Padre Sebastián Englert, is named for the German priest who dedicated his life to improving conditions on Rapa Nui and who is buried beside the church. It provides an excellent summary of the history of Easter Island and its way of life, as well as its native flora and fauna. Here, too, is one of the few female moai on the island and the replica of a coral eye found during the reconstruction of an ahu at Playa Anakena (the original is in storage after an attempted robbery). Texts are in Spanish and English. Note that the museum can easily overcrowd given its small size. ⊠ *Tahai s/n, Hanga Roa* ☎ *3/2255–1020* ⊕ *www.museorapanui.gob.cl* ☉ *Closed Mon.*

Tahai
HISTORIC SIGHT | The ancient ceremonial center of Tahai, where much of the annual Tapati Rapa Nui festival takes place, was restored in 1968 by archaeologist William Mulloy, who is buried nearby. Tahai consists of three separate ahus facing a wide plaza that once served as a community meeting place. You can still find the foundations of the boat-shape

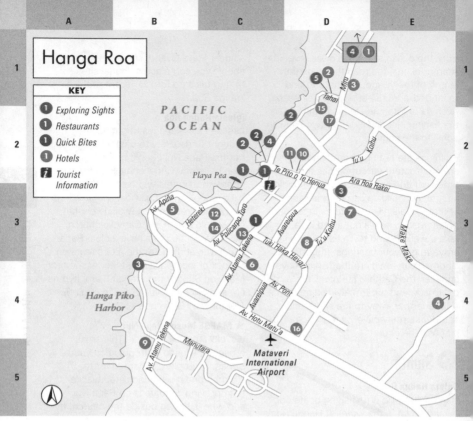

Hanga Roa

KEY

- **1** Exploring Sights
- **1** Restaurants
- **1** Quick Bites
- **1** Hotels
- **i** Tourist Information

PACIFIC OCEAN

Playa Pea

Te Pito o Te Henua

Tuki Haka Hevari

Hanga Piko Harbor

Mataveri International Airport

Sights ▼		Restaurants ▼		Quick Bites ▼		Hotels ▼	
1 Caleta Hanga Roa	C2	1 Amigo Secreto	C2	1 Café Caramelo	C3	1 Altiplánico Rapa Nui	D1
2 Cementerio	D2	2 La Kaleta	C2	2 Mikafe	C2	2 Cabañas Manatea	D1
3 Iglesia Hanga Roa	D3	3 Tataku Vave	B4			3 Chez María Goretti	D1
4 MAPSE Museo Rapa Nui	D1	4 Te Moana	C2			4 Explora Rapa Nui	E4
5 Tahai	D1					5 Hangaroa Eco Village & Spa	B3
						6 Hare Aukara	C4
						7 Hostal Taniera	D3
						8 Hotel Gomero	D3
						9 Hotel Iorana	B5
						10 Hotel Manavai	D2
						11 Hotel O'Tai	D2
						12 Hotel Taha Tai	C3
						13 Hotel Taura'a	C3
						14 Hotel Tupa	C3
						15 Mana Nui Inn	D2
						16 Puku Vai	D4
						17 Vai Moana	D2

Boats float in Hanga Roa's small jetty.

dwellings where religious and social leaders once lived. In the center is Ahu Tahai, which holds a single weathered moai. To the left is Ahu Vai Uri, where five moai, one little more than a stump, cast their stony gaze over the island. Also here is Ahu Kote Riku, with a splendid moai and red topknot intact; this is the only moai on the island to have its gleaming white eyes restored.

■ **TIP→ This is an especially good place to come to see the island's blazing yellow sunsets.** ✉ *On coast near Museo Antropológico Sebastián Englert, Hanga Roa.*

Beaches

Playa Pea

BEACH | **FAMILY** | Hanga Roa has only two tiny beaches: Playa Pea, a stretch of sand near the bay where surfers go to catch waves, and another small beach on the northern edge of the town with a sea pool for swimming. Both are popular among local families with small children. **Amenities:** food and drink. **Best for:** snorkeling; sunset; swimming. ✉ *Policarpo Toro, Hanga Roa.*

🍴 Restaurants

Amigo Secreto

$$$$ | **BELGIAN** | This Belgian-Polynesian restaurant serves some of Easter Island's best food from the fish- and meat-based menu. Try the seared tuna with Tahitian vanilla sauce and one of the many chocolate-based desserts. **Known for:** ocean views; classy and eclectic dishes; buzzy atmosphere. [$] *Average main: pesos15000* ✉ *Av. Policarpo Toro s/n, Hanga Roa* ☎ *3/2255–2060.*

La Kaleta

$$$$ | **SEAFOOD** | This restaurant draws in patrons with its unbeatable, secluded views from the point of Caleta Hanga Roa, seen from the deck by the breaking waves. Seafood dishes can include prawn curry, warm fish salad, and the grilled catch of the day. **Known for:** spacious patio; excellent seafood; panoramic view of the beach. $ *Average main: pesos14000* ✉ *Caleta Hanga Roa, Hanga Roa* ☎ *3/2255–2244* ⊕ *www.lakaletarestaurant.com.*

Tataku Vave

$$ | SEAFOOD | At Hanga Piko, the next bay south from Hanga Roa, this delicious, all-fish restaurant is worth the 15-minute walk. At 6,000 pesos, the set main course at lunchtime is a good value, but the large portions of ceviche to share are even more popular. **Known for:** amazing ocean views; fresh seafood; turtle-spotting on the restaurant grounds. $ *Average main: pesos7500* ✉ *Hanga Piko Jetty, Hanga Roa* ☎ *3/2255–1544* ▭ *No credit cards.*

★ **Te Moana**

$$$ | SEAFOOD | If you stay any length of time on Easter Island, you may find yourself returning to this inviting blue and wood restaurant on the waterfront with an expansive ocean view. The portions of fish, meat, and pasta are generous, and the service is efficient. **Known for:** nice cocktails and beer list; wonderful views; great ceviche and Thai fish soup. $ *Average main: pesos9000* ✉ *Policarpo Toro s/n, Hanga Roa* ☎ *3/2255–1578* ☾ *Closed Sun.*

☕ Coffee and Quick Bites

Café Caramelo

$ | CAFÉ | This airy, colorful café serves the island's best homemade cakes, including a fantastic cheesecake and fruit pie. The coffee is also better than most on the island, with beans sourced from major international roasters. **Known for:** great coffee and smoothies; excellent pastry selection; quick breakfasts. $ *Average main: pesos3500* ✉ *Av. Atanu Tekena, Hanga Roa.*

Mikafe

$ | CAFÉ | FAMILY | This coffee shop with outdoor seating down on the jetty does swift business with hungry divers coming off the boats, locals needing coffee, and kids in search of after-school ice cream for 1,500 pesos. Those ice-cream flavors include strawberry and cream, the unusual *pepino* (a melonlike fruit), and occasionally, island-specific flavors like *tipanie* (a flower). **Known for:** classic sandwiches for lunch; unique ice cream flavors; nice tea selection. $ *Average main: pesos5000* ✉ *Caleta Hanga Roa, Hanga Roa.*

Hotels

Altiplánico Rapa Nui

$$$$ | HOTEL | This hotel, part of a chain of boutique hotels in popular Chilean vacation spots, has minimalist design—beds are mattresses on a cement platform, and some rooms have indoor-outdoor showers—and rooms that are really more like standalone cabins, each one painted with a pattern representing the eye of a moai. **Pros:** Aka Pu moai visible from the hotel; expansive coastal views; total peace and quiet. **Cons:** pricey for what you get; car or taxi needed to get elsewhere on the island; 40-minute walk from Hanga Roa. $ *Rooms from: pesos275100* ✉ *Sector Hinere s/n, Easter Island* ☎ *3/2255–2190* ⊕ *www.altiplanico. cl/altiplanico-rapa-nui-isla-de-pascua* ⇆ *17 cabins* ⊚⫱ *Free Breakfast.*

Cabañas Manatea

$ | B&B/INN | These four cabins couldn't be more basic, with just a bed, a shower, and a shared kitchen, but they're spotlessly clean. **Pros:** great budget option; right beside the Tahai moai, it's the perfect place to watch an Easter Island sunset; airport transfer included. **Cons:** shared common spaces; very basic; 15-minute walk or a 3,000-peso taxi ride from Hanga Roa. $ *Rooms from:*

Mysteries of the Moai

Most people are drawn to Easter Island by the moai, the stone statues that have puzzled and intrigued outsiders since the first Europeans arrived there over three centuries ago. These squat, minimalist figures with oversize heads are believed to have been the crowning glory of a family shrine, standing on an ahu—or stone platform—beneath which ancestors were buried and transmitted their mana, or power, to the living family chief. They most likely overlooked the settlements that erected them.

Most of the moai were carved at the Rano Raraku quarry in the east of the island, where many can still be seen at different stages of completion. That, in itself, was a mammoth task, with only stone tools to chisel the statues laboriously out of the volcanic hillside. It was, however, nothing compared to transporting the finished statues to their ahu. Oral tradition used to claim the moai "walked" to their destination, but most archaeologists believe they were either dragged on wooden platforms or rolled along on top of tree trunks. It's not clear how they could have been moved miles without damaging the statues en route, though the eye sockets were not carved until they arrived at the ahus.

Once the moai arrived at their ahu, how were they lifted into place? In 1955, Norwegian explorer Thor Heyerdahl and a team of a dozen men were able to raise the single moai on Ahu Ature Huki in 18 days. In 1960, archaeologists William Mulloy and Gonzalo Figueroa and their men raised the seven moai at Ahu Akivi. They struggled for a month to lift the first, but the last took only a week.

Both teams used the same method—lifting them with a stone ramp and wooden poles. This technique would be unwieldy for lifting the larger moai, however. It also fails to explain how the *pukao* (topknots) were placed on many of the heads.

Why were the moai subsequently toppled? The reason posited by some is that creating them required a tremendous amount of natural resources, particularly wood, and as these were depleted, family groups that had once worked in harmony began to squabble, attacking the source of their opponent's mana—their moai.

That, at least, is the theory put forward by Jared Diamond in his book *Collapse: How Societies Choose to Fail or Succeed*. If that is the case, the moai are not only Easter Island's glory but, as the island was deforested, the cause of the decline of the civilization that created them. But, in a way, the moai are still serving their original purpose. Mana meant prosperity, and the moai continue to bring this today in the form of tourism.

It is unlikely that any additional moai will ever be stood back up. Archaeologists, such as Sergio Rapu, are looking at the possibility of leaving them where they are and using digital platforms to show both past (moais upright) and present (moais toppled) without damaging the statues.

pesos53000 ✉ *Sector Tahai s/n, Hanga Roa* ☎ *92/7746–2432* 💳 *No credit cards* 🛏 *4 cabins* 🍴 *No Meals.*

Chez María Goretti

$ | **B&B/INN** | The beautiful garden and lovely, airy, plant-filled dining room are the main attractions of this guesthouse on the northern edge of town between Hanga Roa and Museo Antropológico Padre Sebastián Englert. **Pros:** friendly atmosphere; newer rooms are good value. **Cons:** about a 10-minute uphill walk from town; older rooms could use a paint job. [$] *Rooms from: pesos68000* ✉ *Av. Atamu Tekena s/n, Hanga Roa* ☎ *3/2210–0459* 🛏 *20 rooms* 🍴 *Free Breakfast.*

Explora Rapa Nui

$$$$ | **RESORT** | This luxury property is built with local volcanic stone and imported wood and curves along a hillside overlooking the island's south coast in an emulation of the ceremonial village at Orongo. **Pros:** superb service; well-guided hikes; excellent food. **Cons:** incredibly expensive; somewhat isolated; a 15-minute drive from Hanga Roa. [$] *Rooms from: pesos1227100* ✉ *Sector Vaihu s/n, Hanga Roa* ☎ *2/2395–2800* 🌐 *www.explora.com* 🛏 *30 rooms* 🍴 *All-Inclusive.*

★ Hangaroa Eco Village & Spa

$$$$ | **RESORT** | Green initiatives meet traditional architecture and hospitality at this peaceful retreat on the coast. **Pros:** incredible spa; fantastic luxury; environmentally sustainable. **Cons:** expensive; minimum three-night stay; dinner menu doesn't vary much. [$] *Rooms from: pesos728600* ✉ *Av. Pont s/n, Hanga Roa* ☎ *2/2957–0300* 🌐 *www.hangaroa.cl* 🛏 *75 rooms* 🍴 *All-Inclusive.*

★ Hare Aukara

$$ | **B&B/INN** | Located just behind the LATAM airline office, this *residencial* is owned by a history professor and a local sculptor, whose work is displayed in the adjacent art gallery. **Pros:** airport transport included; tours available; contact with local artists in the workshop. **Cons:** credit cards not accepted; early booking is essential; few rooms and high popularity make it difficult to get a space here. [$] *Rooms from: pesos99700* ✉ *Av. Pont s/n, Hanga Roa* ☎ *3/2210–0539* 🌐 *www.aukara.com* 💳 *No credit cards* 🛏 *5 rooms* 🍴 *Free Breakfast.*

Hostal Taniera

$ | **B&B/INN** | The guest book of this little house, located by the side of the church, testifies to more than a decade of satisfied customers. **Pros:** environmentally friendly; awesome garden of coffee, cotton, and different varieties of banana trees; attractively decorated. **Cons:** might be too intimate for some; no free breakfast; very basic rooms. [$] *Rooms from: pesos50000* ✉ *Simón Paoa s/n, Hanga Roa* ☎ *3/2210–0491* 🌐 *www.taniera.cl* 💳 *No credit cards* 🛏 *3 rooms* 🍴 *No Meals.*

Hotel Gomero

$$$$ | **HOTEL** | A drive lined by palm and papaya trees leads to this charming small hotel. **Pros:** impeccably tidy; an inviting swimming pool sits in a beautifully attended garden; owners run a tour service. **Cons:** design is basic; pool is a bit small; on the outskirts of town and up a hill. [$] *Rooms from: pesos129500* ✉ *Av. Tu'u Koihu s/n, Hanga Roa* ☎ *3/2210–0313* 🌐 *www.hotelgomero.com* 🛏 *17 rooms* 🍴 *Free Breakfast.*

Hotel Iorana

$$$ | **HOTEL** | Perched high on a cliff jutting out into the ocean, this hotel entices its visitors with unmatched views. **Pros:** airport transfer available; lovely setting; rooms are attractively, if simply, decorated. **Cons:** can be crowded with tour groups; 15- to 20-minute walk from town; more expensive than other similar midrange hotels. [$] *Rooms from: pesos201200* ✉ *Ana Magaro s/n, Hanga Roa* ☎ *2/2698–1960* 🌐 *www.ioranahotel.cl* 🛏 *52 rooms* 🍴 *Free Breakfast.*

Hotel Manavai
$$$ | **HOTEL** | **FAMILY** | This hotel has 30 simple wood-paneled rooms around a long garden that's perfect for kids to play in. **Pros:** knowledgeable hosts; perfect for families; peaceful garden. **Cons:** no free breakfast; simple decor; no ocean view from rooms. [$] *Rooms from: pesos164700* ✉ *Av. Te Pito o Te Henua, Hanga Roa* ☎ *3/2210–0670* 🌐 *www.hotel-manavai.cl* 🛏 *30 rooms* 🍴 *No Meals.*

Hotel O'Tai
$$$ | **HOTEL** | Although the hotel is right in the center of town, its beautiful gardens make you feel like you're miles from anywhere. **Pros:** views of the ocean; great location; good value for money. **Cons:** no free Wi-Fi; bar not open at night; some of the standard rooms could do with an update. [$] *Rooms from: pesos190400* ✉ *Av. Te Pito o Te Henua s/n, Hanga Roa* ☎ *3/2210–0250* ✉ *otairapanui@entelchile.com* 🌐 *www.hotelotai.com* 🛏 *42 rooms* 🍴 *Free Breakfast.*

Hotel Taha Tai
$$$ | **HOTEL** | Open and airy, this hotel seems to have sunlight streaming in from everywhere. **Pros:** private bungalows are a nice option; rooms are spacious, clean, and comfortable; staff are friendly and helpful. **Cons:** basic decor; small bathrooms; a 10-minute walk from the center of town. [$] *Rooms from: pesos197000* ✉ *Av. Apina Nui s/n, Hanga Roa* ☎ *3/2255–1192* 🌐 *www.hoteltahatai.cl* 🛏 *30 rooms, 10 bungalows* 🍴 *Free Breakfast.*

Hotel Taura'a
$$ | **HOTEL** | This lovely hotel on Hanga Roa's main street is owned by Bill Howe, an Australian, and his Rapa Nui wife, Edith Pakarati. **Pros:** owners run a tour service; good breakfasts—they're different every day of the week—and coffee (a rarity on Easter Island); airport transport available. **Cons:** decor a bit basic; no air-conditioning in rooms; no pool. [$] *Rooms from: pesos113000* ✉ *Av. Atamu Tekena s/n, Hanga Roa* ☎ *9/6622–8129* 🛏 *17 rooms* 🍴 *Free Breakfast.*

Hotel Tupa
$$$ | **HOTEL** | Owned and managed by local archaeologist and former governor of the island, Sergio Rapu, this hotel has three kinds of rooms: budget, garden, and beach. **Pros:** very connected and knowledgeable owners; lovely location overlooking the Hanga Roa bay; owner-run tour service. **Cons:** no Wi-Fi in rooms; some areas not in perfect repair; long, twisty hallways. [$] *Rooms from: pesos205200* ✉ *Taniera Teave s/n, Hanga Roa* ☎ *3/2210–0225* 🛏 *40 rooms* 🍴 *Free Breakfast.*

Mana Nui Inn
$$ | **B&B/INN** | The seven rooms and three simply furnished cabins are laid out in a grassy yard with paved paths, banana trees, and blooming bougainvillea and hibiscus. **Pros:** free airport transfer; friendly owner; ocean-view breakfast room. **Cons:** basic accommodations; breakfast is included only in rooms and not cabins; the 10-minute walk from town on a dirt road gets muddy in the rain. [$] *Rooms from: pesos95200* ✉ *Sector Tahai s/n, Hanga Roa* ☎ *3/2210–0811* 🛏 *10 rooms* 🍴 *Free Breakfast.*

Puku Vai
$$$ | **HOTEL** | Within walking distance of the airport, Puka Vai is clean, airy, bright, and spacious. **Pros:** owners have a good relationship with taxi companies, car rental, and tour agencies; clean, efficient construction. **Cons:** few elements of Easter Island culture present; 15-minute walk from town. [$] *Rooms from: pesos199000* ✉ *Hotu Matu'a s/n, near the airport, Hanga Roa* ☎ *3/2255–1838* 🌐 *www.pukuvaihotel.com* 🛏 *13 rooms* 🍴 *Free Breakfast.*

Vai Moana
$$$ | **RESORT** | The name of this lodging means "blue sea," and it's easy to see why, as a long stretch of azure ocean can be seen from just about everywhere. **Pros:** great views; owner is interested in the living culture (not just historical culture) of Easter Island; very art centric.

Cons: no Wi-Fi in rooms; basic rooms; a 15-minute walk from the center of Hanga Roa. $ *Rooms from: pesos181000* ⊠ *Av. Policarpo Toro s/n, Hanga Roa* ☎ *9/3423–7070* ⊕ *www.vaimoana.cl* ⤷ *26 rooms* ❍❘ *Free Breakfast.*

Nightlife

You're in for a late night if you want to sample the scene in Hanga Roa. There are two sets of nightlife: one that goes on at restaurants until around midnight, and a second one that starts at around 2 am at the few clubs on the island. These are mainly frequented by locals, as tourists tend to go to sleep early to make the most of daylight hours on the island.

DANCE CLUBS
Tao'a Bar Piriti
DANCE CLUBS | This dance club close to the airport appeals to both locals and visitors. The soundtrack is a mix of Latin and pop early in the night; later on at around 2 or 3 am, live bands play. There are two parts of the club: the outer, rustic part, and the inside, which could be a disco anywhere in the world. ⊠ *Av. Hotu Matu'a 196B, Easter Island* ☎ .

Performing Arts

DANCE SHOWS
Ballet Cultural Kari Kari
BALLET | The island's longest-running dance group spends most of the show getting members of the audience on the stage to dance with the performers. It's done with little technology (no flashing lights or microphones) and is in a fairly small space on the main street. Members also perform a very good *sau sau,* the island's famous courtship dance. They perform on Monday, Tuesday, Thursday, and Saturday. ⊠ *Av. Atamu Tekena, Hanga Roa* ☎ *32/2210–0767* ⤳ *15000 pesos.*

Grupo Maori Tupuna
FOLK/TRADITIONAL DANCE | One of three traditional dance groups on the island, this one performs at the Vai te Mihi cultural center next to Amigo Secreto restaurant. Part of every show involves willing participants pulled up onto the stage to dance with the traditional Rapanui dancers. The dances are supposed to be among the least influenced by other Polynesian styles and feature traditionally (read: barely) clad, body-painted men and women telling stories through dance. They perform Monday, Thursday, and Saturday.

■**TIP**➜ **If you'd like to be pulled up on stage, increase your chances by sitting in the front row for 199,000 pesos extra (you need a reservation).** ⊠ *Vai te Mihi, Policarpo Toro s/n, Hanga Roa* ☎ *3/2255–0556* ⊕ *www.maoritupuna.cl* ⤳ *From 16000 pesos.*

Peu Te Puna Tongariki (Tongariki Cultural Center)
FOLK/TRADITIONAL DANCE | This cultural center is aimed at the island's school-aged children to keep Rapa Nui traditions, including songs, poetry, and dance, alive. Performances are frequent (often by the children themselves) and free to the public. You can usually find the kids rehearsing in the garden outside. ⊠ *Policarpo Toro s/n, Hanga Roa* ☎ *3/2210–0226* ⊕ *www.culturarapanui.cl.*

Te Ra'ai
FOLK/TRADITIONAL DANCE | This dance group brings participants off the tourist track right to the host's home, where there is traditional face painting, an explanation of the ceremonial type of cooking called *umu par,* and finally a dance performance put on by the Haha Varua Collective (you can also just attend the dance performance). The dance is traditional Polynesian and Rapa Nui and interactive with the audience. Performances take place Monday, Wednesday, and Friday. ⊠ *Av. Kaituoe s/n, Hanga Roa* ☎ *3/2255–1460* ⊕ *www.teraai. com* ⤳ *Dance performance 20000 pesos; performance and dinner 50000 pesos.*

🛍 Shopping

Souvenir shops line Hanga Roa's two main streets, Avenida Atamu Tekena and Avenida Te Pito o Te Henua. The most popular souvenirs and gifts are reproduction stone moai in a variety of formats (keychain size to the length of your forearm) and shell necklaces. Go farther afield to the sculptor Bene Tuki's workshop at Aukara Lodge, or visit Amaya Vai's art studio two streets back from Atamu Tekena on Tu'u Koihu.

Amaya Art Gallery

ART GALLERIES | Originally from mainland Chile, Amaya Vai has lived on Easter Island for almost 30 years and creates colorful paintings, some on paper made from local products. Her work tends toward natural designs, flowers, and some from the petrolyphs found on the island, in acrylic, watercolor, and mixed media. ⊠ Tu'u Koihu, Hanga Roa ☎ 9/9136–6102.

Anakena Natural Products

OTHER SPECIALTY STORE | This natural products store founded by German transplant Petra Klimsch is filled with everything from soaps made from guava or seaweed, and scented oils to jams, candy, and the world's healthiest honey. English, Spanish, and German are spoken.

■TIP➔ Pick up some white and dark chocolate moai here. ⊠ Ana o Ruhi s/n, Hanga Roa ☎ 9/9876–3689 ⊕ www.rapanuishop.com.

Hare Umanga Rapa Nui

CRAFTS | Formerly known as the Feria Municipal, the town's fruit, vegetable, and fish market has substantially upped its crafts section to include more than 70 artisans and is now known as Hare Umanga Rapa Nui. ⊠ Av. Atamu Tekena, Tu'u Maheke, Hanga Roa ☎ 3/2255–2049.

Mercado Artesanal

CRAFTS | Next to the church is the Mercado Artesanal, a large building filled with crafts stands. Here, local artisans whittle wooden moai and string together seashell necklaces. It's open daily 9–8 (until 7. May–October). When specific vendors step out briefly, they cover their wares with a blanket. ⊠ Ara Roa Rakei s/n, Hanga Roa ☎ 3/2255–1346.

🏃 Activities

Haka pei, or sliding down hillsides on banana trunks, is one of the more popular activities during the Tapati Rapa Nui festival. Another is racing across the reed-choked lake that's hidden inside the crater of Rano Raraku.

Visitors who take to the water usually prefer swimming at one of the sandy beaches or snorkeling near one of the offshore islets. The astroturf soccer pitch is usually filled with teams practicing, but if it's an informal game, you might be able to join in.

DIVING

The crystal-clear waters of the South Pacific afford great visibility for snorkelers and divers. Dozens of types of colorful fish as well as turtles flourish in the warm waters surrounding the island's craggy volcanic rocks. Some of the most spectacular underwater scenery is at Motu Nui and Motu Iti, two adjoining islets just off the coast.

Mike Rapu Diving Center

SCUBA DIVING | This center arranges first dives (no certification necessary) for 65,000 pesos, and for those with NAUI or PADI certification (they are a PADI partner), it's 35,000 pesos. A photographer can be provided for an additional 10,000 pesos. Snorkeling trips are available as well for 25,000 pesos. ⊠ Caleta de Hanga Roa, Hanga Roa ☎ 3/2255–1055 ⊕ www.mikerapu.cl.

Orca Diving Center

SCUBA DIVING | This place will provide a boat, guide, and gear for 40,000 pesos per person or 45,000 for a night dive. The outfitter also rents snorkeling masks and fins if you'd like to go out independently, but the guided boat trips let you see much more. ✉ *Caleta de Hanga Roa, Hanga Roa* ☏ *3/2255–0877, 3/2255–0375* ⊕ *www.orcadivingcenter.cl.*

HIKING

The breezes that cool the island even in the middle of summer make this a perfect place for hikers, and because such a large part of the island is a national park, you can walk more or less wherever you want without worrying if you might be on private property. Be careful, though, as the sun is much stronger than it feels. Slather yourself with sunblock and take plenty of water.

Numerous hikes leave from Hanga Roa. You can take a short walk roughly north along the coast and onto the grassy field before it takes you to Ahu Tahai. More strenuous is the hike on the unpaved road from Ahu Te Peu to the seven moai at Ahu Akivi, about 10 km (6 miles) north of town. One of the most rewarding treks is along a rough dirt path on the northern coast that leads from Ahu Te Peu to Playa Anakena. The six-hour journey around Terevaka takes you past many undisturbed archaeological sites that few tourists ever see. CONAF (the parks service) recommends a guide for this route. If you insist on going without one, pick up an *Easter Island Trekking Map* at any local shop.

HORSEBACK RIDING

One popular way to see the island is on horseback, which typically costs around 40,000 pesos for a half-day or 80,000 pesos for a group tour with a guide, but you may get a discount if you pay cash. Trips past Ahu Akivi and up to Terevaka (the highest point on the island) are popular, and full-day tours of the north coast are also possible. Some outfitters may offer multiday tours, with a minimum of two passengers.

MOUNTAIN BIKING

Mountain biking is a great way to get around Easter Island's sights. Most car rental agencies also rent mountain bikes for 13,000 pesos for 8 hours or 15,000 pesos for 24 hours. Remember to pack water, as you won't find much (if any) outside of town.

SURFING

When the weather is right, you can find surfboard rentals near Playa Pea for about 20,000 pesos for the board or 25,000 pesos with a lesson. Alicia Ika, at Easter Island Travel, teaches surfing as well. Vendors at beachfront stands near SERNATUR (the local tourism office) can also take you out.

The Southeastern Circuit

Most archaeological sites on the island line the southeastern coast. Driving along it, you pass many ahus where moai once stood, most of which have not been reconstructed and most likely never will be. Busloads of tourists hurry past these on their way to Rano Raraku, the volcanic quarry where around 400 moai wait in stony silence, and Ahu Tongariki, where 15 moai famously stand in line.

Heading out of Hanga Roa along the island's southern coast, the road leads to Ahu Vaihu, with its eight fallen moai; Ahu Akahanga, the burial site of the island's first ruler; and Ahu Hanga Tetenga's large unfinished moai. Farther along, at Ahu Tongariki, encounter your first standing moai, but that's just a warm-up for the jackpot at Rano Raraku quarry where the moai were carved out of the hillside. Grab a guide to take you to the caverns of Ana O Keke and Ana O Neru; then, visit the magnetic "navel of the world" stone at Ahu Te Pito Kura and the beautiful pink-sand Playa Ovahe before ending the day at Playa Anakena.

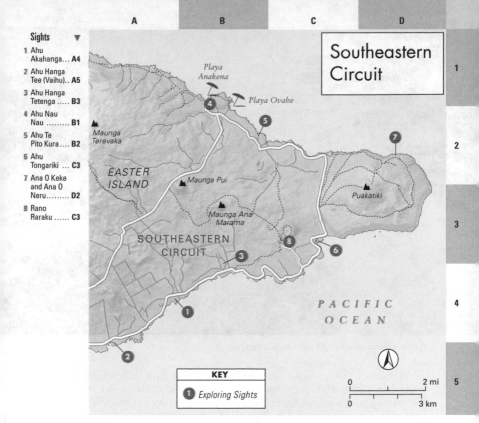

Sights ▼

1 Ahu
  Akahanga... **A4**
2 Ahu Hanga
  Tee (Vaihu).. **A5**
3 Ahu Hanga
  Tetenga **B3**
4 Ahu Nau
  Nau **B1**
5 Ahu Te
  Pito Kura.... **B2**
6 Ahu
  Tongariki ... **C3**
7 Ana O Keke
  and Ana O
  Neru......... **D2**
8 Rano
  Raraku **C3**

Southeastern Circuit

Playa Anakena

Playa Ovahe

▲ *Maunga Terevaka*

EASTER ISLAND

▲ *Maunga Pui*

Puakatiki

▲ *Maunga Ana Marama*

SOUTHEASTERN CIRCUIT

PACIFIC OCEAN

KEY

1 *Exploring Sights*

0   2 mi
0   3 km

Sights

Ahu Akahanga

HISTORIC SIGHT | Tradition holds that this is the burial site of Hotu Matu'a, the first of the island's rulers. The 13 moai lying facedown on the ground once stood on the four long stone platforms. There are also several "boat houses," oblong, boat-shaped outlines that were once the foundations of homes. ⊠ *5 km (5 miles) east of Ahu Vaihu on coastal road, Easter Island.*

Ahu Hanga Tee (Vaihu)

HISTORIC SIGHT | Eight fallen moai lie facedown in front of this ahu, the first you encounter on the southern coastal road. Three reddish topknots are strewn around them. Even after the ahu was destroyed, this continued to be a burial chamber, shown by the rocks piled on the toppled moai. ⊠ *10 km (6 miles) southeast of Hanga Roa on coastal road, Easter Island.*

Ahu Hanga Tetenga

HISTORIC SIGHT | Lying here in pieces is the largest moai ever transported to a platform, measuring nearly 10 meters (33 feet). The finishing touches were never made to its eye sockets, so researchers believe it fell while being erected. ⊠ *3 km (2 miles) east of Ahu Akahanga on coastal road, Easter Island.*

Ahu Nau Nau

HISTORIC SIGHT | Beside the swaying palm trees on Playa Anakena stand the island's best-preserved moai on Ahu Nau Nau. Buried for centuries in the sand, these five statues were protected from the elements. Minute details of the carving—delicate lips, flared nostrils, gracefully curved ears—are still visible.

Five mysterious moai statues stand on Ahu Nau Nau.

On their backs, fine lines represent belts. It was here during a 1978 restoration that a white coral eye was found, leading researchers to speculate that all moai once had them; a replica of that eye is now on display at the Museo Antropológico Padre Sebastián Englert; the original is in storage for safekeeping following an attempted robbery. Staring at Ahu Nau Nau is a solitary moai on nearby Ahu Ature Huki, the first statue to be re-erected on its ahu. Thor Heyerdahl conducted this experiment in 1955 to test whether the techniques islanders claimed were used to erect the moai could work. It took 12 islanders nearly three weeks to lift the moai into position using rocks and wooden poles. ✉ 1 km (about 1 mile) west of Playa Ovahe, at Playa Anakena, Easter Island.

Ahu Te Pito Kura

HISTORIC SIGHT | The largest moai ever successfully erected stands at Ahu Te Pito Kura. Also here is the perfectly round magnetic stone (believed to represent the navel of the world) that Hotu Matu'a

is said to have brought with him when he arrived on the island. ✉ 9 km (6 miles) north of Ahu Tongariki on coastal road, Easter Island.

★ Ahu Tongariki

HISTORIC SIGHT | One of the island's most breathtaking sights is Ahu Tongariki, where 15 moai stand side by side on a 200-foot-long ahu, the longest ever built. Tongariki was painstakingly restored after being destroyed for the second time by a massive tidal wave in 1960. These moai, some whitened with a layer of sea salt, have holes in their extended earlobes that might have once been filled with chunks of obsidian. They face an expansive ceremonial area where you can find petroglyphs of turtles and fish, and the entrance is guarded by a single moai, which has traveled to Japan and back for exhibition. ■TIP➔ **The perfect morning sunrise behind the moai at Tongariki lasts only from December 21 to March 21.** ✉ 2 km (1 mile) east of Rano Raraku on coastal road, Easter Island.

Ana O Keke and Ana O Neru

CAVE | Legend has it that young women awaiting marriage were kept here in the Caves of the Virgins so that their skin would remain as pale as possible. You need an experienced guide to find the caverns, which are accessible only on foot and hidden in the cliffs along the coast. Take a flashlight to see the haunting petroglyphs of flowers and fish thought to have been carved by these girls. ⊠ *Reached via dirt road through ranch on Poike, Poike.*

★ Rano Raraku

HISTORIC SIGHT | When it comes to moai, this is the motherlode. Some 400 have been counted at the quarry of this long-extinct volcano, both on the outer rim and clustered inside the crater. More than 150 are unfinished, some little more than faces in the rock. Among these is El Gigante, a monster measuring 22 meters (72 feet). Also here is Moai Tukuturi, the only statue in a kneeling position; it's thought to predate most others. Look out also for the moai with a three-masted boat carved on its belly; the anchor is a turtle. CONAF checks but does not sell tickets here. They are sold at the airport upon arrival or at the CONAF office near the Anthropological Museum, paid in dollars. The same ticket gives access to all archaeological sights on the island.

■ **TIP→ It's best to buy your national parks ticket upon arrival at the airport.** ⊠ *5 km (3 miles) east of Ahu Hanga Tetenga on coastal road, Easter Island* ⊠ *US$80 for non-Chileans.*

Beaches

★ Playa Anakena

BEACH | FAMILY | Easter Island's earliest settlers are believed to have landed on idyllic Playa Anakena. Legend has it that the caves in the cliffs overlooking the beach are where Hotu Matu'a dwelled while constructing his home. It's easy to see why the island's first ruler might

have selected this spot: on an island ringed by rough volcanic rock, Playa Anakena is the widest swath of sand. Ignoring the sun-worshipping tourists are five beautifully carved moai standing on nearby Ahu Nau Nau. On the northern coast, Playa Anakena is reachable by a paved road that runs across the island or by the more circuitous coastal road. For 20,000 pesos (or ask your hotel to negotiate a better price), a taxi will take you from Hanga Roa and pick you up at the agreed-upon time later. ■ **TIP→ Bring snacks and water from Hanga Roa. Amenities:** parking; toilets. **Best for:** snorkeling; swimming. ⊠ *Easter Island.*

Playa Ovahe

BEACH | A lovely strip of pink sand, Playa Ovahe isn't as crowded as neighboring Playa Anakena. The fact that most tourists pass it by is what makes this secluded beach so appealing. Families head here on weekends for afternoon cookouts, but swimming is dangerous because of strong undercurrents. The cliffs that tower above the beach were once home to many of the island's residents. Locals proudly point out caves that belonged to their relatives. ■ **TIP→ Come in the morning if you want to sunbathe; the position of the sun means that by afternoon, you'll be sitting in the shade. Amenities:** none. **Best for:** solitude; sunrise. ⊠ *Easter Island.*

The Western Circuit

On the western tip of the island are the cave paintings of Ana Kai Tangata and the petroglyphs near the ceremonial village of Orongo. You'll also be treated to a spectacular view of the crater lake inside the long-dormant volcano of Rano Kau as well as the three islets or motu in the ocean below.

Divide this circuit into two, with a break for lunch in Hanga Roa. In the morning, start by visiting Ahu Vinapu, with its unusual masonry, before heading up the

The crater of Rano Kau volcano measures a full mile across.

Rano Kau volcano, with its water-filled crater and wonderful views, to Orongo. On the way down, consider stopping by the cave paintings at Ana Kai Tangata. After lunch, visit the Puna Pau quarry, origin of the moai's red topknots, and the inland moai at Ahu Huri a Urenga, before carrying on north to Ahu Akivi's seven moai, the underground caverns at Ana Te Pahu, and the remains of the so-called boathouses at Ahu Te Peu.

Sights

Ahu Akivi

HISTORIC SIGHT | These seven stoic moai—believed by some to represent explorers sent on a reconnaissance mission by King Hotu Matu'a—are among the few that gaze out to sea, though researchers say they face a ceremonial site. Others say the oral history of the explorers has morphed into stories about the moai, and that there isn't an actual connection between statues and explorers. Archaeologists William Mulloy and Gonzalo Figueroa restored the moai in

1960. ⊠ *Past Puna Pau on road branching north from paved road to Playa Anakena, Easter Island.*

Ahu Huri a Urenga

HISTORIC SIGHT | One of the few ahus to be erected inland, Ahu Huri a Urenga appears to be oriented toward the winter solstice. Its lonely moai is exceptional because it has two sets of hands, the second carved above the first. Archaeologists believe this is because the lower set was damaged during transport to the ahu. ⊠ *3 km (2 miles) from Av. Hotu Matu'a on paved road to Playa Anakena, Easter Island.*

Ahu Te Peu

RUINS | As at Ahu Vinapu, the tightly fitting stones at the unrestored Ahu Te Peu recall the best work of the Incas. The foundations for several boat-shape houses, including one that measures 40 meters (131 feet) from end to end, are clearly visible. From here you can begin the six-hour trail-less hike around the island's northern coast to Playa Anakena. CONAF (national parks service)

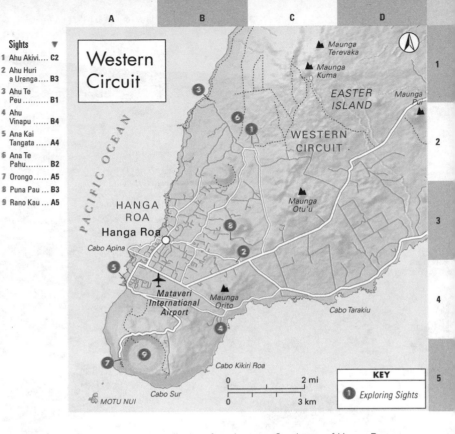

Sights ▼

1 Ahu Akivi.... **C2**
2 Ahu Huri a Urenga.... **B3**
3 Ahu Te Peu **B1**
4 Ahu Vinapu **B4**
5 Ana Kai Tangata **A4**
6 Ana Te Pahu......... **B2**
7 Orongo **A5**
8 Puna Pau ... **B3**
9 Rano Kau ... **A5**

Western Circuit

KEY

1 Exploring Sights

---

recommends a guide, as you may walk past many of the archaeological sites without one. ⊠ *Past Ana Te Pahu on gravel road branching north from paved road to Playa Anakena, Easter Island.*

Ahu Vinapu

HISTORIC SIGHT | The appeal of this crumbled ahu isn't apparent until you notice the fine masonry on the rear wall. Anyone who has seen the ancient Inca city of Machu Picchu in Peru can note the similar stonework. This led Norwegian archaeologist Thor Heyerdahl to theorize that Rapa Nui's original inhabitants may have sailed here from South America. By now it has been established that the first settlers were Polynesian, though evidence points to contact with South America early on. The moai here still lie where they were toppled, including one face up, which is unusual, as most were knocked facedown. ⊠ *Southeast of Hanga Roa along Av. Hotu Matu'a, Easter Island.*

Ana Kai Tangata

CAVE | A small sign just past the entrance of Hotel Iorana points toward Ana Kai Tangata, a seldom-visited cavern on the coast that holds the island's only cave paintings. Directly over your head are images of red and white birds in flight. Dramatic cliffs shelter the cave from the crashing surf. ⊠ *South of Hanga Roa, Easter Island.*

Ana Te Pahu

CAVE | A grove of banana trees marks the entrance to these underground caverns that once served as dwellings. Partly shielded from the blazing sun, a secret garden of tropical plants thrives in the fissure where the caves begin. Below ground is a passage leading to a second cave where the sunlight streams through a huge hole. ■TIP→ Bring a

Did You Know?

More than 400 moai have been counted at the extinct volcano Rano Raraku, on the outer rim and inside the crater.

flashlight, and be careful of dripping water if it's rained in the past week. ✉ *Past Ahu Akivi on gravel road branching north from paved road to Playa Anakena, Easter Island.*

★ Orongo

RUINS | A small museum kick-starts the story of the ceremonial village of Orongo, likely constructed in the late 1600s and used by locals until 1866; the 48 oval stone houses here were occupied only during the ceremony honoring the god Make-Make. Many of these abodes have since been reconstructed. The high point of the annual event was a competition in which prominent villagers sent servants to Motu Nui, the largest of three islets just off the coast. The first servant to find an egg of the sooty tern, a bird nesting on the islets, would swim back with the prize tucked in a special headdress. His master would become the *tangata manu,* or birdman, for the next year. The tangata manu was honored by being confined to a cave until the following year's ceremony. Dozens of petroglyphs depicting birdlike creatures cover nearby boulders along the rim of Rano Kau. CONAF checks but does not sell tickets here. They are sold at the airport or at the CONAF office near the MAPSE Museu Rapa Nui and are good for all archaeological sites on the island. ✉ *South of Hanga Roa on Rano Kau, Easter Island* 🚩 *US$80 for non-Chileans.*

Puna Pau

NATURE SIGHT | Scoria, the reddish stone used to make topknots for the moai, was once excavated at this quarry. About two dozen finished topknots are still here.
■TIP→ **The views of the island from the top of the hill are worth the short climb.** ✉ *Off road branching north from road to Playa Anakena, signposted "Puna Pau" and "Ahu Akivi," Easter Island.*

★ Rano Kau

VOLCANO | This huge volcano on the southern tip of the island affords wonderful views of Hanga Roa. The crater, which measures a mile across, holds a lake nearly covered by reeds. The opposite side of the crater has crumbled a bit, revealing a crescent of the deep blue ocean beyond. Entering the crater is forbidden, except in signposted areas. It is protected, and the ground is unstable. ✉ *South of Hanga Roa, Easter Island.*

Index

A

Aduana de Arica, *210*
Afrigonia ✕, *367–368*
Ahu Akahanga, *429*
Ahu Akivi, *432*
Ahu Hanga Tee (Vaihu), *429*
Ahu Hanga Tetenga, *429*
Ahu Huri a Urenga, *432*
Ahu Nau Nau, *429–430*
Ahu Te Peu, *432–433*
Ahu Te Pito Kura, *430*
Ahu Tongarikí, *430*
Ahu Vinapu, *433*
Air travel, *32, 52*
  Central Coast, *114*
  Chiloé, *301*
  Easter Island, *416*
  El Norte Chico, *154*
  El Norte Grande, *184*
  Lake District, *245*
  Santiago, *58*
  Southern Chilean Patagonia and Tierra del
    Fuego, *362*
  Southern Coast, *325*
Alfa Aldea (observatory), *161*
Algarrobo, *110, 136–139*
Altiplanico Lakes, *202*
Alto Atacama Desert Lodge & Spa
  ⌘, *196–197*
Alto Maipo, *101–103*
Ambrosia Bistro ✕, *94*
Ana Kai Tangata, *433*
Ana O Keke and Ana O Neru, *431*
Ana Te Pahu, *433, 436*
Ancud, *298, 301, 303–306*
&Beyond Vira Vira ⌘, *260*
Antigua Casa Beban, *398–399*
Antiques, shopping for, *70, 90*
Antofagasta, *180, 186–188*
Arica, *180, 183, 209–212*
Art galleries. ⇨ See Museums and
  galleries
Arts. ⇨ See Nightlife and the arts
Ascensor El Peral, *117*
Ascensor Reina Victoria, *117*
Atacama Desert, *183, 208*
Athletic clubs and spas, *99*
ATMs, *39–40*
Aubrey, The ⌘, *83*
Aurora Austral (dog-sledding
  trips), *257*
Auto Museum Moncopulli, *277*
Avenida Alonso de Córdova, *87*
Avenida Bernardo O'Higgins, *54,
  71–74*
Avenida Valpariaíso, *130*

B

Bahía Inglesa, *150, 176–178*
Banks, *39–40*
Baños Colina (hot springs), *105*
Baños Morales (hot springs), *105*
Bar del Tio, *126*
Barrio Concha y Toro, *84–85*
Barrio Paris-Londres, *71*
Beaches
  Central Coast, *113, 115, 122, 131, 136,
    137–139, 143, 145–146, 147–148*
  Chiloé, *317*
  Easter Island, *421, 431*
  El Norte Chico, *150, 157–158, 177*
  El Norte Grande, *205, 210–211*
  Lake District, *265, 281, 292*
Bellas Artes and Lastarria, *54, 74–77*
Bellavista and Parque Metropoli-
  tano, *54, 80–84*
Biblioteca Nacional, *71–72*
Bicycling
  Easter Island, *428*
  El Norte Grande, *199*
  Lake District, *290*
  Santiago, *99*
  Southern Chilean Patagonia and Tierra del
    Fuego, *393, 407–408*
  Southern Coast, *339*
Bird watching
  Central Coast, *142, 147*
  Central Valley, *234*
  Chiloé, *303, 306, 317*
  El Norte Chico, *150, 170–172, 174–175,
    178*
  El Norte Grande, *180, 193, 202*
  Lake District, *287*
  Southern Chilean Patagonia and Tierra del
    Fuego, *372–373, 379, 388, 399, 400*
  Southern Coast, *349, 350–351*
Blue Jar ✕, *67*
Boat and ferry travel, *32–33, 52*
  Chiloé, *301–302*
  Southern Chilean Patagonia and Tierra del
    Fuego, *362*
  Southern Coast, *325*
Boating
  Central Coast, *128*
  Lake District, *288, 290*
  Southern Chilean Patagonia and Tierra del
    Fuego, *358, 391, 401*
  Southern Coast, *346, 348, 349*
Bocanáriz ✕, *75*
Bolsa de Comercio, *72*
Books, shopping for, *77, 198*
Books on Chile, *27–28*
Boragó ✕, *88*
Bouchon Family Wines, *236*
Breweries, *269*
Bus travel, *33, 52*
  Central Coast, *114*
  Central Valley, *219*
  Chiloé, *302*
  El Norte Chico, *154*
  El Norte Grande, *184*
  Lake District, *245*

Santiago, *58*
  Southern Chilean Patagonia and Tierra del
    Fuego, *362–363*
  Southern Coast, *325*

C

Cabañas Ensenada ⌘, *289*
Café Amaranthine ✕, *304*
Cajón del Maipo, *105–106*
Calama, *180, 189–191*
Caleta Angelmó, *292*
Caleta de Zapallar, *147*
Caleta Hanga Roa, *419*
Calle Baquedano, *204*
Camping, *392, 406*
Campo Antilco, *262*
Canal Beagle, *399*
Canal Fun, *399*
Car travel and rentals, *33–35, 52*
  Central Coast, *114*
  Central Valley, *220*
  Chiloé, *302*
  Easter Island, *416–417*
  El Norte Chico, *154*
  El Norte Grande, *184*
  Lake District, *245*
  Santiago, *59*
  Southern Chilean Patagonia and Tierra del
    Fuego, *363*
  Southern Coast, *325–326*
Carretera Austral, *329*
Casa Bouchon ⌘, *237*
Casa Escuela, *163–164*
Casa Higueras ⌘, *124*
Casa-Museo Isla Negra, *140–141*
Casa Silva, *225*
Casa Silva Restaurant ✕, *226*
Casa Valdes ✕, *284*
Casa Valle Viñamar, *135*
Casablanca Wine Valley, *110,
  134–135*
Casas del Bosque, *135*
Cascada de las Animas (hot springs),
  105–106
Casino Dreams Puerto Varas, *287*
Casino Viña del Mar, *128*
Casinos, *128, 287, 344*
Castillo San Sebastián de la Cruz,
  267
Castro, *298, 301, 310–314*
Catedral de Nuestra Señora del
  Rosario, *267*
Catedral de Puerto Montt, *292*
Catedral de San Mateo Apostol, *277*
Catedral de Temuco, *247*
Catedral San Juan Bautista, *189*
Catedrals de Marmol, *349–350*
Caves
  Central Coast, *137*
  Easter Island, *431, 433, 436*
  El Norte Chico, *167*
  El Norte Grande, *207*
  Lake District, *258*

Southern Chilean Patagonia and Tierra del
    Fuego, 367
Southern Coast, 349–350
Celeta Hanga Roa, 419
Cementerio (Easter Island), 419
Cementerio General (Santiago), 85
Cementerio Municipal (Punta Arenas),
    377
Central Coast, 14, 110–148
beaches, 113, 115, 122, 131, 136, 137–139,
    143, 145–146, 147–148
festivals and events, 113–114
hotels, 115, 124–126, 132–133, 135, 139,
    143–144, 146, 148
nightlife and the arts, 126–127, 133
price categories, 115
restaurants, 114–115, 122–124, 131–132,
    136, 139, 141, 143, 146, 148
shopping, 120, 127–128, 133–134
sports and the outdoors, 128, 134, 136,
    139, 144, 146–147
timing the visit, 113–114
tours, 117, 134
transportation, 114
Central Maipo, 101
Central Valley, 14–15, 216–240
festivals and events, 219
hotels, 220, 224–225, 227, 232–233, 235,
    237, 240
nightlife and the arts, 240
price categories, 220
restaurants, 220, 224, 226–227, 231–232,
    237
shopping, 233, 240
sports and the outdoors, 225, 240
timing the visit, 219
tours, 221
transportation, 219–220
Centro (Santiago), 54, 62–71
Centro Artesanal Pueblito Los
    Dominicos, 93
Centro Cultural El Austral, 267
Centro Cultural Estación Mapocho,
    77, 79
Centro Cultural La Moneda, 72
Centro Tursitico Capel, 161
Cerro Castillo National Park, 339, 342
Cerro Concepción (Valparaíso), 117
Cerro de la Virgen (Vicuña), 161
Cerro Fitzroy, 394
Cerro la Virgen (Talca), 236
Cerro San Cristóbal, 80
Cerro Santa Lucía, 72
Cerro Tololo Observatory, 160
Cerro Torre, 394
Cerros Pintados, 207
Cerveceria Kunstmann (brewery), 269
Chacabuco, 180, 188–189
Chaitén, 322, 326–330
Chez Manu ✕, 402
Chile Nativo (tours), 360
ChileTrout (fishing trips), 339
Chiloé, 15, 298–320
beaches, 317
festivals and events, 301
hotels, 302, 305, 308, 310, 313–314,
    315–316, 317, 318, 319
nightlife and the arts, 305

price categories, 303
restaurants, 302, 304, 306–307, 309,
    312–313, 315, 319
shopping, 305, 308–309, 314, 320
sports and the outdoors, 305–306, 314, 320
timing the visit, 301
tours, 306, 320
transportation, 301–302
Chiloé Natural (tours), 306
Cholchol, 247–248
Chonchi, 298, 314–317
Chorillo del Salta, 394
Chucao Lodge 🔾, 328
Chuquicamata (copper mine), 189–190
Churches
Central Valley, 222, 228
Chiloé, 307–308, 309, 311, 314–315
Easter Island, 419
El Norte Chico, 156–157, 161, 166, 173
El Norte Grande, 189, 193, 210
Lake District, 247, 267, 292
Santiago, 63, 65, 72
Southern Chilean Patagonia and Tierra del
    Fuego, 367
Climate, 43
Climbing, 262, 296, 396
Clos Apalta Residence 🔾, 232
Clothing, shopping for, 71, 90, 127, 212
Cloud forests, 150, 169–170
Club de Yates Algarrobo, 137
Cocha Resbaladero, 207
Cochamó, 242, 295–296
Comandancia en Jefe de la Armada,
    121
Como Agua Para Chocolate ✕, 82
Concón, 110, 141–144
Confitería Torres ✕, 68
Contacts, 52.⇨ See also Visitor
    information
Copiapó, 150, 153, 173–174
Copper mines, 173, 189–190, 222
Correo Central, 63
Costanera Center (mall), 93–94
Cotelé ✕, 293
Coyhaique, 322, 338–345
Crafts, shopping for
Central Coast, 133
Central Valley, 233, 240
Easter Island, 427
El Norte Chico, 159, 174
El Norte Grande, 198, 212
Lake District, 252, 278, 295
Santiago, 90
Southern Coast, 344
Credit cards, 40
Cruceros Australis, 358
Cruises, 32–33, 52
Lake District, 291–292
Southern Chilean Patagonia and Tierra del
    Fuego, 357–360, 363–364, 377, 398
Cueca clubs, 70
Curacautín and environs, 242,
    253–254
Curicó, 216, 233–234
Curicó Valley, 218
Cuisine, 16–17, 122
Currency exchange, 40–41

D

Dalcahue, 298, 307–309
Damiana Elena ✕, 380
Dance, 70, 98, 426
Dance clubs
Central Coast, 126, 133
Easter Island, 426
El Norte Chico, 159
El Norte Grande, 206, 211
Lake District, 261, 295
Santiago, 76, 84, 89, 97–98
Southern Chilean Patagonia and Tierra del
    Fuego, 404
Department stores, 128, 133
Destilería Mistral, 164
Dining. ⇨ See Restaurants
Distilleries, 161, 162, 164, 165
Diving, 136, 139, 178, 427–428
Dog-sledding trips, 257

E

Easter Island, 15, 412–436
beaches, 421, 431
festivals and events, 415
hotels, 417, 422, 424–426
nightlife and the arts, 426
price categories, 418
restaurants, 417, 421–422
shopping, 427
sports and the outdoors, 427–428
timing the visit, 415–416
tours, 418
transportation, 416–417
visitor information, 418
Ecotourism, 273, 320, 352
El Calafate, Argentina, 354, 357,
    384–393
El Chaltén, Argentina, 354, 357,
    393–396
El Chiringuito ✕, 148
El Galpón ✕, 277
El Growler (pub), 272
El Mercadito ✕, 312
El Mirador de Guadal 🔾, 350
El Morro de Arica, 210
El Museo de Historia Natural y Cul-
    tural del Desierto de Atacama, 190
El Norte Chico, 14, 150–178
beaches, 150, 177
health and safety, 155
hotels, 154–155, 158–159, 162–163,
    165–166, 168–169, 174, 175–176,
    177, 178
nightlife and the arts, 159, 163, 166,
    169, 178
price categories, 155
restaurants, 154, 158, 162, 165, 168,
    174, 177
shopping, 159, 166, 174
sports and the outdoors, 176, 178
timing the visit, 153–154
tours, 155, 156, 163, 175
transportation, 154
El Norte Grande, 14, 180–214
beaches, 205, 210–211
festivals and events, 183
health and safety, 185

hotels, 185, 188, 190, 196–197, 205–206, 211
nightlife and the arts, 188, 190, 198, 206, 211
price categories, 185
restaurants, 184–185, 187, 190, 194, 196, 205, 207, 211
shopping, 188, 191, 198, 206, 212
sports and the outdoors, 198–200
timing the visit, 183–184
tours, 192–193, 204, 210
transportation, 184
El Nuevo Arriero ✕, 187
Electricity, 37
Elqui Domos ⛺, 165–166
Elqui Valley, 153
Embassies, 52
Emergencies, 37, 52, 62
Emiliana Organic Vineyards, 135
Endemiko ⛺, 254
Ensenada, 242, 288–289
Entre Hielos Lodge ⛺, 350
Eolo ⛺, 389
Espacio y Tiempo Hotel de Montaña ⛺, 335
Estación Central (Santiago), 85
Estadio Nacional Julio Martinex Prádanos, 72
Estancia Bahía Esperanza, 366–367
Estancia Cristina ⛺, 390
Estancia Harberton, 399–400
Estancias, 392
Ex Congreso Nacional, 63
Expediciones Chile, 334

F
Farellones Ski Area, 106–108
Fauna Hotel ⛺, 124–125
Feria Fluvial, 269
Festivals and seasonal events, 50–51
Central Coast, 113–114
Central Valley, 219
Chiloé, 301
Easter Island, 415
El Norte Grande, 183
Lake District, 245
Santiago, 57
Film, 76, 93, 383
Films on Chile, 27–28
Fishing
Lake District, 262, 266, 287–288
Southern Chilean Patagonia and Tierra del Fuego, 407
Southern Coast, 328, 334, 339, 346
Flamingos, 180, 202
Food, shopping for, 93
Forts
Chiloé, 303
El Norte Grande, 193, 210
Lake District, 267, 269, 270
Southern Chilean Patagonia and Tierra del Fuego, 383–384
Frutillar, 242, 281–283
Fuego Patagon ✕, 256
Fuente Toscana ✕, 168
Fuerte Bulnes, 383–384
Fuerte de Niebla, 269

Fuerte de San Antonio, 303
Fundación Chol-Chol, 252
Fundo Los Nichos, 164
Funiculars, 80, 117
Futaleufú, 322, 332–334
Fly-fishing, 262, 287–288

G
Gabriela Mistral Cultural Center (GAM), 63
Galería de Arte (Temuco), 248
Galería Municipal de Arte (Valparaíso), 117
Galleries. ⇨ See Museums and galleries
Gardens
Central Coast, 131
Chiloé, 306
El Norte Chico, 157
Lake District, 269
Santiago, 80
Gemini South Observatory, 160
Geoglyphs, 180, 207, 208
Geysers del Tatio, 180, 200–202
Gigante de Atacama, 180, 208
Gifts, shopping for, 90, 233, 383
Glaciar Martial, 400
Glaciar Perito Moreno, 386–387
Glaciar Upsala, 387
Glaciarium, 386
Glaciers
Southern Chilean Patagonia and Tierra del Fuego, 354, 357, 372–373, 375, 384–388, 400
Southern Coast, 328, 338, 348–349
Golf, 134, 146–147
Granja Alfarera Greda, 104

H
Hacienda Santa Cristina ⛺, 168
Handicrafts, shopping for
Central Coast, 133
Central Valley, 233, 240
Easter Island, 427
El Norte Chico, 159, 174
El Norte Grande, 198, 212
Lake District, 252, 278, 295
Santiago, 90
Southern Coast, 344
Hang gliding, 147
Hanga Roa, 412, 418–428
Hangaroa Eco Village & Spa ⛺, 424
Hare Aukara ⛺, 424
Health and beauty products, shopping for, 251
Health issues, 37–38
El Norte Chico, 155
El Norte Grande, 185
Southern Chilean Patagonia and Tierra del Fuego, 365
Hiking and walking
Chiloé, 306, 320
Easter Island, 428
El Norte Grande, 176, 199
Lake District, 262, 264, 273, 288, 296

Southern Chilean Patagonia and Tierra del Fuego, 392, 396, 410
Southern Coast, 349
History, 25–26
Horse racing, 99, 134
Horseback riding
Central Coast, 144
Central Valley, 240
Chiloé, 314
Easter Island, 428
El Norte Grande, 200
Lake District, 262, 288
Southern Chilean Patagonia and Tierra del Fuego, 392
Hostal Ovalle Suite Boutique ⛺, 168–169
Hostal Valle Hermoso ⛺, 162–163
Hot springs
Central Valley, 223–224
El Norte Chico, 167–168
El Norte Grande, 201–202, 206, 207
Lake District, 258, 279
Santiago, 105–106
Southern Coast, 337
Hotel Ayacara ⛺, 282
Hotel Boutique Casadoca ⛺, 143
Hotel Cabo de Hornos ⛺, 382
Hotel Del Mar ⛺, 132
Hotel Dreams Pedro de Valdivia ⛺, 271
Hotel Ismael 312 ⛺, 76
Hotel Magnolia ⛺, 76
Hotel O'Higgins, 130
Hotel Orly ⛺, 96–97
Hotel Plaza San Francisco ⛺, 69
Hotel Río Serrano ⛺, 373, 376
Hotels, 36–37
Central Coast, 115, 124–126, 132–133, 135, 139, 143–144, 146, 148
Central Valley, 220, 224–225, 227, 232–233, 235, 237, 240
Chiloé, 302, 305, 308, 310, 315–316, 317, 318, 319
Easter Island, 417, 422, 424–426
El Norte Chico, 154–155, 158–159, 162–163, 165–166, 168–169, 174, 175–176, 177, 178
El Norte Grande, 185, 188, 190, 196–197, 205–206, 211
Lake District, 246, 250–251, 253, 254, 256, 260–261, 263, 265–266, 271–272, 273–275, 278, 280–281, 282–283, 285–286, 289, 290, 294–295, 296
price categories, 60, 115, 155, 185, 220, 246, 303, 326, 365, 386, 418
Santiago, 60, 69, 76, 83, 89, 91–92, 96–97, 107
Southern Chilean Patagonia and Tierra del Fuego, 364–365, 369–371, 373, 376, 382–383, 389–391, 394–395, 403–404, 410
Southern Coast, 326, 328–330, 332, 333–334, 335, 336–337, 338, 343–344, 346, 350, 351
Houses, historical
Central Coast, 120, 140–141
El Norte Chico, 163–164
El Norte Grande, 204
Lake District, 267
Santiago, 73, 80–81

Southern Chilean Patagonia and Tierra del Fuego, 380, 398–400
Huella Andina Expeditions, 288
Huilo Huilo, 242, 273–274
Huilo Huilo ⊡, 273–274
Humberstone, 204

I

Ice-trekking, 392–393
Iglesia Catedral, 156
Iglesia de la Immaculada Concepción, 161
Iglesia de la Merced, 222
Iglesia de Nuestra Señora de Gracia, 309
Iglesia de Nuestra Señora de los Dolores, 307–308
Iglesia de San Carlos, 314–315
Iglesia de San Francisco (Castro), 311
Iglesia de San Marcos, 210
Iglesia de San Pedro (Quicaví), 307
Iglesia de Santa María de Loreto, 309
Iglesia de Tenaún, 307
Iglesia Hanga Roa, 419
Iglesia Nuestra Señora del Rosario, 173
Iglesia Parroquial
Puerto Natales, 367
Santa Cruz, 228
Iglesia San Francisco
Copiapó, 173
La Serena, 156
Santiago, 72
Iglesia San Pedro (San Pedro de Atacama), 193
Iglesia San Vicente Ferrer, 166
Iglesia Santo Domingo, 157
Ilo Mapu ✕, 131
Iquique, 180, 202–206
Isla de Aucar, 306
Isla Huapi, 276
Isla Negra, 110, 139–141
Isla Quinchao, 298, 309–310
Isla Seca ⊡, 148
Islote Pájaros Niños, 137
Itineraries, 46–49

J

Jardin Botánico (Valdivia), 269
Jardin Botánico Mapulemu, 80
Jewelry, shopping for, 98
José Ramón 277 (pub), 76

K

Kayaking, 273, 288, 306, 314, 334, 393
Ko'Kayak, 288
Kume Yeal ✕, 274

L

La Alameda, 54, 71–74
La Araucanía, 244
La Bicicleta Verde (tours), 99
La Caperucita y El Lobo ✕, 124
La Cervecería Chaltén ✕, 394
La Chascona, 80–81
La Chiminea (club), 70
La Cuisine ✕, 380
La Junta, 322, 335
La Mar ✕, 88
La Marmita ✕, 381
La Mulata ✕, 205
La Parrilla de Thor ✕, 270
La Parva, 107
La Pista del Andino ⊡, 406
La Sebastiana, 120
La Serena, 150, 155–159
La Silla Observatory, 160
Lago Chungará, 213
Lago Escondido, 400
Lago General Carrera and environs, 322, 349–350
Lago Ranco and environs, 242, 274–276
Lago Roca, 387–388
Lago Vichuquén, 216, 234–235
Lago Yelcho, 328
Laguna Chaxa, 193
Laguna del Desierto, 394
Laguna Nimez Reserva Natural, 388
Laguna Salada, 193
Lagunas Cotacotani, 213
Lake District, 15, 242–296
beaches, 265, 281, 292
festivals and events, 245
hotels, 246, 250–251, 253, 254, 256, 260–261, 263, 265–266, 271–272, 273–275, 278, 280–281, 282–283, 285–286, 289, 290, 294–295, 296
nightlife and the arts, 251, 257, 261, 272, 283, 287, 295
price categories, 246
restaurants, 245–246, 250, 256, 258–259, 265, 270–271, 274, 277, 280, 282, 284–285, 289, 293
shopping, 251–252, 257, 269, 278, 295
sports and the outdoors, 257, 261–262, 264, 266, 272–273, 275–276, 278–279, 287–288, 290, 296
timing the visit, 244–245
tours, 246, 255, 273, 275, 290
transportation, 245
Lakutaia Hotel ⊡, 410
Land Rover excursions, 393
Language, 44–45
Las Campanas Observatory, 160
Las Condes, 54, 90–94
Lastarria, 54, 74–77
Le Rêve ⊡, 97
Libraries, 71–72, 198
Librería del Desierto, 198

Lican Ray, 242, 265–266
Liguria ✕, 96
Limarí Valley, 153
Lodge El Taique ⊡, 280
Lodge Valle Chacabuco ⊡, 351
Lodging. ⇨ See Hotels
Londres 38 Espacio de Memorias, 63
Loreto Hotel ⊡, 83
Los Caiquenes Hotel Boutique ⊡, 286
Los Cauquenes Resort and Spa ⊡, 404
Los Cerros ⊡, 395
Los Glaciares National Park, 354, 357, 384–393
Los Lagos and Los Ríos, 244
Lutier Bistro ✕, 259

M

Mail and shipping, 39
Maitencillo, 110, 144–147
Malls and shopping centers
Central Coast, 133, 134
Chiloé, 383
El Norte Chico, 159
El Norte Grande, 206
Santiago, 71, 93–94
Mamiña, 180, 206
Mamma Gaucha ✕, 342
Mano del Desierto, 187
Mantagua Wetlands at Posada del Parque, 142
MAPSE Museo Rapa Nui, 419
Mapu Lahual, 278–279
Mapuche people, 249
Maracuyá ✕, 211
María Elena (factory), 189
MaríaMaría ✕, 124
Markets
Central Coast, 120
Chiloé, 305, 308–309, 314, 320
Easter Island, 427
El Norte Chico, 159, 174
El Norte Grande, 188, 198, 212
Lake District, 251, 269, 272
Santiago, 67, 74, 79–80, 84, 93
Southern Chilean Patagonia and Tierra del Fuego, 383
Martial Glacier, 400
Martin Pescador ✕, 333
Matucana 100 (theater), 86
Maule Valley, 217
Memorial en Homenaje a los Detenidos Desaparecidos y Ejecutados Políticos de la IV Región, 157
Mercado Central, 79
Mercado La Recova, 159
Mercado Puerto, 120
Mercato ✕, 250
Metropolitan Cathedral, 63, 65
Mina El Teniente and Sewell, 222
Miñeques Lake, 202

Ministerio de las Culturas, las Artes y el Patrimonio, *121*
Mirador (Queilón), *318*
Mirador Cerro la Cruz, *377, 379*
Miscanti Lake, *202*
Mistral, Gabriela, *161, 163–164*
Moais, *423, 429–430, 431, 432, 433*
Money matters, *39–41*
Monolith, *384*
Monumento al Ovejero, *342*
Monumento de los Héroes de Iquique, *121*
Monumento Nacional Isla Cachagua, *147*
Monumento Natural Cerro Ñielol, *248*
Monumento Natural Cueva de Milodón, *367*
Monumento Natural Islotes de Puñihuil, *303*
Monumento Natural Los Pingüinos, *379*
Monumento Natural Pichasca, *167*
Morro Lobos, *306*
Motels, *37*
Mountain climbing, *262, 296, 396*
Muelle Prat (Valparaíso), *120–121*
Multisport, *262, 288, 306*
Municipalidad de Santiago, *65*
Museo a Cielo Abierto, *121*
Museo Antropológico Martín Gusinde, *409*
Museo Arqueológico de La Serena, *157*
Museo Arqueológico de San Miguel de Azapa, *210*
Museo Artequín, *85*
Museo Chileno de Arte Precolombino, *65–66*
Museo Colonial Alemán, *281*
Museo Colonial de Vichuquén, *235*
Museo Corbeta Esmeralda, *204*
Museo de Antofagasta, *187*
Museo de Arqueológio a Historia Francisco Fonck, *130*
Museo de Arte Colonial San Francisco, *73*
Museo de Arte Contemporáneo (Santiago), *79*
Museo de Arte Contemporáneo (Valdivia), *269*
Museo de Arte Moderne de Chiloé, *311–312*
Museo de Artes Visuales, *74*
Museo de Bellas Artes, *121*
Museo de Ciencia y Tecnologia, *85*
Museo de Colchagua, *228–229*
Museo de Historia Natural de Valparaíso, *121*
Museo de la Exploración Rudolph Amandus Philippi, *269*
Museo de La Memoria y Los Derechos Humanos, *86*
Museo de la Moda, *87*
Museo de las Armas, *210*

Museo de las Tradiciones Chonchinas, *315*
Museo del Fin del Mundo, *400–401*
Museo del Mar, *210*
Museo del Recuerdo, *379*
Museo Ferroviario, *86*
Museo Gabriela Mistral, *161*
Museo Histórico de Puetro Montt, *292*
Museo Histórico Ethnográfico de Dalcahue, *308*
Museo Histórico Gabriel González Videla, *157*
Museo Histórico Municipal (Puerto Natales), *367*
Museo Histórico Nacional (Santiago), *66*
Museo Histórico y Antropológico Maurice van de Maele, *270*
Museo Histórico y Arqueológico de Villarrica, *255*
Museo Mapuche de Cholchol, *248*
Museo Maritimo, *401*
Museo Mineralógico (Copiapó), *173*
Museo Mineralógico Ignacio Domeyko, *157*
Museo Municipal de Castro, *312*
Museo Municipal Osorno, *277*
Museo Nacional de Bellas Artes, *79*
Museo Nacional de Historia Natural, *86*
Museo Nacional Ferroviario Pablo Neruda, *248*
Museo Naval y Maritimo (Punta Arenas), *379*
Museo Naval y Maritimo de Valparaíso, *121*
Museo Regional de Ancud, *303–304*
Museo Regional de Atacama, *173*
Museo Regional de Aysén, *342*
Museo Regional de Iquique, *204*
Museo Regional de la Araucanía, *248*
Museo Regional de Magallanes, *379*
Museo Regional de Rancagua, *222–223*
Museo Salesiano de Maggiorino Borgatello, *379–380*
Museo San José del Carmen de El Huique, *229*
Museums and galleries
Central Coast, *117, 121, 127, 130, 136, 140–141*
Central Valley, *222–223, 228–229, 235*
Chiloé, *303–304, 308, 311–312, 315, 318*
Easter Island, *419, 427*
El Norte Chico, *157, 161, 163–164, 173*
El Norte Grande, *187, 190, 204, 210*
Lake District, *248, 255, 269–270, 277, 281, 292, 295*
Santiago, *63, 65–66, 72, 73, 74–75, 79, 85–86, 87, 90*
Southern Chilean Patagonia and Tierra del Fuego, *367, 379–380, 386, 399–401, 409*
Southern Coast, *342*

Music
Central Coast, *127*
El Norte Chico, *178*
Lake District, *272, 283, 295*
Santiago, *70, 83, 97, 98*
Southern Coast, *344*

N

Neruda, Pablo, *80–81, 120, 140–141, 248*
Nightlife and the arts
Central Coast, *126–127, 133*
Central Valley, *240*
Chiloe, *305*
Easter Island, *426*
El Norte Chico, *159, 163, 166, 169, 178*
El Norte Grande, *188, 190, 198, 206, 211*
Lake District, *251, 257, 261, 272, 283, 287, 295*
Santiago, *60–61, 70, 76–77, 83–84, 89, 93, 97–98*
Southern Chilean Patagonia and Tierra del Fuego, *383, 404–405*
Southern Coast, *344*
Nitrate Pampa, *183*
Northern Beaches (Central Coast), *113*

O

Observatories, *160, 161–162, 225*
Observatorio Cerro Mamalluca, *161–162*
Ocio Territorial Hotel 🗙, *313*
Ojos del Caburgua, *258*
Olam 🗙, *91*
Orongo, *436*
Osorno, *242, 276–279*
Outdoor activities. ⇨ See Sports and the outdoors; specific activity
Ovalle, *150, 166–169*

P

Packing, *41*
Palaces
Central Coast, *130*
El Norte Grande, *204*
Santiago, *73*
Southern Chilean Patagonia and Tierra del Fuego, *380*
Palacio Astoreca, *204*
Palacio Cousiño, *73*
Palacio de la Moneda, *73*
Palacio de los Tribunales de Justicia, *66*
Palacio Rioja, *130*
Palacio Sara Braun, *380*
Pan-American Highway, *329*
Pangue Observatory, *162*
Parinacota, *213*
Parks and reserves
Central Coast, *142, 147*
Central Valley, *223, 234*
Chiloé, *298, 303, 306, 316–317, 318–319*
El Norte Chico, *150, 157, 169–172, 174–176, 178*

El Norte Grande, 180, 202, 207–208,
  212–214
Lake District, 242, 252–253, 258, 262–264,
  276, 277, 278–280, 289–290, 292
Santiago, 54, 66, 72, 77–86, 94
*Southern Chilean Patagonia and Tierra del
  Fuego*, 354, 357, 366–367, 371–376,
  379, 380, 384–393, 405–410
Southern Coast, 322, 330–332, 337–338,
  339, 342, 348–349, 350–352
Parque Ahuenco, 306
Parque Cuarto Centenario, 277
Parque Cuevas Volcanicas, 258
Parque de las Esculturas, 94
Parque Etnobotánico Omora, 409–410
Parque Forestal, 54, 77–80
Parque Futangue, 276
Parque Japones, 157
Parque Metropolitano, 54, 80–84
Parque Nacional Alerce Andino, 292
**Parque Nacional Bosques de Fray
  Jorge** (cloud forest), 150, 169–170
Parque Nacional Chiloé, 298, 316–317
Parque Nacional Conguillio, 242,
  252–253
Parque Nacional Huerquehue, 242,
  262–263
Parque Nacional La Campana, 142
Parque Nacional Laguna San Rafael,
  322, 348–349
Parque Nacional Lauca, 180, 212–213
Parque Nacional Llanos de Challe,
  150, 171–172
Parque Nacional Los Glaciares, 354,
  357, 384–393
**Parque Nacional Nevado Tres
  Cruces,** 150, 174–176
Parque Nacional Pan de Azúcar,
  150, 178
Parque Nacional Patagonia, 322,
  350–352
**Parque Nacional Pumlín Douglas
  Tompkins,** 322, 330–332
Parque Nacional Puyehue, 242,
  279–280
Parque Nacional Queulat, 322,
  337–338
Parque Nacional Radal Siete Tazas,
  234
Parque Nacional Tierra del Fuego,
  405–409
Parque Nacional Torres del Paine,
  354, 371–376
**Parque Nacional Vicente Pérez
  Rosales,** 242, 289–290
Parque Nacional Villarrica, 242,
  263–264
Parque O'Higgins (Santiago), 66
Parque Quinta Normal area, 54, 84–86
Parque Tantauco, 318–319
Paseo 21 de Mayo (Valparaíso), 121
Passports and visas, 41–42
Patagona Excursions, 339
Patagonia Big Five (tours), 352
Patagonia Camp ☒ , 376
Patio Bellavista ✕ , 81
Penguins, 147, 150, 170–171, 379

Pérgola de las Flores, 79
Perito Moreno Glacier, 386–387
Persa Bío Bío (market), 67
Petroglyphs
Easter Island, 430, 436
El Norte Chico, 168
El Norte Grande, 206, 208
Pica, 180, 207
Pisco distilleries, 161, 162, 164, 165
Pisco Elqui, 150, 163–166
Pisquera Aba, 162
Pizzas de Fabio ✕ , 333
Playa Anakena, 431
Playa Cavancha, 205
Playa de Queilén, 317
Playa El Canelo, 138
Playa El Sol, 131
Playa Las Machas, 177
Playa Lebun, 317
Playa Ritoque, 143
Playa Totoralillo, 158
Playa Zapallar, 147–148
Plaza Anibal Pinto, 248
Plaza de Armas
Coyhaique, 342
Curicó, 234
Ovalle, 167
Puerto Natales, 367
Santa Cruz, 229
Santiago, 66
Plaza de la Ciudadania, 73
Plaza de la Constitución, 73
Plaza de los Héroes, 223
Plaza José Francisco Vergara, 130
Plaza Mar Bravo, 147
Plaza Muñoz Gamero, 380
Plaza Prat, 204–205
Plaza Sotomayor, 121
Plaza Tupahue, 81–82
Plaza Victoria, 122
Plazuela del Tren, 312
Pomaire, 103–105
Posada Queulat ☒ , 338
Pottery workshops, 104
Price categories
Central Coast, 115
Central Valley, 220
Chiloé, 303
Easter Island, 418
El Norte Chico, 155
El Norte Grande, 185
Lake District, 246
Santiago, 60
*Southern Chilean Patagonia and Tierra del
  Fuego*, 365, 386
Southern Coast, 326
Providencia, 54, 94–99
Pucón, 242, 257–262
Pueblito Expediciones, 273
Puerto Aysén, 322, 345–348
Puerto Chacabuco, 322, 345–348
Puerto Hambre, 354, 383–384
Puerto Montt, 242, 290–295
Puerto Natales, 354, 356–357, 365–371
Puerto Octay, 242, 280–281
Puerto Puyuhuapi, 322, 335–337

Puerto Varas, 242, 283–288
Puerto Williams, 354, 409–410
Pukara de Quitor, 193
Pukara del Cerro Inca, 206
Pulpería Santa Elvira ✕ , 68
Puna Pau, 436
Punta Arenas, 354, 357, 376–383

Q

Queilén, 298, 317–318
Quellón, 298, 318–320
Quemchi, 298, 306–307
Quicaví, 298, 307
Quinta Vergara, 131
Quintay, 110, 135–136
Quintay Whaling Station, 136

R

Raices Andinas (tours), 210
Rain forests
Chiloé, 306, 318–319
Lake District, 278–279
Southern Coast, 337–338
Ramal Talca-Constitución, 236
Rancagua, 216, 222–225
Rancho Espantapajaros ✕ , 280
Rano Kau, 436
Rano Raraku, 431
Rapel Valley, 218
Refugio de Navegantes, 318
Refugio de Navegantes ☒ , 308
Refugio Lo Valdés, 106
Refugio Maricunga ☒ , 175–176
Refugio Pullao ☒ , 313–314
Reloj de Flores, 131
Remota ☒ , 371
Reserva Nacional Coyhaique, 342
Reserva Nacional Laguna Parrillar,
  384
Reserva Nacional Las Vicuñas, 180,
  213–214
Reserva Nacional los Flamencos,
  180, 202
Reserva Nacional Magallanes, 380
**Reserva Nacional Pampa del
  Tamarugal,** 180, 207–208
**Reserva Nacional Pingüino de
  Humboldt,** 150, 170–171
**Reserva Nacional Río de los
  Cipreses,** 223
Reserva Nacional Río Simpson, 342
Residenciales, 36–37
Restaurant Kiel ✕ , 293
Restaurants, 36
Central Coast, 114–115, 122–124,
  131–132, 136, 139, 141, 143, 146, 148
Central Valley, 220, 224, 226–227,
  231–232, 237
Chiloé, 302, 304, 306–307, 309, 312–313,
  315, 319
cuisine, 16–17, 122
Easter Island, 417, 421–422
El Norte Chico, 154, 158, 162, 165, 168,
  174, 177

El Norte Grande, 184–185, 187, 190, 194, 196, 205, 207, 211
Lake District, 245–246, 250, 256, 258–259, 265, 270–271, 274, 277, 280, 282, 284–285, 289, 293
price categories, 60, 115, 155, 185, 220, 246, 303, 326, 365, 386, 418
Santiago, 59–60, 67–69, 75, 81, 82–83, 88–89, 91, 94–96, 103, 104–105
Southern Chilean Patagonia and Tierra del Fuego, 364, 367–369, 380–382, 388–389, 394, 402–403
Southern Coast, 326, 328, 333, 336, 342–343

Restrooms (Santiago), 66
Ristorante Vino Bello ✕, 232
Roca Oceánico, 142
Rodeos, 225
Ruta del Vino (Curicó), 234
Ruta del Vino de Casablanca, 134
Ruta del Vino de Colchagua, 229

S

Safety, 42
El Norte Chico, 155
El Norte Grande, 185
Santiago, 61–62
Southern Chilean Patagonia and Tierra del Fuego, 365
Sala Museo Arqueológico de Santiago, 74–75
Salar de Surire, 180, 214
Salar de Tara, 193
Salar de Uyuni, 193
Salsa clubs, 84
Salvador Cocina y Café ✕, 68
San Clemente, 236
San Fernando and environs, 216, 225–227
San Jose Mine, 173
San Pedro de Atacama, 180, 183, 191–200
Sandboarding, 200
Santa Cruz, 216, 227–233
Santiago, 14, 54–108
emergencies, 62
festivals and events, 57
hotels, 60, 69, 76, 83, 89, 91–92, 96–97, 107
nightlife and the arts, 60–61, 70, 76–77, 83–84, 89, 93, 97–98
price categories, 60
restaurants, 59–60, 67–69, 75, 81, 82–83, 88–89, 91, 94–96, 103, 104–105
safety, 61–62
shopping, 61, 67, 70–71, 74, 77, 79–80, 84, 90, 93–94, 98
side trips, 99–108
sports and the outdoors, 99, 108
timing the visit, 57–58
tours, 62, 99
transportation, 58–59
visitor information, 62
Santiago Centro, 54, 62–71
Santiago Wine Club, 77
Santuario El Cañi, 264
Scenic flights, 408
Scuba diving, 136, 139, 178, 427–428

Se Cocina ✕, 282
Sheraton Miramar 🛏, 132–133
Shopping.⇨ See also Markets
Central Coast, 120, 127–128, 133–134
Central Valley, 233, 240
Chiloé, 305, 308–309, 314, 320
Easter Island, 427
El Norte Chico, 159, 166, 174
El Norte Grande, 188, 191, 198, 206, 212
Lake District, 251–252, 257, 269, 272, 278, 295
Santiago, 61, 67, 70–71, 74, 77, 79–80, 84, 90, 93–94, 98
Southern Chilean Patagonia and Tierra del Fuego, 383
Southern Coast, 344
Singular, The 🛏, 76
Singular, The ✕, 369
Singular Patagonia, The 🛏, 371
Ski & Outdoor Volcán Osorno, 290
Skiing and snowboarding
Lake District, 262, 264, 290
Santiago, 99, 106–108
Southern Chilean Patagonia and Tierra del Fuego, 408–409
Southern Coast, 345
Soccer, 72, 99, 128, 134
Sonesta Hotel Osorno 🛏, 278
Southeastern Circuit (Easter Island), 412, 428–431
Southern Beaches (Central Coast), 113
Southern Chilean Patagonia and Tierra del Fuego, 15, 354–410
health and safety, 365
hotels, 364–365, 369–371, 373, 376, 382–383, 389–391, 394–395, 403–404, 410
nightlife and the arts, 383, 404–405
price categories, 365, 386
restaurants, 364, 367–369, 380–382, 388–389, 394, 402–403
shopping, 383
sports and the outdoors, 357–361, 391–393, 396, 407–409, 410
timing the visit, 362
tours, 357–361, 385–386, 391, 401, 410
transportation, 362–364
visitor information, 365
Southern Coast, 15, 322–352
hotels, 326, 328–330, 332, 333–334, 335, 336–337, 338, 343–344, 346, 350, 351
nightlife and the arts, 344
price categories, 326
restaurants, 326, 328, 333, 336, 342–343
shopping, 344
sports and the outdoors, 334, 335, 337, 345, 346, 348, 349, 352
timing the visit, 325
tours, 327–328, 330, 333, 335, 339, 349, 352
transportation, 325–326
Spanish vocabulary, 44–45
Spas, 99
Sports and the outdoors, 20–21.⇨ See also specific activities
Central Coast, 128, 134, 136, 139, 144, 146–147
Central Valley, 225, 240
Chiloé, 305–306, 314, 320
Easter Island, 427–428

El Norte Chico, 176, 178
El Norte Grande, 198–200
Lake District, 257, 261–262, 264, 266, 272–273, 275–276, 278–279, 287–288, 290, 296
Santiago, 99, 108
Southern Chilean Patagonia and Tierra del Fuego, 357–361, 391–393, 396, 407–409, 410
Southern Coast, 334, 335, 337, 345, 346, 348, 349, 352
Stargazing, 160, 200
Subway travel (Santiago), 59
Surfing, 147, 428

T

Tagua Tagua Observatory, 225
Tahai, 419, 421
Talca, 216, 235–237, 240
Taxes, 42
Taxis
Easter Island, 417
El Norte Chico, 154
Santiago, 59
Te Moana ✕, 422
Teatro del Lago, 283
Teatro Municipal
Iquique, 205
Santiago, 70, 73–74
Teatro Municipal de Viña del Mar, 130
Tembeta Tours, 156
Temuco, 242, 246–252
Termas de Cauquenes, 223–224
Termas de Puritama, 201–202
Termas de Socos, 167–168
Termas Geométricas, 258
Termas Mamiña, 206
Theater
Central Coast, 127, 130
El Norte Grande, 205
Lake District, 283, 295
Santiago, 70, 73–74, 76–77, 86, 98
Tierra Chiloé 🛏, 314
Tierra del Fuego.⇨ See Southern Chilean Patagonia and Tierra del Fuego
Timing the visit, 43
Tipping, 43
Torre Reloj
Antofagasta, 187
Iquique, 205
Torreón Los Canelos, 270
Torres del Paine, 356–357
Tours
Central Coast, 117, 134
Central Valley, 221
Chiloé, 306, 320
Easter Island, 418
El Norte Chico, 155, 156, 163, 175
El Norte Grande, 192–193, 204, 210
Lake District, 246, 255, 273, 275, 290
Santiago, 62, 99
Southern Chilean Patagonia and Tierra del Fuego, 357–361, 385–386, 391, 401, 410
Southern Coast, 327–328, 330, 333, 335, 339, 349, 352

Train travel, 35
Central Coast, 114
Central Valley, 220, 236
Southern Chilean Patagonia and Tierra del
Fuego, 401
Transportation, 32–35
Travesia ✕, 312–313
Trawen Restaurant ✕, 259
Trekking, 264, 288, 392–393
Tren del Fin del Mundo, 401
Tres Marias Excursions, 401
Tulor, 193–194
Turismo Alma Atacama, 175
Turismo Migrantes, 163

U

U.S. Embassy, 52
Upsala Glacier, 387
Ushuaia, Argentina, 354, 357, 396–405

V

Valdivia, 242, 266–273
Valle de la Luna, 194
Valle de la Muerte, 194
Valle del Encanto, 168
Valle del Maule Ruta del Vino
Office, 236
Valle Nevado, 107
Valparaíso, 110, 113, 116–128
Vega Chica and Vega Central, 79–80
Vertiente del Radium, 206
Vicuña, 150, 159–163
Villarrica, 242, 254–257
Viña Antiyal, 102
Viña Balduzzi, 236
Viña Casa Donoso, 236–237
Viña Cavas del Valle, 162
Viña Concha y Toro, 102–103
Viña De Martino, 101
Viña del Mar, 110, 113, 128–134
Viña Gillmore, 237
Viña Lapostolle-Clos Apalta, 229–230
Viña Laura Hartwig, 230
Viña Matetic, 135
Viña Miguel Torres, 234

Viña Montes, 230
Viña MontGras, 231
Viña San Pedro, 224
Viña Santa Cruz, 231
Viña Santa Rita, 103
Viña Tabalí, 168
Viña Tipaume, 224
Viña Undurraga, 101
Viña Vik, 226
Viña Vik Hotel 🍴, 227
Viña Viu Manent, 231
Viñedos de Alcohuaz, 164–165
Viñedos Torreón de Paredes, 224
Vineyards.⇨ See Wine and wineries
Visas, 41–42
Visitor information, 43, 52
Easter Island, 418
Santiago, 62
Southern Chilean Patagonia and Tierra del
Fuego, 365
Vitacura, 54, 86–90
Vocabulary, 44–45
Volcán Puyehue, 279
Volcanoes
Easter Island, 436
El Norte Grande, 202
Lake District, 253, 258, 263–264, 279,
289–290
Southern Coast, 330, 332

W

Walking.⇨ See Hiking and walking
Water sports, 178, 333
Waterfalls
Central Valley, 234
Lake District, 258
Southern Chilean Patagonia and Tierra del
Fuego, 372, 394
Southern Coast, 330, 332, 337–338, 342
Weather, 43
Western Circuit (Easter Island), 413,
431–436
Whaling factory, 136
Wilderness Travel, 360
Wildlife spotting
Central Coast, 137, 142, 147
Central Valley, 234

Chiloé, 303, 306, 317
El Norte Chico, 150, 169–172, 174–175,
178
El Norte Grande, 180, 193, 202, 212–214
Lake District, 287
Southern Chilean Patagonia and Tierra del
Fuego, 372–373, 379, 388, 399, 400,
405–407
Southern Coast, 339, 342, 349, 350–351
Wine and wineries, 18–19, 228
Central Coast, 110, 134–135
Central Valley, 224, 225, 226, 229–231,
233, 234, 236–237
El Norte Chico, 162, 164–165, 168
Santiago, 77, 90, 101, 102–103
WineBox Hotel 🍴, 125
Wines and Barrels Travel (tours), 221

Y

Yelcho Glacier, 328

Z

Zapallar, 110, 147–148
Zapato Amarillo 🍴, 281
Zip lining, 290
Zoológico Nacional, 82

Photo Credits

Front Cover: Kseniya Ragozina / Alamy Stock Photo [Description: The Mano de Desierto is a large-scale sculpture of a hand located in the Atacama Desert in Chile] **Back cover, from left to right:** Diego Grandi/Shutterstock. Tetyana Dotsenko/Shutterstock. David Ionut/ Shutterstock. **Spine:** Lisastrachan/Dreamstime. **Interior, from left to right:** Tifonimages/ Dreamstime (1). Millionstock/Shutterstock (2-3). **Chapter 1: Experience Chile:** Sernatur (6-7). Helder Geraldo Ribeiro/Shutterstock (8-9). Casadphoto/Dreamstime (9). Padchas/Dreamstime (9). Sernatur (10). Viu Manent Winery (10). Pierre-Jean Durieu / Shutterstock (10). Dliv/ Dreamstime (10). Diegograndi/Dreamstime (11). Sunsinger / Shutterstock (11). Atosan/ Dreamstime (12). Vladimir Krupenkin / Shutterstock (12). Abriendomundo/Shutterstock (12). Sernatur (12). Diego Fontecilla/Fundación imagen de Chile (13). Sernatur (13). Fotosdelalma/ Shutterstock (13). Jeremy Richards/Shutterstock (13). Larisa Blinova/Shutterstock (16). Nishihama/Shutterstock (16). Daniel Subiabre/Shutterstock (16). Hlphoto/Shutterstock (17). Barmalini/iStockphoto (17). Cephas Picture Library / Alamy Stock Photo (18) Vladgalenko/ Dreamstime (18). Leonardo Spencer/Dreamstime (18). Diegograndi/ Dreamstime (19). Bodegas RE (19). Oleg Senkov/Shutterstock (20). Tito Alejandro Alarcón Pradena (20). D. Joseph Meyer/Shutterstock. (20). Vaclav Sebek/Shutterstock (20). Ibrester/Dreamstime (20). Jose Luis Stephens (21). Pichugin/Shutterstock (21). Kavram/Shutterstock (21). Alberto Loyo (21). Birdiegal/Shutterstock (21). **Chapter 3: Santiago:** F11photo/Dreamstime (53). Diegograndi/Dreamstime (65). Cge2010/ Shutterstock (67). Toniflap/Dreamstime (75). Carriagada/Shutterstock (81). Javier Volcan/Shutterstock (89). Antiyal (102). Richard Yukio/Shutterstock (104). **Chapter 4: The Central Coast:** Wastesoul/Dreamstime (109). Tomelitte/Dreamstime (116). Diegograndi/Dreamstime (120). Brizardh/Dreamstime (130). Nature's Charm/Shutterstock (138). Paulette Paiyee/Shutterstock (142). Felipe Ahumada Arroyo/Shutterstock (144). **Chapter 5: El Norte Chico:** R.M. Nunes/Shutterstock (149). Viennetta/iStockphoto (164). Marcela Lefort Valenzuela/Shutterstock (169). Spencer Arquimedes/Shutterstock (170). Martin Schneiter/iStockphoto (175). Jess Kraft/Shutterstock (176). **Chapter 6: El Norte Grande:** RPBaiao/Shutterstock (179). Delpixel/Shutterstock (192). MarcioDufranc (195). Skouatroulio/iStockphoto (196). Helder Geraldo Ribeiro/Shutterstock (201). Dmitry Chulov/Shutterstock (212). **Chapter 7: The Central Valley:** Free Wind 2014/ Shutterstock (215). Claudio Arriagada/iStockphoto (223). Agent Wolf/Shutterstock (226). Hoberman Publishing / Alamy Stock Photo (230). JTav/Shutterstock (238-239). **Chapter 8: The Lake District:** Jose Arcos Aguilar/Shutterstock (241). Cavan-Images/Shutterstock (252). Marktucan/iStockphoto (259). Jonas Tufvesson/Shutterstock (263). Guaxinim/Shutterstock (275). Vika12345/Dreamstime (279). Fotosdelalma/Shutterstock (291). Alex Maldonado Mancilla/Shutterstock (294). **Chapter 9: Chiloé:** Tifonimages/Dreamstime (297). Mathes/Dreamstime (304). Marcelicagaray/ Dreamstime (308). Mathes/Dreamstime (310). Fotos593/Shutterstock (315). Michal Knitl/Shutterstock (316). **Chapter 10: The Southern Coast:** Albertoloyo/Dreamstime (321). Erlantzperezr/Dreamstime (331). Jose Arcos Aguilar/Shutterstock (336). Olga Gauri/Shutterstock (340-341). Dudarev Mikhail/Shutterstock (343). Steve Allen/Shutterstock (348). **Chapter 11: Southern Chilean Patagonia and Tierra del Fuego:** Saraporn/Shutterstock (353). Esinel | Dreamstime.com (371). Henner Damke/ Shutterstock (387). Saiko3p | Dreamstime.com (395). Saiko3p/Shutterstock (397). Padchas/Dreamstime (399). Fyletto/iStockphoto (407). **Chapter 12: Easter Island:** Martin Vanek/iStockphoto (411). Lyaschock/Dreamstime (421). Abriendo mundo/iStockphoto (430). Evenfh/iStockphoto (432). Abriendo mundo/iStockphoto (434-435). **About Our Writers:** All photos are courtesy of the writers.

Every effort has been made to trace the copyright holders, and we apologize in advance for any accidental errors. We would be happy to apply the corrections in the following edition of this publication.

Fodor's ESSENTIAL CHILE

Publisher: Stephen Horowitz, *General Manager*

Editorial: Douglas Stallings, *Editorial Director*; Jill Fergus, Amanda Sadlowski, Caroline Trefler, *Senior Editors*; Kayla Becker, Alexis Kelly, *Editors;* Angelique Kennedy-Chavannes, *Assistant Editor*

Design: Tina Malaney, *Director of Design and Production*; Jessica Gonzalez, *Graphic Designer*

Production: Jennifer DePrima, *Editorial Production Manager*; Elyse Rozelle, *Senior Production Editor;* Monica White, *Production Editor*

Maps: Rebecca Baer, *Senior Map Editor*; Mark Stroud (Moon Street Cartography), *Cartographer*

Photography: Viviane Teles, *Senior Photo Editor;* Namrata Aggarwal, Payal Gupta, Ashok Kumar, *Photo Editors;* Eddie Aldrete, *Photo Production Intern*

Business and Operations: Chuck Hoover, *Chief Marketing Officer;* Robert Ames, *Group General Manager;* Devin Duckworth, *Director of Print Publishing*

Public Relations and Marketing: Joe Ewaskiw, *Senior Director of Communications and Public Relations*

Fodors.com: Jeremy Tarr, *Editorial Director;* Rachael Levitt, *Managing Editor*

Technology: Jon Atkinson, *Director of Technology;* Rudresh Teotia, *Lead Developer;* Jacob Ashpis, *Content Operations Manager*

Writers: Mark Johanson, Jimmy Langman, Matt Maynard, Sorrel Moseley-Williams

Editors: Kayla Becker, Lola Augustine Brown

Production Editor: Jennifer DePrima

2nd Edition

ISBN 978-1-64097-357-2

ISSN 2576-0432

All details in this book are based on information supplied to us at press time. Always confirm information when it matters, especially if you're making a detour to visit a specific place. Fodor's expressly disclaims any liability, loss, or risk, personal or otherwise, that is incurred as a consequence of the use of any of the contents of this book.

SPECIAL SALES
This book is available at special discounts for bulk purchases for sales promotions or premiums. For more information, e-mail SpecialMarkets@fodors.com.

PRINTED IN CANADA

10 9 8 7 6 5 4 3 2 1

About Our Writers

Mark Johanson is a Santiago-based journalist whose stories about travel, food, culture, and sustainability have appeared in *National Geographic*, *Travel + Leisure*, *Condé Nast Traveler*, *AFAR*, *Food & Wine*, *Men's Journal*, and *The Economist*, among others. He is the co-author of a dozen guidebooks to destinations across the Americas and Southeast Asia. You can find his work at www.markjohanson.com. Mark updated the Central Coast, Central Valley, and Travel Smart chapters.

Jimmy Langman lives in southern Chile, where he is executive editor of *Patagon Journal*, a magazine about travel, nature, culture, and outdoor sports in the Patagonia region of Chile and Argentina. Since 1998, he has also worked as a freelance journalist, writing regularly for *Newsweek*, *National Geographic News*, *Globe and Mail*, the *Independent* (London), and other publications in the United States, Canada, and Britain. Jimmy updated the Lake District, Chiloé, Southern Coast, and Southern Chilean Patagonia and Tierra del Fuego chapters.

Matt Maynard is based in the Andean foothills above Santiago, where he works as an adventure photographer and investigative environmental journalist. His stories from 6,000-meter summits and remote wilderness areas are published by *Geographical*, *The Guardian*, and *Outside* magazine among others. You can find his work at www.matt-maynard.com. He updated the El Norte Chico and El Norte Grande chapters.

Based in Argentina since 2006, award-winning freelance journalist **Sorrel Moseley-Williams** is also a sommelier who writes about luxury and budget travel, food, and wine for an array of publications including *Decanter*, *Monocle*, the *Guardian*, the *Independent* and *Condé Nast Traveller* among other publications. She updated the Experience, Santiago, and Easter Island chapters this edition.

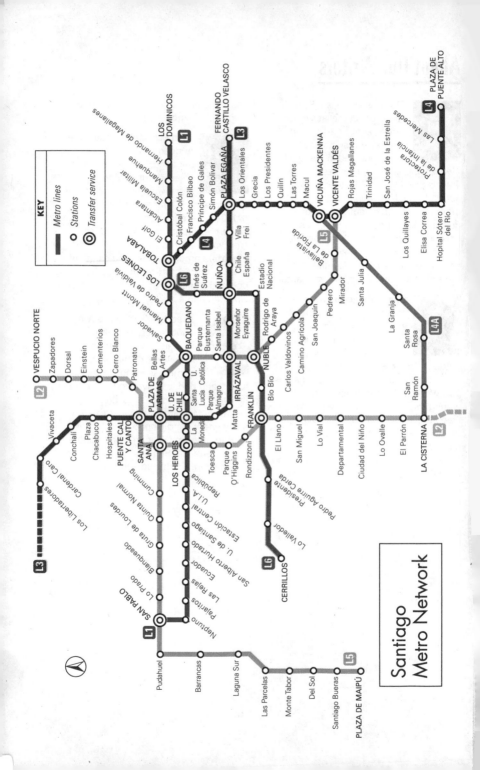

Santiago
Metro Network